GLOBAL ECONOMIC INTEGRATION AND INEQUALITY

GLOBAL ECONOMIC INTEGRATION AND INEQUALITY

Editor:
SIDDHARTHA SARKAR

SERIALS PUBLICATIONS
NEW DELHI

First Published - 2007

ISBN: 978-81-8387-130-3

Published by

SERIALS PUBLICATIONS
4800/24, Ist Floor, Ansari Road
Darya Ganj, New Delhi-110002 (India)
Phone : 23245225. Fax : 91-11-23272135
E-mail: serials@satyam.net.in

PREFACE

Globalization may be understood to connote major increases in worldwide trade and exchanges in an increasingly open, integrated, and borderless international economy. In a world overwhelmed by divergence, globalization probably has a net negative impact. Conversely, in a cooperative world, globalization probably has a net positive impact and thus, it represents a foremost challenge and, at the same time, an unprecedented opportunity in terms of possibilities for conflict or cooperation. While the globalization process is a multifarious and multidimensional phenomenon, some of its most discernible and prominent aspects are economic in character. The world economy has become more unequal over the last two centuries. That inequality is characterized by widening economic gaps between nations, but not necessarily within nations. During this same period, the world economy has become more integrated globally. This leads some economists to suggest a relationship between global economic integration and economic inequality. Increasing globalization has probably mitigated the effects of inequality between nations that participate in global markets. The nations that gained the most from globalization are those poor countries that changed their policies to exploit it, while the ones that gained the least did not, or were too secluded to effectively revise economic and political policy.

Citing enormous integrated economies such as those found in the United States, Japan, and the European Union, it may be considered whether a corresponding colossal world economy with only negligible barriers to trade, migration, and capital movements would make for a more unequal world economy. Such an integrated world economy would be less unequal than today's barrier-filled, partly globalized world economy and such a globalized world would have immense regions with inferior education and chaotic legal institutions and would be more unequal than societies found in economies such as the United States or the European Union. However, the source of that inequality would be poor government and non-democracy in the lagging countries, not the effects of globalization. The challenge will be to build up such new modes of cooperation and new institutions to enhance the benefits and reduce the costs of globalization as opposed to denouncing it or praising it uncritically. Benefits of such global cooperation include ensuring equity and stability in a globalized world; economic growth and stability; economic development for the poorer nations and alleviating non-economic costs of globalization. Establishing new political arrangements and institutions could go a long way to solving inequality, including the economic and other challenges stemming from globalization.

Therefore globalization has changed the world economic system and it poses both opportunities and challenges such as the technological, policy, institutional, ideological, and cultural developments that led to globalization still active and these trends toward greater globalization will likely continue or even accelerate in the future.

Dr. Siddhartha Sarkar

PREFACE

CONTENTS

THE ROLE OF LIQUIDITY FOR THE UK COMPANIES: A PANEL COINTEGRATION AND CAUSALITY APPROACH

*Nicholas Apergis**, *Katerina Lyroudi & Daniel Mccarty*

ABSTRACT

This study investigates the role of certain liquidity indicators for large UK companies listed on the London Stock Exchange in terms of causality relationships with respect to profitability and indebtedness. To this end, a panel approach is employed along with new techniques in the panel cointegration and panel causality literature. The results demonstrated that all three measures of liquidity, i.e. the current ratio, the quick ratio, and the cash conversion cycle play a specific role in terms of causality relationships between liquidity on one hand and profitability as well as indebtedness on the other hand. Each measure of liquidity provides useful information regarding the company's liquidity position as well as the company's profitability and leverage status. Thus, it is recommended to use all three measures in order to get better insights and efficiency in the cash management of a company.

JEL Classification System: *G31; G32*

Keywords: *Liquidity indicators; profitability; indebtedness; panel data; cointegration*

I. INTRODUCTION

According to Brealey and Myers (1996) the determination of a firm's liquidity value is one of the 10 unsolved problems in finance. In the relevant literature certain liquidity indicators, such as the current and quick ratios have been recognised as the traditional appropriate measures of the liquidity position of a firm. However Largay and Stickney (1980) and Aziz and Lawson (1989) have criticised, these ratios as static. Other researchers, as Richards and Laughlin have suggested the cash conversion cycle (CCC) as the appropriate measure of liquidity. The CCC measures the actual time between cash outflows and cash inflows. An increase indicates the deterioration of the firm's liquidity. Therefore, the goal of the company is to decrease the CCC as much as possible without hurting operations. Moreover, the longer the CCC, the greater the need for external financing; this implies that a lower CCC will also improve profits. By reducing the time that funds are invested in working capital, the company will be capable of operating more efficiently. In other words, the CCC adds the cash flow concept (time dimension) to the liquidity analysis against the static analysis of other liquidity ratios, i.e. the current and quick ratios. This makes the former a financial flexibility measure, while the latter are financial solvency measures. [Maness and Zietlow (2002)].

* Department of Financial & Banking Management, University of Piraeus, Piraeus, Greece.

** Department of Accounting and Finance, University of Macedonia, Thessaloniki, Greece.

*** Department of Finance and Real Estate, Florida Atlantic University, Florida, USA.

If we compare the empirical results with the respect to the relationship between liquidity, profitability and leverage, on one hand, and the cash conversion cycle, the current and quick ratios for US and UK companies, on the other hand, in some studies the relationship turns out to be positive [Richards and Laughlin (1980), Moss and Stine (1993), Gallinger (1997), Lyroudi (1999) while in other studies it turns out to be negative [Kamath (1989), Lyroudi and McCarthy (1993)]. According to the theoretical analysis, this relationship should be negative, since a low cash conversion cycle and a high current and quick ratio indicate a good liquidity position. This controversy indicates the need for further research.

Considering the size of the examined firms, it could not be a factor that leads to this controversy, since the Richards and Laughlin (1980), the Kammath (1989), the Moss and Stine (1993) and the Lyroudi *et al.* (1999) study refers to large UK firms. Neither can be the companies industrial sector, since the abovementioned studies regarding US firms analysed firms all from different results. Hence we are faced with a puzzle or a paradox. Therefore, one could wonder whether the methodological approach is a differentiating factor for the controversial results.

There are no a priori reasons that the authors feel it would make liquidity analysis materially different between countries of similar economic and political conditions. Given that there are no conceptual reasons to expect liquidity differences between similar countries like the US and the UK, the analysis for UK firms could shed liquidity more insights to the analysis of liquidity for US companies also.

By applying the novel methodology of panel cointegration and causality, the objective of this study is to investigate the appropriateness of certain liquidity indicators in terms of the relationship among them and in terms of causality with respect to profitability and indebtness. The paper is divided into the following sessions: Session 2 reviews the literature. Section 3 describes the empirical analysis and discusses the results, while Session 4 concludes the paper.

II. LITERATURE REVIEW

Almost all the literature that is presented in this section refers to the US companies, corporate liquidity except one study. The issue of the cash conversion cycle was initially presented by Hager (1976). Nordgren (1981) introduced a cash cycle analysis, based on the asset conversion cycle and the liability cycle. After that, several empirical studies followed examining the cash conversion cycle to determine which variables were affecting it the most. Another group of studies examined, among other issues, the relationship of the CCC with the traditional CR and Ratios.

Belt (1985) examined for US companies the trends of cash conversion cycle and its components during the period 1950-1983. He found that retailing and wholesaling firms both had cash conversion cycles shorter than those of manufacturing firms. Mining firms had the shortest cash conversion cycle because this type of industry has the longest payment deferral period of all the major business types. Finally, Belt found that cyclical phenomena were apparent. The cash conversion cycle increased during periods of recession. The non-durable goods cash conversion cycle had declined persistently, while the durable goods cash conversion cycle had been unstable but declining for the examined time period. Besley and Meyer (1987) evaluated empirically the interrelationships among the working capital accounts and cash conversion cycle, the firm's industry classification and the rate of inflation for US companies for the period 1969-1983. Using the Spearman rank correlation coefficient they found that the cash conversion cycle was most correlated with the average age of inventory and least correlated with the age of spontaneous credit. This conclusion suggested that inventory activity was the most important input to the cash conversion cycle for their sample. Finally, the authors found that there was no significant correlation between the value of cash conversion cycle and the rate of inflation.

Another group of studies examined among other issues the relationship of the cash conversion cycle with the traditional current and quick ratios. In particular, Schilling (1996) supported that the cash conversion cycle is a working capital evaluation technique, which depicts a company's average liquidity position. The advantage of this technique is that it can be used to evaluate changes in circulating capital and thereby facilitate the monitoring and controling of its components.

The issue of the cash conversion cycle was initially presented by Hager (1976). After that several empirical studies followed examining the CCC to determine which variables were affecting it most and Nordgren (1981) introduced a cash cycle analysis, based on the asset conversion cycle and the liability cycle. Richards and Laughlin (1980) suggested that a cash conversion cycle analysis should be used to supplement the traditional but static liquidity ratio analysis because it provides dynamic insights. Based on their results, they concluded that there is a positive relationship between the current and quick ratios and the cash conversion cycle.

Kamath (1989) tested empirically the hypothesis of conflicting signals between current and quick ratio analysis and cash conversion cycle analysis. He also examined whether the net trade cycle is a good approximation of the cash conversion cycle and the relationships between the three above liquidity measures and a measure of the firm's profitability. Focusing on US large firms in six retail industries for the period 1970-1984 he found that: (1) current and quick ratios were negatively correlated with the cash conversion cycle; (2) current and quick ratios were positively related to the profitability ratio; (3) the net trade cycle provided the same information as the cash conversion cycle and (4) both cycles were found to be negatively correlated with the profitability measure. In conclusion, Kamath stated that each measure can provide both useful information and misleading clues regarding the firm's liquidity position, therefore, he suggested to use all three measures.

Lyroudi and McCarty (1993) examined the empirical relationship of the cash conversion cycle and the current and quick ratios for small (capitalization under $1 million) US companies, for the period 1984 to 1988. Their results indicated that the cash conversion cycle was negatively related to the current ratio, to the inventory conversion period and to the payables deferral period, but positively related to the quick ratio and to the receivables conversion period. Furthermore, their results showed differences between the concept of CCC in manufacturing, retail, wholesale and service industries, with the latter having the higher CCC.

Moss and Stine (1993) examined the relationship between the length of the CCC and the size of US retail firms from 1971 to 1990, based on the Standard and Poor's COMPUSTAT data. They also examined the relationship of the CCC and the other liquidity measures. Their results indicated that larger retail firms had shorter CCCs, which implies that smaller companies should try to manage better their CCC. The relationship between the CCC and the current and quick ratios was found positive and significant, indicating that although strong current and quick ratios are generally desirable, they could imply a large investment in working capital which could lead to problems if not taken into consideration.

Gallinger (1997) suggested the abandonment of the traditional liquidity measurements and select the cash conversion cycle. He argued that longer operating policies that result in a longer cash conversion cycle produce a larger commitment to cash and non-cash current asset investments and a lesser ability to finance these investments with current liabilities. The implication is that higher values for the current and quick ratios are usually the result of a greater commitment of resources to less liquid forms of working capital and not an indication of a good liquidity position.

III. EMPIRICAL ANALYSIS

1. The Data and Testable Hypotheses

To explore liquidity concepts of UK firms, we created a sample of non-financial corporations listed on the London Stock Exchange. The corporations selected can be found in the National Index as well as in the Extel Database. This index contained 637 corporations. However, those corporations that had data only for three years or less were excluded from the sample, hence the final sample is composed of 225 corporations. These are the firms listed on the FTSE-100 and FTSE-250 indices, i.e. the top 350 corporations based on their asset size of the London Stock Exchange. The time period under examination is from 1993 to 1999 and the industries included in the sample are the following: (1) Retail Services (96 firms), (2) General Manufacturing (87 firms), and (3) Consumer Goods (42 firms). Annual data on the following variables were obtained: The main indicators of liquidity are the current (CR) ratio measured as the ratio between current assets to current liabilities and the quick (QR) ratio measured as the ratio between the sum of cash, marketable securities and receivables, to current liabilities. The cash conversion cycle (CCC) is defined as the sum of the receivables conversion period (RCP) measured as 360/Accounts receivable turnover, plus the inventory conversion period (ICP) measured as 360/Inventory turnover, minus the payment deferral period (PDP) measured as 360/Payables Turnover. Thus,

$$CCC = (360\ AR/Sales) + (360\ Inv/CGS) - (360\ CL/X)$$

where CL defines current liabilities, CGS defines cost of goods sold, and X is defined as: CGS + General Expenses + Interest + Labor + Advertising + Insurance + Travel + Salaries - Depreciation. To measure profitability, data on return on investment (ROI), return on equity (ROE), and net profit margin (NPM) were also obtained. Finally, data on leverage ratios, e.g. the debt to assets ratio (DAR), the debt ratio (DR), and a reserve relationship with the times interest earned ratio (TIE) were also used. In this paper, small letters express variables in natural logarithms.

A priori, there has to be a relationship between the current and quick ratios and the cash conversion cycle but the relationship may be positive as Richards and Laughlin (1980) argue, or negative as Lyroudi and McCarty (1993) have found. A reduction in the cash conversion cycle can be obtained by decreasing the average collection period, the average inventory age, or by increasing the average accounts payable period. Suppose accounts receivable were to decrease. Since such accounts receivable appear in the numerator of the current ratio, the quick ratio, and the cash conversion cycle, then all three should fall. For a reduction in inventory, the same results occur. For example, a reduction in either inventory or receivables may also suggest a reduction in short-term financing. If short-term financing is reduced, then current ratio, quick ratio and cash conversion cycle may or may not fall. Any change must depend on the relative magnitudes of change in short-term asset and liability changes. A change as suggested by Richards and Laughlin (1980) could occur only if receivables and inventory were totally financed with long-term funds. According to Lyroudi and McCarty (1993), the relationship of the cash conversion cycle with the current ratio was found negative, and only with the quick ratio the relationship was positive.

On the other hand, an increase in the cash conversion cycle can be "achieved" by increasing the receivables conversion period, or the inventory conversion period, or by decreasing the payment deferral period. So if inventories are about to increase and because inventories appear in the numerator of the current ratio, the quick ratio, and the cash conversion cycle, all three measures should rise, suggesting that the current and quick ratios indicate an improvement in a firm's liquidity position, and the cash conversion cycle indicates exactly the opposite. For an increase in accounts receivable the same results would occur. Also, if payables decrease, because they appear in the denominator of the current and the quick ratio, the two liquidity indicators would increase, (suggesting an improvement in liquidity), while the cash conversion cycle would also increase, because the payment deferral period decreases (suggesting a deterioration in liquidity).

When managerial decisions about working capital are required, the CR, QR and CCC will all likely change. Management might decide to reduce short-term financing by increasing long-term financing. In this case, the CR, QR and CCC will rise but different liquidity implications result; the traditional ratios suggest an improvement in liquidity but the CCC indicates a reduction in the firm liquidity. Any change in credit standards, terms of sale or collection policy and/or inventory variables that change the levels of receivables or inventory require a management decision. Unless an off-setting decision is made to other assets or liabilities, changes in CR, QR and CCC are not predictable.

Likewise, the relationships between these liquidity ratios and profitability must depend on a careful analysis. There maybe no reason to suspect any changes in liquidity or profitability ratios for exogenous changes in sales. If one assumes firms use the optimal order quantity models for assets level determination, then any managerial decision that changes receivables, inventory and/or current liabilities must decrease profitability ratios regardless of the impact on liquidity ratios. Optimal order quantity models suggest that for a given change in sales, the optimal level of working capital items will change but less than in proportion to the change in sales. Profit maximisation is still maintained but the CR, QR and CCC will change in some unpredictable way.

If it is assumed that the current and the quick ratios are such that current assets and liabilities are at the optimal level for the specific firm, then any managerial decision that changes the levels of current assets and liabilities, moves the firm away from the profit maximisation levels. Specifically, if the current ratio increases, by either an increase in current assets or a decrease in current liabilities or both, this suggests that current assets move above the optimal level and current liabilities move below it, causing the firm to incur higher costs in its operations, reducing therefore, its profits and finally the value of its shareholders' wealth.

The first hypothesis investigates the causal relationship of the three liquidity measures under examination with the company's profitability. The results of these tests will be helpful guides for managers because they will be able to see which variables are affected, if any, by managerial decisions.

1. The Liquidity/Profitability Hypothesis: The company's liquidity as measured by the variables: current ratio (CR), quick ratio (QR) and the cash conversion cycle (CCC), is expected to have a causality effect on its profitability as measured by the variables: return on investment (ROI), return on equity (ROE) and net profit margin (NPM) and vice versa.

The second hypothesis examines the causal relationship of the three liquidity measures under consideration with the company's debt position. The more liquid a firm is, the lower its short-term debt obligations should be and the higher its short-term debt capacity. This issue is very useful for the managers of the firms to guide them for their financial planning as well as for the various financial institutions that are considering to granting loans to the examined firms.

2. The Liquidity/Leverage Hypothesis: The company's liquidity as measured by the variables: current ratio (CR), quick ratio (QR) and the cash conversion cycle (CCC), is expected to have a causality effect on its indebtedness as measured by the variables: debt to assets ratio (DAR), debt ratio (DR) and the times interest earned ratio (TIE) and vice versa.

2. Dynamic Heterogeneity

The dynamic heterogeneity, i.e. variation of the intercept over countries and time, across a cross-section of the relevant variables can be assessed in a number of ways. In the first step, an ADF(n) equation for each relationship in the panel is estimated; then, the hypothesis of whether regression parameters are equal across these equations. Next, a similar test of parameter equality is performed by estimating a n-order autoregressive model for each relationship under study. Standard Chow-type F tests under the null of parameter equality across all relationships are also performed. If the results reject the null, this indicates heterogeneity in cross-sectional parameters. Finally, homogeneity error variance across groups is also examined as another measure of dynamic heterogeneity. White's tests for group-wise heteroscedasticity are employed to serve this objective. The results are reported in Table 1 and they indicate that the relationships under investigation are characterised by heterogeneity of dynamics and error variance across groups. The demeaning procedure, proposed by Im, Pesaran and Shin (1995), reduces the presence of dynamic heterogeneity significantly.

3. Panel Integration and Cointegration Analysis

The null hypothesis of non-stationarity versus the alternative that the variable is stationary is tested using the group mean panel unit root test (or 't-bar' test) of Im *et al.* (1995). This test is based on the Augmented Dickey-Fuller (ADF) statistic for each country (Dickey and Fuller, 1981) and allows each member of the cross section to have a different autoregressive root and different autocorrelation structures under the alternative hypothesis. The results are reported without and with a trend and are presented in Table 2. The hypothesis that variables cr, qr, ROI, ROE, NPM, rcp, icp, pdp, DR, dar, TIE, and CCC (in levels) contain a unit root cannot be rejected at the 1% significant level. When first differences are used, unit root nonstationarity is rejected at the 1% significant level, suggesting that the above variables are I(1) variables. This result opens the possibility of cointegration among certain variables commensurate on the testable hypothesis.

Table 1
Tests of Dynamic Heterogeneity Across Groups

The ADF(3) column reports the parameter equality test (F test) across all relationships in the panel. The AR(4) column reports the F test of parameter equality conducted in a fourth-order autoregressive model of the relationships under study. Finally, the White's test reports White's test of equality of variances across the investigated relationships in the panel. The White's test was computed by regressing the squared residual of the ADF(3) regression on the original regressor(s) and its(their) square(s). The test statistic is (NT) x R^2, which is x^2 distributed with the number of regressors in the second regression as the degrees of freedom.
* statistical significance at the 1% level.

	ADF(3)	*AR(4)*	*WHITE'S TEST*
Panel 1. The profitability hypothesis			
cr – ROI	19.65*	15.33*	32.79*
cr – ROE	17.68*	14.19*	27.82*
cr – NPM	16.93*	17.36*	29.15*
qr – ROI	16.12*	16.83*	34.84*
qr – ROE	18.77*	19.91*	32.26*
qr – NPM	20.04*	22.39*	36.77*
CCC – ROI	15.63*	17.80*	26.79*
CCC – ROE	17.88*	18.93*	28.71*
CCC – NPM	18.09*	19.83*	29.04*
Panel 2. The leverage hypothesis			
cr – dar	19.18*	21.28*	31.47*
cr – DR	17.73*	19.05*	25.83*
cr – TIE	18.61*	20.95*	29.93*
qr – dar	23.35*	26.84*	37.03*
qr – DR	20.58*	27.05*	36.41*
qr – TIE	19.44*	25.58*	34.06*
CCC – dar	16.21*	18.83*	27.02*
CCC – DR	15.09*	16.55*	18.92*
CCC – TIE	17.73*	18.06*	20.14*

Table 2
Panel unit root tests

Figures in brackets denote the number of lags in the augmented term that ensures white-noise residuals.
* statistical significance at the 1% level.

Variables	*Without Trend*	*With Trend*
CCC	−1.81(4)	−1.97(3)
DCCC	−20.9(3)*	−25.8(2)*
cr	−1.13(3)	−1.32(3)
Δcr	−19.6(3)*	−24.4(1)*
qr	−1.01(3)	−1.39(4)
Δqr	−20.4(2)*	−26.5(2)*
ROE	−1.15(4)	−1.38(4)
ΔROE	−21.4(4)*	−29.8(2)*
NPM	−1.26(3)	−1.32(3)
ΔNPM	−21.9(2)*	−25.2(1)*
ROI	−1.25(3)	−1.39(2)
ΔROI	−21.4(1)*	−29.5(1)*
rcp	−1.24(2)	−1.32(4)
Δrcp	−21.5(1)*	−34.6(2)*
icp	−1.26(3)	−1.39(3)
Δicp	−21.7(2)*	−29.9(1)*
pdp	−1.26(2)	−1.32(3)
Δpdp	−20.8(2)*	−24.5(1)*
dar	−1.19(4)	−1.35(4)
Δdar	−21.5(2)*	−23.9(2)*
DR	−1.23(3)	−1.46(3)
ΔDR	−21.5(1)*	−29.2(2)*
TIE	−1.13(2)	−1.42(3)
ΔTIE	−21.6(2)*	−27.8(2)*

Once the order of stationarity has been established, we can move to a panel cointegration approach developed by Pedroni (1999). The panel cointegration technique makes use of a residual-based ADF test. The specific cointegrating relationships estimated are:

Panel 1. The profitability hypothesis

$$cr_{it} \text{ or } qr_{it} \text{ or } CCC_{it} = \beta_{01i} + \beta_{1i}\, ROI_{it} \text{ or } ROE_{it} \text{ or } NPM_{it} + \varepsilon_{it} \quad (1)$$

Panel 2. The leverage hypothesis

$$cr_{it} \text{ or } qr_{it} \text{ or } CCC_{it} = \beta_{010i} + \beta_{10i}\, dar_{it} \text{ or } DR_{it} \text{ or } TIE_{it} + \varepsilon_{it} \quad (2)$$

where i runs from 1 to N corporations and t runs from 1 to T observations. These relationships only estimate the long-run path, they do not make any assumptions about the direction of causality. The term e_{it} estimates the deviation from the modelled long-run relationship. If the series are cointegrated, this term will be a stationary variable. In other words, stationarity can be achieved by establishing whether ρ_i in:

$$\varepsilon_{it} = \rho_i\, \varepsilon_{it-1} + \xi_{it} \quad (3)$$

is unity. The null hypothesis, associated with Pedroni's test procedure is that $\rho_i = 1$. In other words, the null hypothesis associated with Pedroni's test procedure is equivalent to testing the null of nonstationarity (no cointegration) for all i. Pedroni (1995, 1997) developed four panel cointegration statistics and three group mean panel cointegration statistics. The cointegration results are provided in Table 3. The results confirm that in both testable hypotheses the panel is stationary. In other words, the results indicate that commensurating on the hypothesis tested and accounting for dynamic heterogeneity the variables share a long-run cointegrating relationship.

Table 3

Panel Cointegration Tests

* Rejection of the null hypothesis of no cointegration at the 1% level.

Panel 1. The profitability hypothesis			
	cr-ROI	cr-ROE	cr-NPM
Panel v-stat	-3.1589*	-3.3499*	-8.8812*
Panel rho-stat	-13.6231*	-13.4156*	-11.1036*
Panel pp-stat	-3.9886*	-3.6818*	-8.7927*
Panel adf-stat	-3.2138*	-3.8829*	-6.5551*
Group rho-stat	-11.8601*	-11.8435*	-10.7105*
Group pp-stat	-5.8467*	-5.8508*	-3.6326*
Group adf-stat	-4.8681*	-4.8096*	-3.4121*
	qr-ROI	qr-ROE	qr-NPM
Panel v-stat	-9.2829*	-9.6462*	-5.2409*
Panel rho-stat	-11.9302*	-11.6961*	-10.5764*
Panel pp-stat	-9.9787*	-9.9557*	-8.8145*
Panel adf-stat	-8.3972*	-5.4762*	-3.4082*
Group rho-stat	-16.0717*	-19.0416*	-10.8934*
Group pp-stat	-5.4842*	-5.4984*	-4.0031*
Group adf-stat	-4.2931*	-5.3821*	-3.5651*
	CCC-ROI	CCC-ROE	CCC-NPM
Panel v-stat	-6.6136*	-8.4189*	-3.0884*
Panel rho-stat	-12.2151*	-12.1259*	-7.4192*
Panel pp-stat	-5.7816*	-5.7530*	-5.4981*
Panel adf-stat	-4.7751*	-4.6869*	-4.9056*
Group rho-stat	-15.6166*	-15.4664*	-8.8368*
Group pp-stat	-3.7804*	-5.1262*	-5.9623*
Group adf-stat	-3.0274*	-4.2328*	-3.4233*
Panel 2. The leverage hypothesis			
	cr-dar	cr-DR	cr-TIE
Panel v-stat	-3.572*	-6.7044*	-4.6496*
Panel rho-stat	-12.8374*	-15.2987*	-12.0330*
Panel pp-stat	-5.1883*	-5.0195*	-5.0939*
Panel adf-stat	-4.3232*	-4.3011*	-4.7907*
Group rho-stat	-12.1173*	-13.8969*	-18.8631*
Group pp-stat	-5.1932*	-7.1147*	-7.4109*
Group adf-stat	-4.4557*	-6.7659*	-5.8927*

Table 3 contd.

	qr-dar	qr-DR	qr-TIE
Panel v-stat	-9.877*	-3.7345*	-9.4506*
Panel rho-stat	-15.8561*	-11.9841*	-20.7384*
Panel pp-stat	-8.8912*	-9.9676*	-3.9895*
Panel adf-stat	-6.6304*	-6.3991*	-3.3683*
Group rho-stat	-16.1586*	-19.0927*	-19.7393*
Group pp-stat	-4.4368*	-5.4659*	-5.6908*
Group adf-stat	-3.3049*	-4.2861*	-5.2781*
	CCC-dar	CCC-DR	CCC-TIE
Panel v-stat	-3.4072*	-3.8626*	-8.9428*
Panel rho-stat	-10.1289*	-9.4818*	-9.3463*
Panel pp-stat	-6.385*	-5.9694*	-6.0257*
Panel adf-stat	-4.3894*	-3.9365*	-5.7984*
Group rho-stat	-19.9925*	-9.1692*	-16.2738*
Group pp-stat	-11.1709*	-9.6693*	-7.3528*
Group adf-stat	-8.2465*	-3.5718*	-4.3290*

4. Panel Causality

As cointegration is confirmed, we proceed to estimate causality using the Pooled Mean Group (PMG) estimator of Pesaran, Shin and Smith (1999) to account for the panel data causal relationships. This provides justification for examining the direction of the causal links among the variables under consideration through an error correction VAR (ECVAR) model. The PMG estimator was obtained through the methodological software analysis proposed by Pesaran *et al.* (1999). The error-correction coefficients are negative and statistically significant (Table 4), implying that the error-correction mechanism will eventually bring back the relevant series to its long-run equilibrium after a shock. The error-correction coefficients represent the proportion by which the long-run disequilibrium (or imbalance) in the dependent variables are corrected in each short-term period. Table 4 investigates (in two panels) the two main testable hypotheses. First, whether the company's liquidity is expected to have a causality effect on the company's profitability (and vice versa) and, second, whether the company's liquidity is expected to have a causality effect on the company's indebtedness (and vice versa). Moreover, the results in Table 4 report the sign of the correlation between liquidity and profitability as well as between liquidity and leverage. The sign of that association is given through the δ_{11} coefficient. The results yielded:

Panel 1. The profitability hypothesis

Considering that the cointegration equation is:

ROI_{it} or ROE_{it} or $NPM_{it} = \theta_{0i} + \theta_{1i}\, cr_{it}$ or qr_{it} or $CCC_{it} + u_{it}$

and the associated autogressive distributed lag equation is described by an ARDL (1,1,1) model:

ROI_{it} or ROE_{it} or $NPM_{it} = \mu_i + \delta_{10i}\, cr_{it}$ or qr_{it} or $CCC_{it} + \delta_{11i}\, cr_{it}$ or qr_{it-1} or $CCC_{it-1} + \lambda_i\, ROI_{i,t-1}$ or $ROE_{i,t-1}$ or $NPM_{i,t-1} + \varepsilon_{it}$

The error correction equation yields:

Table 4
Long-run causality tests

Figures in parentheses denote t-statistics while those in brackets p-values. LM is a serial correlation test, RESET is a functional misspecification test, NO is a normality test, and HE is a heterogeneity test, *statistical significance at the 1% level (reject the null hypothesis of no causality).

Dependent Variable	*Error Correction Coefficient, (φ)*
Panel 1. The profitability hypothesis	
Δcr	−0.296(-5.67)*
LM = 1.59[0.25] RESET = 2.39[0.14] NO = 1.37[0.31] HE	= 2.04[0.18]
ΔROI	- 0.127(-12.6)*
LM = 2.61[0.22] RESET = 2.92[0.19] NO = 3.59[0.12] HE	= 0.08[0.77]
δ_{11} = 0.156(4.17)*	
Δcr	- 0.114(-2.15)*
LM = 1.65[0.23] RESET = 0.94[0.35] NO = 1.99[0.16] HE	= 1.76[0.21]
ΔROE	- 0.274(-13.3)*
LM = 0.02[0.99] RESET = 1.16[0.28] NO = 2.59[0.45] HE	= 0.01[0.92]
δ_{11} = 0.179(4.63)*	
Δcr	- 0.132(-2.51)*
LM = 2.42[0.27] RESET = 0.08[0.78] NO = 1.37[0.39] HE	= 1.25[0.48]
ΔNPM	- 0.511(-13.3)*
LM = 0.68[0.41] RESET = 0.08[0.78] NO = 2.56[0.26] HE	= 0.01[0.94]
δ_{11} = 0.218(5.09)*	
Δqr	- 0.194(-1.66)
LM = 1.67[0.21] RESET = 2.41[0.31] NO = 2.89[0.27] HE	= 0.66[0.52]
ΔROI	- 0.134(-14.3)*
LM = 0.98[0.32] RESET = 2.92[0.15] NO = 2.34[0.19] HE	= 0.05[0.82]
δ_{11} = 0.112(4.14)*	
Δqr	- 0.161(-1.39)
LM = 1.53[0.27] RESET = 2.38[0.18] NO = 2.71[0.12] HE	= 1.69[0.22]
ΔROE	- 0.278(-12.4)*
LM = 0.05[0.82] RESET = 0.74[0.39] NO = 2.69[0.21] HE	= 0.01[0.91]
δ_{11} = 0.181(4.77)*	
Δqr	- 0.359(-3.09)*
LM = 1.35[0.31] RESET = 2.37[0.19] NO = 2.94[0.12] HE	= 0.47[0.59]
ΔNPM	- 0.051(-12.2)*
LM = 0.11[0.74] RESET = 0.12[0.73] NO = 2.61[0.17] HE	= 0.01[0.94]
δ_{11} = 0.127(3.97)*	
ΔCCC	- 0.045(-1.34)
LM = 0.78[0.38] RESET = 2.38[0.44] NO = 1.51[0.64] HE	= 1.57[0.62]
ΔROI	- 0.011(-0.32)
LM = 2.72[0.19] RESET = 2.78[0.16] NO = 3.47[0.17] HE = 0.78[0.38]	
δ_{11} = - 0.038(1.61)	
ΔCCC	- 0.024(-0.41)
LM = 0.67[0.41] RESET = 2.55[0.19] NO = 1.42[0.39] HE	= 2.01[0.27]

Table 4 contd.

ΔROE	- 0.025(-1.97)*
LM = 0.26[0.61] RESET = 3.42[0.14] NO = 2.66[0.24] HE	= 3.08[0.11]
δ_{11} = - 0.143(4.18)*	
ΔCCC	- 0.072(-0.45)
LM = 0.41[0.52] RESET = 1.29[0.26] NO = 1.59[0.54] HE	= 2.75[0.27]
ΔNPM	- 0.049(-0.75)
LM = 0.01[0.94] RESET = 1.04[0.74] NO = 2.57[0.26] HE	= 1.56[0.38]
δ_{11} = - 0.029(1.45)	
Panel 2. The leverage hypothesis	
Δcr	- 0.487(-0.92)
LM = 1.76[0.19] RESET = 1.82[0.18] NO = 1.18[0.28] HE	= 2.38[0.13]
Δdar	- 0.468(-11.6)*
LM = 0.11[0.75] RESET = 2.23[0.14] NO = 2.86[0.11] HE	= 0.23[0.63]
δ_{11} = - 0.264(4.08)*	
Δcr	- 0.156(-3.02)*
LM = 1.98[0.15] RESET = 1.95[0.16] NO = 1.49[0.24] HE	= 2.41[0.11]
ΔDR	- 0.134(-13.3)*
LM = 0.02[0.89] RESET = 0.28[0.59] NO = 1.46[0.27] HE	= 0.09[0.88]
δ_{11} = - 0.189(5.17)*	
Δcr	- 0.102(-1.92)*
LM = 1.64[0.18] RESET = 1.39[0.24] NO = 1.28[0.29] HE	= 2.46[0.11]
ΔTIE	- 0.063(-13.4)*
LM = 0.38[0.54] RESET = 0.05[0.94] NO = 1.59[0.26] HE	= 0.01[0.98]
δ_{11} = - 0.258(4.90)*	
Δqr	- 0.321(-2.77)*
LM = 1.58[0.22] RESET = 2.54[0.12] NO = 2.94[0.09] HE	= 0.45[0.63]
Δdar	- 0.443(-10.9)*
LM = 1.56[0.21] RESET = 3.18[0.08] NO = 2.84[0.12] HE	= 0.01[0.93]
δ_{11} = - 0.177(4.63)*	
Δqr	- 0.087(-8.77)*
LM = 1.25[0.29] RESET = 2.55[0.14] NO = 1.16[0.37] HE	= 0.41[0.63]
ΔDR	- 0.111(-11.3)*
LM = 2.96[0.16] RESET = 2.78[0.19] NO = 1.33[0.31] HE = 0.01[0.97]	
δ_{11} = - 0.275(5.11)*	
Δqr	- 0.221(-1.89)*
LM = 1.39[0.23] RESET = 2.39[0.12] NO = 2.91[0.08] HE	= 0.56[0.55]
ΔTIE	- 0.063(-13.3)*
LM = 0.59[0.44] RESET = 0.04[0.84] NO = 2.61[0.19] HE = 0.01[0.93]	
δ_{11} = - 0.281(4.20)*	
ΔCCC	- 0.058(-5.74)*
LM = 1.64[0.24] RESET = 0.81[0.37] NO = 2.63[0.15] HE	= 1.94[0.19]
Δdar	- 0.397(-9.71)*
LM = 2.71[0.18] RESET = 0.62[0.43] NO = 2.85[0.12] HE	= 0.11[0.75]
δ_{11} = - 0.306(5.24)*	

Table 4 contd.

ΔCCC	-0.292(-2.87)*
LM = 2.59[0.19] RESET = 0.87[0.35] NO = 2.79[0.15] HE	= 2.06[0.24]
ΔDR	-0.131(-13.5)*
LM = 1.78[0.18] RESET = 0.34[0.56] NO = 1.53[0.23] HE	= 0.02[0.96]
δ_{11} = -0.294(4.82)*	
ΔCCC	-0.054(-5.02)*
LM = 1.99[0.18] RESET = 1.39[0.24] NO = 1.87[0.2] HE	= 2.84[0.12]
ΔTIE	-0.059(-12.6)*
LM = 2.22[0.14] RESET = 2.22[0.14] NO = 2.53[0.11] HE	= 0.02[0.96]
δ_{11} = -0.372(5.29)*	

ΔROI_{it} or ΔROE_{it} or $\Delta NPM_{it} = \varphi\,(ROI_{i,t-1}$ or $ROE_{i,t-1}$ or $NPM_{i,t-1} - \theta_{0i} - \theta_{1i}\, cr_{it}$ or qr_{it} or $CCC_{it}) - \delta_{11i}$ Δcr_{it} or Δqr_{it-1} or $\Delta CCC_{it} + \varepsilon_{it}$

The results, reported in Table 4 (Panel 1), yielded:

- Current Ratio (cr): In all cases the EC term, (φ), is statistically significant, indicating that liquidity (cr) does cause profitability (ROI, ROE, and NPM). At the same time, profitability also causes liquidity. In other words, there are feedback effects between liquidity and profitability in the long-run. Finally, the relationship between liquidity and profitability is shown to be positive and statistically significant in all three cases.

- Quick Ratio (qr): In all cases the EC term, (φ), is statistically significant, indicating that liquidity (qr) does cause profitability (ROI, ROE, and NPM). By contrast, profitability causes liquidity only with respect to the NPM variable. In other words, there are not explicit feedback effects between liquidity and profitability in the long-run. Finally, the relationship between liquidity and profitability is shown to be positive and statistically significant in all three cases.

- Cash Conversion Cycle (CCC): This time the EC term, (φ), is statistically significant only with respect to the ROE variable. In other words, we cannot assure whether liquidity causes profitability. Moreover, feedback effects are not present in all three cases. Finally, the relationship between liquidity and profitability is shown to be negative and statistically significant only in the case of the ROE variable.

Panel 2. The leverage hypothesis

Considering that the cointegration equation is:

dar_{it} or DR_{it} or $TIE_{it} = \theta_{0i} + \theta_{1i}\, cr_{it}$ or qr_{it} or $CCC_{it} + u_{it}$

and the associated autogressive distributed lag equation is described by an ARDL (1,1,1) model:

dar_{it} or DR_{it} or $TIE_{it} = \mu_i + \delta_{10i}\, cr_{it}$ or qr_{it} or $CCC_{it} + \delta_{11i}\, cr_{it}$ or qr_{it-1} or $CCC_{it-1} + \lambda_i\, dar_{it}$ or DR_{it} or $TIE_{it} + \varepsilon_{it}$

The error correction equation yields:

Δdar_{it} or ΔDR_{it} or $\Delta TIE_{it} = \varphi\,(dar_{it}$ or DR_{it} or $TIE_{it} - \theta_{0i} - \theta_{1i}\, cr_{it}$ or qr_{it} or $CCC_{it}) - \delta_{11i}\, \Delta cr_{it}$ or Δqr_{it-1} or $\Delta CCC_{it} + \varepsilon_{it}$

The results, reported in Table 4 (Panel 2), yielded:

- The Current Ratio (cr): In all cases the EC term, (φ), is statistically significant, indicating that liquidity (cr) does cause indebtedness (dar, DR, and TIE). At the same time, indebtedness causes liquidity only for the cases of the DR and TIE variables.

- The Quick Ratio (qr): In all cases the EC term, (φ), is statistically significant, indicating that liquidity (qr) does cause indebtedness (dar, DR, and TIE). At the same time, indebtedness causes liquidity in all cases. In other words, there are feedback effects between liquidity and indebtedness in the long-run.

- The Cash Conversion Cycle (CCC): In all cases the EC term, (φ), is statistically significant, indicating that liquidity (CCC) does cause indebtedness (dar, DR, and TIE). At the same time, indebtedness also causes liquidity. Thus, there are feedback effects between liquidity and indebtedness in the long-run. In all three cases, the relationship between liquidity and leverage turns out to be negative and statistically significant.

5. Discussion of the Profitability Hypothesis

We investigate the role of three liquidity indicators as determinants of the firm's liquidity. Two of these indicators are the traditional liquidity measures, the current and the quick ratio and the third one is the cash conversion cycle. We explore causality relationships between the firm's liquidity as it is determined by these three measures and the firm's profitability and indebtedness, in order to determine which indicator is the most appropriate for measuring corporate liquidity and to plan accordingly the most efficient working capital management strategy for the firm's value maximisation.

Based on the current and quick ratios we found that liquidity causes profitability in terms of return on investment, return on equity and net profit margin. Moreover, the association between profitability and both ratios turns out to be positive. In other words, when a firm is liquid enough, it is very likely that it has no need for external financing. It can meet all its mature obligations in time, keeping the cost of external financing low. Hence, the interest expenses are low, increasing the firm's net income, in other words, causing the firm's profitability to increase. However, there are a variety of other reasons that could also explain this result. For instance, higher liquidity could allow the firm to invest in better technology to control costs or the liquidity could allow the firm to undertake higher margin investments. A high liquidity position will be determined by a high current ratio and a high quick ratio, implying a large investment in liquid assets (cash, marketable securities, receivables and last, inventories), and low short-term obligations.

Regarding the current ratio as liquidity indicator, there are feedback effects while there are not any regarding the quick ratio. The profitability measures under examination are causing the current ratio. This means that as profitability increases measured by the net profit margin, the company's net earnings will be available to be invested in more future investment opportunities that have positive net present value. As Kim, Mauer and Sherman (1998) have found, there exists a positive relationship between investment in liquid assets and forecasts of future economic conditions. Therefore, the more prospective the investments are, the higher the increase in liquid assets, causing both the current and the quick ratio (which contains the more liquid assets between the two ratios) to increase.

Furthermore, the return on investment and the return on equity are found to cause the current ratio but not the quick ratio. The difference between the two ratios is the exclusion of the inventories (the less liquid form of the current assets of a firm) in the quick ratio. If we analyse these two profitability ratios we see that they contain the NPM and some other variables:

$$ROI = \frac{EAT}{TA} = \frac{EAT}{S} * \frac{S}{TA} = NPM * \frac{S}{TA}$$

$$ROE = \frac{EAT}{E} = \frac{EAT}{S} * \frac{S}{TA} * \frac{TA}{E} = NPM * \frac{S}{TA} * \frac{TA}{E}$$

where: EAT are the earnings after taxes, S are the sales, TA are the firm's total assets and E is the firm's equity capital.

Based on this analysis, there is no causality relationship between ROI and ROE and the quick ratio, because the latter does not include inventories having only the most liquid assets and probably this fact disturbs the causality relationship. As profitability increases due to increases in sales and not earnings, the need for liquid assets to take more profitable investment projects will increase, as we saw previously. Therefore, the current assets of the firms will increase. However, if sales increase, then all the accounts that are directly tied to sales will increase. This means that not only current assets but also current liabilities will increase. The current ratio includes all current assets and current liabilities, while the quick ratio does not include inventories, which also increase by a sales increase. Profitability does not affect the indicator of the firm's most liquid condition.

Liquidity, measured by the CCC, affects only the return on equity, or we can say that it does not cause profitability in terms of the net profit margin and the return on investment. The longer the CCC is, the greater the need for external financing, since the firm will have lower levels of cash and marketable securities to meet its mature obligations [Kim, Mauer and Sherman (1998)]. Equivalently, a shorter CCC will imply that the firm's liquidity is in a better position and that either the average age of inventories has decreased, or the average collection period has decreased, or both have decreased and/or the payables deferral period has increased. In the latter's case, the short-term financing of the firm will increase leaving the equity capital and the long-term external financing intact. In this aspect, a change in the CCC can affect the capital and financial structure of the firm, affecting also the ROE, since a change in the capital structure is a long-term decision. Moreover, there are no feedback effects. None of the profitability ratios can affect the CCC in a causality sense. As we have explained previously, a firm can be profitable but might have a shortage of cash hence, it might need external financing, since the cash and marketable securities are tied up in operations.

Summarising the above analysis, we see that liquidity affects profitability, while a high (low) level of liquidity drives higher (lower) profitability, due to lower (higher) costs of external financing. On the other hand, in some instances profitability also affects liquidity, since an increase in profitability will imply more internal funds available for investment projects, which will imply higher levels of liquid assets, as future investment projects increase. However, in some instances profitability has no causal relationship with liquidity, since higher profitability could be due to increases in credit sales, which by no means affects, or improves the firm's liquidity status. The management of a company should be careful with its terms of sale and its receivables collection policies in order to improve its liquidity position.

6. Discussion of the Leverage Hypothesis

This study, in an effort to determine the most appropriate liquidity measure, the issue of what drives the relations between liquidity and leverage has also to be investigated. Does liquidity influence leverage? Based on the empirical results, it has been observed that liquidity affects the leverage position of a firm according to all three liquidity indicators and influences all three of the leverage indicators. In addition, the relationship between liquidity and leverage has turned out to be negative in all cases. According to the trade-off hypothesis, between the benefits of having too many liquid assets and the costs [Opler, Pinkowitz, Stulz and Williamson (1999)] the management of firms prefers to hold even more than optimal liquid assets to keep the firm's leverage low in case of a deficit of internal funds (to finance investment projects, or operating losses), as well as when outside funds are expensive and to be able to invest when cash flows are low relative to investments.

Specifically, the current and the quick ratios affect the debt to assets ratio (DAR), the debt ratio (DR) and the times interest earned ratio (TIE). As liquidity increases, the current and quick ratios increase, due to either an increase in the current assets variable, or a decrease in the current liabilities, or both. As current assets increase, it means that total assets increase and the DAR declines. As current liabilities decrease, it could mean that either the company is using more long-term external funds hence, affecting the debt ratio, or it could mean that the firm has paid-off its mature obligations affecting the TIE ratio, since the interest expenses will have decreased, adjusted to the new external financing and the two debt ratios, since the total liabilities will be reduced by the reduction in the current liabilities.

On the other hand, leverage also influences liquidity. The relationship between them is negative according to Kim, Mauer and Sherman (1998). As leverage increases, driving up the debt and the debt to assets ratio, the cost of capital increases in general, as default risk increases, and in particular the cost of funds invested in liquid assets increases, reducing the firm's liquidity and the current and quick ratios, by increasing the current liabilities. Furthermore, as the debt ratio increases, according to John (1993), this implies that the firm has access to debt markets and the debt ratio is a proxie for that, the higher leverage can be used as a substitute for maintaining more liquid assets. Hence, the level of current assets decreases, decreasing the current and quick ratios. Regarding the TIE ratio, as leverage increases, the interest expense increases, driving down this ratio that means that a firm has enough operating income to cover its interest expenses. This ratio also affects the current and quick ratios, since as leverage increases and interest payments increase, the firm's most liquid assets decline to cover these expenses.

Regarding the third measure of liquidity, the CCC, our results indicate that this measure affects all three leverage ratios. Furthermore, there are feedback effects from all three leverage ratios on the liquidity measure of CCC. A good liquidity position implies that there is less need for external financing since the firm has cash tied up in operations, as a lower CCC indicates. Hence, the indebtedness of the firm will also be low. A lower CCC leads to lower debt and debt to assets ratios and to a higher TIE ratio, since the interest expenses are reduced.

With respect to the causality relationship from leverage to liquidity, the three leverage measures affect the CCC. The more leverage a firm has, the higher its external financing is, the higher will be the payables deferral period and the higher will be the firm's default risk, driving upwards the cost of capital, and the interest payments. According to an alternative view to the trade-off hypothesis, the financing hierarchy hypothesis [Shyam-Sundèr and Myers (1998)] explains changes in leverage that lead to changes in liquid assets. They support that there is no optimal amount of cash, but instead there is an optimal amount of net debt. As long as a firm has the optimal amount of net debt, it is a matter of indifference for the firm whether it has high cash holdings and high debt, or low cash holdings and low debt. Debt and cash increase mechanically as the firm has more funds available. Hence, in this sense leverage causes liquidity.

Summarising the above analysis, we see that liquidity affects the firm's leverage position, since a high level of liquidity drives the indebtedness of the company lower, as the firm has enough cash to pay-off its mature obligations and the precautionary motive for holding cash by management is strong as Opler, Pinkowitz, Stulz and Williamson (1999) have found. On the other hand, we see that the indebtedness or the firm's leverage affects the firm's liquidity. In particular, higher leverage provides the firm with extra funds to operate smoothly, causing a temporary increase in liquidity since the firm has more cash inflows. However, this external financing will have to be paid off at maturity, and the increased interests will have to be paid on time, causing a depletion in the firm's cash reserves and decreasing its real liquidity. Furthermore, the default and bankruptcy risk of the firm increases driving upwards the cost of capital and reducing the firm's value and the owners' wealth. Also, the agency costs of debt increase as a firm uses more leverage and it becomes difficult and expensive to raise additional funds needed for its operations and its future investments. Therefore, the firm's management should be careful with its degree of indebtedness not to reach uncontrollable levels. It should choose a low level of leverage, which would mean that it should hold a high level of cash.

IV. CONCLUSIONS

This paper investigated the causality relationships between certain liquidity measures of the company and the company's profitability, as well as between these liquidity measures and the company's indebtedness. The study focused, for the first time, on a panel sample consisting of large non-financial UK companies listed on the London Stock Exchange and made use of advanced econometric techniques, i.e. panel cointegration and panel causality.

The empirical results indicated that although in the relevant literature the cash conversion cycle measure of liquidity has demonstrated certain advantages over the static measures of liquidity, i.e. the current ratio and the quick ratio, all three measures have been shown to play a specific role in terms of causality relationships between liquidity on one hand and profitability as well as indebtedness on the other hand in both the short- and the long-run. In other words, each measure can provide useful information regarding the company's liquidity position as well as the company's profitability.

We could say that our empirical results on causality give an answer to the suggestion for future research of Opler, Pinkowitz, Stulz and Williamson (1999) as to what extent a firm's liquidity and its leverage are two faces of the same coin. Their results indicated that variables making debt costly for a firm were also making cash advantageous, since the determinants of liquidity were closely related to the determinants of leverage. We have found that liquidity causes debt and that debt causes also liquidity based on the indicators we used for each variable, hence we can state that at least, empirically, cash holdings and debt are two faces of the same coin.

Thus, it is recommended to use all three measures in order to get better results and efficiency in the cash management of a company. For future research, a next step could be the partition of this sample by industry sector and examine the same relationships according to specific firm characteristics and industry level differences, if there are any found. Cross-sectional analysis could shed more light and insights in the study of corporate liquidity.

References

Aziz, A. and Lawson, G. (1989), Cash Flow Reporting and Financial Distress Models: Testing of Hypotheses, *Financial Management*, 55-63.

Belt, Brian (1985), The Trend of the Cash Conversion Cycle and its Components, *Akron Business and Economic Review*, 48-54.

Besley, Scott and R. L. Meyer (1987), An Empirical Investigation of Factors Affecting the Cash Conversion Cycle, Paper Presented at the Annual Meeting of the Financial Management Association, Las Vegas, Nevada.

Brealey, A.and S. Myers (1996), *Principles of Corporate Finance*, Fifth Edition, New York, NY: McGraw-Hill Book Co.

Dickey, David A. and Fuller, Wayne A. (1981), Likelihood Ratio Statistics for Autoregressive Time Series with a Unit Root, *Econometrica* 49, 1057-1072.

Engle, Robert F. (1978), Testing Price Equations for Stability Across Spectral Frequency Bands, *Econometrica,* 46, 869-881.

Gallinger, George, W. (1997), The Current and Quick Ratios: Do they Stand up to Scrutiny?: Drop the Current Ratio-pick up the CCC, *Business Credit*, 24-25.

Gentry, James, Vaidyanathan, A. R., and Lee, Hei Wee (1990), A Weighted Cash Conversion Cycle, *Financial Management*, 90-99.

Granger, Clive W., Robbins, Richard, P. and Engle, Robert F. (1986), Wholesale and Retail Process: Bivariate Time-Series Modeling with Forecastable Error Variances, in Belsley and Kuhn (Eds.), *Model Reliability*, Cambridge, Mass.: MIT Press.

Hager, H. C. (1976), Cash Management and Cash Cycle, *Management Accounting*, 19-21.

Im, Kyung S., Pesaran, M. Hashem, and Shin Yonacheol (1997), Testing for Unit Roots in Heterogeneous Panels, Revised Version of Working Paper 9526, Department of Applied Economics, Cambridge University.

Im, Kyung S., Pesaran, M. Hashem, and Shin Yonacheol (1995), Testing for Unit Roots in Heterogeneous panels, Working Paper 9526, Department of Applied Economics, Cambridge University.

John, T.A. (1993), Accounting Measures of Corporate Liquidity, Leverage, and Costs of Financial Distress, *Financial Management*, 91-100.

Kamath, R. (1989), How Useful are Common Liquidity Measures?, *Journal of Cash Management,* 24-28.

Kim, C., Mauer, D.C. and Sherman, A.E. (1998), The Determinants of Corporate Liquidity: Theory and Evidence *Journal of Financial and Quantitative Analysis* 33, 335-359.

Kmenta, Jan (1986), *Elements of Econometrics*. New York: MacMillan Publishing Co.

Largay, James A. and Stickney, Cycle, P. (1980), Cash Flows Ratio Analysis and the W. T. Grant Company Bankruptcy, *Financial Analysts Journal*, 51-54.

Lyroudi, Katerina and McCarty, Dan (1992/93), An Empirical Investigation of the Cash Conversion Cycle of Small Business Firms, *The Journal of Small Business Finance* 2, 139-161.

Lyroudi, K., McCarty, D., Lazaridis, T., Hatzigagios, T. and Papanikolaou, V. (1999), An Empirical Investigation of Liquidity: The case of UK firms, presentation 1999 Annual Meeting of the Financial Management Association in Orlando, Florida, US.

Maness, Terry S. and Zietlow, John T. (2002), *Short-term Financial Management, Second Edition,* South-Western Thomson Learning.

Moss, D. J. and Stine, B. (1993), Cash Conversion Cycle and Firm Size: A Study of Retail Firms, *Managerial Finance* 19, 25-34.

Opler, T., Pinkowitz, L., Stulz, R. and Williamson, R. (1999), The Determinants and Implications of Corporate Cash Holdings, *Journal of Financial Economics* 52, 3-46.

Pedroni, P. (1999), Critical Values for Cointegration: Tests in Heterogeneous Panels with Multiple Regressors, *Oxford Bulletin of Economics and Statistics*, 653-670.

Pesaran, H., M., Shin, Y., and Smith, R., P. (1999), Pooled Mean Group Estimation of Dynamic Heterogeneous Panels, *Journal of the American Statistical Association* 94, 621-634.

Phillips, Peter C. B. and Moon, Hyungsik R. (1999), Linear Regression Limit Theory for Nonstationary Panel Data, *Econometrica* 67, 1057-1112.

Richards, Verlyn, D. and Laughlin, Eugene, J. (1980), A Cash Conversion Cycle Approach to Liquidity Analysis, *Financial Management*, 32-38.

Schilling, George (1996), Working Capital's Role in Maintaining Corporate Liquidity, *TMA Journal*, 4-7.

Shulman, J. M. and Cox, R. A. K. (1985), An Integrative Approach to Working Capital Management, *Journal of Cash Management*, 64-67.

Shyam-Sunder, L. and Myers, S.C. (1998), Testing Static Trade-off Against Pecking Order Models of Capital Structure, *Journal of Financial Economics* 51, 219-244.

Zellner, Arnold (1962), An Efficient Method of Estimating Seemingly Unrelated Regressions and Tests for Aggregation Bias, *Journal of American Statistical Association* 57, 348-368.

A COMPARATIVE ANALYSIS OF TOURISM PERFORMANCE IN THE MEDITERRANEAN REGION: A MULTICRITERIA APPROACH

Jehad Mitwasi, George Baourakis** &*
*Costantin Zopounidis****

ABSTRACT

The aim of this study is to develop and implement a new integrated methodology for the evaluation of the overall tourism performance of selected countries of the world. In this paper, the Multicriteria analysis outranking-method (PROMETHEE II) will be used to examine six Mediterranean countries, namely Turkey, Spain, Italy, Portugal, Egypt and Greece. The analysis result of an overall ranking of the examined countries will be provided by identifying the strong and weak points of each country. This study will also prove that the adopted Multicriteria evaluation and ranking methodology can be successfully used in a comparative study among countries based on different criteria. Assessment of the analysis results is essential to enable tourism professionals to make recommendations regarding marketing strategies, government policies and economic strategies. The study will conclude with a discussion of how future research might be directed.

Keywords: *Tourism performance, Multicriteria decision aid, PROMETHEE method, Mediterranean Region, marketing strategies and policies.*

I. INTRODUCTION

Tourism is emerging as a leading global economic driver for the twenty-first century. "The contribution of tourism to the economic growth of many areas, especially regional ones, is very important to the country." (Zopounidis C., Pardalos P. and Baourakis G., 2001). In the Mediterranean Region it is already as important contributor to employment and wealth creation, with a huge flow-through effect that touches all sectors of the economy. The Mediterranean region is home to a population of 467,049,138 people, it covers an area of 8,602,023 (sq. km) and generates $7,246.951 billion of GDP (The World Factbook, 2005). So, it has enormous potential as a catalyst for future economic and social development throughout the entire Mediterranean region.

* Department of Business Economics and Management, Mediterranean Agronomic Institute of Chania, Greece, *E-mail: jmitwasi@maich.gr*

** Department of Business Economics and Management, Mediterranean Agronomic Institute of Chania, Greece, *E-mail: baouraki@maich.gr*

*** Department of Production Engineering and Management, Financial Engineering Laboratory, Technical University of Crete, Greece, *E-mail: kostas@ergasya.tuc.gr*

Moreover, WTO World Tourism Organization predicts that international tourist arrivals will grow at an average rate of 4.1 percent from 1995-2020, with WTO's Tourism 2020 Vision forecasts that international arrivals are expected to reach over 1.56 billion by the year 2020. Of these worldwide arrivals in 2020, 1.2 billion will be intraregional and 0.4 billion will be long-haul travelers. WTO estimations show that the total tourist arrivals by region indicates that by 2020 the top three receiving regions will be Europe (717 million tourists), East Asia and the Pacific (397 million) and the Americas (282 million), followed by Africa, the Middle East and South Asia.

For this reason, the Mediterranean Region, today, still continues to lead the world in both inbound and outbound international tourism, and will continue to do so in the short and medium term. The factors that have propelled tourism growth in the Mediterranean region include: sunny, hot climate, accessible wildlife, varied and impressive scenery, unspoiled areas, diverse cultures, healthy food, a well developed infra-structure and virtually unlimited opportunities for special interest activities such as hunting, diving, golf, hiking, skiing and so on.

Moreover, some important changes that led to the growth in this region such are the increasing elimination of border formalities, the growing integration of transport systems, cultural relations, increasing intra-regional trade and the development of a dense network of tourism-related enterprises.

As we enter the twenty-first century, many new and exciting opportunities await us in the tourism industry. The advent of globalization has coincided with the boom in the tourism sector. This boom has presented new and exiting challenges. One objective of this study was to give a clear picture of the tourism situation in the Mediterranean region in order to develop a new strategies and policies to remain competitive within the international tourism industry.

The main purpose of this research is to introduce a new approach for evaluating the tourism performance of selected countries from the Mediterranean Region. The assessment procedure utilizes the techniques of multicriteria analysis method (PROMETHEE II method). The case studies used for conducting the empirical research are: Turkey, Spain, Italy, Greece, Portugal and Egypt. The results of the multicriteria analysis are used to estimate the tourism parameters which would determine the tourism weaknesses and the strength which the examined countries face nowadays and will also formulate an operational modeling framework for the evaluation and prediction of tourism performance. First the methodological framework for this research is outlined. Then the results and relevant discussion issues are presented. The article ends with suggestions for further lines of research.

II. THE METHODOLOGICAL FRAMEWORK

Multicriteria methods were found to be useful tools to support decision-making in carrying out a comparisons evaluation. A great number of multicriteria algorithms are now available: Refer to Zadeh, 1965; Quinl, 1993; Ripley, 1996; Greco *et al.*, 2002, mathematical programming (Stam, 1997) and MCDA (ELECTRE TRI, UTADIS and MHDIS methods); Roy and Bouyssou, 1993; Doumpos and Zopounidis, 2002; Zopounidis and Doumpos, 2000, 2002. The algorithms differ in fundamental ways. In addition to the algorithms also the implementation of the valuation technique is important for the outcome.

The focus of multicriteria analysis is on the development of appropriate methodologies for the evaluation of a set of alternative solutions. Within the context of this study, the PROMETHEE II multicriteria method (Preference Ranking Organization Method of Enrichment Evaluations; Brans and Vincke, 1985) techniques will be used to assess the performance of six Mediterranean countries with respect to their tourism activities.

III. THE PROMETHEE METHOD

The analysts Roy and Vincke (1981) reported that: before the development of the Multicriteria analysis, the problems of decision-making were well stated involving the optimization of an economic function or a *n* utility function. For instance, the following problem:

Max $\{f(a) \mid a \in K\}$, (K = the set of alternative solutions), is a well-stated problem because the determination of an optimal solution ã, so that $f(\tilde{a}) \geq f(a)$, $\forall$ a $\in K$, makes sense. We obtain a complete graph by considering the actions of K as nodes, and for all, a and b $\in K$, and arc(ab) if $f(a) \geq f(b)$.

On the other hand, the Multicriteria problem:

Max $[f_1(a), f_2(a), \ldots f_h(a), \ldots f_k(a) \mid a \in K]$, where $f_h(a)$, h = 1, 2, 3, ...k are k criteria, in general will not induce a general preorder on K. The problem is no longer well-stated because the notion of the optimal solution makes no sense. In general, there exist no solution ã so that $f_h(a) \geq f_h(b), \forall h \in \{1, 2, 3, \ldots k\}$, on at least of the inequalities being strict. We consequently obtain on K a partial order (transitive relation) called dominance order. If the action of K are again supposed to be the nodes of a graph, called dominance graph. Each arc (ab) represents the dominant character of a over b. The dominance order is, in general, very poor, even when only few criteria are considered, so the dominance graph does not have many arcs. It frequently occurs that the dominance order is empty. In order to support the decision maker who must solve Multicriteria problems, some methods were essentially considered, Fande and, Spronk (1983) presented the following distinctions:

- Multiattributive utility theory (MAUT)
- Outranking methods
- Interactive methods

The PROMETHEE method originates from the outranking relations concept, which was found and developed by Roy (1968) and then it was firstly introduced by Brans *et al.* (1984). "The outranking approach is based on pair-wise comparisons between potential actions, using a binary, so-called outranking relation" (Vincke, 1992). A big advantage of the PROMETHEE approach is its fairly low degree of mathematical complexity which should make its results transparent for decision makers who are often non-experts.

"The outranking method approach brings less intense results than the value function methods as there is usually no ranking of best to worst options. It does not introduce mathematical hypotheses and demands less information from the decision maker". (Vincke, Gassner and Roy, 1989).

Furthermore, with the most important publications being those of Brans and Vincke (1985), and Brans, Vincke and Mareschall (1986), the main principles upon which the PROMETHEE method is based are:

1. Extension of the notion of criteria
2. Valued outranking relation
3. Exploitation of outranking relation

The extension of the criterion notion is based on the introduction of a preference function giving the preference of the decision-maker for an action a with regard to b. This function is defined separately for each criterion, its value lies between 0 and 1. The smaller the function, the greater the indifference of the decision-maker; the closer to 1, the greater his preference. In case of strict preference, the function will be 1.

There are 6 so called generalized criteria, which according to the analysts, cover most cases in practical applications. Let H (d) be a function which is related directly with the preference function P, then for two alternative solutions a and b, H (d) is defined as follows:

$$H(d)=\begin{cases} P(a,b), d\geq 0 \\ P(b,a), d\leq 0 \end{cases}$$

The H function can be of various different forms, depending upon the judgment policy of the decision maker. Generally, six forms of the H function are commonly used as presented in Table 1 (Appendix I).

1. Calculating the Preference Index

On the basis of the six types of the generalized criteria defined in the aforementioned table, a preference index is calculated by the following mathematical formula:

$$\prod(a,b)=\frac{\sum \Pi_i \, p_i(a,b)}{\sum \Pi}$$

Where Π_i is the weight for each criterion f_i ($i = 1, 2, 3, ...k$), $\Pi(a, b)$ represents the intensity of the preference for the alternative a with regard to b, when the criterion are considered simultaneously. The weight increases with the importance of the criterion. The criteria's weights constitute the basis for the assessment of the degree of preference for alternative a over alternative b. The preference index for each pair of alternatives (a,b) ranges between 0 and 1. $\Pi(a,b)\approx 0$ means weak preference of the alternative solution a with regard to b, for all the criteria. $\Pi(a,b)\approx 1$ means strong preference of the alternative solution a with regard to b for all the criteria.

As for the exploitation of the outranking relation for the rank of the alternatives, two flows are defined; the outflow is calculated as follows:

$$\phi^{+}(a)=\sum_{b=k}\Pi(a,b), \quad K = \text{the set of alternatives}$$

And the inflow is calculated:

$\phi^-(a)=\Pi(a,b)$

A high value of $\phi^+(a)$ means that the alternative a outranks the other alternatives of the set K, while the smallest value of $\phi^-(a)$ means that the alternative action a is dominated by the other alternatives. We can then consider that for each action $a \in K$ the net-flow:

$\phi(a)=\phi^+(a)-\phi^-(a)$

As a matter of fact, there are five PROMETHEE methods but the most well-known are PROMETHEE I and PROMETHEE II. PROMETHEE I realizes the partial ranking of the actions, while PROMETHEE II realizes the complete ranking of the actions. In addition, PROMETHEE II is relatively simple in the involvement of criteria importance (weights) and in the computational procedure. Therefore, in our case, only PROMETHEE II will be used. The version labeled PROMETHEE II provides a complete ranking of the alternatives on the basis of the net flow:

$\phi(a)=\phi^+(a)-\phi^-(a)$

Therefore, we have:

- a outranks *bif* $\phi(a) > \phi(b)$ if
- a and b are indifferent alternatives if $\phi(a) = \phi(b)$

2. The Weights

We have decided that the type of generalized criteria chosen in this study, is the Gaussian type (see Table 1, Appendix I). Now, the next step is to decide on the weights. The weights are very important parameters in the application of the PROMETHEE method. The decision as to what weights to use is the exclusive responsibility of the decision-maker. If the decision maker considers that specific criteria are relatively more important than the others, then the weight coefficient of this ratio will be higher than that of others, and vice versa. In this way, the alternative that has a high performance on this ratio will have an advantage compared with the others that do not have such high performances. In our study, we did not have any decision-maker that could specify the weights of the tourism criteria. Therefore, the robustness of the results is analyzed for different settings of the weights. This is carried out by taking into consideration the different weighting scenarios. In particular, in this study 50 weighting scenarios are implemented. In each scenario, the criteria's weights are considered as uniformly distributed random variables in [0, 1], normalized so that the sum adds up to 1. In this way, different cases for the relative importance of the criteria are analyzed and the stability/robustness of the results is explored. In addition to the weight scenarios, different specifications of the σ parameter of the Gaussian generalized criterion are also analyzed. In particular, 10 settings are considered for σ, ranging from 0.25s up to 2.5s, where s is the standard deviation of the pairwise differences of the alternatives on each criterion.

3. The Criteria Modeling

A criterion is a qualitative or quantitative expression that permits a judgment of the consequence or the performance of an alternative for an objective or a constraint. A criterion must be useful and reliable. In our case, criteria were intended to provide a tool for determining the user-established preference in relation to the alternatives. The selection of criteria was based on information gathered from the Euromonitor International Company (2006) pertaining to the "Tourism Parameters" that allowed judgment of the performance of one alternative in comparison to another.

The criteria should be clearly defined and directly relevant to the assessment because it is necessary to ensure a meaningful outcome of the implementation of the PROMETHEE method. For this reason, and after digging deeper in the description of the selected criteria, we discovered that some of the criteria required some adjustments as it is described below.

The following criteria are used in our evaluation of the countries:

(1) The incoming number of arrivals of a country is a positive preference and it is adjusted to the size of the population in that country, because it indicates the maximum capacity of tourists that can visit the specified country. For illustration purposes, Greece is a country of approximately 11 million people and had about 14 thousand incoming arrivals for the year 2003, and Turkey is a country of approximately 68 million people and also has about 14 thousand incoming arrivals; therefore, in this example, Greece is preferred to Turkey in terms of the incoming number of arrivals, as Turkey has the capacity to welcome more tourist in terms of hotels, rooms, beds, transportation, etc.

To adjust for this criterion, the following ratio must be calculated:

$$\text{Criterion 1} = \frac{\textit{Incoming number of arrivals of acountry}}{\textit{Population of that country}}$$

(2) The outgoing number of departures of a country reflects a negative preference on the specified country. In other words, the more the departures are, the more the spending outside the country. However, we don't know how much exactly each tourist departures from his country will spend outside the country. For example, 5,000 departures from Turkey might spend less than 1,000 departures from Spain and so on.

The same also applies to the total number of domestic trips, but the domestic trips give a sign of active domestic tourism inside the specified country; therefore, it reflects a positive preference.

For this reason, out of these two criteria, we can make a ratio that represents the travelers outside and inside the specified country; thus, we refer to the dynamicity of tourism inside the specified country without referring to how much they spend, as follows:

$$\text{Criterion 2} = \frac{\textit{The outgoing number of departures in a country}}{\textit{Total number of domestic trips in that country}}$$

(3) Incoming per capita expenditure is not adjusted and has a positive preference for the evaluation. Therefore:

Criterion 3 = Incoming per capita expenditure of the country

(4) Outgoing per capita expenditure is adjusted and has a negative preference for the evaluation, adjusted as follows:

Criterion 4 = Outgoing per capita expenditure of the country * –1

(5) Per capita expenditure per domestic trip is not adjusted and has a positive preference for the evaluation. Therefore:

Criterion 5 = Per capita expenditure per domestic trip in the country

(6) Total tourism spending has a positive preference to the evaluation and is adjusted to the size of the incoming tourists as well as domestic tourist of the population in the specified country; thereby, it is calculated as follows:

$$\text{Criterion 6} = \frac{\textit{Total tourism spending of the country}}{\textit{The number of incoming tourists and domestic tourists of that country}}$$

(7) Accommodation spending has a positive preference to the evaluation and is also adjusted to the size of the incoming tourists as well as domestic tourists of the population in the specified country; thereby it is calculated as follows:

$$\text{Criterion 7} = \frac{\textit{Accommodation spending of the country}}{\textit{The number of incoming tourists and domestic tourists of that country}}$$

(8) Holiday taking is a percentage of the population considered as holiday takers; it needs no adjustment and has a positive preference to the evaluation. Thereby:

Criterion 8 = Holiday Taking (% of the population) in that country

By using the methodology that is described above, the PROMETHEE II contributes significantly towards making an integrated and rational evaluation and assessment of the performance and viability of the tourism countries examined in this study, by specifying the impact of all those factors (Tourism Parameters) on them.

IV. THE APPLICATION OF THE PROMETHEE II

This is a quantitative research and the completion of this research demanded quality information and particular data that is used for the analysis of this study. This information is accessible only by a limited number of international companies; therefore, a lot of money is required. However, fortunately, we have acquired this information from the Euromonitor International Company.

So, upon deciding on the alternatives, criteria and the weights, we prepared the data for the criteria that we acquired from the Euromonitor International Company. I got the data for five consecutive years for each of the selected countries; that is from 1999 till 2003. The data were organized and set in tables in excel sheets and executed in the PROMETHEE II software.

1. The Results

The results of evaluating the tourism performance of the six countries are displayed in the following tables.

Table 2
PROMETHEE Results

1999		*2000*	
Value	*Country*	*Value*	*Country*
1.782122	Italy	1.207682	Italy
1.22898	Greece	1.171958	Greece
0.142434	Spain	0.333325	Spain
-0.90532	Turkey	-0.68937	Turkey
-1.05123	Egypt	-0.99632	Egypt
-1.19699	Portugal	-1.02727	Portugal

2001		*2002*	
Value	*Country*	*Value*	*Country*
1.109583	Italy	1.276083	Italy
0.9788	Greece	1.139551	Greece
0.26591	Spain	0.267881	Spain
-0.42136	Turkey	-0.52518	Turkey
-0.95326	Egypt	-0.73089	Portugal
-0.97967	Portugal	-1.42744	Egypt

2003		*Average*	
Value	*Country*	*Value*	*Country*
1.300918	Italy	1.335278	Italy
1.216617	Greece	1.147181	Greece
0.25465	Spain	0.25284	Spain
-0.64635	Portugal	-0.67067	Turkey
-0.81209	Turkey	-0.91095	Portugal
-1.31374	Egypt	-1.11213	Egypt

The aforementioned table is simplified in another table that would make it easier to understand. The table presents a comparative ranking in relation to the chosen criteria used in the evaluation for five consecutive years. Moreover, the table shows the average tourism performance of the five years (see Table 3, Appendix I).

2. Discussions of the Results

Italy: The results from Table 5 reveal that the best ranked firm, throughout the years and for all the scenarios is Italy. Italy represents one of the most attractive international destinations for all age bands, from low budget, young backpackers to high-income old couples. In fact, the tourism infrastructure, although quite expensive, especially in the most popular arts cities (such as

Florence or Venice) and in the most exclusive seaside resorts (such as Capri or Portofino), allows a quite broad range of solutions.

Greece: Greece and Spain have the largest number of incoming arrivals ratio (Criterion 1), but the reasons that allowed Greece to rank in second place is that it kept on being the first in terms of per capita expenditure per domestic trips (Criterion 5) and total tourism spending (Criterion 6) throughout all the years, supporting the fact that Greeks would like to take domestic trips and spend a lot of money on leisure.

Spain: There are several reasons that led Spain to come in third place. The accommodation spending (Criterion 7) and total tourism spending (Criterion 6) by tourists and locals comes in third place. Actually, the global economic slowdown and the drop in the number of German tourists visiting the country were significant factors constraining further growth, especially during the latter years of the review period. Also, the per capita expenditure per domestic trips (Criterion 5) is relatively low; the major cause is due to the increasing trend towards taking shorter breaks. This occurs because many of the trips of fewer than four days are made by Spaniards to their second homes. These trips are frequently made at weekends. In Spain, over one fourth of all households own second homes, in most cases located in the same region as their main home. This demonstrates that tourism spending is not high enough inside Spain but still active.

Turkey: Turkey comes in the fourth place for all the years except for the year 2003 when it ranked fifth. This happened due to several reasons. First, Turkey's per capita expenditure of incoming arrivals (Criterion 3) has dramatically decreased from the year 2002 up to the year 2003. As a consequence of currency fluctuations the total amount spent can vary considerably from one year to another. "A remarkable change of inflation rate, down to 55.7% is noticed from the year 1999 to 2004. (The World Factbook, 2005)". This shows that the Turkish economy is developing strongly and the Turkish lira has regained much ground against the major foreign currencies, and this has made Turkey a relatively expensive country for those coming from developed countries.

Portugal: Portugal has had, relatively speaking, the lowest performance from 1999 to 2001. The main reason for this is that the outgoing per capita expenditure (Criterion 4) has been very high compared to the other six countries. The prices of flights leaving Portugal fell substantially over the review period in real terms, reflecting an increasingly competitive airline sector. This encouraged Portuguese holidaymakers to take more holidays abroad and to choose increasingly exotic locations. Portuguese international travelers are increasingly flying to non-European destinations, which added considerable value to outgoing tourism expenditure, as non-European trips tend to be longer and the number of days spent away higher. During the year 2002, Portugal ranked in fifth place, the availability of budget and time to take holiday trips (Criterion 8) has been gradually increasing. This growth principally reflects increasing levels of affluence, a more cosmopolitan population and the increasing availability of budget holidays, which also led to the raise of the dynamicity of the tourism environment (Criterion 2). Also, the per capita expenditure per domestic trips (Criterion 5) increased, underpinned by an increase in luxury tourist facilities such as golf and leisure clubs and 5-star hotels. In 2003, growth in accommodation sales was supported by the rising number of hotels at the luxury end of the market, which commanded higher prices. So, Portugal moved to the fourth place.

Egypt: Egypt ranked in fifth place in the year 1999, 2000 and 2001. Egypt relatively maintained the lowest number of incoming arrivals ratio (Criterion 1). The availability of budget and time to take holiday trips (Criterion 8) has been very low because only a small portion of the population is financially able to travel. There is a decline in the per capita expenditure per domestic trips (Criterion 5) due to financial constraints and altered expenditure priorities. In the year 2002 and 2003, the incoming per capita expenditure (Criterion 3) incurred a sharp decrease, as one-week package holidays from Europe are available at ever lower prices, resulting in declining per capita expenditure amongst incoming tourists. Also, accommodation spending (Criterion 7) and total tourism spending (Criterion 6) by tourists and locals have been steadily decreasing throughout all the years, lower spending on accommodation in 2002 and 2003 is attributed to the price-slashing tactics employed by the management of hotels in an attempt to lessen the blow in the aftermath of 11 September 2001, which led Egypt to move to the sixth place.

V. CONCLUDING REMARKS

The use of the PROMETHEE method is a first experimental effort undertaken in order to evaluate the tourism performance of the examined countries. Replications of the proposed methodology are suggested, which might utilize other multicriteria decision aid techniques, (ex. ELECTRE[1] by Roy, (1991)) that allow one to introduce the veto effects which could be important for modeling real preferences.

The results of the current study enhance our understanding concerning examined countries tourism performance. It can be considered as a first step towards building a tourism decision-making tool that can provide interesting tourism insights to scholars, researchers and professionals working in the tourism sector. Thus, they can have clearer indications of whether or not to revise the countries tourism strategies and possibly the market behavior. Through increased tourism performance evaluation both up and downstream, a country may raise the specter of the traditional servicing, producing, processing and marketing companies' role in counterbalancing tourism and market power.

All the selected countries in this study have the skills and resources for successful tourism development and growth, but it is a matter of identifying the strengths and the weaknesses of tourism behavior, so we could develop our strategies and policies accordingly. As a matter of fact, planning for tourism provides improvements of tourism performance. However, planning does not guarantee a stable tourism performance, as there are always other external or internal factors which have not been considered in our plans that may arise in the future of any country, but it does guarantee that if anything happen in this matter, the country would have the strong background for a quick recovery.

References

Brans J., Vinke P. and Mareschal B. (1984), PROMETHEE: A New Family of Outranking Methods in Multicriteria Analysis, in J.P. Brans, ed., Operations Research '84, Elsevier Science Publishers, pp. 477-490.

Brans, J. and Vincke P. (1985), A Preference Ranking Organization Method: The PROMETHEE Method for Multiple Criteria Decision-making. *Management Science* 31, pp. 647-656.

Brans J., Vincke P. and Mareschal B. (1986), How to Select and How to Rank Projects: the PROMETHEE Method, *European Journal of Operational Research* 24, pp. 228-238.

Doumpos M. and Zopounidis C. (2002), Multicriteria Decision Aid Classification Methods. Kluwer Academic Publishers, Dordrecht.

Fandel G. and Spronk J. (1983), Multiple Criteria-Decision Methods and Applications, Springer Verlag, Berlin.

Greco S., Matarazzo B. and Slowinski R. (2002), Multicriteria Classification. In: Klogsen, W., Zytkow, J. (Eds.), Handbook of Data Mining and Knowledge Discovery, Oxford University Press, Oxford, pp. 318-328.

Quinlan J. (1993), C4.5: Programs for Machine Learning, Morgan Kaufmann Publishers, Los Altos, CA.

Ripley B. (1996), Pattern Recognition and Neural Networks, Cambridge University Press, Cambridge.

Roy B. (1968), Classement et choix en pre´sence de points de vue multiples: La me´thode ELECTRE. In R.I.R.O, volume 8, pp. 57-75.

Roy B. and Vincke P. (1981), Multicriteria Analysis: Survey and New Directions, *European Journal of Operational Research,* volume 8, pp. 207-218.

Roy B. (1991), The Outranking Approach and the Foundations of ELECTRE Methods. Theory and Decision 31, pp. 49-73.

Roy B. and Bouyssou D. (1993), Aide Multicrit_ere _a la D_ecision: M_ethodes et Cas, Economica, Paris.

Stam A., (1997). Nontraditional approaches to statistical classification: Some perspectives on lp-norm methods, Annals of Operations Research 74, pp. 1-36.

Vincke P., Gassner M. and Roy B. (1989), Multicriteria Decision Aid, Wiley & Sons, West Sussex.

Vincke P. (1992), Multicriteria Decision Aid. John Wiley, New York.

Zadeh L. (1965), Fuzzy sets. Information and Control 8, pp. 338-353.

Zopounidis C. and Doumpos M. (2000), Building Additive Utilities for multi-group Hierarchical Discrimination: The MHDIS Method, Optimization Methods and Software 14 (3), pp. 219-240.

Zopounidis C. and Doumpos M. (2002), Multicriteria Classification and Sorting Methods: A Literature Review, *European Journal of Operational Research* 138 (2), pp. 229-246.

Zopounidis C., Pardalos P. and Baourakis G. (2001), The Tourism Industry in Crete: The Identification of New Market Segments. *Fuzzy sets in Management, Economics and Marketing*, World Scientific, P. 116.

Websites

Euromonitor Internaltional. Travel and Tourism. Available from http://www.euromonitor.com/. Accessed 4 January 2006.

The World Factbook. Available from http://www.cia.gov/cia/publications/factbook/. Accessed 11 February 2006.

World Travel and Tourism Council. Available from http://www.wttc.org/. Accessed 27 April 2006.

World Tourism Organization. Available from http://www.world-tourism.org/. Accessed 29 April 2006.

APPENDIX I

Table 1
Forms of the preference function

Criteria Name	*Graphical Form*	*Function Form*	*Parameter*
1. Usual criterion		$H(d)=\begin{cases}0 \text{ if } d=0\\ 1 \text{ if } d\neq 0\end{cases}$	–
2. Quasi-criterion		$H(d)=\begin{cases}0 \text{ if } -q\leq d\leq q\\ 1 \text{ if } d<-q \text{ or } d>q\end{cases}$	q
3. Criterian with linear preference		$H(d)=\begin{cases}d/p \text{ if } -q\leq d\leq q\\ 1 \text{ if } d<-p \text{ or } d>p\end{cases}$	p
4. Level criterion		$H(d)=\begin{cases}0 \text{ if } \lvert d\rvert\leq q\\ 1/2 \text{ if } q<\lvert d\rvert\leq p\\ 1 \text{ if } q<\lvert d\rvert\end{cases}$	q.p
5. Criterion with linear preference and indifference area		$H(d)=\begin{cases}0 \text{ if } \lvert d\rvert\leq q\\ (\lvert d\rvert-q)/(p-q) \text{ for } q<\lvert d\rvert\leq p \ q.p\\ 1 \text{ for } p<\lvert d\rvert\end{cases}$	q.p
6. Gaussian criterian		$H(d)=1-\exp\{-d^2/2\sigma^2\}$	σ

Source: Brans, Vinke and Mareschal, 1986.

Table 3
The Tourism Performance Evaluation Results for the Years 1999-2003

Rank/Year	*1999*	*2000*	*2001*	*2002*	*2003*	*Average Rankin[2] 1999-2003*
1.	Italy	Italy	Italy	Italy	Italy	Italy
2.	Greece	Greece	Greece	Greece	Greece	Greece
3.	Spain	Spain	Spain	Spain	Spain	Spain
4.	Turkey	Turkey	Turkey	Turkey	Portugal	Turkey
5.	Egypt	Egypt	Egypt	Portugal	Turkey	Portugal
6.	Portugal	Portugal	Portugal	Egypt	Egypt	Egypt

Source: Compiled by the authors, 2006.

ASYMMETRIC VOLATILITY AND STOCHASTIC BEHAVIOR OF THE BOMBAY STOCK EXCHANGE

*Mazhar M. Islam**

ABSTRACT

This paper applies the family of ARCH models to examine the asymmetric volatile behavior of Bombay Stock Exchange (BSE) Price Index. The data include daily observations for BSE 30 price index covering the period from July 1, 1997 through February 27, 2005. The data are obtained from the MSCI, and are based on closing adjusted daily series. Empirical results show that GARCH (2,1) model can adequately describe the BSE indicating that BSE. The estimated TARCH and EGARCH parameter s show that the impact of news is symmetric, indicating there is no existence of the leverage effect in future prices of the stock. The overall results indicate the long-run components converge very rapidly to the steady state, and the short run volatility components appear to be insignificant.

I. INTRODUCTION

A significant amount of empirical research has been conducted to investigate the behavior of asset return volatility over time. Attempts to explain this volatility in stock markets have focused in recent research on the issue of modeling time-varying volatility and the implied stochastic prices for expected returns. This phenomenon of securities' volatility has important implications for security pricing and risk management. Among the most popular techniques currently used to capture the clustering effect and to forecast future volatility, belong to the family of Autoregressive Conditional Heteroskedastic (ARCH) models. Engle (1982) introduced ARCH model that permits a changing conditional variance. This model was subsequently extended by Bollerslev (1986) as GARCH process that allows for more flexible structure in the model. The ARCH models are designed to model and forecast the variance of the dependent variable. There are several reasons that we may need to forecast volatility. First, we may need to deal with volatility to understand the risk of holding a stock. Second, forecast confidence intervals may be time varying so that more accurate intervals can be obtained by modeling the variance of the errors. Third, more efficient estimators can be obtained if heteroskedasticity in the errors is handled appropriately. Schwert (1989) has undertaken an extensive study of stock market volatility by using historical data back to the 19th century. His findings show that the stock market volatility tends to increase dramatically during financial crises and periods of uncertainty.

* Professor of Finance & Director of Research, School of Business, Alabama A&M University, Huntsville, *E-mail: mazhar.islam@email.aaamu.edu*

This paper was presented at the Academy of Finance annual meetings in Chicago, March 2006.

Moreover he finds that volatility, once risen, shows some inertia in that it reverts only slowly to its previous, low level. Shiller (1981) argues that stock prices are more volatile than what is justified by time variation in dividends. Schwert (1989) also concludes that stock market volatility cannot be fully explained by changes in economic fundamentals. Campbell et al. (2001) argues that stock market volatility is related to structural change in the economy. They also find that the volatility has significant predictive power for real GDP growth. Lamoureux and Lastrapes (1990) employ a GARCH model to examine the impact of information flow on the volatility of stocks.

While the behavior of other securities markets has been examined extensively, little attention has been paid towards an extensive analysis of the volatility of the emerging stock market of India. Indian economy has been characterized by a diversified industrial base, a growing, world-class IT and software development sector, and a relatively large and sophisticated financial sector. India has been gradually transforming its economic base from agrarian to industrial and commercial. The agricultural sector accounts for 23.6 percent of GDP, the industrial sector 28.4 percent, and services sector 48 percent. Rapid economic progress has often been the precursor to political reform and liberalization. During the Persian Gulf conflict in 1991, India faced a financial crisis because of rising oil prices, which stimulated economic reforms and liberalization. These reforms removed most of the government regulations on investment, including many on foreign investment, and eliminated the quota and tariff system. Government also deregulated a number of industries and privatized many public enterprises. GDP grew at an average of more than six percent through the year 2000. Private investment has been the fuel for India's recent economic success; domestic savings and investment is now about 22 percent of GDP. While foreign direct investment reached a record high of US$3.6 billion in 1997, 20 times higher than it was in the last decade. In recent years the economy has been growing over six percent. The inflation rate is under control. India's balance of payments has been characterized by modest current account deficits and financial account surpluses sufficient to finance the current account and allow the country to more than double its international reserves to over US$44 billion as of year-end 2001. The volume of financial flows into and out of India is also small in relation to the size of the economy. India's large population and a stable democratic institution offer excellent environment for foreign investors. (*Sources: World Bank (www.worldbank.org) and IMF (www.imf.org) Ministry Of Finance(India), Reserve Bank of India and Asian Development Bank (www.adb.org).*

This study attempts to model the time-varying properties of volatility of the Indian stock market along the lines of Engle (1982) and Bollerslev (1986). The Bombay Stock Exchange 30 (BSE) is used as a proxy for the Indian market. The remainder of this paper is organized as follows. Section II discusses the data and the methodology. The empirical results is discussed in section III, while section IV concludes the paper.

II. DATA AND METHODOLOGY

The data include 1,844 daily observations for BSE 30 price index covering the period from July 1, 1997 through February 27, 2005. The data are obtained from the MSCI, and are based on closing adjusted daily series.

ARCH Models

ARCH models are widely used in various branches of econometrics, especially in financial time series analysis. We use ARCH to refer to both ARCH and GARCH models. An ARCH model requires to consider two distinct specifications—one for the conditional mean and one for the conditional variance. The most widely used ARCH modeling group in finance is GARCH (1,1) where today's variance depends on three factors: a constant (long term average), yesterday's news about volatility which taken to be the squared residual from yesterday (the ARCH term) and yesterday's forecast variance (the GARCH term). This specification makes sense in the stock market where investors predict today's variance by forming a weighted average of a long term average (or constant variance), the forecast from yesterday (GARCH term), and what was learned from yesterday's news (ARCH term).

In the standard GARCH (1,1) specification:

$$y_t = x_t\gamma + \varepsilon_t \tag{1}$$

$$\sigma_t^2 = \omega + \alpha\varepsilon_{t-1}^2 + \beta\sigma_{t-1}^2 \tag{2}$$

The mean equation (1) is written as a function of exogenous variables with an error term. Since σ_t^2 is the one-period ahead forecast variance based on past information, it is called the *conditional variance.* The conditional variance equation (2) is a function of three terms: the mean ω; news about volatility from the previous period, measured as the lag of the squared residual from the mean equation ε_{t-1}^2 (the (ARCH term); and the last period's forecast variance $\sigma\frac{2}{t}$ (the GARCH term). The (1,1) in GARCH (1,1) refers to the presence of a first-order GARCH term and a first-order ARCH term. An ordinary ARCH model is a special case of a GARCH specification in which there are no lagged forecast variances in the conditional variance equation. This specification is often interpreted in a financial context, where an agent or trader predicts this period's variance by forming a weighted average of a long term average (the constant), the forecasted variance from last period (the GARCH term), and information about volatility observed in the previous period (the ARCH term). If the asset return was unexpectedly high in either the upward or the downward direction, then the trader will increase the estimate of the variance for the next period. This model is also consistent with the volatility clustering often seen in stock returns data, where large changes in returns are likely to be followed by further large changes.

The GARCH (p, q) model is:

$$\sigma_t^2 = \omega + \sum_{i=1}^{q} \alpha_i \varepsilon_{t-i}^2 + \sum_{i=1}^{p} \beta_i \sigma_{t-i}^2 \tag{2a}$$

where $\omega > 0$, $\alpha_i \geq 0$, $\beta_i \geq 0$,

$$\sum_{i=1}^{q}\alpha_i + \sum_{i=1}^{p}\beta_i < 1$$

σ_t^2 is the conditional variance, ω, α and β are the constant parameters, $\sum_{i=1}^{p}\alpha_i\varepsilon_{t-i}^2$ (the ARCH terms) are news about volatility from the previous periods, and $\sum_{i=1}^{q}\beta_i\sigma_{t-i}^2$ (the GARCH terms) are past period's forecast variances. For the conditional volatility of the model to be well defined, all parameters are required to be non-negative, and the sum of all α and β must be less than unity. This model can effectively deal with the volatility clustering displayed by many financial time series, where large changes are often followed by further large changes. The specification decision, i.e., the determination of the optimal lag structure (p, q), is made by applying the Schwarz Bayesian Criterion (SBC). Among the different GARCH (p, q) models, the GARCH (1,1) specification is found to be the best.

The TARCH Model

In the financial markets, it is found that downward movements are often followed by higher volatilities than upward movements of the same magnitude. The basic GARCH model cannot capture this asymmetry and more models are developed. Among all the models that allow for asymmetric shocks to volatility, we consider both TARCH and EGARCH models. Since these models allow for the leverage effect, we would expect them to be superior to the basic GARCH models. TARCH models was proposed independently by Glosten, Jaganathan, and Runkle(1993) and Zakoian (1994). The TARCH (p, q) specification is:

$$\sigma_t^2 = \omega + \sum_{i=1}^{q}\alpha_i\varepsilon_{t-i}^2 + \sum_{i=1}^{p}\beta_i\sigma_{t-i}^2 + \gamma(\varepsilon_{t-1})^2 d_{t-1} \tag{3}$$

where $d_t = 1$ if $\varepsilon_{t-1} < 0$, and 0 otherwise. In this specification, good news and bad news would have different effects on the conditional volatility. If $\gamma \neq 0$, then there exists asymmetric effect: good news ($\varepsilon_{t-1} > 0$) has an impact of α, while bad news ($\varepsilon_{t-1} < 0$) has an impact of $\alpha + \gamma$. The optimal lag structure is found to be (1,1), hence the TARCH(1,1) specification is selected.

The EGARCH Model

An exponential version of the GARCH model, or EGARCH, was proposed by Nelson (1991). The EGARCH specification for the conditional volatility is:

$$\log\sigma_t^2 = \omega + \sum_{i=1}^{p}\beta_i\log\sigma_{t-i}^2 + \sum_{i=1}^{q}\left(\alpha_i\left|\frac{\varepsilon_{t-i}}{\sigma_{t-i}} - \sqrt{\frac{2}{\pi}}\right| + \gamma_i\frac{\varepsilon_{t-i}}{\sigma_{t-i}}\right) \tag{4}$$

the parameter g gives the asymmetry in this model. The log term implies that the leverage effect is exponential and that the conditional variance is guaranteed to be nonnegative, i.e., no restrictions on the parameters are necessary to ensure $\sigma_t^2 \geq 0$. Like TARCH models, this EGARCH model allows good news ($\varepsilon_{t-i} > 0$) and bad news ($\varepsilon_{t-i} < 0$) to have a different impact on volatility. The asymmetric effects would depend on the sign of the γ term. If $\gamma = 0$, there is no asymmetry. If $\gamma < 0$, good news reduce volatility. If $\gamma > 0$, good news increase volatility.

III. EMPIRICAL RESULTS

The data used for the analysis were 1843 daily observations for the period of July 1997 to February 2005. The data were obtained from the MSCI website data base. Graph 1 shows the random behavior of the stock price series. Graph 2 of the return series clearly shows volatility clustering, while Graph 3 exhibits the GARCH of conditional variance of the stock price series.

Descriptive statistics are reported in Table 1. The number of observation is 1843. The mean is 6.23. Volatility (measured as a standard deviation) is 0.275. The positive skewness indicates that the upper tail of the distribution is thicker than the lower tail, that is, the index increases occur more often than its declines. The J-B tests reject the normality hypothesis indicating fat tail.

Graph 1: Behavior of Bombay Stock Prices

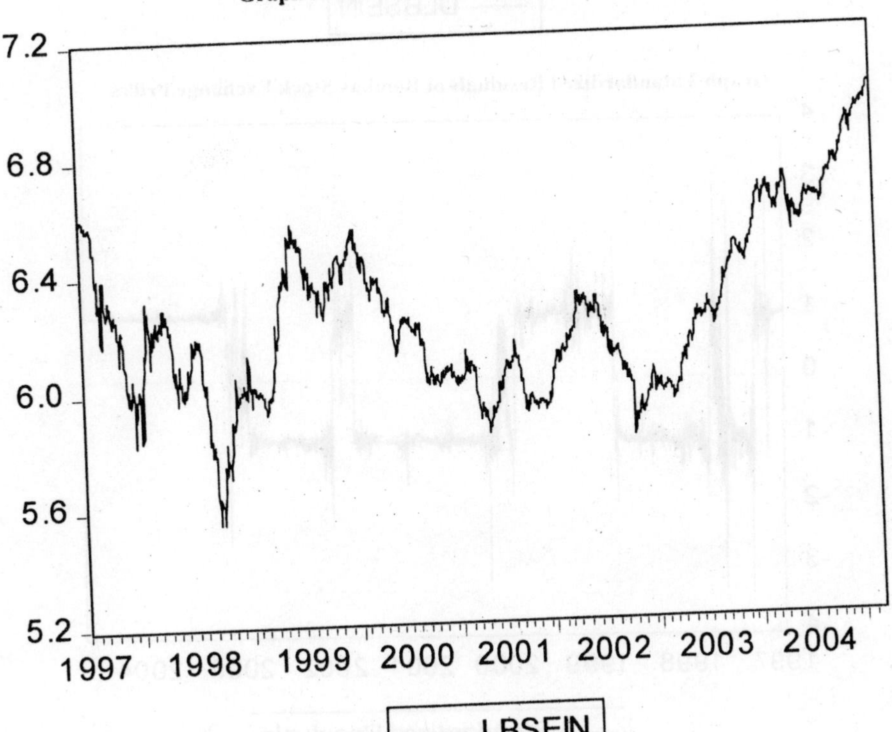

Graph 2: Behavior of Bombay Stock Exchange Stock Returns

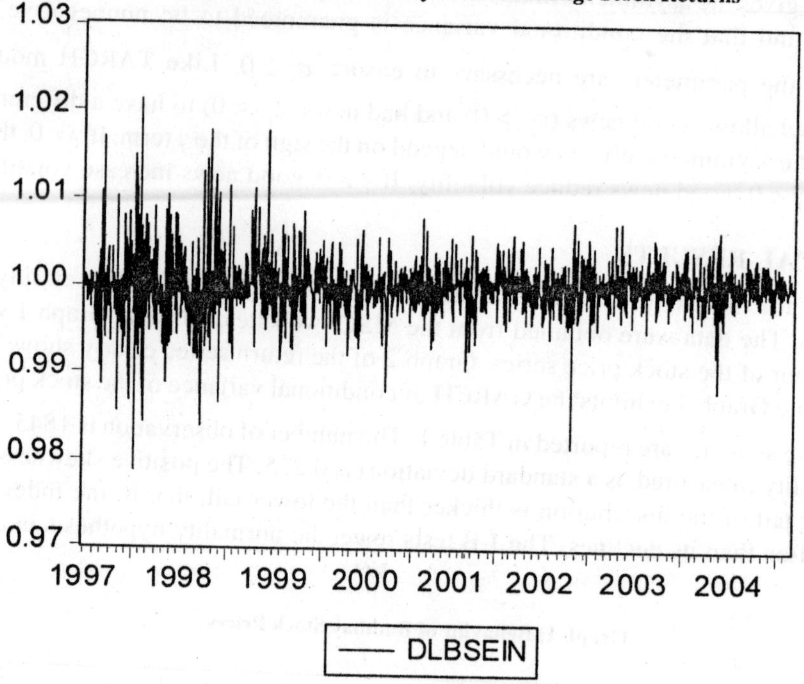

Graph 2 Standardized Residuals of Bombay Stock Exchange Prices

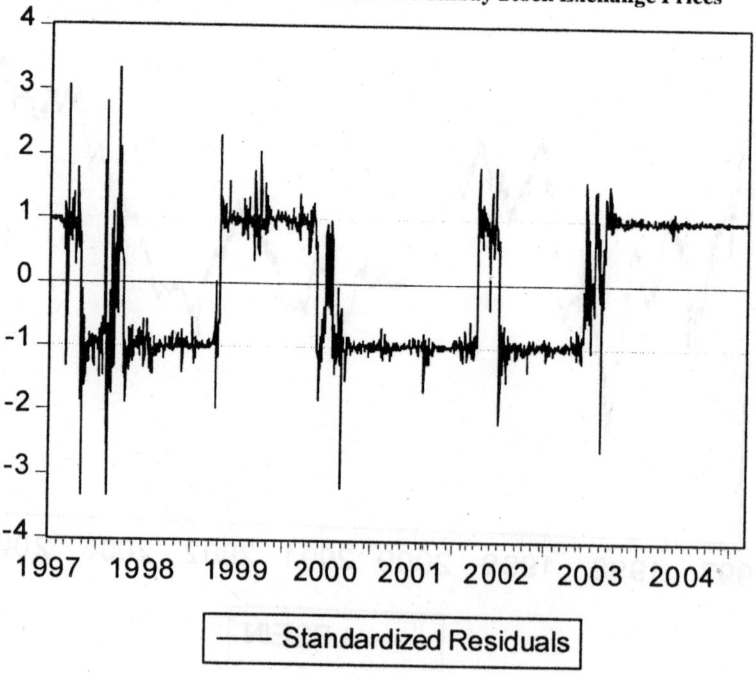

Graph 3: GARCH Conditional Variance of Stock Prices

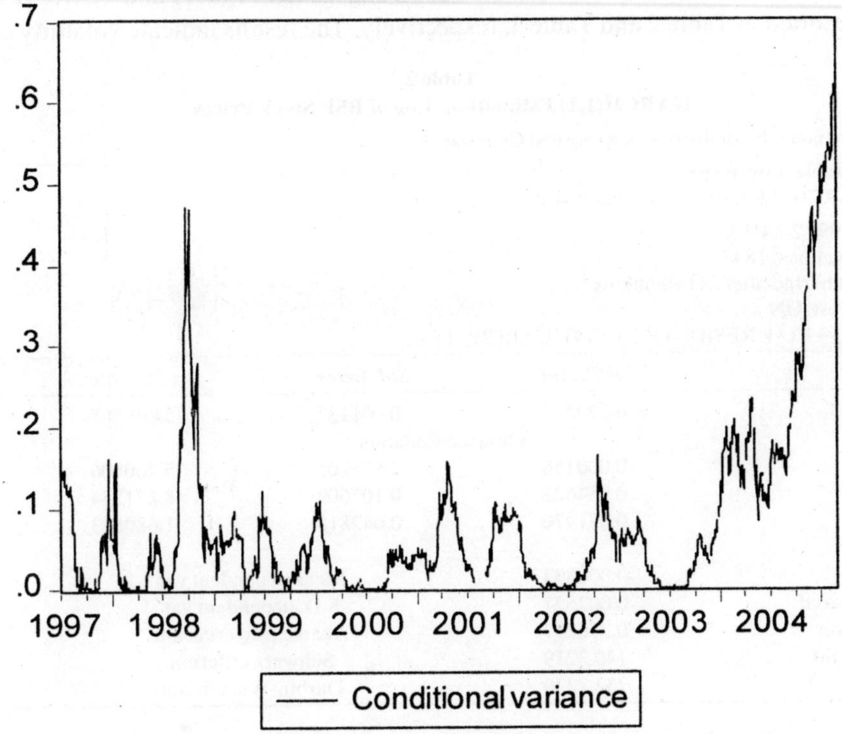

Table 1
Descriptive Statistics of Bombay Stock Exchange Prices

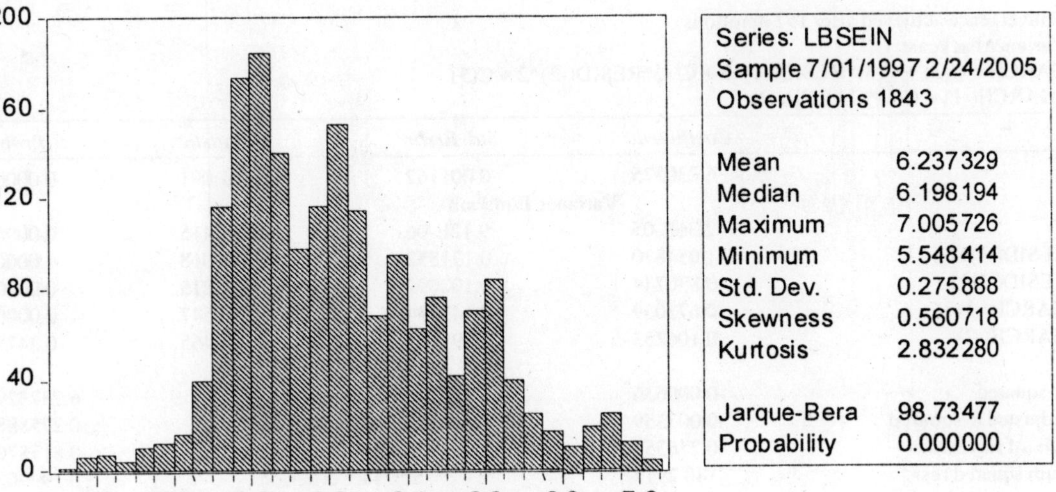

The results of the volatility clustering effect using GARCH (1,1) and GARCH (2,2) test results are reported in Table 2 and Table 3, respectively. The results indicate volatility clustering

Table 2
GARCH(1,1) Estimation: Log of BSE Stock Prices

ARCH in Mean–none. Error distribution–normal Gaussian

Dependent Variable: Log(BSE)
Method: ML-ARCH (Marquardt)-Normal distribution

Sample: 7/01/1997 2/24/2005
Included observations: 1843
Convergence achieved after 211 iterations
Variance backcast: ON
GARCH = C(2) + C(3)*RESID(-1)^2 + C(4)*GARCH(-1)

	Coefficient	*Std. Error*	*z-Statistic*	*Prob.*
C	6.229082	0.001137	5479.867	0.0000
		Variance Equation		
C	0.000156	2.97E-05	5.260506	0.0000
RESID(-1)^2	0.954622	0.107609	8.871234	0.0000
GARCH(-1)	0.071970	0.042818	1.680823	0.0928
R-squared	-0.000894	Mean dependent var		6.237329
Adjusted R-squared	-0.002527	S.D. dependent var		0.275888
S.E. of regression	0.276237	Akaike info criterion		-0.811962
Sum squared resid	140.3279	Schwarz criterion		-0.799983
Log likelihood	752.2230	Durbin-Watson stat		0.005020

Table 3
GARCH (2,2) Estimation: Log of BSE Stock Prices

ARCH in Mean–none. Error distribution–normal Gaussian

Dependent Variable: Log(BSE)
Method: ML-ARCH (Marquardt)-Normal distribution

Convergence achieved after 157 iterations
Variance backcast: ON
GARCH = C(2) + C(3)*RESID(-1)^2 + C(4)*RESID(-2)^2 + C(5)
*GARCH(-1) + C(6)*GARCH(-2)

	Coefficient	*Std. Error*	*z-Statistic*	*Prob.*
C	6.230375	0.001162	5361.091	0.0000
		Variance Equation		
C	2.36E-05	9.12E-06	2.592415	0.0095
RESID(-1)^2	1.054820	0.131852	8.000018	0.0000
RESID(-2)^2	-0.830744	0.102092	-8.137215	0.0000
GARCH(-1)	0.673039	0.145694	4.619547	0.0000
GARCH(-2)	0.106253	0.091877	1.156465	0.2475
R-squared	-0.000636	Mean dependent var		6.237329
Adjusted R-squared	-0.003359	S.D. dependent var		0.275888
S.E. of regression	0.276351	Akaike info criterion		-0.817870
Sum squared resid	140.2917	Schwarz criterion		-0.799902
Log likelihood	759.6670	Durbin-Watson stat		0.005022

effect. The results also show that the sum of the coefficients for ARCH and GARCH is unity implying that shocks to volatility are persistent and therefore have a slower decaying rate such that the shock will eventually return to normal. Volatility is persistent as indicated by the significant lagged ARCH (2) variables implying it has a significant impact on stock prices. On the other hand the significant ARCH variables implies volatility clustering.

As discussed earlier for stocks, it is often observed that downward movements in the market are followed by higher volatilities than upward movements of the same magnitude. To account for this phenomenon, Engle and Ng (1993) describe a News Impact curve with asymmetric response to good and bad news. Here we estimate two models that allow for asymmetric shocks to volatility: Threshold ARCH (TARCH) model , introduced by Zakonian (1990) and Glosten, Jaganathan, and Runkle (1993), and the exponential GARCH (EGARCH) model proposed by Nelson (1991). For the TARCH (1) model in Table 4, the TARCH term is positive, but is not found to be statistically significant, indicating bad news does not increases volatility. The news impact is symmetric. Table 5 reports the estimation results for the EGARCH model with asymmetric order 1. The positive sign without statistically significance implies that good news would result in more volatility than bad news of the same magnitude, which is consistent with the finding from the TARCH model.

Table 4

TARCH(1) Estimation of Log of BSE Stock Prices

ARCH in Mean–none. Error distribution–normal Gaussian

Dependent Variable: Log(BSE)
Method: ML-ARCH (Marquardt)-Normal distribution
Convergence achieved after 132 iterations
Variance backcast: ON
GARCH = C(2) + C(3)*RESID(-1)^2 + C(4)*RESID(-1)^2*(RESID(-1)<0) + C(5)*GARCH(-1)

	Coefficient	*Std. Error*	*z-Statistic*	*Prob.*
C	6.229053	0.001229	5068.327	0.0000
		Variance Equation		
C	0.000157	2.98E-05	5.246552	0.0000
RESID(-1)^2	0.944274	0.157248	6.004982	0.0000
RESID(-1)^2*(RESID(-1)<0)	0.018865	0.200129	0.094266	0.9249
GARCH(-1)	0.071916	0.042852	1.678252	0.0933
R-squared	-0.000900	Mean dependent var		6.237329
Adjusted R-squared	-0.003079	S.D. dependent var		0.275888
S.E. of regression	0.276313	Akaike info criterion		-0.810921
Sum squared resid	140.3288	Schwarz criterion		-0.795948
Log likelihood	752.2635	Durbin-Watson stat		0.005020

Table 5
EGARCH (1) Results of Log of BSE Stock Prices

Asymmetric order 1
ARCH in Mean–none.
Error distribution–normal Gaussian

Dependent Variable: Log (BSE)
Method: ML-ARCH (Marquardt)-Normal distribution
Convergence achieved after 123 iterations
Variance backcast: ON
LOG(GARCH) = C(2) + C(3)*ABS(RESID(-1)/@SQRT(GARCH(-1))) + C(4)*RESID(-1)/@SQRT(GARCH(-1)) + C(5)*LOG(GARCH(-1))

	Coefficient	*Std. Error*	*z-Statistic*	*Prob.*
C	6.214716	0.000710	8749.052	0.0000
		Variance Equation		
C(2)	-1.895993	0.246279	-7.698548	0.0000
C(3)	1.592170	0.176877	9.001584	0.0000
C(4)	0.016597	0.091787	0.180822	0.8565
C(5)	0.900560	0.028849	31.21647	0.0000

R-squared	-0.006722	Mean dependent var	6.237329
Adjusted R-squared	-0.008913	S.D. dependent var	0.275888
S.E. of regression	0.277115	Akaike info criterion	-0.775315
Sum squared resid	141.1450	Schwarz criterion	-0.760342
Log likelihood	719.4528	Durbin-Watson stat	0.004991

IV. CONCLUSIONS

This study attempts to model the time-varying properties of volatility of the Indian stock market along the lines of Engle (1982) and Bollerslev (1986). The Bombay Stock Exchange 30 (BSE) is used as a proxy for the Indian market. The data used for the analysis were 1843 daily observations for the period of July 1997 to February 2005. The data were obtained from the MSCI website data base. Empirical results show that GARCH (2,1) model can adequately describe the Bombay stock market behavior. The negative and significant coefficient of ARCH(2) indicates that the current period volatility is smaller if the past period had large disturbances. Estimation results of the TARCH (1) parameters show that the impact of news is symmetric, indicating no existence of the leverage effect in future returns of the stock. The estimated parameter of EGARCH (1) model also shows the significance of symmetry of order 1. The overall results indicate the long-run components converge very rapidly to the steady state, and the short run volatility components appear to be insignificant. For diagnostic checking of the estimated ARCH model, we applied several tests on the standardized residuals of the stock returns. All residual tests confirm that series are not normally distributed and show leptokurtic. Estimation results of the asymmetric ARCH models (TARCH and EGARCH) show that the news impact is symmetric (confirmed by TARCH parameter estimate) and there is no existence of the leverage effect in future returns of the stock during the sample period.

References

Baldauf, B. and G.J. Santoni (1991), "Stock price Volatility: Some Evidence from the ARCH Model", *Journal of Futures Markets*, Vol. 11, No. 2, 191-200.

Bera, A., E. Bubyns, and H. Park (1988), "Conditional Heteroskedasticity in the Market Model and Efficient Estimates of Betas", *Financial Review*, Vol. 23. No. 2, 201-214.

Bollerslev Tim (1986), "Generalized Autoregressive Conditional Heteroskedasticity", *Journal of Econometrics*, 31: 307-327.

Bollerslev T. (1987), "A Conditional Heteroskedastic Time Series Model for Speculative Prices and Rates of Return." *The Review of Economics and Statistics*, 59: 542-547.

Campbell, John Y.; Lettau, Martin; Malkiel, Burton G and Xu, Yexaio (2001), "Have Individual Stocks Become More Volatile? An Empirical Exploration of Idiosyncratic Risk." *Journal of Finance*. February, Vol. 56. No. 1. pp. 1-43.

Engle, Robert F. (1982), "Autoregressive Conditional Heteroskedasticity with estimates of the Variance of UK Inflation", *Econometrica*, Vol. 50. No. 4. 987-1007.

Engle R. F., and Bollerslev T. (1986), "Modeling the Persistence of Conditional Variance", *Econometric Reviews*, 5, 1-50.

Engle, R. F. and Victor K. Ng. (1993), "Measuring and Testing the Impact of News on Volatility," *Journal of Finance*, 48: 1022-1082.

Errunza, V., K. Jr., O.Kini, and P.Padmanabhan (1994), "Conditional Heteroskedasticity and Global Stock Returns Distribution", *Finance Review*, Vol. 29, No. 3:293-317.

Islam, Mazhar M. (2003d), "Conditional Heteroscedasticity and the Distribution of Stock Returns in the Emerging Market of Oman", *Journal of International Business and Economics*. Vol. 2, No. 1, Fall 2004. pp. 152-60.

Lamoureux, C.G. and G.D. Lastrapes (1990), "Heteroskedasticity in Stock Return data: Volume Vs GARCH Effects." *Journal of Finance*. Vol. 45. No 1. 121-229.

Poterba, J. and L. Summers (1986), "The Persistence of Volatility and Stock Market Fluctuations." *The American Economic Review*, Vol. 76 pp. 1142-1151.

Schwert, G. (1989), "Why Does Stock market Volatility Change Over Time?" *Journal of Finance* 44(5): pp. 1115-53.

Shiller, Ribert J. (1981), "Do Stock Prices Move Too Much To be Justified by Subsequent Changes in Dividends?" *American Economic Review*, June. Vol. 71, No. 3. pp. 421-36.

STOCHASTIC CONVERGENCE IN A GROWTH TRIANGLE: SOME EMPIRICAL EVIDENCE USING PANEL UNIT ROOT TEST

Muzafar Shah Habibullah, A.M. Dayang-Affizzah,***
W.N.W. Azman-Saini & M.T. Hirnissa**

ABSTRACT

The Brunei Darussalam Indonesia Malaysia and the Philippines - East ASEAN Growth Area (thereafter BIMP-EAGA) comprises of Brunei; the Indonesian provinces of Kalimantan, Sulawesi, Maluku and Irian Jaya; Sabah and Sarawak and the Federal Territory Labuan in Malaysia; and Mindanao and Palawan in the Philippines. The purpose of the present study is to answer empirically the question of economic convergence in regional per capita GDP across BIMP-EAGA for the period between 1983 and 2003 using a time-series framework. Based on the stochastic convergence definition suggested by Bernard and Durlauf (1995) and three commonly used panel unit root testing procedures proposed by Levin et al. (2002), Im et al. (1997) and Maddala and Wu (1999), our findings strongly support stochastic convergence hypothesis for BIMP-EAGA for the period after the financial crisis, that is, for the years 1998 to 2003. An important implication of this study is that BIMP-EAGA regional policies, on average, have positive impact on income per capita in all of the seventeen regions.

I. INTRODUCTION

The study of economic convergence has received much attention in the last decade. However, most of the empirical analyses have tested convergence in international economic contexts. The main contention of the convergence analysis is to answer the question of whether poor economies tend to converge towards rich ones or else to diverge over time which is a very important issue that has attracted the attention of policy-makers and academics alike for some decades. Economic convergence or divergence is a topic of considerable interest and debate, not only for validating or otherwise the two leading and competing growth models (the neoclassical and the endogenous growth approaches) but also for its policy-oriented implications. The Solow's (1956) neoclassical growth model, which postulated that differences in initial income do not have long term effects on growth with initially poorer economies are able to

* Department of Economics, Faculty of Economics and Management, Universiti Putra Malaysia, Selangor, Malaysia.

** Department of Economics, Faculty of Economics and Business, Universiti Malaysia Sarawak, Kota Samarahan, Kuching, Sarawak, Malaysia.

catch up with the richer economies. Most empirical tests of the convergence hypothesis have utilized cross-sectional data to investigate the relationship between initial per capita income and growth rates in cross-country and cross-regional studies. Studies that support convergence among countries, among others include Baumol (1986), Barro and Sala-i-Martin (1991, 1992, 1995), DeLong (1988), Dowrick and Nguyen (1989), Grier and Tullock (1989), and Mankiw *et al.* (1992).

However, the traditional testing for convergence has been questioned by Quah (1993), Evans (1998) and Bernard and Durlauf (1995). They suggest using time-series methods (the so-called stochastic convergence) to evaluate convergence since the cross-sectional approach is subject to bias. In a time-series approach, stochastic convergence asks whether permanent movements in one country's per capita income are associated with permanent movements in another countries' income, that is, it examines, whether common stochastic elements matter, and how persistent the differences among countries are. Thus, stochastic convergence implies that income differences among countries cannot contain unit roots. In other words, income per capita among countries is stationary. Empirical studies on testing stochastic convergence, among others include Bernard (1991), Bernard and Durlauf (1995), Campbell and Mankiw (1989), Cogley (1990), Greasly and Oxley (1997), St. Aubyn (1999), Cellini and Scorcu (2000) and Carlino and Mills (1993).

Thus, the objective of this paper is to test the present of stochastic convergence in an emerging growth triangle–the Brunei Darussalam Indonesia Malaysia and the Philippines– East ASEAN Growth Area (BIMP-EAGA). The sample period selected for this study consist of 21 annual data ranges from 1983 to 2003. The BIMP-EAGA has been considered as Asia's largest regional grouping, involving territories of four ASEAN countries comprising a land area of roughly 1.54 million square kilometres. EAGA comprises the entire sultanate of Brunei Darussalam; 10 provinces in the Indonesian islands of Kalimantan (East, Central, South and West), Sulawesi (Central, North, South and South-East), Maluku, and Irian Jaya; Sabah, Sarawak, and Labuan in Malaysia; and 5 regions in the Philippines island of Mindanao (West, North, South and Central) and Palawan.

The paper is organised as follows. In the next section, we discuss the method used to estimate stochastic convergence for the seventeen regions in BIMP-EAGA. Section 3 discusses the empirical results and the last section contains our conclusion.

II. METHODOLOGY

Following Bernard and Durlauf (1995), stochastic convergence occurs if relative log per capita GDP, y_{it}, follows a stationary process, where $y_{it} = \log Y_{it} - \log Y_{qt}$, and Y_{it} is the log of real per capita GDP for country i, and Y_{qt} is log of real per capita GDP of a benchmark country, and both series is $I(1)$. Stochastic convergence is tested by using the conventional univariate augmented Dickey-Fuller (ADF) regression of the following form

$$\Delta y_{it} = \alpha_i + \beta_i y_{it-1} + \sum_{j=1}^{p} \theta_{ij} \Delta y_{it-j} + \varepsilon_{it}, \qquad t = 1,\ldots,T \tag{1}$$

for $i = 1,..., N$ series, and $j = 1,..., p$ ADF lags. The null hypothesis is that y_{it} follows a non-stationary process and the series do not converge stochastically.

However, one important drawback of the univariate ADF unit root test procedures is that the power of the test is quite low. Some authors recognised that the power could be significantly improved if panel data are used instead of a univariate time-series (Levin *et al.*, 2002; Im *et al.*, 1997). For the panel unit root test procedures, Levin *et al.* (2002) proposed to perform the augmented Dickey-Fuller tests based on the following regression model. For a sample of N groups observed over T time periods, the panel unit root regression of the ADF test is written as

$$\Delta y_{it} = \alpha_i + \beta_i y_{it-1} + \sum_{j=1}^{p_i} \gamma_{ij} \Delta y_{it-j} + \varepsilon_{it}, \qquad i = 1,..., N, \qquad t = 1,..., T \tag{2}$$

where α_i, β_i *and* γ_{ij} are parameters and the error terms ε_{it} are uncorrelated across regions. The Levin-Lin-Chu tests for the $H_0 : \beta_i = 0$ against $H_a : \beta_i < 0$. Under the null hypothesis, they show that the test statistics, t^* is asymptotically distributed according to the standard normal distribution.

On the other hand, Im *et al.* (1997) extent the work of Levin *et al.* (2002) to allow for heterogeneity in the value of β_i in Equation (2). Im *et al.* (1997) proposed a *t*–bar statistic, which is based on the average of the individual ADF *t*–statistics.

The null hypothesis of a unit root in the panel data is defined as

$$\beta_i = 0, \text{ for all} \tag{3}$$

against the alternatives that all series are stationary processes

$$\beta_i < 0, i = 1,2, ..., N_1; \beta_i = 0, i = N_1 + 1, N_2 + 2,...., N. \tag{4}$$

This equation of the alternative hypothesis allows for $\beta_i = \beta < 0$ for all i. To test the hypothesis, Im *et al.* (1997) propose a standardised bar statistic given by

$$\Psi_{\bar{t}} = \frac{\sqrt{N}\left\{\bar{t}_{NT} - (1/N)\sum_{i=1}^{N} E\left[t_{i,T}(p_i,0) \mid \beta_i = 0\right]\right\}}{\sqrt{(1/N)\sum_{i=1}^{N} Var\left[t_{i,T}(p_i,0) \mid \beta_i = 0\right]}} \tag{5}$$

where

$$\bar{t}_{NT} = \frac{1}{N}\sum t_{i,T}(p_i, \beta_i) \tag{6}$$

and $t_{i,T}(p_i, \beta_i)$ is the individual *t*–statistic for testing $\beta_i = 0$ for all $E\left[t_{i,T}(p_i,0) | \beta_i = 0\right]$ and $Var\left[t_{i,T}(p_i,0) | \beta i = 0\right]$ are reported in Table 2 of Im *et al.* (1997). Under the null hypothesis, the standardised *t*–bar statistic $\Psi_{\bar{t}}$ is asymptotically distributed as a standard normal distribution ($\Psi_{\bar{t}} \sim N(0,1)$). The Im *et al.* (1997) panel unit root test is derived assuming that the series are independently generated, and they suggested subtracting cross-sectional means to remove common time specific effects. This assumes the error term in Equation (2) consists of two random components, $\varepsilon_{it} = \delta_t + v_{it}$ where v_{it} is the idiosyncratic random component, and δ_t is a stationary time-specific effect that accounts for correlation in the errors across economies.

Another commonly used panel unit root test is the one based on Fisher (1932). Maddala and Wu (1999) propose the test statistic which is based on combining the *p*-values of the test statistics (of β_i) of *N* independent ADF regressions from Equation (1). The test statistic (the Fisher test $P(\lambda)$) is as follows

$$P(\lambda) = -2\sum_{i=1}^{N} \log\ (\pi_i) \qquad (7)$$

where π_i is the *p*-value of the test statistic for unit *i*. The Fisher test statistic $P(\lambda)$ is distributed as a chi-squared distribution with 2*N* degree of freedom.

Sources of Data

In this study, we are using real per capita regional gross domestic product (proxy for regional income) for the seventeen regions in BIMP-EAGA for the period 1983 to 2003 in US$. To derive at each of the real regional income per capita, each of the nominal (domestic currency) regional GDP was divided by the regional population and consumer price index. To convert to income of common currency we deflate all real per capita regional gross domestic products with US currency. All data were converted in natural logarithm for estimation throughout the study.

Data for nominal regional GDP, consumer price index, population and exchange rate (domestic per US$) for the regions in the East ASEAN growth area were compiled from various sources as follow: (a) Sabah and Sarawak from various issues of the respectively Sabah Statistical Yearbook and Sarawak Statistical Yearbook published by the Department of Statistics Malaysia; (b) 10 provinces of the Indonesian island from BPS Statistics Indonesia website available at *http://www.bps.go.id*; (c) 4 regions of the island of Mindanao were compiled from NSCB website available at *http://www.nscb.gov.ph*; and (d) data for Brunei from various issue of the Brunei Darussalam Statistical Yearbook published by the Statistics Division, Department of Economic Planning and Development, Ministry of Finance, Brunei Darussalam.

III. EMPIRICAL RESULTS

Before testing for stochastic convergence by using the panel unit root test of Levin et al. (2002), Im *et al.* (1997) and Maddala and Wu (1999), it is essential to determine the order of integration for each of the region's real per capita income series. The standard ADF tests are used to test for the presence of unit roots in the logarithm of regional per capita income. The results of the ADF test are reported in Table 1. In general, the results indicate that all regional income in BIMP-EAGA are stationary in levels can be rejected at the five percent significance level as shown in columns 2 and 4 in Table 1. Columns 6 and 8 clearly suggest that all regional income is stationary in first differences. In other words, all regional income in BIMP-EAGA are integrated of order one, that is, they are all processes.

Table 1
ADF Unit Root Tests for the Order of Integration

Real per capita regional GDP series	*Series in levels*				*Series in first-differences*			
	Constant	*p*	*Constant & trend*	*p*	*Constant*	*p*	*Constant & trend*	*p*
Brunei	-2.56	0	-2.56	0	-4.67*	0	-4.84*	0
Eastern Kalimantan	-0.75	0	-2.09	0	-4.71*	0	-4.57*	0
Central Kalimantan	-0.93	0	-2.06	0	-4.59*	0	-4.45*	0
Southern Kalimantan	-0.89	0	-1.98	0	-4.49*	0	-4.37*	0
Western Kalimantan	-0.92	0	-2.06	0	-4.74*	0	-4.64*	0
Maluku	-0.40	0	-1.60	0	-3.83*	0	-3.79*	0
Irian Jaya	-0.81	0	-2.08	0	-4.48*	0	-4.37*	0
Central Sulawesi	-1.05	0	-2.09	0	-4.98*	0	-4.85*	0
Northern Sulawesi	-1.13	0	-2.06	0	-4.66*	0	-4.52*	0
Southern Sulawesi	-0.98	0	-2.00	0	-4.49*	0	-4.36*	0
South Eastern Sulawesi	-0.85	0	-2.04	0	-4.62*	0	-4.50*	0
Sabah	-1.57	0	-2.07	0	-3.71*	0	-3.68*	0
Sarawak	-2.80	0	-2.81	0	-5.13*	0	-4.96*	0
Western Mindanao	-2.92	0	-3.05	3	-3.16*	0	-3.57	0
Northern Mindanao	-1.22	3	-2.35	3	-4.35*	2	-3.83*	2
Southern Mindanao	-1.74	0	-3.17	0	-4.02*	0	-4.03*	0
Central Mindanao	-2.91	2	-3.19	0	-3.06*	0	-3.36	0

Having determined that all regional income series are integrated of the same order, we then proceed for the testing of stochastic convergence by using Equation (1) employing the panel unit root test. We do this by employing the ADF unit root test on the differential between each region per capita GDP and the leading country, Brunei's per capita GDP. The result is presented in Table 2. In Table 2 we report the results of the three panel unit root tests for the whole sample period 1983-2003 as well as four sub-samples: period 1983-1991 to represent the years before the inception of the BIMP-EAGA; periods 1992-2003, 1993-2003, 1994-2003, 1995-2003, 1996-2003, 1997-2003, and 1998-2003 to evaluate the performance of the BIMP-EAGA initiatives since 1992 which is the year the concept of such growth triangle was discussed until its establishment in 1994. The year 1995 to 1997 represent the infancy stage until the disruption of the financial crisis in 1997. Thus, in this study the years from 1992 and moving through 2003 will provide the robustness of the empirical findings and also the progress of the BIMP-EAGA initiatives.

We report the estimated *t*-star statistics of the Levin-Lin-Chu (LLC) test, *t*–bar statistics for the Im-Pesaran-Shin (IPS) test and λ-values for the Fisher $P(\lambda)$ test with their accompanying *p*-values. For the period 1983 to 2003, the result clearly indicates that there is no convergence among the seventeen regions in BIMP-EAGA. All three panel unit root tests suggest that the null hypothesis of unit root cannot be rejected at the one percent significance level. This implies

Table 2
Result of Panel Unit Root Tests

Sample period	*Levin-Lin-Chu test, t^{*a}*	*Im-Pesaran-Shin test, $\psi_{\bar{T}}^{a}$*	*Maddala-Wu test, $P(\lambda)^b$*
1983-2003	-1.09 (0) [0.13]	0.44 (0) [0.67]	28.28 (0) [0.65]
1983-1991	-3.97 (0) [0.00]*	-1.74 (0) [0.04]	45.29 (0) [0.06]
1992-2003	0.43 (0-1) [0.66]	2.35 (0-1) [0.99]	19.06 (0-1) [0.96]
1993-2003	-0.48 (0-1) [0.31]	1.59 (0-1) [0.94]	20.52 (0-1) [0.94]
1994-2003	-0.77 (0-1) [0.22]	1.99 (0-1) [0.97]	17.19 (0-1) [0.98]
1995-2003	-1.36 (0-1) [0.08]	1.44 (0-1) [0.92]	17.66 (0-1) [0.98]
1996-2003.	-2.05 (0-1) [0.01]	1.07 (0-1) [0.85]	19.41 (0-1) [0.96]
1997-2003	-3.69 (0-1) [0.00]*	-0.32 (0-1) [0.37]	34.77 (0-1) [0.33]
1998-2003	-39.56 (0) [0.00]*	-20.35 (0) [0.00]*	211.59 (0) [0.00]*

Notes: aUnder the null hypothesis, the standardised bar statistic (the IPS test statistic) is asymptotically distributed as a standard normal distribution. Lag length chosen is based on SIC which is automatically selected by EViews5.1. The numbers in parentheses denote the range of lag length and those in square brackets are p-values. The p-values are estimated from the one-tail test of the standardised normal distribution. bUnder the null hypothesis, the Fisher test statistic P( ) is distributed as a chi-squared distribution with 2N degree of freedom. Lag length chosen is based on the basis of SIC automatically selected by EViews5.1. The p-values are estimated from a chi-squared distribution with 2N degree of freedom. Asterisk (*) denotes statistically significance at 1% level.

that for the 21 year period, on average, regional policy coordination has failed or has not been able to show any impact on regional economic convergence in this growth area.

By splitting the period into periods before and after BIMP-EAGA, we found some interesting results. The results for the period before BIMP-EAGA initiative, which is from 1983 to 1991, the panel unit root test suggests that regional convergence can be rejected at the one percent significance level. This is expected as regional cooperation has not been taken place between the four governments of the BIMP-EAGA. Next we estimate the period after the BIMP-EAGA initiative starting from 1992 and move on to 1998 to 2003. The results of the panel unit root test clearly indicate that the periods 1992-2003, 1993-2003, 1994-2003, 1995-2003, 1996-2003 and 1997-2003 has not shown any tendency towards regional convergence. However, only for the period 1998-2003 that regional convergence is convincingly presence. The null hypothesis of unit root for the period 1998-2003 can be easily rejected at the one percent significance level.

IV. CONCLUSIONS

The study of economic convergence has received much attention in the last decade. Most of the empirical analyses have tested convergence in international economic contexts. Majority of those study employed cross-sectional data analysis to inferred economic convergence among nations. However, Bernard and Durlauf (1995) and others have criticized the used of cross-sectional data and instead suggested the use of time series approach in testing economic convergence.

The objective of the present study is to test empirically the question of regional economic convergence in per capita GDP across the BIMP-EAGA for the period between 1983 and 2003 using a time-series framework. Upon testing the time-series properties of the regional per capita GDP by using the standard ADF test, we found that all regional income series are $I(1)$ processes.

Based on the stochastic convergence definition suggested by Bernard and Durlauf (1995) and three commonly used panel unit root testing procedures proposed by Levin *et al.* (2002), Im *et al.* (1997) and Maddala and Wu (1999), our findings support stochastic convergence hypothesis for the seventeen regions of BIMP-EAGA for the period 1998 to 2003. An important implication of this study is that it appears that the BIMP-EAGA regional policies have an impact on the relative positions of the seventeen regions in terms of their share of EAGA's GDP.

References

Barro, R., and Sala-i-Martin, X. (1991), Convergence across states and regions. *Brookings Papers of Economic Activity*, 1, 107-182.

Barro, R., and Sala-i-Martin, X. (1992), Convergence. *Journal of Political Economy*, 100, 223-251.

Barro, R., and Sala-i-Martin, X. (1995), *Economic Growth*. New York: McGraw-Hill.

Baumol, W.J. (1986), Productivity Growth, Convergence and Welfare: What the Long-run Data Show. *American Economic Review*, 76, 1072-1085.

Bernard, A.B. (1991), Empirical Implications of the Convergence Hypothesis. Working Paper. Stanford University: Center for Economic Policy Research.

Bernard, A.B., and Durlauf, S.N. (1995), Convergence in International Output. *Journal of Applied Econometrics*, 10, 97-108.

Campbell, J.Y., and Mankiw, N.G. (1989), International Evidence on the Persistence of Economic Fluctuations. *Journal of Monetary Economics*, 23, 319-333.

Carlino, G.A., and Mills, L.O. (1993), Are U.S. Regional Incomes Converging? A Time Series Analysis. *Journal of Monetary Economics*, 32, 335-346.

Cellini, R., and Scorcu, A. (2000), Segmented Stochastic Convergence Across the G-7 Countries. *Empirical Economics*, 25, 463-474.

Cogley, T. (1990), International Evidence on the Size of the Random Walk in Output. *Journal of Political Economy*, 98, 501-518.

DeLong, J.B. (1988), Productivity Growth, Convergence and Welfare: Comment. *American Economic Review*, 78, 1138-1154.

Department of Statistics Malaysia. *Sabah Statistical Yearbook*, various issues.

Department of Statistics Malaysia. *Sarawak Statistical Yearbook*, various issues.

Dowrick, S., and Nguyen, D.T. (1989), OECD Comparative Economic Growth 1950-1985: Catch-up and Convergence. *American Economic Review*, 79, 1010-1030.

Evans, P. (1998), Using Panel Data to Evaluate Growth Theories. *International Economic Review*, 39, 295-306.

Evans, P., and Karras, G. (1996), Convergence revisited. *Journal of Monetary Economics*, 37, 249-265.

Fisher, R.A. (1932), *Statistical Methods for Research Worker*. Edinburgh: Oliver and Boyd.

Greasley, D. and Oxley, S. (1997), Time-series Based Tests of the Convergence Hypothesis: Some Positive Results. *Economics Letters*, 56, 143-147.

Grier, K.B. and Tullock, G. (1989), An Empirical Analysis of Cross-national Economic Growth: 1951-1980. *Journal of Monetary Economics*, 24, 259-276.

http://www.bps.go.id

http://www.brunet.bn/org/bimpeabc/welcome.htm

http://www.nscb.gov.ph

Im, K., Pesaran, M.H. and Shin, Y. (1997), Testing for Unit Roots in Heterogenous Panels. Working Paper No. 9526, Department of Applied Economics, University of Cambridge.

Levin, A., Lin, C.F., and Chu, C.S.J. (2002), Unit Root Tests in Panel Data: Asymptotic and Finite-Sample Properties. *Journal of Econometrics*, 108, 1-25.

Maddala, G.S., and Wu, S. (1999), A Comparative Study of Unit Root Tests with Panel Data and a New Simple Test. *Oxford Bulletin of Economics and Statistics*, 61, 631-652.

Mankiw, G., Romer, P., and Weil, D.N. (1992), A Contribution to the Empirics of Economic Growth. *Quarterly Journal of Economics*, 107, 407-437.

Ministry of Finance Brunei Darussalam. *Brunei Darussalam Statistical Yearbook*, various issues.

Quah, D. (1993), Galton's Fallacy and the Tests of the Convergence Hypothesis. *Scandinavian Journal of Economics*, 95, 427-443.

Solow, R.M. (1956), A Contribution to the Theory of Economic Growth. *Quarterly Journal of Economics*, 70, 65-94.

St. Aubyn, M. (1999), Convergence Across Industrialised Countries (1890-1989): New Results Using Time Series Methods. *Empirical Economics*, 24, 23-44.

IMPACT OF PARENTAL EDUCATION ON FAMILY SIZE: A CROSS-SECTIONAL INVESTIGATION

Shahid Ahmed*

ABSTRACT

This article examines the effects of first-, second-, and third level of parental education on the family size. The study further examines the effect of sex composition, particularly son's preference, on family size. The present study is based on primary data and decomposes the effect of male and female education in choosing the family size. The results indicate that education of both male and female are negatively related to family size. In case where both parents are educated, they have more preference for small family compared to single educated parents. It also indicates the male dominance in choosing the family size. The study further reveals that large families on an average found positively associated with favourable male sex ratio in the family. It may be suggested that the education requires positive discrimination in favour of education among Muslims to break the vicious circle of low education, large family size, low per capita income and low education in next generation.

***JEL Classification:** O1, I2, N3.*

The relationship between education and fertility has been a recurrent theme in the demographic literature (Jain,1981; United Nations, 1987; Martin, 1995). Most of the studies until the mid-1970s was consonant with the classic model of the demographic transition, which hypothesized a steady fertility decline concurrent with the process of socio-economic development. The existing studies reveal that the association between education and fertility is not static over the course of the demographic transition (Kasarda, 1979; Martin; 1995). The influence of education on fertility is assumed to derive from various dimensions of the education experience. Schooling provides literacy skills, enables pupils to process information, stimulates cognitive development and bring attitudinal change. In addition to cognitive development and attitudinal change, education opens up economic opportunities and provides vehicle for social mobility. (Kasard *et al.*, 1986; Martin, 1995).

The position of women within the family and the society has been recognized as a crucial factor in determining fertility patterns. Among the various dimension of women's status, education has drawn the most attention. In literature, the relationship between education and fertility is a complex one. A growing awareness of the complexity of the relationship between education and fertility led to a change in the focus of research. Education was shown to affect a

* Reader, Department of Economics, Jamia Millia Islamia (A Central University), New Delhi, India, *E-mail: shah_ec_jmi@yahoo.co.in*

wide range of behaviours, most of which have depressing impact on fertility, but some of which have the potential to raise it. First, women's education affects her preferences for children by widening women's horizons. Second, by increasing the productivity of her time in the market relative to her time in the home, it creates incentives to spend more time working and less for child care (Hashimoto, 1974). Education may also increase home productivity (Leibowitch, 1974). Finally, education may also affect the efficiency of fertility control by increasing women's knowledge and use of birth control techniques, thereby lessening the divergence between desired and actual family size. This aspect has also been highlighted by Michael (1973). Education level affects age at marriage, which in turn may affect family size. Education affects the quantum and tempo of fertility partly through its impact on age at marriage (Smith, 1983)[1].

Education have often been cited as one of the major avenues through which reductions in fertility can be achieved. The cross-national studies have consistently found negative correlations between fertility and education. Fore example, using national data Adelman (1963), Heer (1966), Friedlander and Silver (1967), and Janowitz (1971), all found negative correlations between education and fertility. On the sub-national level, Collver *et al.* (1967), Schultz (1969), Drakatos (1969), and Cain and Weiinger (1973) found negative correlations for Taiwain, Puerto Rico, Greece, and the United States, respectively. Whereas Kamerschen (1971) found positive correlation between education and fertility for the United States while Heer and Boynton (1971) found no significant correlation.

The evidence from the developing world, however, is mixed. Some of the studies reported a negative relationship between family size and educational attainment in Thailand, Brazil and Vietnam. (Psacharopoulos and Arriagada 1989; Knodel, Havanon and Sittitrai, 1990). In Botswana and Kenya, on the other hand, the reverse is true: educational attainment has a positive relationship with family size (Gomes 1984; Chernichovsky 1985). Among Israeli Jews, family size has a negative relationship with educational attainment while among Israeli Muslims, who are less advantaged socio-economically, live in less urban settings and have much higher fertility rates, family size and educational attainment are not negatively related (Shavit and Pierce 1991).

Female education has powerful effects on the total fertility rate (and hence on population growth), the infant mortality rate, and on child health and nutrition. By contrast, statistical analysis shows that male schooling has relatively much smaller effects on these important social outcomes (Strauss and Thomas, 1995). In similar exercise by Murthi, Guio, and Dreze (1997) for India, using district level aggregated data, shows that whereas the district female literacy rate had a strong inverse correlation on the district average total fertility rate, on under-five child mortality rate, and on the female disadvantage in child survival, the district male literacy rate had no significant effect on each of these outcomes. In the words of Dreze and Murthi (2001), female education can be expected to reduce desired family size for number of reasons, ranging from greater autonomy in defining fertility goals to enhanced receptives to modern social norms, reduced dependence on sons for social status and old age security, and higher opportunity cost of time for educated women.

Most of the literature emphasizes the fertility-reducing role of female education and does not highlight equally important role of male education except few (Price-Bonham, 1977; Griffith,

1975; Marciano, 1979). A study by Price-Bonham (1977), in fact, shows a positive relationship between the importance of a decision and the husband's power in making that decision. When Griffith's findings are viewed in this perspective, one perceives a set of most important family decisions (such as fertility) relatively insulated from negotiation or influence by external pressure. In developing country like India, male plays an important role in deciding the desired and actual size of the family. The focus by demographers upon female correlates of fertility-particularly those of female education; labour market participation and religion-may suppress or conceal a fertility variable of the male preference for children. The class, education or religion may be related to the number of children a married couple will have, the decision to have children at all, and the timing of the first conception, are strongly influenced by male preference (Marciano, 1979). Male's education is also expected to reduce desired family size for number of reasons, ranging from greater autonomy in defining fertility goals to enhanced receptiveness to modern social norms, reduced dependence on sons for social status and old age security, and higher opportunity cost of time for educated men. In view of this, the present study tries to analyse the influence of education of both sexes on family size..

The remaining paper is organized as follows: Section 2 presents fertility by religion and education. Section 3 presents educational and economic status of Muslim men and women, Section 4 deals with data and hypotheses to be examined, Section 5 describes the methodology used, Section 6 analyses the empirical results and finally, Section 7 provide concluding remarks.

II. EDUCATIONAL STATUS OF MUSLIMS

The religious Muslim minorities, which constitute 13.5% (Population Census, 2001) of the entire population of the country, is ėconomically and educationally worst off. Educational and economic backwardness of the Muslims has been established by number of reports and surveys. The Gopal Singh Report (1983), the Reports of 43rd round, 1987-88 and the 55th round of the National Sample Survey, 1999-2000 clearly show that the Muslim minority is educationally the most backward segment of the nation in general and women in particular. If a community is educationally backward, it also becomes economically backward and the economic backwardness leads to social and educational backwardness. The linkage between parents' education and family size is well established fact in economic and demographic literature.

The literacy levels of Muslims are skewed towards the bottom. There is a significant difference between figures for Hindus, Muslims and other religious communities in India. Looking at the urban Male literacy rate as per NSSO-55th round, 26 per cent people are illiterate among Muslims while only 12.9 and 6 per cent people are illiterate among Hindus and Christians respectively in India. 27.4 per cent people are literate & upto primary which is higher than the national average of 20 per cent which indicates relatively better education upto this level among Muslims. However, only 7.3 per cent are educated upto higher secondary compared to 12.1 and 13.1 per cent among Hindus and Christians respectively. As far as higher education in Muslims is concerned, the situation is dismal. Only 6 per cent attained higher education while 17.4 and 18 per cent attained in other communities. Similar story emerges when we look at the rural male literacy (table 1).

Table 1

General Education	*Per 1000 Distribution of Rural Male of Age 15 Years and Above by General Education Level for Main Religious Groups in India (1999-2000)*				*Per 1000 Distribution of Urban Male of Age 15 Years and Above by General Education Level for Main Religious Groups in India (1999-2000)*			
	Hinduism	*Islam*	*Christianity*	*All**	*Hinduism*	*Islam*	*Christianity*	*All**
Not Literate	36.8	40.9	24.1	36.9	12.9	25.9	6	14.6
Literate & Upto Primary	25.5	30.3	30.7	26	18.7	27.4	14	19.8
Middle	18	15.3	22.4	17.8	19	19.7	21.8	19.2
Secondary	10.8	8.2	14.5	10.8	19.7	13.7	26.3	19.1
Higher Secondary	5.3	3	4.9	5.1	12.1	7.3	13.8	11.5
Graduate & Above	3.5	2.1	3.4	3.3	17.4	6	18	15.8
Secondary & Above	19.6	13.4	22.7	19.2	49.2	26.9	58.2	46.3
All (Including N.R.)	100	100	100	100	100	100	100	100
	Per 1000 Distribution of Rural Female of Age 15 Years and Above by General Education Level for Main Religious Groups in India (1999-2000)				*Per 1000 Distribution of Urban Female of Age 15 Years and Above by General Education Level for Main Religious Groups in India (1999-2000)*			
Not Literate	65.8	66.4	37	64.8	30.6	44.5	12.2	31.8
Literate & Upto Primary	16.9	19.9	25.9	17.5	18.8	24.5	15.9	19.4
Middle	9.6	8.9	16.5	9.8	16	14	20	15.8
Secondary	4.8	3.2	12.3	5	14.5	9	22.2	14.1
Higher Secondary	1.9	1	4.9	1.9	9	4.5	14.6	8.6
Graduate & Above	0.9	0.4	3.3	0.9	10.9	3.4	15	10.1
Secondary & Above	7.7	4.7	20.5	7.8	34.4	16.9	51.8	32.8
All (Including N.R.)	100	100	100	100	100	100	100	100

Source: Employment and Unemployment Situation Among Religious Groups in India, NSS Report No. 468, 55th Round (July 1999-June 2000).

Note: Figures are in per centages.

Looking at the literacy rate among Muslim women as per NSSO-55th round, there is a little difference between figures for Hindu and Muslim women's primary education for rural India. However, there is a discernible gap between Christian and Muslim women. For the distribution of rural female of age 15 years and above by general education level for main religious groups in India, there are only 0.5 and 1 per cent of Muslim women who received education up to higher secondary, against 1.2 and 1.9 per cent of Hindu women and 4 and 4.9 per cent of Christian women during 1993-94 and 1999-2000 respectively. In case of higher education, only 0.2 and 0.4 per cent got education up to graduation and above against 0.5 and 0.9 per cent of Hindu women and 1.8 and 3.3 per cent of Christian women in 19993-94 and 1999-2000 respectively. The gap between education of Christian and Muslim women in rural areas has widened at faster rate. A similar pattern is observed in other educational categories (i.e., secondary and middle). A similar trend is observed for figures for women's education in urban India (table 1).

This educational disadvantage of men and women in Muslim communities mandates attention. An improvement in the overall literacy rates for Muslims would not just lead to a corresponding increase in Muslim enrolment in universities and professional courses but also ensure more social opportunities for Muslim women (and men). The low literacy and high fertility seems correlated and requires statistical investigation. To the best of my awareness, there is no in-depth statistical analysis of educational attainment of the parents and family size among Muslims in India. However, there is lot of politically charged statement regarding family size among Muslims. There is no serious effort on the part of scholars to study the demographic characteristics among Muslims. There is need of analyzing causes of Muslim educational attainment of parents and the family size. Because there is a lack of secondary data on community basis in India, any reliable study can be based only primary data.

III. DATA AND HYPOTHESES

Data

To test the hypotheses about the family size and parental education, a primary survey are conducted. The sample of 490 households is taken from the Muslim areas in Delhi and Aligarh (U.P) in the month of September 2004. Half of the respondents to this survey are from Delhi and other half are from Aligarh. A preliminary analysis separating the respondents from Delhi and Aligarh indicate insignificant difference between the two groups; hence they are combined so that we have more degrees of freedom in our statistical analysis. The respondents are currently married and cohabiting women aged 15-44 years and their husbands. Only data for women aged 35-44, those nearing the end of their childbearing age are included in the analysis. A wide range of descriptive statistics for all quantitative variables such as Mother's Education (ME), Father's Education (FE) and Family size (FS) are shown in Table 2.The sample moments indicate that the empirical distributions of variables are all skewed when compared with normal distributions. This is reinforced by the highly significant Jarque-Bera statistics.

Hypotheses

We formulated the following hypotheses tests:

Ho: There is no impact of parent's education (mother and father's education) on family size.

Ho: There is no mean difference of family size in educated and uneducated families.

Ho: There is no impact of son's preference on family size.

Table 2
Descriptive Statistics of Quantitative Variables

	Family size	*Mother's Education*	*Father's Education*
Mean	4.680328	6.450820	10.06967
Median	4.000000	5.500000	12.00000
Maximum	14.00000	19.00000	20.00000
Minimum	-1.000000	0.000000	0.000000
Std.Dev.	2.057872	6.518227	6.443108
Skewness	1.044252	0.273237	-0.536844
Kurtosis	5.516594	1.457716	1.864396
Jarque-Bera	108.7335	27.21897	24.83108
Probability	0.000000	0.000001	0.000004

IV. METHODOLOGY

The methodology for the present study basically consists of specifying and estimating bivariate correlation functions, partial correlations and linear regression. The bivariate correlation has been used for detecting the linear relationship between family size and mother and father's education. The simple correlation is measured using the following formula.

$$r_{x_i y_i} = \frac{\sum_{i=1}^{N}(x_i - \bar{x})(y_i - \bar{y})}{\left[\sum_{i=1}^{N}(x_i - \bar{x})^2 \sum_{i=1}^{N}(y_i - \bar{y})^2\right]^{1/2}} \quad (1)$$

In the two variable cases, the simple r had a straightforward meaning. It measured the degree of (linear) association (and not causation) between the two variables but once we go beyond the two variable cases, interpretation of simple correlation becomes difficult. To avoid this problem, we estimated partial correlation coefficient. It gives the coefficient of correlation between Y and X keeping all other variables (say Z) constant. The Partial Correlation Functions (PCF) are calculated as:

$$r_{x_i y_i . z_i} = \frac{r_{yx} - r_{yz} r_{xz}}{\left[(1 - r_{yz}^2)(1 - r_{xz}^2)\right]^{1/2}} \quad (2)$$

For finding out the causal relation between family size and mother and father's education, we applied regression technique. Hetrocedesticity consistent estimates were obtained by OLS using White's correction method for hetrocedesticity. To test the level of significance of the parameters of the equation-3, t-test is used.

$$FS_i = \beta_0 + \beta_1 X_1 + \ldots\ldots + \beta_K X_K + u_i \quad (3)$$

Where FS denotes family size and FE and ME stands for father's education and mother's education respectively. The variable P is used as a dummy variable and constructed to capture male sex ratio in the family as:

$$P = \frac{S}{S + D} \quad (4)$$

Where S stands for number of sons and D stands for number of daughters in the family. The values for dummy variable are assigned as per the following rule:

is $P > 0.5 \Rightarrow 1$, otherwise 0.

To find out the mean difference in the families where only father (F) is educated, only Mother (M) is educated and both parents (FM) are educated,, dummy variables are used in regression.

$$FS_i = \beta_0 + \beta_1 F_i + \beta_2 M_i + \beta_3 FM_i + u_i \quad (5)$$

Similarly, to differentiate the effect of first-, second-, and third level education (Primary Education, Secondary Education (5 To 12), Tertiary Education) on the family size, we applied the regression technique using dummy variables.

$$FS_i = \beta_0 + \beta_1 D_1 + \beta_2 D_2 + \beta_3 D_3 + \beta_4 D_4 + \beta_5 D_5 + \beta_6 D_6 + u_i \quad (6)$$

where D stands for dummy variables. Explanation for each dummy variable is given below the table 5 and table 6.

V. EMPIRICAL ANALYSIS

The analysis has been conducted for the sample of 490 households. The bivariate zero order correlation coefficient is calculated to find the association between the variables. The results are presented in Table 3. The study reveals that the correlation among FS and ME, FS and FE are negative and significant at one per cent level. The coefficient of correlation between the pair of FS and ME, FS and FE is -0.38 and -0.37 respectively. The correlation coefficient shows that there is a negative association between FS and ME, FS and FE but interpretation of simple correlation in more than two variables becomes difficult. To avoid this problem, we estimated partial correlation coefficient. It gives the coefficient of correlation between FS and ME, FS and FE one by one keeping all other variables constant. The Partial Correlation Functions (PCF) is also shown in Table 3. It is observed that partial correlation between FS and ME (-0.223) and FS and FE (-0.195) are negative and significant which imply that the parental education in the family is negatively associated with family size.

As discussed above that there are significant association between family size and parental education. We proceed to multivariate analysis to find out the causal relation between family size and parental education (Mother and Father's Education). We applied regression technique. The regression coefficients are presented in Table 4. The results show that there is a significant causal relation between the family size and parental education. Other things being equal, education level of parents determine the family size norms, which in turn plays crucial role in shaping fertility behaviour. On an average, the one unit change in education of father brings - 0.070 units change in family size while the one unit change in education of mother brings - 0.079 units change in family size.

Table 3
Correlations

	FS	*Bivariate Correlations*	*Partial Correlations*
ME	Pearson Correlation	-0.379**	-0.2228**
	Sig. (2-tailed)	0000	0000
FE	Pearson Correlation	-0.365**	-0.1951**
	Sig. (2-tailed)	00000	0.002

** Correlation is significant at the 0.01 level (2-tailed).
* Correlation is significant at the 0.05 level (2-tailed).

Table 4
Regression Co-efficient

Dependent Variable: FS

Variable	*Coefficient*	*t-Statistic*	*Prob.*
INTERCEPT	5.904439	26.42136	0.0000
FE	-0.070375	-3.088174	0.0022
ME	-0.079905	-3.547258	0.0005
P	0.587255	2.458505	0.0147
R-squared			0.18174
Adjusted R-squared			0.169736
F-statistic			25.83897
Prob(F-statistic)			0.000000

Note: ME= Education of the Mother; FE= Education of The Father; FS= Family Size

The dummy variable P is found to be significant and positive. It implies that favourable male sex ratio has positive effect on family size. The reason may be preference of sons (who could be a source of income for households throughout his life), inheritance laws and customary laws of inheritance favouring sons, neglect of girl child leads to higher mortality, more income needs to be set aside for marriage and dowry purposes for girls and therefore higher preference of male child in the family. The son preference refers to the attitude that sons are more important and more valuable than daughters. Sex composition of children in large families goes in favour of male gender. The above findings are contrary to the results reported by Clark (2000) where data from India show that smaller families have a significantly higher proportion of sons than larger families.

Differential in the desired family size across educational groups are considerably smaller than differentials in actual fetility level. Although uneducated parents typically have more children than their educated counterparts, their family size ideals may not be far apart. To find out the mean differences in the actual family size, we applied dummy variable regression. The results are given in table 5. The average family size is 6 where both mother and father are illiterate. The family size is less than five where only father is educated and mother is illiterate. We could not

Table 5
Dependent Variable: FS

Variable	*Coefficient*	*Std. Error*	*t-Statistic*	*Prob.*
C	6.068442	0.251256	24.15244	0.0000
F	-1.112554	0.340631	-3.266153	0.0012
M	-0.955188	0.635420	-1.503239	0.1341
FM	-2.132538	0.298534	-7.143372	0.0000
R-squared				0.178898
Adjusted R-squared				0.168634
F-statistic				17.43003
Prob(F-statistic)				0.000000

C = INTERCEPT; F = ONLY FATHER EDUCATED; M = ONLY MOTHER EDUCATED; FM = BOTH FATHER AND MOTHER EDUCATED.

substantiate statistically any significant difference where mother is educated and father is illiterate. However, the study reveals that family size is smallest in the families where both father and mother educated. The existing divergence in the reproductive behaviour may partly reflect a highly polarized social structure, in which the educational standards of the upper social strata contrast with those of the lower strata. Income level and educational standard seems to be multicollinear.

Table 6
Dependent Variable: FS

Variable	*Coefficient*	*Std. Error*	*t-Statistic*	*Prob.*
C	6.113929	0.252631	24.20102	0.0000
D1	-0.713452	0.540314	-1.320441	0.1880
D2	-1.156565	0.364812	-3.170302	0.0017
D1	-1.153896	0.374271	-3.083050	0.0023
D4	-0.878264	0.442335	-1.985517	0.0482
D5	-0.894574	0.335416	-2.667053	0.0082
D6	-1.264572	0.383162	-3.300360	0.0011
R-squared				0.184083
Adjusted R-squared				0.163427
F-statistic				8.911772
Prob(F-statistic)				0.000000

C=INTERCEPT;D1= DUMMY FOR FATHER'S PRIMARY EDUCATION; D2= DUMMY FOR FATHERS SECONDARY EDUCATION (5 TO 12);D3=DUMMY FOR FATHERS TERTIARY EDUCATION; D4= DUMMY FOR MOTHER'S PRIMARY EDUCATION; D5= DUMMY FOR MOTHER'S SECONDARY EDUCATION(5 TO 12);D6=DUMMY FOR MOTHER'S TERTIARY EDUCATION.

To examine the effects of participation of parents in first-, second-, and third level of education on the family size, dummy variable regression technique is applied. The results are presented in table 6. The study indicate that second-, and third level of father's education has significant negative effect on family size while first-, second-, and third level of mother's education has significant effect. The study reveals that there is no decline in family size where father is educated only upto primary level. However, female's education upto primary has significant negative effect on fertility. Male's education upto 12th standard has significant negative effect. The negative association emerges only after a critical level of schooling of male, usually after completion of primary level, is reached. There is no gain in declining fertility through the higher education of male. However, in case of female's education, the effect of first-, second-, and third level of education on family size is in ascending order, i.e., higher the female education lower the fertility. When women at the upper and lower end of the educational range are contrasted, fertility levels are seen to be substantially lower among the higher educated. The pattern of lowest fertility among highly educated strata holds for all societies and Muslims are not exception to this. Higher female education has been shown to lead to a postponement of marriage and, thereby, to later family formation.

VII. CONCLUDING REMARKS

This article examines the empirical relationship of family size and parental education in Muslim families and the effects of participation of parents in first-, second-, and third level education on the family size. The study further examines the effect of sex composition, particularly son's preference, on family size. Various important lessons and confirmations emerge from the results presented in this paper. Family educational background can have important impact on family size. The results indicate that both education of male and female are negatively related to family size. In case of both educated parents, they have more preference for small family compared to single educated parents. Male dominance in choosing the family size has also been reflected. The study further reveals that the large families on an average found positively associated with favourable male sex ratio in the family.

The study suggests that there is need of special emphasis on education because it acts as the checks on population explosion. The education of male and female is essential of demographic transition to the third stage in Muslim families. Education in Muslim Male is essential upto secondary to reduce the fertility. At the same time, higher the female education lowers fertility. It may also be suggested that the education requires positive discrimination in favour of education of (both girls and boys) in Muslim families to break the vicious circle of low education, large family size, low per capita income and low education in next generation. It requires the need for public awareness about the intrinsic and instrumental value of education. The question of over all educational development, thus, should be taken in its entirety where the Muslim community, the government and civil society have to work in close co-ordination in word and sprit.

Given the small sample size and the number of omitted variables in the study, there is need of further testing; and other analytical frameworks must be examined for their appropriateness in explaining relative spousal influence on fertility.

Notes

1. In most societies, childbearing takes place within the context of a conjugal union, nuptiality patterns closely linked to fertility patterns.

References

Adelman, I. (1963), "An Econometric Analysis of Population Growth", *American Economic Review*, 53, 314-339.

Cain G. G. and Weiinger, A. (1973), "Economic Determinant of fertility: Results from Cross Sectional aggregate data", Demography, 10, 205-223.

Chernichovsky, D. (1985), "*Socioeconomic and Demographic Aspects of School Enrollment and Attendance in Rural Botswana*", Economic Development and Cultural Change, 33: 319-332.

Clark, S. (2000), "Son Preference and Sex Composition of Children: Evidence from India", Demography, 37, 95-108.

Collver, A., Speare, Jr., and Liu, P.K. (1967), "Local Variations in Fertility in Taiwan", Population Studies, 20, 329-342.

Drakatos, C.G. (1969), "The Determinant of Birth Rate in Developing Countries: An Econometric Study of Greece", *Economic Development and Cultural Change*, 17, 596-603.

Dreze, J. and Murthi, M. (2001), " Fertility, Education, and Development: Evidence from India", Population and Development Review, 27, 33-63.

Employment and Unemployment Situation Among Religious Groups in India, NSS Report No. 468, 55th Round, July 1999-June 2000.

Friedlander, S. and Silver, M. (1967), "A Quantitative Study of Fertility Behavior", Demography, 4, 30-70.

Gomes, M. (1984), "*Family Size and Educational Attainment in Kenya*", Population and Development Review, 10, 647-660.

Gopal Singh Report on Minorities (1983), Govt. of India.

Griffith, J. (1975), " Social Pressures on Family Size Intentions", in UK Kammeyer (ed.), Population Studies (2nd ed.), Chicago: Rand McNally.

Hashimoto, M. (1974), " Economics of Post War Fertility in Japan: Differentials and Trends", *Journal of Political Economy*, 82, S170-S194.

Heer, D. M. (1966), "Economic Development and Fertility", Demography, 3, 423-444.

Heer, D. M. and Boynton, W. (1971), " A Multivariate Regression Analysis of Differences in Fertility of United States Countries, Social Biology, 17,180-194.

Jain, A. K. (1981), "The Effect of Female Education on Fertility: A Simple Explanation", Demography, 18, 577-595.

Janowitz, B.S. (1971), " An Empirical Study of the Effects of Socoieconomic Development on Fertility Rates", Demography, 8, 319-330.

Kamerschen, D.R. (1971), " The Statistics of Birth Rate Determinants, *Journal of Development Studies*, 7: 293-303.

Kasarda, J. D. (1979), "How female Education Reduces Fertility: Models and Needed Research", Mid-American Review of Sociology, 4, 1-22.

Kasarda, J., Billy J.O.G. and West, K. (1986), " Status Enhancement and Fertility: Reproductive Responses in Social Mobility and Educational Opportunity, Academic Press, New York.

Knodel, J., Havanon, N. and Sittitrai, W. (1990), "*Family Size and the Education of Children in the Context of Rapid Fertility Decline*", Population and Development Review, 16:31-62.

Leibowitz, A. (1974), " Education and Home Production", *American Economic Review Papers and Proceedings*, 64, 243-250.

Marciano, T.D. (1979), " Male Influence on Fertility: Needs for Research", The Family Coordinator, 28, 561-568.

Martin, T.C. (1995), "Women's Education and Fertility: Results from 26 Demographic and Health Surveys", Studies in Family Planning, 26, 187-202.

Michael, R.T. (1973), " Education and Derived Demand for Children", *Journal of Political Economy*, 81, S128-S164.

Murthi , M., A. Guio, and J. Drèze (1997), "*Mortality, Fertility, and Gender Bias in India*", in J. Drèze and A.Sen (eds.), *Indian Development: Selected Regional Perspectives,* Oxford University Press.

Population Census (2001), Ministry of Home Affairs, Govt. of India.

Price-Bonham, s. (1977), " Martial Decision-making: Congruence of Spouses' Responses, Sociological Inquiry, 47, 119-126.

Psacharopoulos, G. and Arriagada, A.M. (1989), "The Determinants of Early Age Human Capital Formation: Evidence from Brazil", *Economic Development and Cultural Change,* 37, 683-708.

Schultz, T. P. (1969), "An Economic Model of Family Planning and Fertility", *Journal of Political Economy*, 77, 153-180.

Shavit, Y. and Pierce, J. L. (1991), "Sibship Size and Educational Attainment in Nuclear and Extended Families: Arabs and Jews in Israel", *American Sociological Review*, 56, 321-330.

Smith, P.C. (1983), " The of Age at Marriage and Proportions Marrying on Fertility", In Determinants of Fertility in Developing Countries, Eds. Rodolfo A. Bulatao and Ronald D. Lee, New York: Academic Press, 2, 473-531.

Strauss, J. and Thomas, D. (1995), "Human Resources: Empirical Modeling of Household and Family Decisions", in J. Behrman and T.N. Srinivasan (eds.), *Handbook of Development Economics*, Vol III.

United Nations (1987), " Fertility Behaviour in the Context of Development: Evidence from the World Fertility Survey", Population Studies, No. 100, New York.

WHY DO FOREIGN BANKS INVEST IN TURKEY?

Ahmet Faruk Aysan [*] ***& Şanli Pinar Ceyhan***

Abstract

Sound macroeconomic policies, increasing global liquidity and higher real returns in developing countries played an important role in canalizing capital towards developing markets. Recent improvement in the developing Turkish economy brought the issue of foreign entry to the foreground. High growth potential backed by an increasing population, falling inflation rates and the birth of the mortgage sector made Turkey an ideal place to expand into. This article is not concerned about whether foreign entry is good nor does it discuss the subsequent effects. Rather, it attempts exclusively to shed light on the motivations behind entry to Turkey utilizing recent entry cases.

Key Words: *Globalization of Banking, Turkish Banking Industry, Foreign Bank Entry.*

JEL Codes: *F20, F36, G0, G21.*

I. INTRODUCTION

Recently, financial markets of developing countries have been receiving high amounts of funds thanks to their successful economic policies, increase in global liquidity, and relatively lower real returns in developed countries. It is forecasted that in 15 years mega banks will emerge in global scale, and foreign penetration will preserve its importance. In this kind of an economic picture, Turkey, as a developing country, has been among the major actors with an increasing amount of foreign entry.[1] Latest figures show that foreign asset share (participation banks included) in the Turkish financial sector is 17.5 per cent as of May, 2006.[2] Foreign share in consumer credits is found out to be 42.6 per cent while they occupy 41.7 per cent share in the mortgage sector. Additionally, foreigners have been net debtors with debts to banks and to other financial institutions constituting 48.2 and 45.7 per cent of the sector, respectively.

In the literature, it is mostly the case that foreign entrants introduce their relatively higher-level technology to the host country market. However, this study shows that the entrants also expect to benefit from the technological potential of the Turkish financial sector. In fact, one factor creating synergies between NGB and Finansbank is the optimization of the Southeastern European cost base in areas such as IT. In addition to technological improvement, foreigners choose Turkey as a base to increase their product and service range. This is evident in the decision of NBG to purchase part of Finansbank attracted by its high quality retail products like consumer loans and insurance.

---

* Boğaziçi University, Department of Economics, Istanbul, Turkey, E-mail: *ahmet.aysan@boun.edu.tr*

Not only does Turkey have a geo-strategic advantage due to its position at the intersection of Europe and Asia, but it also has a promising financial market with an increasing population of approximately 70 million as of the end of 2005 and GDP growing at 4.3 per cent per year on average between 2001 and 2005. Especially the improving macroeconomic picture of Turkish economy reflected in single digit inflation numbers and declining interest rates is a frequently pronounced reason for foreign bank entry into Turkey. The improvement in the banking sector can be seen in Table-1. Taking 1999 as the base year, for which the index is 100, one facet of improvement is shown to be the increasing profitability in the sector from 93.6 at the end of 2000 to 107 in May, 2005 with a small decrease following the 2001 crises. The same pattern is also observed in the other indicators. Financial strength, for instance, increases moderately after the crisis period reaching to 110.5 in May, 2005 from 97.4 at the end of 2001.

Table 1
Strengthening Turkish Banking Sector

	Asset Quality	*Profitability*	*Capital Adequacy*	*Financial Strength*
1999	100	100	100	100
2000	93.4	93.6	98.9	94.3
2001	73.3	87.8	113.9	97.4
2001	85.8	104.0	126.7	102.5
2003	101.0	105.7	144.0	109.2
2004	109.6	105.4	145.0	111.3
2005 May	112.6	107.0	143.0	110.5

Source: Central Bank of Turkey
Index, 1999=100

When the improving Turkish financial sector is compared to those of the European countries in terms of the asset share of banks with foreign capital in the banking sector, it can be seen that the share of 15.8 per cent lies below all but Spain and Germany, with 9.7 per cent and 10.5 per cent, respectively, indicating the high growth potential in Turkey. The details are depicted in the Table 2. Among the countries listed, some late comers to the European Union, namely

Table 2
Asset Share of Banks with Foreign Share in the European Union Countries

Country	*2001*	*2002*	*2003*	*2004*	*2005*
Germany	4,7	6	5,9	6,2	10,5
Austria	19,8	21;5	19,5	19,2	19,8
Denmark	31,8	30,6	315,9	30,7	30,7
Finland	77	78	61	63	59
Spain	11	7,8	8,3	8,8	9,7
Litvania	85	96,1	95,6	90,8	91,7
Luxemburg	92,3	92,1	93,5	93,9	94,7
Hungary	-	90,3	87,9	66,4	87,1
Slovak Republic	89,9	95,6	96,3	96,7	97,3
Greece	22,2	24,1	25,3	27,3	30,3
Turkey(*)	3	3,1	2,8	11,8	15,8

Source: IMF, World Bank, Lund and Rasmussen (2006), related countries' authorities
(*) Turkey 2005 data reflects March 2006 data.

Litvania, Hungary and Slovak Republic attract attention with more than 90 per cent asset share as does Luxemburg with a corresponding number of 94.7.

In this study, without exception, all the entrants to the Turkish banking sector express their desire to benefit from the high growth potential in the Turkish financial market. Real GDP growth is forecasted to be 2.1 per cent for Europe, 4.3 per cent for the Central and Eastern European countries while a similar figure for Turkey is five per cent. Moreover, statistics showing this potential such as a more-than-74 per cent-CAGR (Compound Annual Growth Rate) in total assets in the period 1997-2005 was what increased Dexia's appetite for Denizbank. Another mostly cited entry reason is to increase profits escaping from the low profit-financial sector of the parent country. For instance, Fortis, which was an already profitable company, increased its profits by 93 per cent after the purchase of 89.3 per cent of Dışbank shares.

Of course, a bank on its own right is not the ultimate target of foreign entrants. A more important reason of entry is to gain market share in the host country banking sector. This is evident again in the purchase of Dışbank shares by Fortis who could reach more than 1.000.000 new customers, approximately 120.000 new small enterprises and 10.000 new medium-sized enterprises.

Being among more than a hundred countries that will put into practice the Basel II Requirements, Turkey will experience an economic environment with an improved supervision in the banking sector after the new accord becomes effective in 2008. The capital adequacy ratio for the Turkish banking sector, which was higher than the legal limit with 24.2 per cent as of the end of 2005, will decrease to 16.9 per cent with the new arrangement. This prospect will also increase foreign appetite.

Behind foreign bank entry to Turkey, there lies also a demographic reason. People living in different parts of Turkey earn very diverse levels of income and this inequality has given way to migration especially from the Eastern parts of Turkey to big cities whose income per capita is above Turkey's average. This, coupled with the high population of Turkey, resulted in housing problems, and up until very recently, banks were not dealing much with the financing of housing. However, with the improving macroeconomic performance in Turkey, it will be possible for banks to provide mortgages, creating a baby sector with long way to grow.

This paper is organized as follows: While analyzing the issue of foreign entry, in the second section, we will be looking at the pull and push factors mentioned in the literature, and attempt to find correspondences for the Turkish case. The third section deals with the Turkey-specific pull factors covering seven foreign entry cases, the foreign banks being National Bank of Greece (NBG) and EFG Eurobank from Greece, Fortis from Netherlands, Dexia of Belgium, General Electric (GE) from the United States, HSBC of England, and UniCredito from Italy. The last section concludes.

II. UNDERLYING REASONS OF FOREIGN BANK ENTRY

Countries may welcome foreign bank entry either as part of their liberalization process as in Korea, Thailand and China, or when they have high amounts of debt. They finance economic growth at a minimum cost during sudden stops as in the East Asian crisis period when low prices attracted foreign entry.[3] Specifically, due to the insufficiency of the domestic banks during the process of recapitalization of joint venture banks, the Indonesian government increased the foreign ownership share from 85 per cent to 99 per cent. In addition to the increase in number, foreign banks also started to be treated like their domestic counterparts.[4] Similarly, National Bank of Poland tried to consolidate banks in trouble regardless of being domestic or not, and this gave way to foreign entry as long as foreigners could help in restructuring domestic banks.[5]

Increasing foreign trade, improving the technological infrastructure of the domestic banking sector, and increasing the product and service variety are among the expectations of the host country from internationalization. High profit potential (as a result of low level of competition) as well as the low market value of Latin American banks (which make it less costly to gain a high market share), and the Latin American banks' providing increasing returns to financial institutions (because of high intermediation margins) were what pulled foreigners to the host country financial market.[6] While expanding their customer base, foreign banks in Korea were attracted by the fact that they would be treated even better than their domestic counterparts in some banking operations.[7] Moreover, the Single Market Program and the introduction of Euro led to a single banking sector in Europe and entry barriers were eliminated increasing the foreign share in the sector.[8] For the case of Europe, Table 3 compares domestic and foreign banks according to some selected ratios, and indicates the stronger standing of banks with foreign capital. It is shown that nonperforming loans to loans ratio for the banks with foreign capital are lower than those for domestic banks, with figures 1.83 versus 3, respectively. While expenses-to-costs ratio is very much close for the two kinds of banks, profitability ratio of 0.56 for banks with foreign capital exceeds 0.5 of domestic banks. Moreover, tier-1 ratio[9] for domestic banks is found out to be less than that of banks with foreign capital.

Table 3
Selected Ratios for EU-25

EU-25	*Domestic Banks*	*Banks with foreign capital*
Nonperforming Loans (Gross) as a per centage of Loans	3	1,83
General Capital Adequacy ratio	12	15,57
Tier 1 ratio	8	12,4
Expenses /Costs ratio	59,42	59,52
Profitability ratio	0,5	0,56

Note: Banks with foreign capital: Partnerships or subsidiaries controlled by banks with foreign capital as defined by the reporting member country.
Source: EU Banking Sector Stability, Oct, 2005, ECB.

A different view on the issue comes from Coppel and Davies (2003), Weller (2001) and Berger *et al.* (2000) who suggest that deregulation is what attracts foreign entry.[10] Indeed, the low level of foreign entry to the Asian financial markets relative to the Eastern European and Latin American markets is a result of the protectionist economic policies to safeguard the Asian banking sector.[11] As another example, following the initiation of the Convertibility Plan in 1991, Argentina eliminated capital controls, giving way to an increase in the foreign share of the banking sector. Similarly, the process of privatization of the state-owned banks, called PROES, was effective in pulling foreign banks to Brazil.[12] Furthermore, financial liberalization period started in Mexico with the privatization efforts in 1990s.[13]

In addition to the above factors, low profits and regulatory restrictions in home country lead to foreign penetration acting as the "push" factors.[14] Indeed, increasing market competition and thus decreasing profits in the European monetary and economic union, and political and regulatory factors imposing limitations to mergers and acquisitions were two factors pushing European banks abroad.[15] Table 4 lists some other variables motivating EU banks to open abroad. As the net interest margin or the share of net interest income in average assets increases in the EU countries, for instance, EU banks decrease their shares in other countries. On the contrary, increase in total assets, net income or operating income do the reverse effect increasing the share in foreign countries.

Table 4
Factors Affecting the Internationalization Strategies of EU Banks

Descriptive Variables (%)	*Direction of the relation*	*Statistical Significance Level(%)*
Shares /Deposits and other short term funds	-	10
Equity /Assets	-	1
Net Interest Margin	-	5
Net Interest Income/ Average Assets	-	5
Net Loans/ Total Assets	-	10
Total Assets	+	1
Net Income	+	10
Operating Income	+	5

Note: Variable described: Foreign asset share in the total assets of EU banks.
Source: Results of regression analysis conducted by EU Central Bank, EU Banking Structures, Oct, 2005, ECB.

Buch (2000), Green, Murinde and Nikolov (2002) and Lensink and Hermes (2002) suggest that foreign banks go after their customers.[16] In fact, investments of US and Japanese banks, for instance, were found to be positively correlated to the non-bank foreign investments, supporting this view. This has been possible and much easier due to globalization and the removal of entry barriers along with the reforms facilitating their entrance into the host country market.[17] In the past, multinational banks mainly worked for home country customers and provided local firms with access to international financial markets. However, Du (2003)[18] found that while lending, foreign banks give priority to the borrowers other than the ones from the home country. Today, main purpose of these multinational banks is diversification and integration to domestic markets.[19] Risk diversification is possible unless the foreign and domestic markets' business cycles are positively correlated, an example being the expansion of a European bank into Latin America which experience recessions at different times.[20]

III. WHAT IS THE REASON OF FOREIGN PENETRATION INTO TURKEY?

While analyzing the case from the Turkish perspective, we will be looking at the pull and push factors listed below in detail. Seven foreign entry cases have been covered in this study and the related banks are shown in columns. The observations we have gathered from various issues of newspapers and internet sources are summarized in the table. The relevant reasons of entry are indicated with a star for each foreign entry case. For instance, high amounts of debt and increasing foreign trade are factors common to all the cases, supporting what Kraft (2002)[21] suggests.

Table 5
Pull and Push Factors

	Banks						
	NBG-Finans bank	*EFG Euro bank-Tekfen bank*	*Fortis-Dış bank*	*Dexia-Deniz bank*	*GE-Garanti bank*	*HSBC-Demir bank*	*Uni Credito-Koç Group-Yapı Kredi*
Pull Factors:							
High amounts of debt	*	*	*	*	*	*	*
Increasing the international trade	*	*	*	*	*	*	*
Improving technology	*	*			*	*	
Increasing the product and service variety	*		*	*		*	
Growth opportunities	*	*	*	*	*	*	*
Low level of competition in the host country			*				
New customer base	*	*	*	*		*	*
[a]Deregulation							
Push Factors:							
Low profits	*	*	*	*	*		*
Diversification	*	*	*				*
Foreign trade	*	*	*	*		*	
Foreign investment	*	*					
Size of banking sector in the parent country	*	*	*	*			
Going after their customers	*	*				*	
[a]Regulatory restrictions at home							

Source: Authors' tabulation from various newspaper issues and internet sources.
[a]: No evidence with respect to this factor.

Upon foreign entry, it is usually the case that the host country expects to benefit from the superior technological base of the prospective entrants.[22] What we have found out in the Turkish cases, however, is that the reverse could also be the case, in other words, the entrant might be looking for technological improvement after the entry. In fact, NBG, EFG Eurobank, GE and HSBC entered into Turkey hoping also to benefit from the better technological infrastructure that their Turkish partners have compared to their own technology base. Specifically, one factor creating synergies between NGB and Finansbank is reported to be the optimization of the Southeastern European cost base in fields like information technologies. Additionally, GE, which operates in areas from energy, airplane engine, health technology to engineering, suggests that with its superior technological infrastructure Garanti Bank provides a sound base for GE to grow.[23]

Foreign banks are also expected to enhance the product and service variety in the host country banking sector.[24] As in the above discussion, this expectation is shared by the entrants making them choose Turkey as a country to expand into. Finansbank is an example which attracted NBG with its high quality retail products such as car loans, consumer loans, insurance, and checks. HSBC, which provides services such as stock-broking, fund management and investment, insurance, pensions, credit cards to personal, corporate and institutional customers in Turkey, pursued to increase product and service variety through the purchase of Demirbank.

One finding in this study is that without exception, all the banks included reported a desire to take advantage of the high growth potential in the Turkish financial market.[25] Indeed, foreign banks experiencing slow growth in their home countries search for new markets such as the Central and Eastern European market which have high growth potentials marked, for example, by high appetites for credit.[26] Turkey's economy with its increasing population is the biggest and fastest developing one in Southeastern Europe which increases the importance of Turkey for NBG. In accordance with this finding, the high growth statistics such as a more-than-74 per cent-CAGR in total assets for the period 1997-2005 was what increased Dexia's appetite for Denizbank.

Another pull factor we analyze is the low competition level in the financial sector of the host country as Kraft (2002)[27] suggests. Banks stuck at low profit levels due to high degree of competition in their parent countries look for markets with low competition and thus high profits. For instance, stimulated by the strong profit potential, Fortis chose Turkey where there were few foreign competitors and low banking penetration relative to its Western counterparts.

Many foreign banks expand into Turkey intending to buy not merely a Turkish bank but market share, the latter being more difficult to acquire than the former. Indeed, the fact that foreign entrants aim at increasing their customer base, suggested by Kraft (2002)[28], is proved by their inclination to acquire banks with high number of branches. For instance, by purchasing 89.3 per cent of Dışbank shares, Fortis could reach more than 1.000.000 new customers, approximately 120.000 new small enterprises and 10.000 new medium-sized enterprises. Similarly, by purchasing Denizbank, Dexia could reach nearly 1.400.000 retail customers in Turkey. Additionally, HSBC was intending to join its broad corporate client portfolio with the SME client portfolio of Demirbank.[29]

In contrast to the above pull factors, there is also another view suggesting that deregulation is "the" factor that pulls foreigners. Although not explicitly stated in the actual cases included in this study, deregulation in the host country's financial system has an important effect on the foreigners' choice to enter into Turkey. For instance, international agreements were made in order to encourage investment and prevent double taxation. Foreign capital was guaranteed to be nationalized. Moreover, nonresidents could bring the proceeds to their own countries and residents could buy securities that were issued by foreigners via authorized financial institutions, and transfer the foreign exchange to buy these securities abroad. This process deepened the foreign exchange market and increased foreign bank branches in Turkey boosting the competition in the sector. The reflection of this process on figures was an increase in the foreign holdings of shares from less than five per cent in 1990 to more than 50 per cent in 1997.[30]

The first push factor we study is the low profitability in the parent country as indicated in Kraft (2002)[31]. The cases covered in this study revealed that increasing profits is the common motivation in internationalization. Evidence comes from the Garanti-GE deal for which Fitch Rating Agency suggested that the upgraded ratings for Garanti Bank were a result of increased profits accompanying this partnership. Fortis, an already profitable company which purchased 89.3 per cent of Dışbank shares, increased its profits by 93 per cent after the deal. NBG's motivation in purchasing Finansbank shares is no different from these two. Through this transaction, in fact, NBG earns Finansbank's net profits which increased by 68 per cent in one year.

Diversification is another factor, also mentioned in Paula (2003)[32], as to why foreigners decide to expand abroad. It is an integral segment of the expansion strategy of Dexia with more than 40 per cent market share in France and more than 80 per cent market share in Belgium in the public finance area which tries to expand into Europe and the US through partnerships and organic growth. Similarly, GE has operations in more than 100 countries and intends to expand into countries such as Russia, Romania, Netherlands, Turkish Republics and Middle East together with Garanti Bank. One reason to diversify into Turkey is its proximity, both culturally and physically, to the Middle East in the sense that it is easier to reach the Middle East from Ýstanbul than from, for instance, London.[33]

Banks also expand abroad in order to increase international trade and investment. With its expertise in foreign trade, HSBC offers SMEs in Turkey attractive opportunities. The GE's purchase of 25.5 per cent share of Garanti Bank was accompanied by 1.8 billion dollars of American investment, showing the close relationship between trade and investment. Additionally, Fortis plans to set Turkey as the technology base for all of its operations such as telephone banking. In agreement with this, changes are suggested to be made in the law concerning foreigners' property rights in Turkey to increase investments.[34] Greece enters into Turkey in order to make investments in sectors such as industry, tourism and navigation although their main interest lies in the financial sector. Indeed, between 1990 and 2002, Greek investment in Southeastern European countries amounted to five billion Euros one tenth of which were spared for the banking sector.

Foreign banks whose parent countries have relatively small banking sector search for financial markets where they could benefit from greater opportunities. At this point, as the biggest developing economy in the Southeastern Europe, Turkey becomes attractive to banks such as NBG and Fortis.[35] For instance, Greek banking sector with 227,670 billion Euros of asset size as of the end of 2005 is small relative to the Turkish banking sector whose asset size for the same period is 295,844 billion dollars. In fact, Finansbank with its 5.2 per cent share of loans, 208 branches and 1.200.000 active customers is said to be a perfect match for NBG.

It may be the case that banks internationalize following their customers.[36] To give an example, among the seven foreign entry cases examined in this study, banks in Greece are found out to follow Greek industrial and commercial enterprises through Southeast European countries as does HSBC.

The above analysis shows the relevance of the pull and push factors mentioned in the literature to the case of Turkey. Apart from these general factors, there are also Turkey-specific reasons yet to be discussed before reaching a conclusion. Table-6 summarizes our findings related with the pull factors relevant for each foreign entry case.

Table 6
Turkey-specific Pull Factors

	Banks						
	NBG-Finans bank	*EFG Euro bank-Tekfen bank*	*Fortis-Dış bank*	*Dexia-Deniz bank*	*GE-Garanti bank*	*HSBC-Demir bank*	*Uni Credito-Koç Group-Yapı Kredi*
Increasing population and per capita income	*	*	*	*			*
Reforms in the investment area	*		*			*	*
High foreign trade and growth potentials	*	*	*	*	*	*	*
Geopolitical importance	*	*	*	*			
EU accession process	*	*	*	*	*		*
[a]Easy to be taken over							
[a]Small size of Turkish banks							
[a]Equal treatment of Turkish and foreign banks							
[a]No limitation to the foreign ownership of banks							
[a]Easier entrance to the Turkish market							
Lower interest rates	*	*	*				*
Declining inflation rates	*	*	*			*	*
Improving corporate governance system	*			*	*		*
Improving auditing and regulation	*		*	*			
Flexible exchange rate system	*						
Basel II Agreement				*			
Consumer credits and mortgage	*	*	*	*	*	*	*

Source: Authors' tabulation from various newspaper issues and internet sources.
[a]: No evidence found with respect to this factor.

Most of the banks included in this study reported that Turkey is an attractive market with an increasing population and per capita income.[37] Its population of approximately 70 million is expected to reach 82 million in a decade and per capita GDP is expected to grow by more than 4 per cent per annum. Therefore, the banking services and the necessary public infrastructure are supposed to increase in near future. This environment is what pulled Dexia, among others, to Turkey, leading to an agreement as to the purchase of 75 per cent shares of Denizbank.

Foreign banks' consideration of Turkey as a country to expand into is also affected by the structural reforms carried out in the macroeconomic environment.[38] After the Nov. 2000 and Feb. 2001 crises resulting in the contraction of the Turkish economy, Banking Sector Restructuring Program was put in place. As a result, financial risks in the banking sector were alleviated, capital structure was strengthened, bank profitability increased and growth prospects in the sector improved. These improvements in the banking industry became the underlying reason of foreign entry in many cases.

Turkey's high foreign trade and growth potential is the mostly cited Turkey-specific pull factor leading foreigners in their choice of Turkey.[39] After recovering from the 2001 financial crisis, Turkey experienced a 7.6 per cent GNP growth in 2005 and the amount of loans given increased. This financial recovery can also be observed from the different mark-ups in Dışbank and Finansbank sales (since growth outlook is said to be the primary factor used in valuations by analysts). For the 2005-2009 period, while the real GDP growth is forecasted to be 2.1 per cent for the Euro zone and 4.3 per cent for the Central and Eastern Europe, more than five per cent growth for the Turkish case increases foreigners' appetite for Turkey, as was the case in Finansbank-NBG and Denizbank-Dexia agreements.[40] As another case, Fortis, which is an expert in commercial and private banking and in insurance, tries to take place in the promising markets outside of Benelux such as Europe and Asia as part of its overall strategy of ten per cent annual growth. GE reports that Garanti Bank provides a strong base for growth with its high quality workforce, wide distribution network and technological background. Moreover, Koç Financial Services aims to grow in the Turkish credit card and consumer credits market, the purchase of Yapı Kredi shares creating a bank big enough to be able to take part in bank sales in the EU.

Although the EU accession negotiations do not mean that Turkey is strong in absolute sense against possible economic and political risks, the journey towards the Union is what puts Turkey in an attractive position from the viewpoint of foreign investors.[41] This can be observed in NBG's suggestion that its choice of Turkey is related in part to its expansion in Europe. As long as the requirements from the EU side as to the trade restrictions are satisfied, the promising investment environment in Turkey will increase foreigners' appetite for Turkey. The relative attractiveness of the Turkish financial market can be observed from data in Table 7. The share of net interest income in total assets is bigger in Turkey than in EU-25 and the selected EU countries, with 4.61 versus 1.31, pronouncing one more time the high profitability of the Turkish banking sector. In terms of Return on Assets, data show that Turkey has high growth potentials compared to others, having a figure three times as much as that in EU-25 or in the selected countries. Moreover, personnel expenditures to total assets and nonperforming loans to total loans ratios attract attention due to their high levels compared to those of EU-25 and the selected EU members.

In June, 2003, Law No 4875 on Foreign Direct Investment was issued in order for the Turkish foreign investment to comply with international standards. Before this law was passed, founding a new company, new branches, liaison offices or participations required the permission of the Foreign Capital General Directorate. Under this law, however, all but the liaison offices are required to give information and only for statistical purposes. Additionally, foreigners can now make foreign direct investments with no extra burden such as the previous requirement of 50.000 EUR. They no more need to have permission before the establishment stage, and are able to form all types of legal entities that domestic firms are allowed to form and with no limitation. Therefore, differences in the treatment of Turkish and foreign investors are vanishing, and as a result of the simplified process, it has become easier to establish a firm in Turkey encouraging foreign investment.[42]

Improving macroeconomic situation of Turkey is also frequently mentioned by foreign banks among the pull factors.[43] Inflation has seen single digit numbers after long years of high

Table 7
Comparison of Turkey and EU with respect to selected financial ratios:

%	*EU-25*	*Germany*[1]	*Holland*[2]	*Turkey(*)*
Net Interest Income/ Total Assets	1,31	1,18	1,30	4,61
Personnel Expenditure/ Total Assets	0,85	0,57	0,90	1,33
Debt Securities/ Total Assets	19,65	19,90	22,60	36,03
Total Loans/Total Assets	65,72	72,80	54,90	37,80
Nonperforming Loans(gross) / Total Loans	2,73			5,00
Non-cash Loans/ Total Assets	15,28		16,60	16,30
Net Non-interest Income/ Total Income	43,42			19,41
Net Interest Income/ Total Income	56,58	73,40	58,40	80,59
Total Expenses/ Total Income	59,42		71,50	82,56
Managerial Expenses/ Total Expenses	31,40		34,50	36,60
Return on Assets	0,50	0,67	0,50	1,68
Return on Equity	12,21	4,20	9,80	11,81

Note: EU-25 data are as of 2004 and taken from ECB Banking Sector Stability
(*) Turkey data are as of the end of 2005.
[1] Association of German Banks, 2004 data
[2] De Nederlandishe Bank 2004 & 2005 data

and chronic inflation. Interest rates have been low, which, together with increasing income and consumer confidence, increase loans to GDP ratio, and enable banks to perform their mediatory role more effectively. In fact, from May, 2007 on, no tax will be imposed on financial intermediation supporting the recent development.

Foreigners also come to Turkey choosing banks with sound corporate governance.[44] One example is Dexia purchasing 75 per cent of Denizbank which successfully minimized the negative impacts of the crises period through its strong management, and continued its operations without deviating from its steady growth strategies. Another case is the GE- Garanti agreement. Garanti Bank was chosen primarily due to its improved corporate governance in which area GE was placed first in a survey by Financial Times.[45] One underlying reason in the UniCredito-Koç Group and Yapı Kredi deal was to have a clear managerial structure, a better commercial image (there would no more be two banks for the same customer base) and a simpler balance sheet structure.[46]

The fact that the New Basel Accord will be effective in Turkey from 2008 on will create an economic environment with better supervision and market discipline.[47] High capital adequacy ratios in the banking sector will decrease to 16.9 per cent with the new arrangement. The need for consolidation in the sector will be more intensely felt, and thus internationalization of the financial sector will gain popularity.[48] A survey conducted by Turkish Banking Regulation and Supervision Agency on the readiness of the sector for Basel II revealed that with respect to the per centage of assets in the total banking sector, 50.5 per cent is at the beginning level, 45.70 per cent is at the intermediate level, 2.8 per cent is at advanced level and less than one per cent have not yet started the process. When it becomes effective, Basel II will add to banks' transparency and quality of risk management which make Turkey an attractive market to expand into.

Signals for growth in the mortgage industry is an additional factor increasing the popularity of Turkey from the point of view of foreign banks. In this respect, it is beneficial to mention about one other underlying reason for foreign entry. Behind the scene, there lies the fact that high population in Turkey, migration from rural areas to big cities, and high rental fees have created housing problems in Turkey with a burden of 300.000 new demand for houses per year.[49] The severity of the case is better understood by the fact that on its own the city İstanbul welcomes as many migrants in one year as Paris does in 30 years.[50] Additionally, only three per cent of housing has been financed by banks in Turkey during 2002- 2004 period. While the housing financing market constituted 40 per cent of GNP in Europe and 5-15 per cent in developing countries, Turkey lagged behind considerably. Nevertheless, low inflation coupled with falling interest rates recently facilitated the process of change in legislation granting banks the right to offer mortgages.[51] With the new legislation, financing institutions will have been granted tax benefits, foreclosure procedures for mortgage will be shorter and floating interest rates will become considerable. As a result of all these, many foreign banks such as NBG and Dexia, which are experts in mortgage and consumer banking, entered into Turkey to take advantage of this high growth potential in mortgage as well as in consumer credit markets. Moreover, HSBC's motivation was no different from these two as long as the development in the mortgage market is concerned.

IV. CONCLUSION

Out of a need to explore the reasons for the recent spread of foreign banking in Turkey, this research attempts to provide the reader with insight on the issue using information from seven bank entry cases. This study is not concerned about whether foreign entry is good or bad or the subsequent effects of foreign entry, but about the "why" side of the issue trying to compensate for the fact that there is no study on the issue concerning the Turkish case.

While examining the reasons of foreign entry, in the first section, we have listed the pull and push factors given in the literature attempting to find similarities to the foreign entry case for Turkey. Because of our need to delve into the issue for the Turkish case, in the next section, we looked at the Turkey-specific pull factors going over the seven foreign entry cases selected, the foreign parties being National Bank of Greece (NBG) and EFG Eurobank from Greece, Fortis of Netherlands, Dexia from Belgium, General Electric (GE) from the United States, HSBC of England, and UniCredito from Italy.

In our research, most of our findings confirm the reasons spelled in the literature. One frequently pronounced reason of entry is the improving macroeconomic environment in Turkey reflecting itself in low inflation numbers after long years of high and chronic inflation, and declining interest rates. Additionally, Turkey's importance in the geo-political arena together with its increasing population and per capita income make our domestic market attractive.

One other finding of this study is that although foreigners are mostly welcomed on the expectation of a higher level of technology, the Turkish case shows that it may be foreigners who expect technology improvement following the deal. The same situation is also relevant when the relatively richer product and service variety in Turkey is concerned in that foreigners aim to take advantage of the diversity of financial products and services in Turkey.

Apart from this factor, high growth potential in our domestic banking industry is a reason mentioned by all the entrants among their motivators in choosing Turkey. In this growing macroeconomic environment, foreign banks expand into Turkey to buy not only banks per se but also market share, which is more difficult to acquire. Additionally, financial liberalization in the sector increased the depth of the Turkish financial market as a result of more severe competition, and this in turn led to even higher foreign share in the domestic sector.

In addition to many other countries, Turkish financial market will open a new page after Basel II Requirements become effective in 2008. Supervision in the banking sector will be improved and this will create an environment with high level of confidence in the system pulling foreigners to Turkey.

High growth potential in the mortgage sector is another frequently mentioned reason attracting the attention of foreigners. For long years, banks have not been engaged in the task of housing financing. However, problems of housing will be alleviated by banks offering an increasing amount of mortgages thanks to the improving macroeconomic situation in Turkey.

While an increasing foreign share in the Turkish financial market may be attractive as well as beneficial, the issue still deserves to have a closer look. It seems to be the case that Turkey's bank owners give up on a sector that is likely to be a very lucrative market in the future due to high discount rates on domestic banks, i.e., long term gains seem to be sacrificed in search for short term profits.

Notes

1. See Financial Stability Report (June 2006)-Turkish Central Bank, pp. 37-56.

2. This number increases to 33.6 per cent when shares traded in the stock exchange are taken into account. This and the following figures as to foreign share in consumer credits and debts come from various issues released by the BRSA of Turkey.

3. See Vesile Çakar, "Yabancı Sermayeli Banka Girişleri ve Ulusal Bankacılık Sektörleri Üzerindeki Etkileri," TCMB Bankacılık ve Finansal Kuruluþlar Genel Müdürlüğü, TCMB Uzmanlık Yeterlilik Tezi (2003), p.21.

   Ziya Öniş and Ahmet F. Aysan, "Neoliberal Globalization, the Nation-State and Financial Crises in the Semi-Periphery: A Comparative Analysis," *Third World Quarterly* (February 2000), p. 15.

4. See Heather Montgomery, "The Role of Foreign Banks in Post-Crisis Asia: The Importance of Method of Entry," *ADB Institute*, Research Paper Series No: 51, (2003), p.3.; Dietrich Domanski, "Foreign banks in emerging market economies: changing players, changing issues," *BIS Quarterly Review* (2005), p. 71.

5. See Hongyu Liu, "Foreign Participation in Banking Reform: The Poland Experience," *Perspectives*, Vol. 2, No.4, Overseas Young Chinese Forum 2001-2002 (2001), p. 3.

6. See Luiz Fernando Rodrigues De Paula and Antonio J. Alves, Jr. "The determinants and effects of foreign bank entry in Argentina and Brazil: a comparative analysis," (2003), p. 10.

7. See Yongil Jeon, Stephen M. Miller and Paul A. Natke, "Do foreign bank operations provide a stabilizing influence in Korea?," *The Quarterly Review of Economics and Finance*, Vol. 46 (2006), p. 83.

8. See Claudia M. Buch and Stefan M. Golder, "Domestic and Foreign Banks in Germany: Do They Differ?," *Kiel Institute of World Economics*, Kiel Working Paper No. 986 (2000), p. 37.

9. Tier 1 capital is the core measure of a bank's financial strength from the viewpoint of a regulator. Being a measure of the capital adequacy of a bank, it includes financial capital that is considered the most reliable and liquid, primarily Shareholders' equity.Tier-1 ratio equals tier-1 capital divided by risk-adjusted assets.
10. See Jonathan Coppel and Michael Davies, "Foreign Participation in East Asia's Banking Sector," Contribution to the CGFS Working Group on FDI in the Financial Sector of Emerging Market Economies, International Development, Reserve Bank of Australia (2003), p. 22. Christian Weller, "The Supply of Credit by Multinational Banks in Developing and Transition Economies: Determinants and Effects," *United Nations*, DESA Discussion paper No. 16 (2001), p. 12. Allen N. Berger, Robert DeYoung, Hesna Genay and Gregory F. Udell, "Globalisation of Financial Institutions: Evidence from Cross-border Banking Performance," Brookings-Wharton Papers on Financial Service, Vol. 3 (2000), p. 23–158, p. 7.
11. Vesile Çakar, "Yabancı Sermayeli Banka Girişleri ve Ulusal Bankacılık Sektörleri Üzerindeki Etkileri," TCMB Bankacılık ve Finansal Kuruluþlar Genel Müdürlüğü, TCMB Uzmanlık Yeterlilik Tezi (2003), p. 18.
12. See Luiz Fernando Rodrigues Paula, "The Determinants of the Recent Entry of Foreign Banks in Brazil," Proceedings of the 5th Brazilian Congress of Economic History and the 6th International Conference on Business History, No. 023 (2003), p. 10.
13. B. Gerard Dages, Linda Goldberg and Daniel Kinney, "Foreign and Domestic Bank Participation in Emerging Markets: Lessons from Mexico and Argentina," *FRBNY Economic Policy Review*, (Sep. 2000), p. 18.
14. Evan Kraft, "Foreign Banks in Croatia: Another Look," *Croatian National Bank, Zagreb*: Croatian National Bank Working Paper W-10 (2002), p. 7.
15. Luiz Fernando Rodrigues De Paula and Antonio J. Alves, Jr. "The determinants and effects of foreign bank entry in Argentina and Brazil: a comparative analysis," (2003), p. 8.
16. See Claudia M. Buch, "Why Do Banks Go Abroad? Evidence from German Data," *Financial Markets, Institutions & Instruments*, Vol. 9, No.1 (2000), p. 37. Christopher J. Green, Victor Murinde and Ivalyo Nikolov, "The Efficiency of Foreign and Domestic Banks in Central and Eastern Europe: Evidence on Economies of Scale and Scope," *Journal of Emerging Market Finance*, Vol. 3, No. 2 (2002), p. 178. Robert Lensink and Niels Hermes, "The Impact of Foreign Bank Entry on Domestic Banks: Does Economic Development Matter?," *Journal of Banking and Finance*, Vol. 28, No.3 (2002), pp. 553-568.
17. Adrian E. Tschoegl, "Financial Crises & the Presence of Foreign Banks," *Wharton Financial Institutions Center*, Wharton Financial Institutions Center Working Paper Series No: 03-35. (2003), p. 20.
18. Julan Du, "Why Do Multinational Enterprises Borrow From Local Banks?," *Economics Letters*, Vol. 78, No. 2 (2003), p. 287.
19. Luiz Fernando Rodrigues Paula, "The Determinants of the Recent Entry of Foreign Banks in Brazil," Proceedings of the 5th Brazilian Congress of Economic History and the 6th International Conference on Business History, No. 023 (2003), p. 3.
20. Evan Kraft, "Foreign Banks in Croatia: Another Look," *Croatian National Bank: Zagreb*, Croatian National Bank Working Paper W-10 (2002), p. 7.
21. Ibid., p. 14.
22. Vesile Çakar "Yabancı Sermayeli Banka Giriþleri ve Ulusal Bankacılık Sektörleri Üzerindeki Etkileri," TCMB Bankacılık ve Finansal Kuruluþlar Genel Müdürlüğü, TCMB Uzmanlık Yeterlilik Tezi (2003), p.21.
23. Oktay Özdabakoğlu, "Şirketler borsadan da ele geçirilebilmeli," Analiz (October 30, 2005), http://www.referansgazetesi.com/haber.aspx?HBR_KOD=26865&ForArsiv=1 Data come from various issues of BRSA of Turkey.

24. Vesile Çakar, "Yabancı Sermayeli Banka Giriþleri ve Ulusal Bankacılık Sektörleri Üzerindeki Etkileri," TCMB Bankacılık ve Finansal Kuruluþlar Genel Müdürlüğü, TCMB Uzmanlık Yeterlilik Tezi (2003), p. 27.
25. Ibid., p. 41.
26. Carrick Mollenkamp, "Greek Bank to Acquire Turkey's Finansbank for 5.5 billion euros," Wall Street Journal on the Web (April 3, 2006), http://www.eubusiness.com/East_Europe/060329111626.oleml184
27. Evan Kraft, "Foreign Banks in Croatia: Another Look," *Croatian National Bank: Zagreb*, Croatian National Bank Working Paper W-10 (2002), p.14.
28. Ibid., p. 2.
29. Data come from various issues of BRSA of Turkey.
30. Oya Celasun, Cevdet Denizer,Dong He, "Capital Flows, Macroeconomic Management, and the Financial System: The Turkish Case, 1989–97," pp. 1-58.
31. Evan Kraft, "Foreign Banks in Croatia: Another Look," Croatian National Bank: Zagreb, Croatian National Bank Working Paper W-10 (2002), p. 7.
32. Luiz Fernando Rodrigues Paula, "The Determinants of the Recent Entry of Foreign Banks in Brazil," Proceedings of the 5th Brazilian Congress of Economic History and the 6th International Conference on Business History, No. 023 (2003), p.3.
33. Yasemin Kapýyoldaþ, "Bölgesel köprü Türkiye," March 20, 2006 http://www.radikal.com.tr/haber.php?haberno=181867
34. Elif Özmenek, "ABD Büyükelçisi Wilson New York'ta," Voanews , New York (January 11, 2006) http://www.voanews.com/turkish/archive/2006-01/2006-01-11-voa6.cfm.
35. Ufuk Şanlı, "Yunanlar yeniden 'Küçük Asya'da," Aksiyon Haftalýk Haber Dergisi, Sayı: 597 (May 15, 2006), http://www.aksiyon.com.tr/detay.php?id=24235.
36. Claudia M. Buch, "Why Do Banks Go Abroad? Evidence from German Data," *Financial Markets, Institutions & Instruments*, Vol. 9, No. 1 (2000), p. 37.; Christopher J. Green, Victor Murinde and Ivalyo Nikolov, "The Efficiency of Foreign and Domestic Banks in Central and Eastern Europe: Evidence on Economies of Scale and Scope," *Journal of Emerging Market Finance,* Vol. 3, No. 2 (2002), p. 178.; Robert Lensink and Niels Hermes, "The Impact of Foreign Bank Entry on Domestic Banks: Does Economic Development Matter?," *Journal of Banking and Finance*, Vol. 28, No. 3 (2002), pp. 553-568.
37. Begüm Tatari, "Yabancıların Bankacılık Sektörüne İlgisi," İzmir Ticaret Odası (2005),

    http://www.izto.org.tr/NR/rdonlyres/B942DEAC-917E-4200-81F5-2D065174DF75/4914/YabBanka1.pdf; Active ACADEMY Araştırma Merkezi, Bankacýlýkta Yabancý Sermaye Politikasý Doğru Belirlenmeli (Eylül, 2005).
38. Tatari, Begüm, "Yabancıların Bankacılık Sektörüne İlgisi," İzmir Ticaret Odası (2005),

    http://www.izto.org.tr/NR/rdonlyres/B942DEAC-917E-4200-81F5-2D065174DF75/4914/YabBanka1.pdf, p.2.; Active ACADEMY Araştırma Merkezi, ankacılıkta Yabancı Sermaye Politikası Doğru Belirlenmeli (Eylül, 2005), p.3.; Hüseyin Al and Ahmet Faruk Aysan, "Assessing the Preconditions in Establishing an Independent Regulatory and Supervisory Agency in Globalized Financial Markets: The Case of Turkey," forthcoming in the International Journal of Applied Business and Economic Research,Vol. 4, No. 2 (2006), p. 16.
39. Murat Beşinci, "Bankacılıkta yabancı sermaye neden artıyor?," Ekonomistler Bülteni 52. sayı (2005), http://www.bilgiyonetimi.org/cm/pages/mkl_gos.php?nt=609.; Active ACADEMY Araştırma Merkezi, Bankacılıkta Yabancı Sermaye Politikası Doğru Belirlenmeli (Eylül 2005), p. 1.
40. Carrick Mollenkamp, "Greek Bank to Acquire Turkey's Finansbank for 5.5 billion euros," Wall Street Journal on the Web (April 3, 2006), http://www.eubusiness.com/East_Europe/060329111626.oleml184.

41. Begüm Tatari, Yabancıların Bankacılık Sektörüne İlgisi," İzmir Ticaret Odası (2005), http://www.izto.org.tr/NR/rdonlyres/B942DEAC-917E-4200-81F5-2D065174DF75/4914/YabBanka1.pdf, p.1.; Active ACADEMY Araþtırma Merkezi, Bankacılıkta Yabancı Sermaye Politikası Doğru Belirlenmeli (Eylül 2005), p. 1.
42. Hergüner Bilgen Özeke, "Turkey: New Hope for Mortgage Banking," International Financial Law Review , Istanbul (March 2005), http://www.iflr.com/?Page=10&PUBID=33&ISS=14951&SID = 512716 & TYPE =20.; Data come from various issues of BRSA.
43. Begüm Tatari, "Yabancıların Bankacılık Sektörüne İlgisi," İzmir Ticaret Odası (2005), http://www.izto.org.tr/NR/rdonlyres/B942DEAC-917E-4200-81F5-2D065174DF75/4914/YabBanka1.pdf, p. 2.; Active ACADEMY Araştırma Merkezi, Bankacılıkta Yabancı Sermaye Politikası Doğru Belirlenmeli (Eylül 2005), p. 1.
44. Begüm Tatari, "Yabancıların Bankacılık Sektörüne İlgisi," İzmir Ticaret Odası (2005), http://www.izto.org.tr/NR/rdonlyres/B942DEAC-917E-4200-81F5-2D065174DF75/4914/YabBanka1.pdf, p.2.
45. Michael Skapinker, "Different Game, Same Winners," GE in the news, http://www.ge.com/en/company/news/ft_story.htm.
46. Data come from various issues of BRSA.
47. Active ACADEMY Araþtýrma Merkezi, Bankacılıkta Yabancı Sermaye Politikası Doðru Belirlenmeli (Eylül 2005), p. 1.
48. Ziya Öniş, and E. Alper, " The Turkish Banking System,Financial Crises and the IMF in the Age of Capital Account Liberalization: A Political Economy Perspective," *New Perspectives on Turkey*, 30, p. 18.
49. Hergüner Bilgen Özeke, Istanbul, "Turkey: Foreign investment," International Financial Law Review, Istanbul (October 2003), http://www.iflr.com/?Page=10&PUBID=33&ISS=12024&SID=512054&TYPE=20.
50. Yaman Törüner, "İstanbul'a Göç," Milliyet (Eylül 4, 2006).
51. Münür Yayla, Yasemin Türker Kaya, İbrahim Ekmen, "Bankacılık Sektörüne Yabancı Girişi: Küresel Gelipmeler ve Türkiye," BDDK ARD Çalışma Raporları: 2005/6, Araþtırma Dairesi. Ankara: BDDK (2005), p. 36.

CONSERVATIVES, LIBERALS, THE PARTY IN POWER, AND INCOME INEQUALITY

*William R. Dipietro**

Abstract

This paper uses simple time series regressions of income inequality on dummy variables for party affiliation of the prime minister in Australia, Canada, and the United Kingdom to assess the effect of party leadership on income inequality in parliamentary democracies. The results suggest that party leadership matters with regard to the degree of income inequality experienced in these societies.

The central question in this paper is whether, and, if so, to what extent, in a democratic government, the party membership of the top leadership of the central government matters with regard to income equality of a nation. That is to say, disregarding the rhetoric, does the leadership of one party tend to have a superior track record of greater equality when compared to another? For instance, do conservative governments tend to produce greater equality than more liberal governments?

A secondary issue, given the potential trade off between economic growth and equity, is the effect of party leadership on economic growth. The position taken here is that the relationship between growth and inequality depends on the starting position of the economy and the particular set of policies pursued by the government in power. Depending on the starting position of the economy, sometimes the relationship may be positive, sometimes it may be negative, and sometimes there may be no relationship at all.

The study ignores the particulars, the inner workings of one party compared to another with regard to income inequality. .The interest of the paper is on the big picture. The focus is not on the how, the means for modifying inequality that are used by the leadership of one party compared to another. Rather, it is on the outcome of all policies taken together in concert as a group. In other words, the emphasis is on the *total net* effect on income inequality of the entire arsenal of measures employed by the government of one party compared to another.

Looking at the entire picture, disregarding the trees and concentrating on the forest as a whole, for a democracy, does it matter whether the leadership of the country comes from one party or from another with regard to the extent of income inequality in a country?

To see whether the party leadership matters with regard to income inequality and with regard to economic growth in a democratic society, three countries are explored. The countries

* Professor of Economics, Department of Business Administratio, Daemen College, 4380, Main Street, Amherst.

are Australia, Canada, and the United Kingdom. Each of these three countries is a parliamentary democracy. The parliamentary system is selected because there is little question where the locus of power lies. The power is in the hands of the party of the prime minister holding office. The prime minister is the leader of the majority in the house of commons. He rules as long as, and only as long as, he has a majority. In non-parliamentary democracies such as the United States, the locus of power is rather nebulous. It probably shifts over time between the president, the senate and the house. The United States is run by fixed term president, fixed term senators, and fixed term congressmen. Unlike the prime minister in a parliamentary system, the president continues in office even when the majority in the house and the senate are from a different party.

To achieve its goals, this paper is divided into six sections. The first section reviews some of the literature on inequality. The second section outlines some of the sources of income inequality, and identifies the government as an important potential player in income determination. The third section provides inequality profiles for the three countries that are considered here, Australia, Canada, and the United Kingdom. The fourth section looks at the fundamental relationship under investigation—the relationship between income inequality and party leadership. It shows the results of inequality regressions using dummy variables for the party membership of the party holding power. The fifth section uses the same party dummies to look at the potential effects on growth from different party policies. Finally, the last section provides a brief conclusion with potential direction for future research

I. LITERATURE REVIEW

The literature on income inequality, the government's role in determining income distribution, and the trade-off between income equality and economic growth is extensive. The effect of inequality on growth is controversial. In the classic study Kuznets postulates that inequality at first increases with growth but eventually falls with growth when a threshold level of development is achieved (Kuznets 1955). Turning to more recent studies, Perotti, using growth as a function of inequality, finds a negative effect of inequality on growth for his growth equation estimates (Peotti 1996). Similarly, Deininger and Squire find a negative relationship between inequality and growth in their cross country regression analysis when using the data set they developed for measuring inequality for countries around the world (Deininger and Squire 1998).

Although the negative effect of increased growth on income equality is found to be quite small, Scully, however, in his article, "Economic Freedom, Government Policy and the Trade-Off between Equity and Economic Growth", estimates a multi- equation structural model, and finds a positive relationship between growth and income inequality, (Scully 2002). Scully also finds that economic freedom promotes both growth and equity, and that a few assorted government policy variables affect either growth or income equality.

Without denying the possibility of a long-run negative effect of inequality on growth, Forbes uses panel estimation and also finds a positive relationship between income inequality and economic growth over the short and medium term (Forbes 2000).

According to Chang, even when assuming empirically a negative correlation between inequality and growth, without a clearly established theoretical relationship between inequality and growth, a policy dilemma arises in which it is not clear whether or not the government can or should address income inequality through intervention (Chang 1994). Chang reviews the two major classes of theories with regard to growth and inequality-politico economic theories and financial imperfections theories. He stresses the need to identify whether causation runs from equality to growth or from growth to equality.

Turning to the political science literature, Bradley and his co-authors bemoan the fact that so little has been done focusing on the determinants of distributive outcomes in societies (Bradley et al., 2003). Using data from the Luxembourg Income Survey, they find that leftist government is an important determinant of government redistribution.

II. THE GOVERNMENT AS PRIME MOVER OF INCOME INEQUALITY

Within any given country, there are myriads of possible reasons for differences in incomes between individuals. An individual may earn more than someone else simply because he has greater ability and is more productive. Another individual may earn more because of his psychological make-up. For instance, he may, because of an abnormally high level of need achievement, be highly motivated to work hard and long hours. Another individual may earn more because he has greater amounts of human capital in the form of education and training. Someone may command a comparably higher salary because he is employed in a high paying occupation. Different individuals may be at different stages of the life cycle. Some people may save heavily all their life and be just a few years from retirement. As a result of their thrifty ways, they may have accumulated sizable nest eggs, and they may be making substantial amounts of non-wage income. Other individuals may be making very high incomes because of their inherited wealth. Still other individuals may be making little money because they are unemployed, or because they are working in a nonunion zed sectors of the economy, or because they belong to a group that is subject to discrimination. Overall, in a capitalist system anything leading to differences in productivity between individuals or any factor leading to differences in wealth between individuals is a potential cause of inequality. In non-capitalistic systems or to the degree a system is not capitalistic, nonproductive factors such as who you are (by birth or some other ready classification), or who you know (your connections) are major sources of inequality.

It is important to recognize that the government can and does affect any and all of the potential determinants of inequality, and, can directly tamper with income inequality through its policies.

Operationally, there are uncountable ways in which the government can influence inequality by exercising its authority and power. It can establish a minimum wage. It can establish transfer programs of various sorts. It can tax or provide subsidies of various sorts and varieties. It can determine the extent to which bequests are allowable. It can modify welfare programs for the poor, social security for the aged, unemployment compensation, health care, public education, and, directly set wages. The government's reach through legislation, regulation, and rule making is almost unlimited.

In a global sense, the government can affect income inequality in two fundamental ways. First, through taxation, by deciding who it taxes, and, second, through spending, by deciding who it spends on. It can cause income inequality to go up or to go down. At the one extreme, if the government was strictly to tax the poor and spend the money exclusively on the rich, then it would have a pronounced negative effect on inequality. At the other extreme, if the government exclusively taxed the rich and spent all of its money on the poor, then it would act as an agent for reducing income inequality.

Given that the government can have uncountable influences on all of the determinants of income inequality, and given the net effect of government policies as a whole can be positive or negative with regard to income inequality, the central hypothesis of this paper is that whether the government exerts a positive or negative influence on inequality depends on who is running the government. That is to say, the overall effect of the enormous power of the government on income inequality depends on the party in power.

III. THE UPWARD MOVEMENT IN INCOME INEQUALITY

Some people are expressing deep concern over perceived increases in income inequality in society. Are these concerns justified? Should income equality become a major public policy issue? What has been happening to income inequality in Australia, Canada, and Great Britain?

The Texas inequality center constructs Gini coefficients for various countries around the world for the period 1963-1998. The numbers are posted on their website These numbers will be used as our measure of income inequality for the countries throughout the paper.

Figure I show yearly time graphs of income inequality as measured by the Gini coefficient for the three countries, Australia, Canada, and Great Britain. Inequality is plotted on the vertical axis, and time is plotted on the horizontal axis.

A look at figure I clearly show that the grumblings over increased income inequality are well founded. In every one of the three countries, income inequality rose during the 1963-1998 period. The increase in inequality was greatest for the United Kingdom, followed closely by Australia, and then, by a far third, by Canada .In Great Britain, the Gini coefficient started at 29.24 in 1963, and ended at 34.12 in 1998 .In Australia, the coefficient started in 1963 at 31.99, and ended in 1997 with 36.83. Lastly, in Canada, the Gini coefficient started at 35.49 in 1963, and ended at 36.0 in 1998.

While, over the period, the increase in inequality was smallest for Canada, it had the worst record in terms of average inequality between the three countries, and, while the increase in inequality was greatest in the United Kingdom, it had the best record in terms of average inequality between the three countries. For the period, the Gini coefficient averaged 35.15 for Canada, 33.38 for Australia, and 31.29 for the United Kingdom.

In sum, for the period 1963-1998, Canada had the lowest average inequality but the smallest rise in inequality. The United Kingdom had the lowest average inequality and the largest rise in inequality. Australia was in the middle. It fell between Canada and the United Kingdom both in terms of average inequality and the increase in inequality.

Figure I
Trends In Income Inequality In Australia, Canada, And The United Kingdom

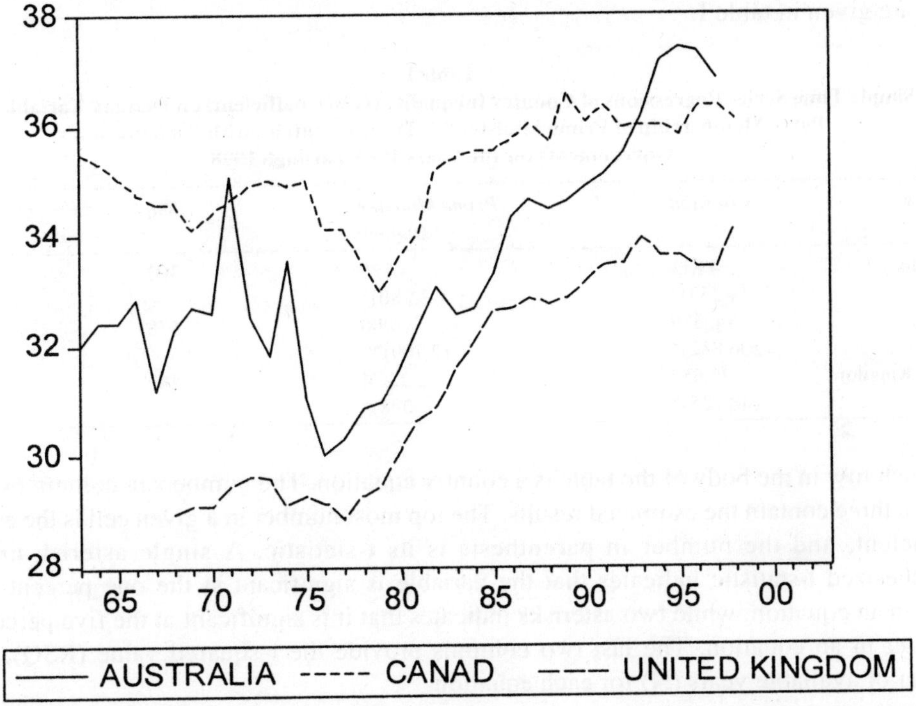

The different inequality profiles provide three unique cases for assessing the effect of party leadership on income inequality in parliamentary democracies.

IV. SIMPLE TIME SERIES REGRESSIONS OF INEQUALITY ON PRIME MINISTER DUMMIES

To see whether differences in party leadership result in quantifiable differences in income inequality for three countries, simple time series regressions using yearly data and dummy variables for party leadership are employed. For the three countries under parliamentary governments (United Kingdom, Canada, and Australia), the GINI coefficient is run on a modified dummy which takes on a value of one when the prime minister for a particular year is from a particular party, zero when the prime minister is not from the selected party, and one-half when it is a transition year resulting in a change in the prime minister ship from one party to another. For the United Kingdom and Canada, the two parties that held the prime ministry during the period are the conservatives and the liberals. In these two countries the prime minister dummy takes on a value of one when there is a conservative prime minister in office. In Australia, the two major parties, in the period under consideration, are the liberal party and the labor party. The prime minister variable dummy for Australia equals one when a liberal party minister is in office, zero when some other party minister is in office, and one-half in a transition year.

The results of the regressions of income inequality, as measured by the Gini coefficient, on the prime minister dummy variable for three parliamentary countries for the years 1963 through 1998 are given in table I.

Table I
Simple Time Series Regressions of Country Inequality (Gini Coefficient) on Dummy Variable for Party Membership of Prime Minister for Three Countries with Parliamentary Governments for the Years 1963 Through 1998

Country	*Constant*	*Prime Minister Dummy*	*Rsq*	*N*
Australia	4.811 (4.253)*	-.128 (-3.780)*	.302	35
Canada	34..889 (206.812)*	.906 (2.709)**	.178	36
United Kingdom	29.652 (48.735)*	2.274 (3.098)*	.242	32

Each row in the body of the table is a country equation. The numbers in column two and in column three contain the estimated results. The top most number in a given cell is the estimated coefficient, and the number in parenthesis is its t-statistic. A single asterisk under the parenthesized t-statistic indicates that the variable is significant at the one percent level or better in an equation, while two asterisks indicates that it is significant at the five percent level or better in an equation. The last two columns provide the r-squared value (RSQ), and the number of available years (N) for each equation.

There is no question whether a government has the ability to change the level of income inequality in a society. The question is not whether, but rather to what extent different parties exercise this power. Looking at table I it is clear that the parties do indeed use the power, and that they use it in a systematic way. In every one of the three country equations in table I, the prime minister dummy is significant at the five percent level of significance or better. For two of the three countries, Australia and the United Kingdom, the prime minister variable is significant at the one percent level or better.

A look at the r-squares for the country equations, reveal that the prime minister dummy explains anywhere from over seventeen percent (Canada) to over thirty percent (Australia) of the total variation of country income inequality over the period.

What story do the signs on the prime minister dummy tell? Two countries, Canada and the U.K., lend support to the hypothesis that more conservative governments are associated with greater inequality, while, one country, Australia, contradicts the hypothesis. Recalling that higher values of the Gini coefficient measure greater income inequality and that lower values of the Gini coefficient mean there is greater income equality, the signs tell us that Liberal party leadership in Australia (the more conservative party in Australia) is associated with greater income equality, while Conservative party (the more conservative party in both Canada and the U.K.) leadership in both Canada and the United Kingdom is associated with greater income inequality.

Regardless of the sign, the sizes of the coefficients on the prime minister variables indicate that the party affiliation of the prime minister exerts a sizable impact on inequality in a democratic society. In Canada, having a prime minister form the Conservative party leads to almost a one point increase in the Gini coefficient. Since the Gini coefficient only varies between zero and one-hundred, this is notable difference in income inequality. In the United Kingdom, a prime minister from the Conservative party, on average, leads to an increase in the Gini coefficient by over two and one half points. Lastly, even in Australia, where the coefficient on the prime minister dummy is the smallest in absolute value terms, leadership by the Liberal party causes the Gini coefficient to drop by over a tenth of a point.

V. POLICIES LEADING TO GREATER INCOME EQUALITY. IS THERE A TRADE-OFF BETWEEN EQUITY AND ECONOMIC GROWTH IN THE OPERATION OF REAL WORLD ECONOMIES?

Alas but, you might say what about economic growth? Traditionally, economists maintain there is a potential sacrifice in efficiency for potential gains in equity. This, however, depends on the initial position of the economy when equity policies are undertaken. The true trade-off assumes that we start at a position of maximum potential output for the initial distribution of income. Realistically, in a real world economy, this is not likely to be the case. Rather, we are likely to be starting from a position within the frontier. From a starting position within the frontier, a variety of outcomes from pursing equity policy are possible. In particular, it is possible for policies to increase income equality and lower growth, or for policies to increase income equality and raise growth, or for policies to increase income equality and leave growth unchanged, or, in the worse case scenario, for policies to reduce income equality and reduce growth.

The situation with regard to the equity growth trade-off is exactly analogous to the cost trade-off relationship between two goods along the production possibilities relationship. The trade-off between two goods only exists when you start at some point on the curve. If you start at a point inside the production possibilities curve, then you can increase one good without reducing the other, or even while increasing the other.

Given the plethora of policy tools the government has at its disposal to effect inequality, and assuming we are somewhere within the equity–efficiency frontier, it is certainly possible for the government to increase equity without reducing growth or even while simultaneously increasing growth. For instance, suppose the government where to subsidize the education of individuals with high IQs from poor neighborhoods. In this case, both equity and potential productivity are likely to be enhanced. A similar result would probably be forthcoming if the government pursued policies to reduce unemployment.

Different parties pursue different policies. The set of policies the government chooses to implement matter. The types of policy pursued by the party in power will determine what happens in the areas of equity and growth. Over time, given that an economy is usually in a suboptimal position, it is possible for one party to fare better on both fronts, on only one of the fronts, or on neither of the fronts when compared to another party.

In section III it was shown that party leadership matters in terms of income distribution for the three countries. To see whether, overall, the policies undertaken by the leadership of one party compared to another differ in terns of economic growth, the prime ministers dummies where once again employed. This time, instead of inequality as the dependent variable, economic growth is used. The data source for the measure for economic growth is the World Bank. The measure is the growth rate of GDP per capita based on constant local currency.

The results of the series of country growth regressions are shown in table II. The table is constructed in an analogous manner as table I.

Table II

Simple Time Series Regressions of Economic Growth (Annual Percentage Growth Rate of GDP Per Capita Based on Constant Local Currency) on Dummy Variable for Party Membership of Prime Minister for Three Countries with Parliamentary Governments for The Years 1963 Through 2000

Country	*Constant*	*Prime Minister Dummy*	*Rsq*	*N*
Australia	2.039	.439	.010	38
	(3.763)*	(.602)		
Canada	2.549	-1.431	.079	35
	(5.923)*	(-1.686)		
United Kingdom	2.087	.111	.001	38
	(3.828)*	(.156)		

Unlike the inequality results of table I, in none of the three countries is the prime minister dummy significant at even the ten percent level or better. The r-square values are dismally low, implying that differences in party leadership have little influence on economic growth.

The implications of the combined results of table I and table II is that, in the real world, a party can pursue policies that change a country's income equality without having an effect on economic growth when compared to other parties. In Australia, the Liberal party reduced inequality without any notable change in economic growth compared to the other parties. In the United Kingdom, the conservative party increased income inequality without much impact on economic growth compared to the Labour party. In Canada, where in table II the coefficient of the prime minister value and its corresponding t-statistic are largest in absolute value compared to the other countries, it even appears that the policies of the Conservative party were detrimental to both income equality and economic growth when compared to its counterpart.

VI. CONCLUSION

What are some of the findings of this study? Three major things come to light.

First, in recent years, income inequality has been rising in the three parliamentary democracies of Australia, Canada, and the United Kingdom. If in these advanced democratic economies the trend in income inequality is upward, then it certainly raises yellow caution flags with regard to the future direction of income inequality for the rest of the world. Second, party leadership appears to be an important factor in determining the extent of income inequality in parliamentary democracies. This means that voters should never be apathetic in their selection of leaders, but rather be very careful who they put in office. The party in office influences how income is distributed. Third, when party leadership policies succeed in improving income inequality, the improvement does not necessarily come at the expense of reduced economic growth. This is welcome news. Perhaps the trade-off is a myth perpetuated to provide justification for maintaining current levels of inequality in the distribution of income.

Where do we go from here? It would be nice to extent the work to include other countries with parliamentary governments. It would also be nice to include countries with democratic forms of government other than parliamentary democracies. Of course, analyzing these governments will probably entail more complicated specifications for the inequality- party leadership equation. For instance, if one where to look at the United, then one would have to consider the party affiliation of the House, the Senate, as well as the President.

References

Bradley, David, Huber, Evelyne, Moller, Stephanie, Nielsen, Francois, and John Stephens (2003), "Distribution and Redistribution in Postindustrial Democracies", *World Politics*, 55(2): pp. 193-229.

Chang, Roberto (1994), "Income Inequality and Economic Growth: Evidence and Recent Theories", *Economic Review-Federal Reserve Bank of Atlanta*, 79(4): pp. 1-10.

Deininger, Klaus and Lyn Squire (1998), "New Ways of Looking at Old Issues: Inequality and Growth", *Journal of Development Economics*, 57(2): pp. 259-87.

Forbes, Kristen (2000), "A Reassessment of the Relationship between Inequality and Growth", *The American Economic Review*, 90(4): pp. 869-888.

Kuznets, Simon (1955), "Economic Growth and Income Equality," *The American Economic Review*, 45: pp. 1-28.

Scully, Gerald W. (2002), "Economic Freedom, Government Policy and the Trade-Off between Equity and Economic Growth", *Public Choice,* 113: pp. 77-95.

Perotti, Roberto. (1996), "Growth, Income Distribution and Democracy", *Journal of Economic Growth*, 1(2): pp. 149-87.

Persson, Torsten, and Guido, Tabellini (1993), "Is Inequality Harmful for Growth?", *The American Economic Review*, 84: pp. 600-622.

The World Bank (2002), World Development Indicators on CD-ROM, Washington, D.C. 2002.

University of Texas Inequality Project, *HTTP://UTIP.GOV.UTEXAS.EDU.*

'OVERWORKED GREEKS? WORKING TIME TRENDS IN GREECE'

Ioannides A. & Mavroudeas S.*

ABSTRACT

Today there is increasing evidence supporting the claim that an increasing number of workers around the world are overworked. Although, many researchers have raised the issue of the longer working time, it is usually considered a non-European phenomenon. This paper disputes this perception with reference to the case of Greece and argues that there is convincing evidence that there is a marked increase in actual working time in Greece from the mid-1980s and onward. This tendency is particularly strong for wage earners having a university degree, who are in many cases being labelled as 'cadres' that do not follow the usual work time regulations concerning eight-hour work, weekends, overtime etc. It is also strong in more traditional categories of workers (manufacturing, construction etc.).

A statistical and econometric evaluation of the official statistical data–despite their significant limitations that tend to underestimate actual working time-confirms this hypothesis.

INTRODUCTION

During recent years the issue of the work-time trends has restarted to receive attention in economics. Till recently there was a widespread belief that there is a permanent secular tendency of the work-time to decline–or at least to remain constant. The case of a contemporary resurge in work time was offhandedly rejected as unrealistic for developed economies. In a nutshell, it was believed–and this continues to be the majority's view–that working time tend to decrease or at least not to increase from the 20th century and onwards. It is true that the early decades of the 20th century witnessed a dramatic decline of average hours per worker as a result of trade unionist struggle against the long work hours and the exhausting conditions of work that prevailed before. Under this pressure capital ceded a portion of the improved labour productivity in the form of reduced work-time. This was reflected in state legislation which first imposed maximum hours constraints (as exemplified in the English Factory Laws and the US Fair Labor Standards Act) and then, in uneven waves, legislated reductions in work-time for the rest of the 20th century. Thus, stability in the level of work hours and standardized work schedules for full-time workers became one of the hallmarks of the postwar era. Consequently, average and median weekly hours remained virtually constant through the 1960s, whereas annual hours continued declining through the 1970s due to the growth in paid holiday and vacation time (see Golden & Figart (2000b), p.2).

* University of Macedonia, Department of Economic Studies, 156 Egnatia St., Thessaloniki, Greece, *E-mail: smavro@uom.gr*

However, a growing number of recent studies have cast doubts on these beliefs. Empirically, there is increasing evidence that sometime after the 1973 crisis the declining work-time trend not only ceased but it has been probably reversed. The advent of 'labour flexibility' is the main culprit for this change. During the last 25 years statutory and collectively bargained limits to the length of the workweek are increasingly either neglected or becoming irrelevant. The organization of time moves from the more or less synchronized hours of work and leisure to more multiple and widely differentiated patterns of flexible working time arrangements. The 'standard' workweek gives way to schemes of hours averaging over longer intervals of time and the eight hours workday is violated for increasing sections of the workforce. These trends bring forth the significance of actual working time, as differentiated from the statutory one. Flexibility and destandardisation make statutory arrangements more or less ineffective. On the other hand actual working time (which incorporates overtime, absenteeism, moonlighting etc.) becomes far more important since it can show the real trends in work-time since in many cases a decline in statutory time can co-exist with an increase in actual work time.

Actual working time appears to be rising in many countries and for increasing segments of the working class; whereas, at the same time, other segments become underemployed. However, the first seems to be the dominant trend. For example, there is significant evidence that actual weekly work hours are rising in the United States, Japan and most of the emerging and less developed market economies (see ILO-KILM (1999)). Particularly the case of overworking in the US has been raised by many researchers (see Schor (2000), Bluestone & Rose (1998), Golden & Figart (2000a) etc.). There is ambiguity on what is happening in Europe, where the greater power of the labour movement and the stronger traditions of the welfare state (despite reversals on both planes during the recent decades) have presented greater resistance to the trend of the increasing work hours. Most studies, influenced by the 35 hours movement and particularly its legislation in France, assume that the postwar downward trend is still effective. However, it is usually neglected that statutory decrease can go hand in hand with actual increase in work time. Furthermore, in Southern Europe the trend towards overworking appears to be more pronounced (see Mutari & Figart (2000)).

This paper studies the case of Greece and argues that there is convincing evidence that there is a marked increase in actual working time in Greece from the mid-1980s and onward. This tendency is particularly strong for wage earners having a university degree, who are in many cases being labeled as 'cadres' that do not follow the usual work time regulations concerning eight-hour work, weekends, overtime etc. It is also strong in more traditional categories of workers (manufacturing, construction etc.). In Mavroudeas & Ioannides (2002) we have argued that official statistical data have significant limitations regarding working time (neglect of changes in the structure of employment, increased moonlighting that goes mainly in the 'black sector' economy, increased 'feminization' of work and the peculiar character of self-employed people) and tend to underestimate actual working time. Despite these limitations, an econometric evaluation of the working time trends in Greece confirmed the hypothesis of the increasing working time. In this paper we extend the statistical and econometric evaluation of this hypothesis.

WORK TIME: EMPIRICAL AND ANALYTICAL ISSUES

Evidence of a rising duration of working time in the last decades has been provided by many studies. Most of them focused on the US and North America. The debate was triggered by Schor's (1991) influential study. Using household surveys of hours from the Current Population Survey (CPS), she found that annual work hours (both paid and unpaid) have increased in the last three decades in the United States. Her claim was echoed by Bluestone & Rose (1998, 2000), who supplemented CPS data with the household survey of the Panel Study of Income Dynamics (PSID) and extended the trend through the mid-1990s. They show that average hours (both weekly and annual) started rising from 1982. This rise has affected both sexes and was stronger among the most highly educated workers.

Other analyses of CPS data gave similar findings. Mishel & Bernstein (1994) and Mishel, Bernstein & Schmitt (1999) have discovered a definite (although smaller than what Schor has calculated) increase of work-time in the USA during the previous three decades. Jacobs & Gerson (1998) agree only partially with Leete & Schor. They argue that it is not the average work-time that is increasing but only the margins of its distribution, i.e. the percentage of those working many hours and the percentage of those working few hours. However, particularly for the USA, they do agree that the percentage of those working more than 50 hours is one of the higher in the world. Heath & Ciscel (1998), also, found that work-time in the USA increased during the 1980s. Additionally, they focused on a rather neglected dimension of this increase: it is total work-time per family that has increased the most and this has serious impact on family and social life.

On the other side, Robinson & Godbey (1997) using time diary evidence argued that total (paid and unpaid) hours have decreased between 1965 and 1995. This triggered a measurement controversy. Robinson & Godbey (1997) argued that time diaries measure actual hours of work more precisely than self-reports as in the CPS and PSID, where workers may overestimate their work time (for example, by systematically neglecting 'on-the-job leisure' during work hours). Schor and others (e.g. Jacobs (1998)) counter-argued that time diaries underestimate actual work time for a number of reasons ('busy person bias', possible neglect of multitasking activities, functional character of 'on-the-job leisure').

Regarding the situation in Europe, certain studies (e.g. Basso (2003)), justifiably argue that it will sooner or later follow the US model. More specifically, Basso (2003: 140-147) – using data from the 'Second European Survey on Working Conditions', which was conducted from the end of 1995 till the beginning of 1996–maintains that there is significant evidence that the tendency of working time to increase is starting to appear in Europe as well. This tendency, as Basso (2003: 144-145) and Mutari & Figart (2000) argue, is stronger and more evident in the less developed EU countries and particularly in the South European ones (Greece, Italy, Portugal). Bosch (1999), also, has reached the conclusion that work-time in Europe has ceased to decline and in some countries it has started to increase as in the USA. Bosch argues that the greater income inequality in these countries has played an important role in this reversal.

The case of overworking might be controversial and conclusions not unanimous. However evaluations of one crucial aspect of actual working time, overtime, are much more unambiguous.

For the US case, it is clearly rising from the 1982 and onwards, even setting aside cyclical fluctuations (Hetrick (2000)). There is another crucial aspect of overtime: its division between paid and unpaid overtime (see Bell *et al.* (2000)). In many cases it is extremely difficult to record the unpaid overtime in labour data for a number of reasons (e.g. legal consequences). However, it is not rare today workers to concede unpaid overtime work because of the pressure of economic difficulties and the fear of loging their jobs in a stringent period.

All these indicate several well-known problems of measurement regarding actual work time. First, the annual rather than the weekly measurement of actual working time gives a more reliable indicator, because it takes into account vacations, holidays and flexible work time arrangements. Particularly the latter create significant measurement problems. For example, in many countries reductions of statutory working time are given by increasing vacations or decreasing annual work time; thus leaving rather unaffected weekly working time. Second, often second jobs are not accounted for, because they are illegal or semi-legal or for tax evasion purposes (moonlighting). Generally, labour supply data do not include much information on hours and wages in secondary job or overtime work. Finally, in some countries statutory work time is compulsory (and thus affects directly actual work time) whereas in others it simply sets a safety net (and affects less actual work time).

There are also a number of analytical issues regarding the study and explanation of work time trends. Neoclassical economics maintain that work hours reflect workers' individual choices between work (and its reward) and leisure. They also tend to consider unpaid work time as a transitory and paranormal case that cannot be sustained in the long run. Thus increases in the length of the working day tend to be analysed assuming corresponding increases in the daily wage rate, and are presumed to reflect changing 'preferences' of workers in favour of increased income as opposed to a preference for leisure.

In contrast, Marxist analyses emphasize the role of class power in determining the 'normal' hours of work. For Marx (1976, p.344) the establishment of a norm for the working day, presents itself as a struggle between *collective* capital and *collective* labour. Hence, normal hours tend to depend upon the work practice in a given industry or manufacturing process, together with the legislation enacted to set limits on working hours and are not the simple aggregate product of free individual choices.

Finally a number of heterodox approaches adopt institutionalist perspectives and take a middle-of-the-road position between Marxism and neoclassicism. They usually try to supplement the neoclassical labour supply model with elements outside the field of individual preferences (see Golden & Figart (2000b)). Thus they maintain that working time is influenced by and influences an array of cultural norms as well as economic forces. The supply of hours depends upon individual and joint preferences within families that reflect societal expectations, roles, and values.

This paper argues that the Marxist perspective is superior to both the other two approaches. It has a conception of the economic dimension that is both social (as against neoclassical individualism) and production-centered (as against both neoclassicism and institutionalism). Additionally it can grasp wider non-economic social relations (culture etc.) and incorporate them in its analysis through a coherent process of layered abstractions instead of simply adding them up in a rather unprincipled manner (as most of the institutionalist approaches do). Within this framework, work time is a fundamental variable since it is the source of value and the basis of the operation of the capitalist system (i.e. the exploitation of wage labour through the appropriation of a portion of it as unpaid labour time). Hence surplus-value reflects this unpaid labour time. Struggles concerning the level of surplus-value are fundamentally struggles concerning work time. Particularly the extraction of absolute surplus-value depends upon the increase of normal work time.

THE GREEK CASE

In Greece a marked increase in actual working time can be identified. This tendency is particularly strong for wage-earners having a university degree, who are in many cases being labeled as 'cadres' that do not follow the usual work time regulations concerning eight hour work, weekends, overtime etc. It is also strong in more traditional categories of workers (manufacturing, construction etc.).

Measurement Problems

Official statistical data have significant limitations that tend to underestimate actual working time. However, despite these drawbacks, even when using the available statistical data, there are significant indications supporting our approach.

The first problem with the data has to do with the change in the structure of employment. With more people working under part-time and part-year contingent contracts, with significant increase in moonlighting, and with substantial increases in overtime (at least in manufacturing), the movement towards 'non-standard' work-weeks and work-years is growing. Yet the standard statistics hardly measure this. In Greece, as elsewhere, the increase of working time is not always happening through the official channels (for example, the extra hours in the private sector are rarely reported in the purpose of saving the insurance charges), therefore it is usually underestimated by the official data.

Second, there is a marked increase of moonlighting in the recent years. These second jobs are usually underreported in order to avoid taxes and social insurance charges. Additionally, a great part of moonlighting takes place in the so-called 'black economy', which is notoriously big in Greece and of course it is not accounted for adequately. However, there is significant evidence that not only part-time work is increasing but also that moonlighting constitutes a great part of it. These moonlighting hours have to be added on top of the officially measured real working time.

A third problem arises from a basic feature of the Greek Economy: the existence of big sectors of economic activity, where self-employment is the main mode of employment. In fact this means that workers have to 'buy' their jobs. During the last years this mode of employment has expanded in new sectors of economic activity. Under this type of employment workers usually work more than average, under fully flexible work schedules. The expansion of this mode of employment indicates an increase on real working time, which is not usually accounted in official data. This Greek peculiarity is enhanced by the universal trend for increasingly blurring boundaries between work and non-work time. Capitalist restructuring (following both traditional and new technology paths) destroys the traditional division of work and family. This process–which affects also 'typical' workers–has even stronger repercussions on this stratum of self-employed workers who become the champions of working time increases.

'Feminisation' of Work

Another important factor is the growing participation of women in the labour market (see Table 1). This participation is more inclined towards flexible work arrangements and in many cases belongs to the informal or 'black' economy (and thus it cannot be easily measured). This growing 'feminisation' of the work force means a major increase in the work time needed for the reproduction of the working class' families since another member of a working class' family performs wage labour and has to recuperate from its attrition. At the same time it contributes additional labour (both paid and unpaid) to the capitalist system.

Table 1
Percentage of Female Labor Force Participation in Greece

Year	*1980*	*1990*	*1995*	*2000*
Labour Force, female (% of total labour force)	28	35	37	38

Source: World Bank (http://devdata.worldbank.org/genderstats)

Work Time Data

Setting aside all these problems of underestimation, a first glance indication is given by the legislation for the daily and weekly working time in combination with the statistics for the real working time per employee. Data about working time are being collected by the Labour Force Survey of the National Statistical Service of Greece (NSSG) from the 1974 and onward. However, there exist similar data from older types of survey of NSSG from the 1960s. From 1981, it is conducted according to the rules of EUROSTAT, which have been revised in 1983. EUROSTAT, ILO (International Labour Organization) and OECD estimations and studies are mainly based on this set of data. NSSG's Labour Force Survey is a household survey covering all the country and conducted yearly. Hours of work refer to the number of hours actually worked during the reference week in first job or business. This includes all hours including extra hours regardless of whether they were paid or not. Persons who have also worked at home (e.g. teachers preparing lessons) are asked to include the number of hours they have worked at home. Unfortunately, the Labour Force Survey provides data for the mean working time in Greece for the year 1987 and afterwards. We have to turn to some other source to collect the data that are necessary for an econometric evaluation of the working time trend. The only statistical survey that can provide such evidence for Greece is the Labour Statistics of the NSSG. They are quarterly surveys investigating wages and occupation in Manufacturing, Mining, Commerce, Energy, Banking and Insurance sectors. They include data only for the paid working time, excluding working time that has been worked but not paid. As mentioned above, this leads to the underestimation both of the working time and the possible upward trend that exhibits. Nevertheless, in the absence of any other set of data covering the last 40 years period in Greece we have to relay upon them, as some ILO and OECD estimations and studies are doing so.

According to these data (Table 2) there is an increase in actual weekly working time in Greek Economy, from 1986 till 1998 (the last available data).

Table 2
Actual Average Work time in Greece

Years	*Average Weekly Hours*
1962	44,08
1963	43,38
1964	43,95
1965	43,78
1966	43,3
1967	43,55
1968	43,7
1969	43,8
1970	44,63
1971	44,13
1972	44,58
1973	43,73
1974	43,8
1975	42,7
1976	41,83
1977	41,05
1978	41,25
1979	41,18
1980	40,7
1981	39,53
1982	38,6
1983	38,53
1984	38,18
1985	39,25
1986	39,2
1987	39,25
1988	41,13
1989	41,1
1990	41,08
1991	41,08
1992	41,08
1993	41,09
1994	41,85
1995	41,13
1996	41,18
1997	40,87
1998	41,13

Source: OECD Statistical Compedium, Labour Statistics NSSG.

ILO's Key Indicators of The Labour Market (Kilm), using the same data set has estimated the actual annual hours worked per employee–broken by males and females-for the period 1990-94. Annual estimations, as explained before, can capture better the contemporary tendency towards flexible labour arrangements. Again, in the case of annual hours, the tendency of the real working time to increase is evident for both sexes.

Table 3
Annual Hours Worked Per person

Years	*Males*	*Females*
1990	819.7	735.7
1991	830.1	738.7
1992	854.8	757.5
1993	860.7	759.8
1994	851.2	755.7

Source: ILO - KILM

Other, less extensive, surveys have similar findings. For example, a survey conducted by the pollster company METRON ANALYSIS, commissioned by the Ministry of Labour found even more pronounced results. The survey–which covered the whole country, was conducted from 14/9/2000 till 29/9/2000, used a three-stage sampling process and had an effective sample of 2.473 persons–found that the average real working time for private sector workers is 44.3 hours, while for public sector workers is 37.8–by far higher than the hours dictated by the 8 hours per day legal limit (METRON ANALYSIS (2000, p.3). A big section of the employees (42.9%) declared that they work more than what is legally provisioned in their main or sole occupation. Additionally, 30% of the employees declared that their overtime work is not paid, while only 13.6% declared that it is paid but not sufficiently enough.

AN ECONOMETRIC EVALUATION OF THE WORKING TIME TRENDS

We assume that if the data exhibit a time trend this would be a deterministic rather than a stochastic one. This is because a great percentage of the driving forces of this process are external to the economic system and they are the outcome of a plan, usually made from governments and/or the employers associations (in high 'correlation' with the working class resistance). This assumption is not indisputable of course, since the trend could also be the outcome of cumulative distortions that take place at the level of every single enterprise.

Under the previous assumption we will show that there is a statically significant time trend in the working time series for Greece and there is also a structural change affecting the slope of the trend.

The data for working time are plotted in Figure 1. We can visually identify two possible break points, the first at the years 1972-1973 and the second between 1984 and 1985. These two possible break points are consistent with important events that affected the economy, such as the oil crisis in 1973 and the announcement of the new economic policy for Greece after the second electoral victory of PASOK in 1985. Since our point is to show a rise in working time during the last years we will check only for the second possible break point.

The equation we use is linear since it is the simplest and more intuitive specification and since we have no economic reason to assume a higher order polynomial. In addition to this is the form of the line graph of the data, plotted in figure1.

Figure 1: Weekly Working Time in Greece

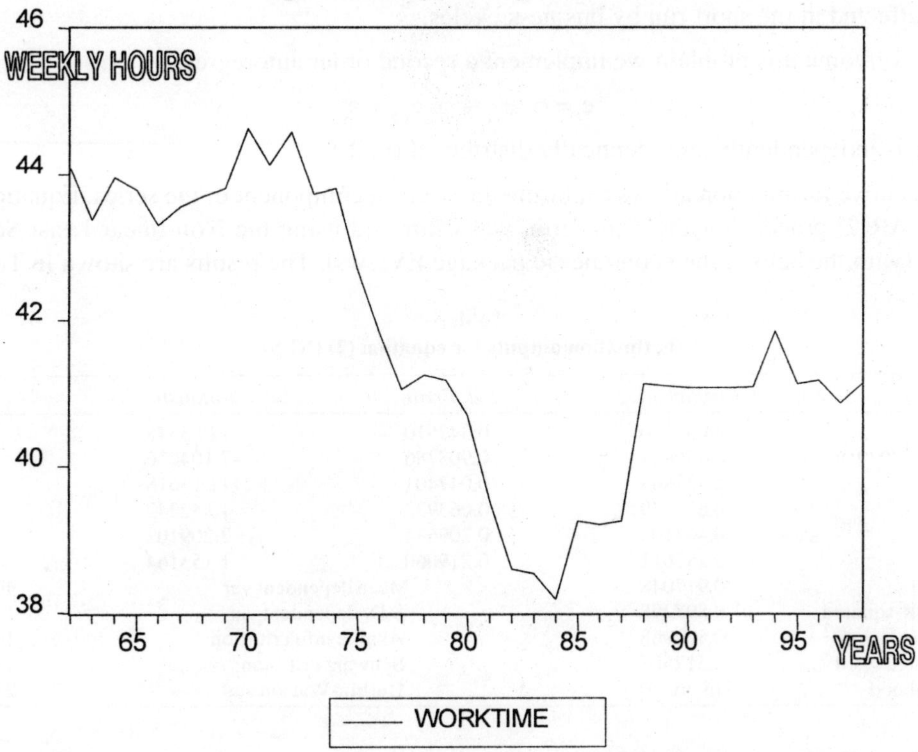

$$Y_t = C(1) + C(3)*t + e_t \quad (1)$$

Where Y_t is the work time

t is for time

e_t is a disturbance term and

C(1), C(3) are the constant term and the slope coefficient to be estimated.

To test for the possible structural change we will use a dummy variable (d) which equals zero for the years before 1985 and one thereafter. So the equation will take the form

$$Y_t = C(1) + C(2)*d + C(3)*t + C(4)*t*d + e_t \quad (2)$$

Where C(2) and C(4) are the coefficients associated with the dummy variable.

The sample we used is from 1972 to 1998. The reason for neglecting previous years is that we mainly want to check the behavior of the working time after the 1973 crisis, since the underlying assumption is that recent trends in working time are generated by the permanent effects and the attempt of overcoming this crisis. This assumption will also help us to use only one dummy variable in our equation, avoiding over specification problems.

The estimation of equation (2) (more specifically the Durbin-Watson statistic) indicates the existence of serial correlation among the residuals. The same conclusion is reinforced by the Q-statistics. In the case of serially correlated residuals the estimators C(1) till C(4) will be biased. The existence of serial correlation in the residuals was rather expected, since working time is affected in the short run by business cycles.

To overcome this problem we implement a second order autoregressive error of the form:

$$e_t = \varphi_1 e_{t-1} + \varphi_2 e_{t-2} + \varepsilon_t \quad (3)$$

where ε_t is independently and identically distributed (i.i.d.).

The above formulation allows capturing the cyclical component of the series. Equation (2), with an AR(2) process for the error term, was estimated using the Non-linear Least Squares method (with the help of the econometric package EViews). The results are shown in Table 5.

Table 5
Estimation outputs for equation (2) (NLS)

	Coefficient	*Std. Error*	*t-Statistic*	*Prob.*
C(1)	44.37380	0.342510	129.5548	0.0000
C(2)	-6.456084	0.908786	-7.104076	0.0000
C(3)	-0.527863	0.047401	-11.13618	0.0000
C(4)	0.672779	0.063932	10.52342	0.0000
C(5)	0.463103	0.209634	2.209102	0.0384
C(6)	-0.252611	0.219060	-1.153164	0.2618
R-squared	0.917048	Mean dependent var		40.96593
Adjusted R-squared	0.897298	S.D. dependent var		1.569459
S.E. of regression	0.502968	Akaike info criterion		1.656548
Sum squared resid	5.312505	Schwarz criterion		1.944512
Log likelihood	-16.36340	Durbin-Watson stat		2.035307

The fit of the equation to the data is now better then in the previous case. The first two coefficients (C(1), C(2)) represent the constant term (before and after the structural change) and have no economic meaning. C(3), which is the slope of the linear equation until the structural change, is negative and statistically significant, as should be expected after viewing the plotted data. C(4) has to be added to C(3), to give the slope of the equation after the break point year of 1985. The statistical significance of C(4) proves that working time does not exhibit a constant trend throughout the period under examination (Mills, 2003, p.16). Further, the absolute value of C(4), which is bigger then the absolute value of C(3), shows that the downward trend of working time is reversed to an upward trend for the years after 1985. The coefficients C(5) and C(6) are the estimators of φ_1 and φ_2 respectively.

Formally, the estimation gives us the following equations describing the phenomenon before and after 1985:

$$Y_t = 44{,}3738 - 0{,}527863 * t + e_t \quad \text{(for t before 1985)} \quad (4)$$

and

$$Y_t = 37{,}917716 + 0{,}1449161 * t + e_t \quad \text{(for t after 1985)} \quad (5)$$

From equations (4) and (5) we can conclude that there was a statistically significant downward trend in working time from 1973 till the change of economic policy in 1985. After that year the trend changes sign (remaining significant), but the upward movement is now to a smaller degree. This was expected, since it is rather easier to reduce than to increase the working time due to political reasons. Besides, we estimate that the major part of the actual rise in working time is most of the times invisible by the official statistics and occurs also through other channels like second job, the rise of number of workers in each family etc.

All these findings confirm the hypothesis of the increasing working time in the Greek Economy.

Work Time Trends in the Basic Productive Sectors of the Greek Economy

In this section we study the available work time data for three major productive sectors of the Greek economy: manufacturing, constructions and transportation–communications. The best available data are from 1987 and onwards. Previous data are incompatible with the new series. The choice of these sectors reflects the Marxian preoccupation with those sectors of the economy where productive labour is performed (as distinguished from unproductive wage labour). It is in these sectors that surplus-value is produced and therefore the increase or not of work time is particularly relevant.

It would be interesting to check also other sectors of the economy and particularly the tertiary sectors because there are empirical signs that overworking affects them as well. Two points are important here. First, that some activities that were considered traditionally as services and unproductive have nowadays changed character. Second, that the unproductive activities have significant macroeconomic effects since they entitle their capitalists to get a share of total surplus-value produced in the economy as a whole. However, the available Greek data are extremely problematic since their classifications have changed radically several times.

1. Manufacturing

The data for the weekly working time in the manufacturing sector are shown in Table 6

Table 6
Weekly Working Hours in Manufacturing

Years	*Actual weekly work hours*
1987	40
1988	41
1989	41
1990	41
1991	42
1992	43
1993	42
1994	42
1995	42
1996	42
1997	42
1998	42*
1999	42
2000	43

* Average of the years 1997 and 1999 because they do not exist data for this year.
Source: NSSG

As we can observe, the data are rounded off to integers. This causes a lack of the appropriate accuracy necessary for our tests. A big part of the work time variations are lost because of this reason. A second problem with the data is the small time period they cover, especially when it is known from the total sectors working time trend that the missing years are important. Finally the 1993 change of classification system, although limited for the examined sectors, affects the continuity of the data. The technique is the same used in the general case, but we don't search for a break point here. The equation under estimation is the following:

$$Y_t = C(1) + C(2)*t + e_t \qquad (6)$$

The type of the correlation of the residuals indicates a first order autoregressive form for the error term and the estimated equation is:

$$Y_t = 41{,}33856 + 0{,}093360*t + e_t \qquad (7)$$

The coefficient C(1) has no economic meaning. The estimated C(2) coefficient is positive and statistically significant at the 87% level of significance. This indicates the existence of an upward trend for weekly working time. The relatively low level of significance may be due to the small sample period, the rounding off and the change of classification system mentioned above, or due to the informal ways through which is achieved the increase in working time.

2. Constructions

The data for the weekly working time in the manufacturing sector are shown in Table 7.

Table 7
Weekly working hours in Constructions

Years	*Actual weekly work hours*
1987	36
1988	38
1989	39
1990	38
1991	40
1992	39
1993	40
1994	40
1995	40
1996	40
1997	40
1998	40.5*
1999	41
2000	41

* Average of the years 1997 and 1999 because they do not exist data for this year.
Source: NSSG

The problems concerning the data, mentioned in the previous case, hold in this case too. The estimation of the equation (6) was conducted with the use of a second order autoregressive form for the error term. The estimated equation is:

$$Y_t = 38,41299 + 0,189033*t + e_t \quad (8)$$

The coefficient C(2) is positive and statistically important at the 99% level of significance. This indicates an upward trend for working time in the construction sector.

3. Transport–Communications

The data for the weekly working time in the transport-communications sector are shown in Table 8.

Table 8
Weekly working hours in Transport-Communications

Years	*Actual weekly work hours*
1987	44
1988	44
1989	44
1990	44
1991	45
1992	45
1993	46
1994	46
1995	46
1996	46
1997	46
1998	46*
1999	46
2000	46

* Average of the years 1997 and 1999 because they do not exist data for this year.
Source: NSSG

Using the same technique as in the manufacturing sector we estimate equation (6) for the sector of transportations and communications. The estimated equation is:

$$Y_t = 44,40448 + 0,143357*t + e_t \quad (9)$$

The C(2) coefficient is positive again and significant at the 79% level of significance. We can't be positive about rejecting the null hypothesis in this case. All the previously mentioned explanations about the quality of data still hold for this sector. One additional explanation is, of course, the already very high level of weekly working time in this sector, which makes a possible upward trend much more difficult to occur and to be counted.

CONCLUSIONS

If the hypothesis of overworking is verified for Greece this, in our opinion, would mark the renewed significance of the extraction of absolute surplus-value. In Mavroudeas & Ioannides (2002) we have argued that contemporary capitalist restructuring, following the 1973 structural crisis and the subsequent long downturn, strives to construct a new era or a new stage of capitalism. This new stage will be based on a new configuration of absolute and relative surplus-value. Contrary to the previous capitalist stage where absolute surplus-value played a lesser role, nowadays absolute surplus-value is upgraded. This does not imply that relative surplus-value ceases to be dominant but rather that the equilibrium between them is changing under the permanent hegemony of relative surplus-value. In the Greek case the increased significance of absolute surplus-value is accentuated by the participation of the Greek economy in the European Union. As Carchedi (1999) has shown, particularly the European Monetary Union (EMU) project of the EU obliges less developed European economies to intensify the extraction of surplus-value and particularly absolute surplus-value.

These developments may support profitability but will definitely worsen labourers' working and pay conditions.

References

Basso P. (2003), *Modern Times, Ancient Hours*, London: New Left Books.

Bell D.& Hart R. (1999), Unpaid Work, *Economica* 66, 271-90.

Bell D., Hart R., Hubler O. & Schwerdt, W. (2000), *Paid and unpaid overtime working in Germany and in the UK*, Bonn: IZA Discussion Paper No. 133.

Bluestone B. & Rose S. (1998), The Unmeasured Labor Force, *Jerome Levy Policy Briefs* no. 39A, May.

Bluestone B. & Rose S. (2000), *'The enigma of working time trends'* in Golden & Figart (eds.) (2000a) 'Working Time: International trends, theory and policy perspectives', London: Routledge.

Bosch G. (1999), Working time: tendencies and emerging issues, *International Labour Review*, Vol. 138 , No. 2, pp. 131-149.

EC (2003), *Employment in Europe 2003*, Directorate-General for Employment and Social Affairs, Luxembourg: Official Publications.

Golden L. & Figart D. (eds.) (2000a), *Working Time: International trends, theory and policy perspectives*, London: Routledge.

Golden L. & Figart D. (2000b), *'Doing something about long hours'*, Challenge, Vol. 43 No. 6.

Heath J., Ciscel D. & Sharp D. (1998), The Work of Families: The Provision of Market and Household Labor and the Role of Public Policy, *Review of Social Economy*, Vol. LVI, No. 4, Winter 1998.

Hetrick R. (2000), *'Analyzing the Upward Surge in Overtime Hours'*, Monthly Labor Review No. 123.

ILO-International Labour Organization (1999), *Key Indicators of the Labour Market-KILM*, Geneva: ILO.

Jacobs J. & Gerson K. (1998), Who Are the Overworked Americans*? Review of Social Economy*, LVI (4).

Leete L. & Schor J. (1992), *The great American time squeeze,* Economic Policy Institute, Washington D.C.

Leete L. & Schor J. (1994), Assessing the time Squeeze Hypothesis: Estimates of Market and Non Market Hours in the United States, 1969-1989, *Industrial Relations* 33(1): 25-43.

Marx K. (1976), *Capital*, Vol. I, London: Penguin Books, 1867.

Metron Analysis (2000), *Survey for employment in Greece*, Athens: Metron Analysis.

Mills T. (2003), *Modelling Trends and Cycles in Economic Time Series*, New York: Palgrave Mcmillan.

Mishel L.& Bernstein J. (1994), *The State of Working America 1994-95*, Armonk, New York: M.E. Sharpe.

Mishel L., Bernstein J. & Schmitt, J. (1999), *The State of Working America, 1998-99*, Economic Policy Institute, ILR Press.

Mutari E. & Figart D. (2000), *'The Social Implications of European Work Time Policies: Promoting Gender Equity?'* in Golden & Figart (2000a) 'Working Time: International Trends, Theory and Policy Perspectives', London: Routledge.

Robinson J. & Godbey G. (1997), *Time for Life: The Surprising Ways Americans Use Their Time*, Pennsylvania: Pennsylvania State University Press.

Schor, J. (1991), *The overworked American*, New York: Basic Books.

Schor J. (2000), Working Hours and Time Pressure: The Controversy about Trends in Time Use, in Lonnie Golden and Deborah Figart (eds): *Working Time: International Trends, Theory and Policy Perspectives*, London and New York: Routledge.

LABOUR PRODUCTIVITY, WAGES AND UNEMPLOYMENT: AN EMPIRICAL INVESTIGATION FOR GREECE USING CAUSALITY ANALYSIS

*Nikolaos Dritsakis**

ABSTRACT

In this paper an effort is made in order to investigate the nexus of dynamic interrelations between the general macroeconomic environment of Greek economy with a special reference to the real wages determination. For the causality analysis among real wages, consumer price index, labour productivity, unemployment rate and gross domestic product a multivariate autoregressive VAR model was used, covering the period 1960:I until 2005:IV. Granger causality tests based on error correction models (ECM) showed that there is a 'strong' Granger causal relation among labour productivity, real wages, rate of unemployment and gross domestic product as well as between real wages and unemployment rate and also among unemployment rate, real wages and gross domestic product.

Keywords*: labour productivity, real wages, unemployment, error correction model, Granger causality.*

JEL C22, E24

INTRODUCTION

The initial formulation of the Phillips curve (1958) suggested the existence of a trade-off between inflation and unemployment through the decrease of aggregate demand. The initial equation related the nominal wage inflation to unemployment. The modern approach on the Phillips curve stems from Friedman (1968). He stated that since employees bargain over real wages, there could not exist a long-run trade-off between inflation and unemployment.

Algebraically Friedman's theory starts from the following equation:

$$w_t - p^e_t = w_{t-1} - p_{t-1} + \Delta prod + a - b_1 u$$

and results in the typical accelerationist Phillips curve:

$$\Delta p_t = \Delta p_{t-1} + a - b_1 u_t$$

Inflation would be a function of unemployment and steady only if unemployment equals to the NAIRU (non accelerating increasing rate of unemployment), which is defined as follows:

$$u^* = a / b_1.$$

* Department of Applied Informatics, University of Macedonia, Economics and Social Sciences, 156 Egnatia Street, P.O. Box 1591, Greece, *E-mail: drits@uom.gr*

The relation between real wages, unemployment, inflation, and productivity has been extensively investigated. One possible equilibrium relationship for the real wages is the following equation:

$$(e-p) = b_1 + b_2 u + b_3 prod + b_4 \Delta e$$

The classical theory of the firm justifies the relationship between productivity and real wages. Insider-outsider models of wage bargaining would consider unemployment as non-significant ($b_2 = 0$) except for the case that it was included in the objective function of the labour unions ($b_2 < 0$). The relationship between inflation and real wages depends on the nature of the wage contracts. Especially, the wage indexation is regarded as one of the major causes of inflation and its retention.

Increases in real wages could lead to unemployment growth if firms financed the cost of these increases exclusively. The wages' growth would increase the participation of the population in the labour force thus leading to unemployment growth even with a stable number of jobs.

Productivity affects unemployment through two different mechanisms: On one hand, an increase in productivity leads to a decrease in the demand for labour for a fixed output level. An increase in unemployment would lead to a decrease in the aggregate demand. On the other hand, an increase in productivity leads to a decrease in the cost of the production and lower product prices. These lower prices could boost the aggregate demand leading to an increase in employment. The above can be described by the following equation:

$$u = b_1 + b_2(e-p) + b_3 prod$$

Traditional empirical studies of the wage equation have specified the rate of unemployment either as a determinant of the change in the wage rate (Phillips curve-effect) or as a determinant of the wage level (wage-curve effect). The Phillips curve specification can be based on the theoretical model of Phelps (1968), where the firm is assumed to set the wages. Knoester and Van der Widt (1987) derive a Phillips curve specification from a wage bargaining process. Usually the specification of the wage–curve is also described as an outcome of a wage bargaining process between employers and trade unions. Today labour economists tend to prefer the bargaining theory to Phelp's theory of wage setting behavior by the firms, for the specification of the wage equation. That is why, from a theoretical perspective, there is some preference to have a wage-curve effect specified in the equation rather than a Phillips-curve effect (Blanchflower and Oswald 1994).

Shapiro and Stiglitz (1984) state that unemployment plays the role of a macroeconomic ''discipline device'' in order to induce employees to intensify their efforts in their job. They are based on the shirking models, where the firm, differentiating from the unemployment salaries, increases the dismissal cost for the employee, thus inducing him to intensify his effort.

Turunen (1998) presents disaggregated wage curve results by individual characteristics, occupations, industries and regions in the United States, using a panel data set of young workers. The results suggest that instead of a strong aggregate wage curve there is a number of different wage curves over time and for different workers groups. The slope of the aggregate wage curve varies over time, with the strongest wage curves appearing in the late 1980s. Wage curves exist for most labour market groups: the wages of the least educated, those in relatively low-skill occupations or service industries are most sensitive to changes in unemployment. Wages of government workers and those in the mining industry increase with unemployment.

Brayton, Roberts and Williams (1999) try to investigate if Phillips curve is valid for the 90's where low inflation and low unemployment coexist. They use quarterly data from the period 1967 to 1998. They suggest that Phillips curve cannot explain low inflation during the last years. The degree of capacity utilisation gives the best results for the last years, but this does not appear in the total sample. They also provide evidence for a significant decrease in the NAIRU after 1995. Finally, they present an (error-correction) adjustment model of prices in conjunction with the long run trend unit labour cost.

Marcelino and Mizon (1999) examine the relationship between wages, prices, productivity, inflation and unemployment. In their paper quarterly data have been used for the period 1965(1) to 1993(1) for Italy, Poland and the UK. They apply a cointegrated VAR model with regime shifts. They analyse the labour markets of these three countries and conclude that there have been significant changes in the structures of the relationships between wages-prices and unemployment - inflation for the period 1979/80. According to the qualitative results they suggest that although there have been some important changes in the labour markets of these three examined economies taking into account a greater degree of flexibility, there are no common characteristics among them. Indeed, this is rationale if someone takes into consideration the different starting points and policies followed in the three examined economies.

Chletsos, Kollias, and Manolas (2000) investigate the relationship between employment, growth rate, labour productivity and wages rate in the case of Greece for the period 1970-93. This period is divided into two sub-periods 1970-1980 and 1981-1993. In the first period they indicate that the employment level is positively related to the growth rate and wages rates are negatively related to the labour productivity. The reverse result is observed in the second period, which is characterized by the restructuring of the Greek economy.

Hsing (2001), based on the augmented Phillips curve and the autoregressive conditional heteroscedasticity model, studied the impact of the union wage increases to non-union wages and found that the growth of non-union wages is positively associated with the expected inflation productivity growth and negatively correlated with the unemployment rate.

Puhani (2002) estimates the changes in the Polish wage and unemployment structures between the years 1994 and 1998 in order to identify the labour market characteristics associated with increasing and decreasing relative demand as well as relative wage rigidities. The evidence of his paper showed that the relative demand for workers with a low level of education has been decreased.

Broersma and Butter (2002) examine the influence of labour market flows on wage formation and they apply the Johansen multivariate cointegration analysis for Netherlands. The estimation results suggest the combination of the outflow from employment to unemployment and the outflow of vacancies as indicators of labour market tightness, qualifying for inclusion into the wages equation.

Dritsakis (2004) attempts to analyze the relationship between productivity and inflation for a transition country of European Union, Romania. For this purpose he uses quarterly data from 1990:IV to 2003:I and the causality analysis, which is based on an error correction model. The results of the empirical analysis showed that there is a causal relationship between inflation and productivity in Romanian economy.

The aim of this paper is to investigate the causal relationship, which might exist between the examined variables, and to answer the following causal hypothesis in order to get useful conclusions.

The examined causal hypotheses are the following:

- Do real wages cause consumer price index?
- Do real wages cause labour productivity?
- Do real wages cause unemployment rate?
- Do real wages cause gross domestic product?
- Does consumer price index cause real wages?
- Does consumer price index cause labour productivity?
- Does consumer price index cause unemployment rate?
- Does consumer price index cause gross domestic product?
- Does labour productivity cause real wages?
- Does labour productivity cause consumer price index?
- Does labour productivity cause unemployment rate?
- Does labour productivity cause gross domestic product?
- Does unemployment rate cause real wages?
- Does unemployment rate cause consumer price index?
- Does unemployment rate cause labour productivity?
- Does unemployment rate cause gross domestic product?
- Does gross domestic product cause real wages?
- Does gross domestic product cause consumer price index?
- Does gross domestic product cause labour productivity?
- Does gross domestic product cause unemployment rate?

The remainder of the paper proceeds as follows: Section 2 describes the data that are used in the causal relationship among real wages, the consumer price index, labour productivity, unemployment rate and gross domestic product, for the Greek economy as well as the specification of the model. Section 3 presents the results of unit root tests. Section 4 summarises the cointegration analysis and Johansen cointegration test. Section 5 analyses the error correction models. Finally, section 6 provides the concluding remarks of this paper.

DATA SPECIFICATION OF THE MODEL

In order to test the causal relationship discussed in the Introduction, we specify the following multivariate VAR model [1]

$$U = (WR, CPI, LP, UR, GDP) \quad (1)$$

where

WR is real wages

CPI is consumer price index

LP is labour productivity

UR is unemployment rate

GDP is gross domestic product

Further, based on the results of the above set of causal hypotheses, the corresponding bi – directional hypotheses have to be examined.

To investigate the causal relationships in a vector autoregressive VAR model popularized by Sims (1980) we formulated the vector U defined in equation (1)[2]. A unique advantage of the VAR model is that it treats each variable in the system as potentially endogenous and relates each variable to its own past values and to past values of all other variables included in the model.

Engle and Granger (1987) and Granger (1988) pointed out that a VAR model in levels with non-stationary variables may lead to spurious results and a VAR model in first differences with cointegrated variables is mis-specified. In the latter case, the error correction term, ECT, which represents the long run relationship between the variables is introduced again back into the VAR and the resulting model is known as the vector error correction model VECM.

A multivariate unrestricted VAR model (with the deterministic term) can be written as:

$$U_t = A_o + A(L)U_t + e_t \quad (2)$$

where

$A(L) = [a_{ij}(L)]$ is a 5 X 5 matrix of the polynomial

$a_{ij}(L) = \Sigma a_{ij1} L^1$

m_{ij} is the degree of the polynomial

$A_0 = (a_{10}\ a_{20}\ a_{30}\ a_{40}\ a_{50})$ is a constant

e_t is a 5 X 1 vector of random errors.

Model (2) can be rewritten as a VECM assuming that there exists at least one cointegrating vector as follows:

$$\Delta U_t = A_0 + A(L)\Delta U_{t-1} + \delta EC_{t-1} + \mu_t \quad (3)$$

where

EC_t is the error correction term

μ_t is a 5 X 1 vector of white noise errors, $E(\mu_t) = 0$ and $(\mu_t \mu_{t-1}) = \Omega$, for t = s and zero otherwise. After normalizing the cointegrating vector, the equation of real wages can be written as:

$$\ln WR_t = \beta_1 \ln CPI_t + \beta_2 \ln LP_t + \beta_3 \ln UR_t + \beta_4 \ln GDP_t \quad (4)$$

The error correction term obtained from equation (4) is:

$$EC_t = \ln WR_t - \beta_1 \ln CPI_t - \beta_2 \ln LP_t - \beta_3 \ln UR_t - \beta_4 \ln GDP_t \quad (5)$$

Finally, the equation of real wages in its detailed form for model (3) is written as:

$$\Delta LWR_t = a_0 + \Sigma a_{1j} \Delta LWR_{t-j} + \Sigma a_{2j} \Delta LCPI_{t-j} + \Sigma a_{3j} \Delta LLP_{t-j} + \Sigma a_{4j} \Delta LUR_{t-j} + \Sigma a_{5j} \Delta LGDP_{t-j} + \delta EC_{t-1} + e_t \quad (6)$$

where EC_{t-1} represents the deviation from equilibrium in period t and the coefficient δ represents the response of the dependent variable in each period to departures from equilibrium.

Granger (1988) pointed out that there are two channels of causality. One channel is through the lagged values of ΔLCPI, ΔLLP, ΔLUR and ΔLGDP, i.e., $a_{i1}, a_{i2}, \ldots a_{im}$ are jointly significant, and the other is if δ is significant. If δ is significant in equation (6) then consumer price index, labour productivity, unemployment rate and gross domestic product, also causes real wages, through the second channel.

The data that are used in this analysis are quarterly, covering the period 1960:I-2005:IV regarding 1996 a base year and are obtained from the database of OECD (Business Sector Data Base), National Statistical Service of Greece, International Monetary Fund (IMF), and Bank of Greece.

All data is expressed in logarithms in order to include the proliferative effect of time series and is symbolized with the letter L preceding each variable name.

If these variables share a common stochastic trend and their first differences are stationary, then they can be cointegrated. Economic theory scarcely provides some guidance about which variables appear to have a stochastic trend and when these trends are common among the examined variables as well.

For the analysis of the multivariate time series that include stochastic trends, the augmented Dickey-Fuller (1979) (ADF) unit root tests are used for the estimation of individual time series, with intention to provide evidence about when the variables are integrated.

Unit Root Tests

Many macroeconomic time series contain unit roots dominated by stochastic trends as developed by Nelson and Plosser (1982). Unit roots are significant in examining the stationarity of a time series because a non-stationary regressor invalidates many empirical results. The presence of a stochastic trend is determined by testing the presence of unit roots in time series data. In this study, unit root test is tested using Augmented Dickey-Fuller (ADF) (1979, 1981).

Augmented Dickey-Fuller (ADF) test

The augmented Dickey-Fuller test (ADF) (1979) refers to the t-statistic of $ä_2$ coefficient ïn the following regression:

$$\Delta X_t = \delta_0 + \delta_1 t + \delta_2 X_{t-1} + \sum_{i=1}^{k} \alpha_i \Delta X_{t-i} + u_t \qquad (7)$$

The ADF regression tests for the existence of unit root of X_t, namely in the logarithm of all model variables at time t. The variable ΔX_{t-i} expresses the first differences with k lags and final u_t is the variable that adjusts the errors of autocorrelation. The coefficients δ_0, δ_1, δ_2, and α_i are being estimated. The null and the alternative hypothesis for the existence of unit root in variable X_t is:

$$H_0 : \delta_2 = 0 \quad H_\varepsilon : \delta_2 < 0$$

This paper follows the suggestion of Engle and Yoo (1987) using the Akaike information criterion (AIC) (1974), to determine the optimal specification of Equation (7). The appropriate order of the model is determined by computing Equation (7) over a selected nexus of values of the number of lags k and has been found that value of k at which the AIC attains its minimum. The distribution of the ADF statistic is non-standard and the critical values tabulated by Mackinnon (1991) are used.

Table I
Tests of Unit Roots Hypothesis

Variables	*Augmented Dickey-Fuller*		
	τ_μ	τ_τ	κ
LRW	-0.87191	-1.0461	4
LCPI	-0.32773	-0.57231	3
LLP	-1.7637	-1.86266	5
LUR	-1.2580	-1.47268	2
LGDP	-0.27394	-0.38564	1
ΔLRW	-2.6713*	-3.9856**	3
ΔLCPI	-3.5531**	-3.7750**	3
ΔLLP	-4.1745***	-4.2911***	4
ΔLUR	-8.9237***	-9.4916***	2
ΔLGDP	-6.7626***	-6.7897***	1

Notes: τ_μ is the t-statistic for testing the significance of δ_2 when a time trend is not included in equation 2 and τ_τ is the t-statistic for testing the significance of δ_2 when a time trend is included in equation 2. The calculated statistics are those reported in Dickey-Fuller (1981). The critical values at 1%, 5% and 10% are –3.61, –2.94 and –2.60 for τ_μ and –4.21, –3.53 and –3.19 for τ_τ respectively.

The lag-length structure of a_ε of the dependent variable x_t is determined using the recursive procedure in the light of a Langrange multiplier (LM) autocorrelation test (for orders up to four), which is asymptotically distributed as chi-squared distribution and the value t-statistic of the coefficient associated with the last lag in the estimated autoregression.

***, **, * Indicate significance at the 1, 5 and 10 percentage levels

Table I presents the results of the ADF test of real wages, consumer price index, labour productivity, unemployment rate and gross domestic product. The results of ADF test are compared with critical values, which we have obtained from Mackinnon (1991) tables. The results of ADF statistic for the examined time series exceed the critical values, because the null hypothesis of a unit root is not rejected. Taking first differences renders each series stationary, with the ADF statistics in all cases being less than the critical value at the 1%, 5% and 10% level of significance.

Cointegration Test

Following the maximum likelihood procedure of Johansen (1988) and Johansen and Juselious (1990), a p-dimensional (p×1) vector autoregressive model with Gaussian errors is expressed by its first-differenced error correction form as:

$$\Delta Y_t = \mu + \Gamma_1 \Delta Y_{t-1} + \Gamma_2 \Delta Y_{t-2} + \ldots + \Gamma_{p-1} \Delta Y_{t-p+1} + \Pi Y_{t-1} + u_t \quad (8)$$

where:

Y_t is a p×1 vector containing the variables.

μ is the p×1 vector of constant terms.

$\Gamma_i = -I + A_1 + A_2 + \ldots + A_i$ (i =1,2...p–1) is the p×p matrix of coefficients.

$\Pi = I - A_1 - A_2 - \ldots - A_p$ is the p×p matrix of coefficients.

u_t is the p×1 vector of the disturbance terms coefficients.

The Π matrix provides information about the long-run relationship between Y_t variables whereas the rank of Π is the number of linearly independent and stationary linear combinations of variables studied. Thus, testing for cointegration involves testing for the rank *r* of Π matrix by examining whether the eigenvalues of Π are significantly different from zero. Johansen (1988) and Johansen and Juselious (1990) propose two test statistics for testing the number of cointegrating vectors (or the rank of Π) in the VAR model. These are the trace *(Tr)* test and the maximum eigenvalue (*L-max*) test. The likelihood ratio statistic for the trace test is:

$$-2\ln Q = -T\sum_{i=r+1}^{p}\ln(1-\hat{\lambda}_i) \quad (9)$$

where $\hat{\lambda}_{r+1}$, $\hat{\lambda}_p$ are the estimated $p-r$ smallest eigenvalues. The null hypothesis to be tested is that there are the most *r* cointegrating vectors. That is, the number of cointegrating vectors is less than or equal to *r*, where *r* is 0,1, or 2... and so forth. In each case, the null hypothesis is tested against the alternative.

Alternatively, the *L-max* statistic is:

$$-2\,In Q = -T\,In(1-\hat{\lambda}_{r+1}) \quad (10)$$

In this test, the null hypothesis of *r* cointegrating vectors is tested against the alternative hypothesis of *r+1* cointegrating vectors. Thus, the null hypothesis *r = 0* is tested against the alternative that *r = 1, r = 1* against the alternative *r = 2,* and so forth. It is well known the cointegration tests are very sensitive to the choice of lag length. The Schwarz Criterion (SC) and the likelihood ratio test are used to select the number of lags required in the cointegration test.

Table II

Cointegration Tests Based on the Johansen and Johansen and Juselious Approach (LWR, LCPI, LLP, LUR, LGDP VAR lag = 5)

	Trace test	*5% critical value*	*10% critical value*
H_0: r = 0	61.0702	34.4000	31.7300
H_0: r ≤ 1	35.2367	28.2700	25.8000
H_0: r ≤ 2	23.5339	22.0400	19.8600
H_0: r ≤ 3	9.0053	15.8700	13.8100
H_0: r ≤ 4	5.2760	9.1600	7.5300

Notes:
- Critical values are taken from Osterwald–Lenum (1992).
- r denotes the number of cointegrated vectors.
- Schwarz Criteria (SC) was used to select the number of lags required in the cointegration test. The computed Ljung – Box Q–statistics indicate that the residuals are white noise.

The results that appear in Table II suggest that the number of statistically significant normalized cointegration vectors is equal to 3 and are the following:

$$LRW = 2.5554\ LCPI + 2.4613\ LLP + 0.0801\ LUR - 1.4269\ LGDP \quad (11)$$

$$LRW = 6.7936\ LCPI + 7.0409\ LLP - 0.00118\ LUR + 5.7755\ LGDP \quad (12)$$

$$LRW = -1.8216\ LCPI - 3.2813\ LLP + 0.17942\ LUR + 3.0230\ LGDP \quad (13)$$

According to the signs of the vector cointegration components and based on the basis of economic theory relationship (12) can be used as an error correction mechanism in a VAR model.

A VAR Model with an Error Correction Mechanism

After determining that the logarithms of the model variables are cointegrated, we must then estimate a VAR model in which we shall include a mechanism of error correction model (MEC). The error correction model (equation 3) is used to investigate the causal relationships among the variables real wages, consumer price index, labour productivity, unemployment rate and gross domestic product. Such analysis provides the short–run dynamic adjustment towards the long–run equilibrium. The significance levels of the F–statistics for the lagged variables and the t–statistics for the coefficient δ of EC_{t-1} are used to test for Granger causality. The numbers in parentheses are the lag lengths determined by using the Akaike criterion.

As discussed earlier in section 2, there are two channels of causality Granger (1988). These are called channel 1 and channel 2. If lagged values of a variable (except the lagged value of the dependent variable) on the right hand side in equation 3 are jointly significant then this is channel 1. On the other hand, if the lagged value of the error correction term is significant, then this is channel 2. The results are summarized in table III.

Table III
Causality Test Results Based on Vector Error–Correction Modeling

Dependent Variable	*F–significance level*					*t–statistic*
	ΔLWR	*ΔLCPI*	*ΔLLP*	*ΔLUR*	*ΔLGDP*	EC_{t-1}
ΔLWR	0.107(2)	0.000(2)***	0.014(3)**	0.073(3)*	0.034(2)**	- 5.2374***
ΔLCPI	0.025(1)**	0.063(2)*	0.125(3)	0.017(2)**	0.087(1)*	-1.2456
ΔLLP	0.245(2)	0.145(3)	0.039(2)**	0.045(2)**	0.345(2)	-1.7413
ΔLUR	0.011(3)**	0.044(3)**	0.028(1)**	0.065(3)*	0.087(3)*	-4.2713***
ΔLGDP	0.147(2)	0.287(1)	0.027(3)**	0.077(2)*	0.095(2)*	-3.4412***

Notes: *, **, and *** indicate 10%, 5%, and 1% levels of significance. Number in parentheses is lag length.

For convenience in discussing the results, let us call the relationships a "strong causal relation" if it is through both channel 1 and channel 2 and simply a "causal relation" if it is through either channel 1 or channel 2.

From the results of table III we can infer that coefficient δ is statistically significant only in case we use as an endogenous variable real wages, the unemployment rate and gross domestic product. In this case we have channel 2 which means that the consumer price index, labour productivity, unemployment rate and gross domestic product affect real wages, consumer price index, labour productivity, real wages and gross domestic product have an effect on unemployment rate as well as consumer price index, labour productivity, unemployment rate and real wages affect gross domestic product. Furthermore, the coefficients of lagged variables are statistically significant in the case where all the variables that are examined in the model are used as endogenous variable (channel 1).

The results of table IV present causality test through these channels

Table IV
Summary of Causal Relations

Variables	*Channels*	*Causal*
WR → CPI	1	Causal relation
WR → LP		
WR → UR	1, 2	Strong causal relation
WR → GDP	2	Causal relation
CPI → WR	1, 2	Strong causal relation
CPI → LP		
CPI → UR	1, 2	Strong causal relation
CPI → GDP	2	Causal relation
LP → WR	1, 2	Strong causal relation
LP → CPI		
LP → UR	1, 2	Strong causal relation
LP → GDP	1, 2	Strong causal relation
UR → WR	1, 2	Strong causal relation
UR → CPI	1	Causal relation
UR → LP	1	Causal relation
UR → GDP	1, 2	Strong causal relation
GDP → WR	1, 2	Strong causal relation
GDP → CPI	1	Causal relation
GDP → LP		
GDP → UR	1, 2	Strong causal relation

From the results of Table IV we can infer that there is a "strong Granger causal" relation between real wages and unemployment rate, as well as between consumer price index and real wages, between consumer price index and unemployment rate, between labour productivity and real wages, between labour productivity and unemployment rate and finally between labour productivity and gross domestic product. The relation between unemployment rate and real wages, between unemployment rate and gross domestic product as well as between gross domestic product and real wages, and also gross domestic product and unemployment rate is "strong Granger causal" relation. Finally, the relation between wages and consumer price index, between wages and gross domestic product, consumer price index and gross domestic product, between unemployment rate and consumer price index, between unemployment rate and labour productivity and also between gross domestic product and consumer price index is simply a "causal relation" as well.

CONCLUDING REMARKS

In this paper an effort was made in order to examine the role of labour productivity, real wages, consumer price index, unemployment rate and gross domestic product in one of the member states of the European Union, Greece, through the analysis of multivariate causality based on an error correction model. For the empirical testing of the above variables, we used the Johansen cointegration test and then continued with Granger causality tests based on a vector error correction model.

The results of the cointegration analysis denote the presence of three cointegration relationships among variables from which only one is used as an error correction in VAR model according to the signs and also according to the economic theory that the components of vector cointegration have. This indicates the presence of a common inclination or of long-run relations among these variables.

The results of causality analysis show that labour productivity cause real wages, unemployment rate and gross domestic product and this causality is characterized as 'strong causal' relationship and the same happens with real wages and unemployment rate, whereas with real wages that cause consumer price index and gross domestic product the causality is characterized as 'simple causal' relationship.

Since the hypotheses set at the beginning of this paper have been answered, as a final concluding remark we can infer that the impact of labour productivity and that of real wages is very prominent in the general macroeconomic environment and also in the Greek economy.

Notes

1. The specification of a multivariate equation in a causality analysis is a major departure from the bivariate equations that have been widely used in the literature to examine the causal relationships. The bivariate studies have been considered to suffer from specification error.
2. Cooley and LeRoy (1985) have criticized the VAR, being a system of unrestricted reduced form equations. See also Runkle (1987) for the controversy surrounding this methodology. However all agree that there are important uses of the VAR model.

References

Akaike, H. (1973), Information *Theory and an Extension of the Maximum Likelihood Principle, In*: Petrov, B. and Csake, F. (eds) 2nd International Symposium on Information Theory. Budapest: Akademiai Kiado, 1973.

Akaike, H. (1974), "A New Look at the Statistical Model Identification", *IEEE Transaction on Automatic Control,* AC-19, pp. 716-23.

Blanchflower, D.C. and Oswald, A.J. (1994), *The wage curve,* MIT Press, Cambmridge, M.A.

Brayton, F., Roberts, J. M., and Williams J. C. (1999), "What's Happened to the Phillips Curve?" *Division of Research and Statistics,* Finance and Economics Discussion Series, Vol. 49, September 1999.

Broersma L., and Butter F. (2002), "An Explorative Empirical Analysis of the Influence of Labour Flows on Wage Formation", *Applied Economics,* Vol. 34, pp. 1583-92.

Chletsos, M. Kollias, Ch and G. Manolas (2000), "The Relationship between Wages, Productivity and Labour Demand in Greece: An Error Correction Approach." *RISEC,* Vol. 47, No1, pp. 95–110.

Cooley, T. F, and LeRoy, S. F. (1985), "A Theoretical Macroeconomics: A Critique", *Journal of Monetary Economics,* Vol. 16, pp. 283–308.

Dickey, D.A., and Fuller, W.A. (1979), "Distribution of the Estimators for Autoregressive Time Series with a Unit Root", *Journal of the American Statistical Association,* Vol. 74, pp. 427–31.

Dickey, D.A., and Fuller, W.A. (1981), "Likelihood Ratio Statistics for Autoregressive Time Series with a Unit Root", *Econometrica,* Vol. 49, pp. 1057–72.

Dritsakis N. (2004), "A Causal Relationship Between Inflation and Productivity: An Empirical Approach for Romania". *American Journal of Applied Sciences,* Vol. 1, No 2, pp. 121–128, 2004.

Engle, R. F, and, C. W. J. Granger (1987), "Cointegration and Error Correction: Representation, estimation and testing". *Econometrica,* Vol. 55, pp. 251–76.

Engle, R.F. and Yoo, B. S. (1987), "Forecasting and Testing in Cointegrated Systems", *Journal of Econometrics,* Vol. 35, pp. 143–59.

Friedman, M. (1968), "The Role of Monetary Policy". *American Economic Review,* Vol. 58, pp. 1-17.

Granger, C. W. J. (1969), "Investigating Causal Relations by Econometric Models and Cross - Spectral Methods". *Econometrica,* Vol. 37, pp. 424-38.

Granger, C. (1988), "Some Recent Developments in a Concept of Causality". *Journal of Econometrics,* Vol. 39, pp. 199–211.

Granger, C. W. J, and P. Newbold (1974), "Spurious Regressions in Econometrics", *Journal of Econometrica,* Vol. 37, pp. 424–38.

Johansen, S. (1988), "Statistical Analysis of Cointegration Vectors", *Journal of Economic Dynamics and Control,* Vol. 12, pp. 231–54.

Johansen, S., and Juselious, K. (1990), "Maximum Likelihood Estimation and Inference on Cointegration With Applications to the Demand for the Money", *Oxford Bulletin of Economics and Statistics,* Vol. 52, pp. 169 -210.

Hsing, Y. (2001), "A Macroeconomic Analysis of the Impact of Union Wage Increases on Nonunion Wages", *Applied Economics Letters,* Vol. 8, pp. 803–06.

Knoester, A., and Van der Widt (1987), "Real Wages and Taxation on ten OECD Countries", *Oxford Bulletin of Economics and Statistics,* Vol. 49, pp. 151- 69.

Mackinnon, J. (1991), Critical Values for Cointegration Tests in Long-run Economic Relationship in Readings in Cointegration (eds) Engle and Granger, Oxford University Press, New York, 267-276.

Marcelino, M, and Mizon, G, E. (1999), "Modelling Shifts in the Wage-price and Unemployment–Inflation Relationships in Italy, Poland and the U.K", IGIER Working Paper, 145, Bocconi University.

Nelson, C.R. and Plosser, C.I. (1982), "Trends and Random Walks in Macroeconomic Time Series: Some Evidence and Implications", *Journal of Monetary Economics*, Vol. 10, pp. 139-62.

Osterwald–Lenum, M. (1992), "A Note With Quantiles of the Asymptotic Distribution of the Maximum Likelihood Cointegration Rank Test Statistics", *Oxford Bulletin of Economics and Statistics*, Vol. 54, pp. 461–72.

Phelps E. S. (1968), "Money-wage Dynamics and Labor-market Equilibrium", *Journal of Political Economy*, Vol. 76, pp. 678-711.

Phillips, A. W. H. (1958), "The Relationship Between Unemployment and the Rate of Change of Money Wage Rates in United Kingdom, 1861-1957", *Economica*, Vol. 25, pp. 283-99.

Phillips, P. C. B. (1986), "Understanding Spurious Regressions in Econometrics", *Journal of Econometrics*, Vol. 33, pp. 311–40.

Puhani P. (2002), "Relative Wage and Unemployment Changes in Poland: Microeconometric Evidence", *Economic System*, Vol. 26, pp. 99–126.

Runkle, D. (1987), "Vector Autoregressive and Reality", *Journar of Economic and Business Statistics*, Vol. 5, pp. 437–54.

Shapiro, C. and Stiglitz, J. (1984), "Equilibrium Unemployment as a Discipline Device", American *Economic Review*, Vol. 74 No. 3, pp. 433–44.

Schwarz, R. (1978), "Estimating the Dimension of a Model", *Annuals of Statistics*, Vol. 6, pp. 461–64.

Sims, C. A. (1980), "Macroeconomics and Reality". *Econometrica*, Vol. 48, pp. 1–48.

Turunen J. (1998), "Disaggregated Wage Curves in the United States: Evidence from Panel Data of Young Workers", *Applied Economics*, Vol. 30, pp. 1665–77.

POVERTY IN KENYA, 1994–1997: A STOCHASTIC DOMINANCE APPROACH

Njuguna F. Mburu & Tabitha W. Kiriti-Nganga***

I. INTRODUCTION

Poverty has been a major concern of many governments world over and many poverty reduction programs have been developed over time and across regions. Despite these efforts, poverty continues to be a key impediment to both human and economic prosperity (OECD, 2000). As put in various policy documents, for instance, the Sessional Paper No. 10 of 1965 on African Socialism and its Application to Planning in Kenya, the Government of Kenya directed its efforts to fighting poverty, disease and ignorance as part of its development objectives.

Consequent to this, various National Development Plans (NDP), Participatory Poverty Alleviation Programs (PPAP), National Poverty Eradication Plans (NPEP) and Poverty Reduction Strategic Papers (PRSP) have spelt out strategies to fight poverty. These policies notwithstanding, poverty levels have continued to increase. For instance in 1971, the number of Kenyans regarded as poor was 3.7 million, increasing to 11.5 million in 1994 and further to 13.3 million in 1997. According to the Welfare Monitoring Survey (WMS) of 1994, the incidence of poverty in Kenya was 47% in the rural areas and 29% in the urban areas. The absolute poverty line was Kshs. 980 per capita per month for rural areas and Kshs.1490 per capita for the urban areas. This has since increased to Kshs. 1239 and 2648 for the urban and rural areas respectively. Mwabu, *et al.* (2002) estimated that the number of poor Kenyans had shot up to 15 million (about 56% of the total populations) in the year 2000.

The government has also established causes, constraints and the processes that engender and entrench poverty but despite these positive developments, poverty alleviation has remained elusive particularly from the 1980s. Poor economic performance has led to increased absolute poverty, i.e., people without adequate food and nutrition, inadequate access to basic services, education, health facilities, safe water and decent housing. This has been blamed on poor policy formulation, initiation, planning and implementation.

The PPAPs have broadened the perceptions of the poor on the phenomenon of poverty. The reports reveal that the poor have been excluded in the formulating of policies aimed at alleviating poverty. With the release of the NPEP (1999-2015), various PRSPs and Millennium Development Goals (MDGs), the government committed itself to reducing by half the number of people living on less than a dollar a day and those living on hunger.

---

* P.O. Box 41512-00100, Nairobi, Kenya, E-mail: *njugs1910@yahoo.com*

** Senior Lecturer, School of Economics, University of Nairobi, Kenya, E-mail: *tkiriti@mail.uonbi.ac.ke; tkiriti@yahoo.co.uk*

Doubtless to say, these endeavours need to be supported by focused policies directed at raising the level of productivity of the economically weak, through close cooperation of the institutions implementing the programs. However, before justifying the targeting of poverty alleviation policies and programs to a category of people or region, there is need for robust evidence to support this.

II. POVERTY

World Bank (2005) categorizes poverty depending on the approach used in measuring it. For example, the income based definition of poverty seeks to specify a level of income per capita in a household below which the basic needs of the family cannot be met. However, it does not acknowledge variations in costs of similar goods for different consumers. The vital importance of non-market household production and non-monetarised exchanges in poor families is not counted.

The basic needs approach involves specifying a set of minimal conditions of life, usually the quality of the dwelling place, degree of crowding, nutrition adequacy and water supply. The proportion of the population lacking these conditions is used to estimate the degree of poverty. The advantage of this approach is that different conditions appropriate to different settings can be specified. However this reduces comparability of estimates in different situations. Similarly, it does not take into account the willingness of people to accept various tradeoffs deliberately, for example, a lower quality of dwelling for reduced transportation time and expense at work.

In the participatory approach, respondents from communities are themselves invited to identify perceptions on their needs, priorities and requirements for minimal secure livelihood. Some sacrifice of comparability of estimates in different communities or at different times is traded off for better information on the identified demands of the individuals themselves. At times, such analyses supplement and reinforce the quantitative measures and at other times they reveal a very different experienced reality.

Despite the many facets of defining poverty, World Bank (2000) admits that we have misconceptions about the poor, why they are poor and what is needed to help them out of this vicious cycle. Regardless of the many definitions of poverty and its multidimensional perspective, we can conclude that overall poverty takes many forms including lack of income and productive resources to ensure sustainable livelihood, hunger and malnutrition, ill health, limited access to education and other basic services, increased morbidity and mortality rates, homelessness and inadequate housing, unsafe environments, social discrimination and exclusion. It is also characterized by lack of participation in decision-making in civil, political, social and cultural life.

According to the participatory poverty assessment study in Tanzania (World Bank, 1997), wealth is associated with the ability to meet basic needs, particularly food. In that study, poverty was associated with skipping meals, cutting meals to one or two per day, involuntary changing diets, sending children to eat at neighbour's homes, and children performing poorly in schools as hunger makes them skip classes and affects their attention in class.

Food poverty is an indicator of the inability of a household to satisfy its basic food requirements for healthy growth and maintenance of the human body. It refers to those whose expenditures on food are insufficient to meet the Food and Agriculture Organisation (FAO) and the World Health Organisation (WHO) recommended daily allowance of 2250 kilocalories per day on food consumption for specific age groups Republic of Kenya, 1998). In 1997, the cost of consuming 2250 kilocalories per person per day was calculated as the equivalent of Ksh.927 per adult per month in rural areas, and Ksh.1254 in urban areas. In 1994, the food poverty line was Ksh.702.99 for rural and Ksh.874.72 for urban areas (Republic of Kenya, 2000a).

Hardcore poverty is an indicator of the inability of a household to meet its basic needs even when all income is spent on food. To measure this, a hardcore poverty line is needed. In 1997, this line was established at Ksh.927 per month per adult in rural areas and Ksh.254 in urban areas (Republic of Kenya, 2000a).

III. MEASUREMENT OF POVERTY CHANGES

1. Poverty Measures

A poverty measure is an index that shows the magnitude of poverty in a society. To form such a measure, an aggregation formula is required that sums up the income dimensions of poverty for a given population (Republic of Kenya, 1997; Mwabu, *et al.* 2000). One poverty measure that has been found manageable in presenting information on the poor in an operationally convenient manner is the FGT (Foster, Greer and Thorbecke) measure developed by Foster, *et al.* (1984). This measure is used to quantify the three well known elements of poverty: the level, depth and severity (also known as incidence, inequality and intensity, respectively) of poverty (Jenkins and Lambert, 1997). The FGT formula that is normally used to measure overall income poverty is shown in equation 1.

$$P\alpha = \frac{1}{N}\sum_{i=1}^{q}\left(1-\frac{Yi}{z}\right)^{\alpha} \qquad (1)$$

Where:

$P\alpha$ is a measure of absolute poverty, including food poverty,

Y_i is the total expenditure of household i, expressed in per adult equivalent (i = 1, .., N),

Z is the poverty line, expressed in per adult equivalent,

N is the total number of households,

q is the total number of poor households, and

α is the FGT parameter, which may be interpreted as a measure of poverty aversion, $\alpha \geq 0$.

$P\alpha = 0$ is the headcount ratio and is the most popular of the FGT measures. Suppose that we have *n* households with income/expenditure $x_1, x_2 \ldots, x_n$ and the poverty line is *z*. Then if *q* households have incomes below *z*, the headcount ratio is simply $H = q/n$. It is the ratio of the number of poor individuals to the total population. This ratio has some shortcomings. First, it does not show how far below the poverty line the poor are: that is, it ignores the inequality among the poor. Secondly, it forces the overall poverty index to be constant even when the welfare of the poor has improved or worsened. Third, with this index, an income transfer from an extremely poor person to a person just below the poverty line (enabling them to cross the line) would show a reduction in poverty despite the decline in the income of the extremely poor. (Poverty here declines because for the same population, there are fewer people below the poverty line, but the poverty gap widens). The headcount index for food poverty, for example, is the number of people whose food expenditure is below the food poverty line, divided by the total population.

The poverty gap P $\alpha = 1$ measures the shortfall of the average income of the poor (in this case, food poor) relative to the poverty line. It can be used to estimate the resources that would bring the expenditure of every food poor person up to the poverty line, thereby eliminating absolute poverty. The main weakness of the poverty gap is that when it is used to assess welfare, it does not differentiate the degree of inequality among the poor.

Inequality refers to the variations in living standards or well being across a whole population. It is the fundamental disparity that permits one individual certain material choices while denying another those very same choices. The Gini coefficient is generally used to measure levels of inequality. It takes on values between 0 and 1 with zero interpreted as no equality. Graphically, the area between the Lorenz curve and the line of equality can easily represent the Gini coefficient (Kuznets, 1955). This is illustrated in Figure 1.

Figure 1
Lorenz Curve of Income Distribution

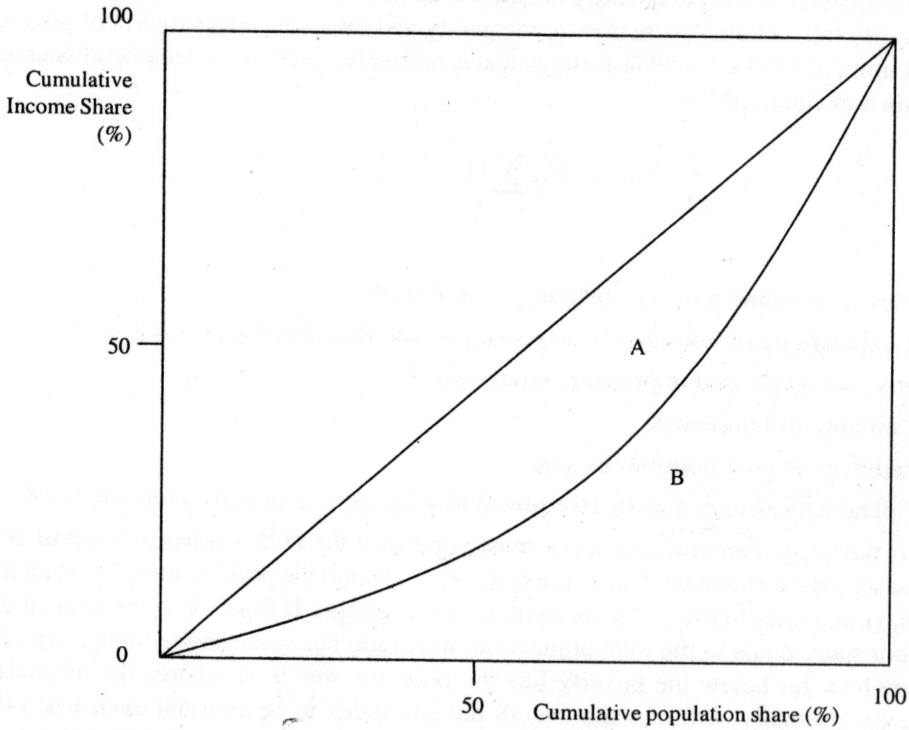

Source: Fields, (2000).

The Gini coefficient is calculated as the area A divided by the sum of areas A and B. If income is distributed completely equally, then the Lorenz curve and the line of total equality are merged and the Gini coefficient is zero.

Poverty severity $P\ \alpha = 2$ is a measure of the severity of poverty among the poor. Poverty severity is measured by the square of the poverty gap, and it increases more than proportionately with the poverty gap. The poverty severity index as measure by $P\ \alpha = 2$ is larger than poverty gap, which indicates that poverty is severest among the very poor.

If poverty lines are available, the FGT indices in equation (1) can be used to measure absolute food poverty and overall absolute poverty. The headcount index for absolute poverty indicates a household's inability to meet all its basic needs (food plus non-food) requirements. Summing the food expenditure required for food energy intake of 2250 kilocalories per day per person and the non-food expenditure allowance gives us the overall poverty line.

Hypothesis testing on $P\ \alpha$ measure can be used to test differences in food poverty between groups (Kakwani, 1993). However, the robustness of poverty comparisons using summary measures can be compromised by errors in living standards data, unknown differences between household consumption level, uncertainties and arbitrariness about the food poverty line and the precise measure. Application of the theory of poverty dominance alleviates this problem (Ravallion, 1992).

2. Methodology of Constructing Poverty Lines

An important aspect in poverty analysis is the setting of poverty lines below which persons are considered to be poor and above which they are not poor. A poverty line may serve other purposes such as monitoring poverty over time, developing poverty profiles, acting as a threshold for entitlement and providing a focus for public debate (Bidani, *et al.*, 2001).

An absolute poverty line has fixed real values over time and space while a relative poverty line has values that rise with average expenditure. Ravallion (1998) argues that a poverty line should always be absolute in the space of welfare for purposes of informing anti-poverty policies. Such a poverty line guarantees that the poverty comparisons made are consistent in the sense that two persons with the same level of welfare are treated the same way.

The traditional techniques for constructing poverty lines are the food energy intake (FEI) and the cost of basic needs (CBN) methods. Both methods anchor the definition of basic needs to food energy requirements.

The FEI aims at finding a monetary value equivalent at which basic needs are met. It presents only the minimum level of basic needs, below which a material lifestyle is not possible. The FEI method sets the minimum food requirement by setting the consumption expenditure level at which food energy intake is just sufficient to meet predetermined average food energy requirement for normal body function. This approach has been widely used by various authors such as Greer and Thorbecke (1986); Ercelawn (1991) and Fambon *et al.* (2000). The advantage with the FEI method is that it automatically includes an allowance for both food and non-food consumption thus avoiding the tricky issue of determining exactly the basic needs of these goods as long as one locates the total consumption expenditure at which a person typically attains the calorie requirement. It also does not rely on price data which can be a problem in many developing countries. It is also parsimonious in its data requirements and it allows for differences between subgroups.

The FEI has inherent weaknesses at the basis for welfare comparisons. The FEI poverty line is computed under the strong assumption that food expenditure and calorie intake are not independently observed (Bouis and Haddad, 1992). As noted by Greer and Thorbecke (1986), the use of fixed food weight to calorie intake factor for the whole country over time and over entire income profile might be inappropriate due to changing food quality and food preparation methods. The method does not allow us to make comparisons across different subgroups of the population using a common yardstick for standards of living because it suffers from inconsistency problems (Ravallion and Bidani, 1994; Bidani et al, 2001). The relationship between food energy intake and total consumption is likely to differ according to differences in tastes, activity levels, relative prices or publicly provided goods.

In the Cost of Basic Needs approach (CBN), the poverty line is constructed by determining a food basket which is assumed to be bought by all households. This approach considers poverty as a lack of command over basic consumption needs and the poverty line as the cost of those needs. The basic food basket is usually set using the nutritional requirements. The bundle is then evaluated at local prices to get the food component of the overall poverty line. The food component of the poverty line is divided by some estimate of the budget share devoted to food to obtain the overall poverty line. The non food component is then got by taking the difference between the overall and the food poverty lines. The problem here is that the determination of the budget share devoted to food is likely not to be a transparent process (Ravallion, 1998).

Due to the intrinsic weaknesses in the FGT measures, the FEI and CBN measures and in general all summary measures of food poverty, what is ideally needed is an approach that is robust to the choice of food poverty line or measure. The theory of stochastic dominance provides such an approach. For example, in Table 1 which gives estimates of food and overall poverty lines for all provinces in Kenya and the whole country, it will be seen that using the different methods same regions in Kenya have different poverty lines.

Table 1
Food and Absolute Poverty Lines by Region

Region	*Food Poverty Lines (Ksh. Per Month per capita)*			*Overall Poverty Lines (Ksh. Per Month per Capita)*		
	CBN	*FEI*	*Sample Size*	*CBN*	*FEI*	*Sample Size*
National	602	571	7834	875	820	7833
Eastern	540	505	1187	810	749	1187
Central	627	640	1471	899	954	1471
Rift Valley	522	551	857	793	858	856
Nyanza	533	543	1360	737	735	1360
Western	594	567	570	836	973	570
North Eastern	707	566	397	951	924	397
Nairobi	852	804	198	1743	1180	198
Coast	731	631	678	1009	828	678
Urban	839	792	1245	1391	1348	1245
Rural	567	536	6589	812	780	6588

Source: Oiro, *et al.* (2004).

There is a lack of consensus on how to measure poverty in general, even though poverty indices and poverty profiles are increasingly being used as guides in targeting resources to reduce poverty. An allocation that is efficient according to one methodology may yield unacceptable results when a different methodology is applied.

Results from poverty studies are also sensitive to the choice of poverty line (the means of identifying the poor) and poverty measure (the measure obtained when aggregating incomes or expenditures of households below poverty line). Since the choices are typically at the discretion of the analyst, this has given rise to the suggestion that the results obtained are not robust. Potentially different results could be obtained by the choice of a different poverty line or measure. Moreover, few conclusions can be drawn if poverty trends differ substantially when different poverty measures are applied or the position of the poverty line is changed.

Analysts have tried to overcome the problem by employing a number of poverty lines/ measures but this only partially overcomes the problem since it may still be possible to obtain different results by the choice of another poverty line. Thus, what is ideally needed is an approach that is robust to the choice of poverty line.

Poverty dominance analysis uses stochastic dominance to provide rankings of distributions in terms of poverty, which are not sensitive to the choice of poverty line. Stochastic dominance, in relation to poverty involves ranking of income/expenditure distributions, i.e. it examines whether one distribution has unambiguously more or less poverty than another over a range of potential poverty lines.

Most of the studies in poverty in Kenya have used the summary measures to determine the extent and level. The robustness of poverty measures using summary measures such as means and variances can be compromised by errors in living standards data, unknown differences between households at similar consumption levels, uncertainties and arbitrariness in both the poverty lines and the precise poverty measure. Dominance conditions are more robust than comparisons based on mean and variances of distributions (Atkinson, 1987; Foster and Shorrocks, 1988; Ravallion, 1984 and Howes, 1994).

Application of the theory of stochastic dominance to poverty analysis permits a more robust comparison of the mean and variance of the variations. It allows poverty comparisons to be made without prior specifications of the poverty line.

In order to compare changes in poverty rates for Kenya, this study tests robustness of the observed changes in the poverty using stochastic dominance analysis, a robust way of ranking distributions. This approach avoids the problem that poverty comparisons may not be robust to the subjective choice of a poverty line. It also avoids the potential that small movements across the thresholds may have large impacts on poverty indices. This is then compared with results from other studies to determine the extent to which conclusions differ and the extent to which the findings are sensitive to the choice of poverty lines. Hence this study tries to answer the following questions. Are the results from poverty studies sensitive to the choice of poverty lines especially when the choice is at the discretion of the analyst? How does this affect their robustness? Does the conclusion differ substantially when summary measures (e.g. mean, variance) and stochastic dominance analysis methods are employed? Do we have an improvement in the levels of poverty in Kenya since 1994? If yes, are they significant?

This paper studies the poverty trends in Kenya using a stochastic dominance approach and data sets from 1994 and 1997 Welfare Monitoring Survey (WMS). Arising from this analysis, focus is placed on the following objectives:

1. Providing an additional set of results by applying robust techniques for comparing income and or expenditure based distributions in addition to standard measures of food poverty.
2. Tracing what has been happening to poverty, living standards and welfare since 1994.
3. Testing for the robustness of poverty comparisons between regions and over time.
4. Determining the extent to which the conclusions differ and the extent to which the findings are sensitive to the choice of the poverty lines.

In this paper, stochastic dominance is applied to a series of regionally representative Kenya household survey data to shed some light on the intertemporal patterns of changes in welfare levels and distribution, across geographical and socio-economic groupings of interest. The study, by capitalising on the time series of Kenya national household survey, makes additional contribution to debate on the trend of poverty and changes in the welfare levels and distribution in Kenya. The use of stochastic dominance to compare distribution of welfare levels across groups over time tests the robustness of changes in poverty that have been reported by other scholars using the same data set.

IV. METHODOLOGY

Poverty dominance analysis is an application of stochastic dominance to distributions of Cumulative Density Functions (CDF), F(x) and G(x) respectively. The CDF of F(x) first order stochastically dominates G(x) if and only if all monotone non-decreasing functions α(x):

$$\int \alpha(x)\,dF(x) \leq \int \alpha(x)\,dG(x) \tag{2}$$

where the integral is taken over the whole range of x. Thus the average value of á is at least as large in distribution F as it is in distribution G, as long as the valuation function is such that more is better, i.e. it is monotone non-decreasing. In this sense, distribution F stochastically dominates distribution G. An equivalent way of expressing this is to say that for all x,

$$G(x) \geq F(x) \tag{3}$$

so that the CDF of distribution G is always at least as large as that of distribution F, i.e. distribution G always has more mass in the lower part of the distribution. In terms of a diagram, the cumulative distribution points H(y), on the vertical axis, are proportional to the area under the curves and to the left of X. As seen in Figure 2, distribution G(x) is everywhere above distribution F(x) and so the probability of getting at least x is higher under F(x) than G(x), thus F(x) first order stochastically dominates G(x).

Suppose it is decided upon a poverty line and denote it as z. If we have n households in total and if q households have income below z, then the headcount ratio, $P_0 = q/n$. In this case, the CDFs are referred to as Poverty Incidence Curves (PICs) and each point on the graph gives the proportion of the population consuming less than or equal to the amount given on the

Figure 2
First Order Stochastic Dominance

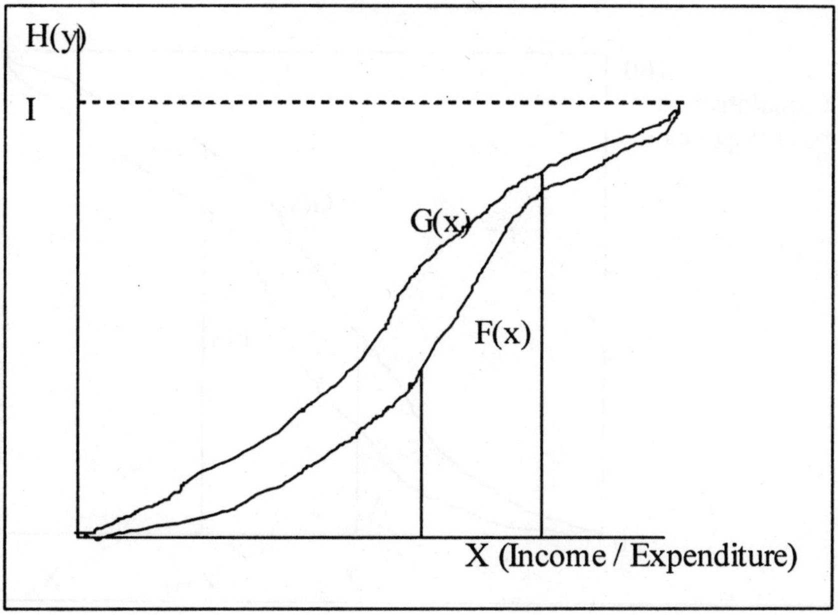

Source: Madden and Fiona, (2000).

horizontal axis. The cumulative distribution points are equivalent to headcount ratios in the sense that they represent the proportion of the population at and below a particular income level. Suppose we do not know the poverty line z, but we are sure that it does not exceed z^{max}. Under these circumstances, poverty will fall between two dates if the poverty incidence curve for the latter date lies above that of the former date, up to z^{max}. This is called the First Order Dominance Condition. In other words, if for all poverty lines up to z^{max}

$$G(x) \geq F(x),$$

Then P_0 will always be higher for the first distribution than the second, i.e. the poverty ranking of two distributions according to the headcount ratio is robust to all choices of the poverty line up to z^{max} if, and only if one distribution stochastically dominates the other. As shown in figure 3, the distribution G(x) is everywhere above that of distribution F(x) and so poverty is higher for G(x) than for F(x), no matter where the poverty line is drawn. This reflects the fact that the proportion of people consuming less than or equal to z^{max} is always greater with distribution G(x) than with distribution F(x). We can conclude that distribution F(x) first order poverty dominates distribution G(x).

If the curves intersect as in Figure 4, then the ranking is ambiguous. For example, if the poverty line was set at Z_b, then the distribution G(x) will lie above distribution F(x). If the poverty line however, is set at Z_a, then the distribution F(x) will lie above distribution G(x). Thus, poverty at Z_b is higher with distribution G(x) but at Z_a poverty is higher with distribution

Figure 3
First Order Poverty Dominance

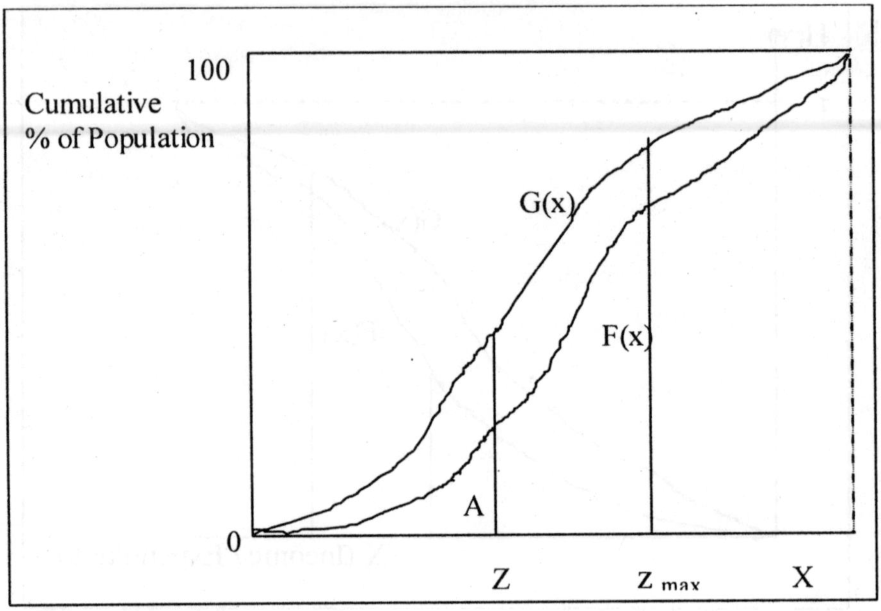

Source: Madden and Fiona, (2000).

Figure 4
Crossing of Poverty Incidence Curves

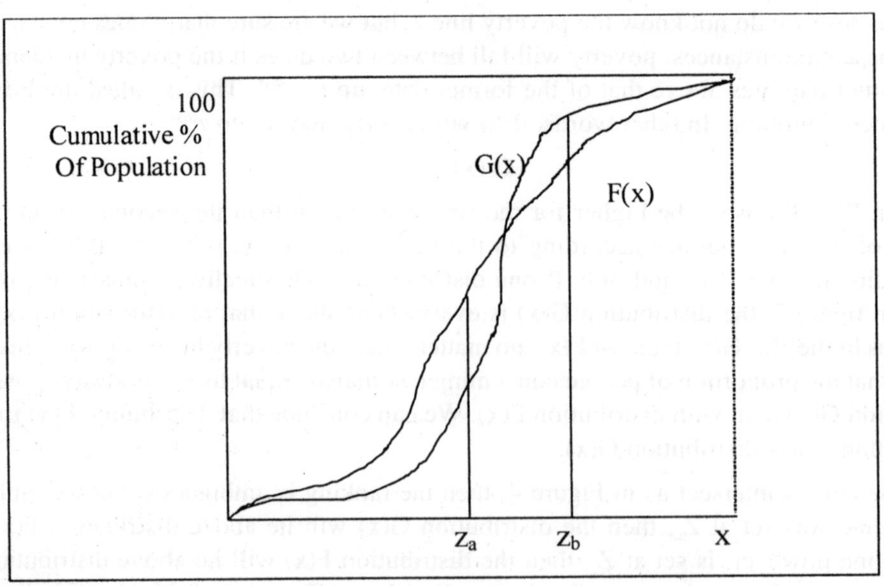

Source: Madden and Fiona, (2000).

F(x). We cannot therefore explicitly state that one distribution exhibits poverty dominance over the other as their ranking in terms of poverty changes depends on where the poverty line is drawn

In this case we impose more structure to our valuation function á(x) and hence equivalently on the range of admissible poverty measures. This leads us on to the second type of stochastic dominance known as second order stochastic dominance. Distribution F(x) second order stochastically dominates distribution G(x) if and only if, for all monotone non-decreasing and concave functions $\alpha(x)$ the previous inequality holds i.e.

$$\int \alpha(x)\,dF(x) \geq \int \alpha(x)\,dG(x).$$

Once again, second order stochastic dominance can be expressed equivalently as

$$D_G(x) = {}^x\!\int G(t)\,dt \geq {}^x\!\int F(t)dt = D_F(x) \qquad (4),$$

So that second order stochastic dominance is checked, not by comparing the CDFs themselves but by comparing the integrals below them. When $\alpha(x)$ is concave, we can interpret the integrals beneath them as additive social welfare functions with $\alpha(x_i)$ being the social valuation (utility) function for individual "i". In the case of poverty analysis, this implies that second order dominance holds for measures that are strictly decreasing and at least weakly convex in the incomes of the poor. i.e. measures that are sensitive to the depth of poverty such as the income gap ratio. We can them employ the second order dominance condition. To examine the robustness of the income gap we must consider the "poverty deficit curve" which can be defined as the area under the CDF or the integrals of the CDF, as discussed above, up to some poverty line z (Figure 5).

Figure 5
Poverty Deficit Curves for F(x)

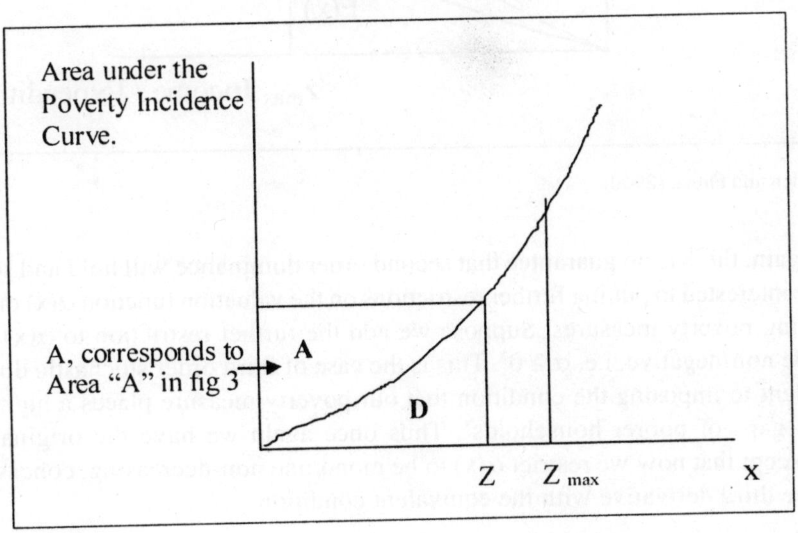

Source: Madden and Fiona, (2000).

In this case a fall in poverty requires that the poverty deficit curve is nowhere lower for the earlier date at all points up to the maximum poverty line and at least somewhere higher (Figure 6). Poverty is thus higher for G(x) as in Figure 6, as its poverty deficit curve is above that for F(x) up to Z_{max}. As previously mentioned, this result will hold for a measure that is sensitive to the depth of poverty such as the income gap ratio but not the head count ratio. Second order stochastic dominance is a concept that is weaker than first order stochastic dominance as first order stochastic dominance implies second order dominance and not vice versa.

Figure 6
Poverty Deficit Curves for F(x) and G(x)

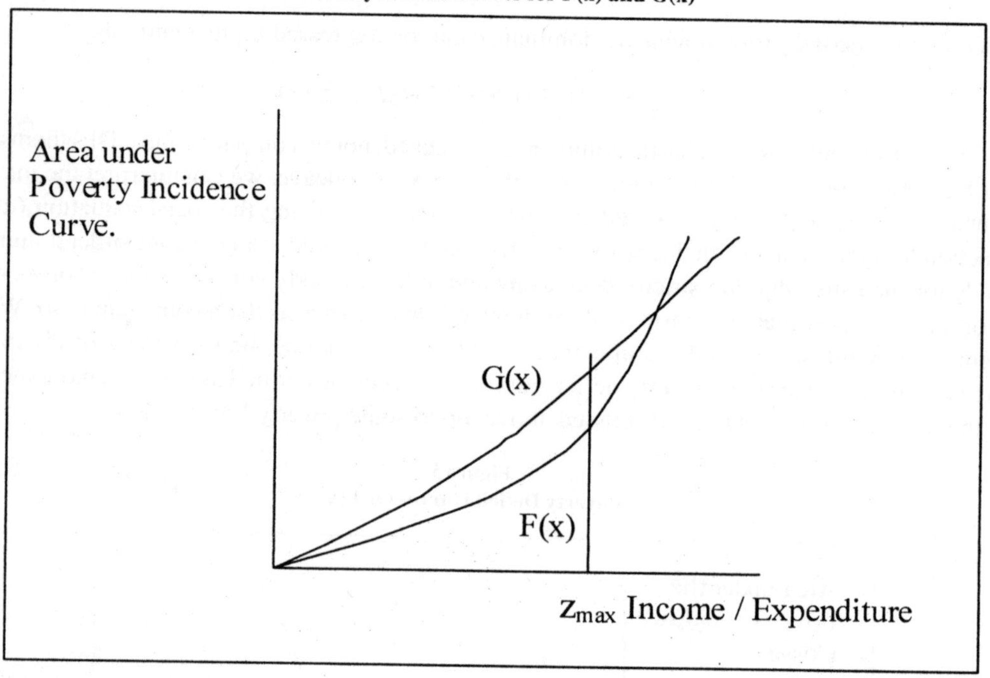

Source: Madden and Fiona, (2000).

Once again, there is no guarantee that second order dominance will hold and so once again, we might be interested in putting further restrictions on the valuation function $\alpha(x)$ or equivalently the underlying poverty measures. Suppose we add the further restriction to $\alpha(x)$ that its third derivative be non-negative, i.e. $\alpha \geq 0$[2]. This is the case of third order stochastic dominance and it is equivalent to imposing the condition that our poverty measure places a higher weight on the poverty gaps of poorer households[3]. Thus once again we have the original dominance condition except that now we restrict $\alpha(x)$ to be monotone non-decreasing, concave and with a non-negative third derivative with the equivalent condition

$$SG(x) = {}^{x}\int D_G(t)\, dt \geq {}^{x}\int D_F(t)\, dt = SF(x) \quad (5)$$

i.e. we are now examining the areas under the poverty deficit curves which we label the poverty severity cure. Figure 7a shows the poverty severity curve for distribution F(x).

Figure 7
Poverty Severity Curves for F(x)

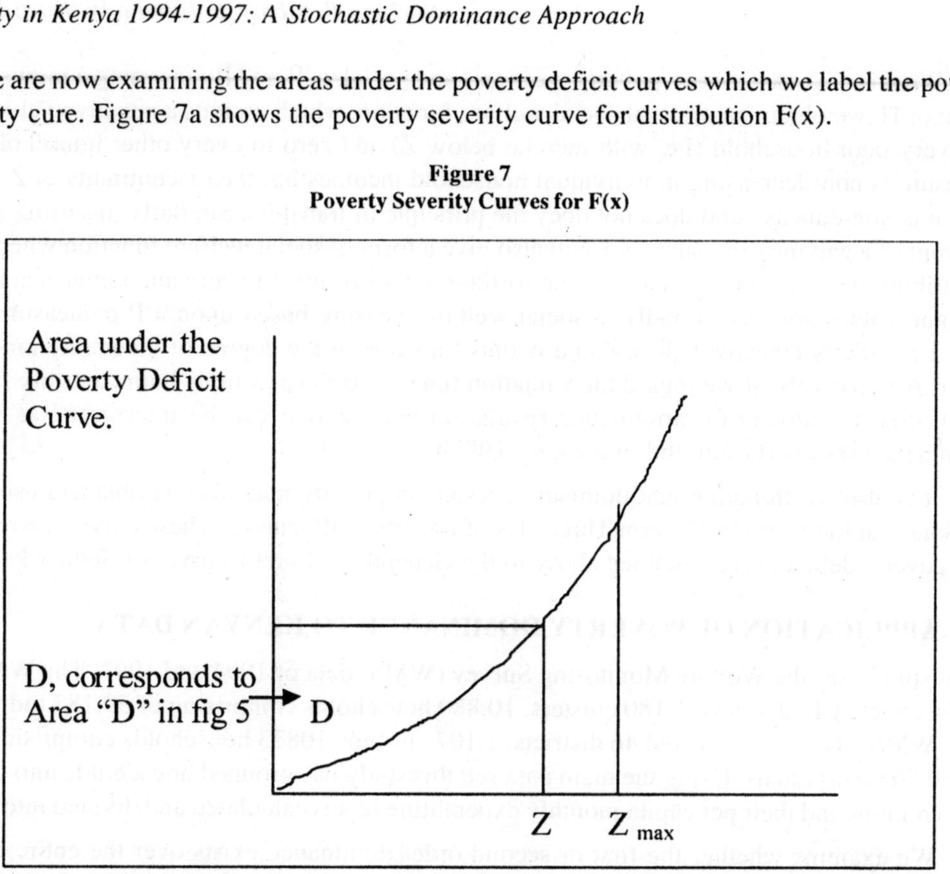

Source: Madden and Fiona, (2000).

In principle, it is possible to examine higher orders of stochastic dominance but in practice, it is rare to go beyond third order. As discussed above, if any given order of dominance does not hold then it is always possible to investigate if a higher order holds. This is equivalent to imposing more restrictions of the valuation function (poverty measure). In the case of poverty dominance, this involves restricting the range of the poverty line over which we search for dominance. Thus, while in general we are interested in the entire distribution of the CDFs up to the maximum value of the poverty line Z_{max}, we may also be concerned with the behaviour of the CDFs between a lower bond estimate, Z_{min} of the poverty line and an upper bound estimate Z_{max}.

It was Atkinson (1987) who first emphasised that in poverty analysis, there is often a lower as well as an upper limit for the poverty line and it may turn out that the distributions do not cross between these limits, so that first order dominance may hold for this range of income/ expenditure if not for all values of Z up to Z_{max}. This leads to another definition of stochastic dominance known as poverty mixed dominance. This definition is a combination of first and second order dominance. Poverty mixed dominance requires that distribution F display second order dominance over distribution G from zero to the lower bound poverty line Z_{min} and first order dominance from Z_{min} to Z_{max} (Ferreira, *et al.*, 1998).

What is the link between poverty measures and social welfare? By inserting a minus sign in front of H, we obtain an unusual social welfare function, which assigns a negative value of 1/n to every poor household (i.e. with income below Z) and zero to every other household. This measure is non-decreasing in individual household incomes but the discontinuity at Z implies that it is non-concave and does not obey the principle of transfers. Similarly, inserting a minus in front of a gap measure such as 1 will also give a form of social welfare function whereby the contribution of each individual to social welfare moves from –1 to zero and remains at zero for income values above Z. Finally, a social welfare measure based upon a P α measure where $\alpha > 1$ is strictly concave below Z and is thus sensitive to the degree of inequality among the poor. Alternatively, if we regard the valuation function α (x) as simply being a utility function u(x), then the stochastic dominance results outlined above can be interpreted as welfare dominance results (Foster and Shorrocks, 1988b).

It is also worth noting that dominance results in poverty may also be obtained using what Jenkins and Lambert (1997) term Three "I"s of poverty (TIP) curves. These curves are related to the poverty deficit curves outlined above to the Generalised Lorenz curves of Shorrocks (1983).

V. APPLICATION OF POVERTY DOMINANCE TO KENYAN DATA

This study uses the Welfare Monitoring Survey (WMS) data of 1994 and 1997. The WMS II of 1994 covered 47 districts, 1,180 clusters, 10,880 households comprising of 59,183 individuals. The WMS III of 1997 covered 46 districts, 1,107 clusters, 10873 households comprising a total of 50,705 individuals. Using the main data set, this study has grouped households into districts, then regions and their per capita monthly expenditure levels calculated and divided into deciles.

We examine whether the first or second order dominance exists over the entire range of expenditure values from zero to the upper bound estimate of the poverty line Z_{max}. We also examine if the first order dominance exists between a lower bound estimate of the poverty line, Z_{min}, and an upper bound estimate Z_{max}. Figure 7b shows the Cumulative distribution Functions of household expenditure for the entire sample for 1994 and 1997.

The x-axis represents equivalent expenditure where expenditure is displayed in Kenya shillings. The y-axis represents the cumulative percentage of the population with at least x amount of per capita monthly expenditure which represents the head count ratio. The points along the horizontal axis, from zero to a maximum level can also be designated as a set of plausible poverty lines. The proportion of the poor is then found by reading off the proportion of the population from the vertical axis that consumes less than the given amount on the horizontal axis. So how do we determine whether dominance holds? One approach is to simply visually inspect the graphs. Clearly, the figure shows that the 1994 dominates the 1997 distribution, i.e. the CDF of 1997 is everywhere above that of 1994. As discussed earlier, if the cumulative distribution or poverty incidence curve for period A lies everywhere above the curve for time B, this represents first order dominance, and it implies that poverty is unambiguously lower in B than A. This shows that there was no improvement in the welfare of Kenyans between 1994 and 1997. In fact there was a worsening of living standards as measured by the consumption per adult equivalent.

Figure 8
Cumulative Distribution Functions of CPAE for Kenya

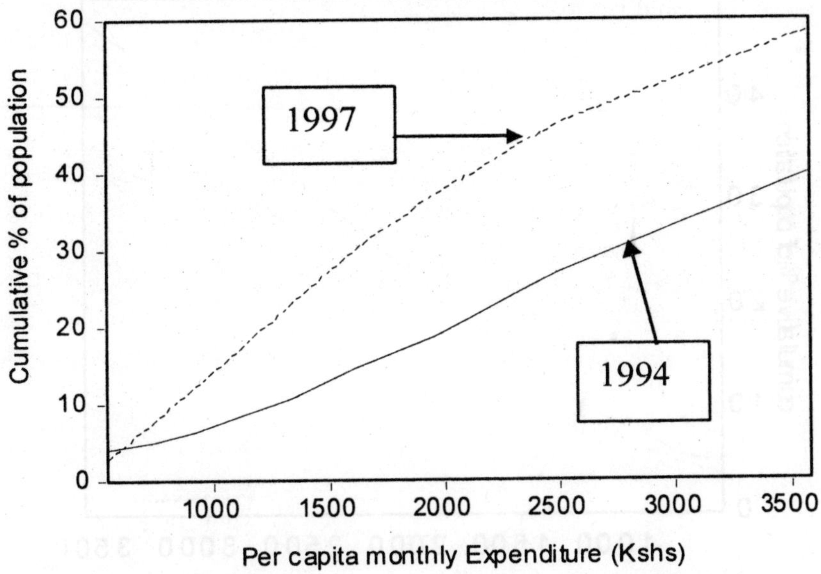

Generally, poverty lines at the very top of the distributions are usually implausible. This implies that it is not necessary to apply stochastic dominance criterion over the entire distribution of consumption expenditure per adult equivalent. We truncate the distribution to include adult equivalent expenditure levels no higher that Ksh. 3,576.09 per month (about twice the poverty line of one dollar per day). Given the increase in poverty over the years, it is not surprising that the dominance analysis reveals that the welfare of the households in this expenditure bracket worsened gradually over time especially over the middle expenditure groups. These results are robust to the choice of poverty line and confirm the results from past studies which show that poverty has been increasing since 1994.

1. Changes in Household Welfare by Region between 1994 and 1997

In this section, we examine whether the changes in national welfare are reflected in the regional levels by conducting stochastic dominance analysis for different regions. We analyse them jointly to provide within year inter-regional comparisons that are robust to the choice of poverty line and individually to highlight inter-temporal changes in welfare distribution within each region. The results for 1994 are shown in Figures 8a to 8d.

The distribution in Figures 8a to 8d confirm the widely known poverty story in Kenya that living standards in Central province dominate those in the rest of the country irrespective of where the poverty line is chosen. The welfare distribution ranking is consistent with findings of previous studies that used specific poverty lines in the sense that Central province enjoys the highest standard of living, followed by Nyanza, Rift Valley, Western, Coast, Eastern and lastly North Eastern in 1994. The results for 1997 are shown in figures 9a to 9e.

Figure 8a

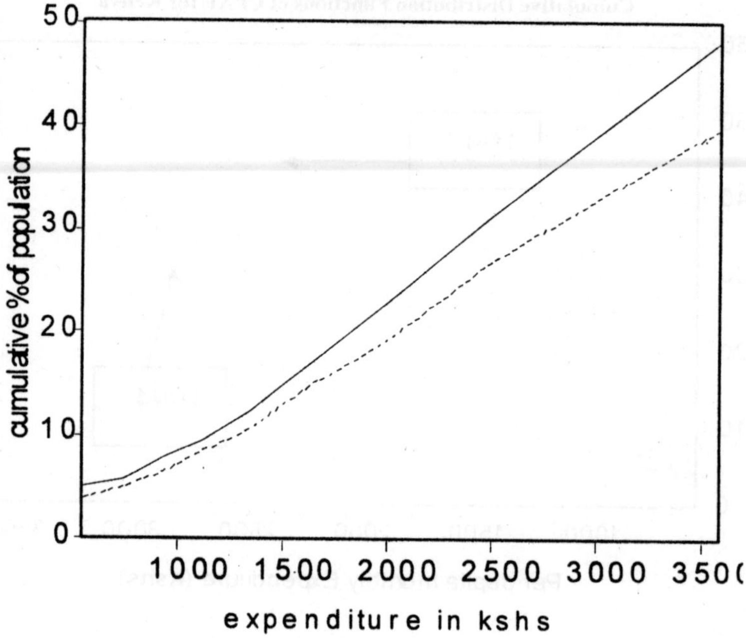

Figure 8b

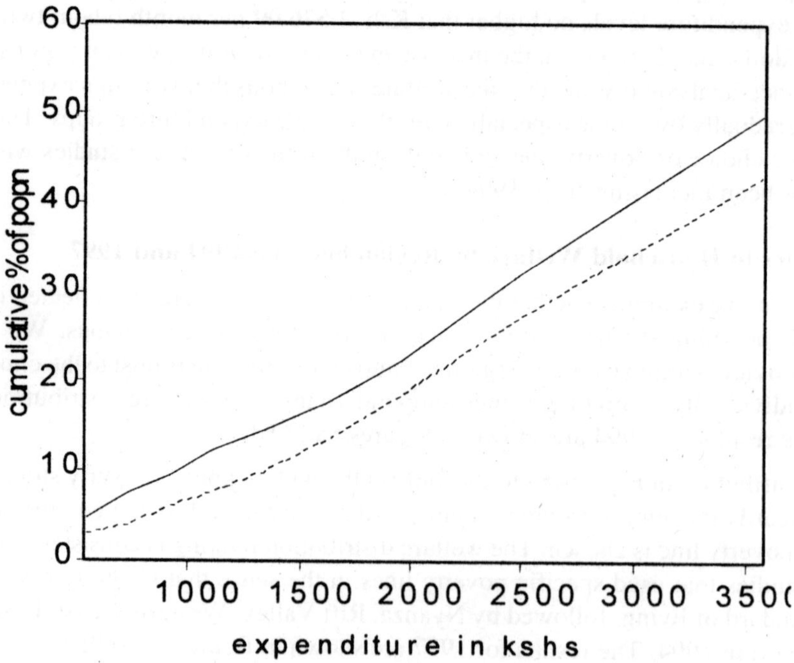

Figure 8c

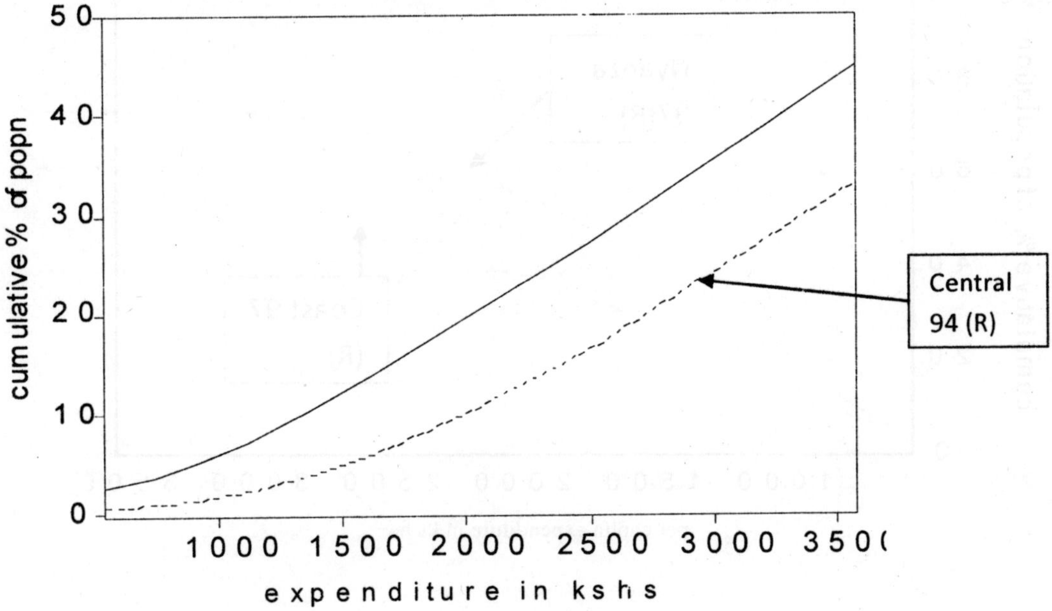

Figure 8d

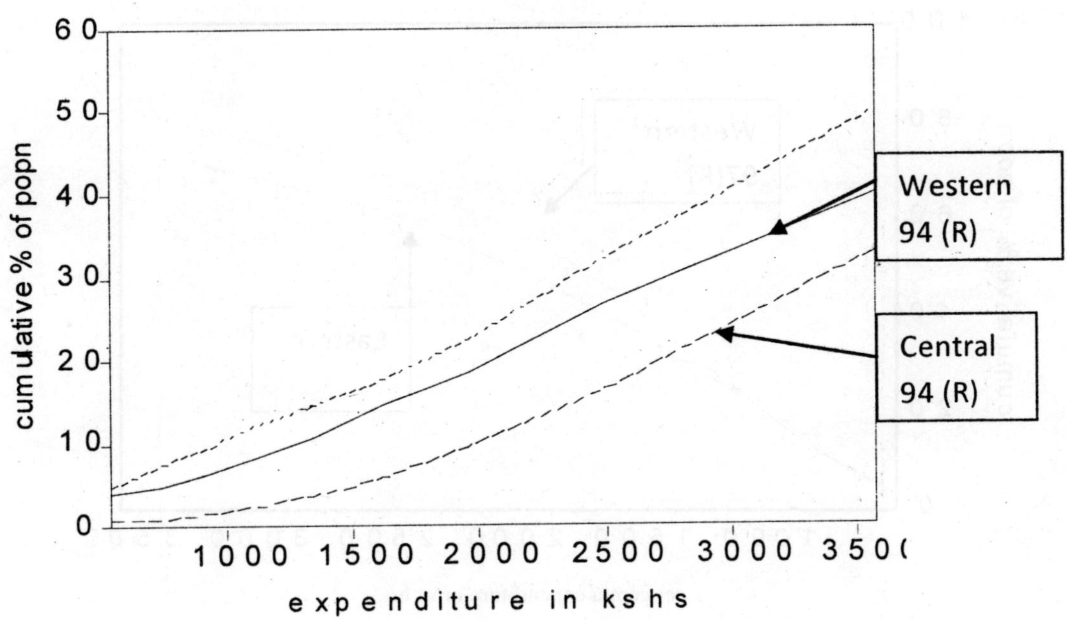

Figure 9a

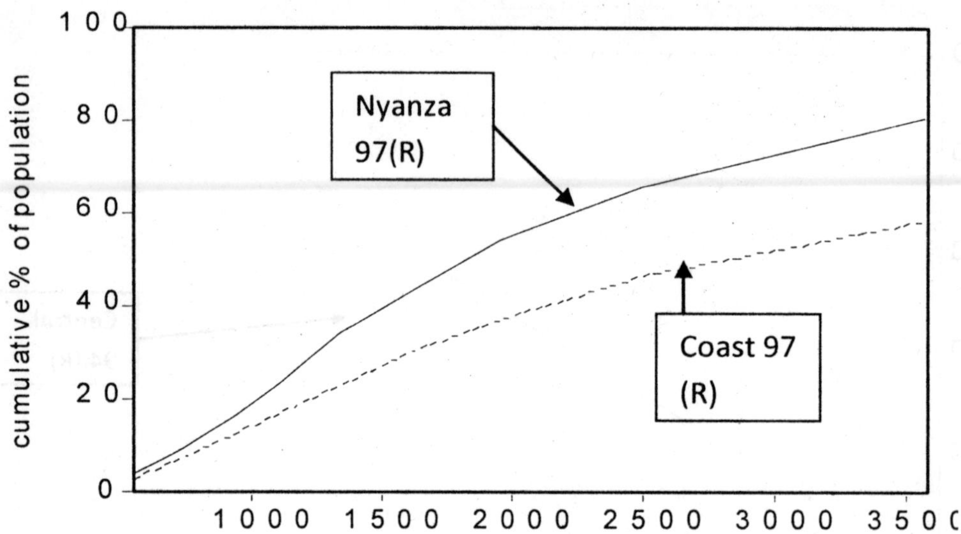

per capita expenditure in ks hs

Figure 9b

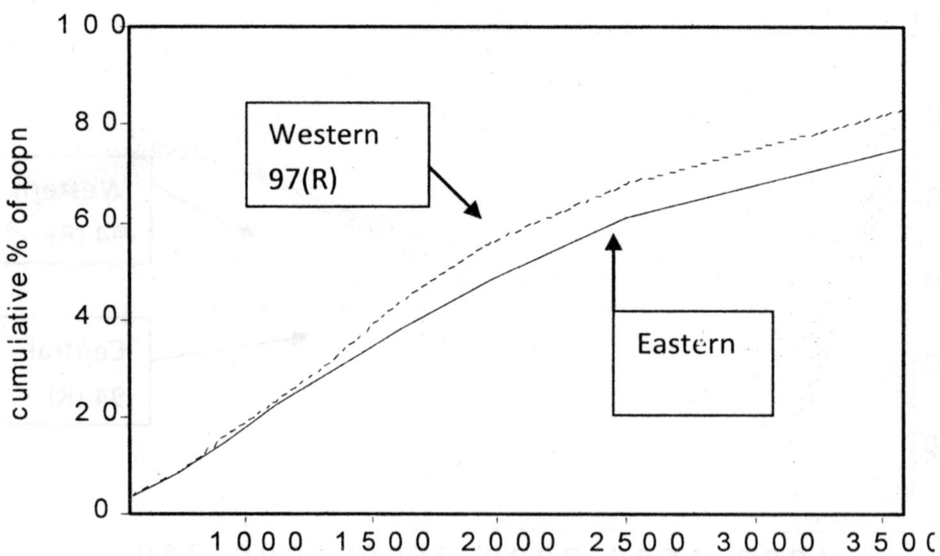

per capita expenditure in ks hs

Figure 9c

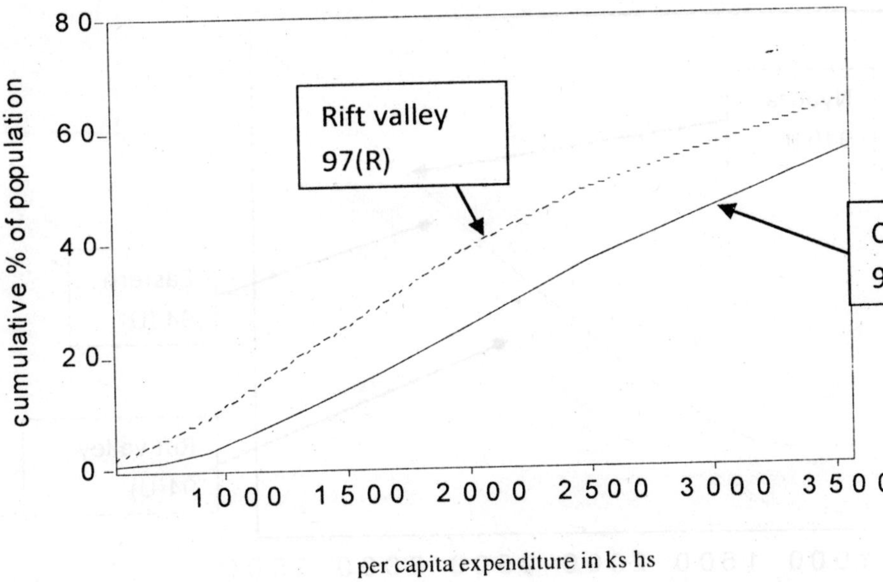

Figure 9d

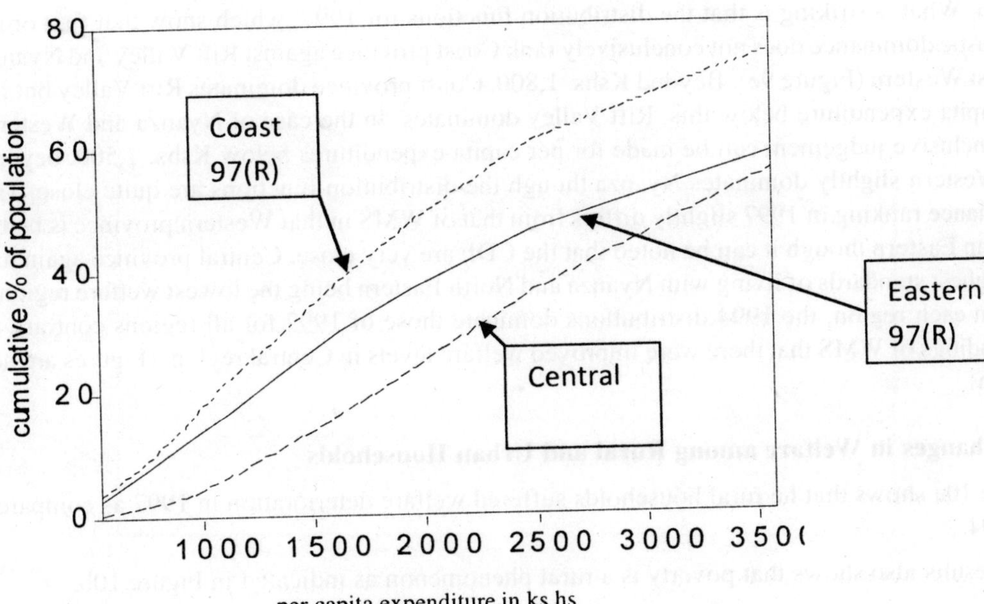

Figure 9e

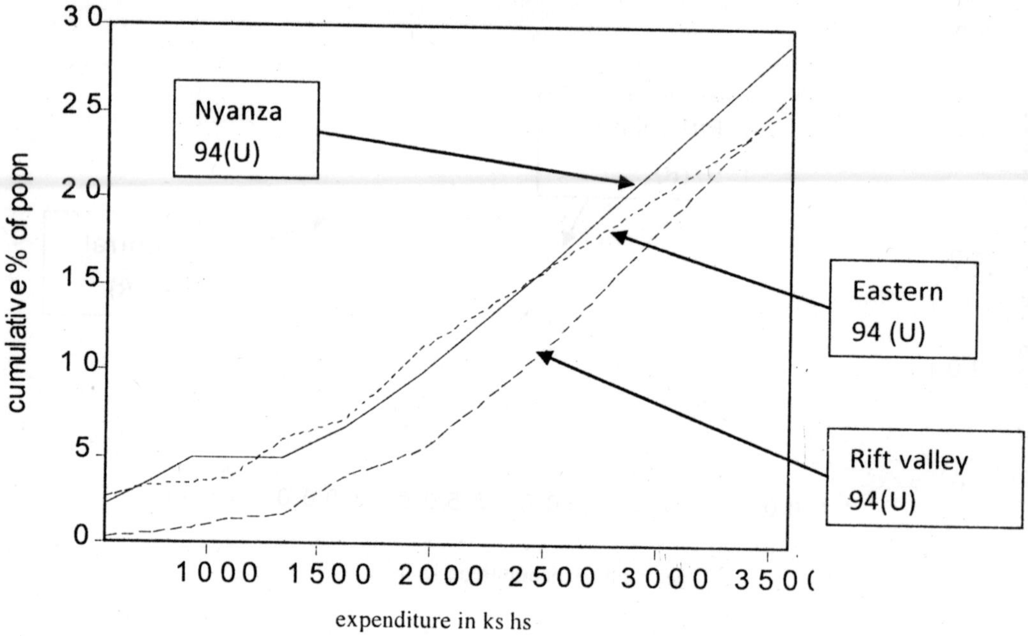

Figures 9a to 9e show the CDF of consumption expenditure per adult equivalent in 1997 by region. What is striking is that the distribution functions for 1997, which show that first order stochastic dominance does not conclusively rank Coast province against Rift Valley and Nyanza against Western (Figure 9e). Beyond Kshs. 1,800, Coast province dominates Rift Valley but for per capita expenditure below this, Rift Valley dominates. In the case of Nyanza and Western, no conclusive judgement can be made for per capita expenditures below Kshs. 1,500, beyond this Western slightly dominates Nyanza though the distribution functions are quite close. The dominance ranking in 1997 slightly differs from that of WMS in that Western province is better off than Eastern though it can be noted that the CDF are very close. Central province again has the highest standards of living with Nyanza and North Eastern being the lowest welfare regions. Within each region, the 1994 distributions dominate those of 1997 for all regions contrary to the findings of WMS that there were improved welfare levels in Central region. (Figures are not shown).

2. Changes in Welfare among Rural and Urban Households

Figure 10a shows that he rural households suffered welfare deterioration in 1997 as compared to 1994.

Results also shows that poverty is a rural phenomenon as indicated in Figure 10b.

In summary, the study has found that first order poverty dominance holds for the years 1994 and 1997 over what can be regarded as a reasonable range of expenditure levels. Thus it

Figure 10a

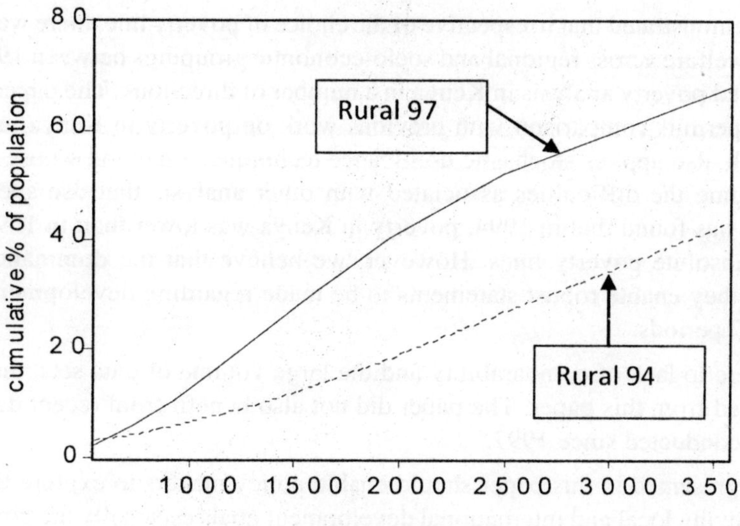

Figure 10b

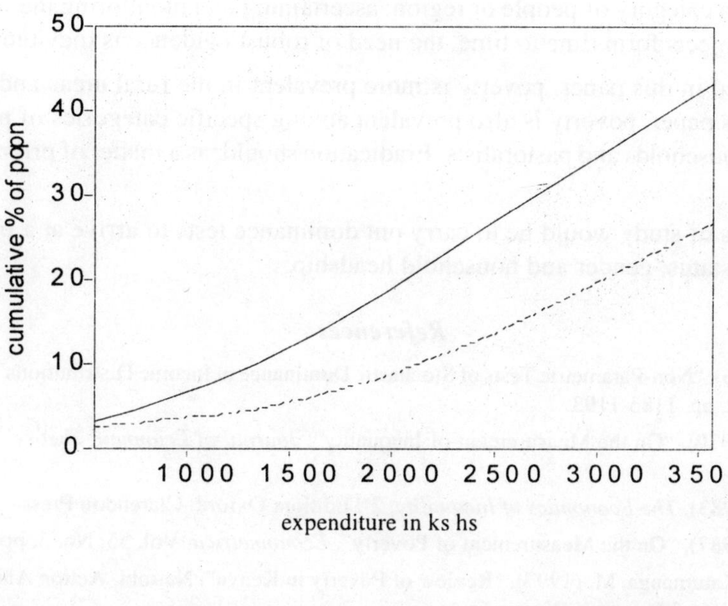

is possible to say with a fair degree of confidence that poverty in 1994 was lower than in 1997. It should also be noted that given the findings of first order dominance, there is no need to search for second or third order dominance since a finding of any degree implies that higher degrees of dominance must also hold.

VI. CONCLUSION AND POLICY RECOMMENDATIONS

This paper has demonstrated that irrespective of the choice of poverty line, there was widespread deterioration in welfare across regional and socio-economic groupings between 1994 and 1997. We have advanced poverty analysis in Kenya in a number of directions. The paper employs the WMS data and permits comparison with previous work on poverty in Kenya using different methodologies. It also applies stochastic dominance technique, a method whose novelty is its ability to overcome the difficulties associated with other analysis that use specific poverty lines. The paper has found that in 1994, poverty in Kenya was lower than in 1997 for a fairly wide range of absolute poverty lines. However, we believe that the dominance results are important since they enable robust statements to be made regarding developments in poverty over the 1994/97 periods.

However, due to lack of comparability and the large volume of data sets, the 1992 WMS data was excluded from this paper. The paper did not also benefit from recent data sets as not WMS has been conducted since 1997.[4]

The results presented in this paper should enable policy makers to explore the challenges involved in achieving local and international development goals especially the goal of reducing poverty by half by the year 2015 as indicated in the Millennium Development Goals (MDGs). The achievement of this goal would allow Kenya to make irreversible progress towards a better life. In the formulation of these goals, justifying the targeting of any poverty alleviation policy and programs to a category of people or region, ascertaining and monitoring the impact of such programs and projects form time to time, the need of robust evidence is inevitable.

As mentioned in this paper, poverty is more prevalent in the rural areas and although not mentioned in this paper, poverty is also prevalent among specific categories of people such as female headed households and pastoralists. Eradication should, as a matter of priority be focused in these areas.

Further areas of study would be to carry out dominance tests to arrive at a poverty profile by employment status, gender and household headship.

References

Anderson, G. (1996), "Non-Parametric Tests of Stochastic Dominance in Income Distributions", *Econometrica*, Vol. 64, No. 9, pp. 1183-1193.

Atkinson, A. B. (1970), "On the Measurement of Inequality", *Journal of Economic Theory*, Vol. 2, pp. 244-263.

Atkinson, A. B. (1983), *The Economics of Inequality*, 2nd Edition, Oxford: Clarendon Press.

Atkinson, A. B. (1987), "On the Measurement of Poverty", *Econometrica*, Vol. 55, No. 3, pp. 749-764.

Ayako, B. A. and Katumanga, M. (1997), "Review of Poverty in Kenya", Nairobi: Action Aid and Institute of Policy Analysis and Research (November).

Ferreira, H. and Litchfield, J. A. (1999), *Inequality, Poverty and Welfare, Brazil 1981-1995*, Mimeograph, London School of Economics.

Ferreira, H., Francisco, J. and Litchfield, J. A. (1998), "Calm after the Storms: Income Distribution in Chile: 1987-1994", *World Bank Policy Research Paper* No 19.

Fields, G. S. (2000), "The Dynamics of Poverty, Inequality and Economic Well being: African Economic Growth in Comparative Perspective", *Journal of African Economies*, Vol. 9, Supp. No. 1, pp. 45-78.

Foster, J. (1998), "Absolute versus Relative Poverty", *American Economic Review*, Vol. 88, pp. 335-341.

Foster, J. E. and Shorrocks, A. F. (1988a), "Poverty Ordering", *Econometrica*, Vol. 56, No. 1, pp. 173-177.

Foster, J. E. and Shorrocks, A. F. (1988b), "Poverty Orderings and Welfare Dominance", *Social Choice Welfare*, Vol. 5, pp. 179-198.

Foster, J. E. and Shorrocks, A. F. (1988c), "Inequality and Poverty Orderings", *European Economic Review*, Vol. 32, pp. 654-662.

Foster, J. Greer, J. and Thorbecke, E. (1984), "A Class of Decomposable Poverty Measures", *Econometrica*, Vol. 52, No. 3, pp. 761-766.

Republic of Kenya (2000a), *Second Report on Poverty in Kenya: Incidence and Depth of Poverty*, Vol. 1. Nairobi: Government Printer.

Republic of Kenya (2000b), *Second Report on Poverty in Kenya: Poverty and Social Indicators*, Vol. 2, Nairobi: Government Printer.

Republic of Kenya (2000c), *Second Report on Poverty in Kenya: Welfare Indicators*, Vol. 3. Nairobi: Government Printer.

Republic of Kenya (2001), *Poverty Reduction Strategy Paper: 2001-2004*, Nairobi: Government Printer.

Greer, J. and Thorbecke, E. (1986), "A Methodology for Measuring Food Poverty Applied to Kenya", *Journal of Development Economics*, Vol. 24, pp. 59-74.

Howes, S. (1994), *Distributional Analysis using Dominance Criteria: With application to Chinese Survey Data*, London School of Economics.

Jenkins, S. P. and Lambert, P. J. (1997), "Three "I"s of Poverty Curves and Poverty Dominance: Tips for Poverty Analysis", *Research on Economic Inequality*, Vol. 8, DP. No. 97, pp. 39-56.

Kenya African National Union (1963), *KANU Manifesto*, Nairobi: Government Printer.

Kuznets, S. (1955), "Economic Growth and Income Inequality", *American Economic Review*, Vol. 45, March, pp. 1-28.

Lambert, P. (1992), "The Distribution and Redistribution of Income", *Journal of Economic Literature*, Vol. 12, (March), pp. 73-84.

Madden, D. and Fiona, S. (2000), "Poverty in Ireland: A Stochastic Dominance Approach", *The Economic and Social Review*, Vol. 31, No. 3, pp. 187-214.

Mwabu, G. Kiriti, T. Ndenge, G. Kirimi, J. Kabubo, J. Gesami, R. Masai, W. Kimuyu, P. Chemengich, M. and Munene, F. (2000), "Poverty in Kenya: Identification, Measurement and Profiles", *Mimeo*, Nairobi.

OECD (2000), *Waging the Global War on Poverty Strategies and Case Studies, http://www.oecd.org/document*

Oiro, M. W. Mwabu, G. and Manda, D. K. (2004), Poverty and Unemployment in Kenya, KIPPRA Discussion Paper No. 33, Nairobi.

Ravallion, M. (1992), "Poverty Comparison: A Guide to Concepts and Methods", Living Standards and Measurement Study, *Working Paper* No. 88, Washington, D. C.: World Bank.

Ravallion, M. (1994), *Poverty Comparisons*, Chur, Switzerland: Harwood Academic Press.

Ravallion, M. and Bidani, B. (1994), "How Robust is a Poverty Profile,? World Bank Economic Review, Vol. 8, No. 1, pp. 75-101.

Ravallion, M. and Chen, S. (1997), "What can New Survey Data tell us about Recent Changes in Distribution of Poverty"? *World Bank Economic Review*, Vol. 11, No. 2, pp. 26-35.

Ravallion and Huppi, M. (1991), "Measuring Changes in Poverty: A Methodological Case Study of Indonesia during an Adjustment Period", *World Bank Economic Review*, Vol. 5, No. 1, pp. 57-82.

Shimelis, A. (2000), "Comments on the State and Path of Poverty in Sub-Saharan Africa: some Preliminary Results by Ali and Thorbecke", *Journal of African Economics*, Vol. 9, Suppl. 9, pp. 41-44.

Shorrocks, A. (1983), "Ranking Income Distributions", *Economica*, Vol. 50, pp. 3-17.

Theil, H. (1967), Economic and Information Theory, Amsterdam: North Holland.

UNDP (2000), *Human Development Report*, New York: Oxford University Press.

World Bank (1997), *Development in Practice: Taking Action to Reduce Poverty in Sub-Saharan Africa*, Washington, D. C.: World Bank.

World Bank (1997), *Voices for the poor: Poverty and Social Capital in Tanzania*, Washington, D. C.: World Bank.

World Bank (2000), *World Development Report*, Oxford: Oxford University Press.

World Bank (2005), *www.worldbank.org/poverty/inequality/index.htm*

THE ENDOGENOUS MONEY HYPOTHESIS: EMPIRICAL EVIDENCE FROM TUNISIA, 1991-2002

*Fatma Siala**

ABSTRACT

This paper tests the endogeneity of money supply in Tunisia during the period 1991-2002, using time series techniques and Granger-causality tests based on co-integration analysis and error- correction models. The main results of the paper are: (i) *The money supply process is endogenously determined.* (ii) *Causality is rather going from bank lending to the monetary base and money supply.* (iii) *Monetary policy should not overlook the behavioural dynamics of banks and thereby the endogenous character of money supply.*

Key words: *endogenous money supply, post-keynesian hypothesis, causality, co-integration, Tunisia.*

I. INTRODUCTION

The traditional analysis of money supply has been considered for a long period as exogenous. Indeed, this hypothesis has been accepted for many decades since it is linked with a uni-dimensional view of monetary regulation. However, post-keynesian economists have seriously questioned the relevancy of such hypothesis and contend in opposite that money supply is rather endogenous. Their argument is an invention based on historical facts and backed by some empirical studies (Howells, 2005 p. 3).

In fact, the neoclassical framework contended that the supply of money is determined by the central bank initiatives which are independent from financial markets considerations. The post keynesian approach reverses such hypothesis and put forward arguments where the growth of money supply is determined by factors linked to credit availability and therefore to financial markets functioning. The implications of this money supply endogeneity are that monetary authorities are not capable alone to control the money stock since this latter is credit-driven and demand-determined.

The literature on money supply endogeneity may be summarized into three strands sharing in common the fact that money supply is influenced by the demand side within the financial markets. We find, *first*, the accomodationnist view where, *second,* the structuralist approach and *finally* the liquidity preference approach.

* Faculté des Sciences Economiques et de Gestion de Tunis (FSEGT), Boulevard 7 Novembre, Tunis, Tunisia, *E-mail: fatma.siala@hexabyte.tn*

The empirical literature on the endogeneity money hypothesis has not provided a clear cut answer for testing this issue. Indeed, the major studies are interested in the case of developed countries: Palley (1994) for the case of United Kingdom and Moore (1988; 1989)) for the american economy. Some other empirical investigations has been carried out for a sample of advanced countries (Howell and Hussein (1998)) or middle income economies (Shanmugam *et al.* (2003), Nell (2001), Vera (2001)) using time series analysis. However, to my knowledge, only very few studies have been reserved to the case of developing countries including those who belong to the Middle East and North African (MENA) region.

The purpose of the paper is to test endogeneity of money hypothesis supply in Tunisia during the period 1991-2002 using Granger causality and cointegration techniques. The choice of Tunisia as a county sample is accounted for by the fact that this country proceeded deliberately to a large financial sector reform including a change in monetary regulation especially during the nineties. In fact, while the reform tends to promote the financial market by providing new direct financing instruments and creating more dynamic capital market, it remains that indirect financing through banking credit constitutes the principal source of finance for economic activities in the country.

To test for money endogeneity hypothesis we use Granger causality tests and cointegration techniques to see the evolution of the variables in the short and the long run. The main results of the paper are: (*i*) the causality is rather going from bank lending to the monetary base and money supply. This result contrasts with the mainstream literature on the topic which considers that causality is going from the monetary base to bank lending. (*ii*) the policy implications of this result is that tunisian monetary authorities should take into account the behavioral dynamics of banking institutions and thereby the endogenous character of money supply.

The outline of this paper is as follows: the theory of money endogeneity is set out in section 2. Section 3 provides an overview of the empirical hypotheses and studies of the money endogeneity. In section 4 we discuss the econometric methodology used to test for causality. Finally, section 5 ends with some conclusions and policy implications.

II. THE ENDOGENEITY HYPOTHESIS

Post-Keynesian economists challenge the conventional money multiplier approach. They argue that money stock is essentially endogenously determined by the demand for credit and not exogenously controlled by the central bank (Moore (1991)). While all post-Keynesians agree that the demand for credit drives the money stock, there exist three theories of the mechanism leading to an endogenous money stock: The so-called "accommodationist view[3], "structuralist view"[4], and the liquidity preference view.

1. The Accommodationist View

According to the monetarist approach the money supply is a multiple of the monetary base and is determined exogenously by the central bank. The Accommodationist approach is considered as the first direct challenge to this orthodox monetarist one and it is found in the seminal contributions of Kaldor (1982) and Moore (1988, 1989). According to this approach, monetary authorities set the cost of short term liquidity and proceed to inject or withdraw reserves according to the demand of banks and the targets fixed for interest rates. In this case, the monetary base and money supply become *"perfectly endogenous, determined by the quantity of bank credit demanded at the interest rate set exogenously by the central bank"* (Moore, 1998, p.176).

According to Moore (1998), monetary authorities *have to* accommodate commercial banks demand for reserves in order to preserve financial system liquidity and to fulfill their role as a last resort lender. In this case, the central bank looses its control over reserves supply but maintains it over the interest rates. Exponents of this approach contend that the money supply function is perfectly interest rate elastic (Moore,1989) and there is no empirical support that the interest rate increase with the level of bank credits.

2. The Structuralist View

For the structuralists, the hypothesis of total accommodation of monetary authorities to reserve demand of the banking system is not fully realistic. They suppose also that bank lending is at least, to some extent, a variable controlled by either the Central Bank or commercial banks (Goodhart, 1989; Davidson 1989). Furthermore, Pollin (1991) and Palley (1994) contend that this accommodation depends, rather, on the attitude of the Central Bank and private banking institutions. In this context, monetary authorities may intervene to place some constraints on banking reserve detention through open market operation. Consequently, the money supply function becomes an upward sloping one with the interest rate.

While the accommodationist view insists on the fact that the central bank has only a *control* over interest rates, an important feature of the structuralist view is that monetary authorities maintain *some control* over the supply of reserves. In this context, the central bank has the possibility to *target* the monetary base as well as the interest rate in implementing policies. It may also use *either* as *instruments* for other objectives (Palley (1998)). Another distinguishing feature of the structuralist endogeneity approach is its focus on the use of liability management practices by banking institutions to get the costless funds. Indeed, this practice allows banks, partially, to go beyond reserve constraints of the central bank. The structuralists emphasize that this liability management does not constitute an adequate supply of reserves to satisfy the demand, although this practice can be presented as a mean to overcome reserve constraints (Pollin (1991)).

3. The Liquidity Preference View

It is an approach that supports mainly the accommodationist's argument relative to the endogenous nature of the money supply. In this theoretical setting, the credit money can never be in a situation of excess supply and that without demand for money there is no supply. Moreover, a situation of excess supply can not occur since according the accommodationist approach there exists an identical supply and demand function (Moore 1991, Kaldor and Trevithick, 1981).

For Howells (1995), the economic agents have different liquidity preferences about their money detention and that there is an independent money demand function. The main debate is about the reconciliation mechanism which ensures the equivalence between the quantity of money demanded and the supply of new deposits generated by new credits. Furthermore, Howells underlines the fact that these suggested mechanisms have some limitations, but he still contends that in the case of insufficiency of supply of deposits with respect to the demand for credits, the individual preferences are likely to modify the relative interest rates. As a consequence, we will attend to a rise of supply of deposits and a reduction in the demand of loans. This variation in the relative interest rate is somewhat seen as mean which ensures the fact that the demand for newly created deposits matches the demand for credits of individuals.

III. THE EMPIRICAL HYPOTHESES AND STUDIES

1. The Hypotheses

According to the accommodationist approach, there is a full accommodation of reserves by monetary authorities and that banking institutions meet all demands for credits. As consequence, we suppose a unidirectional causality from total bank lending (LCR) to the monetary base (LH) and a unidirectional causality from total bank lending (LCR) to the M_3 money supply (LM_3) (Moore, 1989). The use of the monetary aggregate M_3 rather than M_2 is due to the fact that the Tunisian monetary authorities have been moving the monetary target from M_2 to M_3 since 2000.[4]

The structuralist hypothesis is considered as a combination of some ideas belonging to two approaches: the monetarist and the accommodationist views. The orthodox monetarist part of the structuralist model entails a causality running from the base (LH) and the M_3 money multiplier (Lk_3) to bank lending (LCR). The accommodationist part implies causality from bank lending (LCR) to monetary base (LH).

The relationships between these variables may be accounted for, in the structuralist view, by the fact that monetary authorities maintain some control over the reserves of the banking institutions (Palley (1996b, 1998)). Moreover, the structuralists emphasize the liability management practices as a mean to overcome the lack of reserves which constitutes a significant source for loan demand accommodation.

The liquidity preference approach supposes an endogenous money supply hypothesis as suggested by the accommodationist view where the bidirectional causality runs from the bank loans to the money supply. The independence hypothesis of money demand from the loan's

Table 1
The Empirical Hypotheses on Endogenous Money Supply

Accommodationist view (Moore, 1989)	*Structuralist view (Palley, 1996, 1998; Pollin, 1991)*	*Liquidity preference view (Howells& Hussein, 1998)*
$LCR \Rightarrow LH$ $LCR \Rightarrow LM_3$	$LCR \Leftrightarrow LH$ $LCR \Leftrightarrow Lk_3$	$LCR \Leftrightarrow LM_3$

Notes: Definition of variables: LCR=log-level of total bank credit; LH=log-level of monetary base; LM_3=log-level of the M_3 money supply; Lk_3 log-level of the M_3 money multiplier; '$\Rightarrow$' denotes unidirectional causality from left to right, '$\Leftrightarrow$' denotes bidirectional causality.

demand implies that the supply of deposits created by the net bank lending is not necessarily held by new owners of deposits. The amount of money held by these new deposit owners results from their preferences for liquidity. As a consequence, the capacity of credits to create deposits is found constrained by the money demand, and in this case the causality direction runs from the large money supply (LM_3) to the credit (LCR).

2. The Empirical Studies

The manifest importance of the causality issue in the money endogeneity hypothesis has produced substantial empirical evidence since the seminal contributions of Moore (1988, 1989) and Palley (1994). The major empirical studies have focused more on the technical aspects in testing the causal direction between loans and deposits. Moreover, the recent papers have tried to look for eventual long run relationships between these variables (money and credits) with cointegration techniques and to test causality with error correction models (ECM) rather than classical and standard Granger tests. Nevertheless, theses studies are interested in the case of developed and middle-income countries and to my knowledge no studies has encompass the case of a developing economy. The following table summarizes these studies:

Table 2
A Synopsises of the Major Empirical Contributions on the Money Endogeneity Hypothesis

Authors	*Period*	*Causality tests*	*Sample*
Pollin (1991)	1953-1988	Granger Causality	EU
Palley (1994)	1973- 1990	Granger Causality	EU
Howells (1998)	1957- 1992	Error Correction Model	G7
Shanmugam et al. (2003)	1985-2000	Cointegration and Granger Causality	Malaysia
Vera (2001)	1987-1998	Granger Causality	Spain
Nell (2001)	1966-1997	Error Correction Model	South Africa

IV. ECONOMETRIC METHODOLOGY

The objective of this section is to test the endogeneity of the money supply in Tunisia using time series techniques, cointegration and error correction representation. More specifically, we will achieve causality tests for the supply money status in this country. In fact, if we have two variables x_{1t} and x_{2t}, we test Granger causality between these variables by specifying, according theoretical foundations presented below, a bivariate vector autoregression (VAR) as follows:

$$\begin{cases} x_{1t} = \mu_1 + \pi_{11}(L)x_{1t-1} + \pi_{12}(L)x_{2t-1} + \varepsilon_{1t} & (1) \\ x_{2t} = \mu_2 + \pi_{21}(L)x_{1t-1} + \pi_{22}(L)x_{2t-1} + \varepsilon_{2t} & (2) \end{cases}$$

μ_1 and μ_2 are constant drifts and $\pi ij(L)$ are polynomials of order k-1 in the lag operator L. In equations (1) and (2), x_{1t} Granger causes x_{2t}, for example, if the polynomial $\pi_{12}(L)$ is not equal to zero. We can test this hypothesis by using standard methods (example F-test). Nevertheless, the estimation of the above system can not be achieved unless the variables are stationary (or $I(0)$ processes) since causality tests with integrated variables turn to be biased (Granger (1988)).

If the variables are non stationary (or $I(1)$ processes), there may be a long run relationship or a cointegration between the two variables which may lead toward a long run equilibrium state. When the variables are cointegrated, the model (composed of equations (1) and (2)) is rewritten in an equivalent error-correction model (ECM) as follows[5] :

$$\begin{cases} \Delta x_{1t} = \mu_1 + \gamma_{11}(L)\Delta x_{1t-1} + \gamma_{12}(L)\Delta x_{2t-1} + \alpha_1(\beta' X_{t-1}) + \varepsilon_{1t} & (3) \\ \Delta x_{2t} = \mu_2 + \gamma_{21}(L)\Delta x_{1t-1} + \gamma_{22}(L)\Delta x_{2t-1} + \alpha_1(\beta' X_{t-1}) + \varepsilon_{2t} & (4) \end{cases}$$

$\beta' X_{t-1}$ represents a linear combination of x_{1t} and x_{2t}, which are the residuals from the cointegrating vector. The latter system can be rewritten in another compact from in the following equation:

$$DX_t = \mu + \Gamma(L)\,\Delta X_{t-1} + \Pi X_{t-1} + \varepsilon_t \qquad (5)$$

Δ is the first difference operator of the variable, X_t is the vector of the considered variables $(x_{1t}, x_{2t})'$, μ is a vector of constant drifts $(\mu_1, \mu_2)'$, $\Gamma(L) = \{\gamma_{ij}\}$, $\Pi = \alpha\beta'$ with $\alpha = (\alpha_1, \alpha_2)$ and $\beta = (\beta_1, \beta_2)$ and $_t$ is the vector of random variables $\varepsilon_t = (\varepsilon_{1t}, \varepsilon_{2t})'$.

We have to recall that the representation of equation (5) is only relevant in the case of integrated (non stationary). If it is not the case, there is no possibility of cointegration and the relationship between the variables is reduced to the short run. In this case, the Granger causality tests are achieved using first differenced variables in the VAR with no error correction term.

If however, the variables are $I(1)$ processes but cointegrated the attention must be focused on $\Pi = \alpha\beta'$ representing the long run parameter matrix. In this context, when we have one cointegrating vector (the rank of Π is equal to 1, $r = 1$), β are the parameters in the cointegrating vector and α are the adjustment coefficients measuring the strength of the cointegrating relationship in the error correction model (ECM). In this case we have two sources of causation of x_{2t}, by x_{1t}: either through the lagged dynamic terms Δx_{1t} if $\gamma_{21}(L) \neq 0$, or through the lagged cointegrating vector $\beta' X_{t-1}$, if $\alpha \neq 0$.

Indeed, the ECM describes the adjustment of the system in each period towards the long run equilibrium state. In fact, starting from a cointegration state, when we have, in the short run, deviations from the long run equilibrium, we will have (due to the feed back of deviations) changes in the dependant variables in order to converge their movements towards the long run equilibrium state. The coefficients of the error correction terms, α_1 and α_2 represent the proportion by which the imbalance in the dependant variable is adjusted in each short-term period.

The Johanson procedure for testing cointegration focuses, therefore, on the rank of the matrix Π, which determines the number of cointegrating vectors. In a bivariate VAR framework, the number of cointegrating vectors is *one* and the null hypothesis is that there is no cointegrating vector and the alternative one is that we have only one cointegrating vector. To determine the rank of the matrix Π, Johanson and Juselius (1990) developed two likelihood ratio tests. The first one is the Maximum Eigenvalue (ME) test and is given by $J_{ME} = -T\,ln\,(1 - \lambda_r)$, where T is the number of observations and λ_r is the maximal eigenvalue. The aim of this test is to see whether the $rank\,(\Pi) = r-1$ (H_0 hypotheses) against the alternative hypotheses H_a $(r-1)$. The second test is the Likelihood Ratio (LR) test and is based on the trace of the stochastic matrix and given by $J_r = -T\,\Sigma\,ln\,(1-\lambda_i)$ The tests in the current work are carried out using the Likelihood Ratio (LR).

1. Data

We use monthly data spanning from 1991(1) to 2002(12) corresponding the post liberalization period. In fact, although the financial reform has started in 1987, the real implementation of monetary regulation by the public authorities corresponds to the beginning of the nineties. Moreover, the choice of this period avoids, as much as possible, the deep changes that have affected the structure of the banking and financial system since 1987.

The data related to the different aggregates are extracted from the [2]Statistiques Financières[2] of the Banque Centrale de Tunisie (the Central Bank of Tunisia). The money supply is measured by the aggregate M3[6], while the credit variable is approximated by to the total loans granted by the deposit banks to the rest of the economy over their ordinary resources. The monetary base (*H*) corresponds to the currency and reserves held by commercial banks. Finally, the money multiplier (k_3) concerns the aggregate M3. All the variables are transformed into their natural logarithms so that LM_3, LCR, LH, and Lk_3[7].

For all these variables in level the Dickey Fuller tests show that the null hypothesis of unit root can not be rejected at the 5% level of risk. This result indicates that all the variables are nonstationary at levels and stationary in first differences.

V. EMPIRICAL RESULTS

1. Cointegration Tests

Since the announced variables are integrated of order one (I(1)), it is possible now to carry out the cointegration tests between the variables. These tests are achieved using the Johansen procedure which is sensitive to the number of lags[8] used in the VAR model. The optimal number of lags is determined in this paper according to Akaike and Schwarz criteria. Table (3) displays cointegration tests according to the Johanson's maximum likelihood systems procedure.

From the first regression between LM_3 and LCR in Table (1), the trace test shows that it is possible to reject the null hypothesis where there is no cointegration relationship ($r = 0$) at the 5% level of risk. This outcome means that it is not possible to reject the hypothesis assuming that there exists at most a cointegration vector ($r \leq 1$) at the same level of risk. This result is also corroborated by the maximum Eigenvalue value test[9], which tests the null hypothesis that the matrix Π has a rank equal to *r*, against the alternative hypothesis that the rank of Π is equal to $r + 1$.

Table 3
Johansen's Cointegration Tests

Variables	*Trace*	*Statistic*	*Max. Eigenvalue*	*Statistic*
	H_0: r=0	H_1: r ≤ 1	H_0: r = 0	H_1: r ≤ 1
1.3 LM_3, LCR	16.57*	2.75	13.87*	2.74
2.3 LH, LCR	18.76*	0.32	18.44*	0.32
3.3 LH, LM_3	22.06*	2.39	19.67*	2.39
4.3 Lk_3, LCR	16.60*	0.19	16.41*	0.19

*and ** mean statistical significance at the 5%, 1% levels, respectively.

This result shows therefore the existence of a unique cointegration vector indicating a long run relationship between money supply and bank loans. This outcome means that we have a co-evolution between money supply and bank lending which gives in the long run a cointegrating vector or a long run equilibrium state. The short run dynamics of the variables are seen as fluctuations around this long run equilibrium.

The remaining regressions in Table (3) show also the same empirical evidence at a 95% confidence level as in regression (1.3) i.e. a stable long run relationship between the monetary base (LH) and bank credits (LCR), the monetary base (LH) and money supply (LM_3) and the money multiplier (Lk_3) and bank loans (LCR). The presence of cointegration between these variables implies at least one causal direction between the variables of the VAR Granger (1988).

2. Error Correction Estimates

The Error Correction Model (ECM) indicates the degree of adjustment of the system toward the long run equilibrium state. The magnitudes of the coefficients of α vectors (i.e. α_1 and α_2) indicate the speed of adjustment to this long run equilibrium. For example, in the first regression of table (3), the effect of the error correction term (βX_{t-1}) on money supply (LM_3) depends on the signs of the adjustment coefficient α_1 and on the sign of βX_{t-1}.

Table (4) reports the ECM estimates where all terms are stationary. From the first VAR estimation (1.4) which constitutes the core of endogeneity thesis, the results show that the first adjustment coefficient (α_1) is negative (–0.075) and significant at a 5% level of risk while the second (α_2) is not. The estimated coefficient β is also negative and significant and is obtained through the normalization of the cointegrated vectors. According to this coefficient a 1% increase in bank loans (LCR) leads to 1.117% rise in money supply. In this case, the causality is running from the bank loans to the money supply. These results mean that there is a long run relationship between the money supply and bank loans. With the error correction mechanism, the adjustment to lagged deviations from the equilibrium relationship occurs through changes in the money supply only. These results reflect more a change towards the indirect instruments of monetary policy since we have a unidirectional causality from credits to the money supply. In the second VAR equation (1.4), the money variation is not found to exert any effect on bank loans variation in the short run since the coefficient α is not significant even at the 10% level.

The second and third set of regressions in Table (4) show that monetary base (LH) is cointegrated with money supply (LM_3) and with bank lending (LCR) at a 5% level of risk. In both cases, adjustment occurs through changes in monetary base only. All significant loading coefficients have the correct negative sign. The estimated coefficients β show that a 1% increase in bank lending leads to a 0.86 % rise in monetary base and that a 1% increase in supply leads to a 0.73% rise in monetary base.

The fourth set of regressions in Table 4 shows that money multiplier (Lk_3) is cointegrated with bank lending (LCR) at a 5% level of risk .In this case, adjustment occurs through changes in the money multiplier. The estimated coefficient β shows that a 1% increase in bank lending leads to a 0.17% rise in the money multiplier.

Table 4
Vector Error-Correction Model Estimates

	VAR	Regressions	Error term α	Long-run elasticities β	Order of lags
1.4	(LM_3, LCR)	$\Delta LM_3, \Delta LCR$	-0.075 (-2.10)*	1.117 (-16.87)**	1
		$\Delta LCR, \Delta LM3$	-0.03 (-1.6)	-0.89 (-17.8)	1
2.4	(LH, LCR)	$\Delta LH, \Delta LCR$	-0.22 (-4.29)**	0.86 (-17.02)**	2
		$\Delta LCR, \Delta LH$	0.0016 (0.12)	1.15 (-16.87)	2
3.4	(LH, LM_3)	$\Delta LH, \Delta LM3$	-0.16 (-3.17)**	0.73 (-13.77)**	1
		$\Delta LM3, \Delta LH$	-0.026 (-1.65)	1.36 (-16.40)	1
4.4	(Lk_3, LCR)	$\Delta LK3, \Delta LCR$	-0.18 (-3.26)**	0.17 (-3.22)**	1
		$\Delta LCR, \Delta LK3$	-0.004 (-1.49)	1.75 (-4.86)**	1

t statistics between parenthesis.
*and ** mean statistical significance at the 5%, 1% levels, respectively.

3. Granger-Causality Tests

The short-term dynamics of the system is analyzed in bivariate Granger-causality tests between the following pairs of variables: (LCR, LM_3), (LH, LCR), (LH, LM_3) and (LCR, Lk_3). Each test is based on the estimation of an equation that includes 11 lagged differences of one variable, one lagged difference of the other variable and the long-run relationship assessed by the cointegration analysis.

For instance, the Granger- causality test from ΔLM_3 to ΔLCR nests the joint significance of eleven lagged difference of LCR in the following equation.

$$\Delta LM_{3,t} = c + \hat{\alpha}(LM_{3,t-1} + 0.784 - 1.117LCR_{t-1}) + \delta\Delta LM_{3,t-1} + \sum_{j=1}^{11} \hat{\theta}_j \Delta LCR_{t-11} + \varepsilon_t \quad (6)$$

The test consists in carrying out a restriction test on the coefficients θ_j of the loan bank variable (in logarithm) of the VAR representation. In this case the hypotheses are specified as follows:

$H_0: \theta_1 = \theta_2 = \ldots = \theta_{11} = 0$: LCR does not Granger-cause LM_3

And we write $\Delta LCR \Rightarrow \Delta lM_3$.

$H_1: \theta_j \neq 0$ (at least for one j) : LCR Granger- causes LM_3

And we write $\Delta LCR \Rightarrow \Delta lM_3$.

The tests are therefore classical Fisher tests carried out in comparison between a VAR model and a non constrained one. The results of such tests are reported on Table (5):

Table 5
Granger-causality tests based on ECM with Johansen Cointegrating Vectors

Null hypothesis H_0:			*Test statistic*	K_1	K_2
ΔLCR	⇒	ΔLM_3	2.22*	11	117
ΔLM_3	⇒	ΔLCR	1.68	11	117
ΔLCR	⇒	ΔLH	3.66*	11	117
ΔLH	⇒	ΔLCR	1.59	11	117
ΔLM_3	⇒	ΔLH	2.49	11	117
ΔLH	⇒	ΔLM_3	1.18	11	117
ΔLCR	⇒	ΔLk_3	3.13**	11	117
ΔLk_3	⇒	ΔLCR	1.66	11	117

The recorded statistic is the statistic of F. k_1 is the number of restrictions under the null hypothesis, i.e. the degree of freedom of the test. K_2 is the number of observations minus the number of parameters to be estimated in Equation (6), i.e. the degree of freedom of the statistical test at the denominator.*and ** mean statistical significance at the 5%, 1% levels, respectively.

The results of the tests are similar to the previous ones and show clearly that causality is running from bank loans towards money supply which corroborates the endogenous nature of money supply. Indeed, as shown in (Table 5), Granger-causality goes from bank lending to both the monetary base and the money multiplier. This outcome is compatible with both the accommodationist and the structuralist approaches. In this context, since Granger-causality run from bank lending to money multiplier, we cannot reject the hypothesis that liability management practices were a significant device for accommodation of loan demand in Tunisia over the considered period. Moreover, these findings are consistent with those of Moore (1989) and Palley (1994) who investigated the issue for the USA, Vera (2000) for the spainish economy and Shanmugam, Nair and Li (2003) in Malaysia .

VI. CONCLUSION POLICY IMPLICATIONS

In this paper we tested the post-keynesian approach regarding the endogeneity of the money supply. The growth of money supply is determined by factors linked to credit availability and therefore to financial markets functioning. The tests were carried out for Tunisia, with monthly data, for the period 1991-2002 using time series techniques in a bivariate VAR structure.

The Johanson cointegration analysis and the Granger causality tests provide a significant support to the hypothesis that the causality is running from bank loans to money supply. In fact, the significance of the adjustment coefficient in the money supply equation and its insignificance in the bank loans' equation show that adjustment towards equilibrium is mainly derived from the money supply variable. This gives evidence that it is the money supply which is determined by the loans. The money stock movements depend, therefore, on demand factors, especially bank loans availability.

The smallness of this coefficient for Tunisia may be explained by different factors such as the absence of a monthly adjustment tradition. Indeed, while the objectives of the monetary policy in Tunisia are determined on a yearly base, the monetary authorities' concern remains the achievement of the announced goals. Moreover, the markets remain insufficiently developed and the reactions of the different agents are far from being instantaneous.

Moreover, the empirical results may be considered as consistent with the institutional considerations of the monetary policy in Tunisia which highlight some aspects of the endogenous nature of the main component of money supply, namely the monetary base. This form of endogeneity may be explained by the Central Bank's action on the central money supply whenever some variations of the interest rates are considered. This leads to the conclusion that the monetary regulation should take into account the behavioural dynamics of banks and thereby the endogenous nature of money supply.

Notes

1. This group of researchers encompasses among others Moore, Kaldor and Goodhart.
2. The most representative of whom are: Palley, Davidson , Pollin, and Dow.
3. See Hendry *et al.* (1984), Engle and Granger (1987) and Johansen (1988) for more details.
4. M3 = M2 + housing savings + projected savings- investment + Securities. Where M2 = M1 + Quasi-money, where M1 = Fiduciary money + Credit balance of checking accounts + Current accounts opened with the CCP and with registered intermediaries and Quasi-money = Forward deposits + Certificates of deposits + Foreign accounts in foreign currencies opened by residents and non-residents + Sight investments which could not be used directly as a settlement.
5. All the variables are available from author upon request.
6. Boswijk and Franses (1992) have studied the impact of the dynamic specification on the size and power of the different cointegration tests. They have concluded that an insufficient number of lags can lead to an over-rejection of the null hypothesis
7. $\lambda_{max}(r, r+1) = -T \log(1-\lambda_{r+1})$

References

Arestis, P. and Howells, P. (1996), "Theoretical Reflections on Endogenous Money: The Problem with Convenience Lending", *Cambridge Journal of Economics*, 20 (5), 539-51.

Blinder A. S. (1995), "*Central Banking in Theory and Practice*", IMT Press.

Boumedienne, J. and Siala, F. (1997), "Evolution du système monétaire et financier tunisien : vers une nouvelle régulation", *Revue de l'Association des Economistes Tunisiens*, (8), C P U.

Boswijk, P. & Franses, P.H. (1992), "Dynamic Specification and Cointegration", *Oxford Bulletin of Economics and statistics*, 54, (3), 369-81.

Chick, V. (1973), "*The Theory of Monetary Policy*", Oxford: Basil Blackwell.

Cottrell, A. (1994), "Post Keynesian Monetary Economics: A Critical Survey" *The Cambridge Journal of Economics,* 18, 587-605.

Davidson, P. (1989), "On the Endogeneity of money once more", *Journal of Post Keynesian Economics,* XI, 488-490.

Dow, S C. (1988), "Money Supply Endogeneity", *Economie Appliquée,* XLI(1).

Enders W. (1995), "*Applied Econometric Time Series*", John Wiley and Sons.

Engels R. F. & Granger C. W. J., (1987), "Co integration and Error Correction: Representation, Estimation and Testing", *Econometrica*, 55, 251-276.

Fontana, G. (2003), "Post Keynesian Approaches to Endogenous Money: A Time Framework Explanation", *Review of Political Economy*, 15(3), 291-314.

Goodhart, CAE. (1993), "La politique monétaire dans les années quatre-vingt-dix objectifs et moyens d'action ", *Cahiers économiques et monétaires*, 41.

Goodhart, CAE. (1984), "*Monetary Policy in Theory and Practice*". Mc Millan, Londres.

Goodhart, CAE (1999), "The Conduct of Monetary Policy", *The Economic Journal*, 293-346.

Goodhart, CAE. (1991), "Has Moore Become too Horizontal?" *Journal of Post Keynesian Economics*, 12(1), 29-34.

Goodhart, CAE. (2000), "The Organisational Structure of Banking Supervision", *Working Papers*, BIS.

Granger, CWJ. (1988), "Some Recent Developments in a Concept of Causality", *Journal of Econometrics*, 39.

Hergli. M & Mokaddem, M. (1994), "*Monnaie et Mecanismes Monetaires*" ENA, Tunis.

Howells, P. and Hussein, K.A. (1998), "The Endogenous of Money: Evidence From The G7", *Scottish Journal of Political Economy*, Vol. 45(3).

Howells, P. (2005), "The Endogeneity of Money: Empirical Evidence" *Working Paper*, University of the West of England.

Johansen, S. & Julius, K. (1990), "Maximum Likelihood Estimation and Inference on Cointegration_ with Applications to the Demand for Money", *Oxford Bulletin of Economics & Statistics*, 52, 169-210.

Kaldor, N. (1982), *The scourage of Monetarism*, Oxford University Press.

King, M. (1994), "The Transmission Mechanism of Monetary Policy" *Bank of England Quarterly Bulletin*, August.

Moore B. (1988), "Horizontalists and Verticalists. The Macroeconomics of Credit Money, Cambridge University Press, Cambridge.

Moore, B. (1988), "The Endogenous Money Supply" *Journal of Post Keynesian Economics*, spring, 10(3), 372-385.

Moore, B. (1989), "The Endogeneity of Credit Money", *Review of Political Economy*, 1(1), 64- 93.

Moore, B. (1998), "Accommodation to Accommodationism; A note." *Journal of Post Keynesian Economics*, Fall 21 (1), 175-178.

Nell, K. S. "The Endogenous/Exogenous Nature of South Africa's Money Supply Under Direct and Indirect Monetary Control Measures" *Journal of Post Keynesian Economics*, Winter 2000-2001, 23 (2), 313-329.

Niggle, W.C. (1991), "The Endogenous Money Supply Theory: An Institutionalist Appraisal", *Journal of Economic Issues*, XXV(1).

Palley, TI. « The endogenous money supply: consensus and disagreement » *Journal of Post Keynesian Economics*, 1991, Vol. 13, p. 397-403.

—— (1994), "Competing Views of the Money Supply", *Metroeconomica*, 45(1), 68-88.

—— (1996), "Accommodationism Versus Structuralism: Time for an Accommodation" *Journal of Post Keynesian Economics*, 18(4), 585-594.

—— (1998), "Acommodationism, Structuralism, and Superstructuralism", *Journal of Post Keynesian Economics*, Fall 21 (1), 171-173.

Piegay, P. (2000), "The New and Post Keynesian Analyses of Bank Behaviour: Consensus and Disagreement" *Journal of Post Keynesian Economics*, winter, Vol. 22, n°. 2.

Pollin, R. (1991), "Two Theories of Money Supply Endogeneity: Some Empirical Evidence", *Journal of Post-Keynesian Economics*, 13(3), 366-396.

Rochon, L.P. (2001), "Cambridge's Contribution to Endogenous Money: Robinson and Kahn on Credit and money", *Review of Political Economy*, 13. 3, p. 287-306.

Shanmugam, B., Mahendhiran, N. and Ong, W. (2003), "The Endogenous Money Hypothesis: Empirical Evidence from Malaysia 1985-2000", *Journal of Post Keynesian Economics*, summer 25(4).

Siala, F. (1996), "Vers une Régulation Monétaire par les Taux en Tunisie : portée et limites », *Annales d'Economie et de Gestion*, Vol. 3, No. 6.

Vera, A. P. (2001), "The Endogenous Money Hypothesis: Some Evidence From Spain (1987-1998), *Journal of Post Keynesian Economics*, Sping, 23 (3), 509-526.

THE DEMAND FOR MONEY IN GREECE IN THE PERIOD 1858-1938

Erotokritos Varelas[*]

Abstract

The study and the estimation of demand for money have gained popularity in the econometric and economic literature. In the specific case of Greece, numerous articles investigated money, income and the opportunity cost of holding money using quarterly data, mainly of the period after 1960. The objective of the present article is to investigate the long run relationship using annual data and covering the historical period between 1838 and 1938. The results of the used cointegration analysis are presented.

JEL Classification: *C13,C32.*

I. INTRODUCTION

The study and the estimation of demand for money have gained popularity in the econometric and economic literature. In the back drop of structural adjustments entailing financial deregulations and innovations in many countries it seems imperative to establish whether the underlying assumptions and the properties of the money demand function still hold (Mel nick, 1995). One of the important issues confronting the monetary policy is to discover a steady money demand function (Friedman, 1959; Friedman and Schwartz, 1982; Laidler, 1977; Laidler. 1982). Thus,a secure money demand function is a necessary pre-requisite in establishing a one to one relationship between the appropriate monetary aggregates and nominal income.

Laidler (1982) opined that the demand for money holdings is stable when money holdings can be explained by functional relationships which have statistical significance, and that the same equation can be applied to different countries using different data, without it being necessary to change arguments of the relations to achieve satisfactory results. Nevertheless, the empirical evidence for a stable money demand is necessary but not a sufficient condition to uphold the monetarist argument that the money supply is causal in the process of inflation (Kaldor, 1982).

The question for stable and predictable demand function stems from results that traditional models for demand for money function in many industrialized countries showed instability over time in the 1970s. The empirical findings in developing countries faced similar problems in the traditional specification. The problems include but not limited to serial correlation, over prediction or missing money syndromes, misspecification, wrong signs and insignificant

* University of Macedonia, Department of Economics, Egnatia str. 156, 54006 Thessaloniki, Greece. *E-mail: varelas@uom.gr*

coefficients of the important parameters. Friedman (1956) revealed that money demand function assumes that there are a stationary long-run equilibrium relationship between real money balances, real income, and the opportunity cost of holding real balances.

Dickey (*et al.* 1991) opined that time series variables are not stationary individually; one or more linear combinations of the variables are stationary even though individually they are not. Therefore, an econometric model should carry out the property of stationarity on target variables. Unit root test should be performed on univariate time series in order to test order of integration and if individual time series are found to be integrated of the same order after the unit root tests, then these variables may be cointegrated. Cointegration deals with the relationships among a group of variables, where unconditionally each has a unit root. "When this occurs, the time paths of the individual variables are ultimately converged to an equilibrium relationship and are said to be cointegrated. While deviations from equilibrium are possible, they are eventually self revising" (McNown, Wallace 1992).Application of Cointegration test in the estimation of the money demand function are analyzed by Johansen and Juselius (1990), Dickey, Jansen and Thornton (1991), Mehra (1992).

In the case of Greece the determination of a money demand function in a either cointegration or an error correction framework, was the core issue of the empirical work of Arestis (1988), Karfakis (1991), Psaradakis (1993), Papadopoulos & Zis (1997), Ericson & Sharma (1996), Apergis (1999), Apergis *et al.* (1999), Karfakis and Sidiropulos (2000), Brissimis *et al.* (2003), Economidou & Oskooee (2005) and finally Karpetis (forthcoming 2007). These articles used mainly quarterly data covering a period of the Greek economy that extended after the end of the troublesome decade of 1940's. Excemption was the forthcoming paper of Karpetis (2007). In this specific period of time the national economy developed in the absence of major war or historical events, which could greatly affect the evolution of important macroeconomic magnitudes.

The aim of the analysis that is presented in this article is the determination of the long-run relationship among real money (M_1), (M_2), (M_3), real Gross Domestic Product (GDP) and the opportunity cost of holding money using annual data and covering the period between 1858 and 1938. This period of time covers a great part of modern Greek history that is characterized by significant historical and economic evens (see appendix, table 8). The first variable (M_1), is what is usually referred to as money supply in the narrow sense. It consists of the sum of currency circulation and demand (sight) deposits. The second measure of money supply is M_2. This is known as money supply in the broad sense. It consists of M_1 plus time deposits. Finally, the very broad measure of money supply is M_3. Its consists of M_2 plus saving deposits. Given the absence of data concerning the nominal interest rates, we used a proxy named financial innovation as opportunity cost of holding money. It consists of m_2/m_1. We have to note, that inflation is not considered in this period as an alternative cost variable. Examining the plot of the inflation data we note a flat curve. All variables are measured in real values (GDP deflator: 1914 = 100).

The methodology and the data provided by Kostelenos (1995) are used in the second section, in the context of which a cointegration analysis is performed. The results of this analysis are exhibited in this section and the findings concerning the magnitude of the cointegrating coefficients are compared with the empirical findings of the other authors. The conclusions of the realized analysis are presented in the third and final section.

II. INVESTIGATING THE LONG RUN RELATIONSHIP BETWEEN MONEY, INCOME & FINANCIAL INNOVATIONS AS PROXY FOR OPPORTUNITY COST

As it is already mentioned we will investigate in our analysis the relationship between real money demand, real GDP and changes in financial innovations, using annual data and covering a period of the Greek economy raging from 1858 to 1938. The methodology used is the one proposed by Johansen [1988] in the context of which we realize the following four steps.

Step 1: We investigate the stationarity of the following processes

$$\text{(i)}\left\{rm1\right\}_{t=1}^{81},\left\{rm2\right\}_{t=1}^{81},\left\{rm3\right\}_{t=1}^{81}\ \text{(ii)}\left\{ry\right\}_{t=1}^{81}\ \text{and (iii)}\left\{fi\right\}_{t=1}^{81}$$

where:

rm_1: real money supply (*M1*)

rm_2 = real money supply (M2)

rm_3 = real money supply (M3)

ry: Real Gross Domestic Product

fi: Financial Innovations

t = 1 (1858), …. , 81 (1938)

In order to determine their order of integration, we perform an augmented Dickey – Fuller (ADF) test on the level and the first difference of the series. More specifically we estimate using OLS the following, general, equation:

$$\Delta Y_t = a_0 + a_1 t + a_2 Y_{t-1} + \sum_{i=1}^{k} \Delta Y_{t-i} + u_t \qquad (1)$$

where *Y*: the examined time series.

Parameter *k* takes integer values within the interval [0,7] and its value is determined using the sequential method proposed by Perron [1989]. If for the selected value of parameter *k* the residuals are autocorrelated, we increase the value of *k* by one until the problem of autocorrelation is solved. The significance of the unit root null is tested comparing the t – statistic of a_2 coefficient for testing $a_2 = 0$ with the appropriate critical values provided by Fuller [1976].

The results of the unit root tests are presented in the context of table 1. As we see, all three time series are proved to be integrated processes of order 1 [I(1)]. On the basis of this conclusion we proceed to the second step.

Table 1
Unit Root Investigation of Real Money Supply, Real GDP and Financial Innovations

	Variable	*ADF*	*MacKinnon Critical Values*
Levels intercept	rm_t	-1.423	-2.8981
	ry_t	-1.1724	
	fi	-2.4166	
	rm_{2t}	-0.6055	
	rm_{3t}	-0.2524	
LevelTrend and Intercept	rm_t	-2.0258	
	ry_t	-1.0941	
	fi_t	-2.3540	
	rm_{2t}	-2.7945	-3.4669
	rm_{3t}	-1.9884	

Notes: *acceptance of the unit root null at 5% significance level.)

Step 2: We determine the lag length parameter p of the following VAR system

$$\boldsymbol{x_t} = \boldsymbol{A_0} + \sum_{i=1}^{p} \boldsymbol{A_i x_{t-i}} + \boldsymbol{\Psi D_t} + \boldsymbol{e_t} \qquad (2)$$

where $\boldsymbol{A_0}$: $(n \times 1)$ vector of intercept terms, $\boldsymbol{A_i}$: $(n \times n)$ matrices of coefficients, $\boldsymbol{x_t}$ = $= \left(rm_t \quad ry_t \quad dfi_t\right)'$, $\boldsymbol{D_t} = \left(DU_t^{55} \quad DT_t^{55} \quad DU_t^{63} \quad DT_t^{63}\right)'$, $DU_t^j = 0\,(1)$ if $t \leq j$ $(t > j)$, $DT_t^j = 0\,(t - j)$ if $t \leq j\ (t > j)$, with j = 55, 63, and t = 1, 2, …. , 81 , Ψ : $(n \times 4)$ matrix of coefficients, $\boldsymbol{e_t}$: $(1 \times n)$ vector of error terms, $p = 7$ and $n = 3$.

The vector of dummies D_t is included in the right hand side of (4) in order to capture the effects of two major historical events that affected the Greek economy as a whole. The first is associated with the outbreak of the first and second Balkan war in 1912 (observation 55) and 1913 (observation 56), that almost doubled the lands under Greek control. The second event is associated with the outbreak of the Asia Minor campaign in 1920 (observation 63). The defeat of Greece in this campaign against Turkey resulted in the entrance of approximately 1.5 million Greek refuges in Greece, increasing this way country's total population by 26%. The dummies DU_t^j and DT_t^j suggest a change in time series level and trend at $t = j$, as a result of the earlier stated events. At this point it has to be stated that the visual examination of the line plot of the time series indicates the presence of multiple breaks that do not coincide in time Karpetis et. al (2006).

Using the OLS method we estimated (2) as an unrestricted VAR for i = 1 , …. , 7 and determined the values of three information criteria, namely Akaike information criterion (AIC), Schwarz information criterion (SC) and Hannan–Quinn information criterion (HQ). More over we calculated the value of the sequential modified likelihood ratio (LR) statistic proposed by Sims (1980).

The values of the above mentioned information criteria along with the value of LR statistic are presented in table 2. As we see, p = 1 is the lag order selected by all three information criteria and p = 6 is the lag order selected by LR statistic. Although for p = 6 residuals of (4), i.e. the three error terms in e_t, have better properties[1] than for p = 1, we choose p = 1 as the lag order of (4), following Johansen's suggestion (1995) to avoid to many lags and given the relatively small sample used in our analy-sis.

Table 2
VAR Lag Order Selection Criteria for rm_1

Lag	*LR*	*AIC*	*SC*	*HQ*
$0^{a,b}$	NA	47.604	47.974	47.698
$1^{b,c}$	59.442	46.836	47.589*	47.136*
$2^{b,c}$	12.478	46.881	47.917	47.294
$3^{b,c}$	14.406	46.884	48.201	47.409
$4^{b,c}$	8.782	46.973	48.574	47.611
5^{b}	16.470	46.909	48.792	47.659
6^{b}	30.384*	46.548	48.7135	47.411
7^{b}	12.693	46.525	48.972	47.500

Notes: * indicates lag order selected by the criterion (each test at 5% level)

Table 3
VAR Lag Order Selection Criteria for rm_2

Lag	*LR*	*AIC*	*SC*	*HQ*
$0^{a,b}$	NA	52.528	52.808	52.640
$1^{b,c}$	25.0711	49.006	49.566*	49.229*
$2^{b,c}$	11.113	49.078	49.919	49.413
$3^{b,c}$	9.0187	49.176	50.297	49.623
$4^{b,c}$	22.915	49.031	50.432	49.590
5^{b}	3.4414	49.212	50.894	49.883
6^{b}	40.518*	48.691	50.653	49.474
7^{b}	14.428	48.646*	50.888	49540

Notes: * indicates lag order selected by the criterion (each test at 5% level).

Table 4
VAR Lag Order Selection Criteria for rm_3

Lag	*LR*	*AIC*	*SC*	*HQ*
$0^{a,b}$	NA	51.486	51.953	51.672
$1^{b,c}$	18.727	48.961	49.708*	49.259*
$2^{b,c}$	6.8012	49.096	50.124	49.506
$3^{b,c}$	10.445	49.165	50.473	49.687
$4^{b,c}$	20.076	49.056	50.644	49.690
5^{b}	7.0086	49.170	51.038	49.915
6^{b}	49.956*	48.433*	50.582	49.290
7^{b}	11.413	48.439	50.868	49.408

Notes: * indicates lag order selected by the criterion (each test at 5% level).

Step 3: In third step we determine the number of cointegrating vectors (r). In the context of Johansen procedure, the number of cointegrating vectors, if any, is deter-mined with the help of either trace or max–eigenvalue test statistics. The values of these statistics are compared with the appropriate critical values provided by Johansen and Juselius (1990). Given that these critical values assume no exogenous variables in the error correction model (ECM), they can not be used in the context of our analysis in order to determine the number of cointegrating vectors. In this case Juselius (1995) suggests looking at the dynamics of the estimated unrestricted VAR model (2) and in particular whether it converges in the long – run. The magnitudes of the characteristic roots are given in table 5.

Table 5

Roots of Characteristic Polynomial for rm_1		*Roots of Characteristic Polynomial for rm_2*		*Roots of Characteristic Polynomial for rm_3*	
Root	Modulus	Root	Modulus	Root	Modulus
0.9697	0.9697	0.97761	0.97761	0.97406	0.97406
0.7303	0.7303	0.75723	0.75723	0.74677	0.74677
0.1323	0.1323	0.11101	0.11101	0.17582	0.17582

As we ascertain from the data presented in this table, all roots lie within the unit circle and two roots, are quite close to unity. In other words we have that $r = 3 - 2 = 1$, that is there are one cointegrating vector.

Step 4: Given that $r = 1$, we estimate the error correction model allowing for one cointegrating vector. The estimates of the error cointegrating vector are presented in the table below.

Table 6
Vector Error Correction Estimates for rm_1,rm_2 and rm_3

Cointegrating Equation.	*CointEq1*	*Cointegrating Equation.*	*CointEq2*	*Cointegrating Equation.*	*CointEq3*
rm1	1.0000	rm2	1.0000	rm3	1.0000
f1	-523554.5	f1	-.51781.64	f1	-3087293
	(-4.145)		(-2.2556)		(-6.3930)
ry	0.3889	ry	0.6826	ry	0.74711
	(11.139)		(11.598)		(5.3250)
c	78601.08	c	273230.7	c	284371.3
Adj.R-	0.1045		0.1073		0.1083
Akaike AIC	24.554		25.1812		25.4200
Schwarz SC	24.733		25.3611		25.6005
Determ. resid covariance	1.56E+17		2.99E+17		3.94E+17

Note: in ( ) t–statistics.

All cointegrating coefficients have the expected sign and they are statistically significant at 5% level. We have to explain historically the statistical significance of the variables and especially the variable named financial innovations. Starting from the brief (1830s-early 1840s) and rapid recovery from the losses of the War of Independence, a long period of slow growth followed immediately after in Greece, which ended in stagnation in the late 1880s.

During the first and more depressing years of the economic crisis, 1980, the Greek State was unable to contract more loans in order to continue servicing the public debt, while any reform of public finances was almost impossible because of the economic depression. After the crisis of 1893 (Bankruptcy of the Greek economy) forced the country to accept the establishment of a very constraining International Financial Control (Andreades 1939, ii: 453-532). The imposition of the International Financial Control coincided with a dramatic favorable change of the World economic conjuncture. The International Financial Control Committee (IFC) tried to assure, as expected, convenient yields for the bondholders. In order to succeed in its effort, the IFC Committee transformed the whole institutional framework of public finances, imposing a fiscal discipline and a very strict control of the banking system and especially of monetary circulation. The combined consequences of the favorable balance of payments and the fiscal and monetary discipline imposed by the IFC. resulted in the spectacular reevaluation of the drachma, which in very few years reached its gold parity The development of the Greek merchant steam fleet coincided with (and was partly feed of) the increase of transatlantic emigration. The remittances of emigrants and the income created by merchant marine activities soon became very important factors for the balance of payments. The magnitude and the importance of these two kinds of capital transfer were reflected in the accumulation of significant deposits in the Greek Banks. We have to note that migration, which had begun as an act of despair, soon proved to be a rational means for the rapid accumulation of funds many small-owner families needed to meet their small- or long-term obligations. Many (later) migrants did migrate out of choice rather than out of necessity and, in spite of the human cost and personal suffering, emigration coincided in Greece with a period of rapid economic growth, partly financed from the savings of migrant workers.

If we take bank deposits as an indicator of the saving propensity of the Greek Economy, we realize that the era which followed the period of the great depression, characterized by a rapid growth of the Bank deposits, is one of a growing possibility for the Banking system to enlarge its financing activities. It is important here to add that these savings were not created only domestically, but originated from the enterprising Greek Levantine Diaspora, from emigrants in the United States and from those employed in the merchant marine. It is not a coincidence that the Bank of Athens, which was created in the late 19th century, was the first deposit bank in the country and was extensively involved in the Levantine markets. Generally, the banking system gave the possibility through the creations of time deposits (until 1890 the banking system had only savings deposits) to the emigrants to hold money in this form.

The important efforts of modernization in the last quarter of the 19th century were closely linked to the new risks and opportunities the Greek State faced because of the mutations in the international environment. The successive Greek governments begun to exercise a comprehensive foreign policy, siding primarily with Great Britain, and tried to weight actively upon the diplomatic and military developments of the Eastern Question. As a consequence, efforts were made during these years towards the rationalization of civil administration and the formation of a real army organized to fight against other armies and not simply against bandits. Finally, the Greek state tried for the first time to build a communication and transports network: in this way the state expressed its will to penetrate into its territory and to control the populations in ways and by means very different to the previous ones. Although its success in achieving these targets is a matter of debate, we must stress the fact that the first efforts of a real institutional modernization observed during these years had far reaching consequences for the entire Greek economy. To conclude "modernization" of the Greek economy and society became a real issue only in the last quarter of the 19th century, when Greece was transformed both into an active member of the international state system and into a more integrated part of the World Economy.

The recovery of the economy after the imposition of the International Financial Control in combination with a more sound budgetary policy, offered the Greek state the chance to be well prepared for the coming Balkan wars and to profit from the heritage of the Ottoman Empire (Andreades 1939, ii: 533 sq.). Between 1910 and 1918, despite the chronic trade deficit, the balance of payments seems to have behaved rather smoothly, supported by invisible inflows, mainly from shipping and emigrants' remittances, and from income of capital invested abroad (Kostis 1984). The Balkan wars and the First World War yielded wealth, territories, confidence and high expectations. Deposits increased substantially (from internal and external sizes) and the Greek economy seemed invulnerable as the drachma remained solidly at par with the gold franc until 1919. As we have noted, the dramatic increases of the banks deposits is coming from emigrants and from those employed in the merchant marine. In this period the banking system increases the loans to the industrial sector. During the First World War the Greek industry had already profited by the artificial protection created by the disruption of international trade. The industrial units created in this occasion were oriented towards the domestic market (Charitakis 1927, 41 sq.). This multiplier effect-increases of deposits, increases of loans to industry, increases the income demanded- explains the income and the opportunity cost statistically variables in our analysis.

Table 7
Income Elasticities

Analysis	*Period Examined*	*Money Definition*	*Real GDP*
Varelas	1858 ~ 1938	M1	1.348
		M2	1.712
		M3	1.908
Karpetis (2006)	1858 ~ 1938	M1	1.515
Economidou & Oskooee (2005)	1975:1 ~ 2002:4	M1	0.750
		M2	1.450
Brissimis *et al.* (2003)	1975:1 ~ 2000:4	M3	1.674
Karfakis & Sidiropoulos (2000)	1986:1 ~ 1995:4	M1	2.190
Apergis (1999)	1975:1 ~ 1994:4	M1	0.856
Apergis *et al.* (1999)	1978:1 ~ 1995:4	M1	2.438
Papadopoulos & Zis (1997)		M1	1.490
		M2	2.040
Ericsson & Sharma (1996)	1975:1 ~ 1994:4	M3	1.220
Psaradakis (1993)	1961:3 ~ 1989:1	M1	1.451
Karfakis (1991)	1975:1 ~ 1988:3	M1	1.150

Table 7 gives the long-run income elasticities of money demand For real m_1 the long run elasticity is equal 1.348, for real m_2 is equal 1.712 and for real m_3 is 1.908 respectively. Comparing these results with the elasticities derived in the context of other empirical works, it is quite evident that the magnitude of income elasticity derived in the current analysis is quite close to the one derived in the context of the other empirical analysis.

III. CONCLUSIONS

In the context of presented article a cointegration analysis was applied using annual data and covering an era of Greek economic history. The period under consideration was 1858-1938. Financial innovations measured as a proxy for alternative cost of holding money and four dummies were introduced in the error correction model to capture the effects of two major historical events, that is, the first and second Balkan war and the Asia Minor military campaign on the mean and trend of time series used in the analysis. In the context of the performed coitegration analysis one cointegrating vector were derived. In equilibrium, financial innovations was proved to be negative function of real (M_1),(M_2) and (M_3) and a positive function of real income.

APPENDIX

Table 8

Main Economic and Historical Events within the Period 1858~1938

Year	*Obs.*	*Event*
1864	7	Great Britain ceded the seven Ionian Islands to Greece.
1867	10	Greece joins the Latin Monetary Union. As a result, it was obliged to increase drachma's content in precious metal.
1881	24	Annexation of Thessaly and a part of Epirus by Greece.
1882	25	As a result of country's accession to L.M.U. in 1867, the transformation of Greek monetary system is completed. Old coins and foreign currencies used in transactions are withdrawn.
1884	27	The Greek State issues 11000000 gold coins. The New Drachma is put in circulation and coexists with the Old Drachma.
1886	29	Starting from this year, Greek government enters a period of large scale foreign borrowing to finance the budget deficits.
1893	36	Bankruptcy of Greek economy.
1897	40	Greece losses a part of Thessaly after its defeat in the war against Ottoman Empire. The Great Powers establish an International Financial Control over certain Greek finances and guarantee the payment of the war indemnity to Turkey and the country's foreign debt.
1910	53	Passing of the law 3642 under which drachma entered the classical gold standard.
1912	55	Annexation of Crete by Greece. Outbreak of First Balkan War.
1913	56	Outbreak of 2nd Balkan War. Greece annexes Macedonia and the rest of Epirus.
1916	59	Greece enters First World War. As a result of the dispute between Prime Minister, E. Venizelos, and King Constantine regarding the placing of Greece on the side of Entente, the country had two governments until 1917 when King Constantine left the country.
1919	62	Greece recovers Eastern Macedonia, annexes Western Thrace and participates in the reciprocal exchange of national minorities (Neuilly treaty).
1920	63	In accordance to the treaty of Sevres, Greece obtained Eastern Thrace, North & Central Aegean Islands and the region around the city of Smyrna (in Asia Minor).
1921	64	Greece launches the "Asia Minor" military campaign against Turkey.
1922	65	The "Asia Minor front" collapses. Greece is defeated. In accordance to the Lausanne treaty, Greece losses Eastern Thrace and the region around the city of Smyrna. A great number of Greek refugees from Eastern Thrace and Asia Minor enters Greece.
1928	71	Foundation of Central Bank of Greece.
1929	72	The great economic depression.

Notes

1. Residual's autocorrelation is tested via an LM test for 12 lags while their multivariate normality is tested via Jarque–Bera statistic, using Cholesky's orthogonalization method for its determination. Finally, White's heteroskedasticity test (no cross terms) is used in order to test residual's homoskedasticity

References

Apergis N. (1999), "Inflation Uncertainty and Money Demand: Evidence from a Monetary Regime Change and the Case of Greece", *International Economic Journal,* 13,2, pp. 21-30.

Apergis N., Karpetis C., Kotsiopoulou A., Mitakidou E. and Tsakiri Th. (1999), "The Demand for Money in Greece: Evidence Through a Shopping Time Technology Model and Cointegration",*Spoudai*, 49, pp. 3-45.

Andreadis A., (1939), "National Debt and Greek Public Finances", in [Works], Vol. 2, Athens, (in greek).

Arestis P. (1988), "The Demand of Money in Greece:An Application of the Error Correction Mechanism. *Greek Economic Review*, 10, pp. 419-39.

Banerjee, Anindya; Lumsdaine, Robin L.; Stock, James H. (1992), "Recursive and Sequential Tests of the Unit –Root and Trend –Break Hypothesis: Theory and International Evidence", *Journal of Business & Economic Statistics*, 10, 3, July 1992, pp. 271 ~ 87.

Bahmani-Oskooee, M., Economidou, C. (2005), "How Stable is the Demand for Money in Greece?", *International Economic Journal*, 19, 3, 2005, pp. 461-472.

Brissimis S., Hondroyiannis G., Swammy P.A. V.B and Tavlas G. (2003), "Empirical Modelling of Money Demand in Periods of Structural Change: The Case of Greece",*Bank of Greece Working Paper No. 1*.

Charitakis G. (1927), The Greek Industry, (in greek).

Dickey, David A.; Fuller, Wayne A. (1979), "Distribution of the Estimators for Autoregressive Time Series with a Unit Root", *Journal of the American Statistical Association*, 74, 366, pp. 427-31.

Dickey, David A.; Fuller, Wayne A. (1981), "Likelihood Ratio Statistics for Autoregressive Time Series with a Unit Root", *Econometrica*, 49, 4, pp. 1057-72.

Dickey D. A., D. Jansen, D. Thronton (1991), "A Primer Cointegration with an Application to Money and Income" *Federal Reserve Bank of St. Louis*, 58-77.

Ericsson N. and Sharma S. (1998), "Broad Money Demand and Financial Liberalization inGreece", *Empirical Economics*, 23.

Karfakis C.; Sidiropoulos M. S. (2000), "On the Stability of the Long-run Money Demand in Greece", *Applied Economics Letter*, 7, 2, pp. 8386.

Karfakis, C. (1991), "Monetary Policy and the Velocity Money in Greece: A Co-integration Approach", *Applied Financial Economics*, Vol. 1, pp. 123-27.

Karpetis C., Varelas E. and Zikos S. (2006), "Unit Root Investigation of Greek Real Money Supply and GDP", *International Advances in Economic Research*.

Karpetis C., "Money, Income and Inflation in Equilibrium- The Case of Greece", *International Advances in Economic Research,*(forthcoming 2007).

Kostelenos, George C. (1995), "Money and Output in Modern Greece: 1858–1938", pp. 25-31, 337-442, 433-436, 457-459, *Centre of Planning and Economic Research*, Studies 44, Athens.

Kostis C., Petmezas S., Growth and Stagnation in the Greek Economy, 1830-1940 (mimeo).

Kwiatkowski, Denis; Phillips, Peter C. B.; Schmidt, Peter; Shin, Yongcheol (1992), "Testing the Null Hypothesis of Stationarity Against the Alternative of a Unit Root", *Journal of Econometrics*, 54, pp. 159-178.

Lazaretou, Sophia (2003), "Greek Monetary Retrospect: The Adventures of the Drachma", pp. 16-21, *Bank of Greece Working Paper*, No. 2.

Lumsdaine, Robin L.; Papell, David H. (1997), "Multiple Trend Breaks and the Unit–Root Hypothesis", *The Review of Economics and Statistics*, 79, 2, pp. 212-218.

Mehra Y. (1992), " In Search of Stable , Short-run M1 Demand Function", Federal Reserve Bank of Richmond Economic Review.

McNown R., M . Wallace (1992), "Cointegration Tests of L. R. Relation between Money Demand and Effective Exchange Rate", *Journal of International Money and Finance*, 11, 107-114.

N.G., Serena; Perron, Pierre (1995), "Unit Root Test in ARMA Models with Data–Dependent Methods for the Selection of the Truncation Lag", *Journal of the American Statistical Association*, 90, 429, pp. 268-81.

Papadopoulos A., Zis (1997), "The Demand for Money in Greece: Further Empirical Results and Policy Implications", *The Mangester Shool*, 65, 1.

Perron, Pierre (1989), "The Great Crash, the Oil Price Shock and the Unit Root Hypothesis", *Econometrica*, 57, 6, pp. 1361-1401.

Perron, Pierre (1990), "Testing for a Unit Root in a Time Series with a Changing Mean", *Journal of Business & Economic Statistics*, 8, 2, pp. 153-62.

Perron, Pierre (1994), "Trend, Unit Root and Structural Change in Macroeconomic Time Series" in B. B. Rao, ed., *Cointegration for the Applied Economist*, New York: Mac Millan Press, pp. 113-46.

Perron, Pierre (1997), "Further Evidence on Breaking Trend Functions in Macroeconomic Variables", *Journal of Econometrics*, 80, 2, pp. 355-85.

Perron, Pierre, Vogelsang, Timothy J. (1992a), "Testing for a Unit Root in a Time Series with a Changing Mean: Corrections and Extensions", *Journal of Business & Economic Statistics*, 10 , 4 , pp. 467-70.

Perron, Pierre; Vogelsang, Timothy J. (1992b), "Nonstationarity and Level Shifts with an Application to Purchasing Power Parity", *Journal of Business & Economic Statistics*, 10, 3, pp. 301-20.

Perron, Pierre; Vogelsang, Timothy J. (1998), "Additional Tests for a Unit Root Allowing for a Break in the Trend Function at an Unknown Time", *International Economic Review*, 39, 4, pp. 1073-1100.

Phillips, Peter C. B.; Perron, Pierre (1988), "Testing for a Unit Root in Time Series Regression", *Biometrika*, 75, 2, pp. 335-46.

Psaradakis, Z. (1993), "The Demand for Money in Greece: An Exercise in Econometric Modelling with Cointegrated Variables", Oxford Bulletin of Economics and Statistics, 55, 2, pp. 215-236.

Zivot, Eric; Andrews, Donald W. K. (1992), "Further Evidence on the Great Crash the Oil–Price Shock, and the Unit Root Hypothesis", *Journal of Business & Economic Statistics*, 10, 3, pp. 251-70.

DO THE WEAKNESSES IN THE QUALITY OF PUBLIC GOVERNANCE EXPLAIN LOW PRIVATE INVESTMENT IN MIDDLE EAST AND NORTH AFRICA?

Ahmet Faruk Aysan, Mustapha Kamel Nabli** * &*
*Marie-Ange Véganzonès–Varoudakis****

ABSTRACT

This paper shows that, during the 1980s and the 1990s, Middle East and North Africa could have achieved better private investment performances if the region had improved the quality of public governance. This result has been shown for a large number of public governance institutions. This is the case for corruption, quality of bureaucracy, judiciary, security of property rights, regulations and taxation, political stability, as well as political rights and civil liberties. This result is obtained for a panel of 32 countries, by estimating a simultaneous model of private investment and public governance quality, where economic policy and other variables explain concurrently both variables. This empirical model also illustrates that economic reforms, in the form of financial development and trade openness, and human capital affect private investment decision directly, as well as through their positive impact on the quality of public governance.

Keywords: *Public governance, Private Investment, Middle East and North Africa.*

JEL Classification: *P4, E2, E6, D02.*

I. INTRODUCTION

The MENA countries have on average been characterized by a clear deficit in public governance. This shortfall is particularly related to democratic institutions such as political rights, civil liberties, or freedom of the press. The quality of the administration has also been of some concern. These deficiencies have been reported as being responsible for the slow economic activity in MENA (see El Badawi, 2002; and the World Bank, 2004).

Public governance is part of the investment climate of a country. The forward- looking nature of investment underlines the importance of a stable and secure environment "Good" public governance is viewed as reducing these economic uncertainty and as promoting efficiency (see North, 1981). In this respect, and as reported by the World Bank (2004), better public governance improves the investment climate by improving bureaucratic performances and

* Boğaziçi University, Department of Economics, Istanbul, Turkey.

** The World Bank, Washington D.C., USA.

*** CERDI, CNRS, Université d'Auvergne, France.

predictability. This also reduces the cost of doing business. Better public governance also contributes to the effective delivery of public goods that are necessary for productive business. Cross-country correlations using broad proxies for investment climate quality suggest a positive link between the investment climate and private investment decisions[1].

As a part of the reflection on the channel through which public governance may affect economic performance, one strand of the literature has recently reconsidered the role of economic policies in explaining cross-country economic achievements. Recent work on the role of both public governance and economic policies has found that public governance is the dominant factor with little, if any, independent influence of policies[2]. These results, however, stem from endogeneity and specification problems, as pointed out by Sachs (2003). In fact, economic policies are likely to affect cross-country variations in the quality of public governance. There is, in particular, some evidence that greater openness to trade and stronger competition are conducive to better public governance[3]. Given these conditions, economic policies may explain economic performances through their impact on public governance[4]. In the case of private investment, we show that both effects (i.e., direct and indirect) can be brought together if the model chosen is well specified[5]. We estimate in particular a simultaneous model of private investment and of governance institutions, where economic policies concurrently explain both variables.

In this paper, we also address other shortfalls of the empirical literature on public governance and economic performances. We intend, in particular, to categorize what types of governance institutions are more detrimental to entrepreneur investments. To this end, we introduce a large set of governance variables which are not typically used in the literature on the determinants of private investment. Since these indicators are likely to be correlated, we process an aggregated indicator using the principal component analysis methodology. Based on the existing literature, we categorize so called governance institutions in three broad clusters as "Administrative Quality", (*QA*), "Public Accountability" (*PA*), and "Political Stability" (*PS*). We then generate a global indicator of public governance *(GOV)* which summarizes these three aspects[6]. This method allows in a second step to evaluate the contribution of the initial indicators to the private investment's decisions. This information will be useful to understand which factors explain the low investment's performances of the region. In this paper, human development and economic policy variables have been similarly processed.

Our empirical approach relies also on panel data (cross section-time series analysis) which is suitable—contrary to previous studies—to jointly assessing the impact of economic policies and governance institutions on private investments: the time series dimension captures the variability of policies through time and the cross section dimension covers the governance variables which tend to evolve slowly.

This paper also benefits from a newly constructed data set on private investment (see Aysan *et al.*, 2006b). The International Finance Corporation (*IFC*) of the World Bank launched a project which addresses the private investments of various developing countries from 1970 to 1999. Studies using this disaggregated data on private investment show that private and public investment can have very different determinants (Aizenman and Marion, 1999). Building on the IFC series, our new data set covers 99 countries (60 for high quality data) over the period 1970-2002 (see *Annex A1* for the list of countries with high quality data).

Finally, as previously mentioned, our empirical model allows for the simultaneous estimation of private investments and of governance institutions. This model is also justified by the fact that—in addition to economic policies—changes in private investment can influence the quality of public governance[7]. This model of simultaneous equations allows also that some hidden factors affect in parallel private investment and governance institutions. Our empirical results show that governance institutions play a significant role in private investment decisions.

This paper is organized as follows. The second section introduces our classification of governance institutions to determine which institutions are detrimental for entrepreneur investments. The third section presents the other determinants of private investment which will be taken into consideration in our empirical analysis. The fourth section introduces the private investment model tested and the results of the estimations. The fifth section uses this model to determine which factors would boost the level of MENA's private investments in the future. The last section concludes.

II. CLASSIFICATION OF GOVERNANCE INSTITUTIONS

A first step in our analysis has been to differentiate and categorize the numerous different dimensions of public governance. Existing literature on the classification of governance institutions provides some alternatives (see Kaufmann, Kraay and Mastruzzi (2003) and the World Bank (2004) in particular). Our choice of indicators, however, has been limited by the lack of annual data available for a large sample of countries over long periods of time. Considering the existing classifications of governance data, this paper categorizes the public governance variables which are likely to affect individual investors' decision into three broad clusters: "Administrative Quality" (*QA*), "Public Accountability" (*PA*), and "Political Stability" (*PS*).

1. Quality of Administration (*QA*)

The "Quality of Administration" expresses the ability of government to provide investors with an investment-friendly and reliable environment. The "Quality of Administration" is defined by four indicators from the International Country Risk Guide (*ICRG, 1999*): (a) "Control over Corruption", (b) "Quality of Bureaucracy", (c) "Investment Profile", and (d) "Law and Order". These institutions promote investments by reducing the costs and risks of doing business..

Corruption often has adverse effects on economic activities. This fact is well documented and is often described as one of the major constraints facing enterprises in the developing world (see the World Bank 2005). In his cross-country analysis, Mauro (1995) shows that corruption reduces growth. Gupta, Davooli and Alonso-Terme (2002) stress that corruption exacerbates income inequality and poverty. Mo (2001) documents a causal chain of interest for our work, linking corruption to low growth through reduced human and physical capital. In fact, for private investors, corruption increases investment and operation costs, as well as uncertainties about the timing and effects of the application of government regulations. Corruption raises also the investment and operational costs of public enterprises, which are detrimental to private investment through insufficient and low quality infrastructures (see Tanzi and Davooli, 1997). The same conclusions have been reached for the effects of bureaucratic quality on the economic activity (see Evans and Rauch, 2000).

The "Quality of Bureaucracy" index of ICRG summarizes the ability of the government to formulate and implement sound policies. Moreover, the "Quality of Bureaucracy" index indicates that "countries where the bureaucracy has the strength and expertise govern without drastic changes in policy or interruptions in government services. In these low-risk countries, the bureaucracy tends to be somewhat autonomous from political pressure and to have an established mechanism for recruitment and training".

The "Investment Profile" is a measure of the "government's attitude to inward investment as determined by the assessment of four sub-components: risk to operations, taxation, profit repatriation and labor costs". Because investors are making long-term decisions, risks to operations and other uncertainties about future policies are detrimental to investment decisions. Taxation and labor costs have also a first order implication on costs, and therefore on decisions to invest. Although government regulations and taxation are reasonable and warranted in order to protect the general public and to generate revenues to finance the delivery of public services and infrastructures, overregulation and over-taxation deter investments by raising business start-up and operating costs.

In the "Law and Order" index, the law sub-component provides an "assessment of the strength and impartiality of the legal system", while the order sub-component concerns the "popular observance of the law." Although many aspects of the business environment affect investments, the security of property rights is the most important and the better documented issue. Because of the forward-looking nature of investment, investors need institutions that preserve the right of private property, ensure equitable and consistent rule of law in protecting this right, as well as effective incentives to respect and enforce it. A reliable judiciary, in particular, reduces transaction costs for businesses and sends positive signals to investors that rules of law will be equitably and consistently protected and enforced. On the empirical side, the issue of property rights and of rule of law has been widely covered by the literature, and the results of cross-country analysis are robust to various tests and specifications[8].

2. Public Accountability (*PA*)

"Public Accountability" consists in two indicators: "Civil Liberties" and "Political Rights". These indicators are estimated by Freedom House (FH).

Public accountability is part of the investment climate of an economy. Because fixed capital investments are generally irreversible, private investment decisions are highly sensitive to the perception of the credibility and tenacity of the political regime, as well as of policies[9]. An open and participatory political system provides stability of social institutions and ensures a broad public support to policies, which are in this case more sustainable in the long run. Public accountability is a guaranty of transparency and of better availability of information, which also help governments to build credibility. Public accountability provides access to policymakers and can hold them responsible for failures in implementing policies. In particular, freedom of press, free political parties and open elections contribute to government's legitimacy and give voice to citizens in the decision-making process. On the empirical side, the literature on democratic participation has focused on the effects of transparency and accountability on growth, using data on civil liberties, political rights, and freedom of press from various sources. The empirical validation has, however, produced mitigated success[10]. The work of Pastor and Sung (1995) is one of the few to have been able to show a positive effect of various indicators of democratic institutions on private investment in the developing world.

3. Political Stability (*PS*)

"Political Stability" includes the following variables from ICRG (1999): "Government Stability", "Internal Conflict", "External Conflict", and "Ethnic Tensions". Political instability increases the uncertainty in the economy and deters the risk-averse entrepreneurs to take action for profitable investment opportunities. Various authors, using different indicators of political uncertainties, have brought empirical evidence that institutions associated with political instability hamper aggregate investment[11].

All the political and public governance indicators have been aggregated by using principal component analysis (PCA) to account for the multi-collinearity issue in using these potentially correlated variables in the same regression equation. Results of PCA are given in *Annex 2.*

III. OTHER DETERMINANTS OF PRIVATE INVESTMENT AND GOVERNANCE INSTITUTIONS

Although the importance of private investment has been widely developed in the literature, there is less evidence on what induces private firms to invest in developing countries. In fact, developing countries do not operate in a competitive environment and face constraints that are not accounted for in the neoclassical model. This partly explains why most of the economists do not agree on the subject of the determinants of investment in the developing countries[12]. This phenomenon is also the case for MENA economies, for which the empirical literature is very deficient[13]. In this paper, we address some of these constraints. In particular, the ones linked to economic policy and to the quality of public governance will be added to the traditional determinants of private investment, here the expected aggregate demand (the accelerator) and the user cost of capital (Jorgenson, 1963).

1. Structural Reforms

Among the most common constraints faced by developing countries is the deficit in economic reforms. This is the case of the MENA countries which have lagged behind other regions in terms of reforming their economy (Nabli and Véganzonès - Varoudakis, 2007). Structural reforms constitute an important determinant of the actual and future profitability of private investment. We have considered trade policy and financial development as part of our structural reforms index.

By providing more opportunities and incentives for the firms to invest, the financial development is an important part of private investment decisions. A developed financial system mobilizes and allocates resources to the enterprises. A developed financial system is also expected to be more efficient due to an increasing technological specialization, which leads to a better selection of projects and a more advanced diversification of risks. This allows the firms to finance more investment projects and increases the productivity of new investments (see Levine, 1997, for a synthesis). In addition, given the lack of well-functioning financial markets, the neoclassical assumption of the flexible accelerator model about the availability of credit supply by the banking sector cannot be taken for granted in developing countries. This discrepancy also occurs because of the public deficits and public debt, which can lead to financial repression and to eviction of private investment. On the empirical side, the impact of financial development on private investment is now well documented[14]. In his survey of investment functions in developing countries, Rama (1993) presents the positive effect of financial development on private investment in 21 of the 31 papers surveyed.

Trade reforms constitute another factor that can stimulate private investment decisions. Trade openness increases competitiveness and provides access to enlarged markets (Balassa, 1978; Feder, 1982). Trade openness can be at the origin of economies of scale and of productivity gains. In addition, trade openness influences the availability of external credit-considering the general consensus on the role of tradable goods in providing positive externalities in the form of collateral for external financing (Caballero and Krishnamurthy, 2001).

All these factors create favorable conditions for the enterprises to invest. However, as mentioned in the introduction, economic reforms are also expected to affect private investment through their impact on the quality of public governance. There is, in particular, some evidence that greater openness to trade and stronger competition are conducive to public governance improvement[15]. Opening up markets may help to weaken vested interests and reduce rents derived from prevailing economic and institutional arrangements. Trade openness may also lead to demands for governance institutions more suited to an increasingly varied and complex range of transactions (See IMF, 2003).

2. Human Capital

Human capital is part of the investment climate of an economy and is generally considered as a complementary factor of physical capital. Here, we have considered health and education as part of the human capital index. Human capital stimulates private capital formation by raising the profitability of investment. Human capital can also be at the origin of positive externalities[16]. Because skilled workers are better in dealing with changes, a skilled work force is essential for firms to adopt new and more productive technologies[17]. Besides, new technologies generally require significant organizational changes, which are handled better by a skilled workforce[18]. Human capital gives also the opportunity to the enterprises to expand or enter new markets.

Moreover, human capital entails better governance institutions. More educated people with higher life expectancy become more competent bureaucrats and—in addition to better monitoring of the functioning of government officials—demand for better quality of bureaucracy (Galor *et al.*, 2005). In addition, educational attainment reduces the political instability by generating more avenues to reconcile the opposing parties. This idea constitutes one of the classical approaches in the literature to highlight the importance of education in bringing better governance institutions (Lipset, 1959). From the democratic accountability point of view, a more educated society is more likely to be enfranchised in terms of civil rights and liberties (Acemoglu and Robinson, 2001). These considerations justify that human capital also appears as an explanatory factor of private investment through its impact on the quality of public governance.

Although educational attainment has improved in the majority of developing countries, many firms still rate inadequate skills and education of workers as severe obstacles to their operations[19]. This is the case of the MENA region, where progress is still needed in order for the region to catch up with South East Asia and Latin America[20]. To meet this challenge and as pointed out by the World Bank (2004), MENA countries have to gear up their educational system both to improve basic education and to equip the labor force with skills appropriate for enterprises to invest efficiently.

IV. THE ECONOMETRIC MODEL AND ESTIMATION RESULTS

In the empirical model, endogenous variables are the share of private investment and the aggregate measure of public governance (*Gov*). These endogenous variables are simultaneously determined by influencing each other. In order to account for this reverse causality, we establish a system of equations to estimate the share of private investment in GDP (*PI*) and quality of public governance (*Gov*) simultaneously. In the private investment equation, lower quality of public governance is expected to reduce the private investment. In the governance equation, private investment enters on the right side with an expected positive sign. This simultaneous system of equations also enables us to take into account other factors that affect both private investment and public governance.

This system of equations is estimated using three stage least squares by controlling other determinants of endogenous variables. Three stage least square (3SLS) estimation allows to use the links between endogenous variables efficiently. Since endogenous variables appear as regressors in other equations, they have to be instrumented out using exclusion restrictions.

The model estimated is the following:

$$PI_{it} = \alpha_0 + \alpha_1 QI_{it} + \alpha_2 X_{1i} + \varepsilon_{1it} \quad (1)$$

$$Gov_{it} = \gamma_0 + \beta_1 PI_{it} + \beta_2 X_{2i} + \varepsilon_{2it} \quad (2)$$

Where

PI_{it} is the share of private investment in GDP

Gov_{it} represents the aggregate index of public governance

X_{1i} and X_{2i} are the other control variables in private investment (*PI*) and public governance (*Gov*) equations respectively

ε_{1it} and ε_{2it} are the error terms of each equations. i indicates the country and t represents the time of the variable.

The determinants of private investment in the neoclassical flexible accelerator model include the expected aggregate demand (the accelerator) and the user cost of capital. Hence, the private investment equation in our specification incorporates real interest rate (*Realr*) to capture the user cost of capital. It also accounts for the GDP growth rate in last year (*grow*) to control for the accelerator effect. These two variables are excluded from the public governance equation (*Gov*) in order to identify the system.

Both of the equations, on the other hand, take into account the GDP per capita, as well as the variations in structural reform (*SR*) and human capital (*H*). Structural reforms are characterized with trade policy (*TP*) and financial development. Financial development is proxied by the private credit by banks and other depository institutions (*Pcr*). Trade policy is constructed as the commercial openness (calculated by aggregating the export and import in total GDP) from which we have subtracted the exports of oil and mining products, as well as the "natural trade openness" constructed by Frankel and Romer (1999). The trade policy and financial development variables form the structural reform indicators after implementing the principal component analysis (see *Annex 2* for results of PCA). Structural reform is expected to stimulate private investment, as well as the institutional change for the better.

Human capital (*H*) is expressed with life expectancy at birth, and average years of primary, secondary and higher schooling in the total population over 15 years old. These variables are also aggregated with principal component analysis. Human capital is widely considered to enhance the private investment and to lead to better governance institutions. Therefore, human capital variable is expected to have positive coefficients in both of the equations.

GDP per capita is controlled in the investment equation to account for the neoclassical Solow growth model. Countries with lower GDP per capita are expected to gradually catch up with the more developed counterparts by having more capital investment over time. Moreover, GDP per capita accounts for possible externalities, such as greater market size on demand and supply of good and services, and finally on private investment. GDP per capita in public governance equations represents the idea that more developed countries can afford to have better governance institutions (Azariadis and Lahiri 2002). Hence, a positive relationship is expected between GDP per capita and public governance quality.

Oil export as a per centage of total merchandise export also enters into both equations. The typical natural curse hypothesis is taken into account by incorporating this variable into the investment equation. When a country relies more on natural resources extraction in its exports, there can be less incentive to invest for other products. This result, for example, may stem from the increase in the cost of labor (Rodriguez and Sachs, 1999). This variable also has an implication for the quality of public governance. Countries with less reliance on natural resources are expected to form better governance institutions. The natural resource-abounded countries do not need to mobilize the society to enhance aggregate income. The ruling class can control the economy by collaborating with a small number of people in the society. Therefore, the production structure of the country does not generate good governance institutions in favor of the society (Ross 2001, Bellin, 2001). Under these circumstances, the elite is also less inclined to provide better public governance by considering the future effects of today's enfranchisements (Acemoglu and Robinson, 2001) and engage in more rent-seeking activities[21]. Hence, the share of oil export in merchandise export is expected to reduce the quality of public governance.

The tenure of the system (*TenSyst*) from Keefer et al. (2001) is excluded from the investment equation to identify the system of equations. *TenSyst* reports the number of years that an administrative system—regardless of whether autocratic or democratic—lasts in the country. The underlying idea to include this variable in the governance equation is to account for the fact that institutions settle over time. The longer the time passes with the existing system, the better institutions are established. This exclusion restriction is quite reasonable considering that *TenSyst* has a direct impact on the public governance whereas its influence on private investment is more likely to be realized through its effect on these institutions.

Finally, a regional dummy for the Middle Eastern and North African countries (*MENA*) appears as a right hand side variable in both of the equations. One of our primary purposes is to understand the position of MENA countries among the other countries and to see whether MENA substantially diverges from the rest of the world in terms of private investment and of public governance performance.

Equations (1) and (2) have been estimated on an unbalanced panel of 32 developing countries over 1980-2002 using the three stages least square estimations technique (*3SLS*). Tables1 presents the estimation's results of equations (1) and (2).

Estimation results produce quite interesting conclusions. One of the most interesting outcomes concerns the Public governance index which gives a positive and significant coefficient at the 5 per cent level in the investment equation (see Table 1 columns 1 and 3). This result confirms that a low level of corruption, a good quality of bureaucracy, a clear security of property rights, a reasonable risk to operations, a sound taxation and regulation,, better law and order, a stable political situation and a reasonable political accountability are of first importance for the enterprises' decisions to invest. This result makes a real contribution to the empirical literature on governance by validating, over a relatively long period of time, the role of a large set of public governance variables on private economic performance.

Our result is unambiguous and robust to the introduction of other explanatory variables. This is the case of structural reforms which show a significant impact on private investment decisions. The roles of economic policy in explaining cross-country economic achievement has recently been questioned (Easterly and Levine; 2003). Our estimations stress however that, although the quality of public governance constitutes a major factor in the private sector decisions, the role of economic policies cannot be disregarded. Besides, our result confirms that firms in developing countries face constraints that are not accounted for in more developed economies and that deficiencies in trade policy and financial development have a long-term impact on private investment decisions and growth.

Another conclusion of our model consists in validating the neoclassical theory of the firm in the case of developing countries. The accelerator variable has the expected positive sign, which implies that anticipations of economic growth induce more investment. Similarly, the interest rate appears to exert a negative and significant effect on private investment, which is consistent with the user cost of capital theory. Both variables are highly significant, indicating that at the final stage, supply and demand considerations constitute major factors for the entrepreneurs to undertake a new investment project. Our model fails, however, to verify the Solow hypothesis of decreasing return to scale of physical capital accumulation. The coefficient of the GDP per capita variable, although negative, is not significant. As well, human capital does not seem to exert a direct effect on private investment decisions.

Finally, estimation of equation (1) confirms the natural curse hypothesis. The coefficient of the oil export variable as a per centage of total merchandise export is significant and negative. On the opposite, the regional dummy for MENA countries is not significant. This result shows that, after controlling for various explanatory factors, private investment in MENA does not seem to diverge from the rest of the world.

In the "Governance" equation (Table 1, columns 2 and 4), our estimations reveal the positive impact of several factors on the quality of the public governance. These factors have an indirect effect on private investment's decisions by improving the functioning of governance institutions. This is the case of the GDP per capita which means that more developed countries entail better governance institutions. Tenure of system also predicts better administrative quality, as well as human capital. This finding confirms that a higher education level and better health conditions of the population are conducive to an improved quality of public governance. Our results illustrates as well that human capital plays en indirect role on private investment decisions by enhancing the quality of the administration, by helping the political stability, as well as by participating in the democratization process of the country.

An interesting result also concerns the MENA dummy variable which coefficient is significant and negative. This finding confirms the overall low quality of MENA public governance , as already stressed by several authors (see in particular the World Bank, 2004). This result indicates the need for institutional reform in the MENA region, especially considering the positive and persistent role of governance institutions in private investment's decisions.

Our estimations fail, however, to validate the role of private investment in enhancing public governance quality, neither the negative impact of the share of oil export in merchandise export. This result contradicts the fact that countries with less reliance on natural resources form better governance institutions. Structural reforms, also, does not appear to immediately improve the quality of public governance. This result does not confirm that economic reforms can also stimulate private investment by improving the quality of governance institutions.

V. CONTRIBUTION OF VARIOUS GOVERNANCE INSTITUTIONS FOR THE WEAKNESSES OF PRIVATE INVESTMENT IN MIDDLE EAST AND NORTH AFRICA

In this section, we use the model estimated previously to determine which factors account for the low investment's performances of the MENA region. We evaluate, in particular, the contribution of the "Administrative Quality", "Political Stability" and "Public Accountability", which have revealed to have primary importance in explaining firm's decision to invest. For this purpose, we compare the MENA region performance in these aspects– as well as in structural reforms and human capital—to the ones of the more advanced developing economies of our

Table 1
Estimation Results

Explanatory	*Endogenous Variables*		*Endogenous Variables*	
	Priv Inv	*GOV*	*Priv Inv*	*GOV*
Variables	(1)	(2)	(3)	(4)
GOV	2.25 (1.99)**		2.26 (2.00)**	
Private Investment		0.014 -0.667		
Structural Reforms	1.98 *(8.06)****	0.1 *-1.2*	1.98 *(8.07)****	0.13 *-1.46*
Human Capital	0.36 *-1.4*	0.124 *(3.27)**	0.35 -1.36	0.133 *(4.36)****
Oil Exports	-0.035 *(2.97)****	0 *-0.13*	-0.038 *(-3.14)****	-0.001 *-0.49*
GDP per Capita	0 *-0.84*	0.0003 *(8.72)****	0 *(-0.81)*	0.0003 *(8.84)****
MENA Dummy	-0.34 *-0.31*	-0.28 *(1.91)***	-0.32 *(-0.29)*	-0.29 *(2.09)***
Realr	-0.037 *(2.87)****		-0.035 *(3.21)****	
Growth	0.22 *(3.53)****		0.21 *(3.58)****	
Ten Syst		0.015 *(5.75)****		0.016 *(6.44)****
Constant	12.2 *(15.55)****	-0.82 *-2.14*	12.2 *(15.61)****	-0.66 *-9.39*
Numb obs	349	349	349	349

Notes: (*) indicates significance at 10 %; (**) indicates significance at 5 %; (***) indicates significance at 1 %. Sources of data are as follows: the private investment series have been processed from various national and international sources (International Finance Corporation (IFC), World Development Indicators (WDI), Life Data Base (LDB), see section 4.1 for more details). The "Administrative Quality" and "Political Stability" indexes use ICRG (1999) data. The components of the "Public Accountability" indicator come from Freedom House (2002). The "Structural Reforms" index uses data from WDI, but the oil export series entering the trade policy indicator comes from the United Nations. In the "Human Capital' indicator, the numbers of years of schooling are from Barro and Lee (1994) and from Barro (2000a and b), and the life expectancy series is from WDI. All aggregated indicators have been generated after implementing the PCA methodology (see Annex 2 for more details). Interest rates (Rear) have been calculated from IFS and TenSyst comes from Keefer et al. (2001). All other data are from WDI.

sample, like the East Asian economies. We simulate which level of private investment MENA could have achieved if the region had experienced the same growth performances, economic policies and governance institutions as East Asia. This comparison has been done for two time periods–the 1980s and the 1990s respectively–which exhibit, as we will see, quite different characteristics. We use for the calculations the last set of estimations which summarize the effects of the three sub component of public governance (see Table 1 columns 3 and 4).

A first step has consisted in calculating the coefficients of the initial variables which explain the composite governance indicators. The calculation is based on the estimated coefficients of the aggregate indicator in the regression (*GOV,* Table 1 column 3), as well as on the weights of each principal component in the aggregate indicator combined with the loading of the initial variables in each principal component (*Annex* 2)[22]. Coefficients of the initial variables are presented in *Annex 3* and their contributions appear in Tables 2 and 3. In Tables 2 and 3, the contribution of the Quality of Administration index has been calculated by aggregating the contributions of its four sub-components[23]. Same thing has been done for Political Stability[24] and Public Accountability[25] (as well as for Structural Reform[26] and Human Capital[27]).

These simulations show quite interesting results (see Table 2). A first set of conclusions concerns the weaknesses of MENA institutions during the 1980s. This is the case for the "Administrative Quality" which insufficiencies compared to East Asia has cost to the region 1 per cent of private investment to GDP on average per year. These deficiencies have also concerned "Political Stability" which cost has been slightly lower (0.7 per cent of GDP). Private investment could have reached on average 14.2 per cent of GDP (compared to 11.9 per cent observed) if MENA had benefited from the same quality of administration and political stability as East Asia.

Table 2
Private Investment to GDP: Increase with improvement in

% GDP	*Priv Invest (actual)*	*Real Int. Rate*	*Growth*	*Structural Reforms*	*GOV*	QA	PA	PS	*Oil Exports*	*Total Contributions*	*Priv Invest (potential)*
1980	11.9	-0.08	0.39	1.2	2.2	1	0.4	0.7	0.7	4.3	16.3
1990	11.6	0.04	0.31	3.7	0.9	0.3	0.7	-0	1	6	17.6

Source: Authors' calculations

In the 1990s, the gap with East Asia has noticeably reduced and improvement of the "Administrative Quality" and "Political Stability" notably helped investment's decisions, which deficit has only been of 0.2 points of GDP on average per year (see Table 2). This result is in line with the findings of other studies, which acknowledge in the region an improvement in the quality of the administration during the late 1990s (see in particular the World Bank, 2004)[28] However, MENA region has not improved its "Public Accountability" as much as the East Asia throughout the 1990s. In this regard, MENA region could have increased its private investment to GDP ratio by 0.7 per cent on average per year (0.4 per cent in the 1980s).

Our calculations also point out that institutional deficiencies have not been the only reason of the MENA low private investment performances and that the deficit in structural reforms constitutes another major explanatory factor. This has been the case over the whole period, but more importantly during the 1990s. The low trade openness of the region compared to East Asia and the insufficient development of the financial system have reduced private sector investment projects by 3.7 points of GDP in average per year (1.2 during the 1980s). The ratio of private investment could have reached 16.4 per cent of GDP during the 1990s (compared to 11.6 observed) and 15.4 per cent in the 1980s, if both factors (structural reforms and public governance) had been improved to a similar level as East Asia (see Table 2).

A subsequent question has been the one of a more precise diagnostic of which specific factors has contributed to this result. Interesting conclusions first relates to the nature of the weaknesses of the MENA governance institutions during the 1980s. On "Quality of Administration", these weaknesses involve all four sub components: corruption and law and order are two important aspects, but the limitations dues to the low bureaucratic quality, risks to operations, regulations, taxations, and cost of labor have also been of some concern (see Table 3). Our findings are in line with the conclusions of the literature on the role of corruption, as well as of rules of law and property rights in reducing the costs and risks of doing business. Besides, our results bring new empirical evidences on the subject of regulation and taxation and on their impact on the business environment.

Table 3
Private Investment to GDP: Increase with Improvement in

%PIB contr	*QA*	*corruption*	*bur qual*	*inves prof*	*law ord*	*PA*	*pol rights*	*civ lib*	*PS*	*gov stab*	*int confl*	*ext confl*	*ethn tens*	*SR*	*trade pol*	*priv cred*
1980s	1	0.3	0.19	0.2	0.32	0.4	0.2	0.2	1	0.02	0.3	0.5	-0.12	1	1	0.3
1990s	0	0.1	0.23	-0	0.01	0.7	0.4	0.3	-0	-0.05	0	0.08	-0.16	4	1.9	1.9

Source: Authors' calculations

On the side of "Political Stability", the main shortcomings of the region during the 1980s have come from the presence of internal and external conflict which cost respectively 0.34 and 0.50 points of GDP (see Table 3). Our findings corroborate that institutions associated with political instability have a disruptive effect on aggregate investment. However, our results add to the literature by giving specific evidence on which factors are more costly for private investment decisions. In the case of the MENA region, the perception of external and internal conflicts and, to a lower extend, of ethnic tensions have increased the uncertainty in the economy and prevent the creation of a friendly business environment. Finally, on "Public Accountability", concerns about civil liberties and political rights explain both quite well the deficiencies in democratic institutions on both sub periods.

Another striking feature of this new set of calculations relates to the critical concern about trade policy and financial development in the MENA region. Trade policy deficiencies, in particular, have reduced private investment decisions by respectively 1 and 1.9 per cent of GDP on average per year during the two sub-periods. Identically, a better financial system (such as in the East Asian economies) would have stimulated firms' decisions to invest by 1.9 points of GDP yearly during the 1990s (see Table 3). This result makes of structural reforms another important question that MENA governments have to address if the region wants to catch up with more successful developing economies.

1. Contribution of Factors to the Investment Performances: Countries Experiences

Egypt: In Egypt, private investment shows particular low records during the 1990s (See Table 4). Egypt appears to have not improved its governance institutions much, as opposed to other MENA countries in our sample. The main reason for the lack of intuitional reform stems from public accountability, other aspects of public governance having noticeably improved. In the 1980s, corruption appears to be the most important contributing factor for lack of institutional reform. Whereas, most important public governance indicators shift to political rights and liberties in the 1990s (see Table 5). More importantly, private investment in the 1990s primarily suffers from a lack of structural reforms which costs yearly 4.2 points of GDP (compared to 1.3 points in the 1980s, see Table 4).

Iran: In Iran, private investment performed poorly in the 1980s, but potential for improvement is also big in the 1990s. Major obstacles have been the low quality of public governance and the insufficient level of structural reforms. The lack of structural reforms have been felt more in the 1990s, while deficiencies in public governance had been more prominent in the 1980s. Iran could have improved its private investment to GDP ratio by 4.2 and 1.6 per cents in the 1980s and 1990s respectively, if it had reached the same level of institutional quality of East Asian countries (see Table 4). Moreover, the major factor contributing to weak public governance in Iran has been changed from political instability to public accountability in the 1990s. Bureaucratic quality and internal and external conflicts have been of major concern throughout the 1980s. Lack of political rights and civil liberties attract more attention in the 1990s (see Table 5). In the 1990s, however, the deficit of structural reforms has been the most harmful factor to private investment decision, with a cost of 5.9 point of GDP.

Table 4
Private Investment to GDP: Increase with improvement in

1980	*Priv Invest (actual)*	*Real Int. Rate*	*Growth*	*Structural Reforms*	*GOV*				*Oil Exports*	*Total Contributions*	*Priv Invest (potential)*
% GDP						*QA*	*PA*	*PS*			
Egypt	12.6	-0.2	-0.1	1.3	1.7	*1.2*	*0.2*	*0.4*	1.5	4.2	16.8
Iran	9.6		1	2.7	4.2	*1.4*	*0.9*	*1.8*		7.9	17.4
Morocco	12.1	-0.1	0.3	1.9	1.6	*0.9*	*0.1*	*0.5*	-0.4	3.4	15.5
Tunisia	13.6	0	0.4	-1.2	1.6	*0.7*	*0.5*	*0.3*	0.9	1.7	15.3
MENA	11.9	-0.1	0.4	1.2	2.2	*1*	*0.4*	*0.7*	0.7	4.4	16.3

1990 % GDP	Priv Invest (actual)	Real Int. Rate	Growth	Structural Reforms	GOV	QA	PA	PS	Oil Exports	Total Contributions	Priv Invest (potential)
Egypt	8.9	0.1	0.3	4.2	1.7	0.6	0.9	0	1.3	7.5	16.4
Iran	12.7		0.2	5.9	1.6	0.2	1.2	0	2.9	10.6	23.3
Morocco	10.1	-0.1	0.6	3.6	0.4	0.1	0.2	-0	-0.2	4.3	14.4
Tunisia	14.9	0.1	0.1	1.2	0.6	0.2	0.6	-0	0.2	2.3	17.2
MENA	11.6	0.04	0.31	3.7	0.9	0.3	0.7	-0	1	6.2	17.6

Source: Authors' calculations

Morocco: As for other MENA countries, Morocco lack of structural reforms has been more pronounced in the 1990s and its cost for private investment has been of 3.6 points of GDP (compared to 1.9 point in the 1980s). In the 1980s, public governance deficiencies have mainly concerned the low quality of administration—which cost 0.9 points of GDP to the private investment ratio—and more precisely corruption. Morocco, however, has improved its public governance quite significantly in the 1990s (see Table 4) and seems to have alleviated corruption quite well (see Table 5).

Table 5
Private Investment to GDP: Increase with improvement in:

1980s contr % PIB	QA	corruption	bur qual	inves prof	law ord	PA	pol rights	civ lib	PS	gov stab	int confl	ext confl	ethn tens	SR	trade pol	priv cred
Egypt	1.2	0.6	0.17	0.3	0.18	0.2	0.21	0.03	0.4	0	0.26	0.22	-0.1	1.3	0.5	0.7
Iran	1.4	0.1	0.6	0.2	0.41	0.9	0.41	0.53	1.8	0.07	0.6	0.97	0.12	2.7	2.5	0.2
Morocco	0.9	0.4	-0.1	0.2	0.34	0.1	-0.1	0.14	0.5	-0.1	0.3	0.36	-0.08	1.9	0.7	1.2
Tunisia	0.7	0.1	0.09	0.2	0.34	0.5	0.37	0.14	0.3	0.05	0.22	0.44	-0.41	-1	0.1	-0.8
MENA	1	0.3	0.19	0.2	0.32	0.4	0.24	0.21	0.7	0.02	0.34	0.5	-0.12	1.2	1	0.3

1990s contr % PIB	QA	corruption	bur qual	inves prof	law ord	PA	pol rights	civ lib	PS	gov stab	int confl	ext confl	ethn tens	SR	trade pol	priv cred
Egypt	0.6	0.2	0.25	-0.1	0.17	0.9	0.41	0.45	0	-0.1	0.21	0.04	-0.19	4.2	2.1	2.2
Iran	0.2	-0.2	0.15	0.2	0.03	1.2	0.51	0.68	0	-0	0.04	0.17	-0.15	5.9	3.1	2.8
Morocco	0.1	0.1	0.25	-0.1	-0.15	0.2	0.18	0.06	-0	-0.1	0.01	0.09	-0.13	3.6	1.7	2
Tunisia	0.2	0.1	0.25	-0.2	0.01	0.6	0.44	0.13	-0	-0.1	-0.12	0.01	-0.16	1.3	0.7	0.5
MENA	0.3	0.1	0.23	-0	0.01	0.7	0.39	0.33	-0	-0.1	0.04	0.08	-0.16	3.8	1.9	1.9

Source: Authors' calculations

Tunisia: Tunisia performances in terms of private investment, structural reforms and public governance have been the best of our sample of MENA countries. In the 1990s, similar to other MENA countries, Tunisia has done better in term of quality of public governance. Tunisia has especially improved its administrative quality and political stability, whereas the deficiency in public accountability remains almost the same (see Table 4). In fact, in both decades, Tunisia has suffered from a lack of political rights (see Table 5).

VI. CONCLUSION

This paper empirically shows, for a panel of 31 developing countries studied during the 1980s and the 1990s, that public governance constitutes an important part of the investment climate of the developing economies. This result strongly holds for the "Quality of Administration" and confirms that a low level of corruption, a good quality of bureaucracy, a reliable judiciary, a strong security of property rights, a reasonable risk to operations, as well as a sound taxation and regulation contribute significantly to the firms' decision to invest. Our estimations also verify that "Political Stability", by providing a sound and predictable environment to the enterprises, participate as well in a friendly business environment. These results add significantly to the literature on public governance by validating the role of a large set of institutional variables on private economic performances over a relatively long period of time.

Our findings are unambiguous and robust to the introduction of other explanatory variables. This is the case of structural reforms—in the form of trade openness and financial development—and of human capital, which appear to play a significant role in private investment decision. This result confirms that firms in developing countries face constraints that are not accounted for in more developed economies. It also shows that—contrary to recent works which make of governance institutions the dominant factor with little independent influence of economic policies (see Rodrick, Subramanina, and Trebbi, 2002; and Easterly and Levine, 2003).—economic policies and governance institutions both participate in the firms' decisions to invest. We show as well, that structural reforms and human capital contribute to the firms' decisions to invest by also improving the quality of public governance. This conclusion has been reached by estimating a simultaneous model of private investment and public governance, where economic policies and human capital concurrently explain both variables. This conclusion can also be considered as an important contribution to the empirical literature on public governance.

Our estimations find, in addition, some evidence that "Public Accountability" is detrimental for private investment. Although our result have to be considered with caution, they can be regarded as bringing some empirical evidence on the unresolved debate on the potential role of democratic institutions on growth (see Glaeser *et al.*, 2004 and Pastor and Sung, 1995 for more conclusive studies).

In MENA, public governance deficiencies greatly explain the low private investment performances of the region during the 1980s. This is the case for the "Quality of Administration" and "Political Instability", which insufficiencies compared to East Asia has cost on average per year 1.4 point of private investment to GDP. On the side of "Political Stability", the main shortcomings of the region during the 1980s have come from the presence of internal and external conflicts. In the 1990s, the gap with East Asia has noticeably reduced and improvements in the quality of administration and in the political stability of the region have notably helped investment's decisions. "Public Accountability", however, has deteriorated during the same period with a yearly cost of 0.7 point of GDP. This result shows that improvement in democratic institutions is still a key issue in the region.

Public governance deficiencies, however, have not been the only reason of the MENA low private investment performances and the deficit in structural reforms constitutes another major explanatory factor. This has been the case over the whole period, but more importantly during the 1990s. Trade policy deficiencies (compared to Eat Asia) have reduced private investment decisions by 1 and 1.9 per cent of GDP on average per year respectively during the two sub-periods. Identically, a better financial system (such as in the East Asian economies) would have stimulated firms' decisions to invest by 1.9 points of GDP during the 1990s. This makes of structural reforms an important question that MENA governments have also to address if the region wants to catch up with more successful developing economies.

Notes

1. The World Bank (2004) has investigated the correlation between private investment and the ICRG (1999) index of "investment profile". This index is based on measures of contract enforceability, expropriation, profit repatriation, risk of operation, taxation and payment delays.
2. See in particular Rodrik, Subramanina and Trebbi (2002), and Easterly and Levine (2003).
3. For the positive spillover from trade openness on institutions see Berg and Krueger (2003), Islam and Montenegro (2002), and Wei (2000). For the role of domestic competition, see Ades and Di Tella (1999), Djankov and others (2001), and the World Bank (2002).
4. This impact might also be explained by the fact that the measure of institutional quality is most often subjective and an amalgam of policy and institutional factors.
5. In trying to gauge the exogenous contribution of institutions, recent research has given particular attention to the possible role played by geographical and historical influences on institutional formation (see Acemoglu, Johnson and Robison, 2001, and Engelman and Sokoloff, 2002).
6. Various methods of aggregation have been used to categorize different types of institutions. See, in particular, Acemoglu, Johnson, Robinson, and Taicharoen (2003), Kaufmann and others (2003), and the World Bank (2004).
7. See Altmann (2006), Lipset (1959), Glaeser *et al.* (2004), Azariadis and Lahiri (2002), Alesina *et al.* (1996), Isham *et al.* (2002).
8. See Calderon and Chong, (2000), and Acemoglu, Johnson and Robinson (2001) in the context of growth; See North (1981), Knack and Keefer (1995), Easterly and Levine (2003), Rodrik, Subramanian, and Trebbi (2002), and Saleh (2004) in the context of investment.
9. See in particular Rodrik (1991) and Serven and Solimano (1993).
10. See De Haan and Siermann (1996), Prszeworski and Limongi (1993), Prszeworski *et al.* (2000).
11. See in particular Rodrik (1991), Alesina and Perotti (1996), Le (2004), Brunetti and Weder (1994). In the growth context see also Alesina et al. (1996), Svensson (1998), Olson *et al.* (2000).
12. See for example Greene and Villanueva (1991), Blejer and Khan (1984), and Serven (1997).
13. See Shafik (1992) on *Egypt*; Schmidt and Muller (1992) on *Morocco,* as well as Bisat, El-Erian, El-Gamal and Mongelli (1996), and Aysan *et al.* (2006a) on MENA.
14. See for example, McKinnon (1973) and Shaw (1973).

15. For the positive spillover from trade openness on governance quality, see Berg and Krueger (2003), Islam and Montenegro (2002) and Wei (2000). For the role of domestic competition, see Ades and Di Tella (1999), Djankov and others (2001), and the World Bank (2002).
16. See Lucas (1988), Psacharopoulos (1988), and Mankiw, Romer and Weil (1992).
17. See in particular Acemoglu and Shimer (1999).
18. See Bresnahan, Brynjolfsson and Hitt (2002).
19. See the World Bank (2005).
20. See Nabli and Véganzonès -Varoudakis (2007).
21. Aysan (2005) points out that this variable captures the "rentier effect". He notes that "it is easier for the elite to control and capture the rents from 'point source' resources. Resource rents are generally high in oil production. Around 80 per cent of oil income is considered to be resource rent (Gylfason, 2001), while such rents are much lower for other types of products in industry or in agriculture. A small work force is required to extract oil resources. Most of the time, oil is extracted by foreign firms with sophisticated technical skills (Isham et al, 2002). As a result, the ruling elite can exclude the majority of the population in extracting oil reserves. In other words, there exists no incentive on the part of the elite to incorporate the society into increasing aggregate production. Given the lack of economic preconditions, the citizens cannot generate pressure for increased literacy and political influence. This lack of political influence further feeds the vicious cycle by not effectively and peacefully revealing public interest and preferences."
22. See for example, Nabli and Veganzones-Varoudakis (2006) for more details on the methodology.
23. Theses sub-components are corruption, bureaucracy quality, investment friendly profile of administration and law and order (see section 2).
24. Political Stability has been proxied by aggregating the following indicators: government stability, internal and external conflicts, and ethnic tensions.
25. Public Accountability has been calculated by using civil liberties and political rights.
26. The Structural Reform indicator contains trade policy and financial development.
27. Human Capital is defined from life expectancy, and years of primary, secondary and tertiary education.
28. The same studies note, however, that the smaller gap with East Asia is also partly due to a less significant improvement in the quality of institutions in this region.

References

Acemoglu, Daron, and Robert Shimer (1999). "Efficient Unemployment Insurance." *Journal of Political Economy* 107 (5): 893-28.

Acemoglu, Daron, and James A. Robinson (2001), "A Theory of Political Transitions." *American Economic Review* 91(4): 938-963.

Acemoglu, Daron, Simon Johnson, and James A. Robinson (2001), "The Colonial Origins of Comparative Development: An Empirical Investigation." *American Economic Review* 91(5): 1369–401.

Acemoglu, Daron, Simon Johnson, James Robinson, and Yunyong Taicharoen (2003), "Institutional Causes, Macroeconomic Symptoms, Volatility, Crises and Growth." *Journal of Monetary Economics* 89 (September): 49-123.

Ades, Alberto, and Rafael Di Tella (1999), "Rents, Competition and Corruption." *American Economic Review* 39 (September): 49-123.

Aizenman, Joshua, and Nancy P. Marion (1999), "Volatility and Investment: Interpreting Evidence from Developing Countries." *Economica* 66: 157-79.

Agenor, Pierre-Richard, and Peter J. Montiel (1999), *Development Macroeconomics.* Princeton: Princeton University Press.

Alesina, Alberto, and Roberto Perotti (1996), "Income Distribution, Political Instability, and Investment." *European Economic Review* 40: 1203–28.

Alesina, Alberto, Sule Ozler, Nouriel Roubini, and Phillip Swagel (1996), "Political Instability and Economic Growth." *Journal of Economic Growth* 1(2): 189–211.

Altmann, Franz-Lothar (2006), "Promoting Democracy-Building and Security Through Private Investments." Unpublished Manuscript, Stiftung für Wissenschaft und Politik, Berlin.

Aysan, Ahmet F., Gaobo Pang, Marie-Ange Veganzones-Varoudakis (2006a), "Uncertainty, Economic Reforms and Private Investment in the Middle East and North Africa", forthcoming in the *Applied Economics.*

Aysan, Ahmet F., Mustpah K. Nabli, and Marie-Ange Veganzones-Varoudakis (2006b), "Governance and Private Investment in the MENA Countries", *Policy Research Working Paper Series*, N. 3934, the World Bank, Washington D.C.

Aysan, Ahmet Faruk (2006), "The Role of Efficiency of Redistributive Institutions on Redistribution: An Empirical Assessment.", Boğaziçi University Research Papers, ISS/EC 2006-14, Istanbul.

Azariadis, Costas, and Amartya Lahiri (2002), "Do Rich Countries Choose Better Governments?." *Contributions to Macroeconomics* 2(1), Article 4.

Balassa, Bela (1978), "Exports and Economic GrowthFurther Evidence.", *Journal of Development Economics* 5.

Barro, Robert J. (2000a), "International Data on Educational Attainment: Updates and Implications." CID Working Paper 42, Harvard University, Cambridge, Mass.

Barro, Robert J. (2000b), "International Measures of Schooling Years and Schooling Quality." *American Economic Review* 86: 218–23.

Barro, Robert J, and Jong-Wha Lee. (1994), "Panel Data Set Cross Countries." Data Diskette.

Bellin, Eva. (2001), "The Politics of Profit in Tunisia: Utility of the Rentier Paradigm ?." *World Development* 22(3): 427-36.

Berg, Andrew, and Ann Krueger (2003), "Trade, Growth, and Poverty–A Selective Survey." IMF Working Paper 03/30, Washington, D.C.

Bisat, Amer, Mohamed A. El-Erian, Mahmoud El-Gamal, and Francesco P. Mongelli. (1996), "Investment and Growth in the Middle East and North Africa." IMF Working Paper WP/96/124.

Blejer, Mario, and Mohsin Kahn (1984), "Government Policy and Private Investment in Developing Counties." IMF Staff Papers 31(2): 79-403, Washington, D.C.

Bresnahan, Timothy, F. Erik Brynjolfsson, and Lorin M. Hitt (2002), "Information, Technology, Workplace Organization and the Demand of Skilled Labor: Firm-Level Evidence." *Quarterly Journal of Economics* 117 (1): 339-76.

Brunetti, Aymo, and Beatrice Weder (1994), "Political Credibility and Economic Growth in Less Developed Countries." *Constitutional Political Economy* 5(1): 23-43.

Caballero, Ricardo, and Arvind Krishnamurthy (2001), "A Dual Liquidity Model for Emerging Markets.", NBER Working paper 8758, National Bureau of Economic Research, Cambridge, Massachusetts.

Calderon, Cesar, and Alberto Chong (2000), "Causality and Feedback between Institutional Measures and Economic Growth." *Economic and Politics* 12(1): 69-81.

De Haan, Jakob, and Clemens L. J.Siermann (1996), "New Evidence from Historical Accounts and Contemporary Data." *Land Economics* 75 (3): 341-59.

Djankov, Simon, Rafael La Porta, Florencio Lopez-de-Silanes, and Andrei Sheifer (2001), "The Regulation of Entry." CEPR Discussion Paper No.2 953, (September).

Easterly, William, and Ross Levine (2003), "Tropics, Germs, and Crops: How Endowments Affect Economic Development." *Journal of Monetary Economics* 50 (January): 3-39.

El Badawi, Ibrahim, A. (2002), "Reviving Growth in the Arab World." Working Paper Series 0206, Arab Planing Institute, Safat, Kuwait.

Engelman, S., and K. Sokoloff (2002), "Factor Endowments, Inequality, and Paths of Development among New World Economies." *Economia* 3(1): 41–109.

Evans, Peter, and James Rauch (2000), "Bureaucratic Structure and Bureaucratic Performance in the Less Developed Countries." *Journal of Public Economics* 75 (1): 49-71.

Everhart, Stephen, and Mariuzs Sumlinski (2001), "Trends in Private Investment in Developing Countries, Statistics for 1970–2000, and the Impact on Private Investment of Corruption and the Quality of Public Investment," IFC Discussion Paper 44, Washington, D.C.

Feder, G. (1982), "On Exports and Economic Growth," *Journal of Development Economics* 12(1/2).

Frankel, Jeffrey (2002), "Promoting Better National Institutions: The Role of the IMF." Paper presented at the Third Annual IMF Research Conference, Washington, November 7-8.

Frankel, J.A., and D. Romer (1999), "Does Trade Cause Growth." *The American Economic Review* Vol. 89, No. 3.

Fraser Institute, *Economic Freedom in the World,* Vancouver, Canada.

Freedom House (2002), Freedom in the World 2001–2002. Available online at http://www.freedomhouse.org. Accessed 2003.

Galor, Oded, Omer Moav, and Dietrich Vollrath (2005), "Land Inequality and the Emergence of Human Capital Promoting Institutions." *Development and Comp Systems*, 0502018, Economic Working Paper Archive at WUSTL.

Gylfason, T. (2001), "Natural Resources, Education, and Economic Development." *European Economic Review* 45 (May): 847-859.

Glaeser, Edward L., Rafael La Porta, Florencio Lopez-de-Silanes, and Andrei Shleifer (2004), "Do Institutions Cause Growth?." NBER Working Paper #10568.

Greene, Joshua, and Delano Vilanueva (1991), "Private Investment in Developing Countries." IMF Staff Papers 38 (March): 33-58.

Gupta, Sandeev, Hamid Davooli and Rosa Alonso-Terme (2002), "Does Corruption Affect Income Inequality and Poverty." *Economics of Governance* 3(1): 23-45.

Hall, Robert and Charles Jones (1999), "Why Do Some Countries Produces So Much More Output per Workers that Others?." *Quarterly Journal of Economics* 114 (February): 83-116.

Heritage Foundation (2003), Index of Economic Freedom: The Wall Street Journal. http://www.heritage.org/ research/ features/index (accessed December 2004).

ICRG. (1999), *Brief Guide to the Rating System.* International Country Risk Guide, Political Link Service Group, New York.

International Finance Statistics Database (*IFS*). the International Monetary Fund, Washington, D.C.

International Monetary Fund (2003), World Economic Outlook. *Growth, and Institutions*. World Economic and Financial Surveys, Washington, D.C.

Isham, J., Woolcock, M., Pritchett L, and Busby, G. (2002), "The Varieties of Rentier Experience: How Natural Resource Export Structures Affect the Political Economy of Economic Growth.".

Islam, Roumeen, and Claudio Montenegro (2002), "What Determines the Quality of Institutions." *World Bank Policy Research Working Paper No. 2764* (January), The World Bank, Washington , D.C.

Jorgenson, Dale W. (1963), "Capital Theory and Investment Behavior." *American Economic Review* 53(2, May): 247-259.

Kaufmann, Dani, Aart Kraay, and Maximo Mastruzzi (2003), "Governance Matters III, Governance Indicators for 1996–2002." World Bank, Washington, D.C. Processed.

Keefer, Philip (2002), "The Political Economy of Corruption in Indonesia." World Bank, Washington D.C., Processed.

Keefer, Philip, Thorsten Beck, George Clarke, Alberto Groff, and Patrick Walsh (2001), "New Tools in Comparative Political Economy: The Database of Political Institutions." *World Bank Economic Review* 15(1), 165-176.

Knack, Stephen, and Philip Keefer (1995), "Institutions and Economic Performance: Cross Country Tests Using Alternative Institutional Measures." *Economics and Politics* 7(3): 207–27.

Le, Quan V. (2004), "Political and Economic Determinants of Private Investment." *Journal of International Development* 16: 289-604.

Levine, Renelt (1997), "Financial Development and Economic Growth: Views and Agenda." *Journal of Economic Literature* 35: 688-726.

Life Data Base (*LDB*), The World Bank, Washington, D.C.

Lipset, Seymour Martin (1959), "Some Social Requisites of Democracy: Economic Development and Political Legitimacy." *American Political Science Review* 53: 69–105.

Lucas, Robert (1988), "On the Mechanics of Development." *Journal of Monetary Economics* 22(1):1-175.

Mankiw, Gregory, David Romer and David Weil (1992), "A Contribution to the Empirics of Economic Growth." *Quarterly Journal of Economics* 106: 407-37.

Mauro, Paolo. (1995), "Corruption and Growth." *Quarterly Journal of Economics* 110: 681–712.

McKinnon, Ronald I. (1973), *Money and Capital in Economic Development*, Washington, DC: Brookings Institution.

Mo, Park Hūng (2001), "Corruption and Economic Growth." *Journal of Comparative Economics* 29(1): 66-79.

Nabli, Mustapha. and Marie-Ange Véganzonès-Varoudakis (2007), "Reforms and Growth in the MENA Countries: New empirical evidences", *Journal of International Development* 19: 17-54.

Nagaraj, Ratapolu, Aristomène. Varoudakis, and Marie-Ange Véganzonès (2000), "Long-Run Growth Trends and Convergence Across Indian States: The Role of Infrastructures." *Journal of International Development* 12 (1): 45-70.

North, Douglas C. (1981), *Structure and Change in Economic History*. New York: W. W. Norton.

North, Douglas C. (1990), *Institutions, Institutional Change, and Economic Performance*. Cambridge, U.K.: Cambridge University Press.

Political Risk Services (2001), *International Country Risk Guide,* New York: PRS Group. http://www.prsgroup.com (accessed December 2004).

Olson, Mancur, Naveen Sarna, and Anand V. Swamy (2000), "Governance and Growth: A Simple Hypothesis Explaining Cross-Country Differences in Productivity Growth." *Public Choice* 102(3-4), 341 -364.

Pastor, Manuel, and Jae Ho Sung (1995), "Private Investment and Democracy in the Developing World." *Journal of Economic Issues* 29(1): 223-21.

Prszeworski, Adam, and Fernando Limongi (1993), "Political Regimes and Economic Growth.", *Journal of Economic Perspectives* 7: 51–69.

Prszeworski, Adam, Michael Alvarez, Jose Antonio Cheibub, and Fernando Limongi (2000), *Democracy and Development: Political Institutions and Well-Being in the World, 1950–1990.* New York: Cambridge University Press.

Psacharopoulos, George (1988), "Education and Development: A Review." *World Bank Research Observer,* Oxford University Press, 3(1): 99-116.

Rama. Martin (1993), "Empirical Investment Equations in Developing Countries." In *Striving for Growth after Adjustment*, ed. L. Servén and A. Solimano. The World Bank:

Rodriguez, Francisco, and Jeffrey D. Sachs (1999), "Why Do Resource Abundant Economies Grow More Slowly?". *Journal of Economic Growth* 4(3), 277-303.

Rodrik, Dani (1991), "Policy Uncertainty and Private Investment in Developing Countries." *Journal of Development Economics* 36(2): 229-42.

Rodrik, Dani (1999), "Institutions for High-Quality Growth: What They Are and How to Acquire Them." Paper presented at the IMF Conference on Second Generation Reforms, Washington, November 8-9.

Rodrik, Dani, Arvind Subramanian, and Francesco Trebbi (2002), "Institutions Rule: The Primacy of Institutions over Geography and Integration in Economic Development." NBER Working Paper 9305, National Bureau of Economic Research, Cambridge, Massachusetts.

Ross, Michael (2001), "Does Oil Hinder Democracy?". *World Politics* 53: 325–61.

Sachs, Jeffrey (2003), "Institutions Don't Rule: A Refutation of Institutional Fundamentalism." NBER Working Paper. 9490, National Bureau of Economic Research, Cambridge, Massachusetts.

Sachs, Jeffrey, and Andrew Warner (1997), "Natural Resource Abundance and Economic Growth." Center for International Development. Harvard University, Cambridge: Mass. http://www.cid.harvard.edu// ciddata/ ciddata.html (accessed December 2004).

Saleh, Jahangir (2004), "Property Rights Institutions and Investment." The World Bank Policy Research Working Paper Series, 3311, The World Bank, Washington D.C.

Schmidt-Hebbel, Klaus, and Tobias Muller (1992), "Private Investment under Macroeconomic Adjustment in Morocco." In *Reviving Private Investment inDeveloping Countries,* ed. Alay Chhibber, Mansoor Dailami, and Nemat Shafik. Amsterdam: North Holland.

Serven, Luis (1997), "Uncertainty, Instability, and Irreversible Investment: Theory, Evidence, and Lessons for Africa." The World Bank Policy Research Working Paper Series 1722, The World Bank, Washington D.C.

Servén, Luis, and Andrés Solimano (1993), "Private Investment and Macroeconomic Adjustment: A Survey." In *Striving for Growth After Adjustment*, ed. Luis Servén and Andrés Solimano, Washington D.C.: The: World Bank.

Shafik, Nemat (1992), "Modeling Private Investment in Egypt." *Journal of Development Economics* 39 (October): 263-277.

Shaw. E. (1973), *Financial Deepening in Economic Development*, Oxford University Press, New York.

Svensson, Jakob (1998), "Investment, Property Rights and Political Instability: Theory and Evidence." *European Economic Review*, Elsevier, 42(7), 1317-1341.

Tanzi, Vito, and Hamid Davooli (1997), "Corruption, Public Investment, and Growth." IMF Working Papers 97/139, International Monetary Fund, Washington, D.C.

Transparency International (2002), *Global Corruption Report 2003*, Berlin.

Wei, Shang-Jin (2000), "Natural Openness and Good Government." NBER Working Paper 7765, National Bureau of Economic Research, Cambridge, Massachusetts.

World Bank (2002), *World Development Report 2002: Building Institutions for Market*. Oxford University Press, New York.

World Bank (2004), *Better Governance for Development in the Middle East and North Africa: Enhancing Inclusiveness and Accountability*. MENA Development Report. The World Bank, Washington, D.C.

ANNEX 1: LIST OF COUNTRIES WITH HIGH QUALITY DATA (60 COUNTRIES)

Argentina, Bangladesh*, Barbados*, Belize, Benin*, Bolivia*, Brazil*, Bulgaria, Cambodia, Chile*, China*, Colombia*,Comoros, Costa Rica*, Cote d'Ivoire, Croatia, Dominican Rep., Ecuador*, **Egypt Arab Rep.***, El Salvador, Estonia, Ethiopia, Guatemala*, Guinea-Bissau, Guyana, Haiti, Honduras*, India*, Indonesia*, **Iran Islamic Rep.**, Kenya*, Lithuania, Malawi*, Malaysia*, Mauritius*, Mexico, Moldova, **Morocco**, Namibia, Pakistan*, Panama, Papua New Guinea*, Paraguay*, Peru*, Philippines*, Poland*, Romania, Serbia and Montenegro, Seychelles, South Africa*, St. LuciaSt., Vincent and the Grenadines , Thailand*, Trinidad & Tobago*, **Tunisia***, Turkey*, Uruguay*, Uzbekistan, Venezuela*, Yugoslavia (FR).

Due to the lack of corresponding data for some countries, only counties (32 countries) marked with * are included in the final regressions

ANNEX 2: PRINCIPAL COMPONENT ANALYSIS

Table A 2.1
The Public governance Indicator

Component	*Eigenvalue*	*Cumulative R2*
P1	3.94	0.39
P2	1.64	0.56
P3	1.2	0.68
P4	0.91	0.77
P5	0.69	0.84
P6	0.47	0.89
P7	0.43	0.93
P8	0.33	0.96
P9	0.26	0.99
P10	0.13	1

Loadings	*P1*	*P2*	*P3*	*P4*	*P5*	*P6*	*P7*	*P8*	*P9*	*P10*
Corruption	0.25	-0.15	0.61	0.19	0.00	0.53	0.46	0.06	-0.05	0.03
Bureaucracy Quality	0.30	-0.13	0.35	0.51	-0.10	-0.68	-0.13	0.12	-0.10	0.03
Investment profile	0.33	-0.03	-0.43	0.40	0.11	0.02	0.31	-0.63	0.18	-0.08
Law and Order	0.37	-0.31	0.13	-0.12	0.06	0.20	-0.58	-0.05	0.59	-0.05
Political Rights	0.26	0.63	0.08	0.07	0.06	0.09	-0.15	0.11	-0.06	-0.69
Civil Liberties	0.26	0.63	0.04	0.03	0.07	0.08	-0.13	-0.01	0.06	0.71
Government Stability	0.31	-0.20	-0.52	0.24	0.16	0.21	0.01	0.67	-0.16	0.06
Internal Conflicts	0.41	-0.18	-0.03	-0.30	-0.16	0.10	-0.27	-0.31	-0.71	0.03
External Conflicts	0.33	0.07	-0.14	-0.33	-0.73	-0.15	0.34	0.16	0.26	-0.02
Ethnic Tensions	0.31	-0.04	0.08	-0.52	0.61	-0.36	0.34	0.07	0.06	-0.02

GOV = P1*(0.3937/0.7696) + P2*(0.1641/0.7696) + P3*(0.1204/0.7696) + P4*(0.0915/0.7696)

Table A2.2
The Structural Reform Indicator

Component	*Eigenvalue*	*Cumulative R^2*
P1	1.49	0.75
P2	0.59	1
Loadings	P1	P2
Trade Policy	0.71	0.71
Private Credit	071	-0.71
SR = P1		

Table A2.3
The Human Capital Indicator

Component		*Eigenvalue*		*Cumulative R^2*
P1		3.14		0.78
P2		0.38		0.88
P3		0.31		0.96
P4		0.18		1
Loadings	P1	P2	P3	P4
Life Expectancy	0.52	-0.33	0.03	-0.79
H1	0.50	-0.41	0.55	0.53
H2	0.50	-0.05	-0.80	0.32
H3	0.48	0.85	0.23	-0.03
	H = P1			

ANNEX 3: SHORT-TERM COEFFICIENTS OF THE DISAGGREGATED INDICATORS

A.3.1. Direct Effect on Private Investment (1)

Index	*Variables*	*Short-Term Standardized Variables*	*Coefficients Level Variables*
GOV	Corruption	0.49	0.45
	Bureaucracy Quality	0.54	0.52
	Investment Profile*	0.32	0.15
	Law and Order	0.29	0.23
	Political Rights	0.64	0.32
	Civil Liberties	0.63	0.39
	Government Stability	0.14	0.06
	Internal Conflict	0.29	0.11
	External Conflict	0.27	0.12
	Ethnic Tensions	0.22	0.15
SR	Trade Policy	1.40	0.05
	Private Credit	1.40	0.07

Source: Authors' calculations.

Notes: (1) Direct impact is calculated using the estimated coefficient of the aggregated indicators (*GOV* and *SR*, see equation (3), Table (1)), as well as the weights of each principal component in the aggregate indicators, combined with the loading of the initial variables in each principal component (see *Annex* 2).

A.3.2
Indirect Effect on Private Investment (1)

Index	*Variables*	*Short Standardized Variables (a)*	*Term Level Variables (a)*	*Coefficients Level Variables (b)*
H	Life Expectancy	0.06	0.01	0.01
	Primary Education	0.06	0.04	0.09
	Secondary Education	0.06	0.09	0.19
	Tertiary Education	0.06	0.51	1.14

Source: Authors' calculations.

Notes: (1) Indirect impact is calculated using the coefficient of the human capital indicator in the governance equation (column 4, Table 1), multiplied by the coefficient of the governance indicator in the investment equation (column 3, Table 1), in addition to the weights of each principal component in the aggregate indicators, combined with the loading of the initial variables in each principal component (see *Annex* 2).

(a) Coefficient entering the public governance equation (2).

(b) Coefficient entering the private investment equation (1).

SEEKING TO REDRESS THE BALANCE BETWEEN CAPITAL STOCK AND UNEMPLOYMENT: EMPIRICAL EVIDENCE FROM 14 EU COUNTRIES

*Constantinos Alexiou**

Abstract

The spectre of unemployment has been haunting the economies of nearly all countries within the European Union (EU). Despite the vigorous policy measures implemented to tackle the ever so persistent problem, unemployment is still there gathering momentum. In view of the latter, this study attempts to explore the role of two rather neglected variables, capital formation and aggregate demand as potential factors thought to condition employment. Dynamic panel data analysis has been adopted for the econometric investigation, the generated evidence of which suggests that demand-side policies in conjunction with appropriate investment policies should be pursued should a solution to the problem is to be hit upon.

Key words: European unemployment, Panel Data, Capital stock, Aggregate demand.

JEL Classification: B22; E12.

I. INTRODUCTION

Over the last decades reams of academic paper has been used trying to provide useful economic evidence as to how a solution is to be hit upon the ever so pressing problem of unemployment that has crippled the EU economies. While one would expect different economic structures to have affected individual countries differently, in EU the way unemployment has been fluctuating appears to be sharing by nearly all member states. In other words this common experience suggests that the causes and the persistence of high unemployment are related with factors that have influenced all EU countries in a broadly similar manner, rather than in the individual circumstances of each country. Many possible sources of this common problem have been cited and investigated in the literature.[1] Even though a growing body of research focuses on the relationship between capital constraints and unemployment, as well as on the adverse impact the implemented macroeconomic policies in Europe since the late 1970's have had on capital accumulation, it has to be stressed that there still little evidence as to how capital stock affects unemployment.

The main objective of this paper is to empirically examine the relationship between capital stock and unemployment as well as gain expose the appropriate policy mix to surmount the dire

* City Liberal Studies, Affilated Institution of the University of Shefield, Department of Business and Economics, 13 Tsimiski Street Thessaloniki, Greece, *E-mail: c.alexiou@city.academic.gr*

state that the EU economies are experiencing. The rest of the paper proceeds as follows: Section 2 offers a substantive review regarding the channels through which macroeconomic policy might have caused capacity constraints on employment in the EU region. Section 3 empirically tests our hypothesis, while section 4 concludes.

II. A GLANCE AT THE CURRENT MACROECONOMIC FRAMEWORK

Economic policy within the EU has been dominated by the dogmatic implementation of deflationary-type policies thought to stimulate economic growth. Demand-side policies have been regarded as inappropriate, often held culpable for the inflationary pressures that have arisen in a number of economies over the years.

The emerging economic dogma as this is reflected by the respective treaties and regulations put forward over the last fifteen years, has caused the entire region to experience unprecedented fluctuations in economic activity. The new economic orthodoxy adheres to a set of rules and regulation that promote what is perceived as the panacea to the current economic stagnation.

Within this context, the role of the state has been downplayed, assuming a secondary role in the process of stimulating economic activity. It is further suggested, that the key to success lies in the way the market operates i.e. free from any control.

Inflation has been identified as the major culprit for the plight of the EU economies experienced over the last decades. Thereby, restrictive money and credit policies in conjunction with tight fiscal policies have been fostered towards the elimination of inflation. Full employment policies on the other hand, have been sidelined, exacerbating even further the already turbulent labour market. Unemployment has been ascribed to labour market rigidities, which together with poor education, and motivation are preventing the unemployed from getting work on existing capital stock (Layard & Nickell, 1986; Layard & Jackman, 1991)[2]. The implication of the latter is that capital stock is treated as a rather irrelevant variable in neoclassical models[3].

In contrast, an alternative nexus of scholars argue that in all likelihood, deflationary policies have caused industrial capacity to erode imposing a significant constraint on the EU economies to employ their labour force fully. (e.g. Rowthorn, 1995; Smith, 1996; Kitson & Michie, 1996; Arestis & Sawyer, 1998). Arguably, reductions in unemployment call for additional investment in productive capacity. Dwindling investment in manufacturing in many European countries has been a significant factor behind the dramatic rise in European unemployment[4].

Possible Channels

Prior to proceeding to the econometric exploration it is imperative that we identify the potential channels through which restrictive macroeconomic policies have negatively affected productive capacity and unemployment. The prolonged implementation of restrictive macroeconomic policies is likely to have contributed to a productive investment failure in the EU. Lack of investment, in turn, has constrained technological progress and the expansion of demand to the levels required to restore full employment. The cumulative effect of this process has caused capacity problems. As Scott (1992) argues, any type of investment creates new investment opportunities and *visa versa*.

From a Keynesian perspective investment responds to demand and the expectations of the growth of demand.[5] Smith (1996) advances this argument by stating that the current economic situation is one where there is a danger that increasing demand will lead to shortages of capacity and inflationary price increases, while unemployment might still remains high. According to him, the rebuilding of lost capacity is therefore a key requirement for restoring full employment.

Firm's decisions to expand capacity are based to a large extent on their assessment of their expectations of future sales and their perception of risk (Smith, 1996; Driver, 1996). Moreover, formation of expectations depends, to a great extent, on the understanding of government's policy objectives. Such a risk becomes evident in so far as demand may not expand sufficiently to meet the capacity's expansion. Over the last two decades, and especially in the 1990's, expectations are formed predominately through the implementation of deflationary policies across the EU. The restrictive nature of macroeconomic policy has had an adverse effect on aggregate demand, sales and in effect firm's investment decision (see table1 below).

Table 1

Aggregate Demand (Average Growth Rates)

Countries	*1961-66*	*1967-72*	*1973-78*	*1979-84*	*1985-91*	*1992-00*	*2001-05*
Germany	1.5	1.7	1.3	0.9	2.1	1.2	0.9
France	2.6	2.4	2.0	1.8	1.5	1.1	1.2
Italy	2.0	2.1	1.6	1.0	1.2	0.9	0.5
Netherlands	2.9	2.5	1.7	0.6	1.3	1.4	1.6
Belgium	1.8	2.2	1.6	0.9	1.3	1.2	1.6
U.K	1.4	1.3	1.4	1.1	1.8	1.5	1.3
Ireland	1.4	2.1	2.4	1.6	2.0	3.0	3.2
Denmark	1.9	1.9	1.5	2.1	1.6	1.5	1.2
Spain	3.3	2.8	1.5	0.2	1.5	1.1	0.7
Greece	3.1	3.3	1.6	0.7	1.7	1.6	2.1
Portugal	2.9	2.8	1.2	1.0	2.3	1.1	1.2
Sweden	1.8	1.5	1.2	1.2	1.4	1.0	1.3
Finland	1.8	2.4	1.2	2.0	1.2	0.9	0.7
Austria	1.9	2.6	1.6	1.2	1.8	1.1	1.2

Source: OECD, Economic Outlook

Smith (1996) points out that firms need to be confident that demand will grow at such a rate as to validate any expansion of their capacity. Negative experiences and information over the stance of macroeconomic policy and the growth rate of demand make managers to be cautious about the possibility of overestimating future sales, since the penalties associated with such practice tend to be much greater than for losing potential business by failing to expand.

The risk of investing in capacity that will not be fully utilised is related to the possibility of sales' failure and the consequent fall in firm's profit, as well as the ability of firm to absorb it. The latter links the demand with the supply side factors that lie behind the capacity limits on employment. To the extent that the cost of expanding capacity are capital costs, the crucial factors that influence decisions to invest in new capacity are the cost and availability of capital (Rowthorn, 1995; Smith, 1996). The implementation of a restrictive monetary policy to combat inflation has created a bias towards high real interest rates. In addition, the higher interest rates (especially the long-term ones) could be partially attributed to the global, monetary and financial environment that emerged after the collapse of the Bretton Woods. Globalization of financial markets and international financial competition in conjunction with a highly mobile and speculative capital have increased volatility in government bond prices, which in conjunction with exchange rate instability and currency speculation have increased the risk premium on lending. The high interest rates might have inhibited start-up projects and further discouraged investment and business confidence. Interest rate policies since the 1980s have been identified as the main government policy, which has impeded the growth of firms (Kitson & Michie, 1996).

Overall, the restrictive macroeconomic policy is likely to have caused detrimental effects on business demand expectations and their strategies of undertaking new, productive investment. A decreasing rate of growth of productive capacity, in turn, might have constrained new job opportunities in the EU area, contributing to the very high levels of unemployment.

III. ECONOMETRIC INVESTIGATION.

An inspection of the tables provided below illustrate the extent to which the unemployment rate, as well as the growth rate of capital stock have behaved in all EU countries over the period 1961-2005.

Table 2
Unemployment Rate (averages)

	1961-66	*1967-72*	*1973-78*	*1979-84*	*1985-91*	*1992-00*	*2001-05*
Germany	0.7	0.8	3.1	5.5	7.2	9.2	8.8
France	1.6	2.5	4.1	7.6	9.8	10.7	9.5
Italy	3.6	4.1	4.7	6.8	9.6	10.6	9.8
Netherlands	N/A	1.3	3.4	7.3	7.4	6.3	5.6
Belgium	2.1	2.3	4.9	10.7	10.5	12.1	10.3
U.K	1.6	2.5	3.7	8.1	8.5	8.0	7.5
Ireland	4.9	5.4	7.3	10.9	15.9	12.7	6.8
Denmark	1.3	1.6	4.6	8.8	8.9	9.5	8.9
Spain	2.4	3.0	4.4	14.9	18.9	21.4	14.6
Greece	5.2	4.3	1.9	5	7.5	9.6	9.4
Portugal	2	3.9	4.7	7.9	6.3	6.3	5.7
Sweden	1.5	2.2	1.9	2.7	2.2	7.4	7.2
Finland	1.4	2.7	3.9	5.2	4.9	15.1	13.4
Austria	1.9	1.5	1.5	2.7	4.6	5.7	5.8

Source: OECD Economic Outlook

As can be discerned, both variables exhibit inverse patterns. More specifically the unemployment rate has rapidly increased whereas the growth rate of capital stock has severely decreased, most evidently in the 1990's. The observed behaviour of the variables in question could be to a certain extent attributed to the emerging neoliberal economic environment that has pervaded economic policy within the European region.

Table 3

Capital Stock (Manufacturing, Average Growth Rates)

Countries	*1961-66*	*1967-72*	*1973-78*	*1979-84*	*1985-91*	*1992-00*	*2001-05*
Germany	9.2	9.6	4.1	4.9	7.1	3.2	2.3
France	6.1	6.4	5.4	4.3	2.3	2.2	1.8
Italy	8.5	7.4	4.9	3.8	2.5	2.1	1.7
Netherlands	11.7	10.1	9.7	2.9	5.2	2.8	2.0
Belgium	11.4	8.4	12.1	1.8	5.1	2.0	1.4
U.K	3.9	3.8	3.3	3.2	1.7	1.0	0.8
Ireland	14.3	17.8	23.7	11.7	4.3	6.8	6.1
Denmark	8.6	7.8	8.1	6.7	5.3	3.1	2.4
Spain	19.4	13.5	19.9	11.1	15.5	2.4	2.8
Greece	13.9	16.2	18.4	16.9	19.7	10.2	3.5
Portugal	10	13.9	23.6	20.8	19.2	6.0	3.8
Sweden	10.9	6.8	10.1	10.8	12	7.7	4.2
Finland	8.7	9.2	9.5	7.5	6.9	5.8	3.6
Austria	10.7	11.9	6.9	4.7	8.1	4.6	3.3

Source: OECD, Flows and Stock of fixed capital.

The Model

Having previously elaborated on the interaction between capital stock and unemployment, we now formulate our argument through a model which is heavily influenced by the Post Keynesian tradition. We therefore estimate an equation, where the unemployment rate is regressed on three key variables i.e. capital stock, aggregate demand and lagged unemployment. In this context, lagged unemployment purports to capture persistence effects. In addition, in an attempt to investigate this relationship in a more comprehensive way, the inclusion of a dummy variable was deemed necessary. Such a practice will seek to capture the effect of the shift in economic policy-fueled by the emergence of the new orthodoxy and reflected by the a significant historically economic development: the ratification of the Maastricht Treaty- on job creation. The following model therefore provides the platform on which the main hypothesis will be tested.

$$u_{it} = \beta_0 + \beta_1 c_{it-1} + \beta_2 ad_{it} + \beta_3 u_{it-1} + \beta_4 D_t + \varepsilon_t \qquad (1)$$

$$(-) \qquad (-) \qquad (+) \qquad (+)$$

$e_t = NID\,(\varepsilon, \sigma^2)$

Where u_{it} is the unemployment rate, and c_{it} is capital stock, ad_{it} is aggregate demand, u_{it-1} is lagged unemployment and D_t is an additive dummy, t is a time subscript and e is a random term, assumed to satisfy the normal requirements.

For the econometric investigation dynamic panel data analysis has been adopted. The data-set employed consists of N cross-sectional units, denoted $i = 1,\ldots,N$, observed at each of T time periods, denoted $t = 1,\ldots,T$. In this context, annual data for 14 EU countries from 1961 to 2005, *(so $N=14$; $T = 45$)* has been used.

Estimation

In an attempt to model the unemployment rate[6] u_{it}, as a function of capital stock c_{it} aggregate demand ad_{it}, u_{it-1} lagged unemployment and the dummy variable D_t, several specifications of equation (1) following a general to specific approach, were estimated.

Prior to estimating the model, a very succinct discussion of the procedure featured in this empirical part will take place. According to Hsiao (1986) and Baltagi (1995) econometric estimates are more efficient when pooling the observations across countries. It has also been sustained that pooling has the advantage of providing more accurate understanding in the adjustment mechanism between dynamic relationships. As it is indicated below the fixed effects model is preferred to the heterogeneous ones. A series of unit root tests were conducted to check for stationarity, and therefore ensure that panel data estimation techniques can be used appropriately. Even though the standard Dickey-Fuller, Augmented (DF) and Phillips-Perron tests are some of the tests that can be used to check for stationarity, we opted for a panel unit roots test proposed by Maddala and Wu (1999)[7]:

$$\zeta = -2\sum_{i=1}^{N} \ln \pi_i \sim \chi^2(2N),$$

where π_i is the p-value of the ADF unit root test for the *i*th country. A quick inspection of the results presented in table 4 suggest that we can proceed with panel data estimation[8] (see table 6 in appendix).

The selection process between pooled models and individual regressions employed, is in line with the one proposed by Smith (2000). More specifically, the Schwarz Information Criterion (SIC) is envisaged to provide the most appropriate model.

$$SIC^{pooled} = MLL^{pooled} - 0.5k^{pooled}\log(NT)$$

$$SIC^{ind.} = \sum_{i=1}^{14} MLL_i - N[0.5k_i \log(T)]$$

where MLL^{pooled} and MLL_i stand for the maximum log likelihood of the pooled and the individual regressions respectively; k^{pooled} denotes the number of parameters estimated in the fixed effects model whereas k_i is the number of parameters estimated in the individual regressions; N stands for the number of countries and T is the time period. The preceding selection process rendered the fixed effects model more preferable[9].

The resulting homogeneous dynamic model generated the following estimates:

$$u_{it} = -0.12\, c_{it-1} - 1.17 ad_{it} + 0.83 u_{it-1} + 2.97\, D_t$$
$$(0.03) \qquad (0.31) \qquad (0.26) \qquad (0.39)$$

(standard errors in parentheses).

$R^2 = 0.96$

On the basis of the results obtained it can be argued the negative and statistically significant coefficient[10] of c_{it-1} suggests that an increase in capital formation will cause the unemployment rate to go down. Bearing in mind that the undertaken investigation concerns capital stock in the manufacturing sector, it could be argued that an increase in capital stock in all sectors will provide an additional stimuli in employment creation. In addition, the negative and statistically significant coefficient of ad_{it} reinforces our argument according to which policies tailored to boost the components of aggregate demand will play an instrumental role in alleviating the persisting problem of unemployment. Moreover, the coefficient on unemployment persistence is statistically significant suggesting that there is strong persistence rather than full hysteresis. As for the dummy variable, it fully reflects the adverse effects that the emergence of the new policy consensus within the EU area–as reflected by both the emergence of neo-liberalism and the deflationary bias of the Maastricht rules-has had on European employment.

IV. CONCLUSIONS

The empirical findings do suggest that a potential factor behind European unemployment is insufficient growth of capital stock. Therefore measures to stimulate productive investment could play an important role in helping to reduce unemployment.

Achieving economic conditions that promote full employment requires an investment strategy that will enable Europe to increase the quality and quantity in terms of both equipment and structure. Training as such can be perceived as being an important tool to enhance industrial performance, however, giving the unemployed skills when they do not have many opportunities to use them is ineffectual.

It has been envisaged that the adoption of demand side policies is conducive to stimulating investment growth in EU. Nonetheless, for such a prospect to be realised, it is necessary that changes in the current, neo-liberal macroeconomic structure take place. This means that macroeconomic policy should aim to ensure a continuous expansion of demand matched, via more productive investment, by increased employment and output rather than by inflation.

Notes

1. For an extensive survey of this literature see Bean (1994).
2. Rowthorn (1995) maintains that this aspect to the unemployment problem has been neglected in the enthusiasm for labour-market issues. The capacity problem is rejected by neo-liberal economists, who regard the problem of job creation as being mainly a matter of encouraging more employment on existing capital stock and not to increase the amount of this stock.
3. Any policy choice is reduced to recommendations for more flexibility in the labour market, wage austerity and lower social standards as means to reduce the cost of labour (CEPR, 1995).
4. For more on this, see for example, Malinvaud, (1985); Bean, (1989), (1994); Rowthorn, (1995), (1999); Smith, (1996), Alexiou & Pitelis, (2003).
5. The important relationship between investment and demand is overlooked in many recent discussions of economic growth, which ignore demand constraints on the level of economic activity. Investment can increase, as well as respond to, the level of demand, affecting the scale of production as well as its structure, organisation and technological efficiency (see Scott, 1992).
6. Whether unemployment rates contain a unit root is subject to extensive debate in economic studies.

7. This test is a nonparametric test based on Fisher (1932).
8. Is has to be noted that in order to see whether it is appropriate to engage in pool data analysis, a selection process based on the Schwarz Information criteria (*SIC*) proposed by Smith (2000) was conducted.
9. The model selection is based on the maximum value of the *SIC*. SIC^{pooled} = 732.23, SIC^{ind}. = 700.56.
10. By taking capital stock lagged once, we want to emphasize the inherent dynamic relationship between the two variables.

References

Alexiou, C. & Pitelis, C. (2003), On Capital Constraints and European Unemployment: A Panel Data Investigation, *Journal of Post Keynesian Economics*, 25(4), pp. 611-638.

Arestis, P. & Sawyer, M. (1998), Keynesian Economic Policies for the New Millennium, *The Economic Journal*, 108, January, pp. 181-195.

Baltagi, B.H. (1995), *Econometric Analysis of Panel Data*, New York, Wiley.

Bean, C.R. (1989), Capital Shortages and Persistent Unemployment, *Economic Policy*, 8, April, pp. 11-53.

Bean, C.R. (1994), European Unemployment: A Survey, *Journal of Economic Literature*, vol. XXXII, June, pp. 573-619.

CEPR (1995), *Unemployment: Choices for Europe*, (Monitoring European Integration).

Driver, C. (1996), Tightening the Reins: The Capacity Stance of UK Manufacturing.

Firms 1976-1995, in J. Michie & J. Smith (eds.), *Creating Industrial Capacity* (Oxford, Oxford University Press)

Fisher, R. (1932), *Statistical Methods for Research Workers,* Edinburgh: Oliver and Boyd.

Hsiao, C. (1986), *Analysis of Panel Data*, Cambridge: Cambridge University Press.

Kitson, M & Michie, J. (1996), Manufacturing Capacity, Investment and Employment in Michie, J. & Smith, G. J. (eds.) *Creating Industrial Capacity* (Oxford, Oxford University Press).

Layard, R. & Nickell, S. (1986), Unemployment in Britain, *Economica*, 53(S), pp. 121-70.

Layard, R. & Jackman, R. (1991), *Unemployment* (Oxford, Oxford University Press).

Maddala, G. and Wu, S. (1999), "A Comparative Study of Unit Root Tests with Panel Data and a New Simple Test", *Oxford Bulleting of Economics and Statistics,* special issue, pp. 631-652.

Malinvaud, E. (1985), *The Theory of Unemployment Reconsidered* (Oxford, Blackwell).

Rowthorn, R. (1995), Capital formation and unemployment. *Oxford Review of Economic Policy*, vol. 11, no. 1, pp. 26-39.

Rowthorn, R. (1999), Unemployment, Wage Bargaining and Capital-labour Substitution, *Cambridge Journal of Economics*, 23, pp. 413-425.

Scott, M. (1992), Policy Implications of a New View of Economic Growth, *The Economic Journal*, 102, pp. 622-632.

Smith, G. J. (1996), Rebuilding Industrial Capacity in J. Michie & J. Smith (eds.) *Creating Industrial Capacity* (Oxford, Oxford University Press).

Smith, R. (2000), Estimation and Inference with Non-stationary Panel Time-series Data, *mimeo.*

APPENDIX

Table 4
Definitions of Variables

u_{it}	Unemployment rate, OECD, Economic Outlook.
c_{it}	Growth rate of capital stock (manufacturing), OECD Flows and Stock of Fixed Capital.
ad_{it}	Growth rate of aggregate demand, OECD, Economic Outlook.
D_t	Dummy Variable. Takes 0 for 1961 to 1991 and 1 for 1992 to 2005 (captures the effect of Maastricht Treaty).

Table 5
Panel Unit Root Tests

$\zeta(u_{it}) = 52.33$	$\zeta(ad_{it}) = 49.55$	$\zeta(c_{it}) = 48.37$

Note: The undertaken test draws on the one coined by Maddala and Wu (1999). 5% is the significance level.

DUALISTIC ECONOMIC STRUCTURE AND UNEMPLOYMENT IN CHINA

Kishore G. Kulkarni and Weijia Huang***

Abstract

China's red-hot economic development in the past three decades can not cover its serious unemployment problem in both urban and rural areas. Poor rural labor surplus keeps flooding into cities to join the employment competition with more than 20 million unemployed urbanite already in the unemployment cadre. Such process compels municipal governments to establish barriers and reinforces the segmentation of rural and urban labor markets. Immediate and effective solutions to unemployment should be taken to facilitate the transformation of Chinese economy from a dualistic one to a unitary one.

Key words: *unemployment, China, dualistic economy, rural and urban laborers*

INTRODUCTION: THE REALITY OF UNEMPLOYMENT IN CHINA

Initiating its far-reaching opening and economic reform from 1978 and achieving an average GDP growth of 9% per year, China's booming economy seems to have painted a spectacular future for the largest population of the world. It is true that reforms in agriculture, urban housing, taxation, medical care and state-owned enterprise have created numerous jobs and considerably enhanced people's living standard. However, the scenery behind the rosy picture is not so stimulating. According to the statistics from World Bank, China's labor force accounts for 26% of the total labor population in the world, while the proportions of China's natural resource and capital resource are less than 10%. Because of the complexity of China's economy structure, during the transition from a central-planning economy system towards a market-oriented one, the demand of various job seekers in both urban and rural areas of China significantly outstrips the supply of new employment opportunities. At the same time, many job openings can not find enough qualified candidates to match them. Severe unemployment situation, both in the rural and urban areas, has reinforced the segmentation between China's urban and rural labor markets and such ingrained division in turn impedes the free flow of labor force from agriculture sector into industrial sector.

On one hand, municipal governments have already faced complicated urban unemployment problems. On the other hand, driven by prospects of higher pay and better life quality in cities, rural surplus laborers continuously flood into urban areas. In the long run, it would become more and more difficult for China's current dualistic economy to transform into a healthy unitary

* Professor of Economics, CB 77, P.O. Box 173362, Metropolitan State College of Denver, Denver.

** Graduate School of International Studies, Gaylord Street, University of Denver, Denver.

one. Therefore, strong and effective measures should be taken to tackle the unemployment problem in both sectors of Chinese economy.

Generally speaking, the unemployment rate is defined as the percentage of unemployed workers to the total labor force. However, the inaccuracy of statistical data tends to heavily underestimate the unemployment problem in China. According to the Ministry of Labor and Social Security of China, during the recent 6 years, the official unemployment rate has risen from 3.1% in 2000 to 4.2% in 2005[2]. Actually, considering the calculation terms and method, these official statistics can be misleading and this data can only be labeled as official urban registered unemployment rate, which is based on local governments' monthly or annual report of labor rather than on scientific surveys. Unemployment populations in several important sectors are omitted. First, and the most important, the great number of laid-off unemployed workers who are receiving minimal living benefits from state-owned enterprises (SOEs) and collectively-owned enterprise (COEs) is not counted.

Second, these data only covered the unemployed who were 16-45 female and 16-50 male and those who had officially registered at local administrative agencies in urban China; and third, the official data also exclude the 150 million rural surplus workers, who are just holding temporary or seasonal jobs or still looking for employment in cities. According to several scholars' estimation and inner governmental data, the real urban unemployment rate in China has exceeded 10%[3].

Serious and complex unemployment is a universal problem in less developed countries (LDCs). However, unlike periodical unemployment in developed countries, which is generated by the lack of aggregate demand, manifested by periodical economic crisis, and can be successfully solved through the expected recovery of economy, unemployment in LDCs has more structural reasons and can not be simply alleviated by rapid economic growth. In the case of China, a striking growth of GDP seems to be incapable of promoting employment. For example in 2003, although its economic growth rate reached a 10%, facing a 240 million of new labor supply, China was only able to satisfy the employment need for 80 million people.

The main purpose of this paper is to analyze the interaction between China's unemployment situation and dualistic economy structure in rural and urban areas, primarily using Lewis Model of dualistic economy. It also defines the types of unemployment in China, presents relative data, and identifies the specific reasons to each one. In the final part, this paper brings out several policy suggestions to tackle the unemployment problem.

SECTION 2: LEWIS MODEL OF DUALISTIC ECONOMY AND LABOR MARKET SEGMENTATION IN CHINA

1. What are the Main Arguments of Lewis Model of Economic Development?

In 1954, American Economist Arthur Lewis (Princeton University, and Nobel prize Winner in Economics) published his famous paper "Economic Development with Unlimited Supplies of Labor" and brought about the model of dualistic structure economy. Lewis claims that there are two distinct economic sectors in a typical developing country, the traditional or agricultural sector and the modern or industrial sector. The former is characterized by abundant labor force, low labor productivity, subsistence level wage rate, slow growth of output and great dependency on natural conditions. The latter one is characterized by advanced technology, fast growth, the positive marginal product of labor and above subsistence level wage rate. In this model, there are serious hidden unemployment and underemployment as in the majority of developing countries. It would be beneficial for the available labor force to join high capital labor ratio industries. Economic development results from structural changes and the expansion of the industrial sector, which entails a continuous influx of labor force from the agriculture sector.

There are several important assumptions in Lewis Model that we should clarify before further explanation is given. The agriculture sector mainly uses labor and land as production factors, while industrial sector uses labor and capital; There is apparent labor surplus in agriculture sector, which provides unlimited labor force for the growing industrial sector. Differences in wage rate is the major reason for labor migration. Increment in total product would be reinvested by industrialists for future industrial expansion.

For economic development to happen, the higher wage rate in industrial sectors keeps attracting surplus labor force from the traditional sector without affecting the total product output in it. Then positive marginal product of labor in manufacturing sector increases the total industrial product and brings more profit to industrialists. Industrialists reinvest in their factories and provide more employment opportunities, which continue absorbing the redundant labor force in agriculture sector. This cyclical process will keep going until surplus labor force in agriculture has been fully transferred to the industrial sectors and marginal product of labor, wage rate in both sectors have reached the same level. In the long run, the proportions of savings, profit and capital accumulation in gross domestic product will all go up. Finally, such a dualistic structure in economy will disappear. Based on the observation of history, Lewis Model can be empirically verified. If deep structural economic reform and a health economic growth are desirable, the free flow of labor force between rural and urban labor market should never be harnessed and the creation and allocation of employment opportunities would never be over-emphasized.

2. Formation and Current Situation of China's Dualistic Economy

With a more than 75% rural population and distinctions in the production and lifestyle between the traditional sector and modern sector, Chinese economy is a typical dualistic one. In the rural area, where labor is the primary factor of production, people make a living by participating agricultural or handcraft work and sometimes sell their product in the markets of cities and towns, receiving a miserable and unstable income. In the urban area, where industrial infrastructures have been fully developed during the past 50 years and capital is more available, workers in factories and employees in companies enjoy a much higher wage rate as well as necessary welfare and benefits provided by their employers and the government.

Tracing back contemporary Chinese history, the formation process of China's dualistic economy can be owed to the adoption of Soviet Union Model and heavy industry–oriented development strategy, which was pursued vigorously during the central planning period. After the foundation of PRC in the 1950s, besieged by domestic socioeconomic turmoil and isolation by western powers, the central government identified urgent needs to establish a reliable and complete modern industry to ensure the solidity of a newly-born regime. Yet at the beginning of industrialization process in China, the proportion of industrial output in GDP was so low and the industrial product categories were so limited that it was impossible to accumulate enough capital for further development by solely depending on industrial production itself. Therefore, the dominant traditional agriculture of China became the main source to accumulate capital for generating the industrial sector. Considering there were no existent means to transfer the capital through market-embedded channel, the procurement of capital could only be realized by implementing a biased transfer policy. Such policies include restricting and cutting down the prices of agriculture product, limiting rural residents consumption with subsistence level of wage rate, and taking advantage of the huge scissors gap between industrial and agriculture products. According to National Bureau of Statistics (NBS), from 1953 to 1978, the government received 510 billion Chinese yuan (about 63.75 billion dollars) from the scissors gap between prices of industrial and agriculture products[4]. China governments high-intervening development mode has succeeded in establishing its basic industrial system within a surprising short time. What was to blame is government's unawareness to shift its strategic focus to other economic sectors after the establishment of industrial sector. Under this circumstance, the agriculture sector was so heavily deprived of that the formation of two separate economy sectors was inevitable.

Based on economic development analysis of the world, there are mainly three ways for the transformation of dualistic economy into a unitary one. The first one is called the natural industrial growth mode, which was implemented by the US and Britain. In their cases, along with continuous economic growth, dualistic economy would automatically and eventually disappear. The second way is through input of large amount of foreign capital into the productive industrial sector. Development policies concentrated on the growth of the modern sector, while leaving the rural area still undeveloped. This mode is also illustrated in Brazil. The last way is intensifying government's intervention in economic development. In which case agriculture and manufacturing, urban and rural sectors appear to be two completely separate domains. First traditional sector is heavily deprived of, and then it is saved by a mature and productive modern sector. China fits into this model well[5].

3. The Segmentation of China's Urban and Rural Labor Markets

Above analysis informs us that for the elimination of dualistic economy structure in LDCs, the influx of labor force from agriculture sector into industrial sector is a crucial and necessary historical phase. Yet there exists evident segmentation between China's urban and rural labor markets, which have markedly impeded the flow of rural labor into the urban economic sectors. Although rural and urban sectors are forcefully connected by the potential gains from trade between them, the two labor markets are still treated as separate entities. The division between state and non-state ownership sectors, social security (including medical coverage, pensions and unemployment insurance), and related topics such as housing, education, and other social services all differ drastically between China's rural and urban economies.

Motivated by income and welfare incentives, many redundant rural laborers began to flood into urban area. However, facing the heavy burden of existing urban unemployment, municipal government laid out a series of restrictive policies to reinforce the barrier between rural and labor markets. Some characteristic policies include imposition of various taxes and fees on migrant laborers, implementation of enormous discrimination employment policies in urban area and strict administration of urban household registration system. Details of each means are given below.

Arbitrary enhancement of labor cost by local government. Financial deprivations have always been viewed as most instrumental measure to check the migrant labor flood. Many fast developing cities of China have formulated regulations and policies to charge directly rural labor or indirectly their employers different items of fee and tax, such as fee for the issuance of employment license, temporary residence fee in cities, mandatory physical check-up fee and migrant population birth control fee. For instance, a survey conducted by economic research center in Beijing University in late 1990s found that, enterprises in Shanghai are requested to pay the government, for each rural worker they hire an annual miscellaneous fee amounted to 890 yuan, equal to 20% of a worker's annual wage. What is even worse is some municipal authorities manipulate these policies to extract migrant workers' income[6]. So many enforcements deteriorate the life quality of migrant laborers and greatly enhance the employment cost for urban employers.

Government has also implemented discriminatory employment policies to exclude migrant workers from certain professions in urban sectors. In some cases occupational stratification has been institutionalized. On one hand, some municipal governments have implemented regulations to protect urban residents by reserving specific job categories for them and make sure they are not underpaid compared to outsiders. This is especially true for employment opportunities in those profitable monopolistic professions such as power supply and telecommunication, where urbanite enjoy preemptive rights to get hired. For instance, in late 1990s, the labor bureau of one of Beijing's district stipulated that 35 types of jobs should not be opened to migrant workers[7] On the other hand, the range of employment opportunities for rural labor has been restricted to positions featured by "four most undesirable" (most tiresome, most dirty, most dangerous and most humble) for urban citizens. And usually, migrant workers receive a much lower wage compared to urban workers holding similar jobs.

Implemented as a traditional basis of social system since ancient China, strict regulation of household registration also plays a vital part in the segmentation of labor markets. In the central-planning economic period, even for visiting urban relatives, peasants should apply for permission letters from the administration office in their villages, let along for job-hunting in the cities. Nowadays, a more market oriented economy still has inherited such a powerful regulatory means. Without an urban household registration, migrant workers would encounter numerous unexpected difficulties in their urban life. Such examples are getting into qualified primary or middle schools for their children, or receiving adequate medical benefits from employers and government. As a result, rural and urban labor forces are actually participating in a gravely unfair competition for limited jobs.

All in all, the governmental actions to control the flow of rural labor are generated by a purpose to allocate more jobs for urban workers and give priority to solve urban unemployment problems. Thus, to clarify the scenario behind such a severe segmentation between rural and urban labor markets, analysis should be made in both terms of the rural labor supply and demand of labor in urban sector. Not only rural unemployment but also urban unemployment have contributed to the perplex problem. The following section will concentrate on the issues of unemployment in both traditional and modern sectors, and further identify the reasons of each type of unemployment within China's transformational economy structures.

III. ANALYSIS AND CLASSIFICATION OF UNEMPLOYMENT IN RURAL AND URBAN CHINA

With a huge population base, the annual increment of new laborers (those who become legally old enough to be counted into labor force) in recent China is estimated to be 9 million, almost equal to the population of a medium-size European country. Also considering 11 million laid-off workers and 150 million redundant rural laborers, China is experiencing unprecedented heavy unemployment pressure.

Four Types of Urban Unemployment of Contemporary China

(1) Systematic Unemployment:

Laid-off workers from State-owned Enterprises (SOEs)

One of the main causes of unemployment in China today stems from the restructuring of SOEs. Before the reform, state ownership was dominant in the modern sector. These relics of the planning economic system once promised cradle-to-grave job security for their employees, and enjoyed massive state funding and support. China used to be proud of its low urban unemployment rate in the former central-planning economy, when employment was wholly arranged by the administrative dictation from government and operational aim of all-level enterprises was the maximizations of employment and output. In this sense, by sacrificing business profits, enterprises (mainly the SOEs) undertook the responsibility of allocating employment which was supposed to be adjusted by a market system, Consequently, redundancy and saturation of employment in SOEs brought vital drawbacks such as debt burdens, corruption, out dated production and most seriously, large amount of hidden unemployment into Chinese economy. Since China's strategic introduction of market economic mechanism, SOEs' vulnerability in fierce market competition became more apparent. The transformation of operational aim to profit maximization entails previous hidden unemployment inside SOEs to change into open unemployment. Thus, trimming excess staff stood out to be the first step for SOEs to establish modern management system and prepare for competition with private enterprises, joint ventures and foreign-funded companies in a globalized market. From 1998 to the end of 2002, the accumulative statistical number of laid-off workers is 26 million, many of whom are women workers, workers older than 45 and those with limited skills.

For example, China's two largest oil producers, PetroChina, has cut about 63,000 jobs since 2000. China Petroleum has also cut 22% of its workforce[8]. These people have lost not only their so called "iron-bowl" (food and clothes expenses source) but also social security benefits all together. Although re-employment assistance centers were founded (but later removed in 2004) in the majority of SOEs to help laid-off workers seek new employment, only a small minority have received substantial help (e.g in-time training for new skills) from re-employment institutions. Although massive amounts of state funding has been allocated to SOEs to slow the process of laid-off restructuring and to alleviate the hardship of laid-off workers' life conditions, pervasive corruptions in management led to the rare materialization of retrenchment compensations for laid-off labor. The re-employment rate among laid-off labor has not exceeded 50% in recent ten years.

Structural Unemployment due to industrial updating and global competition

Structural unemployment is defined as the mismatch between job requirement and skills or availability of labor force. Frequent adjustment in industrial structure, which includes continuous emergence of new industries and the washout of old industries, always accompanies rapid economic growth. For contemporary China, especially after its entry into WTO, such extensive adjustment has aggravated unemployment. The phenomena "lack of jobs for many people" and "lack of people for many positions" coexist in some professions. First, China's traditional resource-consuming production mode has resulted in the unduly exhaustion of many natural resources.

For example, among China's 426 mineral-based cities, more than 50 have been fully utilized by 2000. Some munitions factories and old industrial bases also went bankruptcy because of inadequate supply of raw materials and isolated location. Secondly, demand of domestic competent professionals is very urgent in some brand new industries such as international trade, finance and banking, biological engineering and informational technology, where job openings are usually occupied by imported qualified talents from abroad. Last but not the least, operating on the principle of fair competition, a WTO membership has forced China to face the reality of international specialization of labor. Those industries which do not have comparative advantage over foreign competitors, such as automobile and software industries, have encountered most significant impact from the shrinkage of their market share and short of innovation impetus. Employment in these industries has reduced.

Frictional Unemployment (especially common in young job-waiters)

This type of unemployment is always present in an economy, resulting from temporary transitions between jobs, professions and locations made by workers and employers or from workers and employers having inconsistent or incomplete information. Currently, the most severe and complicated frictional unemployment happens among fresh college graduates. Since the reform of high education system in 1999, dramatic enlargement of public colleges' enrollment (almost with an annual increment of 0.7 million) and proliferation of private colleges have made college education much more available. Nevertheless, limited qualified faculty, outmoded infrastructure and obsolete curriculum have not secured the competency of college graduates in their future careers. On one hand, high college tuition and traditional self-esteem idea as social pillars among college students increase graduates' expectation of future jobs (e.g in propensity of location, salary, social status, welfare). On the other hand, the absence of career planning instructions results in graduates' inefficiency of job hunting and unrealistic self-position. Requirement of previous work experience from employers and lack of position mobility inside some enterprises have also contributed to the employment trap for college graduates. For instance, this year 4.13 million college and university graduates from flooded into employment, yet by this July, only 49% of them have registered as employed. According to the statistics from Ministry of Education, the unemployment rate among 2005 college graduates has reached 30%, 7% higher than that of 2003. Together with veteran youth and other youth lower-diploma holders, currently there are 3 million unemployed youth in urban China, constituting 23% of a 13 million urban unemployment population.

Voluntary Unemployment related to the above three types of unemployment

This category of unemployment consists three parts: laid-off workers who hold a traditional central distribution view about employment and passively wait for jobs regulated by government or their former "work unit"; workers in less competitive industries who are unwilling to acquire new skills for future employment; recent college graduates and other migrating labor who would rather stay idle than to work in rural areas, at a so-called disgracing social status, or with a much lower salary rate compared to their expectations.

Following is the recent calculation and estimation of urban unemployment rate (1995-2002)[9]

Population (million) Rate(percent)

Year	*1995*	*1996*	*1997*	*1998*	*1999*	*2000*	*2001*	*2002*
Registered Unemployment (Population/ Rate)	5.20 2.9%	5.53 3.0%	5.77 3.1%	5.75 3.1%	5.95 3.1%	6.30 3.6%	6.81 3.6%	7.70 4.0%
Laid off unemployment Population	3.38	3.56	8.15	8.77	9.37	10.0	11.0	
Migrant workersunemployment population	0.55	0.60	0.88	0.93	1.06	1.00	1.2-1.50	
College and university graduate unemployment	N/A	N/A	N/A	N/A	N/A	0.70	0.80	
Actual unemployment Urban Population	8.01-9.13	9.66	14.73	15.41	16.18	17.65	18.81-19.11	19.00
Actual Unemployment Rate	4.1-4.7%	5.0%	6.2%	7.5-8.5%	7.9-8.9%	9.0%	9.1-9.5%	10.5%

2. Hidden Unemployment in Rural China

Hidden unemployment is defined as phenomenon that workers maintain nominal labor relationship with employers, but actually do not work at all or do not work for enough hours. The fundamental roots for unemployment in rural areas of China, basically hidden unemployment, are the serious lack of arable land, low literacy of rural population, improvement in agriculture technology, poor implementation of birth control policy and the weakness for town and village enterprises (TVEs) to absorb labor force, compared to a large surplus rural labor force. Here we can describe it as "five people plow a piece of land providing a three-people workload". From 1990 to 2003, the employment rate in town and village population decreased from 73.7% to 65.6%. It is estimated that within 20 years, the unemployment population in rural China would rise from 150 million to 200 million.[10]

In the former central planning economy, when the management organization in rural China was People's communes and annual output was fixed by governmental agriculture plan tasks, farmers incentives for higher production were generally restricted by the commune's purpose to evade higher task requirements from authorities in the next year if output had exceeded the assigned number. Thus, much land was wasted and left idle, labor force became more abundant. After 1978, although the replacement of the household contract responsibility system in agriculture had endowed farmers freedom to make their own output plan, the undue increase of rural population and rapid shrinkage of arable land in process of rural construction even worsened rural hidden unemployment. Governmental permission of TVEs once helped to solve part of the labor surplus, however, difficulties in finance, technology update, and managerial improvement made TVEs' contribution only temporary and trivial. Large discrepancy between rural and urban wage levels and life styles keeps attracting rural labor. The most effective therapy to rural unemployment still lies in the eradiation of barriers between rural and urban labor markets.

IV. POLICY SUGGESTIONS TO UNEMPLOYMENT PROBLEM OF CHINA

Threats to a healthy transformation from dualistic economy to a unitary one and the social unrest that could result from current high unemployment rates compel that the government should devote considerable attention to this issue. A prosperous economy is just the prerequisite for the increment of employment, yet the alleviation of unemployment can not simply depend on economic growth, pragmatic employment policies are more necessary and effective. Economic development includes not only economic growth in terms of GDP output but also optimization of economic structure and enhancement of economic quality. To successfully cure the unemployment in China, the initiative should be taken by the urban sector first.

1. Promoting the Growth of Tertiary Industry

Creating jobs is a fundamental solution to China's unemployment problems. However, once the scale of economy has taken on in mass-production stage of primary and secondary industries, reduction of employment is inevitable. With same amount of investment, tertiary industry is capable to provide much more employment opportunities than primary and secondary sectors and its skill requirement for workers is also lower. Hence, employment potential in tertiary industry should be fully utilized. During the past two decades, the tertiary sector (or service sector), which includes restaurants, retailing, leisure, transport and entertaining industries, is the only sector that has experienced consistent increase in employment. Its employment share increases from 12.2% in 1978 to 27.7% in 2001, with an annual growth rate of employment of 5.9% compared to counterparts of -1.2% and 2.4% in primary and secondary industries.

Yet viewing the experience of other countries, China's service industry can still be described as undeveloped. In US, the output of tertiary sector contributes more than 70% of the total employment, even in developing countries such as Indonesia, the share is also between 35% to 40%. For China's tertiary industry to facilitate employment, efforts can be made in two aspects. One is promotion of urbanization and wholesome of market system because spread out of service sector depends on a mature market economy in urban areas. Another means is diversification of the category of service sectors. Both governmental authorities and investors should not confine themselves with the traditional idea of service such as hospitality and retailing, they should be encouraged to explore new territories such as managerial consulting, microfinance, insurance and so on.

2. Increase Financial Support and Favorable Policy for Non-state Sector, Especially Small and Medium-sized Companies in Private Sector

Non-state sector in China basically includes private companies, joint ventures, foreign-funded companies. It has been playing an active part and become the main source in the re-employment of laid off workers. From 1997 to 2001, SOE jobs decreased by forty three million, and the private sector and non-state sector jobs increased by 16.5 million.11 In Shanghai, 85% of the employment increment from 2004 to 2005 was attributed to non-state sector. But consider the unsolved unemployment population, the non-state sector is just not growing fast enough to satisfy the employment need. One reason is the unbalanced distribution of state funds among SOEs and business in other property forms.

Worrying about several common drawbacks among private companies such as lack of strong corporate governance system, poor risk-resistance ability, low credit rate and moral constraint, commercial banks are unwilling to provide loans to private sector and roughly three-fourths of bank loans in China has gone to SOEs in order to rescue them from bankruptcy. Actually, the default rate of loans from commercial banks to small and medium companies is as high as 32.11% in 2003, much higher than the average rate among all businesses. Thus, to avoid the vicious cycle of lack of funding and high default possibility in private companies, effective measures should be sought to provide more loans for the expansion of private sectors. For example, gearing to the characteristics of private companies, commercial banks can make positive changes in their credit rating, transaction procedures and risk management. While the government should make efforts to formulate a complete set of regulations and laws in microfinance and build up social credit system to increase the transparency of financial information. Moreover, an efficient social security system should be fully established both in governmental level and inside private companies, to provide benefits such as medical care, housing subsidy pension and insurance to non-state employees. In this way, the feeling of insecurity for non-state sector employment would decrease

3. Readjust Employment Concept and Prepare Laborers with Practical Job Training and Education

This is particularly necessary for majority of laid-off workers and college graduates who can be categorized into frictional or voluntary unemployment. In the first case, because of the relative low literacy and limited skills among laid-off populations, they tend to encounter more failures during their search for re-employment. At the same time, influenced by traditional concept of labor and employment, the "iron-bowl" provided by government, many old-aged laid-off workers have also lost initiatives to search for other forms of employment by themselves. Pride generated by once being employed by the government, fear of competition and great intensity of labor, insecurity of life without various welfare and propensity to permanent jobs drive them to give up any employment opportunities other than jobs from SOEs. They only passively depend on the re-employment centers in their former work units in hope of a distributed job from government in the future. In the second case, considering their expensive investment in higher education, lacking career planning instructions and mature perspective of employment, college graduates would rather wait at home than lower their requirements about a decent job positions. Both dilemmas entail a significant transformation in the concept of the meaning of employment the two groups, which calls for cooperation among governments, universities, community care centers and SOEs. Lectures and training on job-hunting skills and diversification of employment should be integrated into the curriculum of universities. Employment centers in SOEs should ensure the implementation of benefit funding as well as lead laid-off workers to search jobs actively. Other training programs inside private companies, foreign-funded companies and joint-ventures should also be established. Both education and job training would shift labor supply from the low-demand, low-skill category to another higher-demand, higher skill category, thus improve employability and productivity.

Meanwhile, efforts should also be made to solve rural unemployment. Generally, means can be classified into three forms: with land in villages, without land in villages and without land outside villages. The first one means expanding agricultural capability to absorb laborers by large investment in production means, diversification of agriculture categories from merely plant production to mixture of livestock breeding, fishery and so on. The second one means promoting the development of town and village enterprises (TVEs) in order to allocate more rural laborers into industrial sectors, this entails dissemination of scientific management knowledge and technological updating in rural areas. The last solution means the migration of rural labor workers into urban areas, whose success depends on capital accumulation and creation of new jobs in urban areas.

V. CONCLUSIONS AND SUMMARY

There are four principle goals for governmental policies in macroeconomics: economic output growth, stability of prices, full employment and balance of international payments equilibrium. Theoretically, all of them should be concerned in the policy-making process of government. But at different stages of economic development, policies should have different emphasis in these four goals. In the soft landing period at early 1990s, China's primary macroeconomic policy was stabilizing prices and controlling inflation. After 1997, the policy focus shifted to the priority of economic growth.. According to the most recent five-year plan work outlines from Labor and Social Security Bureau of China in November 2006, by 2010, the total number of China's labor force would exceed 830 million. In the near future, full employment should be pursued as the most fundamental state policy

As a typical dualistic economy, Chinese economy can be described and predicted by Lewis Model of economic development. Because of its large population and imbalanced distribution of labor in rural and urban areas, the marginal productivity of rural labor is almost zero and the supply of rural labor for industrial growth seems to be unlimited. The transfer of labor force from rural to urban areas is unavoidable historic period for the modernization of China. To eliminate the barriers of labor transfer and build up a united labor markets throughout the country, it is necessary for municipal governments to gradually loosen the strict regulation of labor flow. What is more important is a proper settlement to both urban and rural unemployment problems. Solutions for laid-off , structural, frictional and voluntary unemployment in urban areas lies in industrial capital accumulation, proliferation of non-state sectors and the rationalization of employment concept and improvement in labor qualities. As supplementary means, diversification in agriculture production and expansion of TVEs can also contribute to reduce the absolute surplus of rural laborers. Each policy would not have a big impact on the unemployment problem, but with all of them working together, the overall result can be significant.

Notes

1. China Labor E-Bulletin. 2004"An Overview of Unemployment in China 2003" IssueNO.16 .http://www.china-labour.org.hk/public/contents/article?revision%5fid=18273&item%5fid=8544
2. Wang Nan.2006. "Some thoughts about China's unemployment problem". Contemporary Economics and Finance. March Issue. 39-41.
3. Li Shi, Hiroshi Sato(editors) 2006 "Unemployment, Inequality and Poverty in Urban China" Routledge Studies on the Chinese Economy volume 19. Taylor and Francis Group.
4. Wikipedia, the free encyclopedia "Economic History of China" http://en.wikipedia.org/wiki/Economic_history_of_China#The_First_Five-Year_Plan.2C_1953-57.
5. Heping Gan, Zhong Jian. 2005 "Using Lewis Model to analyze the transformation of Chinese Economy" Value Engineering No. 2 19.
6. Xuguan Feng. 2001 "Segmentation of China's labor markets and hidden unemployment in rural China" Economics Scholoars, Fudan University.
7. Shuifeng Song.2003 "Policy Issues of China's Urban Unemployment". Contemporary Economic Policy. Volume 21, No. 2.
8. China Labor E-Bulletin. 2004"An Overview of Unemployment in China 2003" Issue NO.16 .http://www.china-labour.org.hk/public/contents/article?revision%5fid=18273&item%5fid=8544
9. Angang Hu. 2002.05.17 "the Largest Employment Competition in the World: Gravity of China's Unemployment". Century China. http: / / www.cc.org.cn/
10. New Beijing News. 2006. "2010: a future of unemployment for 10 million new laborers". Nov 08th. http://finance.163.com/06/1109/08/2VFM6DDR00251OB6.html
11. China Labor E-Bulletin. 2004"An Overview of Unemployment in China 2003" Issue NO.16 .http://www.china-labour.org.hk/public/contents/article?revision%5fid=18273

References

Angang Hu. 2002.05.17 "the Largest Employment Competition in the World: Gravity of China's Unemployment". Century China. http: / / *www.cc.org.cn/*

China Labor E-Bulletin (2004), "An Overview of Unemployment in China 2003" Issue NO.16 .http://www.china-labour.org.hk/public/contents/article?revision%5fid=18273&item%5fid=8544

Heping Gan, Zhong Jian. 2005 "Using Lewis Model to analyze the transformation of Chinese Economy" Value Engineering No.2 19-22.

Ingrid Nielsen, Russell Smyth and Mingqiong Zhang (2005), "Unemployment Within China's Floating Population: Empirical Evidence from Jiangsu Province Data". Department of Economics, Monash University, Monash, Australia.

Jeffrey Sachs, Xiaokai Yang, and Dingsheng Zhang (2000), "Globalization, Dual Economy and Economic Development" China Economic Review. No.11 189-209.

Li Shi, Hiroshi Sato (editors) (2006), "Unemployment, Inequality and Poverty in Urban China" Routledge Studies on the Chinese Economy volume 19. Taylor and Francis Group.

Mei Yang (2004), "Analysis of Unemployment Problem in Current China." Information of Economics and law. Issue 2. 24-26.

New Beijing News (2006), "2010: A Future of Unemployment for 10 Million New Laborers". Nov 08th. http://finance.163.com/06/1109/08/2VFM6DDR00251OB6.html

Xuguan Feng (2001), "Segmentation of China's Labor Markets and Hidden Unemployment in Rural China" Economics Scholoars, Fudan University.

Shuifeng Song (2003), "Policy Issues of China's Urban Unemployment". Contemporary Economic Policy. Volume 21, No. 2.

Wang Nan (2006), "Some Thoughts about China's Unemployment Problem". Contemporary Economics and Finance. March Issue. 39-41.

Wikipedia, the free encyclopedia "Economic History of China" *http://en.wikipedia.org/wiki/Economic_history_of_China#The_First_Five-Year_Plan.2C_1953-57.*

Zhang Wei (2003), "Analysis of China's Unemployment Problem". Forum of Finance and Economics No. 12.

Zuyuan Xiong, Dong Yu. (2004), "Feasible Methods to the Statistics about China's Unemployment Problem" Statistics Research No. 7.

ANALYSIS OF EFFICIENCY AND QUALITY ACROSS PUBLIC AND PRIVATE SECTOR OF HIGHER EDUCATION INSTITUTES IN PHILIPPINES

K.V. Ahir [*] **&** ***K.M. Joshi*** [**]

ABSTRACT

The higher education in the Philippines is characterized by high private enrollments, particularly in non-sectarian (for-profit & non-profit), more than the sectarian. Disciplines respond more to the demands from foreign labor markets than the domestic demand. An excess of graduates in certain fields, causes a mismatch in the labor market, employees doing job within and outside the country for which they are over-qualified. Private sector performs better than the Public sector on the criteria set to measure the quality and efficiency of higher education institutions. The low estimates of return to higher education for the Philippines can be reasoned out to the low private rates of returns resulting from high tuition fees accompanied with cheap Philippines skilled labor in the international market.

INTRODUCTION

It has been confirmed by the Growth Economists, ever since the 1950s that the difference in earnings between people relates to the differences in access to education and health and that an investment to enhance these educational capabilities leads to an increase in human productivity, which in turn leads to a positive rate of return (Schultz 1961).

In 2000, World Bank President James D. Wolfensohn wholeheartedly endorsed the conclusions of the World Bank and the United Nations Educational, Scientific, and Cultural Organization (UNESCO) report—that tertiary education is important in building capacity and reducing poverty. Rising labor productivity accounted for half of GDP per capita growth in most OECD countries between 1990 to 2000 (Perkinson, 2006). The knowledge-based society requires every citizen in every field, to be equipped with the latest knowledge, technology and vocational skills. Therefore, the new paradigm has to be developmental, human centered, environmentally sound and all-inclusive–preparing the learners to be contributors to knowledge and not just mere recipients of knowledge. It has thrown new challenges and opportunities for the centers of higher education and learning–public, private, privatized–national, transnational or multinational, they may be. Higher education, which is growing at the rate of 20% per annum worldwide, is being counted as one of the most important ingredients in knowledge-based economies (Gupta, 2005). A World Bank study (Dollar and Collier, 2001), describes how 24

* Department of Economics, Bhavnagar University, Bhavnagar, India.

** Department of Economics, Bhavnagar University, Bhavnagar, India.

developing countries that integrated themselves more closely into the global economy experienced higher economic growth, a reduced incidence of poverty, a rise in the average wage, an increased share of trade in gross domestic product, and improved health outcomes. These countries simultaneously raised their rates of participation in higher education.

The developing countries face severe public revenue sources crunch, for which critical demands compete. Particularly, higher education is observed to reap more private rates of returns than social, as compared to other levels of education, so the 'user charges' should be levied-is given as one of the justifications for inviting private investments in higher education. Since the methods of financing the education, and in particular higher education, have become a globally debated topic because of the practical and ethical problems encountered with the same, it would be inevitable to focus on the issue of *privatization* and the nature of this good. 'Privatization means changing from an arrangement with high government involvement to one with less. The most important privatized arrangements from a policy perspective are the free market, franchise, contract, voucher and voluntary arrangements. Government can privatize individual and toll goods that it produces by divesting or withdrawing from the activity and allowing the market to supply them' (Savas, 2001).

Higher education meets many of the conditions identified by Barr (1993) as characteristic of a private good, amenable to the forces of the market. First, higher education can not be treated as a purely collective / public good, because it exhibits conditions of rivalness (limited supply), excludability (often available for a price), and, rejection (not demanded by all)- all of which do not meet the characteristics of a purely public good, but reflect at least some important conditions of a private good. Second, the consumers of higher education are reasonably well informed and the providers are often ill informed- thus creating the conditions which are ideal for market forces to operate.

The nature of higher education in terms of its characteristics as a public good to merit good and private good has raised an issue of cost sharing while considering the benefits perceived by an individual in long run. Cost-sharing refers to sharing of the costs of higher education by both the Private entities (students, parents, philanthropists, alumni, service-takers of education like the industry, and communities) –so far happening in the lesser extent and presently predominated Public entities (central and state governments). According to D. Bruce Johnstone, (2001) Cost-sharing is inevitable now in those countries where it is still predominantly a Public monopoly for the following reasons:

Demand Side: Higher Education is being demanded more now in the 21st century, both by Public (to become knowledge-based economies, and induce speedier growth and development) and Private entities alike (higher returns to the higher educated, rising population, and growing number of secondary school pass-outs).

Supply Side: There has occurred a failure in supply of Higher education as a Collective/ Public good because sources of generating Government revenues are both scarce and difficult to be generated, either politically (regressive taxes and increased money supply) or economically (progressive taxes, hampering entrepreneurial spirits). Also, the hard-earned government revenues have competing ends to be prioritized against higher education, specially in the developing countries that are still struggling to provide some basic amenities to its citizens like public health, internal and external security of life, housing and sanitation, public infrastructure, basic education to all, social and economic safety nets, etc. Further ahead, the ever increasing per unit cost of higher education makes it unaffordable for the government to provide it to masses that wish to enroll in higher education, leaving it to be a privilege of the elitist only. Higher education has become expensive because of the increasing expenditures of the infrastructure, ever-increasing numbers of students enrollments, increasing faculty salaries, and increasing operational expenses.

Cost Sharing of Higher Education: Some Pragmatic Reflections

Public funding of higher education would make governments non- responsive and unaccountable towards the tax-payers as they are not the direct beneficiaries of these funds, instead parents and students can held the institutes accountable for the fees paid by them.

If the autonomy to set fees is not given, then due to increased pressures of rising costs, faculty salaries and there by higher education quality suffers. If the student's higher education expenditure including the lodging and boarding are borne by the government their graduation rates become lethargic.

The social rates of returns in Primary education are more than the social rates of returns in higher education (Psacharopoulous and Woodhall, 1985), justifying larger share for primary education from the public treasury. According to George Psacharopoulous and Maureen Woodhall (1985), the private rates of returns to higher education are more than the social rates of returns. The expenses incurred by the government on the higher education are very high .On the other hand the salaries earned by the individuals having completed higher education are notably high. So it is argued out that cost sharing should happen so that more alignment can be observed between those who 'pay' and those who 'benefit'. Without cost sharing it's the tax payers who pay for the benefits enjoyed by the ones with higher education in the form of salaries.

Despite the remarkable rate of change that marks our world today, six forces are undeniably spurring the spread of privatization in higher education: the rise of an information-based economy, changes in demographics, an increase in public scrutiny, the advent of new technologies, the convergence of knowledge-based organizations, and a decline in public trust in government. Governors can help state postsecondary education systems respond to these forces by helping define academic quality and student achievement, eliminating overlap and duplication, ensuring accountability, and more efficiently utilizing the capacity of private providers of postsecondary learning (Levine, 2006).

When globally *Private Higher Education* (PHE) system is discussed, a mention of Philippine higher education system is inevitable. It is one of those very few countries where, the private sector has played a dominating role in the higher education, even since pre-independence. A comparative study of public and private sector higher education, with reference to quality and efficiency aspects needs to be assessed. This paper has been broadly divided into three main parts. The first part gives a brief background of the Philippine higher education, followed by a regressive discussion regarding the quality and efficiency issues, and last part extends some analytical conclusions.

BACKGROUND ABOUT PHILIPPINE HIGHER EDUCATION

The Philippine Private HE sector developed historically because of the increasing demand for the same, lack of sufficient government resources compiled with rising demand for the government treasury and the commitment from the Filipinos to preserve their culture through Filipino orientation.

So, before proceeding with the discussion of efficiency and quality, let's briefly discuss here the Peculiar Characteristics of Philippines Private Higher Education:

I. Dominance of Private Higher Education

When most of the developed countries are also shying out from opening up the Higher Education sector for Private entities, (even-though government revenue generation is getting difficult, the stake holders demanding out of the public treasury are rising and liberalization and globalization are becoming the norms) then the noticeably huge share of Private sector in the Philippines is worth mentioning:

(a) Dominance of Private Higher Education in terms of Number of Institutes and Enrollments

Ever-since the evolution of private higher education in Philippines in 1959-1960, till the academic year 2003-2004, the number of private higher education institutes (PHEIs) as a per centage of total higher education institutes has always ranged from 94% to 64%, but mostly 75%+ (CHED, 2003-2004).These institutes do not get any subsidies from the government. Going by the PROPHE International Database, this is comparable to few countries in the world sharing similar figures; like that of Japan 86.3% (2000), South Korea 87% (2002), Brazil 88.9% (2003), Chile 93.3% (2000) Indonesia 96% (2001); but instead is even higher than most of the other countries in the world like USA 59.4% (2000), Russia 37% (2003), Germany 29.5% (2003),India 42.9% (2005-2006). (other references 3)

Also the enrollments in PHEIs have ranged from 79% to 66% since 1994-1995 till 2003-2004. (CHED,2003-2004).These impressive numbers too are in comparison with few countries like Japan 77,1% (2000), South Korea 78.3% (1994), Brazil 70.8% (2003), Chile 71.0% (2000) Indonesia 71.4% (2001); but instead is even higher than most of the other countries in the world like USA 23.2% (2000), Russia 12.1% (2003), Germany 3.7% (2003),India 30.7% (2005-2006). (other references 3).

Thus, the private sector of Philippines is proportionally the largest of any major country, which allows a rich research of the study of PHE over a long time period, thereby enriching the research conclusions.

(b) Dominance of Private Higher Education in terms of Funding, as compared to Public Sector Funding

As compared to other countries, Philippines (55.5%) ranks second only to the Republic of South Korea (82.6%) and is instead followed by USA (53.2%) as per the private higher education/ total education expenditure, 1997-1998. Also in the measurement of PHE as a per centage of GDP, Philippines (1.05) rank third after Republic of Korea (1.52) and the USA (1.35), in 1995-

1996. The total (National and Local) budget for tertiary education as a per centage of total education budget at all levels is a meager 18.7% and the same allocation as a % of GNP is a mere 0.69% . In contrast, the Household Expenditure on Tertiary Education in 1992-1993 as indicated below is almost 2.5 times in Private as compared to the Public (Valsino, 2000).

Compared with public sector tuition, on average, the expenditure per student at an expensive private university costs three times or more, between $1,600 and $4,000 per term. There are only a handful of highly expensive educational institutions since only a small proportion of the population is well off and can afford them. In most of the public tertiary institutions tuition typically amounts to between $400 and 1,000 per term and any additional fees are usually less than what students would pay at a private institution (Gulosino, 2003). These details have been presented in comparative form in table 1.

Table 1
Higher Education Expenses Borne by Parents and Students [National currency Philippine Peso converted to $US by 1998 PPP estimate $1 = P12.13]

		Public		*Private*	
		Low	*High*	*Low*	*High*
Instructional Expenses	Special "One-Time" or "Up Front" Fees	P200 ($16)	P350 ($29)	P400 ($33)	P500 ($41)
	Tuition	P8,400 ($692)	P12,600 ($1,039)	P19,300 ($1,591)	P50,000 ($4,122)
	Other Fees	P4,850 ($400)	P8,000 ($660)	P12,000 ($989)	P24,000 ($1,979)
	Books & Other Educational Expenses	P2,000 ($165)	P3,000 ($247)	P3,000 ($247)	P4,000 ($330)
	Subtotal Expenses of Instruction	P15,450 ($1,274)	P23,950 ($1,974)	P34,700 ($2,861)	P78,500 ($6,472)
	Lodging	P7,200 ($594)	P36,000 ($2,968)	P7,200 ($594)	P36,000 ($2,968)
	Food	P8,000 ($660)	P26,000 ($2,143)	P8000 ($660)	P26,000 ($2,143)
	Transportation	P7,500 ($618)	P2,500 ($206)	P7,500 ($618)	P2,500 ($206)
	Other Personal Expenses	P8,800 ($725)	P13,200 ($1,088)	P8,800 ($725)	P13,200 ($1,088)
	Subtotal Expenses of Student Living	P31,500 ($2,597)	P77,700 ($6,406)	P31,500 ($2,597)	P77,700 ($6,406)
	Total Cost to Parent & Student	P46,950 ($3,871)	P101,650 ($8,380)	P66,200 ($5,458)	P156,200 ($12,877)

Source: http://www.gse.buffalo.edu/org/IntHigherEdFinance/region_asia_Philippines.html

Private institutions are funded predominantly by tuition fees which with other fees range from 97% to 82% (Joshi, 2006). Other Private resource generation includes that from capital investments, contributions, grants, loans, subsidies, and other income sources in accordance with government legislation but contribute very less to total revenue.

Thus this kind of extremely private sector dominated funding has dual conclusions that, on one hand there is a considerable financial autonomy in raising financial resources, allocating the same and also qualitative aspects related autonomy like implementation of curriculum programs, students and faculty selections. Especially the setting of Tuition-fees is subject to only a few regulatory conditions like private tertiary institutions are required to allocate 70 per cent of any tuition fee increase for teacher compensation, 20 per cent for overhead costs and 10 per cent for return on investment.

On the other hand, only those of the households belonging to the upper or higher-middle classes can afford to put their children in elite, expensive and generally quality associated higher education institutes, but the masses have to be satisfied with either low quality Public higher education institutions, or cheap private higher education institutions, forced by lack of affordability.

II. SECTARIAN, NON-SECTARIAN ENROLLMENTS DISTRIBUTIONS

The private higher education sector in the Philippines is divided into sectarian and non-sectarian institutions. Sectarian institutions are run by religious groups or orders- dominated by the Christianity. In the Catholic sector, there are many institutions managed by Jesuits, Dominicans, Recollects, Augustians, Oblates and other religious orders. In comparison, there are fewer institutions run by protestant missions, but they are considered to be still many, considering that Protestants constitute only 10% of the population. Non-sectarian institutions are also known as proprietary institutions. Some of them are family enterprises. Sectarian institutions are strictly non-stock/non-profit, whereas non-sectarian institutions are either for-profit or non-profit. The EDCOM report (1993) presented a useful distinction to describe the governing structure of private tertiary institutions in the Philippines: First, 'non-stock/foundation' consists of non-profit institutions where share of ownership is not sold, and where surplus are reinvested back to the institutions. Second, 'stock institutions' are proprietary businesses that distribute dividends to stockholders.

Over the last decade from 1994-1995 to 2003-2004, the share of sectarian institute student enrollment as a per centage of total private enrollment has ranged from 30% to 32%, leaving the remaining three-fold share for the non-sectarian enrollments. Thus this shows the willingness on the part of the parents and students, to opt for not-cheap higher education, even-though the economic indicators of the citizens are only comparable to developing countries.

III. MARKET FORCES DOMINANCE IN PRIVATE SECTOR PROGRAM/ DISCIPLINE SELECTION

Considering the above mentioned fact of Private dominance, it is quite logical to expect these institutes to behave in response to the market demand for skill formation. Tuition-fees setting, curriculum program setting and much other autonomy along with the demand behaviour of the markets, as per the 'invisible-hand' concept, determine the program choices of the private HE institutes. The mismatch between the demand and supply cannot be ignored (Morada and Manzala, 2001). But in case of the Philippines, the failure of the state in framing an effective precise policy for higher education along with the slow industrial development, the private sector follow the programs offering policy influenced by the *foreign labour markets* for immigrants.

It can be observed from the table 2 that Public sector has always enrolled a huge number of students in agricultural, forestry, fisheries and vetenary medicines, with private sector showing lesser interest. Whereas the enrolments in discipline groups like religion and theology and specifically service trades have increased, in the medical and allied discipline at least private enrollments have not been given away to Public sector institutes. Rest of the disciplines have all lost private enrollments as a share of total enrollments to public enrollments, like private enrollments from 90% to 86% in Law and jurisprudence and from 78% to 5% in home economics.

Table 2
Historical Enrollment by Discipline Group, Academic Year and Sector

Sr. No.	*1994-1995* Public	% of Total	Private	% of Total	Total	*2003-2004* Public	% of Total	Private	% of Total	Total
1	51,916	87	7,484	13	59,400	71,991	92	6,210	8	78,201
2	4,688	22	16,977	78	21,665	8,341	38	13,849	62	22,190
3	85,710	16	460,272	84	545,982	143,015	26	414,540	74	557,555
4	102,056	43	134,408	57	236,464	212,437	53	191,641	47	404,078
5	73,095	25	214,726	75	287,821	170,947	48	181,720	52	352,667
6	1,789	22	6,477	78	8,266	3,942	38	6,418	62	10,360
7	29,669	26	83,617	74	113,286	18,607	47	21,161	53	39,768
8	557	22	2,020	78	2,577	5,243	95	302	5	5,545
9	1,321	22	4,784	78	6,105	10,188	36	18,076	64	28,264
10	1,542	10	13,408	90	14,950	2,568	14	15,964	86	18,532
11	2,296	22	8,318	78	10,614	10,225	37	17,554	63	27,779
12	3,693	4	94,160	96	97,853	70,565	27	190,061	73	260,626
13	21,085	8	253,856	92	274,941	26,975	8	292,799	92	319,774
14	3,998	22	14,477	78	18,475	15,911	61	10,232	39	26,143
15	-	-	7,713	100	7,713	-	-	7,426	100	7,426
16	1,543	22	5,591	78	7,134	3,456	20	13,684	80	17,140
17	5,877	22	21,281	78	27,158	28,721	39	45,775	61	74,496
18	43	22	152	78	195	1,367	100	-	-	1,367
19	8,745	7	122,303	93	131,048	24,682	15	144,263	85	168,945
	399,623		1,472,024		1,871,647	829,181		1,591,675		2,420,856
	21.35%		78.65%		100.00%	34.25%		65.75%		100.00%

Source: CHED, Commission on Higher Education, Statistical Bulletin, 2003-2004.

Quality and Efficiency Issues–A Region wise and Discipline wise Analysis

Educationist, have different approaches of measuring- the quality of education. One approach tries to measure the quality of education in terms of inputs like, faculty, student's intake, basic infrastructure and instructional facilities, accreditation, curricular considerations, etc. While the other approach, measures the quality of education in terms of educational outcomes, like performances in National level exams, graduation and survival rates, educated unemployed, etc. When quantitative data on both the inputs and outcomes are available, a more regressive approach, like that of rates-of-returns & cost-effectiveness can be carried out.

In the present study, the indicators based on first two approaches, being readily available, the analysis have been attempted here, but the third approach requiring more rigorous quantitative data, only a literature review has been done. Moreover the higher education in Philippines is very systematically categorized in different regions (geographical clusters of Districts) and different disciplines.

INPUT–based Approach

Instructional inputs can be broadly categorized into three main categories, faculty, student's intake and basic infrastructure. But like in many countries, Philippines higher education regulating body CHED has also appreciated accreditation, the granting of Center of Excellence/Center of Development status and curriculum innovation, so these also form an important part of the present discussion. Each of them have been examined below:

(a) Faculty

A review of thirty-two studies in developing countries found evidence that teacher qualifications are important, and concluded that the evidence here suggest that trained teachers do make a difference. (Husen, Saha and Noonan, 1978). High instructional quality is indicated by (i) a high proportion of faculty with advanced degrees, (ii) higher faculty salaries, (iii) lighter teaching loads, (iv)lower faculty student ratio, (v) high proportion of full-time to part-time faculty.

As a matter of policy CHED requires Master's degree as the minimum qualification of a faculty in the tertiary level with a minimum of fifty (50) per cent, in the area of specialization. Besides, they also need to be members of professional organizations or licensed practitioner of their field, as per the program need. Also Civil Service Commission, CSC, have set Qualification Standards.(Biglete, Garcia, Bustos, and Salazar, 2000). In the year 1997-1998, faculties with Masters degree were 23,685 and Doctorals were 7,056, out of a total of 93,671 faculties (32.8% were actually fulfilling the criteria set by CHED). But in the year 2003-2004, the Master's were 34,330 and Doctorals were 10,526, out of 113,716 total faculties (39.4% with necessary qualifications).

Region-wise Comparison: (see Table 3) Going by this criteria if we compare the Public and Private sector intake of faculty with highest credentials, it can be clearly observed that the faculty with masters and doctorals are employed in Private sector more than two-third (2/3rd in Public sector, except Region IV B. Maximum qualified faculties are employed in the region NCR(in Private – four times more than Public), followed by Region VI and IV-B & IV-A. Many reasons have been quoted for the same – faculties are paid much higher in the Private sector, and the concentration of higher education institutes is generally in Central and Urban areas of the country.

Discipline-wise Comparison: (see Table 4) Among various disciplines, education and teacher training employs the maximum number of faculties, followed by business administration and related and engineering and technology. But in all these three private institutes employ on an average double the faculties than in Public. This is logically related to the number of students' enrolment in these disciplines being more than the others. Worth noticing is the gap of faculty employed in the disciplines like medical and allied, and mathematics and computer science. The reasons for this are same as discussed above.

Table 3
Faculty by Region, AY 2003-2004 Highest Educational Credential and Sector

Region	*Public*						*Private*					
	Masters		*Doctors*				*Masters*		*Doctors*			
	1	*2*	*1*	*2*	*Grand Total*	*% of total*	*1*	*2*	*1*	*2*	*Grand Total*	*% of total*
I	725	587	256	397	2,280	2.00	1,653	690	215	295	3,729	3.28
II	410	477	348	333	1,817	1.60	753	553	195	235	2,416	2.12
III	721	773	294	346	2,913	2.56	2,429	1,640	471	517	7,144	6.28
IVA	1,255	568	303	494	3,545	3.12	2,737	1,865	557	831	7,713	6.78
IVB	523	208	70	50	1,196	1.05	313	154	70	44	865	0.76
V	1,081	599	405	367	2,804	2.47	1,293	812	237	423	4,036	3.55
VI	1,763	764	409	327	3,647	3.21	1,812	1,120	257	193	5,278	4.64
VII	482	257	137	187	1,258	1.11	1,915	1,892	340	542	6,388	5.62
VIII	879	555	295	326	2,441	2.15	724	274	40	99	1,950	1.71
IX	726	278	152	93	1,544	1.36	740	389	61	94	2,373	2.09
X	345	387	116	168	1,391	1.22	1,034	916	174	316	3,393	2.98
XI	168	215	72	80	579	0.51	1,373	1,107	229	156	4,082	3.59
XII	179	183	38	50	509	0.45	655	438	159	92	2,109	1.85
NCR	1,291	1,389	337	925	6,000	5.28	6,911	5,211	1,602	1,952	23,833	21
CAR	205	319	120	195	1,029	0.90	477	486	126	153	2,276	2
ARMM	30	168	13	40	366	0.32	107	145	26	41	544	0.48
CARAGA	370	253	92	74	931	0.82	431	307	135	91	1,337	1.18
Grand Total	11,153	7,980	3,457	4,452	34,250	30.12	25,357	17,999	4,894	6,074	79,466	69.9

Note: 1 refers to Total w/units and CAR
2 refers to Total Holder

Table 4
Faculty Employed in Various Disciplines in Public and Private Sector for 2003-04

Sr. No.	*Discipline Group*	*Public*		*Private*	
		Total	*% of Total*	*Total*	*% of Total*
1.	Agricultural, Forestry, Fisheries, Vet Med.	2,941	2.59	381	0.34
2.	Architectural and Town Planning	245	0.22	455	0.40
3.	Business Admin. and Related	3,188	2.80	13,663	12.02
4.	Education and Teacher Training	13,324	11.72	20,929	18.40
5.	Engineering and Technology	3,046	2.68	6,191	5.44
6.	Fine and Applied Arts	180	0.16	286	0.25
7.	General	1,396	1.23	1,837	1.62
8.	Home Economics	249	0.22	120	0.11
9.	Humanities	1,986	1.75	3,980	3.50
10.	Law and Jurisprudence	360	0.32	2,189	1.92
11.	Mass Communication and Documentation	231	0.20	777	0.68
12.	Mathematics and Computer Science	1,493	1.31	5,872	5.16
13.	Medical and Allied	1,352	1.19	9,950	8.75
14.	Natural Science	1,381	1.21	1,691	1.49
15.	Religion and Theology	10	0.01	1,105	0.97
16.	Service Trades	16	0.01	247	0.22
17.	Social and Behavioral Science	1,282	1.13	4,584	4.03
18.	Trade, Craft and Industrial	95	0.08	160	0.14
19.	Other Disciplines	1,475	1.30	5,049	4.44
	Grand Total	34250	30.12	79,466	69.88

Source: CHED, Statistical Bulletin, 2003-2004.

But, as shown in Diagram 1 and 2, both in public and private, the number of eligible teachers in every region is hardly 50% and particularly so in the public sector, where even the total teachers and of them eligible teachers, are both less. One reason can be brain-drain, since the immigration from Philippines has been highest as per ILO. Nearly 10% of population is abroad. But ironically, the conclusions reached at by Charisse Gulosino (2003) suggests that 'the large per centage distribution of Associate Professors and Assistant Professors in public institutions suggests that their academic staff is predominantly employed on fulltime contracts, while staff in private institutions are predominantly on part-time contracts.' This gives a very grim situation of the instructional efficiency.

Diagram 1
Regionwise Faculty Credentials in Private Sector in 2003-04

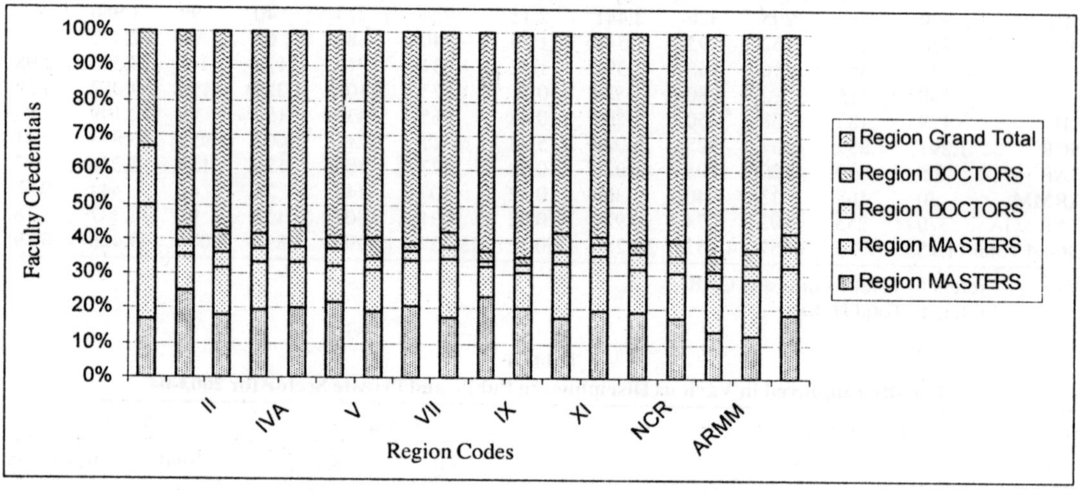

Source: CHED, Statistical Bulletin, 2003-2004.

Diagram 2
Regionwise Faculty Credentials in Public Sector in 2003-04

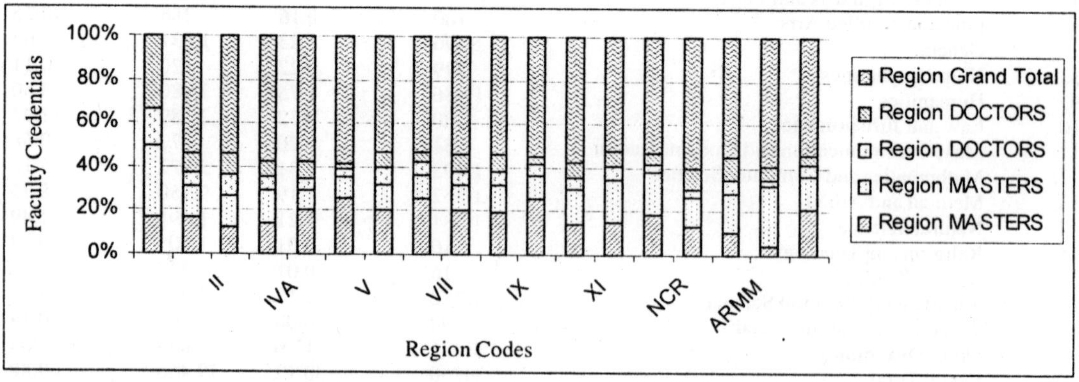

Source: CHED, Statistical Bulletin, 2003-2004.

(b) Student's Intake

Student selectivity indicators refer mainly to admissions requirements, such as: (i) NCEE cut off scores and high school grade point requirement, (ii) entrance examinations (iii) the ratio of admissions to applicants.

In Philippines, entrance to universities and other institutions of higher education is dependent on the possession of a high school ***Certificate of Graduation*** and in some cases on the results of the *National Secondary Achievement Test* (NSAT), or in many colleges and universities the results of their own entrance examinations. NSAT is administered to fourth-year high school students to gauge the quality of the individual institutions they are attending, it was not designed or intended as an admission test, but has nonetheless served that purpose for some institutions. Privately administered testing programs through the Center for Educational Measurement (CEP) are also widely used by colleges for admissions purposes. The two most common ones are the *College Scholastic Aptitude Test* (CSAT) and the *Admission Test for Colleges and Universities* (ATCU). From 1973 to 1994, the National College Entrance Examination (NCEE) was used for admission to post-secondary degree programs; it was abolished and replaced by the NSAT because it was considered by many not to be discriminative enough. The *Philippine Education Placement Test* (PEPT) is a national examination designed to evaluate the grade level of students returning to the school system or seeking admission to college based on knowledge and skills gained through formal and non-formal methods. Thus, two national public examinations are given at the secondary level. These are as follows:

(a) *The National Secondary Assessment Test (NSAT)* The National Secondary Assessment Test is administered to graduating high school students. The NSAT tests abilities and skills in four subject areas: Communications Arts in English and Filipino with 70 and 30 items, respectively, science with 75 items, mathematics with 75 items, and aptitude in technical-vocational fields with 50 items. Except in Filipino Communication Arts, all tests are in English. The NSAT assesses the competencies to have been developed in second, third and fourth years in high school. Competencies assessed in the NSAT were jointly specified by the Bureau of Secondary Education and the National Education Testing and Research Center (NETRC), but the development of the test was solely done by the latter. NSAT was administered to the fourth year high school population nationwide from 1994 to 1996 and to a representative sample from 1997 to 1998.The specific objectives of NSAT are similar with that of the NEAT, except in the school level, covered the secondary schools. Both tests are administered annually.

(b) *The Philippine Education Placement Test (PEPT)* The Philippines Educational Placement Test (PEPT) is the principal instrument used in the Accreditation and Equivalency Program (AEP) which was first established in 1977. The main objective of the AEP is to retrieve out-of-school youths and place them in the formal school system, if they so desire, and to place over-aged in-school youth in the grade/year level corresponding to their ages. The PEPT tests the competencies gained through formal, informal, and non-formal education which are equivalent to those developed in five subject areas—communication arts in English and Filipino, science, mathematics and social studies—from first grade in the elementary school to fourth year in the secondary school. Each subject area test includes 120 test items in a multiple-choice format. The regular PEPT is administered in designated testing centers throughout the country, usually on the last Sunday of November, in special examination centers in April and May, and in walk-in examinations in the NETRC anytime during the year.

The best students prefer to go to the most selective and reputed private institutions and public institutions (especially the UP system). The non-sectarian is rather more open, and selects more students with relatively less tuition than the other prestigious private institutions. In order to have more students for achieving the market based profit objective, a trade off between the quality and students flow exists. Even today one can definitely conclude that prestige and financial conditions has strong and consistent relationship with the overall program quality, as observed in the previous studies.

(c) *Basic Infrastructure*: Indicators of the quality of instructional facilities include : (i) Library Facilities, (ii) Laboratory Facilities, (iii) Classroom Buildings, (iv) Campus amenities and (v) Student Service Facilities. Of these, particularly Library quality indicators include, number of books per student and Library Budget per student.

It is observed that majority of the private institutions are in deplorable conditions in terms of library facilities along with low utilization rates of books. The positive aspect with regard to instructional facilities is that internet access is being widely available across majority of the institutions, which can help in overcoming the poor endowment of libraries partially (Joshi, 2006).

(d) *Accreditation*: Accreditation signifies that an institution meets certain minimum standards of Instructional capability. Accrediting agencies set standards for faculty, library, laboratory, physical infrastructure and also covers the non-teaching function of 'community involvement'. Accreditation is voluntary in Philippines and has a positive effect on the quality of higher education in terms of its effectiveness in stimulating institutional improvement. A coordinating and umbrella organization, the Federation of Accrediting Agencies of the Philippines (FAAP) was established in 1977 with the three agencies accrediting private associations as members. These organizations are: (1) Philippine Accrediting Association of Schools, Universities and Colleges (PAASUC) for Catholic institutions; (2) Philippine Association of Colleges and Universities Commission on Accreditation (PACU-COA) for non-sectarian institutions and (3) Association of Christian Schools and Colleges – Accrediting Agency, Inc. (ACSC-AAI) for other religious institutions. The accreditation is more focused for the programs and not for the institution as whole. The criteria possibly differ from agency to agency as might the application, but the scope of the review based on the areas covered by the standards of each agency is almost identical (Phelps, 2001). The accreditation process consists of self-study by the institution followed by an on-site review by a team of accreditors. The accreditation is divided into four levels: Level I refer to programs/institutions which have undergone a preliminary survey visit and are certified by FAAP as capable of attaining accredited status with in two years. Level II refers to programs

/institutions which have been granted initial accreditation. Level III refers to programs / institutions which have been re-accredited and have met additional criteria set by the FAAP for this level. Level IV refers to the programs/institutions which have attained the distinguished prestige comparable to international universities (Johanson, 1999).

The Federation of Accrediting Agencies of the Philippines (FAAP) as the umbrella organization of accrediting agencies has accredited (see Table-5) a total of 597 higher education programs in 1998-1999 and 743 in 2000-2001, hence, an increase of 24 per cent (Table-8). Of the 743 programs, 643 are baccalaureate, 65 are Master's and 5 are Doctoral. In terms of accreditation level, 152 are Level I, 445 are Level II and 146 are Level III. The number of higher education institutions with accredited programs in 1998-1999 is 152 and 160 in 2000-2001, hence, an increase of 5.3 per cent (CHED, 2003-04).

Table 5
Distribution of Accredited Programs by Region and Level of Accreditation

Region	*Level of Accreditation*			*Total*
	I	*II*	*III*	
I	10	37		47
II	17	11	16	44
III	13	37		50
IV	6	51	4	61
V	9	20		29
VI	14	30	13	57
VII	16	29	35	80
IX	5	3	5	13
X	9	31	4	44
XI	19	30	8	57
XII	3	18		21
NCR	25	116	57	198
CAR	4	16	4	24
ARMM	2	3		3
Caraga		13		15
Total	152	445	146	743

Source: 1998-1999 and 2000-2001 FAAP Directories.

The study conducted by the Task Force on Higher Education (1995) on the role of voluntary accreditation in higher education showed that accreditation has contributed significantly in the improvement of colleges and universities in the area of faculty, instruction, library, laboratories, physical plant and facilities, student and personnel administration, organization and administration, and community and social orientation (Biglete, Garcia, Bustos, and Salazar, 2000).

(e) *COE/COD (Centre of Excellence and Centre of Development):* To strengthen the higher education institutions, public and private, COE/CODs have been established in nine clusters of disciplines, that have consistently exhibited qualities indicating excellence in instructional program quality, strong graduate program and research capability, accreditation level status and performance of graduates in licensure exams. CHED provides each COE a financial assistance of 3 Million Pesos p.a. for a period of three years (except Humanities, Social sciences and communication–1 mln. Pesos) and each COD receive one million Pesos p.a. from CHED's Higher Education Development Fund. The idea is to focus resources on few institutional programs and enhance these programs for them to be a showcase of the Philippine HE system for joining the international higher education arena (Biglete, Garcia, Bustos, and Salazar, 2000).

In the year 2003-2004, (see Table 6), in all 45 disciplines in private and 64 in Government were awarded the COE status, whereas 104 in private and 54 in Government were awarded the COD status (double in private). Since these status are awarded to the most deserving of the institutes, its worth appreciating for the private sector that of the Total COE/CODs, more than 55% belong to the private sector. It should be noted that CHED gives financial assistance only after being awarded the respective status, and not that CHED gives the assistance to develop the status of COE/COD itself. Thus, in this respect the performance of private sector is appreciative, as compared to the public sector, specially considering that the net enrollments in private sector has narrowed down only to 65.75%. Also worth mentioning is the concentration of a huge number of COE/CODs (34.7%) in the National Capital Region NCR. Of these even-though University of Philippines (UP)-a state university, is a major contributor, but also some of the Private universities contribute greatly like, De La Salle University, University of Santo Tomas, Adamson University, Mapua Institute of Technology, etc.

Table 6
COE and COD in Different Sector and Different Regions

Region Codes	*COEs* Private	*COEs* Government	*CODs* Private	*CODs* Government	*Total*
I	0	3	1	2	6
II	3	2	10	5	20
III	0	2	5	6	13
IVA	0	9	1	4	14
IVB	0	2	0	0	2
V	1	2	3	0	6
VI	1	2	11	3	17
VII	5	0	12	0	17
VIII	0	4	1	2	7
IX	0	2	3	2	7
X	3	2	10	3	18
XI	3	0	10	2	15
XII	0	6	0	9	15
NCR	27	28	25	13	93
CAR	2	1	10	3	16
ARMM	0	0	1	0	1
CARAGA	0	0	1	0	1
Grand Total	45	65	104	54	268

Source: CHED, Statistical Bulletin, 2003-2004.

(f) *Curricular Innovations*: Higher Education up gradation should be ensured on a routine basis so that the students who come out of the system is not only capable of handling his expertise knowledge of his respective discipline, but is also able to adjust with this fast evolving globalized surroundings, specially when the country like Philippines has 10% of the population going abroad and that the HE system also tries to cater the foreign labor markets. So CHED as a Policy, updated the General Education Curriculum GEC by, CHED CMO No. 59, s.1996, requiring all Higher Education institutions to offer a 63 units minimum, of General Education GE subjects in all tertiary levels leading to a bachelor degree of four years. The detailed distribution of these 63 marks is as shown below see Table 7. A close observation of the choice of the subjects made here, like English, mathematics, etc. emphasizes the commitment of CHED to retain its production of well-educated global citizenry.

Table 7
Minimum Requirement for the New General Education Curriculum.

I.	Language and literature	24 units
	English–9 units	
	Filipino–9 units	
	Literature–6 units	
II.	Mathematics and Natural Sciences	15 units
	Mathematics–6 units	
	Natural Sciences–6 units	
	Science Elective–3 units	
III.	Humanities and Social Sciences	18 units
	Humanities–6 units	
	Social Sciences–12 units	
IV.	Mandated Subjects 6 units	
	Life and work of Rizal	
	Philippine History	
Total Marks		63 UNITS

Source: CHED, Statistical Bulletin, 2003-2004.

OUTCOMES–Based Approach

If a higher education institutions quality is to be judged by the outputs produced, the basic statistic that needs to checked is the Survival and Graduation rates as compared to the enrollments in the Higher Education System, results in licensure exams and the educated employed statistics. So let's analyze each of them individually here.

(a) Survival and Graduation Rates

For many purposes, measuring output by the number of students who successfully complete a course provides a good first approximation, and comparing this with input measured by the number of pupil-years may be enough to indicate that high rates of wastages and repetition are connected with very low efficiency, judged simply by the length of time needed to produce one qualified school-leaver. (Psacharopolous, and Woodhall, 1985)

As can be observed from the diagram, (see Diagram 3) the enrolment ratio has been consistent at almost 20% since 1995-96, and is much higher than most of the developing countries, but lesser than the developed countries where the similar figures are 50%. According to Maria Asuncion (2006) out of every 100 students enrolled every year in Philippines, 66% complete elementary school, 42% finish their high school and only 14 get their college degree. Going by these figures the situation of Drop-outs seems alarming, and one of the basic reasons quoted are the financial constraints. HELMS III Higher Education and Labor market in the Philippines–a CHED Tracer Study of Parents Income of Graduates in Public and Private Institutions FAPE 1998.–"Approximately, 75% of graduates of Public institutions come from Bottom Quartiles (< 99,000 php), 22% from Middle Quartiles (< 2,99,000 php) and 3% from Upper Quartiles. But in Private the same numbers are respectively, 61%, 33% and 6%. Therefore, the Private Cost of Education can have a negative impact on the demand for education, especially for families from lower Socio-Economic backgrounds. Survival rate between 65% to 70% since 1995-96, shows the grim picture of the amount of wastages caused in the higher education sector. Also the graduation rates have remained between 42% to 48%, except since last two years whereby a drastic rise approximating to 60% graduation rate is applauding. This trend if continues, then it can be called as a sustainable improvement.

Diagram 3
Enrolment, Survival & Graduation Rate

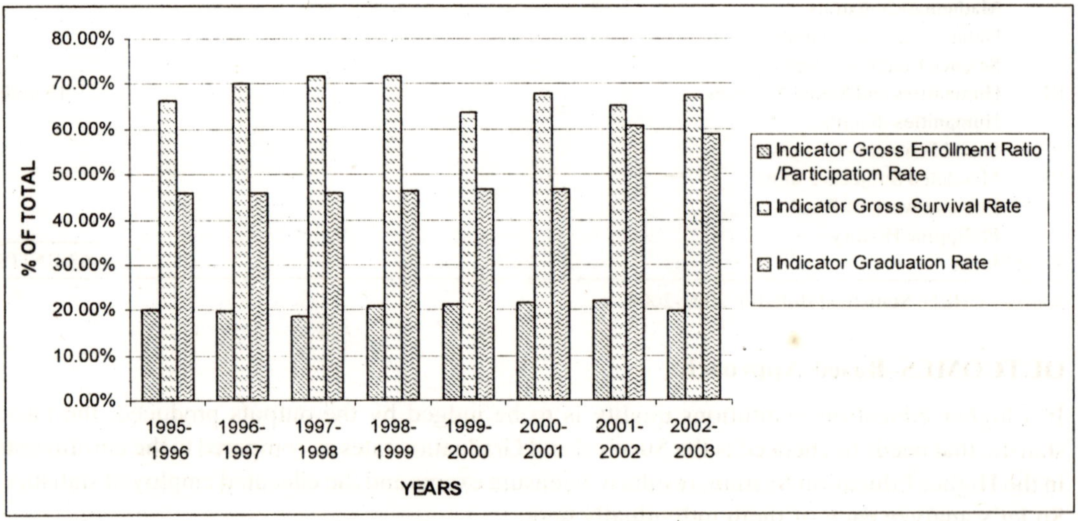

Source: CHED, Statistical Bulletin, 2003-2004.

(b) Results in Licensure Exams

The Professional Regulation Commission PRC administers the Licensure Examinations in the Philippines. Institutions with high per centage of graduates passing the licensure examinations indicate that the kind of education they provide is of good quality. Looking at the available data since 2000 to 2003, it can be observed that on an average the National Passing Rate in the

Licensure Exams has ranged between 41% to 48%. On the basis of disciplines, Geology (86.21%), Metallurgical Engineering (71.43%), Marine Engineering (64.71%) and Marine Transport (60.32%) have done reasonably well. Whereas, discipline wise, Customs Administration (11.8%), Accountancy (19.49%) and Optometry (18.34%) have performed very badly. If on the Licensure Exam results criteria, we are to judge the efficiency of Public and Private Higher Education institutes, then the performance in various disciplines with maximum per centage of Public and Private enrollments should be analyzed. Disciplines with maximum Private enrollments are Medical and Allied, Business Administration and Related, Law and Jurisprudence, etc. and those with maximum Public enrollments are Agriculture, Forestry, Fishery, Environmental Planning and Natural Sciences. The performance of graduates in the Licensure Examination in these disciplines proves public Sector to be more efficient than private Sector. The national per centage of passing in the Licensure Examination proves that the following scores of private sector is just an average performance, whereas those of public sector are more and are increasing over the years. It can be reasoned out to the choices of the low-cost programs on the part of private sector and cheap quality SUCs.

PRIVATE SECTOR :		PUBLIC SECTOR :	
Medical and Allied			
Dentistry	35%	Agriculture	22%
Medical Technology	47%	Forestry	33%
Medicine	56%	Fishery Technology	40%
Nursing	48%	Env.Planning & Sc	47%
Nutrition & Dietetics	50%	Geology	86%
Physical Therapy	26%		
Law and Jurisprudence			
Law	20%		
Criminology	38%		
Customs Administ.	11%		
Business Administration and Related			
Accountancy	19%		

(c) *Educated Unemployed*

According to Maria Asuncion (2006) out of 100 students enrolled in primary education only 14 get the college degree and of these 14 also only 7.7% graduates get employed i.e. only 1 out of every 100 entering into the education system, eventually gets employed. In Philippines in October 2006 about 13.3 % (4.5mln.) people were unemployed. Out of the total unemployed about 40% of them were College Graduates (21%) and College Undergraduates (19%). A striking feature of the tracer studies carried out by CHED - HELMS is that a large proportion of graduates do not enter professions in the fields in which they have been trained. The alarming mismatch in employment of graduates is supported by several cases of accounting and commerce graduates that work as office clerks, bank tellers and sales representatives; of engineers that work as technicians for local and overseas jobs; of doctors and nurses that work as medical representatives; while teacher education graduates, doctors and other professionals (i.e., lawyers, dentists) join the overseas labor market for low-level employment, or in some cases, equivalent jobs. Thus this clearly shows the inefficiency on the part of the higher education sector.

Cost-effectiveness and Rates of Returns

As previously mentioned if very regressive data of both inputs and outputs are available, more complex analysis like calculating rates of returns and cost-effectiveness is possible. Due to the lack of the data here, to complete the discussion of the quality and efficiency, we quote some of the observations made by some of the authors. The Philippine higher educational system is characterized by high attendance rates, implying that unlike other developing countries, there is widespread private interest in educational investments. This feature reflects a rate of return that is more akin to advanced countries than those of its counter parts. The Philippine rate of return has always exhibited an uncommon behavior; in spite of categorized as a developing country its rate of return is more comparable to that of a more developed country, a phenomenon in an educational system with high enrolment rate. The rate of returns estimates in general have been relatively stable during the last few years, though have mostly increased over the eight year period and fallen for the last five years. The private and social rates of return have been around 12 per cent and 11 per cent respectively. Different studies that have utilized varied data sets and cost estimates conclude with the result through out the years, confirming the low estimates of return to higher education for the Philippines (Paqueo and Tan, 1989; Orbeta, 2001).

CONCLUSION

With the expansion of state colleges and universities (SUCs) in the Philippine in recent years, studies have shown that SUCs offer academic programs that duplicate those provided most cost-effectively by private institutions. This has led to the problem of 'crowding out,' that is to say, SUCs tended to draw away students who would otherwise have attended private institutions (Jimenez and Sawada, 2001).

'Over recent decades, however, public provision and financing have expanded rapidly with the establishment by the legislature of many, generally low-quality, public higher education institutions (HEIs). This rapid expansion of publicly funded higher education has required large increases in public funding for higher education. To reverse the resultant trend of a diminishing basic education budget share, the Government has for the last few years pegged the higher education budget at around 15% of the total education budget. However, public higher education spending, as a result, has become increasingly inadequate to support the needs of the continually expanding public sector. Complementary reform strategies are urgently needed to increase cost recovery in public sector institutions, improve efficiency in public spending, and contain or rationalize the growth of the public sector. In the absence of these reforms, further deterioration in the quality and efficiency of public higher education can be expected. At the same time, the viability of private sector institutions will continue to diminish as students are attracted by the low fees of publicly-funded institutions (Duncan, 2002).'

A summary of major findings have been presented in Table 8. It can be clearly observed that private sector clearly outperforms public sector in most of the criterions on which the analysis was possible, or is at least equal. Be it the ratio of enrollments or funding the higher education, till 2003, private sector dominates, though the trend shows a consistent decline in the enrollments in private sector, which should be checked (*crowding-out effect*). Sectarian

Table 8
National Percentage of Passing in the Licensure Examinations (as a % of attempted)

Discipline	*2000*	*2001*	*2002*	*2003*
Accountancy	18.82%	17.74%	18.90%	19.49%
Aeronautical Engineering	27.59%	32.54%	NE	25.12%
Agricultural Engineering	52.34%	51.55%	49.53%	38.04%
Agriculture	-	-	-	22.18%
Architecture	31.13%	36.40%	36.72%	37.25%
Chemical Engineering	44.01%	41.31%	40.27%	39.67%
Chemistry	44.15%	46.73%	50.53%	42.57%
Civil Engineering	30.11%	35.56%	33.45%	36.66%
Criminology	45.18%	49.86%	45.94%	38.29%
Customs Administration	9.09%	9.32%	11.37%	11.08%
Dentistry	38.09%	40.75%	41.50%	35.54%
Electrical Engineering	39.68%	43.88%	43.82%	41.05%
Electronics & Comms. Eng'g.	44.06%	48.57%	40.54%	41.07%
Environmental Planning/Science	66.67%	75.76%	53.85%	47.06%
Fisheries Technology	-	-	-	40.19%
Forestry	28.96%	53.47%	29.49%	33.72%
Geodetic Engineering	43.83%	41.12%	40.80%	37.86%
Geology	70.21%	90.70%	78.79%	86.21%
Interior Design	64.80%	47.42%	51.98%	42.21%
Landscape Architecture	58.33%	56.25%	NE	44.44%
Law	20.84%	32.89%	19.68%	ND
Library Science	53.22%	50.94%	52.44%	51.10%
Marine Engineering	58.64%	45.50%	67.67%	64.71%
Marine Transportation	40.58%	52.35%	81.78%	60.32%
Mechanical Engineering	47.26%	44.11%	41.48%	40.42%
Medical Technology	52.38%	52.58%	49.15%	47.72%
Medicine	65.03%	61.04%	63.18%	56.26%
Metallurgical Engineering	64.52%	70.31%	53.97%	71.43%
Midwifery	51.84%	48.01%	48.26%	49.27%
Mining Engineering	76.92%	86.67%	62.50%	57.14%
Naval Archi. & Marine Eng'g.	64.29%	57.89%	44.83%	40.00%
Nursing	49.64%	53.50%	44.75%	48.22%
Nutrition and Dietetics	55.05%	57.69%	53.08%	50.00%
Occupational Therapy	35.15%	-	35.42%	31.01%
Optometry	15.35%	44.14%	31.09%	18.34%
Pharmacy	62.96%	62.39%	61.43%	59.79%
Physical and Occup. Therapy	-	22.17%	-	-
Physical Therapy	24.91%	-	24.27%	26.25%
Elementary/Secondary Educ.	-	34.41%	-	
Teacher-Elementary	35.56%		35.32%	26.25%
Teacher-Secondary	35.90%	-	36.52%	26.29%
Radiologic/X-Ray Technology	-	-	-	-
Radiologic Technology	36.77%	30.43%	38.76%	38.15%
Sanitary Engineering	50.48%	45.83%	46.02%	44.00%
Social Work	58.20%	64.06%	47.05%	48.00%
Veterinary Medicine	46.83%	48.03%	43.07%	37.33%
Average % of Passing	45.35%	48.30%	44.85%	41.71%

Table 9
Conclusions of the Observations about Quality and Efficiency in the Public and Private Sector.

Sr. No.	*Criteria Selected*	*Private*	*Public*
1	Input-based Approach		
1a	Faculty With Highest Credentials	High	Low
1b	Student's Intake	LOW (Non-sectarian)	LOW (high in UP)
1c	Basic Infrastructure	LOW (exc.INTERNET)	MEDIUM
1d	Accreditation	NA	NA
1e	COE / COD	HIGH	LOW
1f	Curricular Innovation	MEDIUM	MEDIUM
2	OUTPUT -BASED APPROACH		
2a	Survival % Graduation Rate	HIGH	LOW
2b	Results in Licensure Exams	LOW	MEDIUM
2c	Educated Unemployed	LOW	MEDIUM
3	COST-EFFECTIVENESS		

(religion dominated) institutes are able to enroll only 1/3rd of the students in higher education leaving out a whooping 2/3rd for the non-sectarian institutes (including for-profit and non-profit), showing the high acceptance among parents for not-cheap higher education.

Disciplines like Medical and Allied, Trade and Service, etc. being more in demand by the student-cliental, private sector reflect their market-oriented responsiveness towards the same, leaving out the less attractive ones like Agricultural, Forestry, Fisheries and Vetenary Medicines for the public sector.

Private sector has been successful in attracting more than 2/3rd of the eligible faculties, leaving out only 1/3rd for the public sector, but both the sectors are able to employ only about 50% faculties that are eligible by the criteria set by CHED (one of the reasons can be *brain-drain*). Reputed private and public institutes bag more of the selective students, but the non-sectarian institutes are more open to students irrespective of their capabilities judged by the National Secondary Assessment Test (NSAT) and Philippines Educational Placement Test (PEPT).

Basic infrastructure measured by 'library facilities' and 'book utilization rates' mirror a grim situation of the private sector, reluctant to even those sectors that require more of laboratory facilities, external trainings and other large-scale investments.

The number of institutes opting for accreditation is increasing, but as in 2003, most of the institutes were at level II, with fewer numbers at level I and III. A clear dominance of the National Capital Region (NCR) is note worthy, with about 2/7th of accredited institutes in the same.

As for the status of the Center of Excellence - COE and Center of Development COD, the private Sector has proved to be more eligible with about 55% of the total COE/CODs in private Sector. Besides the much reputed University of Philippines (UP), the following private universities have also proved their might: De La Salle University, University of Santo Tomas, Adamson University, Mapua Institute of Technology, etc.

Up gradation of the General Education Curriculum GEC by the CHED (CMO No. 59, s. 1996) is also worth appreciating, representing the consciousness on its part of approaching the globalization policy.

The Participation/enrollment rates are higher than the developing countries, but less than the developed countries (though private sector enrollments are much higher than most of the developed countries, further confirming that the private cost of education can have a negative effect on demand of education), survival and graduation rates being lesser do picturize the higher wastage in the higher education sector.

National Per centage of Passing in the Licensure Examination, at less than 50% gives disturbing conclusions of the quality of higher education. Though inter-disciplinary variations are quite high, sectors with low passing rate are also the ones causing a mismatch in the labor market.

Out of the total unemployed and underemployed, if 40% are college graduates, an obvious result is the mismatch in the labor market, compelling the graduates to do the jobs for which they are either overqualified or under-paid.

Like most of the developing countries, even Philippines faces a fiscal deficit, and is certainly not in a position to share an ever-rising burden of public higher education, specially when the competing ends on the Public treasury need to be prioritized. So, the SUCs illogical growth, to satisfy vested political motives should be checked, in time. At the same time, before re-emphasizing an increased role of private higher education, it needs to be reassured that the capital markets are developed to cater to the needs of demands for private higher education to ensure that the equity issues in participation of higher education is ensured. It should also be duly accompanied by the exploration of more resources of revenue generation by the private institutes like, from the alumni, industries, individual donations, the income generated from auxiliary services by the institutes, etc. Also a proper check on the quality of these institutes, by proper organization, public or private, should be thoroughly ensured, so that the institutes do not become factories producing degrees but is instead in line with the social and ideological ethos associated with the higher education.

Notes

(1) Gross Enrolment Ratio/Participation Rate - % of pre-baccalaureate and baccalaureate students over the schooling age population of 16-21 years old.

(2) Gross Survival Rate - % of 1st year baccalaureate students who were able to reach 4th year, 5th year and 6th year level, 3-, 4- and 5-years ago, respectively.

(3) Graduation Rate - % of 1st year baccalaureate students who were able to graduate.

(4) Region Codes

Region I – Ilocos Region
Region II – Cagayan Valley
Region III – Central Luzon
Region IVA – CALABARZON
Region IVB – MIMAROPA

Region V – Bicol Region
Region VI – Western Visayas
Region VII – Central Visayas
Region VIII – Eastern Visayas
Region IX – Zamboanga Peninsula
Region X – Northern Mindanao
Region XI – Davao Region
Region XII – Cotabato Region
Caraga Region
NCR – National Capital Region
CAR – Cordillera Adminitrative Region

(5) Discipline Codes

Sr. No.	*Discipline Group*
1.	Agricultural, Forestry, Fisheries, Vet Med.
2.	Architectural and Town Planning
3.	Business Admin. and Related
4	Education and Teacher Training
5.	Engineering and Technology
6.	Fine and Applied Arts
7.	General
8.	Home Economics
9.	Humanities
10.	Law and Jurisprudence
11.	Mass Communication and Documentation
12.	Mathematics and Computer Science
13.	Medical and Allied
14.	Natural Science
15.	Religion and Theology
16.	Service Trades
17.	Social and Behavioral Science
18.	Trade, Craft and Industrial
19.	Other Disciplines

Source: CHED, Statistical Bulletin, 2003-2004.

References

Barr Nicholas (1993), The Economics of the Welfare State. London: Weidenfeld and Nicholson.

Biglete A., L. Garcia, A. Bustos, Roderick Salazar (2000), Strategies for Quality and Excellence; (ed. By) Valsino Mona Dumlao, in World Conference on Higher Education and Framework for Priority Action for Change and Development for Higher Education in the 21st century in the Philippines, Higher Education Policy Series No. 1, UNESCO.

Dollar, David, and Paul Collier (2001), Globalization, Growth, and Poverty: Building an Inclusive World Economy. New York: Oxford University Press.

Duncan Wendy (2002), Technical Assistance to the Republic of the Philippines for the Organizational Development of the Commission on Higher Education, ADB and World Bank.

Gulosino Charisse (2003), Evaluating Private Higher Education in the Philippines: The Case for Choice, Equity and Efficiency, Occasional Paper No. 68, NCSPE, Teachers College, Columbia University.

Gupta A. (2005), International Trends in Private Higher Education and the Indian Scenario, Research & Occasional Paper Series: CSHE. Berkeley: University of California. http://cshe.berkeley.edu/

Husen Torstent, Lawrence Saha, and Richard Noonan (1978), Teacher Training and Student Achievement in Less Developed Countries. Washington, D.C.:World Bank Staff Working Paper no. 310.

Johanson, Richard K. (1999), Higher Education in the Philippines. Manila: Asian Development Bank.

Johnstone B. D. (2001), The Economics and Politics of Cost Sharing in Higher Education; Comparative Perspective, an article prepared for a special issue of the Economics of Education Review, 2004, an earlier version of the same was presented to the International Conference on the Economics of Education held at Peking University, Beijing, China, May 2001.

Joshi K M (2006), An Exploration of Private Sector Financing of Higher Education in the Philippines and Its Policy Implications for India. Paper presented in 'Sixth Asia Fellow's Conference', Bangkok, 3-4 July.

Levine Arthur (2006), Privatization in Higher Education. Teacher's College, Columbia University.

Morada Hector B. and Teresita Manzala R. (2001), Mismatches in the Philippine Labor Market. http://www.manila-online.net/bles/download/mplm.pdf

Orbeta A. (2001), Education, Labour Market and Development: A Review of the Trends and Issues in the Past 25 Years. Symposium Series on Perspective Papers for the 25th Anniversary of the Philippine Institute for Development Studies.

Paqueo V. and J.P. Tan (1989), The Economic Returns to Education in Philippines, *International Journal of Educational Development* 9(3).

Perkinson Ron (2006), Trends in Global Higher Education. . . the changing landscape, Presentation to IFC International Investment Forum for Private Higher Education 2nd & 3rd February. www.ifc.org

Phelps Marianne R. (2001), Accreditation and the Quality Assurance System for the Higher Education. Manila: Asian Development Bank.

Psacharopolous G. and Woodhall Maureen (1985), Education for Development-An Analysis of Investment Choices. New York: Oxford University Press.

Savas Emanuel. S. (2001), Privatization and Public-Private Partnerships. New Delhi: Affiliated East-West Press Private Limited.

Schultz T. W. (1961), Investment in human capital, American Economic Review, March.

Valsino Mona Dumlao, (ed.) (2000), World Conference on Higher Education and Framework for Priority Action for Change and Development for Higher Education in the 21st century in the Philippines, Higher Education Policy Series No.1, UNESCO.

World Bank and UNESCO (2000), Higher Education in Developing Countries: Peril and Promise. Washington, D.C.: Report of the Independent World Bank/UNESCO Task Force on Higher Education and Society. Washington, D.C.

Other References:

http://www.answers.com/topic/superpower

http://www.albany.edu/dept/eaps/prophe/data/international.html

http://www.census.gov.ph/data/sectordata/2006/lf060416.htm

AN EXAMINATION OF TIME DEFORMATION IN THE NATIONAL OUTPUT OF ASIAN AND AFRICAN ECONOMIES

Steven Cook & Alan Speight***

Abstract

This paper provides an extension of the literature concerned with testing for asymmetries in the business cycle through the application of diagnostic tests for asymmetry associated with the concept of 'time deformation' (Stock, 1987, 1988) to national per capita GDP data for a wide range of Asian and African economies, totaling 90 in number. This approach is based on the distinction between the economic time scale on which variables evolve and the calendar time scale from which the data are drawn, and the essential proposition under scrutiny is whether national output evolves at a different pace under conditions of expansion and contraction respectively. Time deformation of both cyclical and growth cyclical form is clearly identified on the basis of the test results for 10 of the 22 East Asian economies, 4 of the 15 West Asian economies and 22 of the 53 African economies examined. However, instances of cyclical time deformation are more numerous than those of growth cyclical time deformation for the East Asian economies. This indicates that business cycle asymmetry is more typically related to the sign of the change in output for these countries, and so to periods when output is either rising or falling. The converse is generally the case for instances of test significance amongst the African economies, where there are numerous instances of both cyclical and growth cyclical time deformation, or growth cyclical time deformation alone. Thus, business cycle asymmetry in Africa is more typically related to different regimes associated with whether output is growing above or below its recent average, rather than simply to periods when output is simply rising or falling.

Keywords: *Time Deformation; National Output; Per Capita GDP; Business Cycle Asymmetry.*

JEL codes: *C12; E21; E32.*

I. INTRODUCTION

The possibility of macroeconomic variables displaying some form of asymmetric or non-linear behaviour has a long history in economics. Frequently this has been discussed in connection

* Professor Steven Cook, Department of Economics, School of Business and Economics, University of Wales Swansea, Singleton Park, Swansea, *E-mail: s.cook@swan.ac.uk*

** Professor Alan Speight, Department of Economics, School of Business and Economics, University of Wales Swansea Singleton Park, Swansea, *E-mail: a.speight@swan.ac.uk*

with the business cycle, with asymmetry anticipated in the form of recessionary periods which are relatively sharp in comparison to more gentle and gradual recovery phases. Consideration of this form of asymmetric behaviour can be traced back to the works of Mitchell (1913), Keynes (1936) and Burns and Mitchell (1946). Relatedly, Friedman (1964, 1993) also noted asymmetry in real output, in the sense that the depth of a real output contraction is often strongly correlated with the subsequent expansion, but that the converse does not tend to hold, so that the strength of an expansion is not usually informative as to the depth of the subsequent contraction.

More recently, such asymmetric behaviour in economic time series has been the subject of much attention at an empirical level both in terms of general application and in relation to the business cycle. The variety of alternative methods and tests which have been proposed and applied is apparent from inspection of the literature reviews of Mills (1991) and Mullineux and Peng (1993). In particular, studies of business cycle asymmetry have focused on testing for 'depth' and 'steepness', using the terminology and methodology of Sichel (1993) and Ramsey and Rothman (1996), or on testing for 'time deformation' in the relationship between calendar time and economic (or business cycle) time, using the conceptual framework established by Stock (1987, 1988). This research on national output is of particular interest as it has been shown that asymmetric behaviour has significant implications for the impact of economic policy. Indeed, evidence on the significant impact of asymmetric behaviour for economic policy has been provided for the U.K. by Arden *et al.* (2000), a range of OECD economies by Karras (1996) and the U.S. by Cover (1992) and Rhee and Rich (1995).

However, such empirical studies have tended to focus largely on the analysis of real output data for the United States, and to some extent the industrialized Western economies, but broader international evidence is less prevalent. For example, Goodwin and Sweeney (1993) and Balke and Wynne (1992, 1996) report evidence of depth but not of steepness nor length for a number of OECD economies. Psaradakis (2000) reports similar findings in an empirical analysis of potential asymmetric behaviour in the national output of five major OECD economies, while Razzak (2001) applies a nonparametric test procedure to six industrial countries and finds limited evidence for depth or steepness. In contrast, in the analysis of longer-run annual data for 22 countries spanning the period 1870-1994, Cook (2004) finds far more widespread evidence of business cycle asymmetry using a nonparametric approach.

This paper offers a further extension of the literature concerned with testing for asymmetries in the business cycle through the application of alternative diagnostic tests for asymmetry associated with the concept of 'time deformation' (Stock, 1987, 1988) to national output data for a wide range of Asian (both East and West) and African economies, totaling 90 in number. As noted above, this approach to business cycle asymmetry is based on the distinction between the economic time scale on which variables evolve and the calendar time scale from which the data are drawn. Alternatively, the approach may be considered in terms of latent variables which evolve linearly in economic time but are only observed on the nonlinear transformation of that time scale into calendar time. On either interpretation, the essential proposition under scrutiny is therefore whether national output evolves at a different pace under conditions of expansion and contraction respectively.[1]

The remainder of the paper proceeds as follows. In Section II the concept of time deformation and the associated test procedures are presented. The national output series to be examined are discussed in Section III and, as a precursor to application of tests for time deformation, their orders of integration are examined through a unit root testing procedure. Section IV reports the results obtained from the application of the time deformation tests to the national output series, while Section V summarizes the main findings and conclusions.

II. TIME DEFORMATION

The notion of time deformation, as introduced by Stock (1987), is based upon the distinction between an economic, or operational, time scale (s) within which variables evolve, and the calendar time scale from which observations are drawn (t).[2] Following Stock's (1987) approach, the underlying, or latent, continuous process evolving in *economic* time is specified as $\xi(s)$. The link between economic time and *calendar* time is given by $s = g(t)$. The consequent relationship between the variable of interest (x_t) which is observed at discrete points in calendar time and the latent process is then specified as:

$$x_t = \xi(g(t)) \tag{1}$$

Stock (1987, 1988) considers two forms of time scale transformation based upon the use of Neftci's (1984) switching (or indicator) variable, allowing examination of the possibility that economic time progresses faster during expansions than during contractions. The first, referred to as 'cyclical' expansion/contraction, relates to the sign of changes in the variable of interest, with the relevant indicator variable (z_t) defined as:

$$z_t = \begin{cases} 1 & if \quad \Delta x_t \geq 0 \\ 0 & if \quad \Delta x_t < 0 \end{cases} \tag{2}$$

The second form of time scale transformation, referred to as 'cyclical growth' expansion/contraction, considers changes in the variable of interest relative to its average rate of change. In this second case, the relevant indicator variable (z^*_t) is defined as:

$$z^*_t = \begin{cases} 1 & if \quad \Delta x_t \geq \overline{\Delta x} \\ 0 & if \quad \Delta x_t < \overline{\Delta x} \end{cases} \tag{3}$$

These forms of time deformation therefore consider asymmetry arising due to different speeds of evolution during recessionary and recovery periods. Under cyclical expansion/contraction, the possibility of differing behaviour is permitted when the indicator variable is either increasing or decreasing over the business cycle, whilst under cyclical growth expansion/contraction, differing behaviour is permitted depending upon whether current growth is above or below a long-run average growth rate. In what follows we refer to these two forms of test results as relating to 'cyclical time deformation' and 'growth cyclical time deformation' respectively.

Although the full estimation of time deformation models is computationally demanding, it is relatively straightforward to implement diagnostic tests for the presence of time deformation in the sense of a nonlinear transformation of economic time into calendar time. However, before applying tests of time deformation, it is important to assess the orders of integration of the series under examination, as the correct specification of the testing equation to employ is dependent upon whether the series considered possesses a unit root. When the variables of interest do possess stochastic trends, as will be seen to be the case with the series considered in the present analysis, Stock (1987) proposes the use of the following models:

$$\Delta x_t = \mu + \lambda \Delta x_{t-1} + \sum_{i=1}^{m} \alpha_i \left(z_{t-i} - \bar{z}\right) + \sum_{i=1}^{m} \beta_i \left(z_{t-i} - \bar{z}\right) \Delta x_{t-i} + \varepsilon_t \quad (4)$$

$$\Delta x_t = \mu^* + \lambda^* \Delta x_{t-1} + \sum_{i=1}^{m} \alpha_i^* \left(z_{t-i}^* - \bar{z}^*\right) + \sum_{i=1}^{m} \beta_i^* \left(z_{t-i}^* - \bar{z}^*\right) \Delta x_{t-i} + \varepsilon_t^* \quad (5)$$

The presence or absence of time deformation is then examined formally through testing of the joint significance of the coefficients (α_i, β_i) in (4) under cyclical time deformation and (α^*_i, β^*_i) in (5) under growth cyclical time deformation. The relevant null hypotheses, H_0: $\alpha_i = \beta_i = 0$ in (4) and H^*_0: $\alpha^*_i = \beta^*_i = 0$ in (5), are that time deformation is not present.

III. DATA

The national output series examined are annual observations on real, per capita gross domestic product measured in 1990 International Geary-Khamis dollars over the period 1950 to 2003 for 22 East Asian economies, 15 West Asian economies and 53 African economies.[3] In the interests of brevity, the precise 90 economies are not listed here, but can be seen in the subsequent tabulated results. In all following empirical analyses, the series are considered in their natural logarithmic forms.

As noted above, when performing Stock's (1987) tests of time deformation it is important that the orders of integration of the series under consideration are first determined. Therefore, before considering time deformation, second order augmented Dickey-Fuller (ADF) tests are applied to each series. Denoting the natural logarithmic values of the national output series as y_t, the exact specification of the ADF tests employed is as follows:

$$\Delta y_t = \alpha + \beta t + \rho y_{t-1} + \sum_{i=1}^{2} \gamma_i \Delta y_{t-i} + \varepsilon_t \quad (6)$$

with the calculated test statistic τ_μ given as the *t*-ratio for ρ. Considering the structure of (6), a linear trend is included to increase test power as a result of the trending nature of all the series examined over the sample period. The results obtained from the application of the above test to the 90 economies examined are reported in Tables One to Three. From comparison of the calculated test statistics with the 5% critical value obtained from the response surface analysis provided by MacKinnon (1991), it is apparent that the unit root null hypothesis cannot be rejected for any of the series considered. In light of these results, the time deformation testing equations in equations (4) and (5) above are considered to be the appropriate ones to employ.

Table 1
ADF Unit Root Test Results for East Asian Economies

Economy	*ADF*
Afghanistan	-2.185
Bangladesh	-0.318
Burma	-0.765
Cambodia	-2.319
China	-1.012
Hong Kong	-0.124
India	0.657
Indonesia	-2.196
Japan	-0.269
Laos	-0.544
Malaysia	-3.073
Mongolia	-0.639
Nepal	-0.928
North Korea	-1.128
Pakistan	-1.093
Philippines	-2.356
Singapore	-1.991
South Korea	-1.622
Sri Lanka	-2.068
Taiwan	-0.570
Thailand	-2.793
Vietnam	0.270
5% critical value	-3.498

Notes: The above figures represent calculated ADF(2) test statistics obtained from estimation of equation (6). The 5% critical value was derived from the response surface analysis of MacKinnon (1991).

Table 2
ADF Unit Root Test Results for West Asian Economies

Economy	*ADF*
Bahrain	-1.847
Iran	-1.951
Iraq	-1.708
Israel	-1.172
Jordan	-2.465
Kuwait	-2.164
Lebanon	-2.845
Oman	-1.016
Qatar	-1.863
Saudi Arabia	-1.347
Syria	-2.192
Turkey	-2.099
United Arab Emirates	-1.989
West Bank and Gaza	1.153
Yemen	-1.575
5% critical value	-3.498

Notes: As Table 1.

Table 3
ADF Unit Root Test Results for African Economies

Economy	*ADF*	*Economy*	*ADF*
Algeria	-1.433	Malawi	-1.862
Angola	-2.030	Mali	-2.492
Benin	-2.761	Mauritania	-1.698
Botswana	-2.414	Mauritius	-2.553
Burkina Faso	-2.652	Morocco	-2.065
Burundi	0.051	Mozambique	-1.808
Cameroon	-2.627	Namibia	-2.259
Cape Verde	-1.940	Niger	-2.407
Central African Republic	-3.131	Nigeria	-1.944
Chad	-1.978	Reunion	-1.649
Comoro Islands	-1.907	Rwanda	-1.709
Congo	-1.128	São Tomé & Principe	-0.817
Côte d'Ivoire	-1.292	Senegal	-2.006
Djibouti	-1.738	Seychelles	-2.586
Egypt	-2.040	Sierra Leone	-1.375
Equatorial Guinea	-1.720	Somalia	-3.458
Eritrea and Ethiopia	-1.574	South Africa	-1.911
Gabon	-1.439	Sudan	-2.023
Gambia	-1.580	Swaziland	-1.119
Ghana	-1.582	Tanzania	-1.380
Guinea	-2.028	Togo	-1.393
Guinea Bissau	-1.441	Tunisia	-1.954
Kenya	-0.691	Uganda	-1.136
Lesotho	-2.826	Zaire	-1.336
Liberia	-2.425	Zambia	-2.303
Libya	-1.854	Zimbabwe	-1.203
Madagascar	-2.319		
5% critical value	-3.498		

IV. RESULTS

The results obtained from application of the testing equations in (4) and (5) to the national output series are presented in Tables Four to Nine. In addition to presenting the calculated time deformation test F-statistics under both cyclical and growth cyclical time deformation, asymptotic marginal significance levels (p-values) are provided also. As there is no optimal, or preferred, value provided in the literature for the lag truncation parameter (m) for the terms involving the relevant indicator functions, two values are considered. These values correspond to one and four period lags ($m = 1, 4$). To avoid potential problems resulting from the presence of serial correlation and/or heteroskedasticity, the Newey-West (1987) heteroskedasticity and autocorrelation consistent (HAC) variance-covariance matrix estimator is employed to assess the significance of the alternative F-tests of time deformation.

Considering the results for the East Asian economies presented in Tables Four and Five for the one-period and four-period time deformation testing equations respectively, it can be seen that rejection of the null of no time deformation occurs frequently. More precisely, the null of no time deformation is rejected at the 5% level for 8 East Asian economies (Burma, Cambodia, China, Mongolia, Pakistan, Singapore, Thailand, Vietnam) and at the 10% level for a further 2 economies (North Korea, Sri Lanka).[4] Evidence of time deformation is less prevalent in the results presented for the West Asian economies in Tables Six and Seven, where evidence of time deformation is noted at the 5% level of significance for only three economies (Bahrain, Saudi Arabia, the West Bank and Gaza) and one economy at the 10% level (Lebanon). The results for African economies provided in Tables Eight and Nine, show evidence of time deformation in 18 economies (Benin, Botswana, Cape Verde, Comoro Islands, Gabon, Guinea, Kenya, Lesotho, Libya, Malawi, Mauritania, Mauritius, Morocco, Rwanda, São Tomé & Principe, Swaziland, Tanzania, Zaire) at the 5% level of significance and 4 further economies (Gambia, Namibia, Somalia, Togo) at the 10% level of significance. In summary, time deformation in

Table 4
Time Deformation Test Results for East Asian Economies (m = 1)

	z_t		z^*_t	
Economy	F-stat	p-value	F-stat	p-value
Afghanistan	0.307	0.737	0.307	0.737
Bangladesh	1.098	0.342	1.211	0.307
Burma	2.274	0.114	2.099	0.134
Cambodia	0.891	0.417	0.900	0.413
China**	2.417	0.100	7.186	0.002
Hong Kong	0.302	0.741	0.282	0.755
India	0.400	0.673	0.227	0.798
Indonesia	0.779	0.465	0.939	0.398
Japan	0.621	0.542	0.131	0.877
Laos	N/A	N/A	1.878	0.164
Malaysia	1.673	0.199	1.443	0.246
Mongolia**	6.083	0.004	1.597	0.213
Nepal	0.236	0.791	0.383	0.684
North Korea*	1.427	0.250	2.711	0.077
Pakistan**	2.439	0.098	3.287	0.046
Philippines	1.549	0.223	0.741	0.482
Singapore**	5.037	0.010	2.345	0.107
South Korea	0.643	0.530	0.615	0.545
Sri Lanka*	2.613	0.084	1.873	0.165
Taiwan	0.589	0.559	0.607	0.549
Thailand**	4.782	0.013	0.790	0.460
Vietnam	2.403	0.101	0.930	0.402

Notes: The test results reported are the Stock (1987) statistics for cyclical time deformation, z_t, and cyclical growth time deformation, z_t^*, described in Section II and equations (4) and (5) in particular. The tests are performed using a one period lag (m = 1) for terms involving the relevant indicator function. Figures in parentheses denote asymptotic marginal significance levels (p-values) for the associated F-tests under the null hypothesis that time deformation is not present in the data, using Newey-West (1987) covariance matrix estimation. A single asterisk attached to an economy denotes rejection of the null hypothesis of no time deformation under either or both tests at the 10% significance level. A double asterisk denotes an analogous outcome at the 5% significance level. N/A denotes that due to properties of the series examined, it was not possible to derive a calculated test statistic.

Table 5
Time Deformation Test Results for East Asian Economies (m = 4)

	z_t		z^*_t	
Economy	*F-stat*	*p-value*	*F-stat*	*p-value*
Afghanistan	0.255	0.977	0.255	0.977
Bangladesh	0.861	0.556	0.887	0.536
Burma**	1.851	0.097	2.535	0.025
Cambodia**	3.528	0.004	3.662	0.003
China**	1.631	0.148	2.767	0.016
Hong Kong	1.370	0.240	0.413	0.906
India	0.711	0.680	0.385	0.922
Indonesia	0.277	0.970	0.531	0.826
Japan	0.472	0.869	1.281	0.282
Laos	N/A	N/A	1.594	0.158
Malaysia	0.427	0.898	0.267	0.973
Mongolia**	9.757	0.000	9.313	0.000
Nepal	1.011	0.444	1.658	0.140
North Korea	1.141	0.358	0.949	0.489
Pakistan*	2.080	0.062	1.576	0.164
Philippines	1.503	0.188	1.503	0.188
Singapore*	1.869	0.093	1.043	0.422
South Korea	0.752	0.646	0.348	0.941
Sri Lanka	1.767	0.114	1.108	0.379
Taiwan	0.553	0.809	0.492	0.855
Thailand**	2.221	0.047	1.190	0.330
Vietnam**	2.939	0.011	0.708	0.683

Notes: The test results reported are the Stock (1987) statistics for cyclical time deformation, z_t, and cyclical growth time deformation, z^*_t, described in Section II and equations (4) and (5) in particular. The tests are performed using a one period lag (m=4) for terms involving the relevant indicator function. Figures in parentheses denote asymptotic marginal significance levels (p-values) for the associated F-tests under the null hypothesis that time deformation is not present in the data, using Newey-West (1987) covariance matrix estimation. A single asterisk attached to an economy denotes rejection of the null hypothesis of no time deformation under either or both tests at the 10% significance level. A double asterisk denotes an analogous outcome at the 5% significance level. N/A denotes that due to properties of the series examined, it was not possible to derive a calculated test statistic.

Table 6
Time Deformation Test Results for West Asian Economies (m = 1)

	z_t		z^*_t	
Economy	*F-stat*	*p-value*	*F-stat*	*p-value*
Bahrain**	5.337	0.008	2.849	0.068
Iran	2.279	0.113	0.995	0.377
Iraq	2.080	0.136	2.080	0.136
Israel	1.235	0.300	0.302	0.741
Jordan	0.938	0.399	0.804	0.453
Kuwait	1.062	0.354	1.106	0.339
Lebanon	0.011	0.989	0.011	0.989
Oman	1.002	0.375	1.699	0.194
Qatar	1.678	0.198	1.570	0.219
Saudi Arabia	0.284	0.754	1.177	0.317
Syria	0.565	0.572	0.454	0.638
Turkey	0.598	0.554	0.751	0.478
United Arab Emirates	1.870	0.165	1.888	0.162
West Bank and Gaza**	149.578	0.000	149.578	0.000
Yemen	1.267	0.291	0.363	0.697

Notes: As Table 4.

Table 7
Time Deformation Test Results for West Asian Economies ($m = 4$)

	z_t		z^*_t	
Economy	*F-stat*	*p-value*	*F-stat*	*p-value*
Bahrain	1.480	0.196	1.181	0.335
Iran	1.434	0.214	1.166	0.344
Iraq	1.144	0.357	1.144	0.357
Israel	0.577	0.790	0.565	0.800
Jordan	0.816	0.593	0.337	0.946
Kuwait	0.785	0.619	0.718	0.674
Lebanon*	1.833	0.100	1.660	0.140
Oman	0.931	0.502	1.753	0.117
Qatar	0.898	0.527	1.282	0.281
Saudi Arabia**	2.235	0.045	0.939	0.496
Syria	0.621	0.755	0.315	0.955
Turkey	0.619	0.756	1.677	0.135
United Arab Emirates	0.959	0.481	1.095	0.387
West Bank and Gaza	N/A	N/A	N/A	N/A
Yemen	0.614	0.761	0.307	0.959

Notes: As Table 5.

Table 8
Time Deformation Test Results for African Economies ($m = 1$)

	z_t		z^*_t	
Economy	*F-stat*	*p-value*	*F-stat*	*p-value*
Algeria	1.192	0.312	0.385	0.682
Angola	1.071	0.351	1.136	0.329
Benin**	6.646	0.003	3.900	0.027
Botswana**	4.945	0.011	0.903	0.412
Burkina Faso	1.177	0.317	1.198	0.311
Burundi	0.169	0.845	0.106	0.899
Cameroon	1.122	0.334	1.499	0.234
Cape Verde	0.328	0.722	0.992	0.378
Central African Republic	1.579	0.217	1.594	0.214
Chad	2.114	0.132	2.114	0.132
Comoro Islands**	3.411	0.041	3.760	0.030
Congo	1.618	0.209	1.592	0.214
Côte d'Ivoire	2.077	0.136	2.077	0.136
Djibouti	1.510	0.231	1.377	0.262
Egypt	1.376	0.262	0.203	0.817
Equatorial Guinea	0.460	0.634	1.156	0.323
Eritrea and Ethiopia	0.644	0.530	0.758	0.474
Gabon**	4.142	0.022	4.137	0.022
Gambia*	1.996	0.147	2.533	0.090
Ghana	0.320	0.728	0.297	0.744
Guinea**	2.668	0.080	3.700	0.032
Guinea Bissau	1.371	0.264	1.400	0.257
Kenya**	4.005	0.025	4.645	0.014
Lesotho**	7.783	0.001	7.778	0.001
Liberia	0.094	0.911	0.094	0.911
Libya	2.084	0.136	1.484	0.237
Madagascar	1.346	0.270	1.585	0.215

Notes: As Table 4.

Table 8
Time Deformation Test Results for African Economies (m = 1) (cont'd)

	z_t		z^*_t	
Economy	*F-stat*	*p-value*	*F-stat*	*p-value*
Malawi	1.647	0.203	1.698	0.194
Mali	2.087	0.135	1.511	0.231
Mauritania**	4.295	0.019	3.088	0.055
Mauritius**	0.583	0.562	3.348	0.044
Morocco**	1.927	0.157	5.354	0.008
Mozambique	0.024	0.977	0.190	0.828
Namibia	0.533	0.590	0.521	0.597
Niger	2.065	0.138	1.190	0.313
Nigeria	1.110	0.338	1.041	0.361
Reunion	1.410	0.254	0.891	0.417
Rwanda**	5.710	0.006	4.790	0.013
São Tomé and Principe**	3.950	0.026	3.344	0.044
Senegal	0.929	0.402	0.625	0.539
Seychelles	0.695	0.504	1.484	0.237
Sierra Leone	0.185	0.831	0.181	0.835
Somalia*	1.943	0.154	2.498	0.093
South Africa	0.220	0.803	0.119	0.888
Sudan	0.195	0.824	0.150	0.862
Swaziland	0.160	0.853	0.237	0.790
Tanzania**	7.978	0.001	1.017	0.369
Togo*	1.673	0.198	2.694	0.078
Tunisia	2.188	0.123	1.203	0.309
Uganda	0.176	0.839	0.160	0.853
Zaire	0.246	0.783	0.001	0.999
Zambia	1.731	0.188	2.232	0.118
Zimbabwe	0.367	0.695	0.630	0.537

Notes: As Table 4.

Table 9
Time Deformation Test Results for African Economies (m = 4)

	z_t		z^*_t	
Economy	*F-stat*	*p-value*	*F-stat*	*p-value*
Algeria	0.589	0.781	0.569	0.797
Angola	0.611	0.763	0.670	0.714
Benin**	2.254	0.044	1.452	0.207
Botswana**	2.632	0.021	2.644	0.020
Burkina Faso	1.101	0.384	0.909	0.519
Burundi	1.248	0.298	1.163	0.345
Cameroon	0.810	0.598	0.921	0.510
Cape Verde**	5.379	0.000	1.294	0.275
Central African Republic	0.805	0.602	0.905	0.522
Chad	1.777	0.111	1.777	0.111
Comoro Islands**	2.791	0.015	3.108	0.008

Table contd.

Congo	1.522	0.181	1.541	0.175
Côte d'Ivoire	1.122	0.370	1.122	0.370
Djibouti	1.127	0.367	1.382	0.235
Egypt	0.521	0.834	0.580	0.788
Equatorial Guinea	1.507	0.186	1.451	0.207
Eritrea and Ethiopia	1.119	0.372	0.451	0.882
Gabon	1.737	0.121	1.779	0.111
Gambia	0.824	0.587	1.168	0.343
Ghana	1.493	0.191	1.581	0.162
Guinea	0.939	0.496	0.841	0.573
Guinea Bissau	0.729	0.665	1.503	0.188
Kenya**	2.583	0.023	1.733	0.121
Lesotho**	4.237	0.001	3.216	0.007
Liberia	1.006	0.447	1.006	0.447
Libya**	2.209	0.048	0.766	0.634
Madagascar	0.901	0.525	0.642	0.737

Notes: As Table 5.

Table 9

Time Deformation Test Results for African Economies (m = 4) (cont'd)

	z_t		z^*_t	
Economy	*F-stat*	*p-value*	*F-stat*	*p-value*
Malawi**	3.045	0.009	2.776	0.016
Mali	0.965	0.477	0.439	0.890
Mauritania*	1.788	0.109	1.867	0.094
Mauritius**	1.269	0.288	2.338	0.037
Morocco	1.334	0.256	1.768	0.113
Mozambique	0.153	0.996	0.452	0.882
Namibia*	1.135	0.362	1.854	0.096
Niger	0.755	0.643	0.658	0.724
Nigeria	0.853	0.563	1.127	0.367
Reunion	1.532	0.178	0.863	0.555
Rwanda**	2.371	0.035	2.587	0.023
São Tomé and Principe	0.918	0.512	0.789	0.616
Senegal	0.603	0.769	0.424	0.899
Seychelles	0.654	0.728	1.127	0.367
Sierra Leone	0.431	0.895	0.599	0.773
Somalia	1.603	0.156	1.614	0.152
South Africa	0.239	0.981	0.322	0.953
Sudan	0.554	0.808	0.730	0.664
Swaziland**	3.206	0.007	1.699	0.130
Tanzania**	2.199	0.049	1.391	0.231
Togo	0.660	0.723	0.675	0.711
Tunisia	0.761	0.639	0.570	0.796
Uganda	0.562	0.802	0.610	0.764
Zaire**	2.344	0.037	2.130	0.056
Zambia	0.910	0.518	1.435	0.213
Zimbabwe	0.790	0.614	0.717	0.675

Notes: As Table 5.

national output is present in 10 of the 22 East Asian economies, 4 of the 15 West Asian economies and 22 of the 53 African economies examined.

Time deformation of both cyclical and growth cyclical form is clearly identified on the basis of the test results. However, instances of cyclical time deformation are more numerous than those of growth cyclical time deformation for the East Asian economies. This indicate that business cycle asymmetry is more typically related to the sign of the change in output for these countries, and so to periods when output is either rising or falling, rather than to periods when output is growing above or below trend. The converse is generally the case for instances of test significance amongst the African economies, where there are numerous instances of both cyclical and growth cyclical time deformation, or growth cyclical time deformation alone. Thus, business cycle asymmetry in Africa is more typically related to different regimes associated with whether output is growing above or below its recent average, rather than simply to periods when output is simply rising or falling.

V. CONCLUSIONS

In this paper the issue of testing empirically for business cycle asymmetries in international output data has been extended in various ways, with the analysis undertaken departing from previous research in two main ways. In contrast to most previous studies employing univariate tests of deepness and steepness, an alternative test of asymmetric adjustment is employed based on the concept of 'time deformation' whereby latent variables evolve linearly in economic time but are only observed on the nonlinear transformation of that time scale into calendar time. Previous research is further extended through the empirical examination of a more diverse international data set than considered in this context previously in the literature, covering the per capita GDP of 90 Asian and African economies. Several broad conclusions can be drawn from the results. First, the prevalence of time deformation in national output is diverse regionally. It is present in nearly half the East Asian economies examined and approaching half of the African economies examined, but in only a quarter of the West Asian economies. Second, time deformation of both cyclical and growth cyclical form is clearly identified on the basis of the test results. Third, however, these test results further indicate that business cycle asymmetry amongst East Asian economies is more typically related to the sign of the change in output for these countries, and so to periods when output is either rising or falling. The converse is generally the case for instances of test significance amongst the African economies, where business cycle asymmetry is more typically related to different regimes associated with whether output is growing above or below its recent average, rather than simply to periods when output is simply rising or falling. The full econometric modelling of these business cycle dynamics, including the asymmetric adjustment of output and the underlying nonlinear transformations indicated by the test results reported here, therefore provide interesting and potentially fruitful avenues for further empirical research.

Notes

1. This research therefore adds to the previous studies of Cook (1999a) and Mills (1995) where tests of time deformation were applied to national output data for the UK. While tests of time deformation have been

applied to UK national output, their application more generally to other economic time series has been limited. The exception to this concerns the analysis of U.K. and U.S. consumers' expenditure, where Cook (1999b, 1999c) and Cook and Speight (2006) have explored the relationship between the durability and asymmetry exhibited by components of consumers' expenditure using disaggregated data.

2. Despite the novelty of the framework proposed by Stock (1987), the consideration of alternative time scales does have a precursor in the phase averaging procedures employed at the National Bureau of Economic Research (NBER). The phase averaging procedure employed at the NBER, whereby data are averaged across different phases of the business cycle, has a long history with Burns and Mitchell (1946) and Friedman and Schwartz (1982) offering early and more recent examples of this approach.
3. The series have been downloaded from http://www.ggdc.net/maddison/.
4. As Psaradakis and Sola (2003) show, tests of asymmetry may possess low power when applied to the business cycle component of macroeconomic time series, and we therefore consider test statistic significance up to a threshold of 10% rather than the conventional significance level of 5%.

References

Arden, R., Cook, S., Holly, S. and Turner, P. (2000), 'The Asymmetric Effects of Monetary Policy: Some Results from a Macroeconometric Model', *The Manchester School* 68, 419-441.

Balke, N.S. and Wynne, M.A. (1992), 'Are Deep Recessions Followed by Strong Recoveries?', *Economics Letters*, 39, 183-189.

Balke, N.S. and Wynne, M.A. (1996), 'Are Deep Recessions Followed by Strong Recoveries? Results for the G-7 Countries', *Applied Economics*, 28, 889-897.

Burns, A. and Mitchell, W. (1946), *Measuring Business Cycles*, National Bureau of Economic Research: New York.

Cook, S. (1999a), 'Asymmetry and Non-linearity in UK output', *Applied Economics Letters*, 7, 459-462.

Cook, S. (1999b), 'Time Deformation in UK Consumers' Expenditure', *Bulletin of Economic Research*, 51, 253-258.

Cook, S. (1999c), 'Cyclicality and Durability: Evidence from US Consumers' Expenditure', *Journal of Applied Economics*, 2, 299-310.

Cook, S. (2004), 'On the Detection of Business Cycle Asymmetry in 22 Countries, 1870-1994', *Applied Econometrics and International Development*, 4, 105-120.

Cook, S. and Speight, A.E.H. (2006), 'Time Deformation in UK Consumers' Expenditure: An Analysis of Highly Disaggregated Data', *Applied Economics Letters*, 13, 471-478.

Cover, J. (1992), 'Asymmetric Effects of Positive and Negative Money Supply Shocks', *Quarterly Journal of Economics* 107: 1261-1282.

Friedman, M. (1964), *Monetary Studies of the National Bureau. The National Bureau Enters its 45th Year.* 44th Annual Report, NBER.

Friedman, M. (1993), 'The 'Plucking' Model of Business Fluctuations Revisited', *Economic Inquiry*, 171-177.

Friedman, M. and Schwartz, A. J. (1982), *Monetary Trends in the United States and United Kingdom: Their Relation to Income Prices and Interest Rates, 1867-1975*, Chicago, University of Chicago Press.

Goodwin, T.H. and Sweeney, R.J. (1993), 'International Evidence on Friedman's theories of the Business Cycle', *Economic Inquiry*, 178-193.

Karras, G. (1996), 'Are the Output Effects of Monetary Policy Asymmetric?', *Oxford Bulletin of Economics and Statistics* 58: 267-278.

Keynes, J. (1936), *A General Theory of Employment, Interest and Money*, London: MacMillan.

Mills, T.C. (1991), 'Nonlinear Time Series Models in Economics', *Journal of Economic Surveys*, 5, 215-242.

Mills, T.C. (1995), 'Are There Asymmetries or Nonlinearities in UK Output?', *Applied Economics*, 27, 1211-1217.

Mitchell, W. (1913), *Business Cycles*, Berkeley: University of California Press.

Mullineux, A. and Peng, W. (1993), 'Nonlinear Business Cycle Modelling', *Journal of Economic Surveys*, 7, 41-83.

Neftci, S.N. (1984), 'Are Economic Series Asymmetric Over the Business Cycle?', *Journal of Political Economy* 92, 307-328.

Newey, W. and West, K. (1987), 'A Simple, Positive Semi-definite, Heteroskedasticity and Autocorrelation Consistent Covariance Matrix', *Econometrica*, 55, 703-708.

Psaradakis, Z. (2000), 'P-value Adjustments for Multiple tests for Nonlinearity', *Studies in Nonlinear Dynamics & Econometrics*, 4, 95-100.

Psaradakis, Z. and Sola, M. (2003), 'On Detrending and Cyclical Asymmetry', *Journal of Applied Econometrics*, 18, 271-289.

Ramsey, J and Rothman, P. (1996), 'Time Irreversibility and Business Cycle Asymmetry', *Journal of Money, Credit and Banking*, 28, 1-21.

Randles, R., Fligner, M., Policello, G. and Wolfe, D. (1980), 'An Asymptotically Distribution-free test for Symmetry Versus Asymmetry', *Journal of the American Statistical Association*, 75, 168-172.

Razzak, W.A. (2001), 'Business Cycle Asymmetries: A Deeper Look', *Review of Economic Dynamics*, 4, 230-243.

Rhee, W. and Rich, R. (1995), 'Inflation and the Asymmetric Effects of Money on Output Fluctuations', *Journal of Macroeconomics*, 17, 683-702.

Sichel, D.E. (1993) 'Business cycle asymmetry: A deeper look', *Economic Inquiry*, 31, 224-236.

Stock, J.H. (1987), 'Measuring Business Cycle Time', *Journal of Political Economy*, 95, 1240-61.

Stock, J.H. (1988), 'Estimating Continuous Time Processes Subject to Time Deformation: An Application to Post-war GNP', *Journal of the American Statistical Association*, 83, 77-85.

DOES GLOBALIZATION LEAD TO TRICKLE DOWN GROWTH?

*Siddhartha Mitra**

ABSTRACT

This paper tries to assess the impact of globalization on the trickle down of benefits from economic growth to the poor. In the specific case study of Indian liberalization of 1991 the reforms led to an improvement in the elasticity of poverty to per capita income in both urban and rural areas but a decline in the efficiency of growth in bringing about poverty alleviation in rural areas That is, poverty alleviation, per constant rupee increase in average affluence, actually declined in rural areas.

I. INTRODUCTION

The question of whether liberalization benefits the poor in developing countries has been hotly debated. Academic studies have also differed on this question. An application of the Hecksher-Ohlin Model would imply that gains from trade should flow to the more abundant factor i.e. unskilled labour embodied in the poor of the developing country. However, Don Davis (1996) introduces the notion of local factor abundance to argue that the gains could actually go to owners of capital as these countries might be locally capital abundant i.e. though these countries may be capital scarce relative to the developed countries they might be capital abundant when viewed in the context of the immediate environment in which they operate. The hypothesis of gains to the more abundant unskilled labour has also been challenged by Stiglitz (1970) and Feenstra and Hanson (1997).

Empirical studies have also added to the controversy. Topalova's district based study (2006) has found that Indian districts more exposed to liberalization have exhibited a worse performance in poverty alleviation. Topalova's conclusions do not match with those of a state level study of the Indian case by Hasan, Mitra and Beyza (2005) which looks at the effect of trade protection (through tariff and non-tariff barriers) on poverty alleviation and finds that the existence of protected industries has a negative impact on poverty alleviation. They quite correctly control for labour market flexibility and development expenditure and conclude that trade liberalization has positive implications for poverty alleviation. The differences between Topalova and Hasan, Mitra and Beyza's results could be due to the difference in the unit of analysis (district versus state) and the use of more controls by the latter.

In this paper I try to compare the pre-liberalization experience regarding poverty alleviation with the post liberalization experience through a panel data set with the objective of finding out

* The author is Reader, Gokhale Institute of Politics and Economics, Pune. *E-mail: mitsid@yahoo.com*

whether liberalization impacts the trickle down of benefits of growth to the poor. The data pertain to the state level but separate analyses are undertaken for rural and urban areas. The dependent variable in the econometric exercise measures the responsiveness of poverty to growth of incomes and different variants of this measure are tried. As growth itself is determined by controls such as development expenditure, the need for inclusion of these controls as explanatory variables is not felt. Moreover, we use time itself as a crude index of liberalization, given the difficulty of constructing a composite index of liberalization which includes removal of tariff and non tariff barriers to trade and controls on foreign investment. The fact that the two time periods in our analysis are separated by the implementation of the liberalization process makes such an assumption viable.

The study which is closest in its research objective to this paper is the one by Datt and Ravallion (2002) who look at whether growth after reforms has benefited the poor. Their conclusion is that growth in India has been concentrated in the middle income states and not in the low income states where poverty is concentrated. This result is to be expected as like poverty alleviation growth requires a certain minimum of infrastructure facilities, investment and development expenditure. The present paper does not seek any reasons for the nature of growth patterns. Rather, it takes the existing pattern and spread of regional growth rates as given and then tries to judge how well the benefits from growth have percolated to the poor in the post– reform period relative to the immediate pre-reform period. Unlike Datt and Ravallion, the benchmark for evaluation of post reform performance is not the entire period 1958-91 but a much shorter period of seven years ending in 1992. As Datt and Ravallion themselves acknowledge, certain types of inequality often make marginal poverty alleviation more difficult. To these one should add factors such as political lobby formation and institutions which govern the development process. Obviously, much has changed with respect to these features over the course of the three decades from 1958 to 1991. In ascertaining the impact of liberalization on the poverty alleviating impact of growth the comparison of two periods, which are chronologically adjacent and do not have a large combined time span, prevents distortions through changes in factors other than liberalization such as income distribution and institutions.

II. EMPIRICAL EVIDENCE OF THE IMPACT OF LIBERALIZATION ON POVERTY ALLEVIATION

The period 1993-94 to 1999-00 was a period of significant liberalization for India with removal of both tariff and non tariff barriers and restrictions on foreign direct investment and significant deregulation in sectors (the last process having begun in the eighties). From the data on poverty rates in the initial and final year of this period compiled by Deaton (2003) and state-wise growth of per capita incomes (www.indiastat.com) we can construct absolute measures of poverty alleviation (in percentage points) and the corresponding relative measures (as a percentage of initial incidence of poverty). A similar exercise can be performed for period 1987-1993. The finding of this paper is that both measures of poverty alleviation were positive (for all states except two) and significantly and positively correlated with the growth of per capita income. This suggests that trickle down was associated with growth and more growth meant more trickle down.

Table 1
Urban Poverty Alleviation And Per Capita Income Growth In 1993-99

	Poverty incidence in 1993-94	*Poverty alleviation in 1993-1999 period in percentage point terms*	*Poverty alleviation in 1993-1999 period as percentage of initial incidence of poverty*	*Annual rate of growth of state per capita income*	*Elasticity of annual average poverty alleviation with respect to average rate of growth*
A.P.	17.8	6.5	0.37	4.1	1.31
Assam	13	-0.1	-0.01	0.8	-0.21
Bihar	26.7	0.2	0.01	1.3	0.13
Gujarat	14.7	8.1	0.55	3.6	2.10
Haryana	10.6	5.5	0.52	3.6	2.01
Himachal	3.6	1.9	0.53	4.7	1.56
Karnataka	21.4	9.9	0.46	6.5	1.00
Kerala	13.9	3.4	0.24	3.9	0.94
Madhya	18.5	4.4	0.24	2.3	1.59
Maharashtra	18	5	0.28	2.9	1.45
Orissa	15.2	-0.4	-0.03	1.3	-0.39
Punjab	7.8	3.8	0.49	2.9	2.37
Rajasthan	18.3	7.7	0.42	3.8	1.58
T.N.	20.9	9.8	0.47	5	1.33
U.P	21.7	5.2	0.24	1.8	2.03
West Bengal	15.5	4.1	0.26	5.5	0.71

Table 2
Urban Poverty Alleviation and Per Capita Income Growth In 1987-93

	Poverty incidence in 1987-88	*Poverty alleviation in 1987-1993 period in percentage point terms*	*Poverty alleviation in 1987-1993 period as percentage of initial incidence of poverty*	*Annual rate of growth of state per capita income*	*Elasticity of annual average poverty alleviation with respect to average rate of growth*
A.P	23.4	5.6	0.24	5.0	0.73
Assam	13.6	0.6	0.04	1.3	0.50
Bihar	38.1	11.4	0.30	-0.5	-8.94
Gujarat	16.4	1.7	0.10	6.8	0.24
Haryana	11.8	1.2	0.10	4.4	0.36
Himachal	1.7	-1.9	-1.12	3.8	-3.51
Karnataka	26	4.6	0.18	4.5	0.62
Kerala	21	7.1	0.34	6.0	0.83
Madhya	20.7	2.2	0.11	3.1	0.57
Maharashtra	21.2	3.2	0.15	7.0	0.34
Orissa	20.8	5.6	0.27	2.1	1.94
Punjab	6.6	-1.2	-0.18	2.8	-1.16
Rajasthan	19.8	1.5	0.08	5.4	0.24
T.N.	26.2	5.3	0.20	5.6	0.55
U.P	29.3	7.6	0.26	2.1	1.87
West Bengal	22.3	6.8	0.30	3.0	1.49

Table 3
Correlation of Annnual Growth Rate of PCY at State Level To Poverty Alleviation

Period	*Absolute poverty Alleviation*	*Relative poverty alleviation*
87-93	-.007(.002)	-0.28 (.313)
93-99	.693**(3.58)	.71** (3.77)

The symbol ** represents significance at 1% level. The t statistic is given in parantheses.

Table 4
Fixed Effects Regression of State-wise Urban Elasticities of Poverty Alleviation With Respect to Rate of Growth of PCY on Time

	Regression 1 (all observations available)	*Regression 1 (only observations corresponding to positive elasticities)*
Observations	32	27
F Statistic	4.62 {F(1,15)]	10.46[F(1, 10)]
R-square	0.236	0.511
Coefficient on time	1.43*	.74**
General Remarks	(Hypothesis of all regression coefficients being equal to zero cannot be rejected at 5% level of significance)	(Hypothesis of all regression coefficients being equal to zero cannot be rejected even at 1% level of significance)

Notes: (a) time =1 for the period 1987-1993 and 2 for the period 1993-99. b) ** and * represent significance at 1% and 5% level respectively

Tables 1 and 2 show the average annual rates of per capita income (PCY) growth and urban poverty alleviation (in percentage points) in various large states for the periods 1987-1993 and 1993-99 respectively. The correlations between absolute/relative poverty alleviation (the second measure being the first divided by the incidence of poverty) and the rate of growth of PCY, which are presented in Table 3, are significantly positive only for the second period. Thus, though almost all states exhibit positive poverty alleviation in both periods and growth could be associated with some percolation of benefits to the poor, the evidence for trickle down (i.e. growth directly acting as the cause for these benefits going to the poor) is definitely stronger in the post liberalization period in which growth was significantly and positively correlated with poverty alleviation. Elasticities computed in Table 1 and 2 (relative annual poverty alleviation divided by annual rate of growth) are also regressed on time using a fixed effects model in the following manner

$$E_{it} = \alpha_i + \beta t + u_{it}$$

where t = 1, 2 represents the periods 1987-93 and 1993-99 respectively. Table 4 presents the results for these regressions when all observations are included and when only observations corresponding to positive elasticities are included. The coefficient on "t" is strongly significant in both cases (the significance being stronger in the first case) implying that percentage poverty alleviation per percentage point rate of growth was definitely higher in the second period, thus providing strong evidence for better trickle down in this period relative to the first.

Tables 5, 6 and 7 present the data for rural areas that is similar to that presented by Tables 1, 2 and 3 for urban areas. In this case there is no significant correlation between per capita income growth and absolute/relative poverty alleviation in both the periods, though growth in the case of all the states was associated with positive poverty alleviation. Fixed effects regressions similar to those presented in Table 4 (see Table 8) in this case again show a positive significant change in percentage poverty alleviation per unit rate of growth from the pre-liberalization period to the post liberalization period.

Summarizing, to the extent that evidence for trickle down can be gleaned from statistical data pertaining to the immediate pre and post liberalization periods, it can be concluded that the efficiency with which growth (as measured by the rate of growth of per capita income) resulted in poverty alleviation was stronger in the post-liberalization period in both urban and rural areas.

We now define a more intuitive measure of the efficiency with which resources generated from growth resulted in poverty alleviation. We call this measure the poverty multiplier:

$$M = \frac{\Delta p}{\Delta y} * 1000 = \frac{(P + \Delta P) * \dfrac{\Delta p}{100}}{(P + \Delta P) * \Delta y / 100{,}000}$$

where P denotes population, p denotes percentage incidence of poverty and y denotes per capita income. The symbol Δ is used to denote changes. The numerator gives the number of poor people lifted out of poverty in a given year, assuming that the population replicates itself. The denominator represents the sum total of increase in affluence measured in lakhs (hundred thousands) of rupees. Thus, this measure gives the number of people lifted out of poverty

Table 5
Rural Poverty Alleviation and Per Capita Income Growth in 1993-99

	Poverty incidence in 1993-94	*Poverty alleviation in 1993-1999 period in percentage point terms*	*Poverty alleviation in 1993-1999 period as percentage of initial incidence of poverty*	*Annual rate of growth of state per capita income*	*Elasticity of annual average poverty alleviation with respect to average rate of growth*
A.P	29.2	1.3	0.04	4.1	0.18
Assam	35.4	-0.3	-0.01	0.8	-0.18
Bihar	48.6	9.3	0.19	1.3	2.28
Gujarat	32.5	12.1	0.37	3.6	1.50
Haryana	17	10.5	0.62	3.6	2.32
Himachal	17.1	4.6	0.27	4.7	0.86
Karnataka	37.9	7.6	0.20	6.5	0.48
Kerala	19.5	7.9	0.41	3.9	1.50
Madhya	36.7	5.5	0.15	2.3	1.02
Maharashtra	42.9	12.1	0.28	2.9	1.46
Orissa	43.5	2.2	0.05	1.3	0.64
Punjab	6.2	3.4	0.55	2.9	2.61
Rajasthan	23	6.8	0.30	3.8	1.16
T.N.	38.5	12.9	0.34	5	0.99
U.P	28.7	7.9	0.28	1.8	2.30
West Bengal	25.1	2.4	0.10	5.5	0.28

Table 6
Rural Poverty Alleviation and Per Capita Income Growth in 1987-93

	Poverty incidence in 1987-88	*Poverty alleviation in 1987-1993 period in percentage point terms*	*Poverty alleviation in 1987-1993 period as percentage of initial incidence of poverty*	*Annual rate of growth of state per capita income*	*Elasticity of annual average poverty alleviation with respect to average rate of growth*
A.P	35	5.8	0.17	5.0	0.52
Assam	36.1	0.7	0.02	1.3	0.25
Bihar	54.6	6	0.11	-0.5	-3.51
Gujarat	39.4	7	0.18	6.8	0.41
Haryana	13.6	-3.4	-0.25	4.4	-1.06
Himachal	13.3	3.9	0.29	3.8	1.15
Karnataka	40.8	2.9	0.07	4.5	0.26
Kerala	23.8	4.3	0.18	6.0	0.47
Madhya	43.7	7.1	0.16	3.1	0.82
Maharashtra	44.3	1.4	0.03	7.0	0.07
Orissa	50.4	6.9	0.14	2.1	1.03
Punjab	6.6	0.5	0.08	2.8	0.44
Rajasthan	35.3	12.3	0.35	5.4	0.95
T.N.	49	10.6	0.22	5.6	0.59
U.P	34.9	6.3	0.18	2.1	1.34
West Bengal	36.3	11.2	0.31	3.0	1.53

Table 7
Correlation of Annnual Growth Rate of PCY at State Level to Poverty Alleviation

Period	*Absolute poverty Alleviation*	*Relative poverty alleviation*
87-93	.08 (.30)	.06(.22)
93-99	.201(.26)	.201(.75)

The symbol ** represents significance at 1% level. The t statistic is given in parantheses.

Table 8
Fixed Effects Regression of State-wise Rural Elasticities of Poverty Alleviation with Respect to Rate of Growth of PCY on Time

	Regression 1 (all observations available)	*Regression 1 (only observations corresponding to positive elasticities)*
Observations	32	29
F Statistic	4.2 (p value: 6%)	2.75 (p value: 13%)
R-square	.219	.187
Coefficient on time	.883 (p value: 6%)	.41(p value:13%)

Note : (a) time = 1 for the period 1987-1993 and 2 for the period 1993-99.

Table 9
Poverty Multipliers in Different Periods for Urban and Rural Areas

Year	*Urban poverty multiplier (87-93)*	*Urban poverty multiplier (93-99)*	*Rural poverty multiplier (87-93)*	*Rural poverty multiplier (93-99)*
Andhra Pradesh	9.9	8.6	10.3	1.7
Assam	5.1	-0.8	5.9	-2.4
Bihar	-366.5	-6.6	-192.9	-308.1
Gujarat	1.8	5.7	7.3	8.5
Haryana	1.5	5.3	-4.3	10.2
Himachal Pradesh	-4.1	3.3	8.4	7.9
Karnataka	8.2	13.6	5.2	10.4
Kerala	11.5	3.9	6.9	9.0
Madhya Pradesh	7.5	12.5	24.2	15.6
Maharashtra	2.3	2.4	1.0	5.8
Orissa	30.9	-2.0	38.1	10.7
Punjab	-2.0	5.2	0.8	4.7
Rajasthan	3.1	11.7	25.6	10.3
Tamil Nadu	7.5	10.0	14.9	13.1
Uttar Pradesh	39.9	24.1	33.1	36.6
West Bengal	9.9	8.6	28.6	5.1

Table 10
Correlations

Period	*Urban poverty multiplier and PCY*	*Urban Poverty Multiplier and Initial Urban Poverty*	*Rural poverty multiplier and PCY*	*Rural Poverty Multiplier and Initial Rural Poverty*
1987-93	.28	-0.48**	.19	-0.26
1993-99	.01	0.2	.37	-0.42*

Table 11
Fixed Effects Regression of State-wise Urban and Ruralpoverty Multipliers on Time

	Urban	*Rural*
Observations	32	32
F Statistic	0.83	2.11 (p value: 16.6%)
R-square	0.05	0.12
Coefficient on time	20.72 (p value: 38%)	-10.8 7(p value16.66%)

per hundred thousand rupees of affluence generated. The urban poverty multiplier in 1987-93 was the highest for Uttar Pradesh at 39.9. It continued to occupy first place at 24.1 in the period 1993-99. The second place went to Orissa in the first period and Karnataka in the second period. In the case of rural areas. Orissa and U.P occupied the first and second place in the two periods. Note that these multipliers do not convey how successful these states have been at poverty alleviation but at how successfully they have generated poverty alleviation through resources generated from growth. Overall success in poverty alleviation can be considered to be the product of two factors – resources generated through growth and the poverty multiplier. States like U.P and Orissa have a high poverty multiplier but do not generate enough resources through growth. Thus, their overall poverty alleviation performance is not very good.

Table 10 presents some interesting correlations. Two significant correlations are between the initial urban incidence of poverty and the urban multiplier in the period 1987-93 and that between the rural poverty multiplier and initial rural poverty in 1993-99, both of which are negative. All other correlations in Table 10 are not significant. Table 11 shows that in general the urban poverty multiplier in the second period is not significantly different from that in the first period. The rural multiplier shows a negative time trend.

Table 12
Regresssion of Rural Poverty Multiplier on Urban Poverty Multiplier

	Fixed Effects
Observations	32
F Statistic	68.36(p value<1%)
R-square	0.82
Coefficient on urban multiplier	-.309(p value<1%)

Table 12 illustrates that the relationship between the rural and urban multipliers is significantly negative This illustrates the binding nature of the constraint imposed by growth on poverty alleviation.

CONCLUSION

Globalization leads to trickle down growth to the extent that there is positive growth associated with poverty alleviation. Our data and panel econometrics seem to suggest that trickle down, as measured by elasticities of poverty alleviation with respect to per capita income, has accelerated with liberalization. However, we need to account for the fact that the increase in affluence in absolute terms in the post-liberalization period was much higher than that in the pre-liberalization period. If one considers how efficiently resources generated through growth got translated into poverty allcviation there is not much change in efficiency after liberalization in the case of urban poverty and a somewhat significant fall in the case of rural poverty. There is also some evidence of a trade off between urban and rural poverty eradication which seems to be indicative of a binding constraint on total resources available for poverty alleviation.

References

Deaton, Angus (Jan. 25, 2003), "Prices and Poverty in India, 1987-2000", *Economic and Political Weekly.*

Davis, Donald (1996), "Trade Liberalisation and income distribution" *National of Economic Research Working Paper No.* 5693.

Hasan Rana, Mitra, Devashish and Beyza P. Ural (2006), Trade Liberalization, Labor-Market Institutions and Poverty Reduction: Evidence from Indian States, Mimeo.

Datt Gaurav and Martin Ravallion (2002), "Is India's Economic Growth Leaving the Poor Behind?" *Journal of Economic Perspectives*, 16(3), 89-108.

Feenstra Robert and Gordon Hanson (1997), "Foreign Direct Investment and Relative Wages: Evidence from Mexico's Maquiladoras." *Journal of International Economics*, 42(2), pp. 371-393.

Topalova, Petia (2005), "Trade liberalization Poverty and Inequality: Evidence from Indian Districts," *Mimeo: Department of Economics, Massachussets Institute of Technology.*

Stiglitz, Joseph (1970), "Factor Price Equalization in a Dynamic Economy." *Journal of Political Economy*, 78(3), 456-488.

IT APPLICATIONS, HEALTHCARE AND TARGETING THE POOR

*Kokila P. Doshi**

INTRODUCTION

"A solution is a solution when it is affordable to a common man." Yet, as Prof. C. K. Prahalad states in his book, *Fortune at the Bottom of the Pyramid* [17], selling to the poor is one of the ill-explored areas in business modeling. With urban bias and business focus, globalization and technology bypassed masses of poor in developing nations. However, new innovative business models are being developed today, challenging the "great trade-off illusion"–both in domestic and international context. Increasingly, more and more businesses are demonstrating that targeting the poor is compatible with a sound business strategy and financial success.

With the change in mindset, businesses are reinventing themselves and redefining their role. The earlier belief that corporations serve the rich and that serving the poor is the responsibility of government and non-profit organizations is also changing. Today, a new reality is emerging. As Prof. Hart states in his book, *Capitalism at the Crossroads*, [8] today it is business–more than government and society – that is equipped with the technology, resources, capacity and global reach to lead us toward a sustainable world. Government and non-profit organizations play a collaborative role and develop partnerships with business. Businesses of our times have a tremendous opportunity to pioneer a positive change in society.

In the context of third world countries, businesses that are not necessarily equipped with resources or global reach are also making a difference by addressing some socio-economic problems. It poses more challenges, yet their models are sustainable.

One such business is showcased in this paper, along with the real-life profile of its founder. The study of Narayana Hrudayalaya Hospital (Bangalore, India), demonstrates how a service business contributes to the needs of the poor by leveraging technological advances and developing innovative business models

Bangalore, India, which houses world class IT corporations is also aspiring to become a 'health city' and a hub for quality healthcare for the masses. Leading the positive change is Narayana Hrudayalaya Hospital, a hospital with a heart for the poor. How does this super-specialty hospital 'heal the hearts by remote control' and keep them beating at an affordable cost? The paper describes the driving forces behind the success of Naryana Hrudayalaya Hospital.

* University of San Diego.

ONE MAN'S VISION

Allow yourself to ***dream*** *and you will* ***discover*** *that* ***destiny*** *is yours to* ***design****.*–Jakie Stavros

Dr. Devi Prasad Shetty, a renowned cardiac surgeon and a visionary founder of Narayana Hrudayalaya, dreamt big. His dream is to provide high-tech healthcare to the masses, regardless of their economic status or geographic location. To realize his dream, he designed an innovative business model that is revolutionizing the healthcare system in India. Dr. Shetty believes that the "best business model of all is one that is based on the needs of the poor." [2]

Dr. Shetty's portfolio of achievements is impressive. He founded Narayana Hrudyayalaya hospital in 2001. Prior to that he co-founded Asia Heart Foundation and set up three other hospitals in different regions of India. With his encounter with Mother Teresa, the dream met the divinity and a new sense of purpose was instilled in his work. He is known for his passion for children and poor. He has performed 5000 free heart surgeries for children. In his famous letter to children, he expressed his life mission. "For me this would is such a happy place to live in and in my own small way, I strive to make it happy for others around me, who are not so fortunate." This forms the basic foundation for his model for targeting the poor. The social impact of his work is so vast that he was given "The Social Entrepreneur of the Year 2005" awarded by Schwab Foundation for Social Entrepreneurship.

As described in the literature on Appreciative Inquiry [5, 6] leaders with a social vision view social problems "not as burdens but as compelling business opportunities." Dr. Shetty saw positive possibilities in the midst of the problems posed by India's healthcare system. Reframing the issue, he said in an interview–"Do you see the enormous opportunity? Governments think healthcare is an expense. It is a great way to generate employment. It is an avenue to build the nation." [2]

According to Dr. Shetty, healthcare system must provide the solutions that are affordable and accessible to the poor. Some of the striking features of healthcare system in India include the following:

- There is a mismatch between demand and supply, need and availability of healthcare services- a scenario that is often prevalent in developing countries.
- Almost 70% of the doctors serve the urban area, while 70% of the population of India lives in rural areas.
- India needs 2.4 million heart operations; only 60,000 operations are performed.
- There is an acute shortage of specialists. For a population of over one billion, India trains less than 80 cardiologists while our requirement is 2000-3000 cardiologists. By comparison the U.S. trains 800 cardiologists per year.
- The most important problem of the health delivery system is that it is linked to the affluence.
- Even when state-of-the art facilities are available, hospitals experience high vacancy rates and underutilization of resources due to the lack of ability to pay.
- Only 14% of the population is covered by health insurance, making medical treatments an option for the rich only.
- India produces the largest number of children with heart disease – about 600 a day.

In a personal correspondence with the author, Dr. Shetty expressed his concerns about heart attacks and issues of accessibility as well as the need for specialists. In India, "a heart attack is not a disease of old people, it is the disease of young people who are the breadwinners of the family. Heart disease causes major upheavals in the socio-economic fabric of our country. It is like an epidemic. In our practice, it is not the young son bringing his old father for a bypass grafting operation, it is the old father brining the young son for heart operation." How do we bring high-tech healthcare to the rural masses in remote areas?

NARAYANA HRUDAYALAYA HOSPITAL: TARGETING THE POOR

"You can choose to curse the darkness or light the lamp."

The focus in the design stages is on how to make the dream a reality. With a compelling social vision, the social architecture of Narayana Hrudayalaya hospital has put the poor and children in the center.

Seven simple prescriptions for targeting the poor emerge from the study of Narayana Hrudayalaya hospital and Dr. Shetty's leadership philosophy. This section draws heavily from published interviews of Dr. Shetty [1,2,15] and the author's personal correspondence with him.

First, the problem in developing countries is that healthcare is associated with affluence. It should not be. In the traditional model, healthcare services are typically provided to the urban rich, with the rural poor being the "missing link". A paradigm shift is needed to make the healthcare system broad-based and inclusive. It requires a mindset of providing solutions affordable to the common man. Dr. Shetty observes, "100 years after the first heart surgery, less than 8% of the world's population can afford it".

The study of Narayana Hrudayalaya's operations and strategies demonstrates that "health without wealth" is possible. Equipped with state-of-the-art facilities, the hospital reserves 75% of its beds for the poor. At this world-class hospital, no one is turned away due to the lack of paying capacity. Sixty percent of the treatments are subsidized. Twenty percent of patients are children from different countries. The cardiac diagnostic laboratory has two divisions, one for the poor and one for executives.

Secondly, technological advances offer new tools to target the poor. Technology helps reduce costs and thereby makes certain solutions affordable that previously were beyond the reach of the poor. Technological applications also make such solutions accessible to those who need them and thereby fill the gaps in the healthcare delivery system. "Today, technology and economic tools are making it possible to create a model that will disengage every service business from the concept of affluence." [2] In addition, technology itself has become affordable and scaleable.

The telemedicine project pioneered by Narayana Hrudayalaya hospital is one of the largest projects of its kind in the world. It shows the potential of leveraging technological advances to benefit the poor. To date, 21,000 heart patients are treated using telemedicine technology.

Thirdly, the power of the poor is in the numbers. As Dr. Shetty said in one of his interviews, "the sphere of influence of the poor is phenomenal." Poor people in isolation are helpless. In numbers, they constitute a formidable economic power.

Narayana Hrudayalaya's legendary micro-health insurance plan- Yeshasvini- harnesses the power of the poor. It has insured 2.4 million farmers for the equivalent of 10 cents per farmer per month.

Fourthly, by low margins you can serve the poor. He says, "We do not want to make tons of money." The business model of Narayana Hrudayalaya hospital incorporates this strategy. Large volumes and cost-cutting efforts emphasized by the hospital, in a way, compensate for the low margins.

Fifthly, according to Dr. Shetty, it is possible to build a successful business without the help of the stock market. This is a bold prescription. Western companies are focused on creating value for the shareholders. "What is killing business are expectations from the stakeholders." It is the stock market that leads to bad behavior by executives.

Sixthly, in a service business, one must have a long-term view. This is related to the previous prescription. If success is measured in terms of shareholders' value, management is judged by the short-term stock performance of the organization. At Narayana Hrudayalaya hospital, projects are financed by internal funds, debt, and donations. Debt, rather than equity, is considered the preferred financial option. The seventh prescription is to have a heart for the poor and a mission to make the world a happier place. As George Eby Mathews [15] states, "it is the seventh prescription, in my opinion, that outweighs the other six." Targeting the poor requires compassionate leaders and a social vision. In hiring the team workers, Dr. Shetty emphasizes compassion as the single most important characteristic. Skills and competence will follow.

An eighth prescription can be added in the context of new realities emerging on the global front. That prescription is collaboration with the government, NGO's, universities or other organizations. The global challenges of poverty reduction or healthcare provision require public-private partnerships. As Dr. Shetty mentioned in one of his interviews, "one cannot do this alone…the new buzzword is collaboration." The days of competition are gone.

Narayana Hrudayalaya's ambitious projects have invited partnerships from state governments, NGO's, multinationals such as Hewlett-Packard and the Indian Space Research Organization. Each organization plays a complementary role. Thus, a powerful synergy is created to address the healthcare needs of the community and eliminate one disease at a time, in one village at a time.

TELEMEDICINE PROJECT

"Telemedicine lets ordinary doctors do extraordinary things. It is going to revolutionize healthcare delivery to poor areas around the world." Dr. Devi Prasad Shetty

His background in cardiac surgery, his concern for heart health and his innovative scaleable ideas resulted in a unique Telemedicine Program at Narayana Hrudayalaya Hospital. This telemedicine network is the largest in the world and can serve as a model for developing countries.

With Dr. Shetty's initiative, the telemedicine program was initially established by Narayana Hrudayalaya hospital in 2001. To overcome some infrastructural barriers such as unreliable and expensive phone lines and power outages, a partnership was formed with the Indian Space

Research Organization (ISRO) and the state government. The most important requirement in the telemedicine network according to Dr. Shetty was that the "patient must be able to see the compassionate face of the doctor." The project fully uses Bangalore's IT assets and "marks yet another milestone in ISRO's effort to bring the benefits of space technology to the people at the grassroots level." ISRO provides free satellite connectivity, linking selected super-specialty hospitals with the government hospitals and health centers in remote areas. It is a technological wonder to bring high tech healthcare to the doorstep of the working class population and the poor in remote areas. For many people far removed from the medical capitals, this is all that they have. Local non-specialist doctors are trained to manage coronary care units (CCU). The telemedicine system uses cutting edge technology and provides "customized medical software integrated with computer hardware, along with diagnostic instruments connected to VSAT at each location." The facility enables transmission of patient data, image transfers, and two-way video/audio link between the hub and local stations. Within three minutes, ECGs are read from any corner of the world. Patients in rural areas receive timely consultations from specialist doctors. Once again, the telemedicine program fills in the resource gap by bringing virtual specialists to distant areas and breaks the barriers of distance and time.

The program is 110 centers strong today. Cardiac monitors, defibrillators, ECG machines, and other equipment are provided to government hospitals. The telemedicine program helps these hospitals increase the utilization rate of their infrastructure. "In the context of rural and distant areas, telemedicine-based medicine is also highly cost-effective." General doctors are given ECG machines, with homegrown software, free of cost. To date, 21,000 heart patients have been treated using telemedicine technology.

In personal correspondence, Dr. Shetty writes, "We have mobile vans equipped with echocardiography, defibrillators, treadmills and other outpatient equipment, which go to the villages on weekends and convert rural schools as temporary heart hospitals and offer heart care. This way, we have treated 50,000 patients in Bangalore and Kolkata."

Thus, the telemedicine project run with public-private partnerships helps Narayana Hrudayalaya Hospital to realize the dream of meeting the healthcare needs of the people at a cost that they can afford.

YESHASVINI HEALTH SCHEME

"Yeshasvini is a success because of the pre-existing network of the poor people. And the moral of the story is that unless we organize poor people to come together under one banner, it is very difficult to help them." Dr. Devi Prasad Shetty.

Having solved the problem of accessibility and lack of specialists with the telemedicine projects, Dr. Shetty faced another challenge in terms of affordability of healthcare services. In an informal survey, Narayana Hrudayalaya hospital discovered that the average occupancy of hospital beds in the state was merely 35% and for operation theaters, the utilization rates were much lower. Thus, "it was not the lack of infrastructure but the lack of paying capacity of the working mass and the poor, which was the root cause of the mammoth healthcare problem that India faced." [16].

Only 14% of the population had health-insurance coverage. To break the link between health and affluence, Narayana Hrudayalaya launched an ambitious micro-health insurance scheme- the Yeshasvini Health Scheme. Starting with insuring farmers organized under milk cooperatives in the state, four years after its inception Yeshasvini insures 2.4 million members of the cooperatives at an equivalent of 10 cents per month per member. Under this scheme, members undergo a variety of operations "for the cost of coffee in an upscale coffee bar" at the extensive network of hospitals.

Yeshasvini's success in targeting the poor is reflected in the latest data provided by Dr. Shetty in a personal correspondence:

-No. of free medical consultations: 138,880

-No of free surgeries: 43,317

-No of free heart surgeries: 3,557

According to him, this year's target is to provide coverage to 3 million members

GOODNESS IS GROWING

Narayana Hrudayalaya Hospital, led by Dr. Shetty, has found its positive core. Continuous efforts are underway to "magnify and give life to that goodness "[4]

The organization aims at providing a 'total solution' by providing for complementary needs to have quality healthcare. After developing two model projects, the hospital aims at extending services in different areas and in different ways to bring more people under its wings. The telemedicine links are provided to prisons and airlines. A bone-marrow unit is established at the hospital. The hospital looks for the ways to enjoy the benefits of economies of scope. Dr. Shetty plans to open up a network of rural clinics for primary care, provide free medicine, and provide insurance to the villagers for 50 paise per person per month. The scheme is known as the Arogya Rakhsha scheme. To solve the problem of costly prescription drugs and medicines, a partnership with a leading pharmaceutical firm has been established. Plans are underway to make Bangalore a 'health city'. Narayana Hrudayalaya Hospital, a 780-bed hospital for cardiac care, will be converted into a 5000-bed hospital and serve as a hub to extend its services beyond heart care. In a collaborative program, Narayana Hrudayalaya hospital aims at introducing a Diploma in Cardiology using the network of MBBS doctors to create intermediate level specialists for the rural areas.

He has set up telemedicine links in countries like Malaysia, Pakistan and many more developing countries will be added to the list in the near future. Success feeds on itself and empowers the hospital more and more to deliver the shared vision and make the world a happier place.

SUSTAINABILITY OF THE MODEL

Narayana Hrudayalaya's model for targeting the poor is novel, simple and sustainable. Hosts of factor are responsible for making the model viable:

- **Cross-subsidization**- The clientele mix of 75% poor and 25% rich patients allows the hospital to cross-subsidize the costs.
- **Assembly Line Concept**- A factory model approach is used in which specialists focus only on surgeries. Aravind Eye Care system also used the assembly-line model of McDonald's founder- Roy Kroc to save 2.4 million eyes. The assembly-line approach results in larger output and lower costs. Assembly-line heart surgery aims at reducing the cost of heart surgery by 75 % and achieving zero mortality rates.
- **A Relentless Pursuit of Cost Cutting Across the Value Chain** – Driving the unit cost down without compromising the quality seems to be the mantra at Narayana Hrudayalaya hospital. Achieving larger volumes, economy of scale, increased utilization of medical infrastructure and higher productivity are the tools used by the hospital. Narayana Hrudayalaya hospital performs 24 heart surgery and 25 catheterization procedures a day. An open-heart surgery costs about $100,000 to $150,000 in the U.S. Narayana Hrudayalaya hospital performs it for $1500. It uses strategy of lower margins and larger volume. Diagnostic equipments, operation theatres and labs also get used more reducing the unit costs. For example, instead of 2-5 tests a day, 500 tests are performed on a machine. As Dr. Shetty wrote in a personal correspondence, they worked "with a German company, Schiller to make inexpensive ECG machines costing less than Rs. 10,000 (minus software). We develop the software which is given to the General practitioners free of cost."

The hospital negotiates best deals with the vendors and does not sign long-term contracts. Since the hospital is a larger buyer, it gets 30 –35 % discount on supplies. A largest buyer of heart-valves in the world, Narayana Hrudayalaya hospital uses its buying power to negotiate the price directly with manufacturers. Same logic works for pills and prescription drugs. The hospital maintains zero inventories, thereby shifting risk and responsibility to the suppliers.

In the same way, administrative structures is kept lean and the administrative costs are kept lower with conscious efforts. The hospital uses internal controls and daily accounting system. The hospital is open for business 7 days, as against 5 days in the U.S., getting the maximum return from the capital investment.

- **Human Capital–**At Narayana Hrudayalaya hospital, young doctors in their thirties have performed more than 2000 operations. They gain more heart surgery experience than American heart surgeons have at their retirement. Dedicated teams of compassionate doctors 'breath and live heart-care' just like their visionary leader Dr. Shetty does. They put long hours and work with a sense of purpose.
- **Leveraging Technology**–Narayana Hrudayalaya hospital uses cutting edge technology to provide life–saving treatments to the rural and distance areas. Whether it is the health care application of Space Technology or development of software to reduce the transmission time for ECG data from 48 to 3 minutes, the hospital has mastered the skills of using technological advances to bridge the gaps in existing healthcare system. Telemedicine program supported by Indian Space Research Organization is a sustainable, cost-effective way to reach the poor.

- **Public-Private Partnership**–In order to realize its social vision, Narayana Hrudayalaya hospital forms partnership and collaborations with ISRO, corporations, government agencies, charities and foundations. It allows the hospital to mobilize the resources and exploit complementary strength to provide a 'total solution' to the rural masses.
- **Harnessing the Power of the Poor**–As described earlier the hospital innovated a self-funding insurance scheme–Yeshavini that provides insurance to millions of members of the state co-operatives for 10 cents per month. The scheme is sustainable because;
  - o poor people in large numbers form a 'formidable economic force'
  - o members are organized under one banner for a common purpose (other than health care)
  - o under such a structure, the probability is only .08 that a member will need an operation
  - o upfront payment premium collected from millions of members creates a corpus fund to be used to finance the services
- **Scalability**–The delivery of high-tech quality care to the rural areas involves huge overhead costs. The scalability of the innovative schemes helps spread such costs and increase the coverage. For the telemedicine program, once the groundwork is done it is easy to set up more and more centers. It also applies to the micro–health insurance schemes. Once the mechanics are in place insurance services can be provided to more cooperatives or teachers' union or any other organization that brings the members under one banner.

The model is transferable to other countries also. For the developed countries like U.S. issues such as malpractice lawsuits 'bells and whistles' attitude, share holder's value, infrastructure and lifestyle may pose some challenges in adopting Narayana Hrudayalaya hospital's model effectively. In developing countries, technology infrastructure, extent of government support and availability of skilled healthcare professionals may represent some barriers to the transferability of such a model.

CONCLUSION

In words of UN Secretary General Kofi Annan-" Let us choose to reconcile the creative forces of private entrepreneurship with the needs of disadvantaged and the requirements of future generations." In the 21st century, successful businesses will be the businesses that find business opportunities in alleviating global suffering and pain.

Some of the global challenges such as giving an opportunity. hope and dignity to 1.2 billion people living in deep poverty, deprivation and despair, cannot be faced alone by any one group. It requires collective efforts. Today businesses are best positioned to complement the work of government and become a partner for peace. It requires a paradigm shift, a new level of understanding, new economic models, a sense of purpose, a renewed commitment and above all, compassion, as exemplified in this case study of hospital with a heart for the poor.

References

Bagchi, Subroto (2005), Hero of Our Times–Part I, Indian Express, May 18.

Bagchi, Subroto (2005), Hero of Our Times–Part II, Indian Express, May 19.

Business Week Special Report (2006), "Business Prophet 'How strategy guru C.K. Prahalad is changing the way CEOs think", Business Week, January 23.

Chaffee, Paul (2001), "Claiming the light Appreciative Inquiry and Corporate Transformation," Website of Case-Western Reserve University (*http://ai.cwru.edu*) December 12.

Cooperrider David, Sorensen Jr. P; Diana Whitney and T Yaeger (2000), (Eds). Appreciative Inquiry- Rethinking Human Organization Toward a Positive Theory of Change, Stipes Publishing.

Cooperrider David L. and Diana Whitney (2000), Appreciative Inquiry, Berrett Koehler Communications. San Francisco.

Gullberg, Odd (2006), "The Role of Business in Tomorrow's Society", World Business Council for Sustainable Development, Research Paper. June 2.

Hart, Stuart (2005), Capitalism at the Crossroads, Wharton School Publishing New Jersey.

Khanna, Tarun, V. Kasturi Rangan and Merlina Manocaran (2006), Narayana Hrudayalaya Heart Hospital: Cardiac Care for the Poor–Harvard Business School, Business case 9-505-078, Boston.

Lodge, George C., and Craig Wilson (2006), Multinational Corporations: A Key to Global Poverty Reduction –Part I, Yale Global Online. January 2.

Lodge, George C., and Craig Wilson (2006), Multinational Corporations: A Key to Global Poverty Reduction – Part II, Yale Global Online. January 5.

Lodge G.C. and Wilson C. (2006), A Corporate Solution to Global Poverty: How Multinationals Can Help the Poor and Invigorate Their Legitimacy, Princeton University Press, New Jersey.

Maitland, Alison (2005), "Globalization's Strange Bedfellows", The Financial Times. December 12.

Manville, Brook and Josiah Ober (2003), "A Company of Citizens–What the World's First Democracy Teaches Leaders about Creating Great Organizations". Harvard Business School Press–Boston, Massachusetts.

Mathew, George Ebey (2005), "IT and the Poor–Do we care?" IT toolbox. June 10.

Narayana Hrudayalaya Hospital website *http://www.hrudayalaya.com*

Prahalad, C.K. (2005), "The Fortune at the Bottom of the Pyramid: Eradicating Poverty Through Profits", Wharton School of Business Publishing. New Jersey.

Sachs, Jeffrey (2005), *The End of Poverty: Economic Possibilities for Our Times*. Penguin Press, New York.

Sen, Monalisa (2005), "Making Cardiac Surgery more Affordable for the Poor", Solutions Magazine December 5.

Sood S.P., Bhatia J.S. (2005), "Development of Telemedicine Technology in India: 'Sanjeevani'—An Integrated Telemedicine Application" *Journal of Postgraduate Medicine* Vol. 51, Issue 4.

ENDOGENOUS SEQUENCING OF TRADE POLICIES IN A THREE-COUNTRY EXPORT RIVALRY MODEL+

*Ryoichi Nomura**, *Takao Ohkawa***, *Makoto Okamura**** & *Makoto Tawada*****

ABSTRACT

This paper examines the endogenous sequencing of trade policies in a three-country model where two identical exporting countries give export subsidies and one importing country imposes an import tariff. World welfare and each country's welfare are compared under each possible sequencing of trade policy. The main conclusions are as follows: (i) in equilibrium, the importing country imposes an import tariff first, and both exporting countries gives export subsidies simultaneously, (ii) policy intervention does not improve world welfare as compared to the free-trade level, and (iii) when at least two firms operate in each of the exporting countries, world welfare is maximized with free trade.

Key Words: *Endogenous Sequencing, Export Subsidy, Import Tariff, Free Trade*

JEL Classification Numbers: *L13; F13*

I. INTRODUCTION

The purpose of this paper is to examine the endogenous sequencing of trade policies in the three-country model where two identical exporting countries give export subsidies and one importing country imposes an import tariff. World welfare and each country's welfare are compared under each possible sequencing of trade policy.

In the three-country framework, a number of studies have argued that sequential timing is endogenously determined. Arvan (1991), for example, introduced demand uncertainty into his model and established that the possibility of a sequential move depended on both the degree of demand uncertainty and the number of firms. Similarly, Shivakumar (1993) considered export

---

+ An earlier version of this paper was presented at the annual meeting of Japanese Economic Association (2005 September). We thank Masayuki Hayashibara for his helpful comments. We are responsible for any remaining errors. This work was supported by MEXT.OPEN RESEARCH (2004-2008) and Grand-in-Aid for Scientific Research (no. 17530150). Please send correspondences to: Makoto Okamura, Economics Department, Hiroshima University, Kagamiyama, Higashihiroshima, Hiroshima, Japan, *E-mail: Andrew-uf@w3.dion.nc.jp*

* Research Organization of Social Sciences, Ritsumeikan University.

** Faculty of Economics, Ritsumeikan University.

*** Economics Department, Hiroshima University.

**** Graduate School of Economics, Nagoya University.

quotas as an additional policy instrument for governments, and established that sequential moves may occur when the export quota is chosen and the degree of uncertainty is large. And Ohkawa, Okamura, and Tawada (2002) analyzed the model *without* incomplete information and concluded that the number of firms in each exporting country plays an essential role in determining the timing of trade policies.

It appears that an unsolved problem remains. In the three-country model, previous studies do not address the strategic interaction between an importing country and an exporting country because an importing country does not intervene. We construct a three-country game model: two identical exporting countries give export subsidies and one importing country imposes an import tariff. We examine the endogenous sequencing of trade policies in this model, and make two assumptions: (i) there are no firms in the importing country, and (ii) the exporting countries have the same number of firms. These assumptions lead to clearer results regarding the sequencing of trade policy.

Our main findings are as follows: (i) in equilibrium, the importing country imposes an import tariff first, and both exporting countries give export subsidies simultaneously, (ii) policy intervention does not improve world welfare compared with its free-trade level, and (iii) when at least two firms operate in each exporting country, free trade is efficient from the viewpoint of world welfare.

The paper itself is organized as follows. Section 2 presents a three-stage game to analyze the sequencing of the policy setting. The preliminary results are presented in Section 3. Section 4 investigates the endogenous sequencing of trade policies and compares the welfare for each. Some concluding remarks and directions for future work are provided in the final section.

II. THE MODEL

Consider a trading economy where three countries (first, second and third) exist and a single commodity is traded. The commodity is produced in the first and second countries and exported to the third country. No consumption occurs and n firms operate in the each producing country. All firms have identical production technology with constant marginal cost c.

In the third country, there is no production and consumers purchase the commodity imported from the first and second countries. Let an inverse demand function of the third country be $p = P(Q) \equiv A - Q$, where Q shows the demand for the commodity, p is the commodity price and A indicates market scale and is assumed to be greater than c. Each firm competes *à la* Cournot in the third country market.

The government of each exporting country gives an export subsidy of s_i $(i = 1,2)$ per output so as to maximize the country's national welfare. The government of the third country imposes a specific import tariff of t. Each government then decides not only upon the level of the subsidy or tariff, but also on the sequencing of policy implementation.

We construct the following three-stage game: In the first stage, the government of each country decides the sequencing of its export subsidy and import tariff. In the second stage, each government chooses the level of its export subsidy and import tariff according to the predetermined order. In the third stage, the firms produce and export the commodity under Cournot competition to maximize profits, given the export subsidies and import tariffs set by each government.

III. THE ANALYSIS

We derive the subgame perfect Nash equilibrium as the solution concept of the game by backward induction. Let us begin with the third stage subgame. The firms simultaneously and independently choose their outputs so as to maximize profits given the export subsidy and import tariff set by each government. Firm k's profit in i th country is given by $\pi_{ik} = P(Q)q_{ik} - (c - s_i + t)q_{ik}$ where q_{ik} is firm k's output in the i th country. We focus on the symmetric equilibrium, that is, $q_{ik} = q_i$. The equilibrium output level of each firm in the i th country q_i is given by

$$q_i = \frac{A - c - t + (n+1)s_i - ns_j}{2n+1}, \quad i, j = 1, 2, \quad i \neq j. \tag{1}$$

From (1), total output level in equilibrium is given by

$$Q = \left(\frac{2(A-c) + s_1 + s_2 - 2t}{2n+1}\right)n. \tag{2}$$

For the purpose of simplicity, we normalize $A - c = 1$.

In the second stage, each government of the exporting country sets the level of subsidy s_i in order to maximize national welfare, W_i, defined as the sum of firm profits net of export subsidies:

$$W_i = n(\pi_i - s_i q_i), \quad i = 1, 2.$$

The government of the importing country determines the level of tariff t in order to maximize national welfare, W_3, defined as consumer surplus plus the tariff revenue:

$$W_3 = \frac{1}{2}Q^2 + tQ.$$

The reaction functions of the importing and exporting governments for tariffs and subsidies are given by:

$$t(s_1, s_2) = \frac{2 + s_1 + s_2}{4(n+1)}, \tag{5}$$

$$s_i(t, s_j) = \frac{1 - t - ns_j}{2n(n+1)}. \tag{6}$$

The reaction function of the importing government is upward sloping with s_i, whereas that of the exporting government i, is downward sloping with t and s_j.

We define world welfare as the sum of all countries' welfare:

$$W = W_1 + W_2 + W_3 = \frac{1}{2}Q(2-Q). \tag{7}$$

Because the two exporting countries are identical, there are eight possible sequencing of decisions with trade policy. Table 1 presents these patterns. Note that the i th country does not move later than the j th country.

Table 1
Possible Sequencing of Decisions for Trade Policy

A	All countries act simultaneously.
B	Both exporting countries choose own subsidy level simultaneously, and then the importing country chooses its tariff level.
C	The importing country chooses its tariff level first, and then both exporting countries choose own subsidy level simultaneously.
D	The i th country and the third country act simultaneously before the j th-country choose its subsidy level.
E	The j th country and the third country act simultaneously after the i th country chooses its subsidy level.
F	The i th country is the first mover, the j th country is the second, and the third country is the last.
G	The third country is the first mover, the i th country is the second, and the j th country is the last.
H	The i th country is the first mover, the third country is the second, and the j th country is the last.

From (1) and (3) through (7), we calculate the level of subsidies, s_i^h, and tariff, t^h, the each country's welfare, W_i^h, and world welfare, W^h, in the case of sequencing $h(=A,\cdots,H)$. Tables 2, 3 and 4 summarize the results.

We specify the free trade welfare for each country and the world as benchmarks:

$$W_i^{FT} = \frac{n}{(2n+1)^2}, \quad W_3^{FT} = \frac{2n^2}{(2n+1)^2}, \quad and \quad W^{FT} = \frac{2n(n+1)}{(2n+1)^2}, \quad i=1,2. \tag{8}$$

IV. MAIN RESULTS

First, we examine the equilibrium sequencing for the trade policies. From Table 3, we establish:

Proposition 1: The equilibrium pattern of sequencing is C, that is, the importing country sets its tariff level first, and the exporting countries set their own subsidy level simultaneously.

As shown in Table 3, $W_i^h \geq W_j^h$ in each timing. This means that each exporting country has an incentive to become the leader. In other words, both exporting countries choose simultaneous move in equilibrium. Because pattern D, E, F, G, and H are not equilibriums, only timings A, B, and C are candidates for equilibrium.

We show that each government has an incentive to deviate from timing A, that is each government moves at the same time. Suppose that the importing government becomes the leader. The first-order condition is given by:

Table 2
The level of Subsidies and Tariffs

Sequencing	*Subsidy*		*Tariff*
	s_i^h	s_j^h	t^h
A	$\frac{1}{2n^2+4n+1}$	$\frac{1}{2n^2+4n+1}$	$\frac{n+1}{2n^2+4n+1}$
B	$\frac{1}{(n+2)(2n+1)}$	$\frac{1}{(n+2)(2n+1)}$	$\frac{2n+3}{2(n+2)(2n+1)}$
C	$\frac{1}{2n(n+2)}$	$\frac{1}{2n(n+2)}$	$\frac{1}{2(n+2)}$
D	$\frac{2(2n+1)}{n(4n^2+12n+7)}$	$\frac{2n+1}{n(4n^2+12n+7)}$	$\frac{2n+3}{n(4n^2+12n+7)}$
E	$\frac{4n+1}{(2n+1)(2n^2+5n+1)}$	$\frac{1}{2n^2+5n+1}$	$\frac{2n^2+4n+1}{(2n+1)(2n^2+5n+1)}$
F	$\frac{4}{(2n+1)(2n+5)}$	$\frac{2}{(2n+1)(2n+5)}$	$\frac{2(n+2)}{(2n+1)(2n+5)}$
G	$\frac{2}{n(2n+5)}$	$\frac{1}{n(2n+5)}$	$\frac{1}{2n+5}$
H	$\frac{(2n+1)(4n+3)}{4n(n+1)(2n^2+6n+3)}$	$\frac{2n+1}{2n(2n^2+6n+3)}$	$\frac{4n^2+10n+5}{4(n+1)(2n^2+6n+3)}$

Note: Superscript *h* (= A, ..., *H*) indicates the sequencing of policy decisions.

$$\frac{dW_3^C(s_1,s_2,t)}{dt}=\left[Q\frac{\partial Q}{\partial t}+Q+\frac{\partial Q}{\partial t}t\right]+Q\left[\frac{\partial Q}{\partial s_1}\frac{\partial s_1}{\partial t}+\frac{\partial Q}{\partial s_2}\frac{\partial s_2}{\partial t}\right]+t\left[\frac{\partial Q}{\partial s_1}\frac{\partial s_1}{\partial t}+\frac{\partial Q}{\partial s_2}\frac{\partial s_2}{\partial t}\right]. \quad (9)$$

The first term in (9) represents the direct effect of the tariff. The second (the third) term is the indirect effect through the change in s_1 (s_2). Note that the sign of the second (the third) term

Table 3
Welfare of Each Country

Sequencing \ Country	W_i^h	W_j^h	W_3^h
A	$\frac{n^2(n+1)}{(2n^2+4n+1)^2}$	$\frac{n^2(n+1)}{(2n^2+4n+1)^2}$	$\frac{2n(n+1)^3}{(2n^2+4n+1)^2}$
B	$\frac{n(2n+3)}{4(n+2)^2(2n+1)}$	$\frac{n(2n+3)}{4(n+2)^2(2n+1)}$	$\frac{n(n+1)(2n+3)^2}{2(n+2)^2(2n+1)^2}$
C	$\frac{n+1}{4(n+2)^2}$	$\frac{n+1}{4(n+2)^2}$	$\frac{n+1}{2(n+2)}$
D	$\frac{(n+2)(2n+1)^2}{(4n^2+12n+7)^2}$	$\frac{(n+1)(2n+1)^2}{(4n^2+12n+7)^2}$	$\frac{(2n+1)(2n+3)^3}{2(4n^2+12n+7)^2}$
E	$\frac{n^2}{(2n+1)(2n^2+5n+1)}$	$\frac{n^2(n+1)}{(2n^2+5n+1)^2}$	$\frac{2n(n+1)(2n^2+4n+1)^2}{(2n+1)^2(2n^2+5n+1)^2}$
F	$\frac{n}{(2n+1)(2n+5)}$	$\frac{n(2n+3)}{(2n+1)(2n+5)^2}$	$\frac{8n(n+1)(n+2)^2}{(2n+1)^2(2n+5)^2}$
G	$\frac{n+2}{(2n+5)^2}$	$\frac{n+1}{(2n+5)^2}$	$\frac{2n+3}{2(2n+5)}$
H	$\frac{(2n+1)^2}{8(n+1)(2n^2+6n+3)}$	$\frac{(n+1)(2n+1)^2}{4(2n^2+6n+3)^2}$	$\frac{(2n+1)(2n+3)(5+10n+4n^2)^2}{32(n+1)^2(2n^2+6n+3)^2}$

is negative because of equations (1), (2), (5), and (6). When (9) is evaluated given pattern A, dW_3^C/dt is negative because the first term vanishes. This means that the importing country reduces the level of tariffs from the level of pattern A and thereby enhances own-welfare. It implies that the importing country has an incentive to deviate from pattern A and become the leader.

We next prove that each exporting government has an incentive to become the follower. Suppose that each of them moves second. The effect of the tariff on country i 's welfare is given by:

Table 4
World welfare

Sequencing	*World welfare*
A	$\dfrac{2n(n+1)(n^2+3n+1)}{(2n^2+4n+1)^2}$
B	$\dfrac{n(2n+3)(2n^2+7n+4)}{2(n+2)^2(2n+1)^2}$
C	$\dfrac{(n+1)(n+3)}{2(n+2)^2}$
D	$\dfrac{(2n+1)(2n+3)(4n^2+16n+11)}{2(4n^2+12n+7)^2}$
E	$\dfrac{2n(2n^2+4n+1)(2n^3+8n^2+6n+1)}{(2n+1)^2(2n^2+5n+1)^2}$
F	$\dfrac{4n(n+2)(2n^2+8n+5)}{(2n+1)^2(2n+5)^2}$
G	$\dfrac{(2n+3)(2n+7)}{2(2n+5)^2}$
H	$\dfrac{(2n+1)(4n^2+10n+5)(8n^3+40n^2+52n+19)}{32(n+1)^2(2n^2+6n+3)^2}$

$$\begin{aligned}\frac{dW_i^C}{dt} &= n\left[p'\frac{\partial Q}{\partial s_i}q_i+(p-c-t)\frac{\partial q_i}{\partial s_i}\right]\frac{\partial s_i}{\partial t} \\ &+n\left[p'\frac{\partial Q}{\partial s_j}q_i+(p-c-t)\frac{\partial q_i}{\partial s_j}\right]\frac{\partial s_j}{\partial t} \\ &+n\left[\left(p'\frac{\partial Q}{\partial t}-1\right)q_i+(p-c-t)\frac{\partial q_i}{\partial t}\right].\end{aligned} \tag{10}$$

The first (the second) term is an indirect effect through the change of s_i (s_j). The third term is the direct effect. When (10) is evaluated given pattern A, the first term vanishes; dW_i^C / dt is negative because the sign of the remaining terms are negative [1]. This means that reducing the tariff is profitable for the exporting country i. The exporting government has an incentive to become a follower. This is why the importing (exporting) government becomes a leader (follower).

Proposition 1 shows that the governments of exporting countries move at the same time when the government of the importing country uses an import tariff policy. Proposition 1 [i] in Ohkawa, Okamura and Tawada (2002) also holds when the importing country imposes an import tariff [2].

Next, we compare the equilibrium welfare level with that under free trade for each country. From Table 4, we obtain following results:

Proposition 2: [i] The exporting country's equilibrium welfare is always smaller than the free trade one, but the importing country's equilibrium welfare is always larger than the free trade one. [ii] If $n = 1$, then world welfare in equilibrium is the same as free trade; otherwise, equilibrium world welfare is smaller than that under free trade.

From equation (7), world welfare is an increasing function of Q. From equation (2), if $s_1 + s_2 - 2t > (<) 0$, then the level of Q rises (declines) from the free trade level of welfare; if $s_1 + s_2 - 2t = 0$, it does not change. Also, when $n = 1$, $s_1 + s_2 - 2t = 0$ holds as shown in Table 2. Welfare in the trade policy equilibrium is the same as that under free trade. When $n \geq 2$, the level of tariffs dominates the sum of subsidies, i.e. $s_1 + s_2 - 2t < 0$, and total output reduces from the free trade level. The level of world welfare is lower than that under free trade.

Finally, we examine which policy sequencing maximizes world welfare when all countries intervene in the market, and we compare it with free trade welfare. From equation (8) and Table 4, we obtain:

Proposition 3: [i] The pattern G maximizes world welfare. [ii] If $n = 1$, then the world welfare in pattern G is higher than that under free trade; otherwise, world welfare with pattern G is lower than that under free trade.

Proposition 3 [i] states that the off-equilibrium pattern G is more desirable than the equilibrium pattern C from the viewpoint of world welfare, as long as all countries intervene in the market. Proposition 3 [ii] implies that free trade is efficient from a world welfare viewpoint when there operates at least two firms in each exporting country.

V. CONCLUDING REMARKS

This paper investigates the endogenous sequencing of trade policy in a three-country model where two identical exporting countries give export subsidies and one importing country imposes an import tariff. Our main conclusions are as follows: (i) in equilibrium, the importing country imposes an import tariff first, and both exporting countries give export subsidies simultaneously, (ii) policy intervention does not improve world welfare as compared to the free trade level, and (iii) when at least two firms operate in each exporting countries, world welfare is maximized with free trade.

Two possible directions for future research are indicated. First, one possible direction is to examine situations in which the number of firms in each exporting country differs. Ohkawa, Okamura, and Tawada (2002), for example, showed that if two exporting countries have a different number of firms, the governments of exporting countries move sequentially in a three-country model without the importing country's tariff policy. We would then examine whether hierarchical sequential timing (where all countries behave sequentially) prevails in trade policy. Another direction is to analyze extended model with free-trade agreement.

Notes

1. Calculations are available from the authors.
2. "If the number of firms in both export countries are identical, then the timing of decisions is simultaneous."(Ohkawa Okamura, and Tawada (2002), p.222.)

References

Arvan, L. (1991), "Flexibility versus Commitment in Strategic Trade Policy under Uncertainty," *Journal of International Economics* 31, 341–355.

Ohkawa, T., M. Okamura, and M. Tawada (2002), "Endogenous Timing and Welfare in the Game of Trade Policies under International Oligopoly", in A. D. Woodland (eds.) *Economic Theory and International Trade: essays in honour of Murray C. Kemp*, Northampton: Edward Elgar, 218–231.

Shivakumar, R. (1993), "Strategic Trade Policy: Choosing between Export Subsidies and Export Quotas under Uncertainty", *Journal of International Economics* 35, 169–183.

THE IMPACT OF EXCHANGE RATE VOLATILITY ON INTERNATIONAL TRADE: THE CASE OF SOUTH AFRICA

Guangling (Dave) Liu*

ABSTRACT

This paper investigates the impact of the real effective exchange rate volatility on South Africa's exports for the period from 1978:Q1 to 2005:Q4. A General Autoregressive Conditional Heteroskedasticity (GARCH) model is used to measure exchange rate volatility, and the Johansen cointegration tests and Error Correction Model (ECM) are employed to analyse the long run equilibrium and the dynamic short run relationship between exports and the real effective exchange rate volatility. The empirical evidence indicates that exports is positively related to foreign income and negatively related to the real effective exchange rate in the long run. However, in the short run, the real effective exchange rate volatility is insignificantly related to exports volume. In other words, the volatility does not have impact on South Africa's exports during the study period.

Keywords: *Exchange Rate Volatility; GARCH model; ECM.*

JEL Codes: *F31; C22; C51.*

I. INTRODUCTION

This objective of this paper is to investigate the relationship between the volatility of the real effective exchange rate and international trade in South Africa during the period from the first quarter of 1978 to the fourth quarter of 2005. A General Autoregressive Conditional Heteroskedasticity (GARCH) model is used to measure exchange rate volatility, and the Johansen cointegration tests and Error Correction Model (ECM) are employed to analyse the long run equilibrium and dynamic short run relationship between exports and the real effective exchange rate volatility.

International trade performance in a small open economy (SOE), such as South Africa, plays an important role in its economic growth. The movement of the exchange rate has an important impact on international trade and, hence, the economic growth. During the last three decades, we have seen a substantial increase in the volatility of exchange rates. This trend leads economists to ask whether this volatility hinders trade. According to the traditional international trade theory, a devaluation of exchange rate causes a price competitiveness of export goods in terms of the foreign currency, so that it boosts exports, and vice versa. Therefore, there has been a widespread concern amongst economists and policy makers over the high degree of

* Ph.D. Student, Department of Economics, University of Pretoria, Pretoria, South Africa, *E-mail: dave.liu@up.ac.za*

volatility of the most major exchange rates since the inception of flexible rates in March 1973 (Arize, *et al.*, 2003: 7). Most of this concern stems from the adverse effects of the increased uncertainty from the volatility of exchange rates on international trade.

There is a vast literature that investigates the impact of exchange rate volatility on international trade. However, there is no consensus on this issue. Most of the literature focuses on developed countries (Hooper and Kohlhagen, 1978; Caporate and Doroodian, 1994; Mcken, 1998; Sukar and Hassan, 2001). Seldom studies focus on developing countries especially Sub-Saharan Africa. Arize (1996), Doroodian (1999), and Arize et al (2003) investigate the impact of exchange rate volatility on the volume of international trade in developing countries.

The remainder of the paper is organised as follows. Section 2 explains the importance of this study in developing countries as well as in the South Africa's context. It gives a broad framework of South Africa's volatile currency and international trade performance during the last few decades. Section 3 reviews the recent literature, while Section 4 is devoted to describing the empirical model and measurements. Section 5 describes the data and methodology. Section 6 reports empirical results and the analyses for both long run and short run. Section 7 concludes the paper.

II. THE IMPORTANCE IN THE SOUTH AFRICAN CONTEXT

1. The Increasing Volatility of Exchange Rate

Nominal and real exchange rates became more volatile in the post-Bretton Woods era in both developed and developing countries. Recent empirical literature including West and Cho (1995), Bollerslev and Ghysels (1996), and Kang (1999) investigate the volatility of exchange rate in developed countries. They all find increasing volatility of exchange rates in most OECD countries.

For instance, Kang (1999) estimates and tests several hypotheses with a GARCH model of daily spot nominal exchange rate changes. The author separates the sample period into five sub-periods according to the four episodes during the study period[2], and investigates whether there are statistical significantly structural breaks in their conditional means and variances. If the conditional mean and variance parameters are stable within each sub-period, but become unstable when regime shifts, then instability in conditional means and variances may be attributed to the regime shifts (Kang, 1999:467). The author finds that the unexpected nominal exchange rate changes of the considered currencies[3] exhibited statistically significant structural breaks across the five sub-periods. A further observation is that the volatility of the exchange rates dropped steadily over the first sub sample period and increased over the remaining sub periods (Kang, 1999: 457-462).

The declined use of exchange rate pegs by developing countries has contributed to the increasing volatility of exchange rates. The breakdown of the Bretton-Woods system caused developed countries to shift to floating exchange rates while developing countries continued to use pegs. If the pegs have succeeded in developing countries, there should not be an increasing volatility of exchange rate. Unfortunately, the number of countries opting for pegs was declining dramatically during the last three decades. According to the IMF's *de jure* exchange rate regime record, in the developing world, 86% opted for pegs and 11% opted for more flexible regimes in 1976. However the percentages changed to 45% and 52% in the 1990s. It is a particular experience shared by economies in Latin America during the 1980s and South Asia in the 1990s (Edwards and Savastano, 1999:9).

Some studies have investigated whether the problem of exchange rate volatility is more serious in developing countries than that in developed countries. For instance, Devereux and Lane (2003) investigate the determinants of bilateral exchange rate volatility in developing countries and developed countries by looking at a large cross section of data.

Devereux and Lane (2003) test two hypotheses: The first one is that the higher the level of financial linkages with a creditor country, the lower the level is of bilateral exchange rate volatility. The empirical results suggest that external debt, combining with the balance sheet effects, have a strong negative impact on the movements of the exchange rate (Devereux and Lane, 2003: 110~111). Indeed, as Eichengreen and Hausmann (1999) suggest, developing countries are seldom able to tolerate exchange rate volatility against their major creditors.

The second hypothesis is that "bilateral exchange rate volatility is related to the stock of bilateral financial claims cross-countries" (Devereux and Lane, 2003: 111). Given the domestic budget constraints in developing countries, they have to borrow externally. In this case, exchange rate volatility may have an extra cost, i.e. it is negatively related to bilateral financial claims for developing countries. The exchange rate volatility for both developed and developing countries in their study is summarised in Table 1.

Table 1
Exchange rate volatility

	Full	*DCs*	*LDCs*
Mean	4.21	2.04	4.59
S.D.	5.99	1.06	4514
N	3026	442	2584

Source: summarised from Devereux and Lane (2003)

The results show that both the mean and the standard deviation of exchange rate are much higher for developing countries (LDCs) than developed countries (DCs). In other words, the exchange rate is much more volatile in developing countries than in developed countries.

Greater exchange rate volatility (i.e. the greater exchange rate risk) raises the cost of trading for domestic traders which potentially detrimental implications for the volume of trade. This is because of the time lag in international trade payment. Exchange rate risk for developing countries is generally not hedged because forward or futures markets are either nonexistent or not accessible to all traders. Even if hedging in the forward or futures markets were possible, there are limitations and costs (Arize et al, 2003: 10). Therefore, it is important to investigate the impact of the exchange rate volatility on international trade and find the appropriate solution especially for developing countries. Since this paper focuses on the South African context, it is useful to consider the features of the South African exchange rate regime and experience.

2. The South African Context

According to the IMF's *de jure* exchange rate arrangement, South Africa's exchange rate regime is independently floating (Fischer, 2001). During the data period from 1978-2005, there were several episodes concerning the South African exchange rate that merits particular attention. Bah and Amusa (2003) summarise the exchange rate policy events during the last three decades as follows: South Africa opted for independent managed floating policy between 1974 and 1979. The De Kock commission recommended a dual exchange rate (DRS) in 1979, which consisted of a commercial and financial Rand. The two were unified in 1983. However the financial Rand was reintroduced in 1985 in order to separate the foreign exchange transactions of non-resident portfolio investors on the capital account from all other foreign exchange transactions. The DRS existed until 1995 when the authorities adopted independent floating.

Recently Farrell (2001) investigated both commercial and financial Rand exchange rate volatility by ARCH and GARCH model. His empirical results suggest that the real effective exchange rate volatilities of both commercial and financial Rand were relatively lower during the period of 1985-1995 when the DRS was in place and the volatility of financial Rand was on average higher than the commercial Rand (Farrel, 2001: 14-15)[4]. Since 1995, only the commercial Rand remains in use and this study uses the commercial Rand for consistency purposes. The increasing volatility of Rand motivated economists to investigate the reasons behind it. Recently, MacDonald and Ricci (2003) and Bhundia and Gottschalk (2003) examine the source of the recent fluctuation of Rand.

The Myburgh Commission offered some explanations for the rapid depreciation of the Rand in 2001 and 2002 in their report of August 2002. With regard to Macroeconomic factors, the main factors that the commission emphasised were: a continued slowdown of world economic activity; contagion from the events of debt default in Argentina (both leading to reduced capital inflows to emerging markets including South Africa); a considerable growth in money supply during the third quarter of 2001; a worsening in the current account balance in the fourth quarter of 2001 (shifting from surplus to deficit). All these factors may explain the accelerated depreciation in the end of 2001. The commission also pointed out that the South Africa Reserve Bank's non-intervention policy contributed to depreciation pressure. In short, financial market developments are the most likely source of the depreciation of Rand in 2001 and 2002. Speculation is another important factor that might have exacerbated the Rand's decline, although it itself cannot fully explain the depreciation (Bhundia and Gottschalk, 2003).

Regarding international trade, South Africa has performed increasingly well since 1994. The political transaction and process of trade liberalisation seems to have had a significant beneficial impact on South Africa's international trade performance in 1994. Figure 1 shows how South Africa's exports (including net gold exports) has been increasing during the 1990s, though that performance has slowed down since 2000. The openness of South Africa, measured by the ratio of exports to GDP is shown in Figure 2. It indicates that, on average, South Africa's openness is 16.9% during the sample period. From the measures of one country's openness point of view, a 16.9% of openness indicates that South African economy is neither closed nor particularly open.

South Africa's main trading partners include the following countries: European Community (mainly Germany, United Kingdom, Italy, and France), East Asia and Pacific (Mainly Japan and China including Hong Kong SAR), and North America (mainly United States). Alleyne and Subramanian (2001) show that the respective percentages of South Africa's trade to these four main trading partners are 39%, 24%, 15%, and 11% in 1989. They together accounted for 89% of South Africa's international trade in 1989. This number declines from 89% in 1989 to 79% in 1997. This pattern remains stable in this country's international trade track despite the fact that there is a slight shift from high-income countries to middle-income countries during the 1990s (Alleyne and Subramanian, 2001: 7).

Figure 1: SA Exports 2000=100

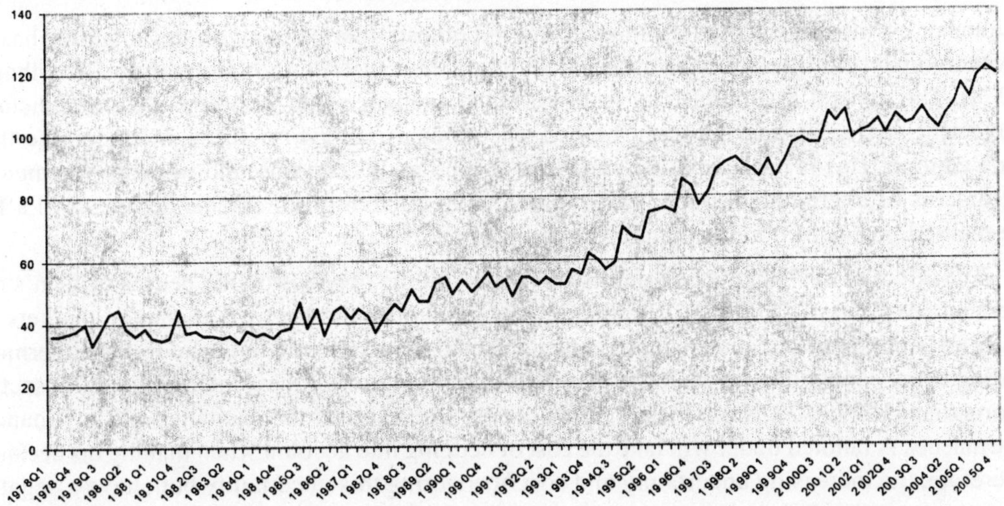

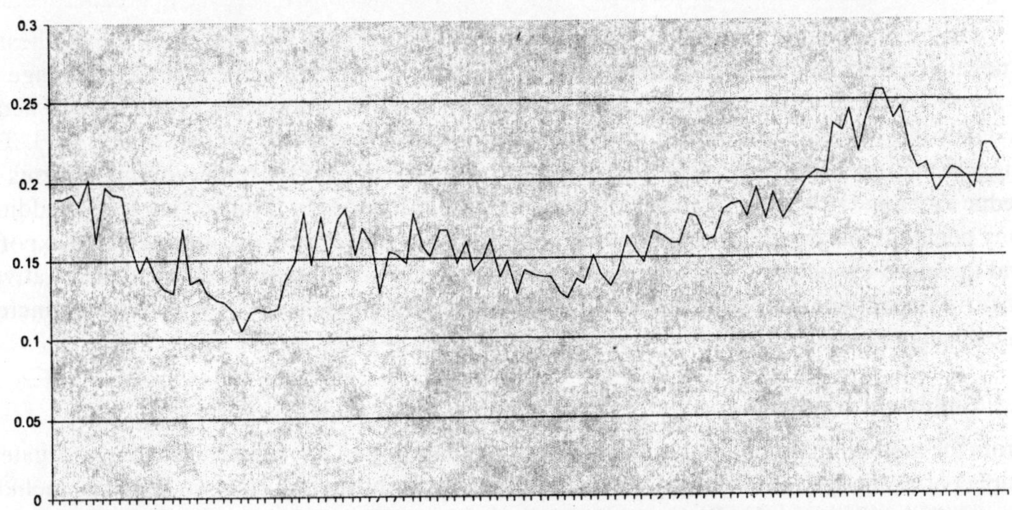

To sum up, it is important and necessary to investigate the impact of exchange rate volatility on international trade in South Africa, a small open economy with a highly volatile exchange rate. Moreover, South Africa is an ideal country for studying the relationship between exchange rate volatility and trade volume in general as it has a high level of exchange rate volatility and a fair level of openness.

III. A BRIEF REVIEW OF THE LITERATURE

Although the literature on this issue is extensive, there is neither theoretical nor empirical consensus on the impact of exchange rate volatility on international trade.

1. Theoretical Survey

A number of theoretical models support the hypothesis that exchange rate volatility has an adverse impact on international trade, including Ethier (1973) and, Hooper and Kohlhagen (1978). The general argument is as follows: If the exchange rate volatility, i.e. unpredictable movement, increases and it cannot be hedged, rational risk-averse firms will decrease their trade volume. This is because of the time lags in both goods delivery and financial payment in the process of international trade. The unpredictable fluctuations in exchange rates will affect the realised profits of trade and therefore the volume of trade.

The effect of exchange rate volatility on trade volume depends on the degree of firm's risk aversion (Arize *et al.*, 2003: 10). In the developing world, the forward exchange markets are either underdeveloped or nonexistent due to their small share of world trade volume. Furthermore, trading firms cannot always plan the magnitude or timing of all their international transaction (Doroodian, 1999:467). Nevertheless, it is not cost-free to cover the exchange risk by financial instruments. A rational trader will take the cost of hedging into account when making his decision. Therefore, the increasing uncertainty and cost of covering this uncertainty both have a negative impact international trade transaction.

On the other hand, Franke (1991) and Sercu and Uppal (2003) argue that the hypothesis of a negative effect results from partial-equilibrium models, which assume that the exchange rate is the sole source of risk for the decision makers, and "either ignores the availability of hedges or takes the prices of the hedge instruments as given" (Sercu and Uppal, 2003: 431). They suggest that exchange rate volatility may not have any impact on trade volume if firms can hedge exchange risk using financial instruments such as forward or futures contracts. In addition, they point out that depreciation or appreciation has opposing effects on importers and exporters and therefore the net effect is ambiguous. Exchange rate volatility may have either negative or positive impact on international trade volume depending on the source underlying the increase in exchange rate volatility.

2. Empirical Evidence

From the methodology point of view, different methodologies have been used to investigate the impact of exchange rate volatility on international trade during the last two decades, including Vector Autoregression (VAR) (Arize, 1995; Samanta and Zadeh, 2003); Autoregressive Moving

Average (ARMA) (Aristotelous, 2001; Bredin et al, 2003). A VAR is a simultaneous-equation system in which each variable is explained by its own lagged values, plus current and past values of the remaining n-1 variables. All the variables in the model are endogenous (Stock and Watson, 2001: 101). An ARMA model, following the Box–Jenkins methodology, allows the dependent variable to be explained by its lagged value and present and lagged stochastic error terms (Gujarati, 2002: 837).

A further group of studies considered cross-sectional data as opposed to the time series data implied above. More recent studies tend to use Autoregressive Conditional Heteroskedasticity (ARCH) and General Autoregressive Conditional Heteroskedasticity (GARCH) model. These include, inter alia, West and Cho (1995), Bollerslev and Ghysels (1996) Mckenzie and Brooks (1997), Mckenzie (1998), Doroodian (1999), So, et al (1999), Sauer and Bohara (2001). The ARCH and GARCH methodologies will be explained precisely in Section 6.

The disagreement in the theoretical literature is matched by a lack of consensus on the empirical side of too. A large number of empirical studies (Arize, 1996; Arize et al, 2000; Bleaney and Greenaway, 2000) have shown negative impacts of exchange rate volatility on total trade, exports, and imports. For instance, Arize *et al.* (2000) investigate thirteen developing countries during the period of 1973-1996.[5] The authors first use Augmented Dickey-Fuller tests and find that the explanatory variables of each individual time series are integrated of order 1.[6] They then find the cointegration between trade volume and exchange rate volatility by the Johansen approach. Their empirical results suggest a statistically significant negative effect of exchange rate volatility on international trade flows in the long run. The dataset they choose for each country covers the current floating exchange rate era. This allows their analysis to address the time-series stability of the estimated dynamic models (Arize *et al.*, 2000: 15).

In contrast, studies by Mckenzie and Brooks (1997), Mckenzie (1998), and Chou (2000), among others, found a positive long run equilibrium relationship between exchange rate volatility and international trade volume. Yet a third group in this literature suggest that there is no significant effect on either exports or imports. For example, Aristotelous (2001) claims that neither exchange rate volatility nor the different exchange rate regimes had affected the exports between United States and British during the period of 1889-1999.

Some studies focus on developed countries while others focus on developing countries or both. Therefore, the empirical studies are not comparable and the impact of exchange rate volatility on international trade is an empirical issue. This is because the data, the study period, the methodology, the measurements, and the specified countries differ widely.

IV. EMPIRICAL MODEL AND MEASUREMENTS

1. Empirical Model

Based on the theoretical and empirical investigation, there are three primary determinants of export demand. The first is an "income effect", the foreign income, measures the economic activity. The second effect is an "exchange rate effect". The "volatility effect", i.e. the exchange rate volatility, should be taken into account as well. The empirical model is the follows.

$$\ln X_t = \alpha + \beta_1 \ln Y_t + \beta_2 \ln REER_t + \beta_3 h_t + \varepsilon_t \quad (4.1)$$

where X_t is exports including net gold exports; Y_t is industrial production; $REER_t$ stands for real effective exchange rate; h_t represents the real effective exchange rate volatility. All the variables are in logarithm form except h_t.

According to the theoretical priors, the volume of exports ought to increase as the foreign income (industrial production) increases, and vice versa. Other things being equal, an increase in the real effective exchange rate reflects a decrease in the domestic costs for tradable goods, thereby stimulates foreign exports demand, and vice versa (Sauer and Bohara, 2001: 137). A rise (fall) in terms of trade will cause the domestic goods becoming less (more) competitive than foreign goods, therefore the volume of exports will decrease (increase). As far as the volatility of real effective exchange rate is considered, the results from recent literature are ambiguous. It can be either positive or negative. Therefore, the expected signs of the parameters in equation (4.1) are: $\beta_1>0$; $\beta_2<0$; $\beta_3<0$, or $\beta_3>0$.

2. Variables Used

Exports X_t

X_t is the volume of exports including net gold exports. Many studies investigate the relationship between volume of exports or imports and exchange rate volatility. Trade volume is preferable to trade value when studying the relationship between exchange rate volatility and international trade (Siregar and Rajan, 2004: 227). Trade volume is obtained by dividing the trade value by its price. The impact of the changing in the value of the currency can be avoided by using volume of trade instead of the value of trade when investigating a country's exports performance. The reason of choosing exports including net gold exports in this study is the following. The gold stock is regarded as a component of a country's foreign reserve. Changes in gold stock have an impact on exchange rate and the country's ability to finance imports, which in turn will affect the exports volume (although this might be out of fashion). In addition, South Africa is the biggest gold producer in the world.

Industrial Production Y_t

Choosing an appropriate measurement in a model is an empirical question. For example, because of the absence of data on real GDP for some of the USA's trading partner countries, Sukar and Hassan choose "the weighted industrial production index of 13 major importers of US goods" (Sukar and Hassan, 2001: 112) as a proxy for the "income effect" when they study the impact of exchange rate on US exports. Michael and Brooks (1997) use both the output of US and Germany to analyse the impact of exchange rate volatility on US–Germany bilateral trade flows. Some authors simply apply world income as an approximate measure, such as Doroodian (1999), Arize (1995), and Bredin et al (2003).

In this study, the index of G7 industrial production is chosen as a measurement of the "income effect" and is used as the proxy for South Africa's main trading partner counties' income. As shown in Section 2, South Africa's major trading partners are Germany, United

Kingdom, United States, and Japan. The percentages of South Africa's trade to these four main trading partners are 39%, 24%, 15%, and 11% respectively in 1989. They together counted for 89% of South Africa's international trade in 1989 (Alleyne and Subramanian, 2001: 4). This pattern remains stable in this country's international trade track despite the fact that there is a slightly shift from high-income countries to middle-income countries during 1990s (Alleyne and Subramanian, 2001: 7). This is the main reason to the industrial production index as a proxy for foreign economic activity. "Although the index of industrial production is a more restrictive measure looking at the level of manufacturing, it should reflect the trend in GDP" (Michael and Brooks, 1997: 76).

Real Effective Exchange Rate $REER_t$

In the case of South Africa, the multilateral real effective exchange rate (REER) is a preferred measure when studying the link between exchange rate and aggregate trade. The measurement of the exchange rate can be nominal or real, bilateral or effective. Most recent literature choose real exchange rate as the measurement since it is the relative price between domestic price and foreign price (PPI or CPI) influencing the volume of trade.

The choice between bilateral and effective exchange rates depends on the type of trade flows being analysed. When aggregate exports are concerned, the relevant measurement of "exchange rate effect" is real effective exchange rate (REER). The real effective exchange rate is calculated as the trade-weighted average of real bilateral exchange rates of South Africa's major trading partners: Germany, United Kingdom, the United States, and Japan. Table 2 shows the weights of the various currencies in the basket of the real effective exchange rate. One should note in Table 2 that the South Africa Reserve Bank substituted the euro for Germany mark when the euro was launched in January 1999. This is due to the important role that euro is expected to play in international financial markets and international trade in goods and services (Walters, 1999: 43). This substitution resulted in a downward adjustment of the weights to all other currencies in the index.

Table 2

Weighted of the various currencies in the basket[7] (%)

	Up to 31 Dec. 1998	*From 1 Jan 1999*
US dollar	51,7	42,8
British pound	20,2	16,7
German mark/euro	17,2	31,6
Japanese yen	10,9	8,9
Total	100,0	100,0

Souce: SARB quarterly bulletin (Note to tables, March 1999)

Volatility of Real Effective Exchange Rate h_t

h_t is the measurement capturing the volatility of the real effective exchange rate. The General Autoregressive Conditional Heteroscedasticity (GARCH) model is employed to specify the second measurement of the real effective exchange rate volatility:

$$\ln REER_t = \theta_0 + \theta_1 \ln REER_{t-1} + \psi_t \qquad \psi_t \sim N(0, h_t) \qquad (4.2)$$

$$h_t = \alpha_0 + \alpha_1 \psi^2_{t-1} + \alpha_2 h_{t-1} + \delta_t \qquad (4.3)$$

where δ_t is a white noise process. The conditional variance h_t in equation (4.3) is a function of three terms: the mean α_0; volatility of previous period measured as squared one-period lagged residual from equation (4.2), U^2_{t-1}; and the previous period forecast error's variance, h_{t-1}.

V. DATA AND METHODOLOGY

1. Data

All the data in quarterly frequencies are taken from South Africa Reserve Bank (SARB) Quarterly Bulletin, except the data for industrial production, which is taken from the International Financial Statistics (IFS). The indices are seasonally adjusted and their basic periods are the year of 2000. The real effective exchange rate (REER) is compiled by averaging the monthly data.

2. Methodology

Regarding to the econometric methodology, the real exchange rate volatility is measured by the generalised autoregressive conditional heteroscedasticity (GARCH) model developed by Bollerslev (1986), Bollerslev and Ghysels (1996) based on Engle's ARCH model.

The mixed results obtained by most of the previous studies using classical regression analysis may be partly due to the nonstationary of the aggregate exports and its determinants (Bredin et al, 2003: 199). Variables such as South Africa's aggregate exports and real effective exchange rate shown in Figures 1 and 2 are naturally nonstationary. Some economic time series data contain a clear upward or downward trend. South Africa's export exhibits an upward trend since 1990. Some exhibit "random walk" behaviour, i.e. neither upward nor downward tendency (Enders, 1995: 137). South Africa's REER falls into this category. Such nonstationary time series disturbs the assumption that the underlying time series is stationary or at least can be made stationary with appropriate transformations for forecasting purpose.

The regression of a nonstationary time series on another nonstationary time series may produce a spurious regression. Therefore, a test for cointegration is as a pre-test to avoid "spurious regression" (Gujarati, 2002: 882). This paper employs the Augmented Dickey-Fuller (ADF) unit root test to test the time series stationarity before the test of cointegration. The ADF test also avoids the argument that "[being] aware that 'eyeballing' the data is not a substitute for formal testing for the presence of conditional heteroscedaticity or nonstationary behaviour" (Enders, 1995: 138).

The Johansen multivariate cointegration procedure is used to test for the long run equilibrium among the variables in equation (4.1). Johansen's multivariate cointegration procedure is becoming an essential tool for cointegration tests on time series models. It does not suffer from the drawbacks of Enger-Granger approach such as small sample bias and inability to test statistical hypotheses (Verbeek, 2000: 295-296). The Johansen multivariate cointegration procedure is optimal in terms of symmetry, unbiasedness, and efficiency. It developed a maximum likelihood estimation procedure to test for the number of cointegrating relations (Verbeek, 2000: 296). If all or most of the variables have unit roots, then Johansen's multivariate cointegration test can be used to find out the existing cointegrating vectors. If there are at least one or more than one cointegrating vector then a long run equilibrium among the variables exists.

Investigating the model's short run structure becomes more important for the information on the short run adjustment behaviours of the explanatory variables (Harris, 1995:11). When estimating a dynamic equation, simply differencing the variables is a misspecification: an omitted variable (error correction term) and massive loss of information about the long run. A vector error-correction model (VECM) is a suitable approach to contain the information on both the short run and long run model. The basic idea of a VECM is the Granger representation theorem: the error correction and cointegration are equivalent representations for any set of I(1) variables (Enders, 1995: 371). I use ECM to investigate the short run dynamics because the exchange rate volatility is I (0), while other variables are I (1)[8].

The following section presents empirical results including the volatility of real effective exchange rate measured by a GARCH (1,1) model, the ADF unit root test results, the cointegration and ECM results.

VI. EMPIRICAL RESULTS AND ANALYSIS[9]

1. Measuring the REER Volatility GARCH (1,1)

The simplest GARCH model is the GARCH(1,1) model written as:

$$\varepsilon_t = z_t \sqrt{h_t} \tag{6.1}$$

$$h_t = \alpha_0 + \alpha_1 \varepsilon^2_{t-1} + \alpha_2 h_{t-1} \tag{6.2}$$

where z_t is independently and identically distributed with zero mean and unit variance. ε_t is conditionally heteroscedastic. The unconditional means of ε_t are equal to zero, i.e. the expected value of ε_t is

$$E\varepsilon_t = E\, z_t \sqrt{h_t} = 0 \tag{6.3}$$

The unconditional variance of ε_t is assumed to be constant. However in this GARCH(1,1) model, the conditional variance of ε_t is given by $E_{t-1}\, \varepsilon^2_t = h_t$ in equation (6.2). In other words, the conditional variance of the shock ε_t in time period t is a function of the squares of past shocks and the first lag of the conditional variance itself (Franses and van Dijk, 2000: 137). Obviously, the conditional variance h_t needs to be nonnegative. In order to guarantee that this is the case for the GARCH(1,1) model, the parameters in equation (6.2) have to satisfy the conditions that $\alpha_0 > 0$, $\alpha_1 > 0$, and $\alpha_2 \geq 0$. The empirical literature suggest that the GARCH(1,1) model is an appropriate model for measuring the volatility of exchange rate. Accordingly, a GARCH(1,1) model is estimated to measure the real effective exchange rate volatility for South Africa. Table 3 reports the result, which is also shown in equation (6.4).

$$h_t = 0.00071 + 0.271553\varepsilon^2_{t-1} + 0.471828h_{t-1} \tag{6.4}$$

The constant and all the parameters are positive and statistically significant.[10] The result indicates that a significant GARCH effect exists, as the parameter of h_{t-1} in the variance equation is statistically different from zero.

Table 3
GARCH model: $h_t = \alpha_0 + \alpha_1 \varepsilon^2_{t-1} + \alpha_2 h_{t-1}$

	α_0	α_1	α_2
Coefficient	0.000711	0.271553	0.471828
s.e.	0.000283	0.14394	0.155171

The real effective exchange rate is characterised by conditional heteroscedasticity because the assumption of a constant variance (homoskedasticity) does not hold. Figure 3 shows high level of the real effective exchange rate volatility during the sample period, especially during the second half of 1980s and from 1996 to 2003.Unlike Farrell's observation[11], the most volatile period of real effective exchange rate was during 1985 to 1988. The reintroduction of DRS induced the high volatility of real effective exchange rate.

Figure 3: Real Effective Exchange Rate Volatility (GARCH) 2000=100

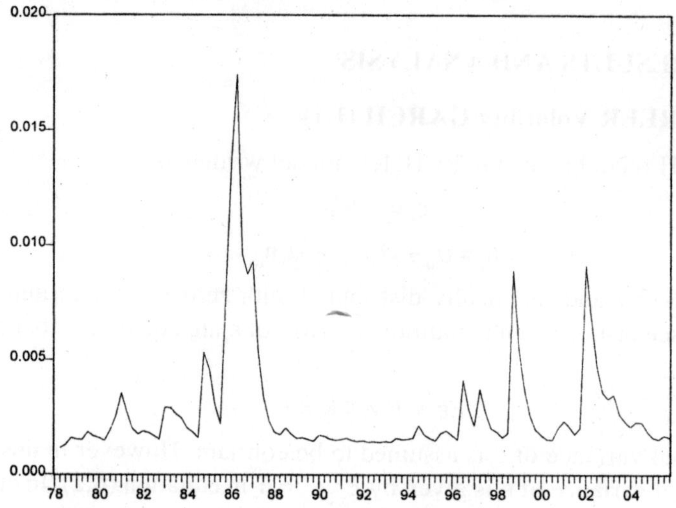

2. ADF–Unit Root Test

The ADF test for a unit root is performed by regressing the first difference of the variable on its lagged value, a constant, and the lagged first difference of the series:

$$\Delta\Psi_t = \omega_0 + \varpi_1 \Psi_{t-1} + \sum_{j=1}^{k} \varpi_i \Delta\psi_{t-j} + \varepsilon_t \qquad (6.5)$$

where Δ denotes the first difference operator; ε_t is a random disturbance term; and k is the number of lags of the first difference on Ψ that is necessary to make ε_t serially uncorrelated. The null hypothesis is that $\omega_1 = 0$, i.e. there is a unit root. The alternative is that the variable is mean stationary (Maddala and Kim, 1998: 75-76).

The null hypothesis of ADF tests is that the series is nonstationary. Both the level and the first difference of the variables in Equation (4.1) are considered in ADF tests. The number of the lagged time periods is often determined empirically (Gujarati, 2002: 817). It is set to four according to the rule of thumb that at least four lagged time periods are chosen for quarterly data. For nonstationary time series, the null hypothesis cannot be rejected regardless the number of lagged time periods.

The results suggest that series X_t, Y_t, $REER_t$ (in logarithm form) are nonstationary, but their first differences are stationary (*I* (1)), while h_t is stationary at level (*I* (0)). The ADF test results on the time series properties of exchange rate volatility are mixed. Some empirical evidence suggests the volatility is *I* (1), while others find *I* (0). It seems to reflect the way by which the exchange rate volatility has been generated (Pattichis, 2003: 2). Regarding the volatility generated by GARCH model, Arize (1995), Suhar and Hassan (2001), and Bredin *et al.* (2003) find GARCH generated measurement of volatility to be *I* (1), while Rahmaltsyah *et al.* (2002) find GARCH generated measurement of volatility to be *I* (0).

3. Cointegration Tests and Long Run Equilibrium

In the main equation (4.1),[12] the volume of exports, the industrial production, and the real effective exchange rate are I(1), while the volatility are I(0). The cointegration tests test whether the linear combination $\ln X_t - \alpha - \beta_1 \ln Y_t - \beta_2 \ln REER_t = \varepsilon_t$ is stationary. If "ε_t" is stationary, then there is long run equilibrium between the component variables and the equilibrium error "ε_t" is transitory in nature. Volatility is not included in the long run equilibrium but in the short run dynamic because the cointegration tests require that all the component variables must be integrated of the same order (Enders, 1995: 358).

The Johansen multivariate cointegration tests indicate that there is one cointegrating vector exists. In other words, there is long run equilibrium between the volume of exports X_t, the industrial production Y_t, and the real effective exchange rate $REER_t$.

The normalised cointegration vectors are reported in Table 4. The cointegrating vector normalised on exports gives the long run income (income effect) and relative price (exchange effect) elasticity for exports demand. The foreign income, measured by industrial production, is positively related with exports volume, while the real effective exchange rate is negatively related with the export volume. The volume of exports is relatively elastic with respect to foreign income and relatively inelastic to the real effective exchange rate.

The model passes the general cointegration tests for all three variables. However, as shown in Table 5, the weak exogeneity tests suggest that exports and foreign income are endogenous in this model.

Table 4
Nornalized Cointegrating Vectors

	lnX	*lnY*	*lnREER*
β	1.0000	-1.5827	0.2747
α	-0.0460	-0.0311	-0.0077

Table 5
General Cointegration Restriction (GCR) and Weak Exogeneity (WE) Tests

	lnX	*lnY*	*ln REER*
GCR	1.2071 (0.2719)	0.74986 (0.3865)	0.09182 (0.7619)
WE	5.3724 (0.0205)*	14.107 (0.0002)**	0.19483 (0.6589)

NB: LR tests: ÷2(1); probability in parenthesis.

4. Error Correction Model (ECM) and Short Run Dynamic

Having established the long run relationship of the export volume, foreign income, and real effective exchange rate, the next step is to examine the short run interaction between all the jointly endogenous variables using Error Correction Model (ECM).

The volatility can be theoretically positive or negative to exports. Evidently, Bredin, et al (2003) find that the exchange rate volatility has no effect on the volume of Irish's exports in the short run but a significant positive effect in the long run. Sukar and Hassan (2001) find a significant negative relationship between US exports volume and exchange rate volatility in long run, but insignificant in the short run. Sauer and Bohara (2001) use panel data for 22 industrialised and 69 developing countries during the 1973-1993 period and show that the trade effect of real exchange rate volatility is more harmful in developing world, particularly in Latin America and Africa, than in OECD or Asian LDCs.

The result of the error correction model (ECM) is reported in Table 6[13]. The most important effects considered here are the effects of real effective exchange rate volatility (h_t) and the error correction term (ECM_{t-1}). The volatility has an insignificant effect on exports in short run.

In the case of South Africa, the main export firms are either multinational corporations or affiliates of multinational firms. This might result in oligopolistic structure in particular product markets. The export firms may respond to real exchange rate volatility by increasing exports in short run, so that their exports in terms of value can still maintain at its equilibrium level. It is notable that it is the exports volume, not value or profit, which is positively but insignificantly related to the real effective exchange rate volatility. Furthermore, exports will only respond to the volatility if the new rate is expected to persist at least for the time that takes to adjust production. Hence, it is not surprising that the volatility has an insignificant effect on the exports volume in the short run (Bredin *et al.*, 2003: 206).

The error correction term (ECM) in ΔlnX equation is statistically different from zero at less than 1% significant level, which indicates a strong error correction effect. The negative coefficient of ECM, -29.8%, contributes a negative value to the change of exports volume in time period t, ΔlnX_t. Therefore, ΔlnX_t will be negative to restore the equilibrium. That is, for instance, if lnX_{t-1} is above its equilibrium value, it will start falling in the next period to correct the equilibrium error. The absolute value of ECM's coefficient decides how quickly the equilibrium is restored. The magnitude of the equilibrium feedback shows that about 29.8% of the disequilibrium between export volume and its associated variables is removed per quarter. The ECM suggests that the adjustment speed towards the elimination of disequilibrium is rapid and statistically significant.

Table 6
ECM results

Variables	*Coefficients*	*Standard errors*	*t-statistics*	*t-prob*
		Equation ΔlnX		
ΔlnYt	0.350444	0.1830	1.920	0.058
ΔlnREERt	-0.199361	0.1223	-1.630	0.106
Δht	-1.06339	1.9570	-0.544	0.588
ECMt-1	-0.297547	0.0707	-4.210	0.000
		Equation ΔlnY		
ΔlnXt	0.095454	0.04984	1.92	0.058
ΔlnREERt	0.060224	0.06436	0.936	0.352
Δht	1.693720	1.009	1.68	0.096
ECMt-1	0.140371	0.03745	3.75	0.000
		Equation ΔlnREER		
ΔlnXt	-0.122660	0.07525	-1.63	0.106
ΔlnYt	0.136038	0.1454	0.936	0.352
Δht	0.469823	1.536	0.306	0.760
ECMt-1	-0.0273115	0.05985	-0.456	0.649
		Equation Δh		
ΔlnXt	-0.00261436	0.004808	-0.544	0.588
ΔlnYt	0.0152791	0.009105	1.68	0.096
ΔlnREERt	0.00187632	0.006135	0.306	0.760
ECMt-1	-0.00360816	0.003770	-0.957	0.341

VII. CONCLUSIONS AND REMARKS

This paper aims to analyse the long run and short run relationship between international trade and the real exchange rate volatility using the techniques of generalised autoregressive conditional heteroscedasticity (GARCH) model, the Johansen cointegratiion approach, as well as Error Correction Model (ECM).

The empirical result suggests that exports volume is positively related to foreign income and negatively related to the real effective exchange rate in the long run. In the short run, the real effective exchange rate volatility is insignificantly related to exports volume. In other words, the volatility does not have impact on South Africa's exports during the study period.

During the sample period, the dual exchange rate policy had been introduced during 1979-1983 and 1985-1995. This raises the Lucas critique: "the parameters of macroeconomic relationships used in policy design can only be invariant to policy adjustments if the policy is itself based on a rule that specifies how future policy adjustments will be made" (Taylor, 1999b). Future investigation, considering tests for exogeneity, for instance, is required to investigate the relevance of this critique for models of exports performance such as that offered here.

Notes

1. For more details, see Kang (1999: 453-454).
2. The Japanese yen, the Canadian dollar, the French franc, the British pound, and the Deutsche mark.

3. This paper's empirical result suggests that the launch of DRS caused a high volatility in the first three years. (see Figure 3).
4. See Arize *et al.* (2000: 12).
5. The regression function: $Q_t = \alpha + \beta_1 W_t + \beta_2 P_t + \beta_3 \sigma_t + \varepsilon_t$. Where Q_t is volume of one country's exports, W_t is a scale variable that captures world demand conditions, P_t is the relative prices and measured by the ratio of that country export price in U.S. dollars to the world export price in U.S. dollars, σ_t is a moving-sample standard deviation, ε_t is a disturbance term. All the variables are in logarithm except ε_t.
6. Weights are based on total trade in merchandise and services and by taking into account the currency denomination of commodities traded on international markets.
7. See Section 6.2.
8. All programmes are performed using PcGive, except for the GARCH model using EViews.
9. a_1 is significant at 10% level and a_2 is significant at 1%.
10. His empirical results suggest the real effective exchange rate volatilities of Rand were relatively lower during the period of 1985-1995 when DRS was in place.
11. $\ln X_t = \alpha + \beta_1 \ln Y_t + \beta_2 \ln REER_t + \beta_3 ht + \varepsilon t$ (4.1)
12. I assume exports is weekly exogenous in the model.

References

Alleyne, T. and Subramanian, A. (2001), What Does South Africa's Pattern of Trade Say About Its Labor Market? Washington. IMF Working Paper. WP/01/48.

Aristotelous, K. (2001), Exchange-rate Volatility, Exchange-rate regime, and Trade Volume: Evidence from the UK–US Export function (1889–1999). *Economics Letters.* 72: 87-94.

Arize, A. C. (1995), The Effect of Exchange Rate Volatility on U.S. Exports: An Empirical Investigation. *Southern Economic Journal.* 62: 34-43.

Arize, A. C. (1996), The impact of Exchange Rate Uncertainty on Export Growth: Evidence from Korean Data. *International Economic Journal.* 10: 49-60.

Arize, A. C., Osang, T., and Slottje, D. J. (2000), Exchange-Rate Volatility and Foreign Trade: Evidence from Thirteen LDC's. *Journal of Business & Economic Statistics.* 18(1): 10-18.

Arize, A. C., Malindretos, J., and Kasibhatla, K. M. (2003), Does Exchange-rate Volatility Depress Export Flows: The Case of LDCs. International Advances in Economic Research. 9(1): 7-21.

Bah, I. and Amusa, H. A. (2003), Real Exchange rate Volatility and Foreign Trade: Evidence from South Africa's exports to the United States. *The African Finance Journal.* 5(2): 1-19.

Bhundia, A. and Gottschalk, J. (2003), Source of Nominal Exchange Rate fluctuations in South Africa. Washington. IMF Working Paper. WP/03/252.

Bleaney, M. and Greenaway, D. (2001), The Impact of Terms of Trade and Real Exchange Rate Volatility on Investment and Growth in sub-Saharan Africa. *Journal of Development Economics.* 65: 491-500.

Bollerslev, T. (1986), General Autoregressive Conditional Heteroscedaticity. *Journal of Econometrics.* 31: 307-326.

Bollerslev, T. and Ghysels, E. (1996), Periodic Autoregressive Conditional Heteroscedasticity. *Journal of Business & Economic Statistics.* 14(2): 139-152.

Bredin, D., Fountas, S. and Murphy, E. (2003), An Empirical Analysis of Short-run and Long-Run Irish Export Functions: Does Exchange Rate Volatility matter? *International Review of Applied Economics.* 17(2): 193-208.

Caporade, T. and Doroodian, K. (1994), Exchange Rate Variability and the Flow of International trade. *Economics Letters*. 46(1): 49-54.

Chen, C. H. (2002), Taiwan's Exports and Trade Imbalance Against US and Japan: An Empirical Investigation Based on Error Correlation Model. *Applied Economics*. 34: 2303-2309.

Chou, W. L. (2000), Exchange Rate Variability and China's Exports. *Journal of Comparative Economics*. 28(1): 61-79.

Devereux, M. B. and Lane, P. R. (2003), Understanding Bilateral Exchange Rate Volatility. *Journal of International Economics*. 60: 109-132.

Doroodian, K. (1999), Does Exchange Rate Volatility Deter International Trade in Developing Countries? *Journal of Asian Economics*. 10: 465-474.

Edwards, S. and Savastano, M. A. (1999), Exchange Rate in Emerging Economics: What Do We Know? What Do We Need to Know? National Bureau of Economic Research, Inc, NBER Working Papers, 7228.

Eichengreen, B. and Hausmann, R. (1999), Exchange rates and Financial Fragility. National Bureau of Economic Research, Inc, NBER Working Papers, 7418.

Enders, W. (1995), Applied Econometric Time Series. U.S.. John Wiley & Sons, Inc.

Ethier, W. (1973), International Trade and the Forward Exchange Market. *American Economic Review*. 63: 494-503.

Farrell, G. N. (2001), Capital Controls and the Volatility of South African Exchange Rates. South Africa Reserve Bank Quarterly Bulletin Occasional Paper No 15, July 2001. Available [on line]: http://www.reservebank.co.za/internet/Publication.nsf/LADV/D6DB6F136AD3104342256B6C003B9E58/$File/occ15.pdf

Fischer, S. (2001), Exchange Rate Regimes: Is the Bipolar View Correct? Lecture delivered at the AEA, 6 January 2001.

Franke, G. (1991), Exchange Rate Volatility and International Trading Strategy. *Journal of International Money and Finance*. 10: 292-307.

Franses, P. H. and van Dijk, D. (2000), Non-linear Time Series models in empirical finance. United Kingdom. Cambridge University Press.

Gujarati, D. (2002), Basic Econometrics. Fourth edition. New York. McGraw-Hill.

Harris, R.I.D. (1995), Using Cointegration Analysis in Econometric Modelling. U.K.. Prentice Hall/Harvester Wheatsheaf.

Harvey, A. (1990), The Econometric Analysis of Time Series. 2nd edition. U.K.. Philip Allan Prentice Hall Europe.

Hooper, P. and Kohlhagen, S. W. (1978), The Effects of Exchange Rate Uncertainty on the Prices and Volume of International Trade. *Journal of International Economics*. 8(4): 483-511.

Kang, I. (1999), International Foreign Exchange Agreements and Nominal Exchange Rate Volatility: A GARCH Application. *North American Journal of Economics and Finance*. 10: 453-472.

Macdonal, R. and Ricci, L. (2003), Estimation of the Equilibrium Real Exchange Rate for South Africa. Washington. IMF Working Paper WP/03/44.

Maddada, G. S. and Kim, In-Moo (1998), Unit Roots Cointegration and Structural Change. United Kingdom. Cambridge University Press.

Mckenzie, M. D. and Brooks, R. D. (1997), The Impact of Exchange Rate Volatility on German-US trade flows. *Journal of International Financial Markets, Institutions and Money*. 7: 73-87.

Mckenzie, M. D. (1998), The Impact of Exchange Rate Volatility on Australian. *Journal of International Financial Markets, Institutions and Money*. 8(1): 21-38.

Myburgh, J. F. (2002), Final Report of the Commission of Inquiry into the Rapid Depreciation of the Rand and Related Matters. Available [on line]: *http://www.gov.za/bodies/myburgh/*

Mohr, P. (2000), Economic indicators. Revised edition. South Africa. Unisa Press.

Pattichis, C. (2003), Conditional Exchange Rate Volatility, Unit Roots, and International trade. *The International Trade Journal. XVII (1)*: 1-19.

Percu, P. and Uppal, R. (2003), Exchange Rate Volatility and International Trade: A General-equilibrium Analysis. *European Economic Review.* 47: 429~441.

Pretorius, A. and de Beer, J. (2004), Contagion in Africa: South Africa and a trouble neighbour, Zimbabwe. Economic Modelling. 21: 703~717.

Rahmaltsyah, T., Rajaguru, G. and Siregar, R. Y. (2002), Exchange-Rate Volatility, Trade and "Fixing for life" in Thailand. *Japan and the World Economy.* 14 (2002): 445-470.

Samanta, S. K. and Zadeh, A., M. (2003), Cross Country Spillover Effects In Foreign Exchange Market: An Empirical Analysis of Six OECD Countries. *The International Trade Journal. XVII* (2): 129-166.

Sauer, C. and Bohara, A. K. (2001), Exchange Rate Volatility and Exports: Regional Differences between Developing and Industrial Countries. *Review of International Economics.* (1): 133-152.

Siregar, R. and Rajan, R. S. (2004), Impact of Exchange Rate Volatility on Indonesia's Trade Performance in the 1990s. *J. Japanese Int. Economies.* 18: 218-240.

So, K. P., Lam, K. and Li, W. K. (1999), Forecasting Exchange Rate Volatility using Autoregressive Random Variance Model. *Applied Financial Economics.* 9: 583-591.

Stock, J. H. and Watson, M. W. (2001), Vector Autoregressions. *Journal of Economic Perspectives.* 15(4): 101-115.

Sukar, A. and Hassan, S. (2001), US Exports and Time-varying Volatility of Real Exchange Rate. *Global Finance Journal.* 12(1): 109-119.

Taylor, J. B. (1999(b), "The New Normative Macroeconomics". Lecture given to the 21st conference of the Brasileiro de Econometrica, 9 December 1999.

Van de Merwe, E. J. (1995), Exchange Rate Management policies in South Africa: Recent Experience and Prospects. SARB Occasional Paper. No. 8, June 1995.

Verbeek, M. (2000), A Guide to Modern Econometrics. U.K.. John Wiley & Sons, Inc.

Walters, S. S. (1999), Note on the Introduction of the Euro and the Revised Weighting Structure of the Nominal Effective Exchange Rate of the Rand. South Africa Reserve Bank Quarterly Bulletin Articles and Notes. 1999. Available [on line]: *http://www.reservebank.co.za/internet/Publication.nsf/LADV/5A46E88FE847E00A42256B6D003A261F/$File/Note0399.pdf*

West, K. D. and Cho, D. (1995), The Predictive Ability of Several Models of Exchange Rate Volatility. *Journal of Econometrics.* 69: 367-391.

HUMAN DEVELOPMENT: A CASE STUDY

*Rudra Prakash Pradhan**

ABSTRACT

The paper prepares a case study on human development, representing the status of India at the global level and national level. The study confirmed that India is in the group of medium human development and its rank is 127 out of 177 countries in the world. Though its status has been increasing over the years, it is considerably low in contrast to other emerging countries in the world. The problem is again more worsening and diverging at the disaggregate level, particularly an existence of large-scale regional variation across its states. While the status of human development is appreciably high in Kerala, Punjab, Haryana and Maharashtra, it is significantly low in Bihar, Orissa, Madhya Pradesh and Uttar Pradesh. The paper finally concludes with some suggestions to improve the status of human development in the economy

I. INTRODUCTION

The achievement of economic progress is one of the outstanding objectives in any countries in the world. There are various measures available to assess the same and that varies with respect to time and needs of the economy (Castles and Henderson, 2005; Meher, 2005; Haq, 2003; Fukuda-Parr, 2003; Maddison, 2001; Sen, 2001; Sen and Anand, 2000; Sen, 1998; Heston and Summers, 1996; Summers and Heston, 1991; Mukherjee, 1980; Morris, 1979; Hicks and Streeten, 1979; Overseas Development Council (ODC), 1977; Adelman and Morris, 1967). Economists generally recognize that 'economic development' involves much more than that of 'economic growth'. While economic growth concentrates narrowly on sustained increases in the flow of goods and services, economic development has conceived as a multi-dimensional process and that involves major changes in the social structures, popular attitudes and national institutions as well as acceleration of economic growth, reduction of inequality and an eradication of poverty (Sachs, 2005; Todaro and Smith, 2003; Seers, 1972). In other words, economic development has often been emphasized the reduction of poverty, inequality and many more rather than simply evoking the average income per se. In this context, the role of social services- especially basic health and education- has received greater attention, although these services have been viewed mainly as the instruments for raising the incomes of poor (Anand and Ravallion, 1993).

But the greatest weakness of economic growth, which is measured by GDP (GNP) per capita, is that it is a uni-directional measure, which captures only economic aspects and fails to

* Assistant Professor, Vinod Gupta School of Management (VGSOM), Indian Institute of Technology (IIT), Kharagpur, India, *E-mail: rudrap@vgsom.iitgp.ernet.in & pradhanrp@yahoo.com*

incorporate other aspects such as cultural, social, political, and many other choices that people can make. The achievement of same is only a means not an end in itself (Fukuda- Parr, 2003a). To put in other way, the achievement of higher GDP (GNP) per capita is not an end in itself but a means to an end, i.e., human happiness. Similarly the Physical Quality of Life Index (PQLI), which is the average outcome of a country with respect to life expectancy, literacy rate and infant mortality rate, is also a one-directional measure of economic development, as it does not incorporate economic indicators and other social indicators as well. The achievement of PQLI is also not an end rather it is a means to an end. Obviously there has been a long search for a comprehensive measure of economic development, which could capture all or many more of the choices people make- a measure that would serve as a better yardstick of the socio- economic progress of nations (Haq, 2003).

It was in the year 1990, the search somewhat came to end when United Nation Development Programme (UNDP) introduced the concept 'human development', which is measured in the form of a composite index called as Human Development Index (HDI). The Godfather of this concept was Pakistani Great *Mehbub Ul Haq* along with a group of fellow development economists like *Paul Streeten, Frances Stewart, Keith Griffin, Sudhir Anand, Meghnad Desai* and many more (Fukuda-Parr, 2003b; Haq, 1995). The newly measure of HDI is not a replacement to GDP per capita or PQLI or any other socio-economic measure of development (Komlos and Snowdon, 2005), rather it reflects an understanding of the real position of a society in several aspects. The new measure of economic development has several advantages in the economy in contrast to other available measures of economic development. Some of the celebrated them are as follows:

- The HDI is a multi-dimensional measure of economic development.
- It merges economic and social indicators, which is one of the distinctive features and chief strengths of HDI.
- The index is important for its choice of capabilities and focus at the national average rather than disparities.
- HDI is very popular for its methodological simplicity and explicit basis in philosophical reasoning.
- It is the long-term outcome of a country with respect to investigation, investment and research.
- The index enhances national priorities and hence, indirectly put pressures on policymakers to improve their performance.
- HDI can be disaggregated by gender, ethnic group or geographical region and in man other ways- to present relevant policy inputs as well as to forecast impending trouble.
- It can reveal the future potential growth of a country. For instance, if a country has built up considerable human capital, it can accelerate its GNP growth by choosing the right macroeconomic policies.
- The index ensures early warnings to the nations with respect to strength, blemishes and tension point.

- HDI is very helpful to trace a meaningful comparison among the countries/ regions in the globe or states/ districts in a country.
- Above all, HDI is neither perfect nor fully developed. It requires continuous analysis and further refinement (Haq, 2003).

Keeping in above backdrop, present paper prepares a case study on human development and highlights the status of India at the global level and national level. The remaining of paper is organized into the following fashion: Section II discusses the methodology and data descriptions. Section III follows results and discussions. Section IV concludes with policy implications thereof.

II. METHODOLOGY AND DATA DESCRIPTIONS

As we have mentioned earlier, the summary measure of human development is represented in the form of a composite index and that's called as a Human Development Index (HDI). The composite index is calculated on the basis of three socio-economic indicators that reflects three major dimensions of human development: longevity, educational attainment, and standard of living (HDR, 2002). Longevity is measured by life expectancy at birth. Educational attainment is measured by a weighted average of the adult literacy (one-third) and the combined- primary, secondary and tertiary- gross educational enrollment ratios (two-thirds). An adjusted GDP per capita (PPP USD) is used as a measure of a decent standard of living. A brief outline of these three basic dimensions and their indicators are presented in Figure 1. As per the UNDP guidelines, HDI estimation for any economy/ region simply represents a weighted average of above three basic dimensions. The construction of HDI follows two step procedures: first, the building of dimension index and second, the edifice of HDI. The dimension index is the ratio of difference between actual value minus minimum value and maximum value minus minimum value. In mathematical,

$$Y_{ij} = \frac{(X_{ij} - X_{\min})}{(X_{\max} - X_{\min})} \qquad (1)$$

Where, Y_{ij} = Dimension index of jth indicator in i[th] country/ state; X_{ij} = Original j[th] indicator in i[th] country/ state; X_{max} = Maximum value of jth indicator; and X_{min} = Minimum value of jth indicator.

$$HDI = \frac{\sum_{j=1}^{n} Y_{ij}}{\sum_{j=1}^{n} j} \qquad (2)$$

Where, HDI is human development index, which is the average of above three dimension indices. The special feature of this index is that its composite value as well as dimension indices

Figure 1: The Structure of Human Development Index

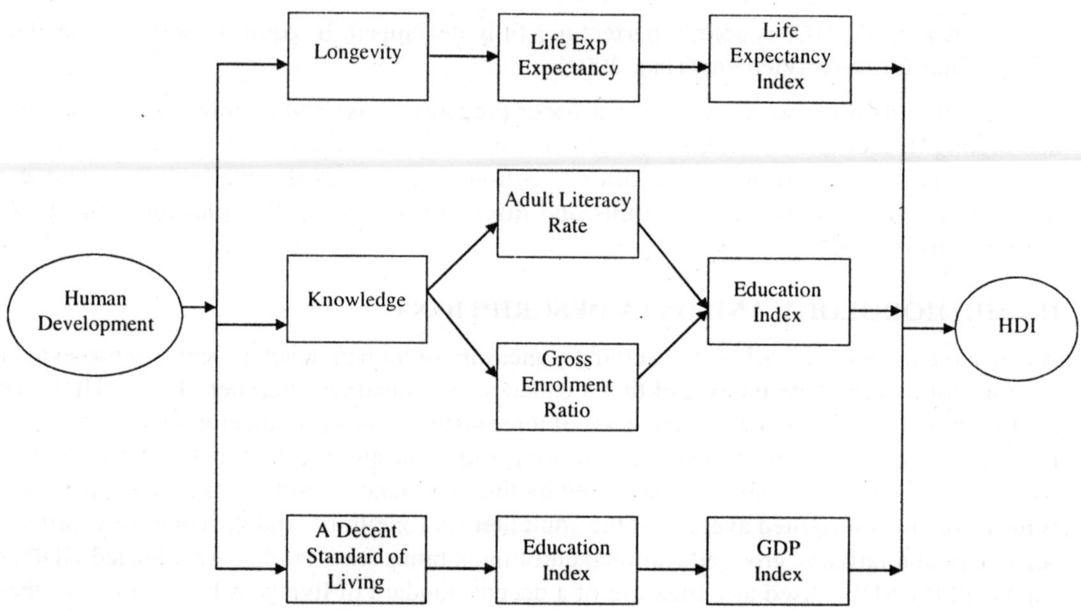

Source: Human Development Report (HDR), 2002

are always positive and lies between zero and one. If the HDI value is closer to one, it indicates a higher level of human development and if the value is closer to zero, it indicates a low level of human development.

But the critics say that indicators used by UNDP are not always appropriate for all situations and for all regions in the world (Mehrotra, 2005; Sahni and Viswanath, 2005; Shanmugam and Bhaduri, 2000; Hirway and Mahadevia, 1999; GOK, 1999). For instance, adult literacy along with gross enrolment ratios are used to capture education index could lead to overestimation of human well being. Similarly, life expectancy for health index could also be an oversimplification of the issues affecting the quality of life. In case of per capita income, it gives an underestimated figure as unpaid work within the family or on a voluntary basis continues and is not included in income accounting. In some situation, there is no proper availability of data at the regional level, as per the UNDP identification.

Consequently many countries have already started preparing detailed HDI estimates in a fairly disaggregated form. Among them, India, South Africa, Philippines, Turkey, Bolivia, Egypt and Bangladesh are celebrated one. In India, the Planning Commission is the sole organ, who prepared HDI for the country and across its states. Its preparation of HDI is almost all same like UNDP methodology but the chosen of parameters are slightly different to each dimension of human development (See Figure 2). In the present paper, we however added two more dimensions such as basic amenity and economic participation to UNDP and Planning Commission measure.

Figure 2: The Structure of Human Development Index

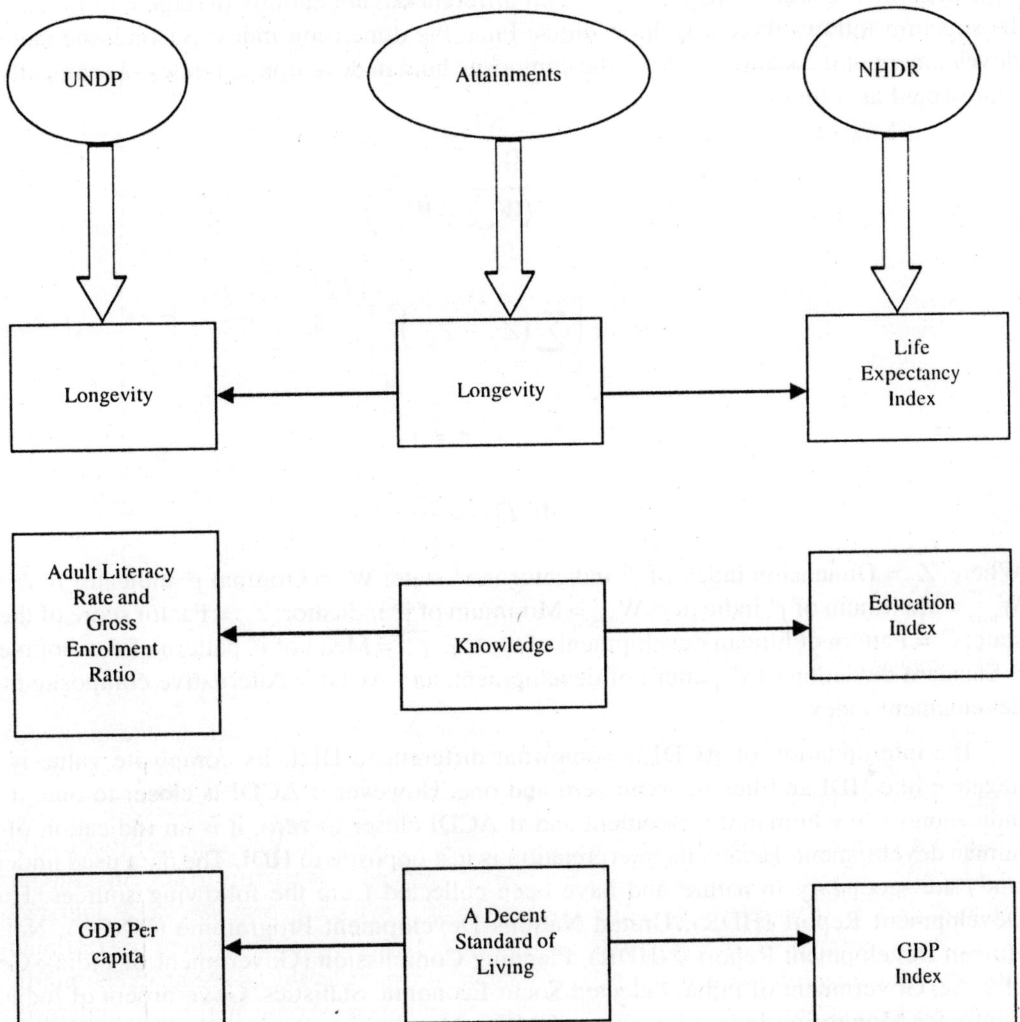

Source: Human Development Report (HDR), 2002; National Human Development Report (NHDR), 2001.

The inclusion of these two dimensions has greater relevance at the regional level, particularly in the country like India. The rationale behind the selection of basic amenity as a component of human development is to measure the access to basic facilities, which are important requirement for better standard of living. Similarly, economic participation, which defines participation of people in economic process, also considerably justified on the ground that it affords people a basis for social dignity and self-respect (HDR, 1993). This also empowers people in terms of decision making and that affects their own life.

The study also used an alternative composite index method to verify the relevance of the first method. The second method is little bit different but not entirely divergent to first method. Its structure follows three step procedures: First, the dimension index; Second, the pattern of development of the state; and third, the composite human development index. Technically, it is represented as follows:

$$Z_{ij} = \frac{(W_{ij} - W_{\min})}{(W_{\max} - W_{\min})} \tag{3}$$

$$C_i = \left[\sum_{i=1}^{n}(Z_{ij} - Z_{0j})^2\right]^{1/2} \tag{4}$$

$$C = \overline{C} + 2S \tag{5}$$

$$ACDI = \frac{C_i}{C} \tag{6}$$

Where, Z_{ij} = Dimension index of jth indicator in i^{th} state; W_{ij} = Original j^{th} indicator in i^{th} state; W_{max} = Maximum of jth indicator; W_{min} = Minimum of jth indicator; Z_{0j} = Factor score of the best state; C_i = Pattern of human development of ith state; $\overline{C}$ = Mean of ith pattern of development; S = Standard deviation of ith pattern of development; and ACDI = Alternative composite human development index.

The interpretation of ACDI is somewhat different to HDI. Its composite value is non-negative like HDI and lies between zero and one. However if ACDI is closer to one, it is an indication of low human development and if ACDI closer to zero, it is an indication of high human development. Hence, its interpretation is just opposite to HDI. The data used under this study are secondary in nature and have been collected from the following sources: Human Development Report (HDR), United Nations Development Programme (UNDP); National Human Development Report (NHDR), Planning Commission (Government of India); Census of India, Government of India; Selected Socio-Economic Statistics, Government of India; and Centre for Monitoring Indian Economy (CMIE), Mumbai.

III. RESULTS AND DISCUSSION

The broad objective of this paper is to trace India's status of human development at the global level as well as national level. While the former follows the country-wise comparison at the globe, the latter follows the state wise comparison in India. The present paper has not done any empirical investigation for the first part of the objective. The discussion of this part has been based on the estimated results of UNDP (See HDR, 2005). On the contrary, the second part of this objective has been empirically investigated by two different composite methods. The first method is directly followed by UNDP as well as Planning Commission (Government of India) methodology, though there is considerable inclusion of some additional dimensions as well as parameters. The second method is more or less same but its interpretation is slightly different to first method. While the first method measures human development by Human Development Index (HDI), the second method measures the same by Alternative Composite Human Development Index (ACDI). The HDI reflects that a state has high human development, if its value is closer to one and has low human development, if its value is closer to zero. On the contrary, ACDI indicates that a state has high human development, if its score is closer to zero and has low human development, if its score is close to one.

The discussion of first followed at the global level; that is the country-wise comparison. As you know UNDP empirically prepared the HDI for 177 countries and the status of each country categorically grouped under three broad heads such as high human development, medium human development and low human development. If the value of HDI for a country/ state is more than or equal to 0.800 (i. e. $X \geq 0.800$), it is grouped under high development. If the HDI score is equal to 0.500 or above but less than to 0.800 (i.e. $0.500 \leq X > 0.800$), the country/ state is in the group of medium human development. And if the HDI score is less than to 0.500 (i.e. ($X < 0.500$), the country/ state is in the group of low hunıan aevelopment.

On the basis of this classification, there are about 57 countries are in the first group, 88 countries are in the second group and rest 32 countries are in the third group. The major countries that stayed in the first group are Norway (0.963), Iceland (0.956), Luxembourg (0.949), Canada (0.949), Sweden (0.949), Switzerland (0.947), Ireland (0.946), Belgium (0.945), USA (0.944), Tonga (0.810), Bulgaria (0.808), Panama (0.804) and Trinidad and Tobago (0.801). However, the first ten country's' HDI score is very closer to one (See Figure 4) and they continue to dominant the other countries in the global economy. The major countries that stayed in the

Figure 3: The Structure of Human Development Index (in the Present Study)

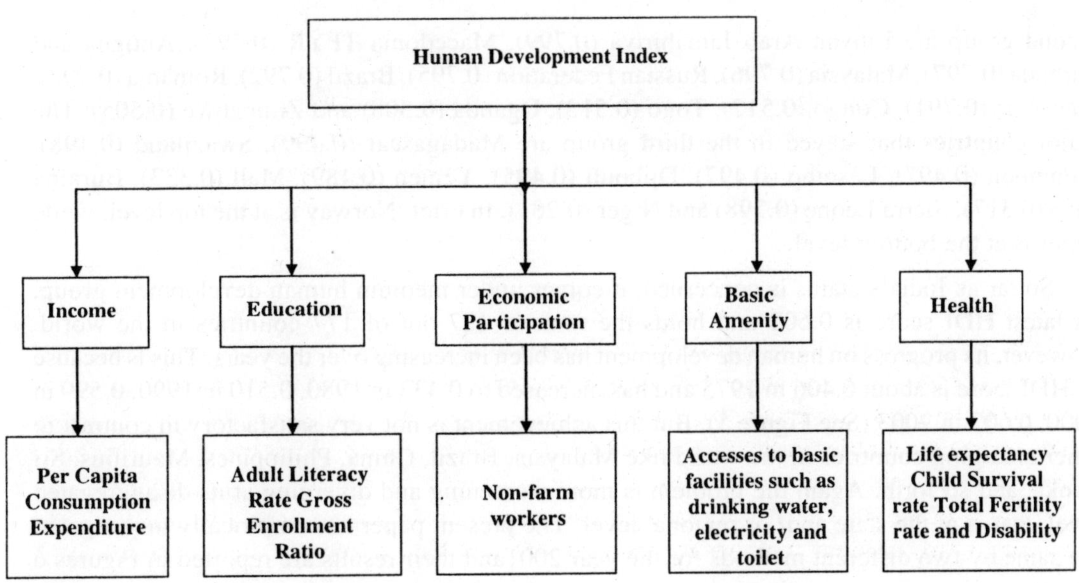

Figure 4: Country-wise Human Development in the Globe

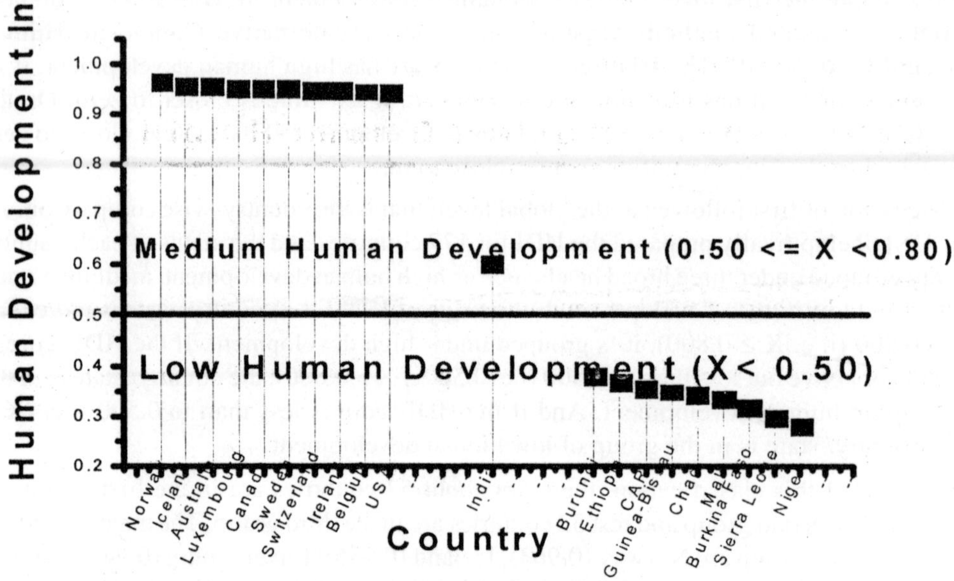

Note:
1. The UNDP provides HDI of 177 countries and their respective ranks.
2. 57 countries are in the high human development group.
3. 88 countries are in the medium human development group.
4. 32 countries are in the low human development group.
5. India is in medium human development group.
6. India's score is 0.602 and its rank is 127 out of 177 countries in the globe.

Source: Human Development Report (HDR), 2005.

second group are Libyan Arab Jamahiriya (0.799), Macedonia TFYR (0.797), Antigua and Barbuda (0.797), Malaysia (0.796), Russian Federation (0.795), Brazil (0.792), Romania (0.792), Mauritius (0.791), Congo (0.512), Togo (0.512), Uganda (0.508) and Zimbabwe (0.505). The major countries that stayed in the third group are Madagascar (0.499), Swaziland (0.498), Cameroon (0.497), Lesotho (0.497), Djibouti (0.495), Yemen (0.489), Mall (0.333), Burkina Faso (0.317), Sierra Leone (0.298) and Niger (0.281). In brief, Norway is at the top level, while Niger is at the bottom level.

So far as India's status is concerned, it comes under medium human development group. Its latest HDI score is 0.602 and holds the rank of 127 out of 177 countries in the world. However, its progress on human development has been increasing over the years. This is because its HDI score is about 0.406 in 1975 and has increased to 0.433 in 1980, 0.510 in 1990, 0.590 in 2000, 0.602 in 2003 (See Figure 5). But this achievement is not very satisfactory in contrast to other emerging countries in the world like Malaysia, Brazil, China, Philippines, Mauritius, Sri Lanka, and so forth. Again the problem is more worsening and diverging at its disaggregated level, that is at the state and/ or regional level. The present paper has empirically investigated the same by two different methods for the year 2001and their results are reported in Figures 6

Figure 5: India's Progress on Human Development

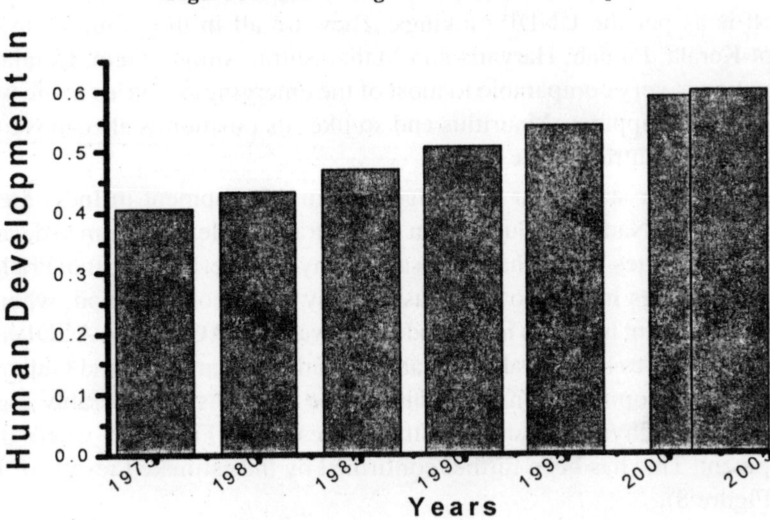

Figure 6: State-wise Human Development Index in India

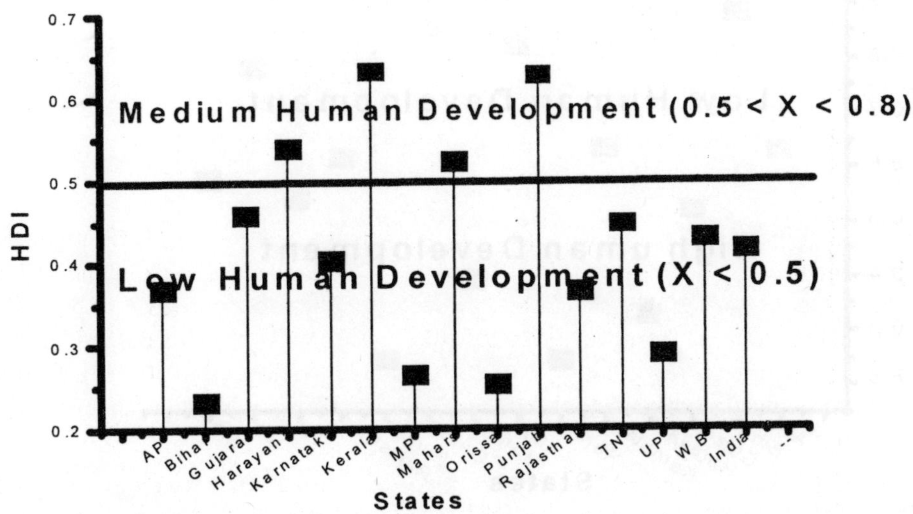

Note: 1. 0 < HDI < 1
2. If HDI is close to one, it is an indication of high human development.
3. If HDI is close to zero, it is an indication of low human development.
4. No state is in high human development group, as per UNDP rankings.
5. The states that have high human development are Kerala, Punjab, Haryana and Maharashtra.
5. The states that have low human development are Bihar, Orissa, Madhya Pradesh and Uttar Pradesh.
5. MP: Madhya Pradesh; TN: Tamil Nadu; UP: Uttar Pradesh; WB: West Bengal; HDI: Human Development Index.

Source: Author's Calculation

and 7. The estimated results confirm that no Indian state is in the group of high human development, which is as per the UNDP rankings. They are all in the group of low human development except Kerala, Punjab, Haryana and Maharashtra. Among them, Kerala is at the top level, whose position is very comparable to most of the emerging countries in the world like Malaysia, China, Brazil, Philippines, Mauritius and so like. Its position is also above than that of average of developing countries in the world.

Besides Kerala, the other states that have high human development in India are Punjab, Haryana, Maharashtra, Tamil Nadu and Gujarat. On the contrary, the level of human development is comparably low in the states like Bihar, Orissa, Madhya Pradesh and Uttar Pradesh (See Figure 6). The above findings have also been justified by the second method, where state's position of human development has been identified by the value of ACDI. The ACDI confirmed that its value is low in the states like Kerala, Punjab, Haryana, Maharashtra and Gujarat, where they have high human development. On the contrary, the ACDI is considerably high in the states like Bihar, Orissa, Madhya Pradesh and Uttar Pradesh (See Figure 7), where they have low human development. This has been further confirmed by the estimated results of Planning Commission (See Figure 8).

Figure 7: State-wise Alternative Composite Development Index in India

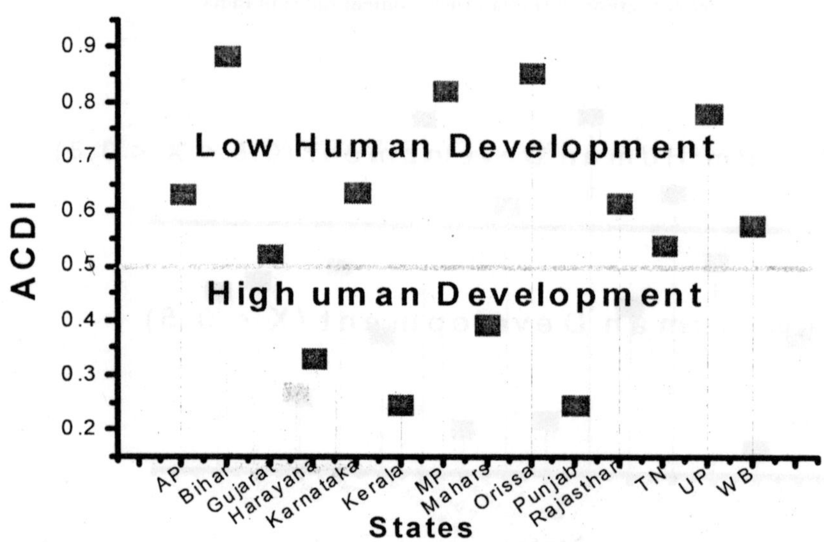

Note:
1. 0 < ACDI < 1
2. If ACDI is close to one, it is an indication of low human development.
3. If ACDI is close to zero, it is an indication of high human development.
4. Like the identification of states by HDI, ACDI clarifies that Kerala, Punjab, Haryana and Maharashtra have high human development.
5. The other states have low human development.
6. ACDI: Alternative Development Index; and
7. Other notations are defined earlier.

Source: Author's Calculation

Figure 8: State-wise Human Development in India

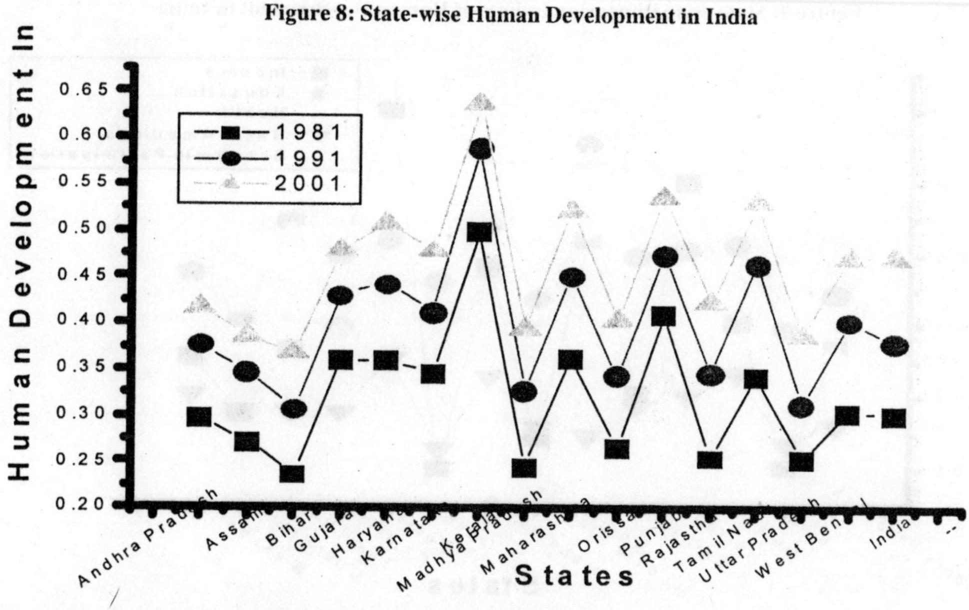

Source: National Human Development Report (NHDR), 2001

But no state is extremely good or bad in all the dimensions of human development. For instance, Tamil Nadu stands second position in education but holds tenth position in basic amenity. Kerala holds first position in education, health and economic participation but holds eleventh position in basic amenity. Similarly, Gujarat is second position in basic amenity but holds eighth position in health. Karnataka is fourth position in health but holds tenth position in income (See Figure 9). In the similar fashion, it can be analyzed for other states also. The above findings confirmed that most of the states move up and down their ranks with respect to different dimensions of human development. But in reality, a high human development needs a substantial step up in all the dimensions simultaneously. This is because they are very inter-related to each other and that has also been statistically verified by calculating correlation coefficients among them (See Table 1). Hence, a single indicator can not bring high human development in the

Table 1

Variance-covariance Matrix of HDI and Its Indices

	X_1	X_2	X_3	X_4	X_5	X_6
X_1	1.000					
X_2	0.491*	1.000				
X_3	0.562*	0.858*	1.000			
X_4	0.681*	0.214	0.277	1.000		
X_5	0.650*	0.887*	0.806*	0.389	1.000	
X_6	0.887*	0.814*	0.838*	0.608*	0.895*	1.000

Note: X_1: Income Dimension Index; X_2: Education Dimension Index; X_3: Health Dimension Index; X_4: Basic amenity Dimension Index; X_5: Economic participation Dimension Index; X_6: Human Development Index; and *: The probability level of significance at 1%.

Figure 9: State-wise Dimension Indices of Human Development in India

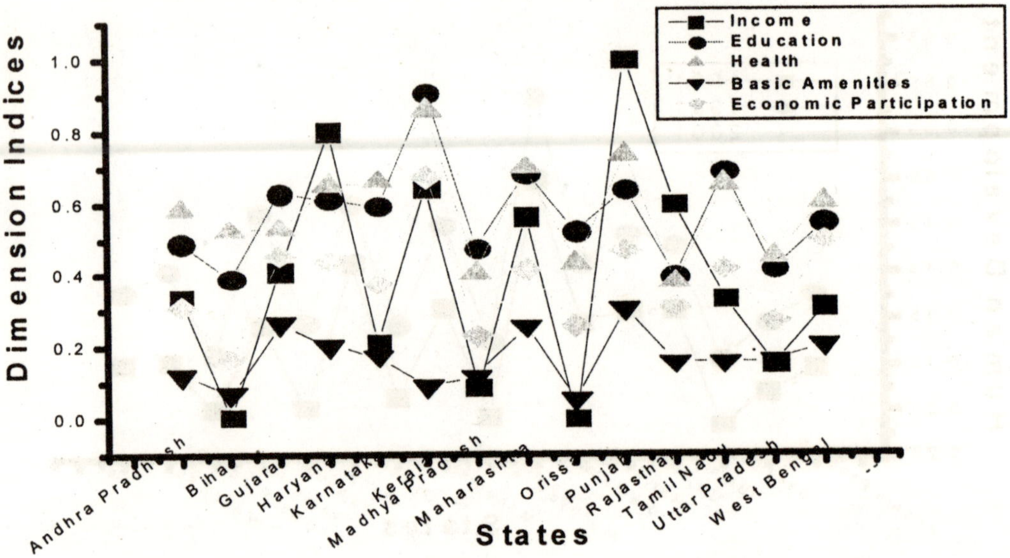

Source: Author's Calculation

state. The lack of one leads to lack of others, resulted overall degradation of human development in the economy. Though India's position is not satisfactory in contrast to other emerging countries in the world, its progress has been increasing over the years. That is not only at the aggregate level (See Figure 5) but also at the disaggregate level (See Figure 8), where all the individual state's position has been significantly improved over the years.

On the whole, the study is very relevant for three grounds: First, it highlights the issue of human development at the global level as well as national level. Second, it incorporates more dimensions of human development in contrast to UNDP and Planning Commission measure. This has very distinctive advantage of underlying the nature of human development as well as for formulating policies and programmes for its further improvement in the economy. Third, the paper studied the case by two different methods.

IV. CONCLUSION AND POLICY IMPLICATIONS

The paper prepared a case study on human development, representing the status of India at the global level and national level. While the first part follows country-wise comparison at the globe, second part follows state-wise comparison in India. The study has not empirically investigated the first part but analyzed the same on the basis of UNDP results. On the contrary, the study empirically investigated the second part by two different composite methods such as Human Development Index (HDI) and Alternative Composite Human Development Index (ACDI). The analysis confirmed that UNDP estimated the HDI for 177 countries in the globe and rank them under three different groups such as high human development, medium human development and low human development. By this classification, 57 countries are in the first group, 88 countries are in the second group and rest 32 countries in the third group. So far as India's status is concerned, it is in the group of medium human development and its rank is 127 out of 177 countries in the world. Though its status has been increasing over the years, it is considerably low in contrast to other emerging countries in the world. The problem is again more worsening and diverging at the disaggregate level, particularly an existence of large-scale regional variation across its states. While the status of human development is appreciably high in the states like Kerala, Punjab, Haryana and Maharashtra, it is significantly low in the states like Bihar, Orissa, Madhya Pradesh and Uttar Pradesh.

But no state is extremely good or bad in all the dimensions of human development. Some states are very good position in some front say education or health but very low position in some other fronts says basic amenity or income. For instance, Tamil Nadu is substantially high performer in health but very low performer in basic amenity. In the similar way, it can be analyzed for the rest of states. The paper finally concludes that for attaining a high human development, a state has to improve all the dimensions of human development simultaneously. This is because they are very interrelated to each other. The lack of one leads to lack of others, resulted overall degradation of human development in the economy. This obviously intimates that government of the concerned state as well as centre has to look the same in a balanced way. It is further suggestive to follow the Five-Point Agenda, as proposed by Professor Sakiko Fukuda-Parr (2003b), to enhance the status of human development in the economy. These are as follows:

- Priority to 'social development' with the goals of expanding education and health opportunities.
- Economic growth that generates resources for human development in its many dimensions.
- Political and social reforms for democratic governance that secures human rights so that people can live in freedom and dignity, with greater collective agency, participation and autonomy.
- Equity in the above three elements with a concern for all individuals, with special attention to the downtrodden and poor, whose interests are often neglected in public policy as well as the removal of discrimination against women.
- Policy and institutional reforms at the global/ national level that create an economic environment more conducive for poor countries/ states to access global/ national markets, technology and information.

The implementation of these points could not be a daunting task, if there is adequate political will in the economy.

References

Adelman, I. and Morris, C. T. (1967), Society, Politics and Economic Development. Baltimore: Jhon Hopkins University Press.

Anand, S. and Ravallion, M. (1993), "Human Development in Poor Countries: On the Role of Private Incomes and Public Services", *Journal of Economic Perspectives*, 7 (1): 135-150.

Castles, I. and Henderson, D. (2005), "International Comparisons of GDP: Issues of Theory and Practice", *World Economics*, 6 (1): 55-84.

Fukuda-Parr, S. (2003a), "Rescuing the Human Development Concept from the HDI: Reflections on a New Agenda", in S. Fukuda-Parr and A. K. Shiva Kumar (eds.), '*Readings in Human Development*'. UK: Oxford University Press.

Fukuda-Parr, S. (2003b), "The Human Development Paradigm: Operationalizing Sen's Ideas on Capabilities", *Feminist Economics*, 9 (2-3): 301-317.

GOI (2001), Provisional Population Totals, Census of India. New Delhi: Government of India (GOI).

GOK (1999), Human Development in Karnataka: 1999, Government of Karnataka (GOK). Bangalore: Planning Department.

Haq, M. Ul. (2003), "The Birth of Human Development Index", in S. Fukuda-Parr and A. K. Shiva Kumar (eds.), '*Readings in Human Development*'. UK: Oxford University Press.

Haq, M. Ul. (1995), Reflections of Human Development. New York: Oxford University Press.

HDR (2005), Human Development Report, United Nations Development Programme (UNDP). New York: Oxford University Press.

HDR (2004), Human Development Report, UNDP. New York: Oxford University Press.

HDR (2002), Human Development Report, UNDP. New York: Oxford University Press.

HDR (1993), Human Development Report, UNDP. New York: Oxford University Press.

HDR (1990), Human Development Report, UNDP. New York: Oxford University Press.

Heston, A. and Summers, R. (1996), "International Price and Quantity Comparisons: Potentials and Pitfalls", *American Economic Review*, 86 (2): 20-24.

Hicks, N. and Streeten, P. (1979), "Indicators of Development: The Search for a Basic Needs Yardstick", *World Development*, 7 (6): 567-580.

Hirway, I. and Mahadevia, D. (1999), Gujarat Human Development Report: 1999. Ahmedabad: Mahatma Gandhi Labour Institute.

Komlos, J. and Snowdon, B. (2005), "Measures of Progress and Other Tall Stories: From Income to Anthropometrics", *World Economics*, 6 (2): 87-135.

Maddison, A. (2001), The World Economy in Millennial Perspective. Paris: OECD.

Meher, S. (2005), "Human Development in Orissa: An Inter-state and Inter-District Analysis", *Journal of Regional Science*, 37 (1): 23-32.

Mehrotra, S. (2005), "Human Capital or Human Development? Search for a Knowledge Paradigm for Education and Development", *Economic and Political Weekly*, 40 (4): 300-306.

Morris, M. D. (1979), Measuring the Condition of the World's Poor: The Physical Quality of Life Index. London: Cass.

Mukherjee, M. (1980), Physical Quality of Life Index. Mumbai: Centre for Monitoring Indian Economy.

NHDR (2001), Notational Human Development Report (NHDR), Planning Commission. New Delhi: Government of India.

ODC (1977), Overseas Development Council (ODC), The United States and World Development: Agenda for 1977. New York: Praeger.

Sahni, R. and Viswanath, S. (2005), "Human Development Index of Maharashtra: A Reality Check", *Economic and Political Weekly*, 40 (4): 4387.

Seers, D. (1972), "What are We Trying to Measure", *Journal of Development Studies*, 8 (3): 21-36.

Sen, A. K. (2001), "What is Development About", in G. Meier and J. E. Stiglitz (eds.), '*Frontiers of Development Economics: The Future in Perspective*', Oxford: Oxford University Press.

Sen, A. K. and Anand, S. (2000), "The Income Component of the Human Development Index", *Journal of Human Development*, 1 (1): 83-106.

Sen, A. K. (1998), "Mortality as an Indicator of Economic Success and Failure", *Economic Journal*, 108 (446): 1-25.

Sachs, J. D. (2005), The End of Poverty: How We can Make It Happen in Our Lifetime. London: Penguin.

Shanmugam, K. R. and Bhaduri, S. N. (2000), "Composite Indices of Basic Human Needs and Income in India", *Artha Vijnana*, 52 (2): 115-126.

Summers, R. and Heston, A. (1991), "The Penn World Table (Mark 5): An Expanded Set of International Comparisons, 1950-88", *Quarterly Journal of Economics*, 106 (2): 327-368.

Todaro, M. P. and Smith, S. C. (2003), Economic Development. New York: Addison Wesley.

APPLICATION OF THE MONETARY POLICY REACTION FUNCTION IN THE ANALYSIS OF OUTPUT FLUCTUATIONS FOR JAPAN

*Yu Hsing**

ABSTRACT

Applying an extended IS-MP-AS model (Romer, 2000, 2006) and the Taylor rule (1993, 1998, 2001), this study finds that the equilibrium real GDP is negatively affected by real depreciation, the world interest rate, and the expected inflation rate, and positively influenced by real government deficit spending, the real stock price, and the real land value. Current low inflation rates and gradual rising stock prices are expected to help the Japanese output. However, record-low land values and gradual rising world interest rates may dampen its economic recovery.

JEL Codes: *F41, E52, O53*

Key Words: *IS-MP-AS model, Taylor rule, Stock values, Land values*

INTRODUCTION

Since the 1990s, the economic growth rate in Japan has been slow or negative. As a result, the unemployment rate rose from a low of 2.10% in 1991 to a high of 5.38% in 2002 and gradually declined to 4.40% in 2005. Since 1999, disinflation has caused concerns about its potential adverse impacts on business operations and other economic activities. The Bank of Japan has pursued expansionary monetary policy by dropping the discount rate to 0.10% since 2001 and the overnight call rate to a very low level of 0.00114% in 2005. To stimulate the slow economy, the authorities engaged in expansionary fiscal policy gradually, and deficit spending as a percent of nominal GDP rose from 2.13% in 1990 to a high of 8.44% in 1999. The exchange rate appreciated from 131.80 yens per U.S. dollar in 2001 to 117.97 in 2005, making Japanese-made products more expensive for other countries to purchase. The stock market reached a record high of 38,916 in December 1989, declined by as much as 79.9% to a low of 7,831 in April 2003, and then gradually rose to 12,595.35 in 2005. The land price index dropped 53.2% from a high of 147.8 in 1991 to 69.1 in 2005. Considerable decreases in real and financial assets are expected to affect consumption and investment expenditures adversely.

This paper attempts to examine output fluctuations in Japan based the IS-MP-AS model (Romer, 2000, 2006; Hsing, 2005, 2006) and has several different aspects. First, the IS-MP-AS

* Charles Blackwell Endowed Professor in Economics, Department of General Business, College of Business, Southeaster Louisiana University, USA, *E-mail: yhsing@selu.edu*

model is extended to include several additional variables such as the stock price, real estate value, the exchange rate, and the world interest rate. Households are likely to increase their consumption spending when assets in the form of real estate or stock values go up because of the wealth effect. Business firms are expected to raise investment spending with increased assets due to Tobin's q theory or the balance-sheet channel. Second, the Taylor rule (1993, 1998, 2001) is applied in formulating the monetary policy reaction function so that the Bank of Japan would target the interest rate based on the inflation gap, the output gap, and the world interest rate. Third, comparative-static analysis is employed to determine the direction and magnitude of a change in one of the exogenous variables on the equilibrium output.

LITERATURE SURVEY

Posen (1998) indicated that the sluggish Japanese economy was attributable to the domestic macroeconomic and financial policies and that it would be appropriate for other countries to take countercyclical measures to increase aggregate demand and stimulate the economy. He suggested that reform in the financial institution, a tax cut or government spending increase, and stabilization of monetary policy are required for Japan to pull out of the slow growth. According to Kuttner and Posen (2001), the output gap for Japan was as high as 11% in 1999; M2 had a relatively persistent impact on prices whereas the monetary base and prices were not cointegrated; an increase in the monetary base led to yen depreciation mostly via its impact on the interest rate; the tax estimated multiplier was 4.84 and the estimated government spending multiplier was 3.53 over a 4-year period; and the impact of a tax cut was temporary whereas the effect of government spending was more enduring. Based a VAR model with output, taxes, and spending for Japan and a sample during 1976-1999, Kuttner and Posen (2002) showed that most of the 1990s were characterized by a contractionary fiscal policy and that a large percent of variation in output growth can be explained by shocks to fiscal policy. They found that the tax multiplier was estimated to be 2.5 and that the government spending multiplier was 2.0 over a four-year period. These are lower than the multiplier of 4.0 due to shocks to a tax cut if the method by Blanchard and Perotti (1999) is applied. Because Recardian-equivalence hypothesis in Japan was not found, an expansionary fiscal policy of more government spending or less tax or both was recommended to pull the Japanese economy out of the recession.

Miyao (2002, 2003, 2005) indicated that a shock to monetary policy had a continual impact on output, that yen depreciation led to insignificant increase in exports but substantial decline in imports due to a structural break after the mid-1980s and may not be as effective as some would expect in stimulating the economy, that since the late 1990s, the close relationship between M2 + CDs and income or the price level has broken down, and that the predictive power of bank loans has declined partly due to large non-performing loans and structural changes.

Saito (2001) investigated the effectiveness of monetary policy in Japan in the 1990s based on the criteria of liquidity and business cycles. He showed that the Bank of Japan was successful in providing adequate liquidity to the market during the Asian financial crisis. However, the Bank of Japan seemed not to provide enough guidance on the disinflation path, the flat Phillips curve, and very elastic money demand. In studying the zero bound and comparing the banking problems and monetary policies between the U.S. in the 1930s and Japan in the 1990s, Sellon

(2003) suggested that the major issue in these two situations was not a zero bound but a weak banking institution that made monetary policy less effective. He suggested that even if the short-term interest rate reaches the zero bound, the Bank of Japan still has other options such as depreciation of the yen, more coordination between fiscal and monetary policy, and direct involvement by the Bank of Japan in promoting the capital market. Ohyama (2004) found evidence of support for the monetarist and Keynesian views that adequate money is needed to reach full employment and that expansionary fiscal policy in the short run and structural reforms in the long run are effective tools in reducing deficiency in aggregate spending.

Hamada (2004) advocated the use of inflation or price-level targeting to address the slow economic growth because of the limited effect of conventional monetary policy due to the zero bound interest rate. In examining the Bank of Japan's monetary policy reaction function based on the VAR model, Hsing (2004) found that the (overnight) call rate in Japan reacted positively to the output gap, the inflation gap, depreciation of the yen, stock market performance, and the lagged call rate. The reaction of the call rate to a shock to exchange rates or stock market indexes lasts longer than the response to the inflation gap or output gap. With the exception of the lagged call rate, the exchange rate and the inflation gap are more influential than stock indexes and the output gap in describing the variation in the call rate.

Baba, Nishioka, Oda, Shirakawa, Ueda, and Ugai, (2005) indicated that the deflation of asset prices instead of the deflation of general prices was responsible for the stagnating economy in the post 1990 period, that the Bank of Japan contained the risk premium by providing liquidity and taking measures with risk to avoid a liquidity crisis, and that the almost zero interest rate policy of the BOJ has reduced the expected short-term interest rate and changed the yield curve.

THE MODEL

Suppose that consumption is affected by disposable income, the real interest rate, the real estate value, and the stock price via the wealth effect (Mishkin, 1995; Kuttner and Mosser, 2002), that investment is influenced by output, the real interest rate, the land value, and the stock price due to Tobin's q theory and the Balance sheet channel (Mishkin, 1995; Kuttner and Mosser, 2002), that the net exports sector is a function of the real exchange rate, that the interest rate in the monetary policy reaction function (MP) is affected by the inflation gap, the output gap, and the world interest rate, and that the inflation rate depends upon the expected inflation rate, the output gap, and the real exchange rate. The extended IS-MP-AS model for Japan can be expressed as

$$Y = C(Y-T, R, L, S) + I(Y, R, L, S) + G + NX(\varepsilon) \tag{1}$$

$$R = R(\pi - \pi^*, Y - Y^*, R^W) \tag{2}$$

$$\pi = \pi^e + \alpha(Y - Y^*) + \beta\varepsilon \tag{3}$$

where

Y = real GDP in Japan,
C = the consumption function,
T = government tax revenues,
R = the real interest rate,
L = the land value,
S = the stock price,
I = the investment function,
G = government spending,
NX = next exports,
ε = the real exchange rate (units of the yen per U.S. dollar times relative prices),
π = the inflation rate,
π^* = the inflation target,
Y^* = potential output,
R^W = the world interest rate,
π^e = the expected inflation rate, and
α, β = parameters with positive values.

Suppose that the above equations have continuous partial derivates. Let

$$C_Y > 0, C_T < 0, C_R < 0, C_L > 0, C_S > 0, I_Y > 0, I_R < 0, I_L > 0, I_S > 0,$$
$$NX_\varepsilon > 0, R_\pi > 0, R_Y > 0, R_{R^W} > 0, \pi_Y > 0, \pi_\varepsilon > 0.$$

The endogenous-variable Jacobian is given by

$$|J| = (1 - C_Y - I_Y) - \alpha R_\pi (C_R + I_R) - R_Y (C_R + I_R) > 0. \quad (4)$$

Applying the implicit-function theorem, we can write the equilibrium value of real output as an implicit function of the following valuables and parameters:

$$\overline{Y} = \overline{Y}(G, T, \varepsilon, S, L, R^W, \pi^e; \pi^*, Y^*, \alpha, \beta). \quad (5)$$

Based on comparative-static analysis, the impact of deficit spending on the equilibrium real output is given by

$$\partial \overline{Y} / \partial G - \partial \overline{Y} / \partial T = (1 - C_T) / |J| > 0 \quad (6)$$

The impact of a change in the real exchange rate on $\overline{Y}$ can be expressed as

$$\begin{aligned} \partial \overline{Y} / \partial \varepsilon &= [NX_\varepsilon + \beta R_\pi (C_R + I_R)] / |J| \\ &> 0 \text{ if } |NX_\varepsilon| > |\beta R_\pi (C_R + I_R)| \\ &< 0 \text{ if } |NX_\varepsilon| < |\beta R_\pi (C_R + I_R)| \end{aligned} \quad (7)$$

Equation (7) suggests that the net impact of real currency depreciation on equilibrium output depends on whether the positive effect of increased net exports would be greater than the negative effects of reduced consumption and investment expenditures due to the increased interest rate made by the Bank of Japan. The respective impacts of a change in the expected inflation rate, stock prices, and land values are given by

$$\partial \overline{Y} / \partial \pi^{e} = R_{\pi}(C_{R} + I_{R})/|J| < 0 \tag{8}$$

$$\partial \overline{Y} / \partial S = (C_{S} + I_{S})/|J| > 0 \tag{9}$$

$$\partial \overline{Y} / \partial L = (C_{L} + I_{L})/|J| > 0 \tag{10}$$

As shown, the magnitude of the negative impact of a higher expected inflation rate on the equilibrium output depends upon the central bank's monetary policy reaction function to raise the interest rate in response to a higher inflation rate and reduced consumption and investment expenditures. A higher stock price or land value is expected to increase the equilibrium output because of positive impacts on consumption and investment expenditures.

EMPIRICAL RESULTS

The sample runs from 1962 to 2005. Annual data are used because of lack of adequate quarterly data for government spending and revenues. Except that G and T were taken from the Ministry of Finance and that the data for land values were obtained from the Japan Real Estate Institute, all other data were collected from the *International Financial Statistics* which is published by the International Monetary Fund. G, T, S, and L are divided by the CPIx100 and expressed in real terms. To reduce multicollinearity, real government deficit D = G – T is used. The real exchange rate equal to the nominal exchange rate times the relative prices. The share stock price index has a base year in 2000. The expected inflation rate is the weighted average inflation rate of the CPI in past four years (Davidson and McKinnon, 1985). Due to its worldwide influence, the U.S. federal funds rate is chosen to represent the world interest rate. Real GDP and government deficit are expressed in billion yens.

According to the ADF or the DF-GLS test, all the variables have unit roots in levels and are stationary in first difference at the 1% or 5% level. The ADF cointegration test shows that the test statistic is 4.94 with p = 1 compared with the critical value is 3.77 at the 1% level. Hence, these variables are cointegrated and have a long-term stable relationship.

The estimated regression is presented in Table 1. The first-difference form is not employed because the long-term relationship may become obscured (Greene, 2003). The Newey-West (1987) method is employed to generate consistent estimates of standard errors and covariance when the forms of autocorrelation and heteroskedasticity are unknown. The value of R^2 suggests that 97.95% of the variation in the equilibrium real output can be explained by the six right-hand side variables. All the coefficients are significant at the 1% level except that the coefficient of the real stock price is significant at the 5% level. The equilibrium real output has a positive relationship with real deficit spending, the real stock price, and the real land value and a negative

Table 1
Estimated Regression for Japan's Real Output

Dependent Variable: $\overline{Y}$
Method: Least Squares
Sample (adjusted): 1962 2005
Included observations: 44 after adjustments
Newey-West HAC Standard Errors & Covariance (lag truncation = 3)

Variable	*Coefficient*	*Std. Error*	*t-Statistic*	*Prob.*
C	252793.0	96684.17	2.614626	0.0128
G-T	5.223156	1.130609	4.619773	0.0000
ε	-619.9182	229.0472	-2.706509	0.0102
S	346.0282	177.2740	1.951939	0.0585
L	1240.945	363.4295	3.414540	0.0016
R^w	-3347.469	744.9461	-4.493572	0.0001
π^e	-7420.061	1536.542	-4.829064	0.0000
R-squared	0.979450	Mean dependent var	345376.8	
Adjusted R-squared	0.976117	S.D. dependent var	138035.5	
S.E. of regression	21332.03	Akaike info criterion	22.91872	
Sum squared resid	1.68E+10	Schwarz criterion	23.20257	
Log likelihood	-497.2118	F-statistic	293.9116	
Durbin-Watson stat	1.168769	Prob(F-statistic)	0.000000	

Notes:
$\overline{Y}$ is the equilibrium real GDP.
G-T is real deficit spending.
ε is the real exchange rate defined as $e(P^f/P)$ where e is the nominal exchange rate.
S is the real stock price index.
L is the real land value.
R^w is the federal funds rate.
π^e is the expected inflation rate.

relationship with the real exchange rate, the federal funds rate, and the expected inflation rate. Specifically, the multiplier of real deficit spending is estimated to be 5.223. An increase in the real exchange rate by 1 unit would hurt real GDP by 619.918 billion yens. A 1 unit increase in the real stock index would raise real output by 346.028 billion yens, and a 1 unit increase in the real land value index is expected to raise real output by 1,240.945 billion yens. When the federal funds rate rises 1 percentage point, real output is expected to decline 3,347.469 billion yens. If the expected inflation rate rises one percentage point, real output will decline 7,420.061 billion yens. Therefore, substantial decreases in real estate values and stock prices had contributed to the economic slowdown in Japan considerably.

A log-linear regression is also estimated to compare with the linear-form regression. The R^2 is 97.34%. The coefficients for real deficit spending, the real stock price, and the real land value are positive and significant at the 1% or 5% level. The coefficients for the federal funds rate and the expected inflation rate are negative and significant at the 1% or 5% level. However, the coefficient for the real exchange rate is negative and insignificant even at the 10% level.

Hence, we may draw a different conclusion regarding the impact of the real exchange rate on the equilibrium output. To save space, the detailed results are not presented and will be available upon request.

SUMMARY AND CONCLUSIONS

This study has examined output fluctuations for Japan based on an extended IS-MP-AS model and the Newey-West HAC method in empirical work. This paper finds that more deficit spending, real appreciation of the yen, a higher real stock price, a higher real land value, a lower U.S. federal funds rate, and a lower expected inflation rate would increase real output. Because of negative inflation rates in recent years, the option to further lower the expected inflation rate would be difficult to pursue. The large multiplier effect of real deficit spending suggests that expansionary fiscal policy is an effective tool as revealed by Kuttner and Posen (2001, 2002). The exchange rate policy may need to be reassessed because real appreciation of the yen would help raise real output and the conventional approach of currency depreciation would hurt real output. As empirical results have demonstrated, asset prices in the form of land values and stock prices would affect consumption, business spending, and aggregate demand. Therefore, the government may need to reduce unnecessary regulation to help the real estate market.

A rising world interest rate is expected to hurt the Japanese economy as the Bank of Japan is expected to react to the world interest rate in the same direction. However, the Bank of Japan may need to evaluate its interest rate policy so that it would leave some room for future changes in either direction. The recent increase of the overnight call rate is an example for the Bank of Japan to conduct monetary policy based on rising world interest rates, declining unemployment rates, rising economic growth rates, and other related factors.

References

Baba, N., Nishioka, S., Oda, N., Shirakawa, M., Ueda, K., and Ugai, H. (2005), "Japan's Deflation, Problems in the Financial System, and Monetary Policy", *Monetary and Economic Studies*, Vol. 23, No. 1, pp. 47-111.

Bernanke, B. and Gertler, M. (1999) , Monetary Policy and Asset Price Volatility, New Challenges for Monetary Policy", *A Symposium sponsored by the Federal Reserve Bank of Kansas City*, Jackson Hole, Wyoming, August 26-28, pp. 77-128.

Blanchard, O. and Perotti, R. (1999), "An Empirical Characterization of the Dynamic Effects of Changes in Government Spending and Taxes on Output", National Bureau of Economic Research Working Paper No. 7269.

Davidson, R. and MacKinnon, J. G. (1985), "Testing Linear and Loglinear Regressions against Box-Cox Alternatives", *Canadian Journal of Economics*, Vol. 18, No. 3, pp. 499-517.

Greene, W. (2003), *Econometric Analysis*. Upper Saddle River, New Jersey: Prentice Hall.

Hamada, K. (2004), "Policy Making in Deflationary Japan", *Japanese Economic Review,* Vol. 5, No. 3, pp. 221-239.

Hsing, Y. (2004), "Estimating the Bank of Japan's Monetary Policy Reaction Function", *Banca Nazionale del Lavoro Quarterly Review*, Vol. 57, No. 229, pp. 169-183.

Hsing, Y. (2005), "Application of the IS-MP-IA Model to the Singapore Economy and Policy Implications", *Economics Bulletin*, Vol. 15, No. 6, pp. 1-9.

Hsing, Y. (2006), "Analysis of Output Fluctuations in Taiwan: An Application of the IS-MP-AS Model," *International Advances in Economic Research*, Vol. 12, No. 2, pp. 203-211.

Ito, T. and Iwaisako, T. (1996), "Explaining Asset Bubbles in Japan", *Monetary and Economic Studies*, Vol. 14, No. 1, pp. 143-193.

Kuttner, K. N. and Mosser, P. C. (2002), "The Monetary Transmission Mechanism: Some Answer and Further Questions", *Federal Reserve Bank of New York Economic Policy Review*, Vol. 8, No. 1, pp. 15-26.

Kuttner, K. N. and Posen, A. S. (2001), "The Great Recession: Lessons for Macroeconomic Policy from Japan", *Brookings Papers on Economic Activity*, No. 2, pp. 93-160.

Kuttner, K. N. and Posen, A. S. (2002), "Fiscal Policy Effectiveness in Japan", *Journal of the Japanese and International Economies*, Vol. 16, No. 4, pp. 536-558.

Mishkin, F. S. (1995), "Symposium on the Monetary Transmission Mechanism", *Journal of Economic Perspectives*, Vol. 9, No. 4, pp. 3-10.

Miyao, R. (2002), "The Effects of Monetary Policy in Japan", *Journal of Money, Credit, and Banking*, Vol. 34, No. 2, pp. 376-392.

Miyao, R. (2003), "The Effects of Yen Depreciation Policy in Japan", *Economic Review*, Vol. 54, No. 2, pp. 114-125.

Miyao, R. (2005), "Use of the Money Supply in the Conduct of Japan's Monetary Policy: Re-Examining the Time-Series Evidence", *Japanese Economic Review*, Vol. 56, No. 2, pp. 165-187.

Newey, W. K., and West, K. D. (1987), "A Simple, Positive Semi-Definite, Heteroskedasticity and Autocorrelation Consistent Covariance Matrix", *Econometrica*, Vol. 55, No. 3, pp. 703-708.

Ohyama, M. (2004), "Effective Demand and National Income: A Microeconomics of the IS-LM Analysis and Its Application to the Stagnation of the Japanese Economy", *Keio Economic Studies*, Vol. 41, No. 2, pp. 1-23.

Posen, A. S. (1998), *Restoring Japan's Economic Growth*. Washington, DC: Institute for International Economics.

Romer, D. (2000), "Keynesian Macroeconomics without the LM Curve", *Journal of Economic Perspectives*, Vol. 14, No. 2, pp. 149-169.

Romer, D. (2006), *Advanced Macroeconomics*. 3rd editon, Boston: McGraw-Hill/Irwin.

Saito, M. (2001), "Monetary Theory and Practice: A Review of the Recent Japanese Experience in Retrospect", *Economic Review*, Vol. 52, No. 2, pp. 97-106.

Sellon, G. H., Jr. (2003), "Monetary Policy and the Zero Bound: Policy Options when Short-Term Rates Reach Zero", *Federal Reserve Bank of Kansas City Economic Review*, Vol. 88, No. 4, pp. 5-43.

Taylor, J. B. (1993), "Discretion Versus Policy Rules in Practice", *Carnegie-Rochester Conference Series on Public Policy*, Vol. 39, No. 0, pp. 195-214.

Taylor, J. B. (1995), "The Monetary Transmission Mechanism: An Empirical Framework", *Journal of Economic Perspectives*, Vol. 9, No. 4, pp. 11-26.

Taylor, J. B. (1998), "Applying Academic Research on Monetary Policy Rules: An Exercise on Translational Economics", *Manchester School*. Supplement, Vol. 66, No. 0, pp. 1-16.

Taylor, J. B. (2001), "Monetary Policy Rules: Introduction", In *Monetary Policy Rules*, ed. John B. Taylor, pp. 1-14, NBER Conference Report series. Chicago and London: University of Chicago Press.

Taylor, J. B. (2000), "Reassessing Discretionary Fiscal Policy", *Journal of Economic Perspectives*, Vol. 14, No. 3, pp. 21-36.

HUMAN CAPITAL AND ECONOMIC GROWTH IN ZIMBABWE

Christopher Mupimpila[*]

Abstract

This study extends the earlier work on human capital and economic growth in Zimbabwe. Previously, it had been established that there is a positive and significant relationship between human capital and economic growth in Zimbabwe. The present study goes a step further and examines the significance of different types of education. The study analyses the effects of primary, secondary, and university education in the economic growth of Zimbabwe during the period 1975-2004. The results show that there is a positive and significant relationship between secondary education and economic growth in Zimbabwe. This is as expected. However, there are plausible explanations of why primary and university education are insignificant in the economic growth of Zimbabwe. Economic theory shades light on these issues.

I. INTRODUCTION

Ncube (1999), found a positive and significant long run relationship between hum n capital and economic growth in Zimbabwe. The present study extends this work. Ncube (1999) used aggregate data, without explaining the sort of education that is significant for economic growth in Zimbabwe. The present study determines whether primary, secondary or tertiary education is most significant. The popular view is that primary education is what matters the most. Wolff and Gittleman (1993) examined the significance of different types of education. They found that, for developed countries, tertiary education is the most significant variable, and for developing countries, primary education is statistically significant. However, according the UNESCO/OECD (2003), upper secondary and tertiary levels of education are significant in order for human capital to have a positive impact on economic growth. The findings of the present study give evidence for the case of Zimbabwe.

The education system in Zimbabwe has been divided into three periods (Ncube, 1999). First, there was the colonial period, when education was racially segregated between the European settlers and indigenous Africans. The settlers benefited greatly from the colonial system. Their education institutions were subsidized by the state while the indigenous Africans had limited access to education. Invariably, the formal education of settlers was superior to that of the indigenous population. Indeed, formal education was a tool to maintain racial segregation, economic and social inequalities in colonial Zimbabwe.

* Senior Lecturer, Department of Economics, University of Botswana, *E-mail: mupimpi@mopipi.ub.bw*

Secondly, there was the period after Zimbabwe became independent in 1980. Then, the new government sought to redress the inequalities of the colonial system. Among other things, the government established many primary and secondary schools. According to Ncube (1999, p.3), the expansion in education "...was more rapid during the first five years of independence." Primary school enrollments rose from 1.2 million in 1980 to 2.2 million in 1985. Secondary school enrollments rose from 74,320 in 1980 to 482,000 in 1985. Thus, between 1980 and 1985, there was nearly an 80 per cent rise in primary school enrollments while secondary school enrollments rose by about 550 per cent. The government also increased the number of vocational and technical colleges. The education boom in Zimbabwe lasted through the 1980s.

Thirdly, there is the current period, which started in the 1990s with the Economic Structural Adjustment Programme (ESAP). During this period, real expenditures on education have declined. The problem has been aggravated by cost recovery measures, but above all, by the long and prolonged recession in the country. As is the case elsewhere in Africa, cost recovery in education is the euphemism for the introduction of school fees. It is an antithesis to the premium that some countries place on education, and it negates measures that are designed to reduce poverty and income inequality. In Zimbabwe, these problems are worsened by stagflation: a period of rising unemployment and inflation. Unemployment was 10 per cent in 1980, but by 1998, it had risen to 40 per cent (Ncube, 1999, p. 2).

This paper consists of two main parts, excluding the introduction. The first part outlines the Solow growth model with labour-augmenting technological progress. Essentially, technological progress improves the efficiency and effectiveness of labour, and this stimulates economic growth. The second part of the paper gives empirical findings on the link between human capital and economic growth in Zimbabwe. The paper analyzes the role of primary, secondary and tertiary education in Zimbabwe.

II. THE MODEL

We assume the aggregate production function is given by the Selow (1957) growth model:

$$Y = F(K, L, t) \tag{1}$$

Where Y, K, L and t represent the amounts of total output, capital, labour and technological progress. Precisely, we assume that technological progress is Harrod-neutral or labour-augmenting (Romer, 2006):

$$Y(t) = F(K(t), A(t)L(t)) \tag{2}$$

Where A(t) is the state of the art, "knowledge" or the "effectiveness of labour," and A(t)L(t) is "effective labour". Differentiating equation (2) with respect to time, we obtain:

$$\dot{Y}(t) = \frac{\partial F}{\partial K}\dot{K}(t) + \frac{\partial F}{\partial L}\dot{L}(t) + \frac{\partial F}{\partial A}\dot{A}(t) \tag{3}$$

Where the dot represents the time derivative of a given variable. Note that $\frac{\partial F}{\partial L} = A\left[\frac{\partial F}{\partial (AL)}\right]$ and $\frac{\partial F}{\partial A} = L\left[\frac{\partial F}{\partial (AL)}\right]$. Dividing both sides of equation (3) by Y(t) and manipulating the results (See Appendix B), we obtain:

$$\frac{\dot{Y}(t)}{Y(t)} = n_k \frac{\dot{K}(t)}{K(t)} + n_L \frac{\dot{L}(t)}{L(t)} + R(t) \qquad (4)$$

Where n_k and n_L are elasticities of output with respect to capital and labour respectively. Equation (4) shows that proportional growth in output depends on three sources: capital, labour and technological progress. In their study, Mankiw *et al.* (1992) augment the Solow model by adding human capital. One of their key findings is that, if human capital is added to the Solow model, the quality of the model is enhanced: the model becomes more robust. This is a basis for the present study. The econometric form model estimated in this study is:

$$RGDP_t = \beta_0 + \beta_1 INVTt + \beta_2 GL_t + \beta_3 PE_t + \beta_4 SE_t + \beta_5 UE_t + \varepsilon_t \qquad (5)$$

Where $RGDP_t$ is real gross domestic product in period t, β_i, i = 0, …, 5 are the coefficients. The variables INVT and GL are, respectively, investment and labour force growth. The human capital variables are PE, SE, and UE; student enrollments at primary, secondary and university levels. It is expected that the variables, INVT, GL, PE, SE and UE all have a positive and significant impact on real GDP in Zimbabwe.

III. DATA AND VARIABLES

The data fitted to the empirical model, equation (5), are for the period 1975-2004. The data are from various issues of the statistical bulletins published by the Central Statistics Office of the Republic of Zimbabwe. The dependent variable, GDP, is real gross domestic product, measured in millions of Zimbabwe dollars. In this study, growth in real GDP is the proxy for economic growth. The growth rated of each variable in the study is the fractional growth rate, and is approximated by the first difference for the logarithm of the variable. The independent variables are as follows. First, the study employs the conventional neoclassical variables of investment (INVT) and labour force growth (GL). Investment is defined as gross fixed capital formation plus changes in stocks. This is real investment in millions of Zimbabwe dollars. Secondly, the proxy for human capital is educational enrolment at primary (PE), secondary (SE), and university (UE) levels. The variable PE is the total number of student enrollment in primary schools during 1975-2004. Similarly, SE represents the total student enrollment in secondary schools during the same period. The variable UE is the total university student enrollment in Zimbabwe during 1975-2004.

There is no consensus among researchers on how best to depict human capital accumulation (Lucas, 1988; Mankiw *et al*, 1992; Benhabid and Spiegel, 1994). Some studies use investment in education to represent human capital formation (McMahon, 1987; Oketch, 2006). However, studies often use literacy and enrollment rates. Ncube (1999) analyses aggregate enrollment data, without explaining the sort of education that is significant for economic growth in Zimbabwe. The present study also uses enrollment data, but attempts to determine whether primary, secondary or tertiary education is most significant.

Appendix A gives the time–series properties of the variables and the error–correction model. The results show that the variables are normally distributed. Unit root tests are employed, the order of integration is established and the error – correction model is specified. The results of the error–correction model for the variable "*LRGDP* established by OLS are presented in section 4.

IV. EMPIRICAL RESULTS

Table 1 gives the empirical results of the present study. The results are labeled as equations 1, 2, 3 and 4. The first three equations are the reduced forms of equation (5) above, while the fourth equation is the full model. The results show that the goodness of fit (Adj. R-squared) is satisfactory, particularly for the full model, the last column of Table 1. The results show that the regressors explain a significant per centage of the variations in real GDP during the period of study, 1975-2004, and a small per centage of growth in GDP remains unexplained. The F-statistics of the four estimated equations reject the null hypothesis that the coefficients of the variables are jointly zero. The Durbin-Watson statistics (DW) indicate that there is no autocorrelation problem. The ECT coefficient gives the speed of adjustment of the endogenous variable towards equilibrium when there is an economic shock, while its sign gives the direction of adjustment towards equilibrium (Hatanaka, 1996). The higher the coefficient is, the faster the speed of adjustment towards equilibrium. The diagnostic tests thus reveal that the models meet the fundamental statistical requirements. Therefore, a meaningful economic interpretation of the results can be carried made.

The results show that the coefficients of the first difference of investment *(DINVT)* and secondary school enrollment *(DLSE)* are significant at the one per cent level and have the expected signs, while growth in labour force *(DLGL)* is significant at the 5 per cent level (Table1, Equation 4). The error-correction term is significant at the one per cent level and has the expected sign. These results suggest that the variables that significant determine economic growth in Zimbabwe are investment and secondary school education, followed by labour force growth. Primary and university education do not significantly influence economic growth in Zimbabwe.

In Equation 1, the reduced form of the model depicts the impact of primary school enrollment. In this case, both secondary school and university enrollments are excluded from the estimation. In the equation, investment, labour force growth and past values of real GDP are significant and have the expected signs. The results also show that the coefficient of the second lag of primary education (*DLPE_2)* is significant only at the 10 per cent level, although it has the expected sign. This results does not support popular notion is that primary education is what matters the most (Easterlin, 1981; Psacharopoulos 1994). Rather, the results confirm the UNESCO/OECD (2003) assertion that, for it to be significant in economic growth, education must reach the critical threshold of upper secondary and tertiary levels.

In Equation 2, the impact of secondary school enrollment *(DLSE)* is considered. In this case, investment is significant at the one per cent level, while labour force growth and the lagged value of real GDP are significant at the 10 per cent level. The coefficient of secondary school enrollment is significant at the one per cent level and has the expected sign. The results show there is a positive and significant relation between secondary education and growth in real GDP in Zimbabwe. These results support earlier findings that suggest that providing people universal primary education is not enough to stimulate economic growth; they need to be educated beyond a critical threshold in order to raise their productivity (UNESCO/OECD, 2003).

Table 1
Regression Results of Education and Economic Growth

Dependent Variable: DLRGDP

Variables	*Equation 1*	*Equation 2*	*Equation 3*	*Equation 4*
Constant	-0.026145	-0.031062 (-1.916400)***	-0.026287 (-1.403127)	-0.054161 (-3.326390)*
DLRGDP_1	0.323979 (2.363323)**	0.246632 (1.914579)***	0.319895 (2.254393)**	0.231288 (1.977414)***
DLGL	1.512457 (2.476867)**	0.714969 (1.905729)***	1.462202 (2.318140)**	1.407287 (2.815896)**
DLINVT	0.175222 (5.364985)*	0.119938 (3.998632)*	0.165607 (5.040832)*	0.127463 (4.916208)*
DLPE_2	0.194907 (1.953037)***			-0.165639 (1.251107)
DLSE		0.316325 (3.983976) *		0.376487 (3.819864)*
DLUE_2			0.073020 (1.468864)	0.067979 (1.737911)***
ECT_1	-0.266919 (-2.880021)**	-0.43554 (-4.269523)*	-0.164682 (-2.241645)**	-0.436650 (-5.033102)*
D-W stat.	2.1437	1.8619	1.9990	2.0002
Adj R	0.6032	0.6737	0.574838	0.766602

(i) The t-statistics are in parenthesis
(ii) Asterisks *, ** and *** denote significance at the 1, 5 and 10% levels.

In Equation 3, university enrollment *(LUE)* is added to the model. In this case, investment is significant at the one per cent level, while labour force growth and the lagged value of real GDP are significant at the 5 per cent level. The human capital coefficient *(DLUE)* is insignificant, contrary to the findings of other studies, which show that university enrollment significantly affects economic growth though increases in labour productivity as a result of improved skills. There are two reasons the coefficient on university education is not statistically significant in the case of Zimbabwe. First, the education boom in Zimbabwe during the 1980s was essentially a rapid growth in secondary education. Ncube (1999, p. 3) states that: "primary schools built doubled in the period 1980 to 1995 while secondary schools increased from 197 to 1540." During the period 1980 to 1985, the increases in enrollments were as follows: primary school, 74 per cent; secondary school, 549 per cent; university, 130 per cent. These figures clearly show that the education boom in Zimbabwe during the 1980s was essentially a boom in secondary education. It is a reason the coefficient of secondary education is statistically significant while those of primary and university education are not.

Secondly, the coefficient of university education is insignificant because the macroeconomic environment in Zimbabwe since the 1990s may have lowered the long- run benefits of university education and thereby reduced university enrollment below its potential. Given a high degree of economic and political uncertainty, secondary education may, in the long run, be more beneficial than university education. As McConnell and Brue (2005, p. 32) succinctly state:

> Deciding to go to college involves weighing future benefits and present costs. The future benefits are higher expected-lifetime earnings. The present costs include *direct costs*, such as tuition and books and *indirect costs* (or *opportunity costs*) of foregoing income that could be earned as a full-time worker with a high school diploma. Students attend college because they expect the long-run benefits of a degree to exceed the short-run costs.

In Zimbabwe, the long run benefits of a degree do not exceed the short-run costs, because there has been precipitous decline in economic conditions in the country since the 1990s. The causes of the decline are many but intertwined. After it attained independence in 1980, Zimbabwe rapidly expanded public expenditures without an accompanying rise in government revenues. The exponential growth in expenditure was caused by, among others, rising social sector spending, subsidies to state companies, the country's involvement in the war in the Democratic Republic of Congo and the land redistribution programme (see for instance, Chemhuru, 2003; Gamariel, 2006). The mismatch between growth in expenditures and revenues resulted in persisted budget deficits, which were financed mainly by domestic borrowing. In turn, domestic borrowing raised interest rates and inflation. Meanwhile, the government debt grew, foreign exchange problems escalated and productivity declined. These problems were exacerbated by the controversial land redistribution programme which the government of Zimbabwe started in January 2000. This programme has variously been dubbed as the land reform programme, the land acquisition programme, or simply the land invasions by "war veterans." Ostensibly, the programme was designed to give land to landless Zimbabweans. Stated by Mutembei (2006, p. 5): "Interestingly, many Zimbabweans are in agreement with President Robert Mugabe's land redistribution programme, but fault the manner in which the whole process was handled. They say, with a lot of conviction that it does not make sense for five per cent of the population to own over 90 per cent of the country's productive land."

The downward economic spiral in Zimbabwe has resulted in galloping inflation, shortages of basic commodities, rising unemployment and the exodus of skilled and unskilled labour to neighbouring countries. It is estimated that there are more than two million Zimbabweans now living in South Africa (ZimOnline, 2007, p.6). Zimbabweans have also migrated to Botswana, Mozambique, Namibia and Zambia in search of better conditions of life. One of the most interesting developments was the so-called 'zero revolution' in Zimbabwe. Moyo (2006, p.4) describes the zero revolution as follows:

> On July 31, 2006 the Bank's Governor Gideon Gono took the nation by surprise when he announced in his mid-term monetary statement that a new family of bearer's cheques would be introduced by midnight that day and further that the new notes would be minus three zeroes. What this means is that if one had a trillion Zimbabwe dollars that was immediately reduced to a billion, if you had a billion that became a million, if you had a million it shrunk to a thousand and if you had a thousand dollars they zeroed to just one dollar.

The zero revolution was essentially a currency reform whereby the Central Bank of Zimbabwe removed three zeroes from the currency. If a person had a bear's cheque of 100,000 Zimbabwe dollars, after the zero revolution this became 100 Zimbabwe dollars. The currency changeover was a sign of the high inflation rate in the country. According to Mutembei (2006, p.4), Zimbabwe's inflation rate in 2006 was close to 1,000 per cent while the parallel exchange rate was 500,000 Zimbabwe dollars to one US dollar. In January 2007, the annual rate of inflation in Zimbabwe reached a new record of 1, 593 per cent and was expected to accelerate further to 4, 096 per cent by the end the year (*The Zimbabwean,* 2007, p. 5).

The Zimbabwean experience is by no means unique. Heckman (2002) shows how labour market distortions in China discourage workers from acquiring skills. These distortions include wage restrictions and educational policy which favours certain regions over others. Heckman argues (p. 7): "Since workers get only a small fraction of their payment for skill, they have weak incentives to acquire skills." The point is; education is a form of investment in human capital. For people to invest in it, education must be profitable. Researchers have tried to identify and measure the returns to education; whether these returns are monetary or non-monetary, social or private (McMahon, 1987; Psacharopoulos, 1989, 1994). The current economic conditions in Zimbabwe are such university education has low discounted long run benefits. Under these circumstances, it should not be surprising that the coefficient of university education in our regression model is statistically insignificant

VII. SUMMARY AND CONCLUSIONS

This study determines whether primary, secondary or university education is significant for economic growth in Zimbabwe. It builds on the work of Ncube (1999), who found a positive and significant relationship between education and economic growth in Zimbabwe. The present study employs an augmented Solow growth model, and provides empirical evidence for the period 1975-2004. The results show that investment and secondary school education are significant at the one per cent level, while labour force is significant at the 5 per cent level. All the variables have the expected signs.

The findings of this study are contrary to the notion that primary education is the most significant human capital variable for economic growth. The results also show that, in Zimbabwe, university education is not statistically as significant as secondary education. This could be due to the fact that the education boom of the 1980s in Zimbabwe was essentially a boom in secondary education. It could also be due to the fact that stagflation in Zimbabwe has reduced the long-term benefits of university education below its potential. Therefore, in the long run, secondary education may be more beneficial than university education. The point is, even under conditions of stagflation, people make rational decisions. As researchers, we must interpret our findings in the light of economic theory. This effort is made here.

APPENDIX

Appendix A: Time – Series Properties and the Error – Correction Model

Time Series Properties

Preliminary tests were carried out on the data to establish its normality and stationarity. Table A.1 shows a summary of the descriptive statistics. It is evident that the data satisfy the normality test as shown by the insignificant Jarque-Bera probability. Two of the series however show low probability values attributed to structural breaks that characterize Zimbabwean data.

Table A. 1
Descriptive Statistics for Variables in Levels

	LGL	*LINVT*	*LPE*	*LSE*	*LUE*	*LGDP*
Mean	2.27488	3.012608	14.46023	12.87964	8.937652	9.815417
Median	2.332994	3.253712	14.63007	13.38338	9.017068	9.853502
Maximum	2.624669	3.900932	14.75212	13.67184	10.71157	10.14266
Minimum	1.778336	-1.267077	13.61655	11.16935	7.211557	9.364262
Std. Dev.	0.253664	1.093666	0.389809	0.942045	1.084875	0.246491
Skewness	-0.417750	-2.692233	-1.420048	-1.035627	-0.053644	-0.458510
Kurtosis	1.886131	10.27600	3.317847	2.361064	1.847796	1.975351
Jarque-Bera	2.423456	102.4158	10.20896	5.872912	1.673855	2.363542
Probability	0.297682	0.000	0.006069	0.053053	0.433039	0.306735
Observations	30	30	30	30	30	30

Unit Root Tests

Economic time series data may exhibit a trend or unit root(s) over time. If this happens, the time series is said to be non-stationary. Non-stationarity implies that their mean and auto-covariances depend on time. Time series data is said to be stationary or mean-reverting if their mean and auto-covariances are independent of time. With unit roots present, there could be spurious regressions- where results may suggest statistically significant relationships, when in reality there are no meaningful relationships between the variables.

This study employed a unit root testing procedure proposed by Philips and Perron which is an alternative to the often used Augmented Dickey-Fuller (ADF) test. The Phillips-Perron (PP) test, however, controls for higher order serial correlation. Even though the ADF has more power than the PP test, the former does not take account of structural breaks such that it may conclude that a unit root exists when it does not.[1] Table A. 2 gives a summary of the unit root test results.

Table A. 2
Results of Unit Root Tests for Data Series in levels

Variable	*Calculated t-statistic*	*Critical value t-statistic (5%)*	*Inference*
LGL	-3.736590	-2.9665	Stationary
LINVT	1.799836	-2.9665	Non-stationary
LPE	-2.089552	-2.9665	Non-stationary
LSE	-1767177	-2.9665	Non-stationary
LUE	-1.100230	-2.9665	Non-stationary
LRGDP	-1.473071	-2.9665	Non-stationary

Critical values produced by EViews

Integration Tests

The order of integration is determined through a series of difference operations which applies the PP tests to the differenced series until stationarity is achieved at some level of differencing. The Johansen cointegration technique requires that the variables be integrated of the same order. In this study the PP tests was conducted on the differenced series in order to determine the order of integration of the variables. The results of the stationarity tests on the differenced series are shown in Table A. 3.

Perron (1989) argued that "standard tests for the unit root hypothesis against trend-stationary alternatives cannot reject the unit root hypothesis if the time series has a structural break." (*pp. 1361-1401*). This was also seconded by Kim (1990) who used Bayesian methods. Zimbabwean annual data may have structural breaks, particularly at 1991, i.e at the inception of economic reform programmes. These breaks may affect data consistency and the quality of statistical inferences. The null hypothesis in the Phillips-Perron (PP) tests is that the variable in question is non-stationary. The test accepts the null hypothesis if the value of the calculated *t*-statistic is more than the critical value of the *t*-statistic that the test generates.

Table A. 3

Results of Unit Root Tests for first differenced Data Series

Variable in first difference	*Calculated t-statistic*	*Critical value t-statistic (5%)*	*Inference*	*Order of Integration*
LINVT	-5.602604	-2.9705	Stationary	I(1)
LPE	-2.954428	-2.6242	Stationary	I(1)
LSE	-2.985354	-2.9705	Stationary	I(1)
LUE	-6.468515	-2.9705	Stationary	I(1)
LRGDP	-3.392986	-2.9705	Stationary	I(1)

Notes: Asterisks* denotes significance at 10% level

Cointegration and Error Correction Model

If variables are integrated of the same order, even though they may be non-stationary, their linear combinations can be stationary (Engle and Granger, 1987). Table 3 shows that the variables are I(1) which forms the basis of cointegration analysis. Cointegration analysis was conducted using the Johansen cointegration test and the results are presented in Table A. 4.

Table A. 4

Johansen's Cointegration Test

Eigen Value	*Likelihood Ratio*	*5% Critical*	*1% Critical Value*	*Hypothesised No. of CE(s)*
0.956768	173.7968	94.15	103.18	None**
0.802979	85.84420	68.52	76.07	At most 1**
0.463732	40.3977	47.21	54.46	At most 2
0.354488	22.91239	29.68	35.65	At most 3
0.063222	1.828647	3.76	6.65	At most 4

** denotes rejection of the hypothesis at 1% level of significance.
L.R Test indicates two cointegrating equations at 5% significance level.

The eigenvalue statistic rejects the null hypothesis that there are no cointegrating vectors or five common trends. The results show the presence of two long run relationships from the 5 series, *LRGDP, LINVT, LSE, LPE* and *LUE.* As such cointegration is accepted and a long run growth function is specified.

Table A. 5
Long-Run Growth Function

LRGDP	1.00000
C	-13.87868
LGL	-1.501725 (0.10548)
LINVT	-0.155104 (0.01261)
LPE	0.758411 (0.08962)
LSE	-0.281300 (0.03818)
LUE	0.069141 (0.02055)

Log likelihood =264.3416

In parenthesis are the standard errors, before the parenthesis are parameter coefficients.

Only one long run equation is however specified and the normalization process was guided by both economic theory, where LRGDP is the regressed, and by statistical reason. The long run equation is presented in Table A. 5.

The residual generated from the long- run growth function was lagged once and used as an error correction term. Thus a dynamic error correction model of the growth rate of real output that reflects both the short run and long run determinants of economic growth as well as convergence of RGDP to its long run equilibrium resulted in a re-specification of the original equation into an Error Correction Model (ECM). The results of the ECM are presented in the following section.

Appendix B
Derivation of the Labour-Augmented Solow Growth Model

The derivation of the Solow growth model with Harrod-neutral or labour-augmenting technological progress is as follows. We assume that the aggregate production function is given by the Solow (1957) growth model:

$$Y = F(K, L, t) \tag{B.1}$$

Where Y, K. L and t represent the amounts of total output, capital, labour and technological progress. Assuming that technological progress is Harrod-neutral or labour-augmenting, equation (B.1) is stated as (Romer, 2006):

$$Y(t) = F(K(t), A(t)L(t)) \tag{B.2}$$

Where A (t) is the state of the art; "knowledge" or the "effectiveness of labour." Differentiating (B.2) with respect to time, we obtain:

$$\dot{Y}(t) = \frac{\partial F}{\partial K}\dot{K}(t) + A\left[\frac{\partial F}{\partial\ (AL)}\right]\dot{L}(t) + L\left[\frac{\partial F}{\partial\ (AL)}\right]\dot{A}(t) \tag{B.3}$$

Where $\dot{Y}(t) = \frac{dy}{dt}$, $\dot{K}(t) = \frac{dk}{dt}$, $\dot{L}(t) = \frac{dL}{dt}$ *and* $\dot{A}(t) = \frac{dA}{dt}$.

Note that in equation (B.3), $A\left[\frac{\partial F}{\partial (AL)}\right] = \frac{\partial F}{\partial L}$ and $L\left[\frac{\partial F}{\partial (AL)}\right] = \frac{\partial F}{\partial A}$. Substituting these terms in equation (B.3) yields:

$$\dot{Y}(t) = \frac{\partial F}{\partial K}\dot{K}(t) + \frac{\partial F}{\partial L}\dot{L}(t) + \frac{\partial F}{\partial A}\dot{A}(t) \tag{B.4}$$

Dividing both sides by Y(t) we obtain:

$$\frac{\dot{Y}}{Y(t)} = \frac{\partial F}{\partial K}\frac{1}{F}\dot{K}(t) + \frac{\partial F}{\partial L}\frac{1}{F}\dot{L}(t) + \frac{\partial F}{\partial A}\frac{1}{F}\dot{A}(t) \tag{B.5}$$

Multiplying the terms on the right-hand side of equation (B.5) by K/K, L/L and A/A respectively, we get:

$$\frac{\dot{Y}(t)}{Y(t)} = \frac{\partial F}{\partial K}\frac{K}{F}\frac{\dot{K}(t)}{K(t)} + \frac{\partial F}{\partial K}\frac{L}{F}\frac{\dot{L}(t)}{L(t)} + \frac{\partial F}{\partial A}\frac{A}{F}\frac{\dot{A}(t)}{A(t)} \tag{B.6}$$

Note that in equation (B.6), $\frac{\partial F}{\partial K}\frac{K}{F} = n_k$, the elasticity of output with respect to capital, and $\frac{\partial F}{\partial L}\frac{L}{F} = n_L$, the elasticity of output with respect to labour. Furthermore, following Romer (2006), let $R(t) = \frac{\partial F}{\partial A}\frac{A}{F}\frac{\dot{A}(t)}{A(t)}$.

Then equation (B.6) becomes:

$$\frac{\dot{Y}(t)}{Y(t)} = n_K\frac{\dot{K}(t)}{K(t)} + n_L\frac{\dot{L}(t)}{L(t)} + R(t) \tag{B.7}$$

Equation (B.7) shows that the growth rate of output depends on the growth rates of capital, labour and technological progress.

References

Benhabib, J. and M. Spiegel (1994), "The Role of Human Capital in Economic Development: Evidence from Aggregate Cross-Country Data," *Journal of Monetary Economics* 34: 143-174.

Bils, M. and P. Klenow (2000), "Does Schooling Cause Growth?" *American Economic Review* 90: 1160-1183.

Chemhuru, S. (2003), *Health Status, Productivity, and Economic Growth: The Case of Zimbabwe*. Unpublished M. A. dissertation, University of Botswana.

Dickey, D. A. and W. A. Fuller (1979), "Distribution of Estimators for Autoregressive Time Series and Unit Roots," *Journal of American Statistical Association* 74 (366): 427-431.

Easterly, R. (1981), "Why isn't the Whole World Developed?" *Journal of Economic History* 41: 1-19.

Easterly, W. and R. Lavine (2001), "What Have We Learned from a Decade of Empirical Research on Growth?" *The World Bank Economic Review* 15 (2): 177-219.

Engle, R. and C. Granger (1987), "Cointegration and Error Correction: Representation, Estimation and Testing," *Econometrica,* 55(2): 251-78.

Gamariel, G. (2006), *Government Expenditure Composition and Economic Growth: The Case of Zimbabwe.* Unpublished M. A. dissertation; University of Botswana.

Gordon, R. J. (2000), "Does the 'New Economy' Measure up to the Great Inventions of the Past?" *Journal of Economic Perspectives* 14 (4): 49-74.

Guisinger, S., J. Henderson and G. Scully (1984), "Earnings, Rates of Return and the Earnings Distribution in Pakistan," *Economics of Education Review* 3 (4): 257-267.

Gujarati, D. (1995), *Basic Econometrics*. New York: McGraw-Hill Publishers.

Hatanaka, M. (1996), *Time-Series-Based Econometrics: Unit Roots and Co-Integration*. Oxford: Oxford University Press.

Heckman, J. J. (2002), "China's Investment in Human Capital," *NBER Working Paper No. 9296* (October): 1-18.

Johansen, S. (1988), "Statistical Analysis of Cointegration Vectors," *Journal of Economic Dynamics and Control* 12: 231-54.

Johansen, S. and K. Juselius (1990), "Maximum Likelihood Estimation and Inference on Cointegration with Applications to the Demand for Money," *Oxford Bulletin of Economics and Statistics* 52: 169-210.

Johnson, T. (1970), "Returns from Investment in Human Capital," *The American Economic Review* 60: 4: 546-60.

Kennedy, P. (1998), *A Guide to Econometrics*. Malden, Massachusetts: Blackwell publishers Inc.

Kruger, A. and M. Lindahl (2001), "Education for Growth: Why and For Whom?" *Journal of Economic Literature* 39: 1101-1136.

Lucas, R. E. Jr. (1988), "On the Mechanics of Economic Development," *Journal of Monetary Economics* 22:3-42.

Mankiw, N. G., D. Romer, and D. N. Weil (1992), "A Contribution to the Empirics of Economic Growth," *Quarterly Journal of Economics* 107: 407-437.

McConnell, C. L., and S. L. Brue (2005), *Economics: Principles, Problems and Policies*, New York: McGraw Hill.

McMahon, W. W. (1987), "The Relation of Education and R&D to Productivity Growth in the Developing Countries of Africa," *Economics of Education Review* 6: 183-194.

Moyo, J. (2006), "The Zero Revolution: Tale of Poor Millionaires in Mugabe Country," *Nation*, Sunday, 3 September: 4 & 5.

Mutembei, P. (200?), "A Few Beers With Friends Saw us Slapped With a Bill of 78 Million Dollars," *Nation*, Sunday, 3 September: 4.

Nelson, R. and E. Phelps (1966), "Investing in Humans, Technical Diffusion and Economic Growth," *American Economic Review* 56: 69-75.

Ncube, M (1999), "Is Human Capital Important for Economic Growth in Zimbabwe?" *African Journal of Economic Policy* 6 (2): 1-14.

The Zimbabwean, 15-21 February, 2007: 5.

UNESCO/OECD (2003), *Financing Education – Investments and Returns: Analysis of the World Education Indicators, 2002 Edition*. Paris: UNESCO-UIS/OECD.

Oketch, M. O. (2006), "Determinants of Human Capital Formation and Economic Growth in African Countries," *Economics of Education Review* 25: 554-564.

Psacharopoulos, G. (1989), "Returns to Education: A Further International Update and Implications," *Journal of Human Resources* 20 (4): 583-604.

Psacharopoulos, G. (1994), "Returns to Education: A Global Update," *World Development* 22 (9): 1325-1343.

Romer, D. (2006), *Advanced Macroeconomics*. New York: McGraw-Hill Companies, Inc.

Siphambe, H. K. (2000), "Rates of Return to Education in Botswana," *Economics of Education Review* 19: 291-300.

Solow, R. M. (1957), "Technical Change and the Aggregate Production Function," *Review of Economics and Statistics* 39: 312–20.

Schultz, T. P. (2002), "Why Governments Should Invest More to Educate Girls," *World Development* 30 (2): 207-25.

Schultz, T.W. (1960), "Capital Formation By Education," *Journal of Political Economy* 68: 571-583.

Wolf, E., and M. Gittleman (1993), "The Role of Education in Productivity Convergence: Does Higher Education Matter?" in A. Szimai, B. van Ark and D. Pilat, ed., *Explaining Economic Growth*, Amsterdam: Elsevier Science Publishers.

World Bank (1994), *Adjustment in Africa: Reforms, Results, and the Road Ahead*. Oxford: Oxford University Press.

ZimOnline (2007), "The Dead's Contribution in Zim," *Botswana Guardian*, 9 February: 6.

Asian-African Journal of Economics and Econometrics, Vol. 7, No. 1-2, 2007: 345-363

INCOME AND PRICE ELASTICITIES OF DEMAND FOR AGGREGATE IMPORTS: ALTERNATIVE ECONOMETRIC TESTS FOR BANGLADESH

Anisul M. Islam*

ABSTRACT

This paper estimates income and price elasticities of demand for imports in Bangladesh using Johansen-Juselius multivariate cointegration analysis along with various tests for non-stationarity. Cointegration results indicate that the import demand function is dominated by income and relative prices. Tests on linear restrictions on the coefficients clearly reject the hypothesis of proportionality between income and imports, while the hypothesis that import prices and domestic prices have coefficients which are equal in magnitude but opposite in sign could not be rejected. The income elasticity coefficient is statistically significant and its magnitude exceeds unity indicating that imports are both "normal" and "luxury" goods in the context of Bangladesh. The relative price variable is found to be significantly negative and its magnitude is less than unity. This variable captures the "substitution" effect in the import demand function. Analysis of the short-run dynamics shows that the short-run import demand function is stable and adjusts to its long-run equilibrium path with a reasonable speed.

INTRODUCTION

As a poor developing country in South Asia, Bangladesh has historically relied heavily on the foreign sector for trade in goods, services, and resources including foreign capital. Prior to its independence [1] in 1971 and immediately after independence up until the late seventies, the country basically followed an *inward-oriented import-substitution* trade strategy. Since the late-seventies and early eighties, however, this country has embarked upon a road to an *outward-oriented export-promotion* regime by liberalizing its internal and external sectors of the economy.

As a direct consequence of this major policy change, the country has been experiencing a greater degree of dependence on the foreign sector. The levels of exports, imports, and foreign capital flows have increased in both absolute and relative terms. As Figure 1 shows, imports have remained consistently above exports, as a result, the country always experienced severe and growing trade deficit problem with the rest of the world since her independence. Although both exports and imports have risen, the latter has increased faster than the former, resulting in

* Professor of Economics, University of Houston-Downtown, One Main Street, Houston, *E-mail: islama@uhd.edu*

Figure 1: Imports, Exports, and Trade Deficit in Bangladesh: 1972-2000

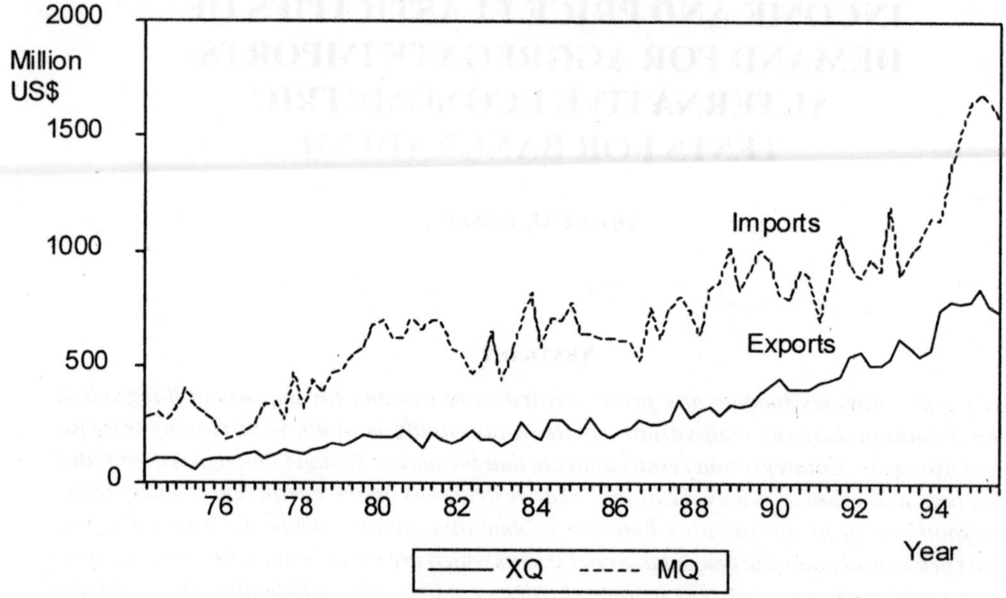

a far greater trade deficit than ever before. Because of this, it is very important to carry out an in-depth empirical study of the demand for imports for Bangladesh in order for the country to develop a sensible trade policy regime to overcome this persistent trade deficit problem.

The primary objective of this paper is to empirically estimate the income and price elasticities of aggregate import demand function for Bangladesh using well-known Johansen-Juselius multivariate cointegration analysis. Although a few previous studies empirically examined the import demand function for this country in the past, with the exception of Dutta and Ahmed (1999), none used quarterly time series data covering a reasonably long period of time as used in this study. Further, this study applies advanced time series techniques such as unit root and cointegration tests in estimating the import demand function for Bangladesh. It is to be noted here that reliable estimates of the parameters of the import demand function are needed for developing appropriate trade and exchange rate policies for developing countries like Bangladesh.

A BRIEF REVIEW OF LITERATURE ON IMPORT DEMAND

A large body of literature exists on the study of import demand functions for both developed[2] and developing[3] countries. However, only a few studies exist for Bangladesh[4]. Most previous studies not only used insufficient data but also suffer from a number of serious theoretical and methodological weaknesses, thus rendering their empirical results highly unreliable.

Like other developing countries, Bangladesh faces severe foreign exchange constraints in meeting its import needs. As a result, any theoretical specification of the import demand function for the developing countries in general and Bangladesh in particular needs to incorporate this important and often binding restriction. A few researchers have recognized that aggregate demand for imports in the developing countries is constrained by the availability of foreign exchange (see Hemphill, 1974; Morgan, 1989; and Emran and Shilpi, 1996; for example). However, in their studies, both Hemphill (1974) and Moran (1989) failed to address this issue in a theoretically consistent manner as was shown by Emran and Shilpi (1996). Most other studies failed to address this issue at all in their studies. Following Emran and Shilpi, this study will incorporate this restriction on the theoretical and empirical specification of the import demand function for Bangladesh in an appropriate manner.

Further, most previous studies on the import demand function for both developed and developing countries applied the standard regression analysis using time series data to estimate the function without prior examination of the time series properties of the variables in their models (for examles, see Shilpi, 1990 for Bangladesh; Sarmad, 1989 for Pakistan; Khan, Rahman and Islam, 1997 for US imports from Mexico; and Hemphill, 1974 and Khan, 1974 for developing countries). The results from the standard regression analysis could be valid if the variables included in the model are stationary, the error term is serially uncorrelated and homoskedastic, and the time period used is of sufficient length to uncover the long-run relationships and the underlying short-run dynamics.

However, most of these studies failed to examine whether the above mentioned conditions hold before applying the standard regression methods, notably the assumption of "stationarity" of the variables in their estimated import demand models. Advances in time series techniques help us to carefully examine the time series properties of the variables before applying the standard regression methods as discussed below.

Since the previous studies did not properly address the issue of foreign exchange constraint in a theoretically consistent manner (except Emran and Shilpi, 1996) and since these studies failed to examine the time series properties of the variables before applying the standard regression methodology (except Emran and Shilpi, 1996 and Dutta and Ahmed, 1999), it is legitimate to raise serious questions about the reliability of their empirical results. These considerations have motivated the current study. The primary objective of this paper is to estimate the import demand function for Bangladesh under foreign exchange constraints using quarterly time series data while overcoming various theoretical and methodological limitations of most previous studies mentioned above.

This objective will be carried out firstly by using quarterly data for a longer time period than previously used; secondly, by using a theoretically consistent framework to deal with the issue of foreign exchange constraints; and thirdly, by applying advanced and more appropriate econometric techniques which were not used in previous studies. More specifically, the advanced econometric techniques that are used in this paper include, among others, unit root tests, cointegration tests, likelihood ratio tests of linear restrictions on parameters, and exogeneity tests. These techniques allow one to examine the long-run relationships hypothesized in the context of the import demand function for this country. In addition, these techniques allow the researchers to conduct hypothesis testing including the study of the short-run dynamics (the speed and direction of adjustment) that occurs within the long-run framework.

THE THEORETICAL FRAMEWORK

In modeling aggregate demand for imports, the conventional theoretical framework has been to include real income and relative prices as arguments in the import demand equation. The real income is used to represent the scale variable, while the price of imports relative to price of domestic goods as the opportunity cost variable in the equation. The problem with this specification is that imports in most developing countries are severely constrained by the availability of foreign exchange. This problem is more severe under a regime of exchange controls where the official rate is normally overvalued resulting in severe foreign exchange rationing. In this situation, the standard model would be mis-specified.

To overcome this problem, some researchers (see Moran, 1989) have added foreign exchange availability as an additional argument in the conventional import demand model. Others such as Hemphill (1974) specified a model solely in terms of variables representing foreign exchange supply. However, the methods used by both Hemphill (1974) and Moran (1989) to incorporate this restriction were severely flawed and devoid of any behavioral interpretations. When foreign exchange availability is used as an argument in the presence of income and relative prices, the resulting function becomes a "near identity" resulting in nonsensical results, which was demonstrated by Emran and Shilpi (1996). They proposed a theoretically consistent methodology to deal with this problem. When income and relative prices are present in the same equation along with the foreign exchange availability to represent foreign exchange rationing, they demonstrated that the resulting near identity problem in this function can be resolved if one uses the ratio of foreign exchange availability to income instead of foreign exchange availability in that function. This paper follows this procedure in estimating the import demand function for Bangladesh under foreign exchange constraints as follows:

In a representative agent economy, agents are expected to maximize a utility function consisting of two composite goods: home goods (H) and import goods (M):

$$U = U(H, M) \tag{1}$$

subject to two budget constraints, a local currency budget constraint and a foreign currency budget constraint given by equations (2) and (3) respectively:

$$H + P \, . \, M \leq y \tag{2}$$

$$M \leq f \tag{3}$$

where:

$y = Y/P_H$ which is nominal GDP (Y) deflated by price of home goods (P_H)

$P = (P_M / P_H)$ which is Import price (P_M) relative to price of home goods (P_H)

f = real foreign exchange availability given by ($F.e / P_M$)

F = Nominal foreign exchange available in foreign currency

e = Exchange rate between local and foreign currency (Taka per US$)

In this framework, if the foreign currency budget constraint (3) is binding, then the volume of imports is identically equal to foreign exchange availability. As a result, the variables in the local currency budget constraint (2) becomes irrelevant if foreign exchange availability is used as a regressor. However, the above constrained maximization problem can be solved under certain reasonable parametric restrictions (such as imports are not Giffen goods) and the following theoretically consistent import demand function can be obtained for estimation purposes (for details of the derivation and interpretation, see Emran and Shilpi, 1996) :

$$M = M(y, P, Z) \tag{4}$$

where Z = (f / y) is the ratio of real foreign exchange availability to real GDP. When this variable is included in equation (4) instead of foreign exchange availability f itself when y and P are also present as arguments in the import demand function, the problem of near identity can be avoided. As a result, the estimated coefficients would be both theoretically sound and empirically consistent (see Emran and Shilpi, 1996, p. 318). After adding a random error term in equation (4), this general function can be rewritten in a constant elasticity form as follows:

$$M = a\, y^{b} P^{c} Z^{d} u \tag{5}$$

Taking natural logarithms (ln) on both sides, equation (5) becomes:

$$\ln M = a + b \ln y + c \ln P + d \ln Z + \ln u \tag{6}$$

with the a priori sign expectations given as follows:

$$b > 0; \quad c < 0; \quad d > 0 \tag{7}$$

where b, c, d are elasticity coefficients with respect to the variables y, P, and Z respectively.

The log-linear form was chosen because it was found to be the most appropriate functional form in different empirical studies (see Boylan, Cuddy and O'Muircheartaigh, 1980; and Khan and Ross, 1977). Further, the estimated coefficients give elasticity values directly. This specification has the added advantage of reducing the problem of heteroskedasticity (if any) in the import function (see Maddala, 1992 and Khan, Rahman and Islam, 1997).

The expected impact of each explanatory variable on the demand for imports is given in equation (7) and is briefly explained below. The impact of the first two explanatory variables are derived directly from the theory of demand. A rational consumer will allocate his/her income among various consumable commodities in such a way so as to achieve maximum possible utility. The amount of imports purchased by this consumer will thus depend on his income, the price of imports and the price of home goods (see Leamer and Stern, 1970, p. 9). A positive sign for the coefficient of the income (y) variable (b > 0) will indicate that imports are "normal" goods. A negative sign, however, would indicate them to be "inferior" goods. Further, if this coefficient exceeds unity, imports could be interpreted as "luxury" goods; on the other hand, if it is less than unity, imports could be interpreted as "necessary" goods.

Home goods and import goods can be considered as imperfect substitutes for each other. As a result, the coefficient of the relative price variable (P) is expected to be negative (c < 0) because as imports become more expensive, rational agents would substitute import goods for home goods, thus reducing the demand for import goods. Finally, the coefficient of Z is expected to be positive (d > 0) because as the foreign exchange constraint is relaxed, imports in a larger quantity are expected to flow into the country (see Hemphill, 1974; Moran, 1989; and Emran and Shilpi, 1996).

In addition to examining the sign of each coefficient, the likelihood ratio statistic can be used to test a number of other hypotheses within the co-integration framework as follows. (a) Since traditional "t" and "F" tests may not be valid, the Likelihood Ratio (LR) test can be applied on each explanatory variable in equation (6) by imposing long-run exclusionary (zero) restriction on these coefficients. (b) LR tests can be conducted by imposing linear restrictions on different parameters in equation (6). One such hypothesis is to examine the proportionality between income and import demand ($H_0 1$: b =1).

Further, it is also possible to examine the hypothesis that the coefficients of import price and domestic price indices are same in magnitude but opposite in sign ($H_0 2$); In the traditional specification of the import demand function, relative price is used instead of import and domestic prices as separate variables under the assumption that consumers do not suffer from money illusion (see Leamer and Stern, 1970, p. 10; and Khan, Rahman and Islam, 1997). The advantage of using this specification of the price variable is that it reduces the problem of multicollinearity between import price and domestic price which otherwise might bias the parameter estimates. More importantly, it reduces the problem of multicollinearity which usually exists between income and domestic price (Khan, Rahman and Islam, 1997). Murray and Ginman (1975), on the other hand, argues that such specification constraints the influence of the two price variables to be equal in magnitude but opposite in sign and they presented evidence that rejects the traditional specification. This is clearly a testable hypothesis which conducted under this null hypothesis. In addition, the two above mentioned hypotheses can be imposed jointly in the import demand function ($H_0 3$: $H_0 1$ and $H_0 2$ holds jointly).

The cointegration techniques are also useful in analyzing the short-run dynamics underlying the long-run equilibrium demand function given by equation (6). More specifically, this analysis will indicate whether the money demand function is stable and, if so, the direction and speed of adjustment towards the long-run equilibrium path.

THE EMPIRICAL FRAMEWORK

Equation (6) can be estimated by the standard regression method if the variables M, y, P and Z are stationary and the residual term u is uncorrelated and homoskedastic. Most previous studies on import demand function for developing countries used the conventional theoretical specification of the import demand function and applied the standard regression method to estimate it without prior examination of the time series properties of these variables (see Shilpi, 1990 for Bangladesh and Sarmad, 1989 for Pakistan). If the variables are non-stationary in their levels, the standard regression method could be inappropriate because the usual "t" and "F" tests become meaningless (see Engle and Granger, 1987). More importantly, the estimated regression coefficients could be "spurious" (see Granger and Newbold, 1974). Therefore, one needs to apply cointegration techniques to estimate the above equation. These techniques are discussed below.

Time Series Properties of the Variables

A stationary series is generally characterized by a time-invariant mean and a time-invariant variance. Several alternative methods are available to test for non-stationarity of a time series.

In this paper, we will apply the following three well-known and widely used techniques for this purpose: (a) The Augmented Dickey-Fuller test (ADF test); (b) The Phillips-Perron test (PP test); and (c) The Likelihood Ratio (LR) test. An elaborate discussion for each of them can be found in Dickey and Fuller (1981), Phillips and Perron (1988), and Hansen and Juselius (1995) respectively. If the variables are found to be non-stationary in their levels, then one needs to apply the cointegration tests which are discussed below. The Johansen-Juselius (JJ) cointegration method along with other relevant tests will be applied if the variables are found to be non-stationary.

Cointegration Tests: The Johansen-Juselius (JJ) Method

The multivariate cointegration techniques developed by Johansen (1988; 1991; 1992) and Johansen-Juselius (1990; 1992) using a maximum likelihood estimation procedure allows researchers to estimate simultaneously the system involving two or more variables to circumvent the problems associated with the traditional regression methods used in previous studies on this issue. Further, this method is independent of the choice of the endogenous variable because it treats all the variables in the model as endogenous within a VAR (vector autoregression) framework. More importantly, this method allows one to estimate and test for the presence of more than one co-integrating vector(s) in the multivariate system. In addition, it enables the researchers to test for various structural hypotheses involving restricted versions of the co-integrating vectors and speed of adjustment parameters using likelihood ratio tests. The main features of this method are discussed below.

Following Johansen (1988) and Johansen and Juselius (1990), a VAR representation of the N-dimensional data vector X_t is specified as follows:

$$X_t = + \Pi_1 X_{t-1} + \ldots\ldots\ldots\ldots\ldots + \Pi_k X_{t-k} + \delta + e_t \quad (t=1,2,\ldots\ldots\ldots\ldots, T) \tag{8}$$

where $e_1, \ldots\ldots\ldots, e_T$ are distributed as N-dimensional i.i.d. normal variables, δ represents a vector of constants, and the X_t is a vector of all the endogenous variables in the system. In this study, the vector X_t is of dimension N = 4 because it contains four endogenous variables [$\ln M_t$, $\ln y_t$, $\ln P_t$, $\ln Z_t$]' which are defined later.

Now using the notation $\Delta = 1\text{–}L$, where L is the lag operator, the VAR system represented by (8) can be rewritten as the Error Correction Model (ECM) as follows:

$$\Delta X_t = \Pi X_{t-1} + \varphi_1 \Delta X_{t-1} + \ldots\ldots\ldots\ldots \varphi_{k-1} \Delta X_{t-k+1} + \delta + e_t, \tag{9}$$

where:

$$\varphi_I = -(I - \Pi_1 - \ldots\ldots\ldots\ldots - \Pi_i) \quad (I = 1, \ldots\ldots\ldots\ldots, k\text{-}1),$$

and

$$\Pi = (I - \Pi_1 - \ldots\ldots\ldots\ldots - \Pi_k).$$

The main focus of the Johansen-Juselius technique is on the parameter matrix Π. The rank "r" of this matrix r (Π), where ($0 < r < N$), will determine the number of co-integrating vectors in the VAR system. If the rank of this matrix is found to be "r", then there are "r" linear combinations of the variables in the system that are stationary and that all other linear combinations are non-stationary. The matrix Π can be rewritten as $\Pi = \alpha\beta'$ where α is the speed of adjustment vector (also called weights or loadings) and β is the co-integrating vector. The dimension of α and β are (N x r) and the system (9) is subject to the condition that Π is less than full rank matrix, i.e. r < N. The procedure boils down to testing for the value of "r" on the basis of the number of significant eigenvalues of Π. For this purpose, the maximum eigenvalue test (λ_{max}) and the trace test (λ_{Trace}) are applied. The λ_{max} and λ_{Trace} test statistics are given by the following equations:

$$\lambda_{max}\,(r, r+1) = -T\ln(1-\lambda_{r+1}) \tag{10}$$

$$\lambda_{Trace}\,(r) = -T\,\Sigma\ln(1-\lambda_i) \quad (I = r+1, \ldots., n) \tag{11}$$

where λ_i is the estimated value of the ith characteristic root (eigenvalue) obtained from the estimated Π matrix, N is the number of variables, and T is the number of usable observations.

The λ_{max} statistic tests the null hypothesis that the number of co-integrating vectors is r against the alternative of (r + 1) co-integrating vectors. If the estimated value of the characteristic root is close to zero, then the λ_{max} will be small. The λ_{trace} statistic, on the other hand, tests the null hypothesis that the number of distinct characteristic roots is less than or equal to r against a general alternative. In this statistic, λ_{trace} will be small when the values of the characteristic roots are closer to zero and its value will be large, the further the values of the characteristic roots from zero. Note that the statistic has a sharper alternative hypothesis than the trace statistic and hence it may be preferred in selecting the number of co-integrating vectors. Also note that in actual test situation, the two statistics may give conflicting results.

Johansen and Juselius (1990) provide the critical values of the λ_{max} and λ_{trace} test statistics using simulation method for determining the rank of the Π matrix. The above mentioned test statistics are distributed as χ^2 with appropriate degrees of freedom (N-r) where N is the number of variables and r is the value of the rank under the null hypothesis. In these likelihood ratio tests, the null hypotheses are accepted if the estimated values are less than the critical values at the appropriate significance level and the degrees of freedom.

The coefficients of the estimated α vector can be interpreted as the weights with which the excess demand for imports (disequilibrium in the import demand function due to random shocks and/or policy intervention) enters the equation in the VAR system. The sign and magnitude of these coefficients will give important information about the short-run dynamics of the system, i.e. its stability as well as the direction and speed of adjustment towards the long-run equilibrium path. If the absolute value of the relevant coefficient in α is less than unity, it will indicate that the system is stable. The magnitude of the coefficient will indicate the average speed with which the system will go back to its long-run equilibrium path. A small coefficient will indicate slow adjustment and a large coefficient will indicate rapid adjustment.which shows the direction and speed of adjustment of the system towards the co-integrating (long-run) relations after a stochastic shock.

As mentioned earlier, Johansen-Juselius method can be used to conduct a number of Likelihood Ratio (LR) tests as follows: (a) to examine stationarity of each variable in the VAR system; (b) to conduct exclusionary restriction on each explanatory variable in the system; this test is useful in making inferences about the significance of different variables in an equation;

(c) to examine exclusionary restrictions imposed on the loadings i.e., the speed of adjustment vector (α). This test can identify weakly exogenous variables in the system; and (d) to test linear restrictions on the co-integrating vector which is useful for testing various economic hypotheses; and (e) to determine jointly the appropriate rank and deterministic components in the data. This test is quite useful first step in selecting an appropriate deterministic components for the cointegration analysis.

DATA AND VARIABLES

The information about the data and measurement of the variables are discussed below.

M = (M' * 100 / P_M) is the dependent variable real imports in equation (6). IP = Industrial production Index (IP); a proxy for y in equation (6). This variable is used instead of real GDP because quarterly data on GDP is not available for Bangladesh. PMCPI = (P_M*100/CPI); a proxy for the relative price P in equation (6). IRY = (IR*100/Y) is the international reserves excluding gold (IR) as a percentage of GDP; a proxy for Z in equation (6). For this transformation, annual GDP series was converted into quarterly GDP series using an interpolation technique. Since quarterly data on total foreign exchange availability for the country are not available, international reserves excluding gold is used as a proxy for this variable. M' stands for nominal value of imports; P_M stands for import price index; Y stands for nominal GDP[5]; CPI stands for Consumer Price Index as a proxy for price of home goods; LM = Natural logarithm of M; LIP = Natural logarithm of Industrial Production index; LPMCPI = Natural logarithm of the relative price variable; LIRY = Natural logarithm of IRY. Data Sources: various publications of the Bangladesh Bank (the central bank of the country) and International Financial Statistics of the IMF. Data Frequency: Quarterly. Time Period Covered: 1974.I to 2000.IV.

THE EMPIRICAL RESULTS

Before proceeding further, it is to be noted here that two econometric software packages such as the EVIEWS (Econometric Views by the Quantitative Micro Software) and the CATS (Cointegration Analyśis of Time Series by Estima) were extensively used in generating the empirical results reported below.

Time Series Properties

Table 1 reports the unit root tests using the ADF and Phillips-Perron tests and Table 6 (section I) provides the Likelihood ratio (LR) test for stationarity for all the variables in the model. The ADF test reveals that the null hypothesis of unit root is accepted for all variables except the relative price (LPMCPI) variable. The Phillips-Perron test reveals similar results except for the relative price and industrial production index (LIP) variables. The null of unit root for the LIP variable can be accepted, however, at the 1% level. For these two tests, McKinnon critical values at 1%, 5%, and 10% significance levels were used. The LR test shows that the null hypothesis of stationarity is rejected for all the variables corresponding to rank =2 (the chosen rank for this study as discussed later). In this test, the calculated values are greater than their critical values at the 5% level thus rejecting the null of stationarity for all the variables. Based on the three different tests above, the variables were found to be nonstationary except for the relative price variable. As a result, the standard regression model is not appropriate in examining the relationships depicted in the import demand function for Bangladesh. In this situation, one has to use the co-integration techniques to uncover the appropriate relationships.[6]

Table 1
Unit Root Tests

Variables	ADF Test *Level*	ADF Test *1st-difference*	Phillips-Perron Test *Level*	Phillips-Perron Test *1st-difference*
LM	-2.23	-6.99***	-2.74	-12.87***
LPMCPI	-4.53***	—	-3.72**	—
LIP	-1.35	-13.16***	-3.44***	-16.25***
LIRY	-2.52	-5.25***	-2.63	-7.09***

Notes: (1) The McKinnon critical values (with intercept and trend) are: (a) 1% = -4.07; (b) 5% = -3.46; and (c) 10% = -3.16 respectively. (2) Without intercept and trend) are: (a) 1% = -2.59; (b) 5% = -1.94; and (c) 10% = 1.62; (2) Both intercept and trend were significant in LMR, LIP, and LIRY equations while neither was significant for LPMCPI; (3) (a) *** = significant at 1% level; (b) ** = significant at 5% level; and (c) * = significant at 10% level.

Selection of Optimal Lag Length and Deterministic Components

Before discussing the characteristics of the Π matrix, we need to specify the appropriate lag length k* of the VAR system so as to make the residuals uncorrelated and homoskedastic. Akaike Information Criterion and the Scwartz Criterion were used in determining the appropriate lag lengths. In this data set, an optimal lag length of k* = 2 was sufficient to make the residuals uncorrelated and homoskedastic.[7] The trace statistics for a preliminary determination of rank and the appropriate deterministic components cases are given in Table 2. In this table, out of the five possible cases with respect to alternative specification of deterministic components (see Hansen and Jeselius,1995) for details), only three were relevant for the current analysis - these are the three intermediate ones: Case 2 (intercepts in the cointegrating relations), Case 3 (Deterministic components in the levels of the variables), and Case 4 (trends in the cointegrating relations).

Table 2
Identifying Rank and Deterministic Components Jointly

Eigenvalues: *rank*	*p-r*	*Case2*	*Case 3*	*Case 4*	*Trace Test:* *Case 2*	*Case3*	*Case4*
0	4	0.3649	0.3639	0.4225	61.00*	54.30*	79.84*
1	3	0.2927	0.2855	0.3631	35.58*	28.97*	49.09*
2	2	0.1621	0.1614	0.2413	16.19	10.14	23.83
3	1	0.1062	0.0051	0.1387	6.29	0.29	8.37

Note: The critical values for the selection of rank and deterministic components jointly for different models are given in Hansen and Juselius (1995). 90% critical values were used. * indicates significance at 10% level.

In a sequential search based on the trace statistics using the LR test, i = 2 (i.e. rank = 2) and Case 2 (intercepts in the cointegrating relations) seems to be the best choice in this data set given that the null hypothesis corresponding to this rank-case combination is the first one to be accepted at both 90% and 95% critical values. Thus the selected rank-case combination becomes m_{ij}, i = 2 (rank 2), j = 2 (case 2). This preliminary analysis indicates that there could be a maximum of two cointegrating vectors (rank = 2) and that intercepts be included in the cointegrating relations. This result also indicates that there are no trends in the variables nor in the cointegrating relations. Further probe on the determination of the exact rank follows.

Determination of the rank of the Π matrix

The previous analysis shows that the maximum rank in this model could be r = 2. However, we need to probe further in determining the exact rank of the Π matrix. Table 3 presents the λ_{max} and λ_{Trace} test statistics for the model along with their 90% critical values. This table shows that the null hypothesis of r (Π) = 0 is clearly rejected by both the λ_{max} and λ_{Trace} test statistics at the 10% significance level. The null hypothesis that r (Π) = 1 is also rejected by the two test statistics. But the null hypothesis that r (Π) = 2 couldn't be rejected by the two test statistics. So, it is be concluded that there are two co-integrating vectors (r = 2) in the VAR system. This result confirms our previous conclusion based on joint determination of rank and deterministic components. This result on optimal rank is used in conducting further empirical analysis in the paper.

Table 3
Determination of the Rank of the Π Matrix

Eigenvalues (λ_i)	λ_{max} *statistic*	λ_{Trace} *statistic*	*Null Hyp: Ho: r*	*critical value* λ_{max} *(90)*	*critical value* λ_{trace} *(90)*
0.3649	25.42*	61.00	0	18.03*	49.91
0.2927	19.39*	35.58	1	14.09*	31.88
0.1621	9.91	16.19	2	10.29	17.79
0.1062	6.29	6.29	3	7.50	7.50

Note: * indicates significance at 10% level.

Residual Analysis

Given the above selection of two co-integrating vectors and the deterministic components model (intercepts in the co-integrating relations), diagnostic tests on the residuals from all the endogenous variables in the VAR system are presented in Table 4. This table reports some descriptive statistics as well as several univariate tests on the residuals of all the endogenous variables. The descriptive statistics include the mean, standard deviation, Skewness, and kurtosis measures of the residuals from each equation of the VAR system. The two univariate tests on the residuals are: (a) the LM (Lagrange Multiplier) tests on residuals obtained for each of the equations of the VAR system using an ARCH (Autoregressive Conditional Heteroskedasticity) process of appropriate lag order in order to test for the hypotheses that the residuals are uncorrelated and homoskedastic. (b) the second univariate test is the test for normality of the residuals using Doornik-Hansen (1994) version of the Shenton-Bowman (1977) test for each of the equations in the VAR system. This table also reports the R^2 values from each equation in the system.

Table 4
Diagnostic Tests on the Residuals

Variables	*Mean*	*St. Dev.*	*Skewness*	*Kurtosis*	*Normality*	*ARCH(2)*	*R-squared*
Δ LM	0.01	0.12	-0.92	5.07	8.78	1.35	0.59
Δ LPMCPI	-0.02	0.07	0.57	4.93	9.96	4.31	0.15
Δ LIP	0.01	0.06	1.03	6.81	16.94	0.46	0.68
Δ LIRY	0.02	0.21	-0.29	2.95	0.62	3.38	0.28

Notes: or ARCH (2), the critical value at the 5% level with 2 degrees of freedom is 5.99. (ii) For normality, the critical value at the 5% significance level is 15.507.

The descriptive statistics show mean values to be close to zero and reasonably low standard deviations for all variables. There appears to be some Skewness in the data which appears to be positive for LPMCPI and LIP variables whereas negative Skewness for LMR and LIRY variables. Excess Kurtosis appears in LMR, LPMCPI, and LIP variables. These results indicate that the residuals from each equation may not follow a normal distribution. The univariate Doornik-Hansen normality tests reported in this table provide evidence of deviations from normality for the LIP variable only (evaluated at the 5% level of significance). This deviation from normality, however, does not render the co-integration tests invalid. Similar deviations from normality were observed by Johansen and Juselius in two of their empirical papers (1990; and 1992).

For carrying out the cointegration analysis, a more important issue is whether the residuals are uncorrelated and homoskedastic. These are tested by the LM tests on the ARCH(2) process and are test results are given in Table 4. The order of 2 for the ARCH process is determined by the optimal lag structure which was earlier determined to be of order $k^* = 2$. The LM tests on each equation suggest that the residuals are uncorrelated as well as homoskedastic in all the equations of the VAR system. Based on this result, one can proceed with the interpretation of the co-integration test results as follows.

Estimated Long-run Relations and Short-run Dynamics

Based on the existence of two co-integrating vectors, the vector which resembles most closely to the import demand function estimated by the Johansen-Juselius maximum likelihood (ML) method (normalized on LM) is presented in Table 5. It also reports the χ^2 statistics for long-run exclusionary restrictions on each of the explanatory variables of the model (see also Table 6, section II). These statistics can be used to make inferences about the significance of the different explanatory variables in the import demand equation. The results show that the null hypothesis of long-run zero restriction is rejected for all the variables at 5% significance level except the constant term which can be rejected at the 10% level. These likelihood ratio test results indicate that all explanatory variables are significant and be included in the import function in Bangladesh.

Based on the estimated coefficients reported in Table 5, the long-run equilibrium import demand function is given by the following equation (written in explicit form):

Table 5
ML Estimates of the Co-integrating Vector (Normalized on LM)

Variables	*Co-integrating vector (β)*	χ^2 *(1)*	*5% Critical Value:* χ^2 *(1)*
LM	1.00	—	—
LPMCPI	0.401	4.11**	3.84
LIP	-1.833	3.87**	3.84
IIRY	0.542	11.65**	3.84
CONSTANT	-0.360	3.78	3.84

Notes: χ^2(1) statistics are derived by imposing exclusionary restrictions on corresponding explanatory variables (β); (ii) Constants were not included in the cointegration space during the estimation of the cointegrating vector (β). (iii) ** indicates significance at 5% level.

Table 6
LR Tests for Stationarity, Long-run Exclusion, and Weak Exogeneity

I: TEST FOR STATIONARITY: LR TEST CHISQ (pr)

Rank	*DGF*	*CHISQ(5%)*	*LM*	*LPMCPI*	*LIP*	*LIRY*
1	4	9.49	18.73	18.53	18.75	13.74
2	3	7.81	12.76	12.58	12.82	10.83
3	2	5.99	3.95	3.66	3.91	7.88

II: TEST FOR EXCLUSION: LR TEST CHISQ (r)

Rank	*DGF*	*CHISQ(5%)*	*LM*	*LPMCPI*	*LIP*	*LIRY*	*CONST*
1	1	3.84	1.95	0.74	2.47	4.79	0.00
2	2	5.99	11.19	4.11	3.87	11.65	3.78
3	3	7.81	14.45	7.58	7.14	15.24	7.01

III: TEST FOR WEAKEXOGENEITY: LR TEST CHISQ (r)

Rank	*DGF*	*CHISQ(5%)*	*LM*	*LPMCPI*	*LIP*	*LIRY*
1	1	3.84	0.01	0.09	4.96	4.51
2	2	5.99	4.01	0.16	5.32	11.81
3	3	7.81	7.46	0.76	7.36	13.57

Note: *** indicates significance at 1% level

$$LM = 0.360 + 1.833 \text{ LIP} - 0.401 \text{ LPMCPI} - 0.542 \text{ LIRY} \quad (12)$$

The elasticity coefficient of the LIP variable is positive; it also exceeds unity. This value clearly indicates that imports are "normal" as well as a "luxury" goods for this country. This result is consistent with the that reported by Emran and Shilpi (1996) and Goldstein-Khan (1985) for different countries. Using annual time series data and real GDP as the scale variable, Emran and Shilpi (1996) obtained a similar large elasticity coefficient (1.58) for Bangladesh. Goldstein-Khan reported that the income elasticity coefficient varies from 1.0 to 2.0 for the advanced industrialized countries in the world. This observed large elasticity coefficient for this country is not surprising given that the residents in many developing countries like Bangladesh tend to emulate the conspicuous consumption patterns observed in the advanced industrialized countries. The need for these luxury consumption goods are normally met through imports. It is clear from this result that at least a significant part of total imports in this country can be considered as luxury goods.

The elasticity coefficient of –0.401 associated with the relative price variable shows the expected negative sign but it is less than unity (inelastic). This result is consistent with the result reported by Emran and Shilpi (1996) and Goldstein-Khan (1985) for different countries. The former reported a value of –0.23 for Bangladesh using annual data and Goldstein-Khan reported values ranging from –0.50 to –1.0 for different industrialized countries in the world.

In a country like Bangladesh where the foreign exchange market is not well-developed and the exchange rate is institutionally controlled, one would expect the LIRY variable to have a positive effect on import demand. However, contrary to this expectation and contradicting the findings reported in Emran and Shilpi (1986), this variable came out with an unexpected negative sign. Initially, we suspected that this result may have been caused by the multicollinearity problem. However, an examination of the correlation matrix shows that the simple correlation coefficient between LIP and LPMCPI was only -0.25, between LIP and LIRY was 0.15, and between LIRY and LPMCPI was -0.26. Therefore, we concluded that multicollinearity could not be an explanation for this unexpected sign.

We went on to investigate further whether the unexpected result could be due to the use of the cointegration technique instead of the standard regression method. We conducted this probe by re-estimating equation (6) by the standard regression method as well as the Engle-Granger two step cointegration method. This exercise is expected to give us a comparison of different results obtained by different methods. These results are reported in Table 7. Columns (2) and (3) of this table give the standard regression results for the equilibrium and disequilibrium versions with correction for first order autocorrelation when appropriate. The fourth column gives results based on the Engle-Granger two step method and the last column reproduces the results obtained earlier from Johansen-Juselius cointegration method.

An examination of these results show that the coefficient of the relative price variable came out with the negative sign and statistically significant in all different estimation methods. However, the LIP variable had the appropriate sign and significance in only the Johansen-Juselius cointegration method. This coefficient came out with the unexpected negative sign in all other methods. With respect to the LIRY variable, it was not satisfactory in any method.

Note that when the variables are non-stationary, the conventional "t" and F tests are not meaningful. More specifically, the Engle-Granger results cannot be evaluated by the conventional test statistics. This equation can be evaluated by the ADF and the Phillips-Perron tests on the residuals from this equation. If the residuals are found to be stationary, then we could conclude that there is a long-run equilibrium relationship among these variables. This was indeed the case as the null hypothesis of unit root could be rejected for residuals based on both ADF and Phillips-Perron tests (see Table 7, the last two rows corresponding the Engle-Granger two-step regression).Although this method shows evidence of cointegration confirming the Johansen-Juselius results, the sign and magnitude of most of the coefficients did not turn out to be satisfactory. Note that the significance of the coefficients obtained from the Johansen-Juselius method were evaluated based on the likelihood ratio test as described earlier.

Table 7
Standard Regression, Engle-Granger (EG) and Johansen-Juselius (JJ) Estimates

Variables	*Standard: Equilibrium model*	*Standard: Disequilibrium. model.*	*Engle-Granger: Equilibrium model*	*Johansen-Juselius: Equilibrium model*
CONS.	10.07***	5.42***	9.76***	0.36*
	(7.04)	(2.73)	(6.67)	
LPMCPI	0.51***	-0.27***	-0.53***	-0.40**
	(4.04)	(-2.41)	(-6.55)	
LIP	-0.22	-0.07	-0.12	1.83**
	(-0.86)	(-0.27)	(-0.45)	
LIRY	-0.001	0.02	-0.06	-0.54***
	(-0.01)	(0.37)	(-1.0)	
LM(-1)		0.42***		
		(3.12)		
AR(1)	0.43***			
	(3.08)			
R^2	0.63	0.62	0.56	
Adjusted R^2	0.60	0.59	0.54	
F	21.89***	20.84***	23.05***	
DW	2.27	2.21	1.15	
ADF Test			-2.96***	
PP Test			-4.87***	

Notes: (1) t-values are given in parentheses below the coefficients; (2) *** significance at 1% level; (3) ** significance at 5% level; and (4) * significance at 10% level; (5) Engle-Granger equation is evaluated by the ADF and the Phillips-Perron test; and (6) JJ estimates are reproduced from table 5; Likelihood Ratio test is used in determining significance of these coefficients.

This comparison clearly indicates that the Johansen-Juselius cointegration method gave the best possible results in this study, a result which is expected because of the superiority of this technique over the other methods. Therefore, these results are considered to be robust and more reliable. The standard regression results are nothing but spurious.

Looking at the short-run dynamics, the results reported in Table 8 show that the speed of adjustment coefficient is -0.39 for the import demand function. This coefficients has the correct negative sign and it is statistically significant at 1% level. The absolute value of this coefficient being less than unity indicates stability of the short-run import demand function. Further, the magnitude of the coefficient seems to be reasonable. Thus, based on this coefficient, we can conclude that the short-run import demand function for Bangladesh is stable and that about 39% of any deviation of the import demand from its long-run equilibrium path is corrected within a quarter.

Likelihood Ratio Tests of Linear Restrictions

Three hypothesis tests based on linear restrictions on the co-integrating vector were conducted in this study. The likelihood ratio test statistics are reported in Table 9. The first hypothesis ($H_0 1$) tested is that of proportionality between industrial production (a proxy for income) and import demand. This hypothesis of proportionality is clearly rejected by the data. The second

Table 8
Short-run Dynamics and The Speed of Adjustment

Variables	*Speed of adjustment*	*t-values*
ΔLM	-0.391***	-2.96
ΔLPMCPI	0.027	0.37
ΔLIP	-0.155**	-2.35
ΔLIRY	0.043	0.19

Notes: *** indicates significance at 1% and ** indicates significance at 5% level.

Table 9
Likelihood Ratio Tests on Linear Restrictions on β

$H_0$1: The LR test:	CHISQ(2) = 14.39***,	pvalue = 0.01
$H_0$2: The LR test:	CHISQ(2) = 3.78***,	pvalue = 0.15
$H_0$3: The LR test:	CHISQ(4) = 19.04***,	pvalue = 0.00

Notes: (1)DGF is degrees of freedom; (2) LR stands for Likelihood Ratio; (3) CHISQ is the theoretical value of ÷ ².

hypothesis is that the import price and the domestic price indices have coefficients which are equal in magnitude but opposite in sign. The likelihood ratio test suggests that this hypothesis could not be rejected. This result supports the traditional specification of using the ratio of import price to domestic price as a composite variable in the import demand function. The third hypothesis tested is the joint restriction that industrial production and import demand are proportional and that the nominal import price and domestic price indices have coefficients which are equal but opposite in sign. This joint hypothesis is clearly rejected by the test statistic for the import demand function. This result is not surprising given the rejection of the first hypothesis.

Finally, we also tested for the hypothesis that the explanatory variables are weakly exogenous. The likelihood ratio test statistics under the null hypothesis that the relevant variables are weakly exogenous are reported in Table 6 (section III). For the selected rank r=2 and evaluated at 5% level of significance, the likelihood ratio tests statistics could not reject the null hypothesis of weak exogeneity for the relative price (LPMCPI) and the industrial production (LIP) variables, while it rejected the null hypothesis for the foreign exchange constraint (LIRY) variable.

CONCLUSIONS

In this paper, we estimated the income and price elasticities of import demand function for Bangladesh under foreign exchange constraints using cointegration techniques. Quarterly time series data were used in the estimation process. Various hypothesis tests were conducted within the Johansen-Juselius cointegration framework. Cointegration results indicate that the import demand function in Bangladesh is strongly dominated by both income (industrial production) and the relative price variables. This result is quite consistent with the conventional demand theory.

The elasticity coefficient with respect to production (income) was found to be highly elastic indicating that imports are both "normal" goods and "luxury" goods for Bangladesh. One implication of this result is that the demand for imports is expected rise faster than the progress of the economy. As a consequence, the share of imports in GDP is likely to increase over time. The relative price elasticity, however, was found to be moderately inelastic. This implies that imports are not very price sensitive for Bangladesh. The implication of this result is that the trade and exchange rate policies may not be as effective in regulating imports and hence reducing trade deficits as generally believed by policy makers.

Test on linear restriction on the coefficients clearly rejects the hypothesis of proportionality between industrial production and imports while the hypothesis that import price and domestic price have coefficients which are equal in magnitude but opposite in sign could not be rejected. Further, the analysis of the short-run dynamics indicate that the short-run import demand function is stable and it normally adjusts to its long-run equilibrium path with a reasonable speed. It is to be noted that the variable representing the foreign exchange constraint came out with an unexpected negative sign. One possible explanation of this result might be that the ratio of international reserve to GDP did not serve as a good proxy for the foreign exchange availability constraint. Therefore, this result does not necessarily negate the importance of this constraint for Bangladesh. Further investigation of this issue in future studies is thus warranted.

Finally, a comparison of the Johansen-Juselius cointegration results with the standard regression estimates and the Engle-Granger two-step cointegration estimates clearly indicate the superiority of the former estimates. The empirical results found in this study are therefore arguably more reliable than those reported in most previous studies with the exception of Emran and Shilpi (1996) which was based on annual data.

Notes

1. Bangladesh achieved political independence from Pakistan in 1971 through a bloody war of independence lasting from March 1970 to December 1971.
2. For an excellent discussion on the import demand functions in developed countries, see Barker (1976), Boylan, Cuddy and O'Muircheartaigh (1980), Goldstein and Khan (1985), Khan and Ross (1977), Murray and Ginman (1975), Stern, Francis and Schumacher (1976), Thursby (1988), Thursby and Thursby (1984), among others.
3. For an elaborate discussion of the import demand functions for developing countries, see Emran and Shilpi (1996), Hemphill (1974), Khan (1974), Moran (1989), Sarmad (1988; 1989), Shilpi (1990) , among others.
4. For studies on Bangladesh, see Shilpi (1990), Emran and Shilpi (1996), and Dutta and Ahmed (1999).
5. The quarterly data on GDP is not available in Bangladesh. However, we needed this variable in order to calculate the ratio of foreign exchange to GDP (Z). A quarterly series for this variable, however, was obtained from Mr. A. Kashem, an officer of the Research Department of the Bangladesh Bank, the central bank of this country. He has compiled this quarterly series using an interpolation techniques.
6. Johansen and Juselius (1992) used stationary domestic and foreign inflation rate variables in their cointegration model for explaining Purchasing Power Parity theory for the U.K. These two stationary variables were included in the cointegrating vector along with the other non-stationary variables.
7. These tables are not reported here because of space limitation; however, they can be obtained from the author upon request.

References

Arestis, P. and G. Hadjimatheou (1982), *Introducing Macroeconomic Modeling*, London: The Macmillan Press.

Barker, T. (1976), "The Determinants of Britain's Visible Imports, 1946-1966: A Program for Growth" in Stern, Francis and Schumacher (eds.), *Price Elasticities in International Trade*, London: The Macmillan Press.

Boylan, T.A., M.P. Cuddy and I. O'Muircheartaigh (1980), "The Functional Form for Aggregate Import Demand Equation" *Journal of International Economics*, v. 10, pp. 561-566.

Buckler, M. and C. Almon (1976), "Imports and Exports in an Input-Output Model", in Stern, Francis and Schumacher (eds.). *Price Elasticities in International Trade*, London: The Macmillan Press.

Caves, R., J. Frankel, J. and R. Jones (1990), *World Trade and Payments*, New York, Harper Collins Publishers.

Dickey, D.A. and W.A. Fuller (1979), "Distribution of the Estimates for Autoregressive Time Series with a Unit Root", *J. of the American Statistical Association*, v. 74, June, pp. 427-31.

Doornik, J.A. and H. Hansen (1994), "An Omnibus Test for Univariate and Multivariate Normality", Working Paper, Nuffield College, Oxford.

Emran, M.S. and F. Shilpi (1996), "Foreign Exchange Rationing and the Aggregate Import Demand Function", *Economics Letters*, vol. 51, pp. 315-322.

Engle, R.F. (1982), "Autoregressive Conditional Heteroskedasticity with Estimates of the Variance of U.K. Inflation", *Econometrica*, Vol. 50, pp. 987-1007.

Engle, Robert F. And C.W.J. Granger (1987), "Co-Integration and Error Correction: Representation, Estimation, and Testing", *Econometrica*, Vol. 55, n.2 , March, pp. 251-76.

Goldstein, M. And M. Khan (1985), "Income and Price Effects in Foreign Trade", in R.W. Jones and B.B. Kenen (eds.), *Handbook of International Economics*, Elsevier, Amsterdam, pp. 1041-1105.

Granger, C.W.J. and P. Newbold (1974), "Spurious Regressions in Econometrics", *Journal of Econometrics* , Vol. 2, n. 1, pp. 111120.

Hansen, H. and K. Juselius (1995), *CATS in RATS: Cointegration Analysis of Time Series*, Evanston, Illinois: Estima Inc.

Hemphill, W. (1974), "The Effects of Foreign Exchange Receipts on Imports of Less Developed Countries", *IMF Staff Papers*, Vol. 21, pp. 637-677.

International Monetary Fund (1999), *International Financial Statistics*, various issues, Washington, D.C.

Johansen, S. (1988), "Statistical Analysis of Cointegration Vectors", *Journal of Economic Dynamics and Control*, Vol. 12, pp. 231-54.

Johansen, S. (1991), "Estimation and Hypothesis Testing of Co-integration Vectors in Gaussian Vector Autoregressive Models", *Econometrica*, Vol. 59, Nov., pp. 1551-1580.

Johansen, S. (1992), "Determination of the Cointegration Rank in the Presence of a Linear Trend", *Oxford Bulletin of Economics and Statistics*, Vol. 54, pp. 383-397.

Johansen, S., and K. Juselius. (1990), "Maximum Likelihood Estimation and Inference on Co-integration with Applications to Demand for Money", *Oxford Bulletin of Econ. & Statistics*, Vol. 52, May, pp. 169-210.

Johansen, S. and K. Juselius (1992), "Testing Structural Hypothesis in a Multivariate Co-integration Analysis of the PPP and the UIP for UK", *Journal of Econometrics*, Vol. 53, May, pp. 211 244.

Khan, M.S. (1974), "Import and Export Demands in Developing Countries", *IMF Staff Papers*, Nov. , pp. 678-693.

Khan, M., M. Rahman, and A. Islam (1997), "Tariff Cuts and Net U.S. Benefits: The Case of the U.S. and Mexico." *Applied Economics*, 29, pp. 1509-1514.

Khan, M.S. and K.Z. Ross (1977), "The Functional Form of the Aggregate Demand Equation", *Journal of International Economics,* Vol. 7, pp. 149-160.

Leamer, E.E. and R.M. Stern (1970), *Quantitative International Economics*, Allyn and Bacon, Inc., Boston.

Maddala, G.S. (1992), *Introduction to Econometrics,* 2nd ed. Macmillan, New York.

Moran, C. (1989), "Imports Under a foreign Exchange Constraint", *The World Bank Economic Review*, Vol.. 3, pp. 279-295.

Murray, T and P. Ginman (1976), "'An Empirical Examination of the Traditional Aggregate Import Demand Model", *Review of Economics and Statistics*, Vol. 58, pp. 75-80.

Phillips, P., and P. Perron. (1988), "Testing for a Unit Root in Time Series Regression", *Biometrika*, Vol.. 75, June, pp. 335-346.

Sarmad, K. (1988), "The Functional Form of the Aggregate Demand Equation: Evidence from Developing Countries", *The Pakistan Development Review*, Vol. 28, pp. 309-315.

Sarmad, K. (1989), "The Determinants of Import Demand in Pakistan", *World Development*, Vol. 17, pp. 1619-1625.

Shenton, L.R. and K.O. Bowman (1977), "A Bivariate Model for the Distribution of b1 and b2", *Journal of the American Statistical Association*, Vol. 72, pp. 206-211.

Shilpi, F.J. (1990), "Estimating Income and Price Elasticities of Imports and Exports of Bangladesh", Research report No. 122, Bangladesh Institute of Development Studies, Dhaka, Bangladesh, Dec.

Stern, R.M., J. Francis and B. Schumacher (eds.) (1976), *Price Elasticities in International Trade*, London: The Macmillan Press.

Szenberg, M., J. Lombardi, and E. Lee (1977), *Welfare Effects of Trade Restrictions: A Case Study of the U.S. Footwear Industry*, New York: Academic Press.

Thursby, J. (1988), "Evaluation of Coefficients in Misspecified Regressions with Applications to Import Demand", *Review of Economics and Statistics*, Vol.. 70, n. 4, Nov., pp. ??.

Thursby, J. and M. Thursby (1984), "How Reliable are Simple Equation Specifications of Import Demand?", *Review of Economics and Statistics*, v. 66, pp. 120-128.

DISTRIBUTION AND GROWTH IN AN ECONOMY WITH HETEROGENEOUS CAPITAL AND EXCESS CAPACITY

*Theodore Mariolis**

Abstract

In a world of heterogeneous capital the aggregate capital-capacity ratio can change in a complicated way as the real wage rate changes and, therefore, nothing useful can be said, a priori, about the relationships between the real wage rate (or the aggregate profit share), the degree of capacity utilization and the rates of profit, capital accumulation and interest.

Key words: *Aggregate capital-capacity ratio, Capacity utilization, Heterogeneous capital, Post-Keynesian theory, Sraffian theory.*

JEL Classifications: *D57, E11, E12.*

INTRODUCTION

In modern post-Keynesian theory (in the tradition of Kalecki-Steindl) the interaction of changes in income distribution and effective demand holds centre stage. In this approach, and contrary to the standard growth theories, the redistribution of income 'has complex, even ambiguous, effect on the level of employment and output' (Bhaduri and Marglin, 1990, p. 375) or, what amounts to the same thing, the interactions between the real wage rate (or the aggregate profit share) and the rates of capacity utilization, profit and capital accumulation are not necessarily monotonic (*ibid.*, pp. 380-4); furthermore, a 'bad income distribution' can be a cause of stagnation (Dutt, 1984).[1]

Sraffian theory, on the other hand, begins with the placement of the produced means of production at the centre of the analysis. Thus, one of the key findings is that in a world of heterogeneous capital goods the traditional neoclassical statements about the relationships between the distribution of income, long-period commodity prices and technical conditions of production are not verified and/or make no sense. In this regard a change in the real wage rate has no longer unambiguous effects on the capital-labour and capital-capacity ratios.[2]

The objective of this paper is to assess the consequences of the presence of heterogeneous capital goods in a system, in which (i) the rates of profit and capacity utilization are uniform; and (ii) the desired rate of capital accumulation is a strictly increasing function of both the degree of capacity utilization and the aggregate profit share.[3] It then follows that the aggregate capital-capacity ratio enters into the determination of the equilibrium between investment and

---

* Department of Public Administration, Panteion University, Athens, Greece, *E-mail: mariolis@panteion.gr*

I am indebted to lefteris Tsoulfidis for helpful discussions and comments on an earlier version of this paper.

savings and, therefore, nothing unambiguous can be said, *a priori*, about the directions of change in the rates of capacity utilization, profit and accumulation when the real wage rate (or, alternatively, the aggregate profit share) changes.

The remainder of the paper is organized as follows. The next section presents a basic model for a multi-sector closed economy with excess capacity of capital, which includes a 'classical savings function'. In our effort to investigate the role of heterogeneous capital we employ rather extremely restrictive assumptions. Thus the analysis is more in the nature of an *exercise*, rather than the formulation of a complete framework. The following section allows for alternative savings assumptions. The final section concludes.

THE BASIC MODEL

Consider a closed economy with excess capacity, which produces many basic commodities (*à la* Sraffa, 1960, pp. 7-8) by linear processes of single production. We further assume that input coefficients are fixed, homogeneous labour is the only primary input and capital goods do not depreciate. There are only two classes, workers, employed in proportion to the level of production, *i.e.*, there is no supplementary or 'overhead' labour, and capitalists, and two kinds of income, wages and profits. Wages are paid at the end of the common production period and there are no savings out of this income, whilst a given and constant fraction of profits, s_p ($0 < s_p \leq 1$), is saved. The growth of the economy is not constrained by the availability of labour. Both within each sector and between the sectors there is a uniform degree of capacity utilization, u ($0 < u \leq 1$), which gives the ratio of actual output to potential output, where the latter is taken to be proportional to the capital stocks in existence. Competitive conditions are taken to be close to free competition. This allows us to interpret the underutilization of productive capacity as caused essentially by an insufficient effective demand (Kurz, 1995, pp. 96-7; see also Kurz, 1994, Sections 3 and 6). The desired rate of accumulation is a strictly increasing function of both the degree of capacity utilization and the aggregate profit share. Finally, we ignore entirely questions of technological change and questions of government expenditure and taxation.[4]

On the basis of these assumptions, we may write the following system of relations:

$$\mathbf{p} = \mathbf{pA}(r/u) + w\mathbf{a} \tag{1}$$

$$\mathbf{pb} = 1 \tag{2}$$

$$\mathbf{x} = \mathbf{Ax}(g^S/u) + c\mathbf{b} \tag{3}$$

$$\mathbf{ax} \equiv 1 \tag{4}$$

$$g^S \equiv S/K = s_p r\,,\; K \equiv \mathbf{pAx}(1/u) \tag{5}$$

$$g^I = F(u,h); F(\mathbf{0}) \geq 0, F_x \equiv (\partial F/\partial x) > 0, x = u,h \tag{6}$$

$$h \equiv 1-(w/\mathbf{px}) = vr/u, \quad v \equiv \mathbf{pAx}/\mathbf{px} \tag{7}$$

$$g^I = g^S \tag{8}$$

$$(s_p h/v) > F_u \tag{9}$$

where **p** denotes the vector of commodity prices, **A** the irreducible matrix of capital coefficients, **a** the vector of labour input coefficients, r the uniform rate of profit, w the uniform money wage rate, **b** a given vector representing the uniform consumption pattern, **x** the vector of outputs per unit of labour, g^S the actual rate of capital accumulation, determined by the amount of savings, S, K the total savings and value of capital stocks per unit of labour, respectively, c the index of consumption per unit of labour, g^I the desired rate of capital accumulation, $F(\bullet)$ a continuous function, h the aggregate profit share, and v the aggregate capital-capacity ratio. Equation (2) fixes the standard of value or *numéraire*. Hence w also symbolizes the level of the real wage rate. Equation (6) defines an investment function. Equation (8) defines the commodities market equilibrium. Finally, relation (9) gives the short-run Keynesian stability condition for the $g^I - g^S$ equilibria (*i.e.*, total savings must increase by more than investment demand when (u rises).

It is quite clear that the system has one degree of freedom. From (1) and (2), *i.e.*, the 'price side' of the system, we obtain

$$\mathbf{p} = w\mathbf{aB}(r/u), \mathbf{B}(r/u) \equiv [\mathbf{I} - \mathbf{A}(r/u)]^{-1} \tag{10}$$

and

$$w = [\mathbf{aB}(r/u)\mathbf{b}]^{-1} \tag{11}$$

where **I** is the identity matrix, and each element in **B** (r/u) is homogeneous of degree zero, positive and increases with r/u, tending to infinity as r/u approaches its maximum feasible value, λ^{-1} (λ denotes the Perron-Frobenius eigenvalue of **A**). Thus equation (11) defines a strictly decreasing '$w-(r/u)$ frontier' for this economy. From equations (3) and (4), *i.e.*, the 'quantity side' of the system, we obtain

$$\mathbf{x} = c\mathbf{B}(g^S/u)\mathbf{b}, \mathbf{B}(g^S/u) \equiv [\mathbf{I} - \mathbf{A}(g^S/u)]^{-1} \tag{12}$$

and

$$c = [\mathbf{aB}(g^S/u)\mathbf{b}]^{-1} \tag{13}$$

where each element in $\mathbf{B}(g^S/u)$ is homogeneous of degree zero, positive and increases with g^S/u, tending to infinity as g^S/u approaches its maximum feasible value, λ^{-1}. Thus equation (13) defines a strictly decreasing '$c-(g^S/u)$ frontier' for this economy. Furthermore, equations (5), (7) and (10)-(13) imply that the aggregate capital-capacity ratio, v, is a complicated expression involving r/u, s_p and technical conditions, that is,

$$v = [\mathbf{aB}(r/u)\mathbf{AB}(s_p r/u)\mathbf{b}][\mathbf{aB}(r/u)\mathbf{B}(s_p r/u)\mathbf{b}]^{-1} \tag{14}$$

Nevertheless, given that $h = vr/u$ and that h is a strictly increasing function of r/u (see Franke, 1999, pp. 46-9, where $u = 1$ holds, by assumption), it follows that (i) $0 < vr/u < 1$ for $0 < r/u < \lambda^{-1}$, and $v = \lambda$ at $r/u = \lambda^{-1}$; (ii) the elasticity of v with respect to r/u is greater than -1; and (iii) the elasticity of v with respect to h is less than 1. Finally, the equality between investment and savings from equations (5)-(8) implies

$$F(u,h) = s_p hu/v \tag{15}$$

and, recalling (9), the local slope of the '*IS* – curve' in $u \times h$ space is given as

$$du/dh = \{[F_h - (s_p u/v)] + (e_v F(\bullet)/h)\}[(s_p h/v) - F_u]^{-1} \tag{16}$$

or

$$du/dh = [F_h - (1-e_v)(s_p u/v)][(s_p h/v) - F_u]^{-1} \tag{16a}$$

where e_v represents the elasticity of v with respect to h. Thus, equation (15) defines a non monotonic, in the general case, '*IS* – curve' for this economy.

Given w from outside the system, (10) and (11) determine a unique solution for ($\mathbf{p}$, r/u). Hence (5), (12) and (13) determine a unique solution for ($\mathbf{x}$, c), (7) determines (v,h), and (15) determines a unique equilibrium value of u. Nevertheless, it is impossible to make any *a priori* prediction concerning the effects of a variation in w on the equilibrium values of u, r and g^S. More specifically, (16) indicates that the movement of the degree of capacity utilization, as a result of a change in the distributive variable, *i.e.*, the wage rate or the aggregate profit share, can be decomposed into the following two distinct effects: (i) the relative response of investment and savings, represented by the term $[F_h - (s_p u/v)]$; and (ii) the response of the aggregate capital-capacity ratio, represented by the term $(e_v F(\bullet)/h)$. Thus, when investment responds relatively weakly (strongly) to changes in h, *i.e.*, $F_h < (s_p u/v)$ ($F_h > (s_p u/v)$), u *may* rise (fall) due to the fact that $e_v >$ (<)0. Differentiation of $r = hu/v$ with respect to h gives

$$dr/dh = (1 - e_v + e_u)(u/v) \tag{17}$$

where e_u represents the elasticity of the '*IS* - curve', or, recalling (16a),

$$dr/dh = [hF_h - uF_u(1-e_v)](1/v)[(s_p h/v) - F_u]^{-1} \tag{17a}$$

Since $e_v < 1$, it follows that $e_u \geq 0$ implies $dr/dh > 0$. However, neither an elastic, negatively sloped '*IS* – curve', *i.e.*, $e_u < -1$ or, equivalently, $hF_h - uF_u < -e_v s_p r$, nor $hF_h < uF_u$, which implies that the elasticity of the desired rate of accumulation with respect to h is less than its elasticity with respect to u, necessarily imply $dr/dh < 0$.[5]

From (7), (9), $e_v < 1$, (16a) and (17a) we may derive the following conclusions:

(i) The model is capable of generating three alternative sets of steady-state equilibria or 'growth regimes':[6] A 'regime of overaccumulation', characterised by $du/dh < 0$ and $dr/dh > 0$, prevails when

$$uF_u(1-e_v) < hF_h < (1-e_v)s_p r \tag{18}$$

A 'regime of underconsumption', characterised by $du/dh < 0$ and $dr/dh < 0$, prevails when

$$hF_h < uF_u(1-e_v) \tag{19}$$

A 'Keynesian regime', characterised by $du/dh > 0$ and $dr/dh > 0$, prevails when

$$(1-e_v)s_p r < hF_h \tag{20}$$

(ii) *Even with* a linear investment function, the effects of a redistribution of income (or of a change in s_p) on the rates of capacity utilization, profit and accumulation are neither known *a priori* nor independent of the initial state of the system. Moreover, nothing rules out the 'reswitching' of growth regimes (see Mariolis, 2004, p. 176, for a pertinent numerical example).

(iii) As is well known, the validity of $e_v = 0$ cannot, in general, be extended beyond a quasi-one-commodity system, that is, the cases in which **a** or **b** is the Perron-Frobenius eigenvector of **A**, and thus $v = \lambda$ (see, *e.g.*, Marglin, 1984, pp. 240-4). Consequently, it must be said that the great complexity of a multi-sector system is due, in the final analysis, to the fact that the aggregate capital-capacity ratio is not given independent of, and prior to, the determination of prices, distribution and growth.

SOME EXTENSIONS

In this section we shall extend the argument to the following cases: (i) there are savings out of wages; (ii) there is a rentier class; and (iii) workers save.

Savings out of Wages

Assume that a given and constant fraction of wages, s_w $(0 < s_w < s_p)$, is saved. Then (5), (9), (16) and (17a) become

$$S/K = s_p r + s_w(w/K)$$

or

$$g^S = (s_p - s_w)r + s_w(u/v) \tag{21}$$

$$A > F_u \tag{22}$$

$$du/dh = [F_h - (s_p - s_w)(u/v) + e_v(Au/h)](A - F_u)^{-1} \tag{23}$$

Thus it follows that when investment 'is hardly affected by the interest rate and the propensity to save out of interest income is relatively low, there may arise regimes of accumulation with positive responses throughout the rates of capacity utilization, accumulation and profit to an increasing interest rate' (Hein, 1999, p. 15). Furthermore, given i, a 'Keynesian regime' prevails iff

$$C \equiv a_1 a_2 \lambda + (a_0 + Bzi)s_p < 0 \tag{31}$$

whilst a 'regime of underconsumption' prevails when $e_u < -1$, namely

$$(s_p h/\lambda a_1) - 1 < (C/\lambda a_1 a_2)^{1/2} \tag{32}$$

Nevertheless, in a multi-sector system the aggregate capital-capacity ratio depends on u, r and g^S, whilst g^S is related to r and to i by (26). Thus nothing useful can be said, *a priori*, about the directions of change in u, r and the rate of accumulation when i (or h) changes.

Finally, the long-run equilibrium is defined as one in which z remains constant over time. Since the percentage rate of growth of the stocks of loans equals $s_R i$, it follows that

$$\dot{z} = (s_R i - g^S)\, z \tag{33}$$

where $\dot{z}$ denotes the first derivative of z with respect to time. Let us first consider a quasi-one-commodity economy. From (27), (29) and (33) we obtain the equation of motion for z:

$$\dot{z} = D_1 z + D_2 z^2 \tag{34}$$

where

$$D_1 \equiv s_R i - a_0 - a_2 h - a_1(a_0 + a_2 h)[s_p(h/\lambda) - a_1]^{-1} \tag{34a}$$

and

$$D_2 \equiv a_3 i - a_1 Bi[(s_p h/\lambda) - a_1]^{-1} \tag{34b}$$

The effects of a variation in w (or i) on the equilibrium value $z = -D_1/D_2$, and therefore on the equilibrium values of the rates of capacity utilization, profit and accumulation are vague (see Hein, 2004, pp. 13-20, for a detailed analysis). Nevertheless, in a world of heterogeneous capital, a redistribution of income influences D_1 and D_2 both by changing r/u and by changing the aggregate capital-capacity ratio. Hence there is a further source of ambiguity.

Workers Save

Suppose the same economy as before. But now assume that (i) s_w represents the workers' saving ratio, and thus Z, $0 < Z < K$, represents the amount of capital per unit of labour that the workers own indirectly (through loans to the capitalists; see Pasinetti, 1974, chs 5-6); and (ii) there is no rentier class. Then (21) (or (26)), (22) (or (28)) and (29) become

$$S/K = s_p[r-(Z/K)i]+s_w[(w/K)+(Z/K)i]$$

or

$$g^S = (s_p - s_w)(r - zi) + s_w(u/v) \tag{35}$$

$$A > a_1 \tag{36}$$

$$u = (a_0 + a_2 h + B_1 zi)(A - a_1)^{-1} \tag{37}$$

where $B_1 \equiv s_p - s_w - a_3$. Furthermore, since the percentage rate of growth of the stocks of loans equals $s_w[i+(w/Z)]$, it follows that

$$\dot{z} = (s_w i - g^S)\, z + s_w (1-h)(u/v) \tag{38}$$

From (27), (37) and (38) we obtain the equation of motion for z:

$$\dot{z} = E_0 + E_1 z + E_2 z^2 \tag{39}$$

where

$$E_0 \equiv s_w[(1-h)/v](a_0 + a_2 h)(A - a_1)^{-1} \tag{39a}$$

$$E_1 \equiv s_w i - a_0 - a_2 h - \{a_1(a_0 + a_2 h) - [s_w(1-h)B_1 i/v]\}(A - a_1)^{-1} \tag{39b}$$

and

$$E_2 \equiv a_3 i - a_1 B_1 i (A - a_1)^{-1} \tag{39c}$$

Thus it can be concluded that this case combines the main features of the previous two cases.[9]

CONCLUDING REMARKS

It has been shown that in a simple model for an economy with heterogeneous capital goods and excess capacity the interaction between distribution and growth is a particularly complex phenomenon. Although the sensitivity of the results to the algebraic expression of the investment function and to the assumptions with respect to savings cannot be disregarded, the principal, and totally independent of the observer, reason for the complexity is that the aggregate capital-capacity ratio cannot be treated as a *datum*. And it need hardly be said that this finding casts doubt on the reliability of income redistribution as a macroeconomic policy concerned with removing stagnation.

Taking the robustness of this conclusion as given, future research efforts should, first, examine the possibility of closing the basic model by an endogenous determination of distribution and second, concretize the analysis by considering the existence of 'overhead' labour, depreciation, alternative production methods and technological change, differential rates of capacity utilization and profit, pure joint products, and government fiscal activity.

Notes

1. See also Sherman (1979), Rowthorn (1981), Dutt (1987a, 1990, 2003) and Lavoie (1992). See Commendatore *et al.* (2003) for a survey on (post-) Keynesian theories of growth, and Lavoie (2006) for a review of the so-called heterodox theories.
2. See Sraffa (1960, chs 3 and 6), and Pasinetti (1974, pp. 132-9, 1977, chs 5-7), Marglin (1984, chs 11-12), Panico and Salvadori (1993, p. xx), Kurz and Salvadori (1995, chs 3-6 and 13-15), *inter alia.*
3. This specification of investment function is due to Marglin and Bhaduri (1990, pp. 160-71). See also Bhaduri and Marglin (1990, pp. 379-80) and Kurz (1990, pp. 218-21). See Lavoie *et al.* (2004) for a theoretical and empirical investigation of the issue at hand. For two-sector models, with homogeneous capital, a uniform rate of profit, mark-up pricing and, therefore, differential degrees of capacity utilization, see Dutt (1987b, 1990, ch. 6, 1997) and Lavoie and Ramirez-Gaston (1997).
4. See Rowthorn (1981, pp. 22-30), Kurz (1990, pp. 226-35), Dutt (1990, pp. 105-7) and You and Dutt (1996) for one-commodity models.
5. This is quite different from the case of a one-commodity model, where $e_v = 0$ and, therefore, $e_u < -1$, $hF_h < uF_u$, and $dr / dh < 0$ are equivalent (see Bhaduri and Marglin, 1990, pp. 382-4).
6. The following terminology is due to Kurz (1990, pp. 222-6), whilst for an alternative terminology see Bhaduri and Marglin (1990, pp. 388-9).
7. See Spaventa (1970, pp. 139-41 and 146) and Marglin (1984, ch. 11); in both analyses $u = 1$ holds, by assumption.
8. See Lavoie (1993, 1995), Hein (1999, 2004, 2006), Hein and Ochsen (2003) for a detailed examination of these assumptions and for relevant one-commodity models. See Dutt (1989) for a Marxian/Post-Keynesian one-commodity model with a rentier class.
9. It is worth noting that this model is *formally* similar to a model for an open economy with excess capacity of capital, which includes a 'classical savings function' (see Mariolis, 2006).

References

Bhaduri, A. and Marglin, S. (1990), "Unemployment and the Real Wage Rate: The Economic Basis for Contesting Political Ideologies", *Cambridge Journal of Economics*, Vol. 14, pp. 375-393.

Commendatore, P., D' Acunto, S., Panico, C. and Pinto, A. (2003), "Keynesian Theories of Growth", in N. Salvadori (ed.), *The Theory of Economic Growth. A 'Classsical' Perspective*, pp. 103-138, Cheltenham, Edward Elgar.

Dutt, A. K. (1984), "Stagnation, Income Distribution and Monopoly Power", *Cambridge Journal of Economics*, Vol. 8, pp. 25-40.

Dutt, A. K. (1987a), "Alternative Closures Again: A Comment on 'Growth, Distribution and Inflation'", *Cambridge Journal of Economics*, Vol. 11, pp. 75-82.

Dutt, A. K. (1987b), "Competition, Monopoly Power and the Uniform Rate of Profit", *Review of Radical Political Economics*, Vol. 19, pp. 55-72.

Dutt, A. K. (1989), "Accumulation, Distribution and Inflation in a Marxian/Post-Keynesian Model with a Rentier Class", *Review of Radical Political Economics*, Vol. 21, pp. 18-26.

Dutt, A. K. (1990), *Growth, Distribution and Uneven Development*, Cambridge, Cambridge University Press.

Dutt, A. K. (1997), "Profit-Rate Equalization in the Kalecki-Steindl Model and the 'Over-Determination' Problem", *The Manchester School*, Vol. 65, pp. 443-451.

Dutt, A. K. (2003), "New Growth, Theory Effective Demand, and Post-Keynesian Dynamics", in N. Salvadori (ed.), *Old and New Growth Theories. An Assessment*, pp. 67-100, Cheltenham, Edward Elgar.

Franke, R. (1999), "Technical Change and a Falling Wage Share if Profits are Maintained", *Metroeconomica*, Vol. 50, pp. 35-53.

Hein, E. (1999), "Interest Rates, Income Shares and Investment in a Kaleckian Model", *Political Economy. Review of Political Economy and Social Sciences*, Issue 5, Autumn, pp. 5-22.

Hein, E. (2004), "Interest Rate, Debt, Distribution and Capital Accumulation in a Post-Kaleckian Model", *WSI Discussion Paper*, No. 133.

Hein, E. (2006), "On the (In-) Stability and the Endogeneity of the 'Normal' Rate of Capacity Utilisation in a Post-Keynesian/Kaleckian 'Monetary' Distribution and Growth Model", *Indian Development Review*, Vol. 4, pp. 129-150.

Hein, E., Ochsen, C. (2003), "Regimes of Interest Rates, Income Shares, Savings and Investment: A Kaleckian Model and Empirical Estimations for some Advanced OECD – Economies", *Metroeconomica*, Vol. 54, pp. 404-433.

Kurz, H. D. (1990), "Technical Change, Growth and Distribution: A Steady-State Approach to 'Unsteady' Growth", in H.D. Kurz, *Capital, Distribution and Effective Demand. Studies in the 'Classical' Approach to Economic Theory*, pp. 211-239, Cambridge, Polity Press.

Kurz, H.D. (1994), "Growth and Distribution", *Review of Political Economy*, Vol. 6, pp. 393-420.

Kurz, H.D. (1995), "The Keynesian Project: Tom Asimakopoulos and the 'Other Point of View'", in G.C. Harcourt, A. Roncaglia and R. Rowley (eds), *Income and Employment in Theory and Practice: Essays in memory of Athanasios Asimakopoulos*, pp. 83-110, New York, St. Martin's Press.

Kurz, H.D. and Salvadori, N. (1995), *Theory of Production. A Long-Period Analysis*, Cambridge, Cambridge University Press.

Lavoie, M. (1992), *Foundations of Post Keynesian Economic Analysis*, Aldershot, Edward Elgar.

Lavoie, M. (1993), "A Post-Classical View of Money, Interest, Growth and Distribution", in G. Mongiovi and C. Rühl (eds), *Macroeconomic Theory: Diversity and Convergence*, pp. 3-21, Cambridge, Cambridge University Press.

Lavoie, M. (1995), "Interest Rates in Post-Keynesian Models of Growth and Distribution", *Metroeconomica*, Vol. 46, pp. 146-177.

Lavoie, M. (2006), "Do Heterodox Theories Have Anything Common? A Post-Keynesian Point of View", *Intervention. Journal of Economics*, Vol. 3, pp. 87-112.

Lavoie, M. and Ramirez-Gaston, P. (1997), "Traverse in a Two-Sector Kaleckian Model of Growth with Target-Return Pricing", *The Manchester School*, Vol. 65, pp. 145-169.

Lavoie, M., Rodriguez, G. and Seccareccia, M. (2004), "Similitudes and Discrepancies in Post-Keynesian and Marxist Theories of Investment: A Theoretical and Empirical Investigation", *International Review of Applied Economics*, Vol. 18, pp. 127-149.

Marglin, S. A. (1984), *Growth, Distribution and Prices*, Cambridge, Harvard University Press.

Marglin, S. A. and Bhaduri, A. (1990), "Profit Squeeze and Keynesian Theory", in S. A. Marglin and J. B. Schor (eds), *The Golden Age of Capitalism: Reinterpreting the Postwar Experience*, pp. 152-186, Oxford, Clarendon Press.

Mariolis, T. (2004), "Distribution, Accumulation and Interest Rates in a Post-Keynesian Multisectoral Model", in K. Sham Bhat (ed.), *Issues in Financial Development*, pp. 164-195, New Delhi, Serials Publications.

Mariolis, T. (2006), "Distribution and Growth in a Multi-Sector Open Economy with Excess Capacity", *Economia Internazionale/International Economics*, Vol. 59, pp. 51-61.

Panico, C. and Salavdori, N. (1993), "Introduction", in C. Panico and N. Salvadori (eds), *Post Keynesian Theory of Growth and Distribution*, pp. xiii-xxxi, Aldershot, Edward Elgar.

Pasinetti, L. (1974), *Growth and Income Distribution. Essays in Economic Theory*, Cambridge, Cambridge University Press.

Pasinetti, L. (1977), *Lectures on the Theory of Production*, New York, Columbia University Press.

Rowthorn, R.E. (1981), "Demand, Real Wages and Economic Growth", *Thames Papers in Political Economy*, Autumn, pp. 1-39.

Sherman, H. J. (1979), "A Marxist Theory of the Business Cycle", *Review of Radical Political Economy*, Vol. 11, pp. 1-23.

Spaventa, L. (1970), "Rate of Profit, Rate of Growth, and Capital Intensity in a Simple Production Model", *Oxford Economic Papers*, Vol. 22, pp. 129-147.

Sraffa, P. (1960), *Production of Commodities by Means of Commodities*, Cambridge, Cambridge University Press.

You J.-I. and Dutt, A. K. (1996), "Government Debt, Income Distribution and Growth", *Cambridge Journal of Economics*, Vol. 20, pp. 335-351.

SHORT-RUN AND LONG-RUN DYNAMICS BETWEEN EXPORTS, FOREIGN DIRECT INVESTMENT AND OUTPUT IN THE MANUFACTURING SECTOR: THE CASE OF MALAYSIA

Mahendhiran Nair* & V. G. R. Chandran

ABSTRACT

This paper aims to investigate the causal relationship between foreign direct investment (FDI), manufacturing exports (ME) and manufacturing output (MO) in Malaysia for the sample period 1970-2003. Using the Unrestricted Error Correction Model (UECM) and the bounds test developed by Pesaran et al. (2001), there is evidence of a long run relationship between MO, FDI and ME. The empirical analysis showed that the long run causality run from FDI and ME to MO. The paper also discusses strategies to enhance the competitiveness of the Malaysian manufacturing sector.

***Keywords:** Granger-Causality, manufacturing sector, foreign direct investment, unrestricted error correction model*

***JEL classification:** L60, N65, 014, 032 and C22.*

I. INTRODUCTION

It has been widely debated that exports and foreign direct investment (FDI) are key to economic growth in developing countries. Access to global markets is important for nations, especially for developing countries where the domestic market is too small for firms to pursue economies of scale. In many developing countries, lack of capital is a major hindrance for socioeconomic development. FDI contributes to national development in the developing world in the following ways: (i) creation of employment, (ii) raise the quality of factor inputs and (iii) enhances the innovative capacity of domestic firms.

Studies examining the impact of exports and FDI on the nation's growth indicate that FDI and exports contribute positively to economic output especially in the developing countries. In addition, with better complementary assets in the host countries, the contribution to economic growth will be stronger. Balasubramanyam *et al.* (1996) using cross sectional data and OLS regression method found that FDI has a positive effect in export promoting countries but not in

* School of Business, Monash University, 2 Jalan Kolej, Bandar Sunway, Petaling Jaya, Selangor, Malaysia, *E-mail: mahendhiran.nair@buseco.monash.edu.my*

** Department of Economics, University Technology MARA, Sagamat, Johor, Malaysia, *E-mail: vgrch679@johor.uitm.edu.my*

the import substituting countries. Similarly, Borensztein et al. (1998) study also supported the FDI led growth proposition whilst concluding that the magnitude of FDI influence depends on the stock of human capital.

More recent empirical studies, Li and Liu (2004) and Bengoa and Sanchez-Robles (2003) indicated that FDI has a significant positive effect on economic growth. In addition, these studies also showed that the magnitude of the effect depends on the host countries economic condition. For instance, Li and Liu (2004) using a panel data of 84 countries found that the effect was stronger in countries with skilled workers. Marwah and Tavakoli (2004) showed a positive linkage between FDI and economic growth in four Asian countries including Malaysia.

There are several other studies that have examined the export and FDI led hypothesis for developing countries using the causality analysis. Mah (2005) showed a long run relationship between export and growth in China. Using the error correction model, the study indicated a bi-directional causality between export and economic growth in China. Conversely, Zhang (2001) using data of 11 developing countries found causality running from FDI to economic growth in five countries. The study also recognized that host countries economic environment is important in accelerating the influence of FDI on growth. Other studies, examining the causality between export and growth include studies by Salvatore & Hatcher (1991) Bahamani-Oskooee & Alse (1993); Doraisami (1996); Ahmad et al. (1997); and Al-Yousif (1999).

In Malaysia, investment liberalisation policies in the 1970s have encouraged the inflow of FDIs into the country. Foreign Multi-National Corporations (MNCs) established plants and subsidiaries in the early 1970s. Most of the MNCs were in the manufacturing sector. These MNCs have played a major role in transforming the economic structure of Malaysia from an agricultural to a manufacturing based economy. To this end, this paper hopes to fill the gap in the literature by empirically examining the relationship between FDI, manufacturing export (ME) and manufacturing output (MO) of the Malaysian manufacturing sector–a sector that has been a key engine of growth for the Malaysian economy since the mid 1980s.

In this study we used the Unrestricted Error Correction Model (UECM) to examine the dynamics between FDI, ME and MO. We also used a new cointegration test called the bounds test developed by Pesaran *et al.* (2001) to establish if the variables are co-moving. This empirical framework has two major advantages over the traditional error correction framework proposed by Engle and Granger (1987), Johansen (1988) and Johansen & Juselius (1992). First, the UECM approach used in this study allows for the explanatory variables to be a mixture of stationary and non-stationary series (that is series with the order of integration of zero and/or one). Second, the bounds test is robust against small sample bias. Hence, gives reliable estimates for small sample studies such as the present study.

The paper is organized as follows. In Section II, the methodology and data used in the study are described. In Section III, the empirical results are discussed. In Section IV, policy implications are examined. In Section V, concluding remarks are given.

II. THE METHODOLOGY AND DATA

In this section, we outline the empirical method and the data used in this study. First, using the Phillips-Perron (PP) unit root test, the order of integration of each of the series were determined.

If the series were found to be stationary, the Ordinary Least Squares will be used to determine the long run relationship between the variables. If the series were found to be non-stationary (order of integration more than zero), the following UECM proposed by Pesaran et al. (2001) will be used to capture the dynamics between the variables:

$$\begin{aligned}\Delta LMA_t &= \alpha_{0M} + \sum_{i=1}^{k1} \beta_{iM} \Delta LMA_{t-i} + \sum_{i=1}^{k2} \xi_{iM} \Delta LFDI_{t-i} + \sum_{i=1}^{k3} \lambda_{iM} \Delta LX_{t-i} \\ &+ \theta_{1M} LMA_{t-1} + \theta_{2M} LFDI_{t-1} + \theta_{3M} LX_{t-1} + \varepsilon_{Mt},\end{aligned} \tag{1}$$

$$\begin{aligned}\Delta LFDI_t &= \alpha_{0F} + \sum_{i=1}^{k1} \beta_{iF} \Delta LFDI_{t-i} + \sum_{i=1}^{k2} \xi_{iF} \Delta LMA_{t-i} + \sum_{i=1}^{k3} \lambda_{iF} \Delta LX_{t-i} \\ &+ \theta_{1F} LFDI_{t-1} + \theta_{2F} LMA_{t-1} + \theta_{3F} LX_{t-1} + \varepsilon_{Ft},\end{aligned} \tag{2}$$

$$\begin{aligned}\Delta LX_t &= \alpha_{0X} + \sum_{i=1}^{k1} \beta_{iX} \Delta LX_{t-i} + \sum_{i=1}^{k2} \xi_{iX} \Delta LMA_{t-i} + \sum_{i=1}^{k3} \lambda_{iX} \Delta LFDI_{t-i} \\ &+ \theta_{1X} LX_{t-1} + \theta_{2X} LMA_{t-1} + \theta_{3X} LFDI_{t-1} + \varepsilon_{Xt},\end{aligned} \tag{3}$$

where *LMA*, *LFDI* and *LX* are the logarithm value of the value-added manufacturing output, manufacturing export and foreign direct investment, respectively. The first difference operator is denoted as Δ. The variables in (1), (2), and (3) are in logarithm so that the coefficients are the elasticities. Information of the short run dynamics are capture in β, ξ and λ. On the other hand, the information of the long run dynamics is in the θs. The residuals are denoted as εs and are assumed to be homoskedastic, not serially correlated and are normally distributed. The above models are also known as the Auto-Regressive Distributed Lag Model, ARDL[*p*,*q*,*r*], where *p*, *q* and *r* are the lag for the respective variables.

In order to test the absence of a long run relationship in (1), (2) and (3), we conduct a Wald-type (F-test) coefficient restriction test, which entail testing the following null hypothesis, respectively:

$$H_0 : \theta_{1M} = \theta_{2M} = \theta_{3M} = 0, \tag{4}$$

$$H_0 : \theta_{1F} = \theta_{2F} = \theta_{3F} = 0, \text{ and} \tag{5}$$

$$H_0 : \theta_{1X} = \theta_{2X} = \theta_{3X} = 0. \tag{6}$$

This test is known as the bounds test (Pesaran *et al.*, 2001) and the computed F-statistics under the null hypothesis (4), (5) and (6) are denoted as *F(LMA|LFDI,LX)*, *F(LFDI|LMA,LX)*, and *F(LX|LFDI, LMA)*, respectively. The asymptotic distributions of the test statistics (F-statistics) are non-standard regardless of whether the variables are *I(0)* or *I(1)*. For this purpose Pesaran *et al.* (2001) computed two sets of asymptotic critical values where the first set assumes variables to be *I(0)* and the other as *I(1)*. These critical values are known as lower bounds (LCB) and upper bounds critical values (UCB), respectively. A decision on whether cointegration exists between the dependent variable and its regressors is then made based on the following criterion given in Table 1.

Table 1

F Statistics	*Decision*	*Meaning*
istics > UCB	Reject	The dependent variable and its regressors are cointegrated
F statistics < LCB	Fail to reject H_0	The dependent variable is not cointegrated with its regressors
LCB <F statistics< UCB	Results inconclusive	

Once both order of integration and cointegration relationship are established, we then use the standard Granger causality tests to confirm the direction of causality. In the case, when series are of order *I(1)* and cointegrated, we conduct the Granger causality with inclusion of the lagged error correction term (ECT) (which is obtained from the long run cointegration relationship) as an additional independent variable in the equation. Thus, the Granger causality relationships are written as Vector Error Correction Models (VECM) given below:

$$\Delta LMA_t = \alpha_{0M} + \sum_{i=1}^{k} \beta_{iM} \Delta LMA_{t-i} + \sum_{i=1}^{k} \xi_{iM} \Delta LFDI_{t-i} + \sum_{i=1}^{k} \lambda_{iM} \Delta LX_{t-i} + ECT_{t-1} + \varepsilon_{Mt} \tag{7}$$

$$\Delta LFDI_t = \alpha_{0F} + \sum_{i=1}^{k} \beta_{iF} \Delta LMA_{t-i} + \sum_{i=1}^{k} \xi_{iF} \Delta LFDI_{t-i} + \sum_{i=1}^{k} \lambda_{iF} \Delta LX_{t-i} + ECT_{t-1} + \varepsilon_{Ft} \tag{8}$$

$$\Delta LMX_t = \alpha_{0X} + \sum_{i=1}^{k} \beta_{iX} \Delta LMA_{t-i} + \sum_{i=1}^{k} \xi_{iX} \Delta LFDI_{t-i} + \sum_{i=1}^{k} \lambda_{iX} \Delta LX_{t-i} + ECT_{t-1} + \varepsilon_{Xt} \tag{9}$$

Likewise, if the series are not cointegrated the Granger causality is conducted without the ECT. We used the Schwarz Bayesian Criterion (SBC) to select the lags for the ARDL cointegration analysis.

In (7), to test whether lagged first differences of LFDI Granger-Cause LMA, we impose restrictions on all the lagged LFDI using the Wald test. This is equivalent to testing the short run causality of LFDI on LMA. To test the significant of the ECT we use the t-statistics. If the ECT is significant then we have evidence of long run causality. The direction of causality for (8) and (9) are conducted in the same way.

The data on manufacturing value added output and manufacturing exports were obtained from *Malaysian Economic Statistics-Time Series* book published by Department of Statistics Malaysia. Data on foreign direct investment (FDI) was obtained from the Malaysian Industrial Development Authority (MIDA). The sample period for this study is from 1970 to 2003.

III. EMPIRICAL RESULTS

The results of the unit root test using the PP test is reported in Table 2. The PP test showed that all the variables are non-stationary (order of integration of the series were greater than zero). That is all the series are integrated of order 1. This implies that using ordinary least square may lead to spurious estimates.

Table 2
Phillip-Perron Unit Root Test

	Log Levels		*Log differences*	
	Without trend	*With trend*	*without trend*	*with trend*
LMA	-1.699	-1.727	-4.757*	-5.163*
LFDI	-2.031	-2.463	-7.045*	-7.235*
LX	-0.567	-1.709	-4.983*	-5.002*

Note: * denote significant at 1% significance level.

Table 3 reports the result of the bounds test for cointegration analysis. It is evident that only when LMA is the dependent variable, there exists a long run relationship between LFDI, LX and LMA. The reported F-statistics (7.324) exceeds the UCB, suggesting the variables are co-moving at the 5% significance level. However, in the case of LFDI and LX serving as the dependent variable, there is no evidence of any long run relationship between the regressors and its determinants.

Table 3
The Bounds Test for Cointegration

	F-Statistics	*Lag*	*95% critical value bounds*	
			LCB: 3.79	*UCB: 4.85*
F_{MA}(LMA|LFDI, LX)	7.324	2		
F_{FDI}(LFDI|LMA, LX)	2.913	3		
F_X (LX|LMA, LFDI)	2.790	4		

Notes: Critical values obtained from Pesaran et al. (2001). The underlying UECM equation passes series of the diagnostic test. Standard regularity conditions (the residuals are homoskedastic, have no serial correlation and satisfy the normality assumption).

The *LFDI* and *LX* appear to be the long run forcing variable for LMA based on the bounds test. However, in the short run, the direction of Granger causality may be different. The direction of causality in the short run is given in Table 4. The results showed that in the short run, none of the lagged differences are significant. This implies none of the variables Granger-Cause one another in the short run.

The long run impact is also captured by the error correction term (ECT). The *ECT* for (7) is -0.317 and was found to be statistically significant at the 5% significance level. This suggests that in the long run both *LFDI* and *LX* Granger-Cause *LMA*. This means that causality runs interactively through the *ECT* from *LFDI* and *LX* to *LMA*. The magnitude of the *ECT* term suggests that a deviation from the equilibrium level of *LMA* during the current period will be corrected by 32% in the next period.

Table 4
Granger Causality Test

	F-Statistics [Probability]			*[t-statistics]*
Dependent Variable	$\Sigma\Delta LMA_{t-1}$	$\Sigma\Delta LFDI_{t-1}$	$\Sigma\Delta LX_{t-1}$	ECT_{t-1}
ΔLMA_t	-	0.329[0.571]	0.038[0.845]	-0.317[-2.55]**
$\Delta LFDI_t$	1.314[0.297]		2.123[0.129]	-
ΔLX_t	1.012[0.430]	0.288[0.882]	-	-

Notes: ** denotes significant level at 5%; selection of lag terms is based on the Schwartz Bayesian Criterion (SBC) which also subjected to series of diagnostic test. The CUSUM plot and CUSUMSQ plot showed that the test statistics was within the 5% significant level. Hence, indicating no evidence of any structural instability. ECT is calculated based on the following equation: ECT = LMA - 0.19278*LFDI - 0.60031*LX - 2.6815*C

From the above empirical analysis, we can conclude that *FDI* and *LX* only influences *LMA* in the long run. The estimated long run elasticities of LFDI and LX on LMA using the UECM are given in Table 5. Based on the Schwartz Bayesian Criterion, the ARDL[1,0,0] was found to be the optimal model. Note that LX and LFDI have positive and significant impact on LMA at the 1% significance level.

Table 5
Long Run Elasticities

Dependent Variable	*LMA*
LX	0.432 [0.003]*
LFDI	0.146 [0.001]*
Trend	0.038 [0.123]

Notes: * denote significant at the 1% significance level. The probabilities are given in [ ]

IV. POLICY IMPLICATIONS

The empirical analysis above showed that the Malaysian manufacturing output is dependent on the export market and foreign direct investment. This imply that the Malaysian manufacturing sector, which is a key engine of growth, is sensitive to the global export market and the flow of FDI. With the entrance of China in the global economy, the competition for the global manufacturing market share has intensified. Nair *et al.* (2005) using the Revealed Comparative Advantage (RCA) method showed that China have comparative advantage over Malaysia in many of the labour intensive manufacturing sector The study also showed that China had also built its comparative advantage over Malaysia in many of the high skilled and technology-intensive manufacturing sectors.

Rapid increase in China's comparative advantage over the last decade was due to the significant investment in research & development and human capital development. These investments have transformed China from a low cost production center to a leading hub for innovation in the manufacturing sector. Today, China is seen as a major producer for new generation manufacturing products, especially in the electrical, electronics and the ICT sector. These developments have eroded the competitiveness of the Malaysian manufacturing sector, both in terms of market share and the inflow of FDI.

In this section, we discuss the strategies for enhancing the innovative capacity and competitiveness of the Malaysian manufacturing sector. Given, the labour force in Malaysia is relatively small compared to China; Malaysian manufacturing industries must move-up the value chain by improving their innovative capacity. To raise the innovative capacity of local manufacturers, two key strategic thrusts should be given special attention. First, the pool of researchers and innovators in the manufacturing sector is relatively low compared to China. The supply of skilled workers and researchers should be increased to match that of China and other regional economies. This can be done by the government giving more scholarships and fee-waivers for candidates qualified for higher degree research programs (Masters and Doctorate) in science, technology and engineering related fields. Further, greater efforts should be made to attract knowledge workers in the region to relocate to Malaysia. Immigration policies should be more liberal for skilled workers from other parts of the world to relocate to Malaysia and contribute positively to Malaysian firms in the manufacturing sector.

Second, Malaysia's R&D spending is significantly lower than that of China. Malaysia's total expenditure on R&D as percentage of GDP in 2003 was 0.69%, while China's was 1.31% (IMD, 2005). In 2003, Malaysian business enterprises spent USD443 million on R&D. On the other hand, business enterprises in China spent USD11.598 Billion on R&D (IMD, 2005). To raise the competitiveness level of the manufacturing sector, Malaysia must increase its R&D spending to levels comparable to that of China and more developed countries (at least 2 percent of the GDP).

V. CONCLUSION

This study investigated the direction of causality between FDI, exports and manufacturing growth in Malaysia. The empirical results showed the existence of a long run relationship between FDI, exports and manufacturing growth. Further, in the long run FDI and exports Granger-Cause manufacturing growth. However, empirical results showed that the relationship between FDI, exports and manufacturing output is not statistically significant in the short run.

In summary, the Malaysian manufacturing output is dependent on FDI and manufacturing export. With increasing competition from countries such as China for the global manufacturing export market and FDI, Malaysia must raise the level of competitiveness of the manufacturing sector. Strategies to raise the competitiveness of the Malaysian manufacturing sector were discussed in this paper.

References

Ahmad, J., Harnhirun, S. and Yang, J. (1997), "Export and Economic Growth in the ASEAN Countries: Cointegration and Causality Tests", *International Review of Economics and Business* 44, 419-30.

Al-Yousif, Yousif K. (1999), "On the Role of Exports in the Economic Growth of Malaysia: A Multivariate Analysis", *International Economic Journal* 13(3), 67-75.

Bahamani-Oskooee M. and Alse J. (1993), "Export Growth and Economic Growth: An Application of Co-integration and Error-correction Modeling", *Journal of Developing Areas*, July, 535-542.

Balasubramanyam, V. N., Salisu, M. and Sapsford, D. (1996), "Foreign Direct Investment and Growth in EP and IS Countries", *The Economic Journal*, 106 (1), 92-105.

Bengoa, M. and Sanchez-Robles, B. (2003), "Foreign Direct Investment, Economic Freedom and Growth: New Evidence from Latin America", *European Journal of Political Economy*, 19(3), 529-545.

Borensztein E., De Gregorio, J. and Lee, J. W. (1998), "How Does Foreign Direct Investment Affects Economic Growth?", *Journal of International Economics*, 45(1), 115-135.

Doraisami, A. (1996), "Export Growth and Economic Growth: A Reexamination of Some Time-series Evidence of the Malaysian Experience", *Journal of Developing Areas*, 223-230.

Engle, R.F. and Granger, C.W.J (1987), "Cointegration and Error Correction: Representation, Estimation and Testing", *Econometrica*, 55, 251-276.

IMD (2005), *IMD World Competitiveness Yearbook 2005*, IMD, Switzerland.

Johansen, S. (1988), "Statistical Analysis of Cointegration Vectors", *Journal of Economic Dynamics and Control*, 12, 231-254.

Johansen, S. and Juselius, K. (1992), "Testing Structural Hypothesis in a Multivariate Cointegration Analysis of the PPP and the UIP for UK", *Journal of Econometrics*, 53, 211-244.

Li X. and Liu X. (2004), "Foreign Direct Investment and Economic Growth: An Increasingly Endogenous Relationship", *World Development*, 33 (3), 397-407.

Mah J. S. (2005), "Export Expansion, Economic Growth and Causality in China", *Applied Economics Letters*, 12, 105-107.

Marwah K. and Tavakoli A. (2004), "The Effect of Foreign Capital and Imports on Economic Growth: Further Evidence from four Asian Countries (1970-1998)", *Journal of Asian Economics*, 15, 399-413.

Nair, M., Vengedasalm, D., Madhavan, K. and Govindaraju, V.G.R.C. (2005), "Trade Dynamics Between China and ASEAN-5: and Empirical Analysis", *Proceedings of the 30th Federation of ASEAN Economic Association Conference on China and India: Challenges and Opportunities for ASEAN*, Makati City, Philippines, 25-26 November.

Pesaran, M.H., Shin Y. and Smith R.J. (2001), "Bounds testing approach to the level relationship", *Journal of Applied Econometrics*, 16, 289-326.

Salvatore, D. and Hatcher, T. (1991), "Inward and Outward Oriented Trade Strategies", *Journal of Development Studies*, 27, 7-25.

Zhang, K.H. (2001), "Does Foreign Direct Investment Promote Economic Growth? Evidence from East Asia and Latin America", *Contemporary Economic Policy* 19(2), 175-185.

THE IMPACT OF PRIVATIZATION ON SERBIAN ENTERPRISES

***Jovana Zelic*[*] & Persefoni V. Tsaliki*[**]**

Abstract

This paper examines the way that various ownership structures, resulted by the five waves of privatization, have affected the growth performance of Serbian enterprises. The analysis takes place for the period 2002-2003 and refers to a sample of more than 15,000 of enterprises with different ownership structure. The empirical findings show that private ownership yields higher investment levels than social ownership, whereas voucher privatization leading to inside ownership provides worse results in terms of investment than privatization by sale. Moreover, enterprises privatized by free distribution still invest more than enterprises that did not go through the process of privatization and, more importantly, the initially private firms outperform all other forms of ownership. Furthermore, the analysis includes numerical variables in an attempt to investigate to what extent the enterprises behave as organized business entities.

***JEL Classification:** L100, L250, L330*

I. INTRODUCTION

Since 1990's, Post-Communist countries are challenged to establish a market economy system. The Former Republic of Yugoslavia (FRY) was, at the beginning at least, an economy with substantially better chances to transform and integrate with the West (Medish, 1997). However, the evidence today show that FRY stands behind from most Central and Eastern Europe Countries which, during this period, undertook serious and systematic reforms (EBRD, 2004; Arsic *et al*, 2001). In contrast, in FRY there was a delay in reforming the structure of the country and the deferral of the privatization process and enterprise restructuring is the most frequently reported obstacle for accelerating GDP growth rates (OECD, 2003; Vukotic and Pejovic, 2002; Djuricin, 1997; Lazovic and Cvjeticanin, 2001).

This paper explores the relationship between different methods of privatization and enterprise performance with the use of relevant data for the FRY economy. Section 2 presents the recent developments of the Serbian economy and reports the various privatization waves that took place in the last years. Section 3 deals with the empirical analysis and investigates the impact that privatization *per se* might have on enterprise's performance in FRY. In the final section we conclude and we make some remarks about future research efforts.

---

* Business Administration and Economics Department, City Liberal Studies, *E-mail: j.zelic@city.academic.gr*

** Department of Economics, Aristotle University of Thessaloniki, *E-mail: ptsaliki@econ.auth.gr*

II. FRY ECONOMY AND ITS FIVE PRIVATIZATION WAVES

While most of the transitional economies undertook serious and systematic reforms[2], today's Yugoslavia, Serbia and Montenegro, is the least reformed economy in the region (EBRD, 2004).[3] At the outset of the transition, Yugoslavia experienced two hyperinflations and the short-run policies implemented by the currency board without adequate structural changes did not help much (Jovovic, 1999; Pitic, 1997). Due to armed conflicts, the economy faced dramatic increase in public consumption coupled with rise in wages and money supply (Jovovic, 1999; Labus, 1997; Pitic, 1997; Penev, 1997). Government kept increasing money supply to stimulate further production growth which, however, resulted only in mediocre production increase and huge rise in general price levels (Gavrilovic, 1995).

Hence, during the 1990's, the FRY economy was an economy with inadequate structure, nonexistent hard-budget constraints, lack of financial discipline by state and socially owned enterprises, delayed privatization process, no structural changes, slow internal and external liberalization of economy, delayed bank restructuring and rehabilitation, and volatile real exchange rate (Penev, 1997). According to Arsic, *et al* (2001), Serbian economy produced less than half of its capacity during the 1990s, and the capacity utilization in most industries dropped to one third, mainly due to international embargo and mismanagement of economy. Since 2000, however, real reforms were undertaken (OECD, 2003; Vukotic and Pejovic, 2002; Lazovic and Cvjeticanin, 2001) and despite the fact that FRY's economy achieved certain level of economic stability; still, its economic growth figures are not as bright as expected.

OECD Economic Survey (2003) records a number of causes that potentially account for the sluggish performance of FRY's economy, with the most important the anemic FDI inflows which are blocked by the delay of large-scale privatisation and enterprise reforms (Penev, 2002)[4]. In general, privatization represents one of the pillars of the new paradigm for economic reforms. Those in favor to privatization argue on the grounds that the competitive economy and the private sector in practice do better than state/public sector in general (Ettori, 2002; Madden and Savage, 1997; Estrin, 1994; Elgar, 1993; Rees, 1984). Those against to privatization argue that public enterprises exist and should exist for their ability to correct market failures (Rees, 1984). It is also argued that it is not the form of ownership but the type of organization and management of companies that determine the economic efficiency and the performance of an enterprise (Kornai, 1995). And, as expected, studies on the public/private sector performance and on the motivating factors for public/private sector managers obtained mixed results (Heinrich, 2002; Hayes, 2000; Estrin, 1994; Elgar, 1993; Khojasteh, 1993; Dornbusch, *et al.* 1991).[5]

Privatisation in FRY mainly implies the abolishment of social ownership of capital through the determination of ownership rights (Djuricin, 1997; Milovanovic, 1990; Phychitko, 1989; Pejovich, 1989). Since 1990, five waves of privatisation took place. The first wave of privatization in Yugoslavia was carried out in 1990 and employees were allowed to buy the firms they were working in at extremely favourable terms. In 1991, Serbia alone regulated privatisation by its own Law according to which employees again had the major role in the privatisation process. New impetus for privatisation came in 1993 with hyperinflation, which drastically decreased the real cost of shares (Lazic and Sekelj, 1997) and privatisation accelerated. In order to induce privatisation further, a new Law was introduced in 1997 according to which approximately 800 enterprises were privatised until 2001, and the majority of them are considered to be the 'best' companies in Serbia (Lazovic and Cvjeticanin, 2001). A new privatisation law was introduced in 2001 in accordance to the suggestions of IMF, World Bank and European Bank for Reconstruction and Development in an attempt to produce positive results in short time period; however, a slowdown in the privatization process is evidenced (OECD, 2003).[6]

III. EMPIRICAL ANALYSIS

With the use of cross sectional data[7] we evaluate the impact of ownership structure on the performance of enterprises in Serbian economy. The database employed in our empirical analysis consists of 15,021 enterprises, out of which 3,151 are socially owned; 10,705 are originally private; 636 are insider owned; and 529 privatised by sale.

The model employed in the analysis is:

$$Y = b_1 - b_2D_2 + b_3D_3 - b_4D_4 - b_5NEW + b_6EQT + b_7SLS + b_8EMP$$

where Y is the log of the sum of net value of fixed assets in 2002 plus purchases of fixed assets in 2003 divided by the net value of fixed assets in 2002; hence, the investment level of the enterprise[8] is used as a proxy to the growth performance of an enterprise. D_2, D_3 and D_4 are dummy variables used to capture the ownership structure of the company. Hence, $D_2 = 1$ if socially owned enterprise and $D_2 = 0$ if otherwise; $D_3 = 1$ if originally private enterprise, $D_3 = 0$ if otherwise; $D_4 = 1$ if insider ownership, $D_4 = 0$ if otherwise. The signs indicate the direction of the expected theoretical relationship.

The model also includes numerical variables in an attempt to investigate to what extent enterprises in FRY behave in a manner predictable by microeconomic theory that is they behave as organized business entities. Hence, *NEW* is the log of Net Fixed Assets in 2002 over the Gross Fixed Assets in 2002 and it is used as a proxy to capture the need of an enterprise to invest. *EQT* equals the difference of Equity in 2002 minus Accumulated Losses in 2002 (Net Equity in 2002) over Net Fixed Assets in 2002 and it is used as a proxy for the financial obligations of the enterprise. *SLS* captures the growth in sales. The *EMP* gives information about the size of the company, which is approximated by the log of the number of employees in 2003. With the exception of the number of employees, we use lagged explanatory variables.

Table 1 summarizes the results of our empirical work. Where appropriate we used White's correction test for robust standard errors and we check for multicolinearity among the independent variables in all models used. In the brackets, the standard errors are given. Additionally, in an attempt to homogenize our sample, a second round of estimations was made in a sample of 2,802 enterprises[9], which included only the enterprises with workforce of more than 50 employees.

Running the proposed equation for all 15,021 observations and making the distinction among privatization methods, we conclude that numerical variables depicting age, level of equity financing and increase in sales exert a significant independent influence on fixed assets growth, alongside with ownership structure explanatory variables. The size variable, *EMP*, of

Table 1
Econometric Results

Sample of 15,023 enterprises

1. $$INV = 0.049 - 0.070D_2 + 0.323D_3 - 0.058D_4 - 0.124NEW + 0.004EQT + 0.004SLS$$
$$(0.022) \quad (0.018) \quad (0.02) \quad (0.02) \quad (0.016) \quad (0.0007) \quad (0.001)$$

Sample of 2,802 enterprises

2. $$INV = 0.113 - 0.120D_2 + 0.220D_3 - 0.082D_4 - 0.202NEW + 0.020EMP$$
$$(0.092) \quad (0.027) \quad (0.044) \quad (0.028) \quad (0.100) \quad (0.008)$$

the company remained insignificant and thus it was excluded from the table. The homogenized sample of the 2,802 enterprises provides similar results. In Model 2, the size variable, *EMP*, is significant whereas, the *EQT* and *SLS* variables have no significant independent impact on the growth of fixed assets and thus were excluded. The results provided in our analysis are in alignment with the theory. The coefficient of determination, however, remains low for all models ($R^2 < 0.15$), although no statistical problems exist in the various models and the sample is large enough.

V. CONCLUDING REMARKS

In this paper we attempted to investigate the determinants of the performance in Serbian enterprises. Our study showed that the sales method is superior to free distribution in the FRY's environment and although voucher privatization has its advantages, privatization by sale is still more suitable (Dornbush, *et al*, 1991; Frydman and Rapaczynski, 1991; Lazovic and Cvjeticanin, 2001; Maksimovic, 2002). We also attempted to analyze the relationship of enterprise growth performance to the age of its fixed assets, its ability to invest from its own resources, its motive for further investment in terms of sales growth and its size.

Our empirical analysis reached to conclusions which are in accordance to theoretical proposals. The five privatization waves experienced by the FRY's economy have influenced enterprises' growth, the extent of which differs among the various privatization methods which led to different ownership structures. We showed that Serbian enterprises are not characterized by chaotic behavior, but instead they perform as organized business units in accordance to microeconomic theory. However, the measures of internal factors affecting enterprises' decision to invest do not capture the whole spectrum of factors that may exert influence on these decisions, as it is evidenced from the low coefficient of determination found in our research. This relatively low strength of the model suggests that other forces, possibly macroeconomic or political (*i.e.* relative political instability, past experience of hyperinflation, lost faith in the banking sector, high interest rates) still influence the entrepreneurs' decision to invest and future research should be conducted to that direction.

Notes

1. Basic constituents for a successful transitional process are considered among others the liberalization of prices, the free foreign exchange operations, the disciplined monetary and fiscal policies, the reduction of inflation, the deep structural adjustments and the belief in market principles (Medish, 1997).

2. This slowdown in reforming of Serbia and other former Yugoslav countries may be attributed to the consequence of political and armed conflicts in the region, which suspended significantly the transition for long periods (Penev, 2002).
3. Voszka (2003) argues that fluctuations in FDI distribution among various countries are largely attributed to the schedule and privatisation methods followed by these countries.
4. Some of these studies argue that the development of a sound private sector in SEE countries does not entail the simple transfer of ownership from state to private, but rather it is the process by which the very institution of property is reintroduced. Further, it is argued that without a sound market economy and extensive private ownership, the danger of a backlash in the democratisation process is always present and privatisation is the best way to create the solid foundation for a viable democracy (Elgar, 1993; UN, 1992; Frydman and Rapaczynski, 1991).
5. This slowdown might be due to that enterprises easily privatized without major restructuring have been already privatized (Ettori, 2002).
6. Time-series analysis in the Serbian economy cannot be conducted because of lack of data for the period 1990-2000. The initial database of our analysis consisted of financial reports from 74,104 enterprises which more or less represent the entire population for FRY. However, companies lacking critical data were excluded from the analysis; such companies are the public and cooperative enterprises. Additionally, companies with less than 5 employees were also excluded from the analysis. The data used in the analysis refer to financial reports for the years 2002-2003 and obtained through the National Bank of Serbia and the Privatisation Agency. For details look at Tsaliki and Zelic (2005).
7. The investment level of a specific company can be measured in few ways, one being the increase in total assets of the company. However, increase in total assets of the company does not necessarily imply growth since it could be generated from the increase in inventory or accounts and other receivables. Instead, increase in new fixed assets directly implies enterprise growth.
8. The sample obtained in this manner consists of enterprises, out of which 249 are privatized by sale, 478 are privatized by free distribution of shares, 520 belong to the initially private sector and 1,552 are socially owned.

References

Arsic, M., Mladenovic, Z. & P. Petrovic, (2001), *Macroeconomic Stabilization in the FRY*, Global Development Network for Southeast Europe: The Vienna Institute for International Economic Studies, Vienna.

Djuricin, D. (1997), "Privatization in FR Yugoslavia's Transition", *Challenges and Opportunities for the Economic Transition in Yugoslavia,* International Conference Proceedings, pp. 15-23.

Dornbush, R., Blanchard, O., Krugman, P., Layard R. & L. Summers (1991), *Reform in Eastern Europe*, The World Institute for Development Economics Research, Helsinki.

Elgar, E. (1993), "The Reasons for Privatization", in *Privatization in Eastern Europe: a Critical Approach,* Mesto Izdavac, pp. 48-111.

Estrin, S. (1994), *Privatization in Central and Eastern Europe,* London: Longman Group.

Ettori, F. (2002), "Privatization: Revolutionary or Reactionary?", *Reporter*, 26/11.

European Bank for Reconstruction and Development (2003), *Transition Report, Integration and Regional Cooperation,* London.

European Bank for Reconstruction and Development (2004), *Spotlight on South-Eastern Europe: An Overview of Private Sector Activity and Investment,* London.

Frydman, R. & A. Rapaczynski (1991), "Markets and Institutions in Large-Scale Privatization: An Approach to Economic and Social Transformation in Eastern Europe', *World Bank Symposium Proceedings.*

Gavrilovic, P. (1995), "Monetary Stability and Economic Growth", in *Perspectives of Yugoslavian Economy after 1994,* Serbian Academy of Sciences and Arts, Belgrade.

Hayes, K. (2000), "Public Sector Performance: Move or Monitor?', *Southern Economic Journal*, 66, 4, pp. 820-829.

Heinrich, C. (2002), "Outcomes-Based Performance Management in the Public Sector: Implications for Government Accountability and Effectiveness', *Public Administration Review*, 62, 6, pp. 712-726.

Jovovic, D. (1999), "Exchange Rate Regimes of Dinar, Macroeconomic Aspects", *Jugoslovensko Bankarstvo*, 5, 6, pp. 36-42.

Khojasteh, M. (1993), "Motivating the Private vs. Public Sector Managers", *Public Personal Management*, 22, 3, pp. 391-402.

Kornai, J. (1995), "The Principles of Privatization", in Z. Poznanski (ed), *The Evolutionary Transition to Capitalism,* Mesto Izdav, pp. 30-201.

Labus, M. (1997), "Financial Sector in Yugoslavia", *Challenges and Opportunities for the Economic Transition in Yugoslavia,* International Conference Proceedings, pp. 32-49.

Lazic, M. & L. Sekelj (1997), "Privatization in Yugoslavia", *Europe-Asia Studies*, 49, 6, pp. 1057-1071.

Lazovic, D. & D. Cvjeticanin (2001), "Internal and External Privatisation in Serbia", *Economist*, 34, 2, pp. 97-107.

Madden, G. & S. Savage, (1997), "Measuring Public Sector Efficiency: A Study of Economic Departments at Australian Universities", *Education Economics*, 5, 2, pp. 153-169.

Maksimovic, I. (1995), "Problems of Economic Growth, Efficiency of Economy and Transformation of Ownership", in *Perspectives of Yugoslavian Economy After 1994,* Belgrade: Serbian Academy of Sciences and Arts.

Medish, M. (1997), 'Opening Speech', in *Challenges and Opportunities for the Economic Transition in Yugoslavia*, International Conference Proceedings, pp. 77-84.

Milovanovic, M. (1990), *Inefficiency of socially Owned Enterprise*, Belgrade: Naucna Knjiga.

OECD Economic Survey (2003), *Federal Republic of Yugoslavia: Economic Assessment*, Belgrade.

Pejovich, S. (1989), "Liberty, Property Rights, and Innovation in Eastern Europe", *Cato Journal*, 9, 1, pp. 57 71.

Penev, S. (1997), "Foreign Investment Opportunities", in *Challenges and Opportunities for the Economic Transition in Yugoslavia,* International Conference Proceedings, pp. 24-32.

Penev, S. (2002), "Foreign Direct Investment Trends and Investment Climate in the Countries of South-East Europe", in *Attracting Private Investment-Putting the Policy Frameworks in Place: Experiences from Slovenia and South-East Europe,* Mesto: The Investment Compact for South East Europe, pp. 67-91.

Pitic, G. (1997), 'Macroeconomic Framework', in *Challenges and Opportunities for the Economic Transition in Yugoslavia,* International Conference Proceedings, pp. 3-15.

Prychitko, D. (1989), 'Horvat Answer Hayek? The Crisis of Yugoslav Self-Management' (Online), *http://www.libertyhaven.com*

Rees, R. (1984), *Public Enterprise Economics*, London: Weidenfeld and Nicolson.

Tsaliki, P. and J. Zelic (2005), "Ownership Structure and Performance of the Serbian Enterprises", *Zagreb International Review of Economics & Business,* 8, 2, pp. 73-82.

Voszka, E. (2003), *Incentives for the Private Investments in the Region*, Budapest: Finance Research Ltd.

Vukotic, E. & S. Pejovic (2002), "*Transition and Institutions: What Now?*", Belgrade: Institute of Social Sciences

VOLATILITY MODELS AND AN APPLICATION FOR EMERGING MARKETS

Oktay Taş, Zeynep İltüzer & Kaya Tokmakçıoğlu

ABSTRACT

In the last quarter of 20th century financial markets went through important crisis which made investors and academics aware of volatility and its adverse effects on securities' risk. Therefore, many methods to understand and model volatility have been developed in research area. During these researches it is realized that financial time series have certain characteristics in common which include volatility clustering, asymmetry, leverage effect and fat tailed distribution and therefore new methods that model financial data and cover these fundamental qualities have been developed. In this study, the concentration is on the volatility patterns of stock markets. This paper describes the effect of volatility on emerging markets' stock exchange by using their national indexes. Firstly, volatility and volatility models are explained briefly. Secondly, ARCH, GARCH, EGARCH, Asymmetrical PARCH and TGARCH are used in order to calculate volatilities of emerging markets. Besides, GED and t-distributions are included in volatility calculation in order to reflect fat tail characteristics of financial time series. In conclusion, differences and similarities of involved markets' volatility characteristics are compared and discussed.

INTRODUCTION

In the last quarter of 20th century financial markets went through important crisis which made investors and academics aware of volatility, which refers to the spread of all likely outcomes of an uncertain variable, and its adverse effects on securities' risk (Poon, 2005, p. 1). Therefore, during the globalization of financial markets risk management is getting important. Because risk management is related with uncertainty, it is obvious that uncertainty has to be measured in order to manage the risk. In that case, uncertainty is measured with volatilities of securities in financial markets (Bolgün & Akçay, 2005, p. 39). Thus, asset price movements in an efficient market can be defined as follows:

$$r_t = \frac{S_t - S_{t-1}}{S_{t-1}} = \mu_t + \varepsilon_t ; \quad E[\varepsilon_t] = 0, \quad Var[\varepsilon_t] = \sigma_t^{\,2}$$

Here, r_t refers to return at time t, which is the percentage change in the asset price S over the period t-1 to t, and is the sum of a nonrandom mean return for period t, μ_t, and a zero mean

* Istanbul Technical University, *oktay.tas@itu.edu.tr*

random disturbance ε_t. In an efficient market, we cannot be sure about the sign of the random component of return in period *t* because past price movements give no information about it (Figlewski, 1997, p. 3). Generally, the return of an asset is calculated from its prices and the volatility from its returns. Simply, the volatility, assumed that it is constant in time, can be estimated as

$$\sigma_n^2 = \frac{1}{T-1}\sum_{t=1}^{T} r_{n-t}^2 ,$$

where r_{n-t} is the daily return.

However, according to empirical tests, volatility changes with time (Soczo, 2003, p. 203). Therefore, a time-varying volatility can be modeled only by adjusting the volatility parameter which changes over time. Hence, the new model can be given as:

$$\sigma_t = [\frac{1}{T-t}\int_t^T \sigma_s^2 ds]^{1/2}$$

VOLATILITY MODELS

Below, volatility models, which are used in this paper to estimate the empirical results, are briefly explained.

ARCH

In 1982, Engle wrote his epoch-making article "Autoregressive Conditional Heteroscedasticity with Estimates of the Variance of United Kingdom Inflation" which meant to be a new era for modeling financial time series. In this article he stated that the ARCH process is a mean zero, serially uncorrelated process with nonconstant variance conditional on the past, but constant unconditional variance (p. 987). ARCH models formulate conditional variance which is defined in ARCH literature as $\sigma_t^2 = h_t$. Then, the return, r_t, is calculated as

$$r_t = \mu + \varepsilon_t$$

$$\varepsilon_t = \sqrt{h_t z_t}$$

where $z_t \approx D(0, 1)$ is a white noise and the distribution D is often taken as normal (Poon, 2005, p. 37). Moreover the ARCH process suggested by Engle can be written as follows:

$$h_t = \omega + \sum_{j=1}^{q} \alpha_j \varepsilon_{t-j}^2$$

with $\omega \rangle 0$ and $\alpha_j \geq 0$ (Figlewski, 1997, p. 33). According to these formulations h_t is known at time $t-1$. If it is assumed that $E[\varepsilon_{t+\tau}^2] = h_{t+\tau}$, the unconditional variance of r_t can be calculated as follows:

$$\sigma^2 = \frac{\omega}{1 - \sum_{j=1}^{q} \alpha_j}.$$

Here, it is important that the sum of the autoregressive parameters is less than one $\sum_{j=1}^{q} \alpha_j < 1$ (Poon, 2005, p. 38).

The ARCH models, namely GARCH, TGARCH, EGARCH, PGARCH, ARCH-M, which are widely used in economics and finance has been derived from ARCH. An important problem confronted in these models is that they require many observations before they behave well (Figlewski, 1997, p. 34).

GARCH

The Generalized Autoregressive Conditional Heteroscedasticity (GARCH) model depends mainly on the article which was written by Bollerslev in 1986. Andersen, Bollerslev, Christoffersen and Diebold assert that GARCH model offers a more convenient and parsimonious framework for modeling key dynamic features of returns, including volatility mean-reversion, long-memory, and asymmetries (2005, p. 23). Engle and Ng (1993) state: "Bollerslev (1986) generalizes the ARCH (*p*) model to the GARCH (*p, q*) model, such that

$$h_t = \omega + \sum_{i=1}^{p} \alpha_i \varepsilon_{t-1}^2 + \sum_{i=1}^{q} \beta_i h_{t-i}$$

where $\alpha_1, \ldots, \alpha_p, \beta_1, \ldots, \beta_p$ and ω are constant parameters" (p. 1752). In this formula p has to be greater than zero and q has to be greater than or equal to zero where p and q are the orders of the processes. Besides, the restriction $\sum \beta_i + \sum \alpha_i < 1$ must also be satisfied to ensure stationarity in the variance equation (Apergis & Eleptheriou, 2001, p. 52). Then, the unconditional variance equals:

$$\sigma^2 = \frac{\omega}{1 - \sum_{i=1}^{p} \alpha_i - \sum_{i=1}^{q} \beta_i} \quad \text{(Poon, 2005, p. 38).}$$

TGARCH (Threshold GARCH)

In 1994, Jean Michel Zakoian published his article about the threshold heteroskedastic model which is a modification of classical ARCH models introduced by Engle (1982). In this model, the conditional standard deviation is a piecewise linear function of past values of the white noise and is calculated as follows:

$$\sigma_t = \alpha_0 + \sum_{i=1}^{p}\left[\alpha_i\left|\varepsilon_{t-i}\right| + \gamma_i D_{i,t-i}\left|\varepsilon_{t-i}\right|\right] + \sum_{j=1}^{q}\beta_j\sigma_{t-j}\,.$$

$$\text{where } D_{t-1} = \begin{cases} 1 \mapsto \varepsilon_{t-1} < 0 \\ 0 \mapsto \varepsilon_{t-1} > 0 \end{cases}.$$

If $\alpha_0 > 0, \alpha_i \geq 0, \alpha_i + \gamma_i \geq 0$ and $\beta_j \geq 0$, for $i = 1,\ldots,p$ and $j = 1,\ldots,q$, the conditional volatility is positive. Furthermore, the process is covariance stationary, in the case $p = q = 1$, if and only if

$$\beta_1^2 + \frac{1}{2}\left[\alpha_1^2 + (\alpha_1 + \gamma_1)^2\right] + \frac{2}{\sqrt{2\pi}}\beta_1(\alpha_1 + \gamma_1) < 1$$ (Poon, 2005, p. 42).

EGARCH

Due to their frequent use in financial area, it was inevitable to make some adjustments in the GARCH models. With the adjustment of Nelson in 1991, it was possible to avoid the negative values of the conditional variance. Thus, it was possible to implement the model logarithmically (Bolgün & Akçay, 2005, p. 342). With this model it was also possible to capture the leverage or asymmetric effect, which occurs when an unexpected drop in price (bad news) increases predictable volatility more than an unexpected increase in price (good news) of similar magnitude, and this effect results in that a symmetry constraint on the conditional variance function in past ε's is inappropriate (Engle & Ng, 1993, p. 1752). Consequently, exponential GARCH (EGARCH) model can be defined as follows:

$$\log h_t = \omega + \beta.\log(h_{t-1}) + \gamma.\frac{\varepsilon_{t-1}}{\sqrt{h_{t-1}}} + \alpha\left[\frac{\left|\varepsilon_{t-1}\right|}{\sqrt{h_{t-1}}} - \sqrt{\frac{2}{\pi}}\right]$$

where ω, β, γ and α are constant parameters. Since γ is typically negative, positive return shocks generate less volatility than negative return shocks. Again, the process is covariance stationary if and only if $\sum\beta < 1$ (Poon, 2005, p. 41). Meanwhile, because of the non-differentiability with respect to $\frac{\varepsilon_{t-1}}{\sqrt{h_{t-1}}}$ at zero, the EGARCH model is often somewhat more difficult to estimate and analyzed numerically (Andersen *et al.*, 2005, p. 22). However, according to the news impact, EGARCH model differs from GARCH model in two main points: First, it allows good news and bad news to have a different impact on volatility, which GARCH model does not. Second, it allows big news to have a greater impact on volatility than the standard GARCH model (Engle & Ng, 1993, p. 1753).

A-PARCH

The Asymmetric Power ARCH (A-PARCH) model is a recent addition to time series models that may be used for predicting volatility. The general A-PARCH (p,q,δ) model

$$\varepsilon_t = z_t h_t$$

where $\{z_t\}$ iş a sequence of independent identically distributed random variables with a symmetric density with zero mean and a nite $2\delta - ht$ unconditional absolute moment. Furthermore,

$$h_t\delta = \alpha_0 + \sum_{j=1}^{p} \alpha_j \left(|\varepsilon_{t-j}| - \phi_j \varepsilon_{t-j}\right)\delta + \sum_{j=1}^{q} \beta_j h_{t-j}\delta$$ (He & Teräsvirta, 1997, p. 3).

THE METHODOLOGY OF THE RESEARCH

In this study, it is tried to examine volatility characteristics of emerging stock exchange markets, whether they have similar patterns or different structures. In this context, 6 countries, Argentina, Brazil, Chile, Colombia, Mexico, Turkey, are chosen to be representative for emerging markets. For each country, the monthly US dollar total returns data between 1986/12-2005/12, 228 observations, are used. These data are obtained from Standard & Poors IFCG indexes in order to overcome difficulties due to different methodologies used for locally produced indexes.

Among a number of volatility modeling methods such as implied volatility model, stochastic volatility model, Arch models are chosen to capture volatility characteristics of these markets. For each market, firstly mean modeling, that is ARMA (p, q) , is performed and than ARCH/GARCH, TARCH, EGARCH, A-PARCH are formed. In addition, GED and t-distributions as well as normal distribution are included in volatility calculation in order to reflect fat tail characteristics of financial time series.

EMPIRICAL ANALYSIS

The logarithmic return of the monthly US dollar total return of stock markets S&P IFGC indexes are used for modeling. By examining the related data of stock exchange markets, mean modeling of markets are found as in Table 1.

Table 1
Mean Models of Stock Exchange Markets

Stock Market		*Mean Model*
Argentina	ARMA(3,3)	LOGRETURN_AR = 0.0129 + 0.6586 AR(3) + 0.5431MA(3) (0.41) (0,00) (0.04)
Brazil	ARIMA(0,1,1)	D(LOGRETURN_BR) = 0.0001 + -0.9924 MA(1) (0.58) (0.00)
Chile	ARMA(0,1)	LOGRETURN_CH = 0.0189 + 0.2373 MA(1) (0.00) (0.00)
Colombia	ARMA(0,1)	LOGRETURN_CL = 0.0136 + 0.3859 MA(1) (0.05) (0.00)
Mexico	AR(0) MA(1) MA(3) MA(4)	LOGRETURN_MX = 0.0169+ 0.4058MA(1) -0.1544 MA(3) + 0.1887MA(4) (0.04) (0.00) (0.01) (0.00)
Turkey	AR(0) MA(3) MA(14)	LOGRETURN_TR = 0.0112 + 0.1636 MA(3)-0.4077MA(14) (0.20) (0.00) (0.00)

As a result of Arma modeling of log returns of stock market, models have reached the white noise process. Later, whether or not series have arch effects should be examined.Table1 shows the ARCH-LM test results and probabilities of each market. According to test results only Chile Stock Exchange market does not have arch effect, and therefore Chile Stock Exchange volatility modeling can not be performed.

Table 2
ARCH_LM Test results, F-statistics and Their Probabilities

Country	*F-statistic*	*Probability*
Argentina	10.21116	0.000000
Brazil	2.070185	0.033576
Chile	1.829450	0.083008
Colombia	11.65518	0.000000
Mexico	18.07674	0.000000
Turkey	12.20012	0.000000

After mean modeling and determining the heteroscedasticity, Arch models for series are performed. Estimation results for the Argentina Stock Market are presented in Table3 in Appendix. Gaussian GARCH (1, 1) model and GARCH (1, 1) with GED error distribution are appropriate models for Argentina volatility characteristic. In GARCH (1, 1) with GED error, there is a little improvement in the AIC, which means that it may be a better model than Gaussian GARCH (1, 1). However these models do not give us asymmetrical effects in the volatility of the market. With this purpose EGARCH, TGARCH, PARCH are examined, findings are as follows: EGARCH (1, 1) model no matter which error distribution is used, that is, normal, student-t and GED, shows no sign of asymmetry. As it is seen from the Table 3 probabilities of δ_2 coefficients in three EGARCH model is insignificant, which means that there is no asymmetry. Another asymmetrical model A-PARCH (1, 1) with those three error distribution is found as invalid as well, because of high probability values showing the insignificance of all coefficient. TGARCH (1, 1) with GED and Student –t error distribution shows also no asymmetrical effect because of insignificance coefficients. However, it is found some evidence of asymmetry in Gaussian TGARCH (1, 1). However contrary to leverage effect, positive events has bigger impact on volatility. As a result, Argentina Stock Exchange Market can be modeled ARMA (3, 3), GARCH (1, 1). In order to determine whether the volatility of Argentina stock market affects the rate of returns of stock, ARCH-M is performed. Related statistics are shown in Table8 and results show that volatility of Argentina Stock Market does not affect the rate of returns of stocks.

Estimation results for the Brazil Stock Market are presented in Table 4 in Appendix. GARCH (1, 1) with normal, student- t and GED errors are appropriate models for Brazil Stock Market. According to coefficients significance level and AIC, GARCH (1, 1) with student-t error distribution is better than other two. It is found some evidence of asymmetry. Gaussian TGARCH (1, 1) shows asymmetry with that probability of coefficient of γ_1 is 0.09. Although it is bigger than %5 level, at %10 significance level it is significant. So if it is not evaluated so strictly, Gaussian TGARCH (1, 1) model shows asymmetrical effect. Therefore, it can be said that, in Brazil Stock Exchange Market negative events cause higher volatility than positive events contrary to Argentina. Gaussian EGARCH (1, 1) has also shows asymmetrical effect with the coefficient of $\delta_2 = 0.0452$, probability = 0.08, which means that it is significant only at %10 significance level as in the case of TGARCH (1, 1). Compared to Gaussian EGARCH (1, 1), there is little improvement in the AIC of Gaussian TGARCH (1, 1). Other than these two asymmetrical models, other asymmetrical models, EGARCH (1, 1) with student-t and GED errors and A-PARCH with normal, student-t and GED errors, includes insignificant coefficients and show no sign of asymmetry. When valid models are compared, the best AIC value of GARCH (1, 1) with student–t error can be considered as a better model. However to determine the best model, it should be compared their forecasting capacity, which is beyond the scope of this study. In order to determine whether the volatility of Brazil stock market affects the rate of returns of stock, ARCH-M is performed. Related statistics are shown in Table8 and strong evidence has found that volatility of Brazil Stock Market has important effect on stocks' rate of return due to high significance level of the coefficients. As a result, ARIMA (0, 1, 1) as mean model and GARCH-M (1, 1) or TGARCH-M (1, 1) may be accepted as explanatory models of Brazil Stock Market.

It can not be performed any ARCH models for Chile Stock Market since it has not arch effect, which means no heteroscedasticity.

Estimation results for the Colombia Stock Market are presented in Table 5 in Appendix. Gaussian GARCH (0, 3) model is appropriate model for Colombia Stock Market due to significance of coefficient and AIC when compared to GARCH (0, 3) with Student-t and GED errors distribution. Since these models do not take into account the leverage effect, when EGARCH, TGARCH, A-PARCH models are examined, findings are as follows: TGARCH (0, 3) with student-t and GED error distribution shows asymmetrical effect by γ_1 's significance

Table 3
Volatility model results of Argentina Stock Exchange

Model	α_1	β_1	γ_1	δ_1	δ_2	δ_3	ϕ_1	ϕ_2	ϕ_3	ϕ_4	Log Likelihood	AIC
GARCH(1,1)- N(*)	0.1843 (0.00)	0.8019 (0.00)									113.8857	-0.958984
GARCH(1,1)-Student	CAN NOT BE PERFORMED											
GARCH(1,1)-GED	0.1753 (0.00)	0.7451 (0.00)									129.2620	-1.086774
TGARCH(1,1)- N(*)	0.3771 (0.00)	0.6837 (0.00)	-0.3373 (0.00)								115.9200	-0.968178
TGARCH(1,1)- Student	0.2404 (0.08)	0.6648 (0.00)	-0.0979 (0.57)								80,52295	-1.135914
TGARCH(1,1)- Ged	0.2781 (0.01)	0.6791 (0.20)	-0.1901 (0.00)								132.2967	-1.104860
EGARCH(1,1)- N(*)				0.2759 (0.00)	0.0479 (0.20)	0.9231 (0.00)					111.2469	-0.926639
EGARCH(1,1)- Student				0.3744 (0.00)	-0.0106 (0.90)	0.8874 (0.00)					136.0423	-1.138154
EGARCH(1,1)- Ged				0.3538 (0.00)	0.0372 (0.63)	0.9083 (0.00)					132.1747	-1.103775
A-PARCH(1,1,1)-N(*)							0.0031 (1)	-0.8077 (0.99)	0.2703 (0.56)	7.6484 (0.47)	121.9735	-1.013098
A-PARCH(1,1,1)-Student							0.0606 (0.69)	-0.4595 (0.61)	0.5885 (0.00)	3.4082 (0.01)	136.3605	-1.132093
A-PARCH(1,1,1)-Ged							0.0034 (0.99)	-0.7006 (0.99)	0.3044 (0.63)	7.2742 (0.58)	134.4828	-1.115402

* Values in Parenthesis Show The Probabilities of Coefficients

** GARCH = C+ α_1 *RESID(-1)^2 + β_1 *GARCH(-1)

*** TGARCH = C+ α_1*RESID(-1)^2 + γ_1*RESID(-1)^2*(RESID(-1)<0) + β_1 *GARCH(-1)

**** EGARCH MODEL: LOG(GARCH) = C + δ_1*ABS(RESID(-1)/@SQRT(GARCH(-1))) + δ_2*RESID(-1)/@SQRT(GARCH(-1)) + δ_3*LOG(GARCH (-1))

***** A-PARCH MODEL: @SQRT(GARCH)^ ϕ_4 = C + ϕ_1*(ABS(RESID(-1)) - Cϕ_2*RESID(-1))^ ϕ_4 + ϕ_3*@SQRT(GARCH(-1))^ ϕ_4

Table 4
Volatility Models' Results of Brazil Stock Exchange Market

MODEL	α_1	β_1	γ_1	δ_1	δ_2	δ_3	ϕ_1	ϕ_2	ϕ_3	ϕ_4	Log Likelihood	AIC
GARCH(1,1)- N(*)	0.1327	0.8463										
	(0.00)	(0.00)									98.95088	-0.82776
GARCH(1,1)-Student	0.1152	0.8785										
	(0.03)	(0.00)									108.8943	-0.90655
GARCH(1,1)-GED	0.1220	0.8583										
	(0.06)	(0.00)									109.2169	-0.90940
TGARCH(1,1)- N(*)	0.0809	0.8475	0.0984									
	(0.06)	(0.00)	(0.09)								99.72520	-0.82577
TGARCH(1,1)- Student	0.0751	0.0561	0.8847									
	(0.31)	(0.00)	(0.48)								109.1139	-0.89968
TGARCH(1,1)- Ged	0.0933	0.0533	0.8582									
	(0.23)	(0.00)	(0.53)								109.4141	-0.90232
EGARCH(1,1)- N(*)				0.2516	0.0452	-0.9430						
				(0.00)	(0.08)	(0.00)					98.51938	-0.81514
EGARCH(1,1)- Student				0.1748	-0.0650	0.9860						
				(0.06)	(0.32)	(0.00)					109.9665	-0.90719
EGARCH(1,1)- Ged				0.2416	-0.0320	0.9673						
				(0.03)	(0.63)	(0.00)					109.7539	-0.90532
A-PARCH(1,1,1)-N(*)							0.1295	0.0661	0.8697	0.8545		
							(0.01)	(0.78)	(0.00)	(0.17)	100.2446	-0.82153
A-PARCH(1,1,1)-Student							0.1074	0.2855	0.8965	0.7051		
							(0.03)	(0.50)	(0.00)	(0.23)	110.3602	-0.90185
A-PARCH(1,1,1)-Ged							0.1117	0.0843	0.8834	0.6153		
							(0.08)	(0.83)	(0.00)	(0.43)	110.2154	-0.90057

* Values in Parenthesis Show The Probabilities of Coefficients

** GARCH = C+ α_1*RESID(-1)^2 + β_1*GARCH(-1)

*** TGARCH = C+ α_1*RESID(-1)^2 + γ_1*RESID(-1)^2*(RESID(-1)<0) + β_1*GARCH(-1)

**** EGARCH MODEL: LOG(GARCH) = C + δ_1*ABS(RESID(-1)/@SQRT(GARCH(-1))) + δ_2*RESID(-1)/@SQRT(GARCH(-1)) + δ_3*LOG(GARCH(-1))

***** A-PARCH MODEL: @SQRT(GARCH)^ ϕ_4 = C + ϕ_2*(ABS(RESID(-1)) - ϕ_2*RESID(-1))^ ϕ_4+ ϕ_3*@SQRT(GARCH(-1))^ ϕ_4

Table 5
Volatility Models' Results of Colombia Stock Exchange Market

MODEL	α_1	β_1	β_2	β_3	γ_1	δ_1	δ_2	δ_3	δ_4	ϕ_2	Log Likelihood	AIC
GARCH(0,3)- N(*)		-0.5148	0.9934	0.4860							262.6639	-2.25143
		(0.00)	(0.00)	(0.00)								
GARCH(0,3)-Student		-1.2206	0.4966	0.7330							266.7388	-2.27841
		(0.00)	(0.28)	(0.00)								
GARCH(0,3)-GED		-1.2700	0.3855	0.6684							265.7618	-2.26984
		(0.00)	(0.49)	(0.02)								
TGARCH(0,3)- N(*)		0.7004	-0.3301	-0.1779	-0.0799						261.7876	-2.23497
		(0.15)	(0.43)	(0.77)	(0.83)							
TGARCH(0,3)- Student		0.8502	-0.7231	0.5854	0.1011						268,6757	-2.2866
		(0.00)	(0.00)	(0.00)	(0.00)							
TGARCH(0,3)- Ged		0.8402	-0.7529	0.5475	0.0848						267.5692	-2.2769
		(0.00)	(0.02)	(0.00)	(0.02)							
EGARCH(0,3)- N(*)						0.2577	0.2349	-0.4142	0.3329		266.7775	-2.27875
						(0.00)	(0.36)	(0.02)	(0.22)			
EGARCH(0,3)- Student						0.0991	1.4655	-1.4163	0.5047		270.8841	-2.30600
						(0.02)	(0.00)	(0.00)	(0.07)			
EGARCH(0,3)- Ged						0.0897	0.6244	0.7798	-0.8403		266.7181	-2.26945
						(0.03)	(0.00)	(0.00)	(0.00)			
A-PARCH()-N(*)												
A-PARCH()-Student												
A-PARCH()-Ged												

* Values in Parenthesis Show the Probabilities of Coefficients

** GARCH = C+ α_1*RESID(-1)^2 + β_1*GARCH(-1) + β_2 *GARCH(-2) + β_3*GARCH(-3)

*** TGARCH = C+ α_1*RESID(-1)^2 + γ_1*RESID(-1)^2*(RESID(-1)<0) + β_1*GARCH(-1) + β_2*GARCH(-2) + β_3*GARCH(-3)

**** EGARCH MODEL: LOG(GARCH) = C + δ_1 *RESID(-1)/@SQRT(GARCH(-1)) + δ_2*LOG(GARCH(-1)) + δ_3*LOG(GARCH(-2)) +δ_4 *LOG(GARCH (-3))

level of 0.00%, 0.02% respectively. It shows that negative events have more effect on volatility than positive events have. In addition, it is found some asymmetry evidence in EGARCH (0, 3) with student-t and GED errors. These four models are compared according to coefficients' significance level and AIC, TGARCH (0, 3) with student–t error distribution is better than others. A-PARCH model can not be performed since ARCH order, which is zero, is smaller than asymmetrical order, which is 1. As a result it can be said that ARMA (0, 1) as mean model and TGARCH (0, 3) with student-t error as volatility model can be used as representative for Colombia Stock Exchange Market. However it should be noted that for a better evaluation, appropriate model should be compared according to their forecasting accuracy, which is beyond the scope of this study. In order to determine whether the volatility of Colombia stock market affects the rate of returns of stock, ARCH-M is performed. Related statistics are shown in Table 8 and like Argentina, volatility of Colombia has also no impact on rate of returns of stocks.

Estimation results for the Mexico Stock Market are presented in Table 6 in Appendix. GARCH (1, 1) with normal, student-t, GED errors are accepted as explanatory models for Mexico Stock Market volatility due to high significance level of coefficients and AICs. EGARCH, TGARCH, A-PARCH models which are used for measure asymmetrical effects show no sign of asymmetry. In TGARCH models, γ_1 's probabilities, which measure the asymmetrical effects, are quite high compared to 5%. In EGARCH models, although δ_1 s, which measure the asymmetrical effects are significant, since δ_1 s are insignificant, models can not be seen as explanatory. In A-PARCH models, again ϕ_1, which measure the asymmetrical effects, are insignificant. As a result, in Mexico Stock Exchange Market No evidence of asymmetry is found, which means that there is no leverage effect in the Mexico Stock Market, and AR(0) MA (1) MA (4) as mean model and GARCH (1,1) as volatility model are for Mexico Stock Market. In order to determine whether the volatility of Mexico stock market affects the rate of returns of stock, ARCH-M is performed. Related statistics are shown in Table 8 and like Argentina and Colombia, volatility of Mexico Stock Market has also no impact on rate of returns of stocks.

Estimation results for the Turkey Stock Market are presented in Table 6 in Appendix. Firstly, GARCH (1, 0) with normal, student –t, GED errors are found as appropriate models for stock market in Turkey. When they are compared according to AIC and coefficients' significance level, it has not been seen evident difference. In addition, no asymmetry evidence in the stock market of Turkey is found such as stock market of Mexico since coefficients, which determine asymmetrical effects, are insignificant with high probability. That is, there is no distinction between positive and negative returns on volatility. In order to determine whether the volatility of Brazil stock market affects the rate of returns of stock, ARCH-M is performed. Related statistics are shown in Table 8 and strong evidence has found that volatility of Turkey Stock Market has important effect on stocks' rate of return due to high significance level of the coefficients like in Brazil. As a result AR (0) MA (3) MA (14) as mean model and GARCH-M (1, 0) as volatility model are for stock market in Turkey.

Table 6
Volatility Models' Results of Mexico Stock Exchange Market

MODEL	α_1	β_1	γ_1	δ_1	δ_2	δ_3	ϕ_1	ϕ_2	ϕ_3	ϕ_4	*Log Likelihood*	*AIC*
GARCH(1,1)- N(*)	0.2720	0.698442										
	(0.00)	(0.00)									193.7725	-1.64712
GARCH(1,1)-Student	0.2098	0.5922										
	(0.00)	(0.04)									207.1777	-1.76471
GARCH(1,1)-GED	0.2135	0.6352										
	(0.00)	(0.04)									202.3561	-1.72242
TGARCH(1,1)- N(*)	0.3021	0.7164	-0.092									
	(0.00)	(0.00)	(0.31)								194.1449	-1.64162
TGARCH(1,1)- Student	0.3497	0.6740	-0.2046									
	(0.10)	(0.00)	(0.32)								207.8853	-1.76215
TGARCH(1,1)- Ged	0.3312	-0.1844	0.7168									
	(0.07)	(0.00)	(0.27)								204.8559	-1.72680
EGARCH(1,1)- N(*)				0.4025	-0.0470	-0.4778						
				(0.00)	(0.55)	(0.00)					182.9592	-1.53473
EGARCH(1,1)- Student				0.4443	0.0817	0.8900						
				(0.00)	(0.38)	(0.00)					208.4608	-1.76720
EGARCH(1,1)- Ged				0.4523	0.0599	0.8886						
				(0.00)	(0.44)	(0.00)					203.4731	-1.72344
A-PARCH(1,1,1)-N(*)							0.0476	-0.2477	0.3500	6.8267		
							(0.66)	(0.03)	(0.27)	(0.17)	194.5890	-1.64551
A-PARCH(1,1,1)-Student							0.1068	-0.2475	0.4328	5.0350	208.5738	-1.75941
							(0.41)	(0.09)	(0.06)	(0.00)		
A-PARCH(1,1,1)-Ged							0.0568	-0.2646	0.3422	6.9584	204.5587	-1.72419
							(0.73)	(0.07)	(0.40)	(0.31)		

* Values in Parenthesis Show the Probabilities of Coefficients

** GARCH = C+ α_1*RESID(-1)^2 + β_1*GARCH(-1)

*** TGARCH = C+ α_1*RESID(-1)^2 + γ_1*RESID(-1)^2*(RESID(-1)<0) + β_1*GARCH(-1)

**** EGARCH MODEL: LOG(GARCH) = C + δ_1*ABS(RESID(-1)/@SQRT(GARCH(-1))) + δ_2*RESID(-1)/@SQRT(GARCH(-1)) + δ_3*LOG(GARCH(-1))

***** A-PARCH MODEL: @SQRT(GARCH)^ ϕ_4 = C + ϕ_1*(ABS(RESID(-1)) - ϕ_2*RESID(-1))^ ϕ_4+ ϕ_3*@SQRT(GARCH(-1))^ ϕ_4

Table7
Volatility Models' Results of Turkey Stock Exchange Market

MODEL	α_1	γ_1	δ_1	δ_2	ϕ_1	ϕ_2	ϕ_3	*Log Likelihood*	*AIC*
GARCH(1,0)- N(*)	-0.0975 (0.00)							81.18829	-0.67709
GARCH(1,0)-Student	-0.0996 (0.00)							80.71244	-0.66414
GARCH(1,0)-GED	-0.0954 (0.00)							81.23749	-0.66875
TGARCH(1,0)- N(*)	-0.0978 (0.00)	0.0581 (0.63)						82.08743	-0.67620
TGARCH(1,0)- Student	-0.1001 (0.00)	0.0902 (0.58)						81.50211	-0.66229
TGARCH(1,0)- Ged	-0.09852 (0.00)	0.0497 (0.70)						82.37526	-0.66995
EGARCH(1,0)- N(*)			-0.2108 (0.28)	0.0335 (0.76)				78.78804	-0.64726
EGARCH(1,0)- Student			-0.1744 (0.42)	0.0249 (0.84)				78.98114	-0.64018
EGARCH(1,0)- Ged			-0.2091 (0.30)	0.0333 (0.77)				78.78880	-0.63849
A-PARCH(1,0,1)-N(*)					-0.0699 (0.49)	-0.2097 (0.76)	1.9906 (0.01)	81.69800	-0.66401
A-PARCH(1,0,1)-Student					-0.0680 (0.54)	-0.2294 (0.77)	1.9853 (0.01)	82.34478	-0.66091
A-PARCH(1,0,1)-Ged					-0.0690 (0.59)	-0.3244 (0.77)	1.8936 (0.00)	80.75519	-0.64697

* Values in Parenthesis Show the Probabilities of Coefficients

** GARCH = C+ α_1*RESID(-1)^2 +

*** TGARCH = C+ α_1*RESID(-1)^2 + γ_1*RESID(-1)^2*(RESID(-1)<0)

**** EGARCH MODEL: LOG(GARCH) = C + δ_1*ABS(RESID(-1)/@SQRT(GARCH(-1))) + δ_2*RESID(-1)/@SQRT(GARCH(-1))

***** A-PARCH MODEL: @SQRT(GARCH)^ ϕ_4 = C + ϕ_1*(ABS(RESID(-1)) - ϕ_2*RESID(-1))^ ϕ_4

Table 8
Coefficients and Their Statistics in Arch-m Models of Argentina, Brazil, Colombia, Mexico, Turkey

	Coefficient	*Std. Error*	*Z-statistic*	*Probability*
ARGENTINA				
GARCH(1,1)-M @SQRT(GARCH)	-0.030216	0.242088	-0.124813	0.9007
GARCH(1,1)-M GARCH	-0.120488	0.573537	-0.210078	0.8336
GARCH(1,1)-M LOG(GARCH)	-0.006258	0.019156	-0.326683	0.7439
TGARCH(1,1)-M @SQRT(GARCH)	0.085479	0.249478	0.342630	0.7319
TGARCH(1,1)-M GARCH	0.076448	0.500382	0.152779	0.8786
TGARCH(1,1)-M LOG(GARCH)	-0.008440	0.024677	-0.342029	0.7323
BRAZIL				
GARCH(1,1)- M @SQRT(GARCH)	0.075188	0.022769	3.302228	0.0010
GARCH(1,1)- M GARCH	0.117734	0.036182	3.253905	0.0011
GARCH(1,1)- M LOG(GARCH)	0.009668	0.003225	2.997691	0.0027
TGARCH(1,1)-M @SQRT(GARCH)	0.085891	0.002574	33.37131	0.0000
TGARCH(1,1)- M GARCH	0.155164	0.041981	3.696055	0.0002
TGARCH(1,1)- M LOG(GARCH)	0.010945	0.000496	22.06529	0.0000
COLOMBIA				
TGARCH(0,3)- M @SQRT(GARCH)	-0.042878	0.083215	-0.515271	0.6064
TGARCH(0,3)- M GARCH	-0.660273	1.776758	-0.371617	0.7102
TGARCH(0,3)- M LOG(GARCH)	-0.003175	0.004427	-0.717190	0.4733
EGARCH(0,3)- M @SQRT(GARCH)	0.785550	0.537060	1.462686	0.1436
EGARCH(0,3)- M GARCH	1.920902	3.353318	0.572836	0.5668
EGARCH(0,3)- M LOG(GARCH)	0.034097	0.021296	1.601094	0.1094
MEXICO				
GARCH(1,1)- M @SQRT(GARCH)	-0.016438	0.013040	-1.260530	0.2075
GARCH(1,1)- M GARCH	-0.757018	0.944766	-0.801275	0.4230
GARCH(1,1)- M LOG(GARCH)	-0.281944	0.236702	-1.191133	0.2336
TURKEY				
GARCH(1,0)- M @SQRT(GARCH)	-1.010204	0.382528	-2.640865	0.0083
GARCH(1,0)- M GARCH	-2.839012	1.479110	-1.919406	0.0549
GARCH(1,0)- M LOG(GARCH)	-0.073197	0.024931	-2.935951	0.0033

CONCLUSION

Volatility characteristic and patterns of financial time series has captured substantial attention for the last quarter of 20th century both in research area and in practice. In this study, it is aimed to find whether emerging markets have similar patterns or not. In this context, stock markets of Argentina, Brazil, Colombia, Chile, Mexico and Turkey have been examined. According to findings, every country has its own volatility characteristics and there is nothing in common for these six countries in terms of volatility patterns. While stock markets have asymmetrical effect in Argentina, Brazil and Colombia, no evidence of asymmetry has been found for stock markets in Turkey and Mexico and in Chile stock market, there is no arch effect, which means that there is no heteroscedasticity. Apart from that, asymmetrical effect in Argentina is against to leverage effect, while asymmetry in Brazil and Colombia favors the leverage effect. That is, negative shocks leads to higher volatility than a positive shock, in Brazil and Colombia, Argentina stock markets show the opposite of this fact. In Argentina, Brazil and Mexico, with GARCH (1, 1) model, markets' volatility are affected from both deviations from expected return of the pervious day and volatility of previous day, however in Turkey, stock market volatility – GARCH (1, 0) is affected only from deviations from expected return of the pervious day while in Colombia – GARCH (0, 3), stock market volatility is affected only from volatility of previous three days. Beside how volatility pattern of these six emerging markets are is an important issue, whether their volatilities have an effect on rate of returns of stock is another important point. Findings show that in terms of effect on returns there is nothing in common among related countries as well. While Volatilities affect stocks' rate of returns in Brazil and Turkey, rate of returns of stocks in Argentina, Brazil and Colombia. Based on the findings of empirical analysis nothing has been found as common for all of the six countries included in the study in terms of neither volatility characteristics of six country nor their effects on rate of returns.

References

Andersen, T. G., T. Bollerslev, P. F. Christoffersen, F. X. Diebold (2005), Practical Volatility and Correlation Modeling for Financial Market Risk Management, paper prepared for "Risks of Financial Institutions", *University of Chicago Press.*

Apergis, N., S. Eleptheriou (2001), Stock Returns and Volatility: Evidence from the Athens Stock Market Index, *Journal of Economics and Finance* 25(1): 50-61.

Bolgün, E., Akçay, B. (2005) Risk Yönetimi, *Scala Yayıncılık.*

Bollerslev, T. (1986), Generalized Autoregressive Conditional Heteröscedasticity, *Journal of Econometrics* 31: 307-327.

Bollerslev, T., R. Y. Chou, K. F. Kroner (1992), ARCH Modeling in Finance, *Journal of Econometrics* 52: 5-59.

Engle, R. F. (1982), Autoregressive Conditional Heteroscedasticity with Estimates of the Variance of United Kingdom Inflation, *Econometrica* 50(4): 987-1008.

Engle, R. F., V. K. Ng (1993), Measuring and Testing the Impact of News on Volatility, *Journal of Finance* 48(5): 1749-1778.

Figlewski, S. (1997), Forecasting Volatility, *Financial Markets, Institutions & Instruments* 6(1): 1-88.

He, C., T. Teräsvirta (1997), Statistical Properties of the Asymmetric Power ARCH Process, *Working Paper Series in Economics and Finance* 199: 1-22.

Poon, S. H. (2005), A Practical Guide to Forecasting Financial Market Volatility, John *Wiley & Sons Inc.*

Soczo, C. (2003), Estimation of Future Volatility, *Periodica Polytechnica* 11(2): 201-214.

Tsay, R. S. (2002), Analysis of Financial Time Series, *Wiley Series.*

DO TECHNOLOGY SHOCKS MATTER IN TAIWAN IN THE 1990S?

Tin-Chun Lin*

ABSTRACT

This paper attempts to test the hypothesis that the real output growth in Taiwan in the 1990s could be traced primarily to exogenous factors, such as technology shocks. The evidence supports the consensus view that human capital growth is important for explaining Taiwan's growth over the sample period 1965-1990, but no longer has significant explanatory power for Taiwan's growth over the sample period 1975-2000. More importantly, this paper emphasizes the contrasting empirical results and draws the inference that economic growth in Taiwan in the 1990s could be traced mainly to exogenous factors. [JEL classification: *O40; J24; I20; C50]*

***Keywords:** Education, Economic Growth, Technology shocks.*

I. INTRODUCTION

The 1990s represent a remarkable era in the information technology revolution that had a significant impact on productivity in the broad spectrum of industries worldwide. In the 1990s, Taiwan's electronics and information sectors expanded rapidly to become the main industries. The electrical and electronics sectors increased their share of production value in the manufacturing industry from 13.3% in 1989 to 30.1% in 1999. As a result, in 1999, 30.4% of Taiwan's exports were electronic, information, and telecommunications products. In addition, between 1990 and 1998, Taiwan's manufacturing industry had become increasingly knowledge-based. Thus, professional information, telecommunications, and networking services have expanded most rapidly, and electronic commerce has become a service trend. For this reason, this paper attempts to test the hypothesis that the real output growth in Taiwan in the 1990s could be traced primarily to exogenous factors, such as technology shocks.

Although a number of recent empirical studies have investigated the effects of education on growth or the impact of social indicators on economic growth in Taiwan (e.g., Armer and Liu [1993], Tallman and Wang [1994], Hsieh and Hsing [2002], and Lin [2003]), no studies have been done of whether or not the economic growth in Taiwan over the last decade were driven mainly by technology shocks. Thus, I attempt to investigate the main sources of Taiwan's economic growth in the last decade. The main contribution of this paper is the comparison of regressions for the earlier period (1965-1990) with those for an overlapping but later period

* School of Business and Economics, Indiana University-Northwest, 3400 Broadway, IN 46408, USA, *E-mail: tinlin@iun.edu*

(1975-2000) to distinguish the relative contribution of education to growth in the two periods, as well as through a complementary test and discussion to determine whether the sources of economic growth were primarily exogenous or endogenous in the 1990s.

This paper is organized as follows. Section 2 develops a production function and describes data measurement. Section 3 reports the empirical analysis and results. Further exploration and discussion are provided in Section 4. Finally, conclusions are found in Section 5.

II. PRODUCTION FUNCTION AND DATA MEASUREMENT

The Cobb-Douglas form is applied to the production function. Therefore, output can be modeled as follows:

$$Y_t = \left(A_0 e^{\xi t}\right) K_t^{\alpha} \left(L_t H_t\right)^{\beta}, \tag{1}$$

where Y is real output, K is physical capital, L is raw labor input, H is the quality of human capital, $(L \cdot H)$ is effective labor, ($A_0 e^{\xi t}$) is an exogenous knowledge and technological factor, α and β are the physical capital and effective labor shares, respectively, and t is time trend.

An individual's income is assumed to rely on his human capital, which is a function of schooling. Thus, the individual's income can be specified as:

$$I\left(h\left(E_t\right)\right) = \varpi \cdot h\left(E_t\right) \tag{2}$$

where I is the individual's income, ϖ is the wage per unit of human capital, and $h(.)$ is the quality of human capital as a function of schooling which is denoted by E. Hence, the estimated general form of the structural earnings function can be specified as:

$$\ln I = \Omega + g\,(E) \tag{3}$$

where Ω is a constant term.

Based upon equations (2) and (3), human capital is implied to be given by:

$$H\left(E_t\right) = e^{g(E)} \tag{4}$$

while Ω corresponds to $\ln(\varpi)$. The standard assumptions about the $g(E)$ are that $g' > 0, g'' \le 0$ (Wills, 1986). For the sake of simplicity, assume that $g\left(E_t\right) = \gamma E_t$, where γ is a constant parameter, and then substitute equation (4) into equation (1). Thus, the production function can be re-expressed as follows:

$$Y_t = \left(A_0 e^{\xi t}\right) K_t^{\alpha} \left(L_t e^{\gamma E_t}\right)^{\beta} \tag{5}$$

Taking natural logarithms of both sides of equation (5), the production function becomes linear:

$$\ln Y_t = \ln A_0 + \xi t + \alpha \ln K_t + \beta \ln L_t + \gamma \beta E_t \tag{6}$$

The Taiwan data for 1964-2000 that are used in this study include annual measures of economic output, physical capital input, labor input, and educational stock compiled mainly from *Statistical Yearbooks of the Republic of China, Statistical Abstract of National Income in Taiwan Area, Monthly Bulletin of Manpower Statistics in Taiwan Area, Education Statistics of The Republic of China*, and *Quarterly National Economic Trends in Taiwan Area.*

Output (Y) is defined as GDP (gross domestic product). This variable is measured in millions of New Taiwan dollars (NT$) at 1996 constant prices. Physical capital (K) is defined as real capital stock, which includes gross fixed capital formation and increases in stocks (e.g., buildings, equipment, and other construction) in the domestic economy, and is also measured in millions of New Taiwan dollars at 1996 constant prices. Labor (L) is measured as the number of people in the economically active population of the employed. This variable is reported in thousands of employed people. Human capital (E) is measured as the average number of years of formal education per person among employed people [i.e., the average number of years of formal education per person = (primary stock x 6 + junior stock x 9 + senior stock x 12 + college stock x 16) / total employed people].

III. EMPIRICAL ANALYSIS AND RESULTS

Based upon equation (6), the econometric model can be specified as follows:

$$\ln Y_t - \ln Y_{t-1} = C_0 + a_K(\ln K_t - \ln K_{t-1}) + a_L(\ln L_t - \ln L_{t-1}) + a_E(E_t - E_{t-1}) + \varepsilon_t \qquad (7)$$

where ε_t is stochastic disturbance terms, assuming a mean 0 and a variance σ^2. In Equation (7), Y stands for real output, K stands for physical capital, L stands for Labor, and E stands for education stock.

In addition, the 1990s were a remarkable decade for the world economy. The information technology revolution in this decade had the most profound effect not only on the United States and other developed countries, but also on developing countries, such as Taiwan. This information motivates us to observe the Taiwan economy of the 1990s from a different perspective. Thus, the first sample period covers 1965-1990, while the second covers the period from 1975 to 2000, leaving us fewer observations in the time series analysis. Splitting the sample period between 1965-1980 and 1981-2000 further reduces degrees of freedom. Under the circumstances, I opted to use two sample periods–one excluding the 1990s and the other including the 1990s. We then observed the differences in the statistical results to draw certain inferences about the 1990s.

Reported in Column 2 of Table 1 are estimated results for the period 1965-1990. The estimate of the average share of education on the effect of output growth is 0.181. Besides, the estimated effect of education is positive and statistically significant at the 5 per cent level, indicating potent effects of education on growth. Both capital and labor shares are estimated to be 0.145 and 0.642, and the effects on output growth are statistically significant at the 1 per cent level. Nevertheless, the coefficient of technical progress is estimated at 2.5 per cent. It is not even statistically significant at the 5 and 10 per cent levels. The R-square is about 37 per cent. The DW and LM tests indicate that autocorrelation does not exist. In addition, it should be noted that the period of 1963–1980 was the most rapid growth in Taiwan's economic development history. Taiwan maintained an annual growth rate of 10 per cent over these 18 years.

Table 1
Estimates of $\ln Y_t - \ln Y_{t-1}$

Explanatory Variables	*1965-1990*	*1975-2000*
Constant	0.025	0.049***
	(1.22)	(4.12)
$\ln K_t - \ln K_{t-1}$	0.145***	0.168***
	(2.76)	(4.09)
$\ln L_t - \ln L_{t-1}$	0.642***	0.852***
	(2.44)	(3.64)
$E_t - E_{t-1}$	0.181**	-0.03
	(2.09)	(-0.49)
R^2	0.376	0.603
Durbin-Watson	1.40	1.85
Autocorelation (LM Test)	No	No

(*t*-value). *** Denote statistical significance of the *t*-statistic at the 0.01 level; ** denote statistical significance of the *t*-statistic at the 0.05 level.

Moreover, the estimated results for the period 1975-2000 are presented in Column 3 of Table 1. Surprisingly, the estimated effect of average education is shown to be negative, but it is not statistically significant at the 5 or 10 per cent levels, indicating no relationship between education and real output growth. However, the effect of technical progress, as shown in the constant, is markedly significant at the 1 per cent level, and the coefficient of the constant, estimated at 4.9 per cent, is extremely higher than the estimate for 1965-1990. Additionally, the R-square of over 60 per cent is remarkably larger than the coefficient in 1965-1990. Finally, both the DW and LM tests show that autocorrelation does not exist. In addition, it should be noted that during the period of 1981–1999, Taiwan's annual growth rate dropped to 7.15% from the near 10% average over the period of 1963–1980. The reasons of the mild slowdown could be a consequence of structural changes in the industrial sector. However, political and social transformations could also be part of the reasons. During that period, the agricultural sector had the lowest performance, but the service sector experienced the highest growth rate.

In short, dramatic differences in the role of education as revealed in the analysis, which divided the sample period between "1965–1990" and "1975–2000", can be attributed to the development of the 1990s. Thus, two questions remain: Why couldn't the growth in Taiwan in the latter period 1975–2000, especially in the 1990s, be explained by formal education? In addition, according to the result, the effect of technical progress on growth, represented by the constant term, in the latter period is remarkably significant. Were economic growth primarily driven by technology shocks in Taiwan in the 1990s? To answer these questions, we need further discussion and exploration.

IV. FURTHER EXPLORATION AND DISCUSSION

In this study, annual data were employed. Their use of annual data means that the effects of annual fluctuations, which are driven more by unspecified demand-side factors, probably dominate the determination of the size and significance of the coefficients, but to an unknown extent. These short-run fluctuations probably swamp the longer slow but steady growth-related side effects from human and physical capital formation. For example, Figures 3 and 5 show dramatic annual fluctuations in the annual growth of physical capital from 1975 through 2000, especially in the earlier part of this later period, and relatively little annual fluctuation in the annual change in education levels in Taiwan.

One would expect that the human capital coefficient would be almost zero and not significant in explaining these sharp fluctuations in annual growth of real GDP in this period, in fact, this is the case. The graphs and empirical results have a lot to say about the sensitivity of physical capital investment to the wild cyclical swings in interest rates in the 1980s, and given that investment demand is an additive component of GDP, about the swings in real GDP, but relatively little to say about longer-run growth effects on production from the supply side. Long-term interest rates in the United States went to 13.9 per cent in 1981 and stayed above 10.6 per cent through 1985 real rates of interest were 9.1 per cent in 1982, which with the globalization of financial markets surely affected Taiwan and investment in physical capital there as well. Average educational attainments are far less affected by this since the base human capital stock is so large and since most education is not financed by borrowing which is sensitive to real interest rate conditions in the financial markets. The fact that GDP growth fell in the 1980s thus may have a lot more to do with Reaganomics than with the lessening significance of human capital to Taiwan's long run growth and welfare.

Moreover, looking at the trends alone, there does appear to be a slowdown in the annual growth rate of real GDP for the entire period (shown in Figure 2 as a per centage annual change), a slowdown in the annual growth rate of physical capital (shown in Figure 3), and a slowdown in the growth rate of raw labor inputs (shown in Figure 4). At the same time there is slightly higher average growth in education levels. For this reason, it is possible to assume that human capital is being substituted for raw labor, and it is also possible that there is some substitution of human capital for physical capital. Thus, a complementarity test is provided to investigate whether or not there is a relationship (i.e., complements or substitutes) between human capital and physical capital as well as raw labor.

The complementarity formation may be modeled using a generalization of the Cobb-Douglas model, the transcendental logarithmic production function, which is:

$$\begin{aligned}\ln Y_t - \ln Y_{t-1} &= C_0 + a_K[\ln K_t - \ln K_{t-1}] + a_L[\ln L_t - \ln L_{t-1}] + a_E[E_t - E_{t-1}] \\ &+ b_{KK}\left[(\ln K_t)^2 - (\ln K_{t-1})^2\right]/2 + b_{LL}\left[(\ln L_t)^2 - (\ln L_{t-1})^2\right]/2 + b_{EE}\left[E_t^2 - E_{t-1}^2\right]/2 \\ &+ b_{KL}[\ln K_t \ln L_t - \ln K_{t-1} \ln L_{t-1}] + b_{KE}[\ln K_t \cdot E_t - \ln K_{t-1} \cdot E_{t-1}] \\ &+ b_{LE}[\ln L_t \cdot E_t - \ln L_{t-1} \cdot E_{t-1}] + b_{D1}D1_t + b_{D2}D2_t + \varepsilon_t ,\end{aligned} \tag{8}$$

where $D1$ and $D2$ are dummy variables to capture the effects of the two oil crises of 1973–1975 and 1979–1982 (indicated as $D1$) and the Asian financial crisis of 1997–1998 (indicated as $D2$). If human capital and physical capital as well as raw labor are substitutes, it should be able to estimate $b_{KE} < 0$ and $b_{LE} < 0$. According to the results shown in Table 2, unfortunately, no remarkable relationship is found between human capital and raw labor; but the finding shows that human capital and physical capital are complements because the effect is positive and statistically significant at the 10 per cent level.

Table 2
Estimates of $\ln Y_t - \ln Y_{t-1}$ (1975-2000)

Explanatory Variables	*Equation (2)*	*Equation (3)*
Constant	0.07682***	0.12062***
	(6.14)	(4.06)
$\ln K_t - \ln K_{t-1}$	39.35*	0.14651***
	(1.85)	(4.43)
$\ln L_t - \ln L_{t-1}$	-57.92	0.4076
	(-0.97)	(1.40)
$E_t - E_{t-1}$	-7.86	0.12448*
	(-0.47)	(1.96)
$\frac{(\ln K_t)^2 - (\ln K_{t-1})^2}{2}$	-0.7669**	
	(-2.23)	
$\frac{(\ln L_t)^2 - (\ln L_{t-1})^2}{2}$	6.385	
	(1.14)	
$\frac{(E_t)^2 - (E_{t-1})^2}{2}$	-0.3481	
	(-1.28)	
$\ln K_t \cdot \ln L_t - \ln K_{t-1} \cdot \ln L_{t-1}$	-1.494	
	(-1.31)	
$\ln K_t \cdot E_t - \ln K_{t-1} \cdot E_{t-1}$	0.6015*	
	(1.72)	
$\ln L_t \cdot E_t - \ln L_{t-1} \cdot E_{t-1}$	-0.3364	
	(-0.38)	
$E_t \cdot t - E_{t-1} \cdot (t-1)$		-0.005858***
		(-2.73)
$D1_t$	-0.03221***	-0.034334***
	(-4.48)	(-4.30)
$D2_t$	-0.00927	-0.009935
	(-0.74)	(-1.01)
R^2	0.897	0.823
Durbin-Watson	2.45	2.19

(t-value) *** Denote statistical significance of the t-statistic at the 0.01 level; ** denote statistical significance of the t-statistic at the 0.05 level; * denote statistical significance of the t-statistic at the 0.1 level.

Figure 1: Average Years of Education per Person Among Employed People (1964-2000)

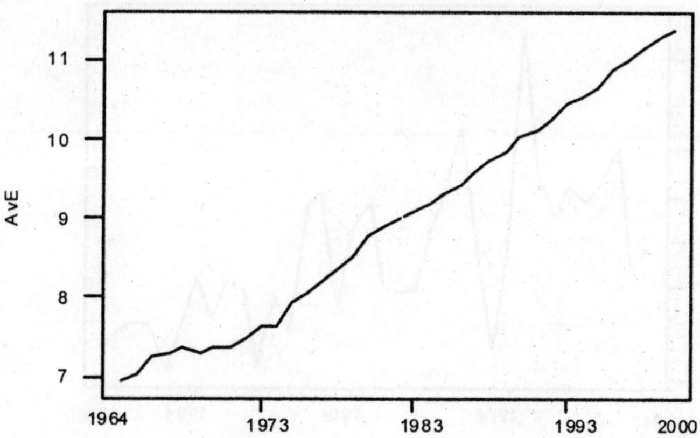

Figure 2: Annual Growth Rate for Real GDP in Taiwan (1965-2000)

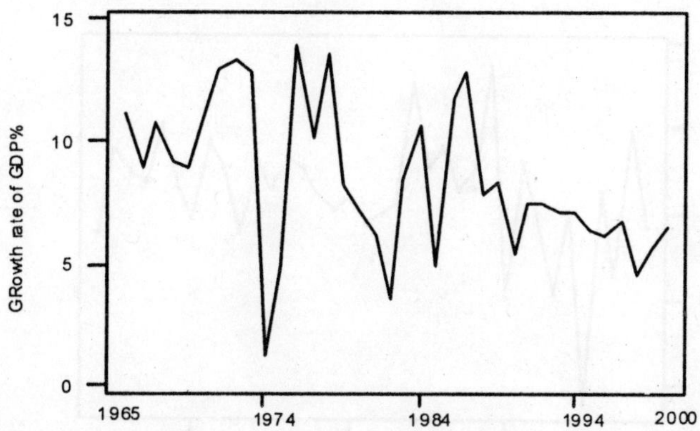

Figure 3: Annual Growth Rate for Capital in Taiwan (1965-2000)

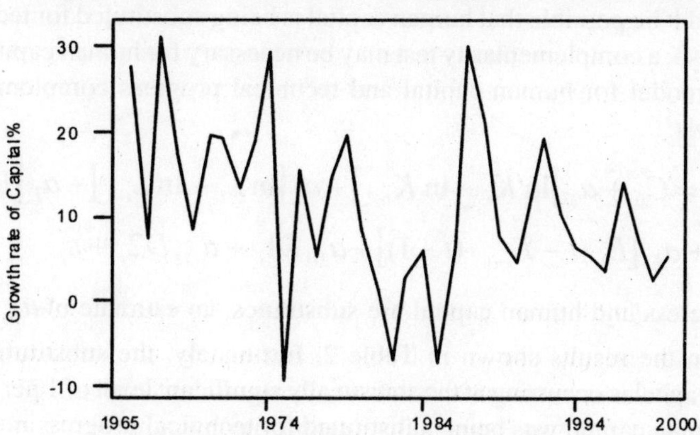

Figure 4: Annual Growth Rate for Labor in Taiwan (1965-2000)

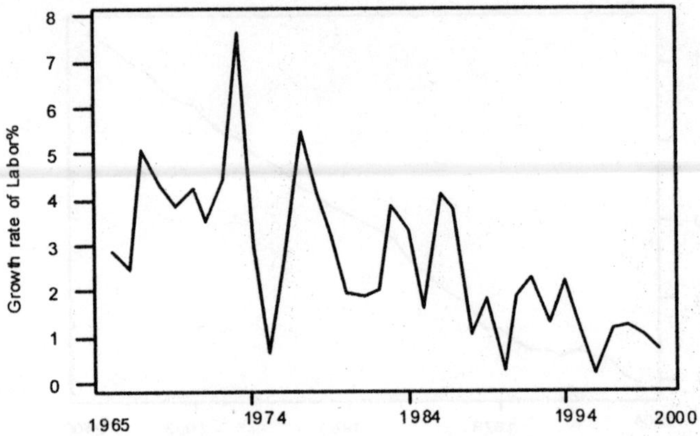

Figure 5: Annual Change for Average Education in Taiwan (1965-2000)

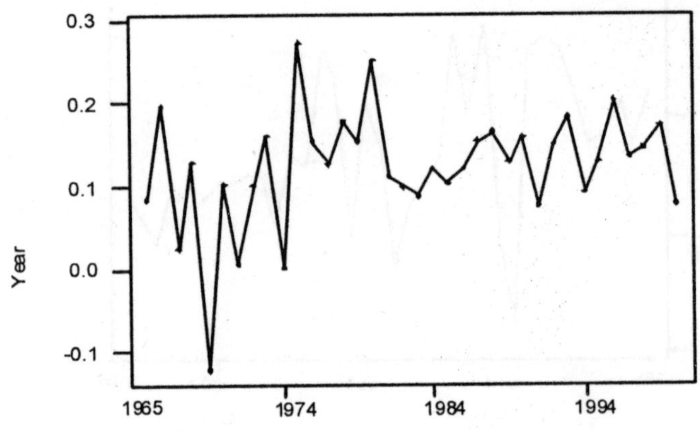

In addition, could it be possible that human capital is being substituted for technical progress in the later period? If so, a complementarity test may be necessary for human capital and technical progress. A simple model for human capital and technical progress complementarity can be constructed as follows:

$$\ln Y_t - \ln Y_{t-1} = C_0 + a_K[\ln K_t - \ln K_{t-1}] + a_L[\ln L_t - \ln L_{t-1}] + a_E[E_t - E_{t-1}]$$
$$+ a_{Et}[E_t \cdot t - E_{t-1} \cdot (t-1)] + a_{D1}D1_t + a_{D2}D2_t + \varepsilon_t . \quad (9)$$

If technical progress and human capital are substitutes, an estimate of $a_{Et} < 0$ should be feasible. Based upon the results shown in Table 2, fortunately, the substitution of technical progress for human capital is occurring at the statistically significant level of 1 per cent. Therefore, it is possible that human capital was being substituted for technical progress in the later period.

In summary of this point, the insignificance of human capital formation in the later period, and the relatively high significance of physical capital in all periods, may largely reflect annual fluctuations. The substitution of technical progress for human capital may also be occurring in this instance. Additionally, prior to the 1960s, Taiwan's economy was primary geared toward agricultural and non-technical production (Liang, K. and Liang, C., 1988; Kim and Lau, 1994). But during the 1960s, Taiwan transformed itself into a newly industrializing country, and the policy priorities of the Taiwan government were industrial production and the education of the population. Investment in education in the following decades provided positive and significant effects on growth. In the 1990s, however, the world saw the New Economy develop as a result of rapidly advancing information technology. Higher productivity led to dramatic increases in total real output in the 1990s. The information technology revolution (Jorgenson, 2001) and quantum rise in productivity affected not only developed countries, but also many developing countries, including Taiwan. Technological advances in Taiwan and their impact on its economic productivity have to be examined from a new perspective. For example, Internet innovation was not invented in Taiwan, but it was carried to Taiwan and led to many Internet-related industries and new jobs, thereby further improving worker productivity. Such innovation in Taiwan obviously exerts an exogenous impact on technology. Therefore, according to the results of this study and analysis, we conclude that exogenous technology shocks could explain much of the real output growth in Taiwan in the 1990s.

V. CONCLUSIONS

In this paper, the empirical work shows that human capital investment through educational achievement is a central source of Taiwan growth. At its core, this paper offers several more observations in the data set and engages in minor alterations of the empirical model. The econometric evidence supports the consensus view that human capital growth is important for explaining Taiwan's growth over the period 1965–1990 and. Most of attention in the paper, though, examines the finding that the human capital measure no longer has explanatory power for Taiwan's economic growth over the sample period 1975–2000.

In addition, according to the results, the coefficient of technical progress is remarkably larger and more significant for the later period (1975–2000) than for the earlier period (1965–1990), implying the larger role of technical progress in the growth that occurred during the 1990s. Therefore, I emphasize the contrasting empirical results and draw the inference that the sources of economic growth in Taiwan in the 1990s could be mostly exogenous.

References

Armer, M., Liu, C. (1993), Education's Effect on Economic Growth in Taiwan. Comparative Education Review 37(3), 304-321.

Barro, R. (2001), Economic Growth in East Asia before and After the Financial Crisis. *NBER Working Paper* 8330.

Hsieh, W., Hsing, Y. (2002), Economic Growth and Social Indicators. *International Journal of Social Economics* 29 (7), 518-617.

Jorgenson, D. (2001), Information technology and the U.S. economy. *American Economic Review* 91 (1), 1-32.

Kim, J., Lau, L. (1994), The Sources of Economic Growth of the East Asian Newly Industrialized Countries. *Journal of Japanese and International Economics* 8(3), 62-78.

Liang, K., Liang, C., Liang, H. (1988), Development Policy Formation and Future Policy Priorities in the Republic of China. Economic Development and Cultural Change 36(3) (supplement), S67-S101.

Lin, T. (2003), Education, Technical Progress, and Economic Growth: The Case of Taiwan. *Economics of Education Review* 22 (2), 213-220.

Park, Y., Lee, J. (2001), Recovery and sustainability in East Asia. *NBER Working Paper* 8373.

Tallman, E., Wang, P. (1994), Human Capital and Endogenous Growth: Evidence from Taiwan. *Journal of Monetary Economics* 34, 101-124.

CORRUPTIONS AND ECONOMIC PERFORMANCES IN SEVERAL AFRICAN COUNTRIES: AN ANALYSIS

Subarna K. Samanta & Thomas P. Breslin*

Abstract

The analysis of corruption in international business is a relatively new phenomenon and for last two decades many research works have attempted to capture the economic impact of corruption in a country. However, most of them have concentrated their analysis to the experiences of only the developed countries. None or very few of the current works have addressed the corruption issue in the context of the developing countries. This work examines theoretically as well as empirically, the incidence of corruption in the context of economic growth and investment in the developing countries; especially for several African countries that signed a treaty indicating to make changes in their business practices.

Keywords: *Corruption; foreign direct investment; developing countries*

JEL Classification numbers: *F2; F21; F23; O16.*

INTRODUCTION

Corruption in international business has recently emerged as a major public policy concern across the globe. Corrupt practices such as bribing public officials to obtain business contracts and favors are not new in human civilization. In the ancient Indian book *Arthasastra*, (in approximately 300B.C.) Chanakya mentions the concept of *utkoch*, meaning bribery. In China, the Qin Dynasty (220BC)) understood the concept of corruption and placed heavy penalties on it. However, the rampant use of corrupt practices is a relatively new phenomenon in modern industrial organizations. Corruption is conceived as a distorting factor in the smooth functioning of the economy, because it tends to disrupt the free and open market economic practices and procedures and consequently can lead to a distorted lower level of social and economic well being for the country as a whole. One of the most unfortunate outcomes of such corrupt practices is the negative impact on the public's respect for the rule of law, and therefore, on the structure and stability of society (Mauro, 1995).

In the last half century, the world has experienced a tremendous growth in the international trade and investment. However, this growth has also ushered in an era of corruption in

* School of Business, The College of New Jersey, Ewing, *E-mail: SSamanta@tcnj.edu*

First draft of this paper was presented at the annual meeting of the Eastern Economics Association in February 2006, Philadelphia, PA.

international business processes. The World Bank estimated that five percent of the exports to developing countries go to corrupt officials (Moss, 1997). The chairman of the U.S. branch of Transparency International, a non-governmental organization dedicated to combating corruption, has noted that many analysts feel "there has been a gradual escalation in bribe paying to influence the decision making of public officials. At one point, five percent of a contract price was standard. That has increased gradually until now it's in the twenty to thirty percent range" (Andelman, 1998). If bribery is a burden to international firms, it is possible that it maybe even more costly to the countries where they operate. It has been further estimated that the income lost as a result of corruption is the largest potential source of funding available to many developing countries aside from foreign direct investment (Hamra, 2000).

The Incidence of corruption is likely to be higher in certain countries. Given the legal prohibition against bribery in US and other OECD countries and their experience in both implementing the law and creating procedures to conform to the law, firms in these countries are less likely to offer bribes to obtain an advantage when deciding to invest in a foreign country[1]. On the other hand, developing countries are in many cases, just beginning the economic transformation or development processes and becoming exposed to the influence of corruption. Many of these developing countries were under different economic or political structure until the middle of the last century. Moreover, in such countries, regulations addressing corruption were generally regarded as inadequate in scope and their implementation. Therefore, after an introduction to the process of economic transformation, it is likely that corrupt practices are going to flourish in those countries. It is little wonder that most of the corrupt countries are perceived to least developed or poor. Economic agents and governmental organizations around the world are aware of the existences of such corrupt practices in these countries (for example the Bofor scandal in India, as well as several recent corruption scandals in Bangladesh[2]). In Kenya, "questionable" public expenditures noted by the Controller and Auditor General in 1997 amounted to 7.6 per cent of GDP (Shah and Schacter 2004).

This experience of corruption in developing countries, has led multilateral financial agencies such as the World Bank, International Monetary Fund and others to become more cautious about granting aid or approving foreign direct investments in such countries. Similarly, multinational corporations and other private firms are also more concerned about unexpected incidents of corruption. Non-governmental organizations such as Transparency International, through its annual rankings of perceived corruption among countries also address this subject. In the same spirit, in 1999, eleven African countries signed a treaty in which that they stated that they would make changes to their administrative and legal systems to reduce corruption. These countries are: Benin, Botswana, Ethiopia, Ghana, Malawi, Mali Mozambique, Senegal, South Africa, Tanzania, and Uganda. The purpose of this paper is to analyze how the incidence of corruption may affect the capital formation, especially its effect on foreign investment and economic growth in these developing countries.

As mentioned earlier, there has been a phenomenal growth in the level of trade and investment by multinational corporations and other firms in foreign countries in the last few decades. For example, foreign direct investment (FDI) of $60 billion in 1968 increased to more than $3.5 trillion by 1998 (International Financial Statistics 2001). It can be seen that the FDI has grown dramatically over the last few decades in many countries including developing countries. The FDI typically refers to money invested abroad for more than one year and involves an element of control over the money invested. It is different form portfolio investment which is often short term and passive. FDI has recently become an important factor for the development strategy of these developing nations. Its importance originates from job creation as well as changing the technological infrastructure of the FDI recipient countries. Many studies have examined the reasons behind FDI and the choice of host countries. The literature addressing this topic is too vast to be comprehensively reviewed here. However, opportunities for growth and profit are the most obvious reasons for the multinational and other firms investing in foreign countries. The change in the economic, structural and regulatory infrastructures in the developing countries is considered to be an important inducement for FDI. For instance, after China liberalized its economy in 1978 and invited the FDI to revive its economy, its economic performance improved tremendously and foreign firms invested enormous sums of capital. Consequently, many countries followed the same policy, as India did in 1991. However, policy efforts to attract FDI have met with differing levels of success across countries. This study analyzes the role of corruption in these efforts, most notably in the form of bribery as an influential factor in FDI. It seems obvious, given the negative aspects resulting from corruption; businesses would hesitate to invest in countries which are perceived to have high levels of corruption. In contrast, firms are likely to invest in countries where they are not expected to pay bribes to conduct business. Habib and Zurawicki (2002) looked at 89 countries over a three year period (1996-98) and concluded that corruption was an obvious impediment to investment.

The organization of this paper is as follows: In the next section, we have developed a model and derive the hypotheses that we want to investigate. In section III, the statistical methodology and the data used for empirical examination of our theoretical propositions are presented. In section IV, a discussion of the implications of our statistical results is presented. In the final section, the conclusion of our findings and the limitations of the study are presented.

MODEL

The existing research indicates that bribery in international business occurs as a result of the interaction of three key variables: economic conditions, cultural factors and social fabrics[3]. However, to analyze the impact of corruption in the economy we start with a very simple and basic model of a firm. We consider a partial equilibrium model of an oligopolistic industry in which there are *n* identical foreign firms. Each foreign firm produces output for both home consumption and exports. For simplicity, the marginal costs are taken to be constant and they are also the average variable costs. The *n* foreign firms compete in the domestic and foreign markets for the sale of the commodities. The inverse demand functions for these commodities are given by,

$$P_i = g_i(D_i),\ g' < 0,\ (i = d, f) \tag{1}$$

where P_i and D_i are respectively the price and the total demand in the i-th market(*d* stands for domestic market and *f* stands for foreign market). For simplicity, the inverse market demand functions are assumed to take the following linear form:

$$P_d = g_d(nx_d) = \alpha_d - \beta_d nx_d \tag{2}$$

is the domestic market clearing price, and,

$$P_f = g_f(nx_f) = \alpha_f - \beta_f nx_f \tag{3}$$

is the foreign market-clearing price. Let x_d and x_f respectively denote the quantities of output produced for the domestic market and for the foreign market respectfully by each foreign firm. Therefore, the aggregate quantity on the domestic market is

$$D_d = nx_d \tag{4}$$

And the aggregate quantity on the foreign market is given by;

$$D_f = nx_f \tag{5}$$

We will assume that the total cost of producing the two homogenous goods x_d and x_f is given by

$$C_i(x_{di} + x_{fi}) = c(x_d + x_f) \tag{6}$$

where c is a fixed constant. In this model, there are no fixed costs and the marginal cost c is assumed to be constant. The firms incur corruption costs for operating in the domestic market. Let t_d capture the unit corruption cost incurred by the firm in producing each unit of output and selling it domestically. So, the profits for each firm is given by,

$$\Pi = g_d(nx_d)x_d + g_f(nx_f)x_f - c(x_d + x_f) - t_d x_d \tag{7}$$

We assume that the number of foreign firms n, is endogenous and the government in the host country can affect this number by being more corrupt or less corrupt (i.e; for a change in the value of t_d). The host country is assumed to be small in the market for FDI, i.e. foreign firms would enter (exit) the host country if the profits they make in the host country, Π_h, are larger (smaller) than the reservation profits, Π_w, they can make in the rest of the world. In the equilibrium therefore, we must have; $\Pi_h = \Pi_w$

If we have a case where $\Pi_h > \Pi_w$, then foreign firms would enter into the host country, and if $\Pi_h < \Pi_w$ foreign firms would exit from the host country. Clearly when $\Pi_h = \Pi_w$, foreign firms would be indifferent. This is the FDI equilibrium situation. The firms are assumed to behave in a Cournot- Nash fashion, therefore, the first order profit maximization conditions are

$$\partial\Pi / \partial x_d = g_d - c - t_d - x_d g_d' = 0 \tag{8}$$

and therefore,

$$g_d - c - t_d = x_d g_d' \tag{9}$$

$$\alpha_d - \beta_d nx_d - x_d \beta_d = c + t_d \text{ or,} \tag{10}$$

$$\beta_d (n+1)x_d = \alpha_d - c - t_d \tag{11}$$

The optimum output for the local market would be

$$x_d = (\alpha_d - c - t_d) / \beta_d (n+1) \tag{12}$$

Noting that this Nash equilibrium quantity x_d is derived under the assumption of symmetry since $x_{d1} = x_{d2} = = = \ldots\ldots\ldots = x_{dn} = x_d$

Similarly, for the foreign market(or rest of the world market),

$$\partial \Pi / \partial x_f = g_f - c - x_f g_f' = 0 \quad (13)$$

and

$$g_f - c = x_f g_f' \quad (14)$$

$$\alpha_f - \beta_f n x_f - x_f \beta_f = c \quad (15)$$

and

$$\beta_f (n + 1) x_f = \alpha_f - c \quad (16)$$

The optimum output level produced for the foreign market is

$$x_f = (\alpha_f - c) / \beta_f (n+1) \quad (17)$$

Similarly we also have for symmetry

$$x_{f1} = x_{f2} === \ldots\ldots\ldots = x_{fn} = x_f$$

It should be noted that we also have;

$$\Pi = (g_d - c - t_d) x_d + (g_f - c) x_f \quad (18)$$

$$\Pi = \beta_d x_d^2 + \beta_f x_f^2 = \Pi_w \text{ (reservation profit)} \quad (19)$$

Next we substitute respectively, output produced for the domestic market and that which is produced for the foreign market, and get

$$\Pi_w = (\alpha_d - c - t_d)^2 / \beta_d (n+1)^2 + (\alpha_f - c)_2 / \beta_f (n+1)^2 \quad (20)$$

From this equation, we get

$$(n + 1)^2 = (\alpha_d - c - t_d)^2 / \beta_d \Pi_w + (\alpha_f - c)_2 / \beta_f \Pi_w \quad (21)$$

Differentiating this equation in terms of *n and* t_d, we get

$$2(n+1) dn = - 2 [(\alpha_d - c - t_d)^2 / \beta_d \Pi_w] dt_d \quad (22)$$

From which we get;

$$dn / dt_d = - [(\alpha_d - c - t_d)^2 / \beta_d \Pi_w (n+1)] < 0. \quad (23)$$

Equation (23) implies that, if t_d(cost of corruption) increases by one unit, then n (the number of foreign firms) will decrease by, $[(\alpha_d - c - t_d)^2 / \beta_d \Pi_w (n+1)]$

Also we get from equation (12)

$$dx_d / dt_d = - 1 / \beta_d (n + 1) < 0 \quad (24)$$

Thus, if the corruption cost increases by one unit, operation of the multinational firm in the host country declines as output and sale decreases.,

From the results above, it is evident that the number of foreign firms or multinational corporations operating in the host country, and the amount of domestic production in the host country will decrease if t_d increases. It also implies that FDI will increase if the t_d decreases (or indirectly, the level of transparency in handling business operations improves) and consequently, the host country's economy will also grow. We can therefore conclude that a corrupt country is worse off compared to a non corrupt country. This theoretical model postulates that when an economy is corrupt-ridden, there is an adverse effect on FDI and on the economy's output. An improved transparency level will drastically reduce corruption cost; with transparency in place, newer openness may lead to a greater marginal gain in FDI inflows and positive effect on the economy. Thus, from this analysis the following propositions are suggested:

Proposition I: Capital Formation is likely to be lower in countries where the perceived level of corruption is high.

Proposition II: FDI is likely to be lower in countries where the perceived level of corruption is high.

Proposition III: Rate of Growth of the economy is likely to affected adversely by that country's level of corruption

Proposition IV: If the country takes a stance against corruption, and develops a more transparent policy, the result will lead to positive effects on these variables and on the economy.

EMPIRICAL METHODOLOGY

In this section, we examine the statistical evidence regarding the relationship between corruption and the economic performances of the developing countries from Africa as suggested in the previous four propositions. We describe the empirical work in several steps: the econometric specification, selection of key independent variables and the regression results. The countries that we have considered in our study are Benin, Botswana, Ethiopia, Ghana, Malawi, Mali Mozambique, Senegal, South Africa, Tanzania, and Uganda. These are the countries that signed a treaty in 1999 to take corrective action to combat corruptions in their economic structures. We also believe that selection of these countries provides a fair representation of the developing countries in the world. The data used are from several issues of the International Financial Statistics, and several publications of International labor Organizations and UNCTAD. The data are annual data for the time period of 1995-2004. Two different models are used in this study to analyze the effects of corruption on FDI of these countries. The first is a pooled Ordinary Least Squares Regression model, which uses all the data together for regression analysis. The second model is a panel data model where fixed effect method and random effect method for these countries over the time period are used to estimate the relation between corruption and the other economic variables. The empirical investigation will be based on the following model of regression:

$$Y_{it} = \delta(corruption)_{it} + \gamma' CV_{it} + \alpha_{it} + \varepsilon_{it;} \quad (25)$$

$$i = 1,2, \ldots, n \text{ and } t = 1,2,\ldots,T$$

Where Y_{it} is the dependent variable (FDI, rate of growth of the economy, and rate of gross capital formation), corruption is the measurement of the corruption in the country and the CV is the vector control variables (i.e. a set of macro variables that are likely to affect the dependent variable). δ γ *and* α are coefficients of interest and ε_{it} is the white noise error term. Control variables included in our analysis are the measurement of GDP, population, political risk of the countries and others such as the rate of inflation, exchange rate stability, a measurement of openness etc. Obviously, the main variable of interest in our analysis is this measurement of corruption. To capture the magnitude of corruption across countries, the indices complied by Transparency International (TI) are used. The index is based on a series of surveys (*www.transparency.org*). The number of surveys used for each country range from 4 to 11. The Index is calculated based on data from the Economist Intelligence Unit (Country Risk Service and Country Forecasts), Gallup International, the Institute for Management Development (World Competitiveness Yearbook), the Political and Economic Risk Consultancy in Hong Kong (Asian Intelligence issue), Political Risk Services (International Country Risk Guide), the World Bank (World Development Report and Private Sector Survey), and the World Economic Forum (Global Competitiveness Survey) collected over the previous three years. All these studies have a section on the problem, prevalence, pervasiveness, extent, and the number of cases of corruption in various countries. As a single composite score, the CPI has increased the reliability of the data of each individual source. While one could have used the scores or rankings provided by several of the surveys used to calculate the CPI, however from our prospective the CPI score is more valid and reliable and best captures the perception of the level of corruption in a country as it affects the international businessperson.

In our analysis Gross Domestic Product, political risk and the population are used as the proxies for market opportunity for the investor; these should have a positive, negative and positive impact on the volume of direct investment. Taking into account these variables, the following reduced form equation is used to examine our proposition about the impact of corruption in the developing countries[4].

$$Y_{it} = \beta_{0it} + \underset{(+)}{\beta_1 CPI_{it}} + \underset{(+)}{\beta_2 GDP_{it}} + \underset{(?)}{\beta_3 Polrisk_{it}} + \underset{(+)}{\beta_4 POP_{it}} + \underset{(+)}{\beta_5 D} + \varepsilon_{it;} \qquad (26)$$

$$i = 1,2, \ldots,10 \text{ and } t = 1,2,\ldots,10 \ (1995\text{-}2004)$$

Where Y_{it} is a measurement of the dependent variables (rate of growth of the economy, FDI, and the Gross Fixed Capital formation). Among the independent variables, CPI is the measurement of corruption (corruption perception index), GDP is the measurement of real gross domestic Product (is a proxy for market size and overall economic performance, GDP divided by consumer price index), POP is the population of the countries (another proxy for market size), Polrisk is the measurement of political risk in the economy (a proxy for bureaucratic and regulatory endeavors), and ε_{it} is a white noise random error. A proxy variable (a dummy variable) D is also introduced for the years after 1999 to capture the announcement effect of the policy changes of these countries regarding business practices to control corruptions. CPI data for Benin was not available for any time period, so we have to exclude it and limit our analysis to 10 countries. In addition to this, on many occasions, we do not have data for all variables which make the estimation process rather difficult and complicated.

ANALYSIS OF EMPIRICAL RESULTS

Basic descriptive statistics for these variables are presented in Table 1. The RATS version 6.3 and SAS software were used for compilation of these statistics, OLS estimation and Panel Data

Estimation. As is seen from the Table, CPI is missing for 34 observations, Government Expenditure (GOV) is missing for 38 observations and we can not use it as an explanatory variable in the model. In Table 2, OLS regression results (the full cross section and time series data pooled together) for the equation (26) are presented. As mentioned before, dependent variables analyzed here are the real foreign direct investment (FDI), rate of economic growth (GRWTH) and the gross fixed capital formation (Capital Formation) in real term. Because of the paucity of relevant data points, estimation are done using only 52 observations for FDI, 58 observations for GRWTH and 54 observations for capital formation. Many other possible explanatory variables can not be used in the estimation process because of inconsistency of data points. We find from the Table 2 that overall model is useful to some extent (F statistics is significant in all cases, at least 5% level of significant in all cases as F values are 4.12, 3.27 and 3.24 with the p-values .0035, 012 and .013 respectively). However, the predictive power of the regression model is not very high (R-square values are .31 for FDI, .24 for GRWTH and .25 for the capital formation). Adjusted R-square values are significantly lower than these, which are reflected by the insignificance of many independent variables. Real GDP is a significant variable for the FDI and capital formation, population is significant for economic growth and CPI (corruption perception index) is significant for the capital formation. According to the definition of the measurement of the index of corruption, the higher the index, the more honest or less corrupt is the country. CPI is not significant for FDI and economic growth; the inference therefore is that corruption is not a significant factor for affecting foreign direct investment and the growth of the economy (at least from the OLS estimation results), but for indigenous capital formation it is a significant factor. Therefore, it does support our stated propositions partly. The dummy variable for signing of the treaty in 1999 is not an important and/or significant variable. However, for FDI and capital formation, it has the expected positive sign. Thus, the transparency decision made by these countries may have some positive impact on the foreign direct investment and indigenous capital formation.

In Tables 3 and 4, we reported the re-estimation results of the equation (26) using Panel Data estimation methodology. The data is not balanced and there are several missing observations.

Table 1
Summary Statistics

Variable	*FDI*	*Capital Formation*	*GRWTH*	*CPI*	*RGDP*	*POP*	*GOV*	*POLRISK*
Mean	3.516	207.77	4.66	3.52	1271.98	24.34	4752.05	63.45
Variance	77.397	209294.21	3.938	1.52	7692759.9	359.76	50408491.4	42.30
Maximum	68.78	2128.09	9.10	6.40	11197.1	75.59	24882.85	78.0
Minimum	0.00	2.99	-1.20	1.90	14.55	1.61	3.31	53.0
Kurtosis	39.45	6.76	0.51	-0.245	5.22	0.546	1.12	-0.408
Skewness	5.97	2.76	-0.65	0.88	2.60	1.145	1.48	0.64
Missing Obs	10	12	15	34	7	0	38	0
Sample* size	90	88	85	66	93	100	62	100

*** because of unavailability of few observations, actual sample observations used in the analysis.**

Table 2
Ordinary Least Square Estimation

Dependent Variable:	*FDI*	*Rate of Growth*	*CapitalFormation*
Constant	-15.40 (-1.05)*	2.36 (0.69)	860.70 (0.94)
CPI	-1.94 (-1.13)	-0.45 (-0.31)	254.82** (2.64)
polrisk	0.37 (1.28)	0.05 (0.77)	-22.02 (-1.27)
GDP	0.0016** (3.61)	0.00001 (0.15)	0.03** (1.45)
Pop	0.022 (0.19)	0.03** (2.45)	-1.86 (-0.35)
Dummy for 1999	0.83 (0.33)	-0.054 (-0.10)	43.89 (0.34)
R-square	0.31	0.24	.25
F stat	F(5,46)= 4.12** (0.0035)***	F(5,52) = 3.27** (0.012)	F(5,48) = 3.24** (0.01)
Sample Obs^	52	58	54

* t-statistics are in the parentheses
** implies significance of at least 5% level
*** p-values for F-statistics
^ Inadequacy of data

Table 3
Panel Estimation
(Fixed Effect Model)

Variable	*FDI*	*Rate of Growth*	*Capital Fprmation*
CPI	-3.12 (-0.73)	0.98* (2.36)	102.90** (1.60)
Polrisk	0.56 (1.23)	0.06 (1.25)	-0.02 (0.003)
GDP	0.003 (0.95)	0.0004 (0.87)	0.05 (0.89)
POP	-0.11 (-0.07)	0.05 (0.45)	2.17 (0.09)
Dummy for1999	2.65 (0.64)	0.48** (1.52)	85.83** (1.35)
R-SQUARE	0.36	0.74	89
F-Stat for the model	F(13,38)=1.64 (0.12)	F(13,44)=13.60** (0.00)	F(13,40)=59.19** (0.00)
F test for no fixed effects	F (8,38) =.37 p-value = (0.93)	F(8,44)=15.50 p-value = (0.00).	F(8,40)=71.54 p-value = (0.00)
Sample obs	52	58	54

t-values in the parentheses_
* Significant at least at 5% level
** significant at least at 10% level

Table 4
Estimation of Panel data model
(Random Effect)

Variable	*FDI*	*Rate of Growth*	*Capital*
Intercept	-16.99	-4.22**	648.85
	(-1.01)	(-1.39)	(1.29)
CPI	-1.82	0.82*	78.66**
	(-1.13)	(2.21)	(1.38)
Polrisk	0.37	0.06	-0.67
	(1.21)	(1.57)	(-0.12)
GDP	0.0016*	-0.0001	-0.04
	(3.62)	(-0.658))	(-0.82)
POP	0.022	0.08**	-5.15
	(0.14)	(1.79)	(-0.50)
Dummy for 1999	.83	0.31	99.29*
	(0.33)	(1.01)	(2.17)
R-square	.31	.22	.25

p-values in the parentheses_
* Significant at least at 5% level
** Significant at least at 10%

Consequently, the estimation process uses only about half of the data. After conducting the standard Hausman test for Fixed Effect model versus pooled OLS model and Random Effect model versus Fixed Effect model, the Fixed Effect Model seems to be appropriate for the GRWTH variable and the Capital Formation variable. Whereas for the FDI variable, the Random Effect model seems appropriate. We have reported both types of estimation results here. Fixed effect estimation results are presented in Table 3. It can be seen from Table 3 that the Hausman test statistics are 0.37, 15.50 and 71.54 (with the p-values of 0.93, .00 and .00) where the null hypothesis is that there is no fixed effect in the model. It seems that the estimation results for the FDI variable are very poor (as is indicated by the low F- value of 1.64 with p-value of 0.12).

However, the examination of the results for the GRWTH and Capital formation reveal somewhat mixed results. The predictive powers of the models have improved significantly over the OLS estimation results. Now, the R-squared values are .36, .74 and .89. We can also find that CPI has a significant positive effect on the gross capital formation and on the growth of the economy. The dummy variable for 1999 is also significant in both cases. It can be seen that population, GDP and the political risk do not have significant effect on the rate of economic growth or on the domestic capital formation. On the whole, the results of the Table 3 support our hypotheses regarding corruption and the transparency in reducing corruption to some extent, as CPI and the dummy for 1999 are statistically significant for both economic growth and capital formation.

In Table 4, Random Effect model estimation results are presented. For the FDI model, GDP seems to be the only significant factor of relation. This corroborates the result from the OLS estimation in Table 2. CPI is again significant for both economic growth and domestic capital formation. The dummy variable for 1999 is also significant for the domestic capital formation.

The empirical results from these three tables suggest that there are many other factors affecting or influencing FDI, economic growth and domestic capital formation in the developing countries (as evident by low values of R-square statistic), not included in the model. But among the variables studied in this research, the level of corruption in those countries was the prime and main interest. Considering all the evidences, it is quite obvious that level of corruption is not an important factor or determinant of the FDI in these countries, but for domestic capital formation and economic growth, it is. Indeed, the treaty signed by these counties to combat corruption in their decision making process does have significant positive effect on their economies.

CONCLUSION

This issue of corruption in international business environment has become a growing concern among the policymakers across countries. This paper has examined the nature and the extent of relationship between the level of corruption and the FDI for the developing countries. The theoretical analysis postulates that corruption has a negative impact on the level of capital formation or on the use of capital in the production process. In other words, foreign direct investment (which is an important part of the capital formation in these countries), will also be negatively impacted by the presence of corruption in their economic infrastructure. Next, data was collected for several developing economies (eleven countries from Africa) over a period of time (1995 to 2004) to examine empirically this relationship. The statistical findings are not quite consistent with our theoretical propositions. The data for this study are obtained from various issues of International Financial Statistics, various ILO publications and Transparency International. SAS software was used to estimate the statistical relation. No conclusive evidence was found that, for the developing countries, corruption is a very serious issue that affects the inflow of foreign direct investment in those countries. Nonetheless, it is suggested that these countries should make utmost effort to root out corruption in their economic infrastructure if they want to advance their economic well being.

This study also suffers from several limitations. The measurement of corruption is perception based, not on real data. Second, other important relevant economic variables should have been included in our estimation methodology; therefore the empirical results may have been affected by an omitted variable bias problem. However, it seems that omitted independent variables are likely to be uncorrelated to CPI; therefore, coefficient estimate of the index of corruption is likely to be unbiased. Limitations of data are also of very serious concern. It is difficult to get consistent data for all developing countries with all relevant explanatory variables. This however, can be rectified in future when newer sets of data are available.

Notes

1. There are exceptions to this also. Recent controversy regarding "Al Yamaha" project in Saudi Arabia where British reportedly paid bribe to get the contract (Economist December 28, 2006). "Corruption Scandal at Siemens May Derail Reconstruction Drive", Wall Street Journal, Dec. 18, 2006.
2. "People pay TK 6796Cr in bribes a year," The Daily Star, April 21, 2005. "As Nigeria Tries to Fight Graft, a New Sordid Tale", New York Times, Nov. 29, 2005.
3. See Sanyal and Samanta (2002, 2004 and 2004).

4. We have used different variations of the model. This seems to be most suitable depending on the nature and availability of the relevant data.

References

Andelman, David (1998), Bribery: The New Global Outlaw. *Management Review*. April, pp. 49-51.

Das, S. P. (1983), Multinational Enterprise Under Uncertainty. *Canadian Journal of Economics,* 16(3) 420-428.

Habib, Mohsin and Zurawicki, Leon (2002), Corruption and Foreign Direct Investment. *Journal of International Business Studies*. 33(2), pp. 291-307.

Hamra, Wayne (2000), Bribery in International Business Transactions and the OECD Convention: Benefits and Limitations. *Business Economics*. 35(4), pp. 33-46.

Husted, Bryan (1999), Wealth, Culture, and Corruption. *Journal of International Business Studies*. 30(2), pp. 339-359.

International Financial Statistics. Washington, DC: International Monetary Fund.

Lambsdorff, J. (1998), Corruption in Comparative Perception. In Jain, A.K., Ed. *Economics of Corruption*. London: Kluwer Academics.

Mauro, P. (1995), Corruption and Growth. *Quarterly Journal of Economics*. 110(3), pp. 681-712.

OECD Observer. September (2000), The Fight Against Bribery and Corruption. OECD: Paris.

Rose-Ackerman, Susan (1997), *Corruption and Development*. Paper Presented at the Annual World Bank Conference on Development Economics. Washington, DC: World Bank.

Sanyal, Rajib and Samanta, Subarna. (March–April 2004), Determinants of Bribery in International Business. *Thunderbird International Business Review*. 45(2), pp 133-149.

Sanyal, Rajib and Samanta, Subarna (2002), Corruption Across Countries: The Cultural and Economic Factors. *Business & Professional Ethics Journal* 21(1), pp. 20-46.

Sanyal, Rajib and Samanta, Subarna (2004), Determinants of Bribe Giving in International Business, *International Journal of Commerce and Management*, 14(2), pp. 1-14.

Shah, Anwar and Schacter, Mark (Dec 2004), Combating Corruption: Look Before You Leap, *Finance and Development*, 41(4), pp. 40-43.

Smarzynska, Beata and Wei, Shang-Jin. (undated). *Corruption and Composition of Foreign Direct Investment: Firm-level Evidence*. Washington, DC: The Brookings Institution.

www.oas.org/oasnews (website of Organization of American States)

www.transparency.org (website of Transparency International, Berlin and data on corruption perception index)

www.undp.org (website of United Nations Development Program and data on human development index)

Wei, Shang-Jin (2000), How Taxing is Corruption on International Investors? *The Review of Economics and Statistics,* 82(1), pp. 1-11.

PERCEPTION OF WOMEN IN SMEs TOWARDS VARIOUS ENTREPRENEURSHIP RELATED ISSUES: A FACTOR ANALYTICAL APPROACH

*Anil Kumar**

ABSTRACT

This paper examines the perception of women in SMEs towards various entrepreneurship related issues in Northern India by taking a sample of 450 respondents from five states of Northern India i.e. Haryana, Punjab, Rajasthan, Himachal Pradesh and Delhi. The factor analytical model has clubbed various issues relating to women entrepreneurs into two factors, one is designated as business related issues and other is separate official machinery. Business related issues can be tackled by enhancing level of awareness in the field of management of small enterprises and imparting training in the field of business. Infrastructure and other facilities need to be strengthened. Requirements of separate support agencies can be tackled by creating special cells under the charge of women officials within different departments. It will help women entrepreneurs in presenting their cases better.

Micro and small enterprises (SMEs) constitute an important segment of the Indian economy. This sector has potential to generate gainful employment opportunities. This sector can assure equitable distribution of income and wealth, balance regional development and also act as nursery for the growth of entrepreneurship among population in general and women in particular.

The female participation in economic activities has seen tremendous improvement at global level during last decade. Women-owned firms represented nearly 40 per cent of all firms in the United States and employed approximately 27.5 million people (NFWBO, 2001). Similarly, rates of self-employment among women are increasing in several EU countries. In Germany, women have created one-third of new businesses since 1990 representing more than one million jobs. In Europe and newly independent states Transition Economics, women are 25 per cent of the business owners. In Great Britain women are one-fourth of the self-employed sector. It has been seen that women out number man by at least two times, particularly when it comes to starting business in China. There are over 5 million women entrepreneurs constituting one fourth of all the entrepreneurs in China (Workshop Proceedings 2000). In Japan too a similar trend has been noticed. The percentage of women entrepreneurs increased from 2.4 per cent in 1980 to 5.2 per cent in 1995 (Shigeko, 2000). In Latin America, women constitute 15 to 20 per

* Reader, Haryana School of Business, Guru Jambheshwar University of Science & Technology, Hisar-125001, Haryana (India) *e-mail: anil_k6559@yahoo.co.uk*

This paper is a part of Major Research Project entitled "Women Entrepreneurship in Northern India" sponsored by UGC. The author is grateful to UGC for providing financial assistance for this project.

cent of all employees, concentrated largely in the commercial and service sector. At present 9.5 per cent women entrepreneurs are managing the small enterprises in India (GOI, 2001).

Information vividly shows that rate of participation of women in business is found to be low when compared with advanced countries of the world. The new economic regime has offered large number of opportunities and challenge to micro and small enterprises of our economy. As a result of this, micro and small-scale sector owned by women entrepreneurs has been confronted with the various issues related to entrepreneurship development. The present study has tried to analyze perceptions of women entrepreneurs in Northern India towards various entrepreneurship related issues by using factor analytical model.

REVIEW OF LITERATURE

The literature cites number of studies in this field.

Taylor and Brooksbank (1995) examined the marketing practices among small New Zealand organisations by taking a sample of 427 small business owners. Findings revealed that the small business firm looks the marketing practices differently from their larger counterparts.

Breen *et al.* (1995) examined financial and family issues by taking a sample of 211 female entrepreneurs from Australia. The study highlighted that female business owners faced the problem of getting finance and started business with low initial capital. On the family front women entrepreneurs faced the problem of supervision and care for sick children.

Caputo and Dolinsky (1998) has examined the role of financial and human capital of household member to pursue self-employment among females. The analysis revealed that business knowledge and cooperation of husband in family matters contribute a lot to pursue the business. Finding further suggested that government should provide necessary skill to women to ensure rapid growth of entrepreneurship.

Bliss and Garratt (2001) has examined the working of organisation for women in Poland. The paper has examined the various activities performed by these associations to promote women entrepreneurs. Information was collected from 12 support organisation for women. Data collected from these organisations highlighted that basic purpose of these organisations has been to provide inputs to women entrepreneurs in the field of professional ethics, protection of rights of women entrepreneurs and their companies, exchange of experience and other activities.

Mambula (2002) analysed major constrains faced by SMEs in Nigeria. A sample of 32 small business entrepreneurs was taken. Analysis of data revealed that majority of SMEs face the problem of finance and infrastructure while managing their businesses. The author recommended that small business entrepreneurs should collaborate with each other to sort out the various problems faced by them. There is need to form alliance of Government, Research Institutions and Financial Institutions to create appropriate training for prospective small business.

Watson (2003) has examined the failure rates among female control business in Australia. The analysis of study highlighted that failure rate of female control business is relatively higher than male controlled business. But the difference is not significant after controlling for the effects of industry.

Tagoe *et al.* (2005) has examined the financial challenged facing by urban SMEs under financial sector liberalisation in Ghana. Main challenges faced by urban SMEs are access to affordable credit over a reasonable period. To manage this challenge SMEs should manage record keeping in an effective manner. Moreover, availability of collateral improves SMEs access to formal credit. But better availability of investment avenues further reduces the accessibility of credit to SMEs.

Above studies touched different areas pertaining to women entrepreneurs, but none of the study seems to have touched the area like perception of women entrepreneurs towards various entrepreneurship related issues at regional level. The present study proposes to fill the gap in existing literature.

OBJECTIVES AND METHODOLOGY

In this study an attempt has been made to analyse the perception of women entrepreneurs towards various entrepreneurship related issues confronted by them. For this purpose 26 statements have been administered to women entrepreneurs of the sample. These are:

Sr. No.	*Label*	*Statement*
1.	X_1	It is difficult to survive without help of husband.
2.	X_2	Women can compete with men.
3.	X_3	Success results in neglect of children, family and home.
4.	X_4	Availing financial assistance from support system is a problem.
5.	X_5	Home is the right place for women.
6.	X_6	Women become entrepreneur out of compulsion.
7.	X_7	Job is better than entrepreneurship.
8.	X_8	Being a women is boon for becoming entrepreneur.
9.	X_9	Marketing of the product is a problem for women entrepreneurs.
10.	X_{10}	Ideal stage to be an entrepreneur is before marriage
11.	X_{11}	Present policy provisions are sufficient for growth of women entrepreneurship.
12.	X_{12}	With reduction of public sector self employment is the only way.
13.	X_{13}	Ignorance of law is an obstacle.
14.	X_{14}	Management should be a compulsory subject at graduate level.
15.	X_{15}	Social and cultural barriers act as hindrance in the growth of business.
16.	X_{16}	Emerging areas have more scope than traditional ones.
17.	X_{17}	EDPs can act as stimulator.
18.	X_{18}	Business family can act as motivator.
19.	X_{19}	Success stories of women entrepreneurs can act as motivator.
20.	X_{20}	Product produced by women entrepreneurs should be given due publicity.
21.	X_{21}	Business incubators should be setup.
22.	X_{22}	Women officials should deal with women.
23.	X_{23}	Women inspectors should deal with women.
24.	X_{24}	Acquiring technical know how is a problem.
25.	X_{25}	Management training is must for women.
26.	X_{26}	There should be separate support agencies for women entrepreneurs.

Likert five degree scale has been used to seek the opinion of women entrepreneurs on the above said statements.

To achieve these objectives, a sample of 450 women entrepreneurs from five states of Northern India i.e. Delhi, Haryana, Himachal Pradesh, Punjab and Rajasthan has been taken. Number of women entrepreneurs from each state has been mentioned in Table 1:

Table 1
State-wise Number of Enterprises Owned by Women Entrepreneurs Taken for Study

State	*Number of Women entrepreneurs*	*Percentage*
Delhi	60	13.33
Haryana	120	26.67
Himachal Pradesh	51	11.33
Punjab	110	24.44
Rajastan	109	24.23
Total	450	100

During the survey it has been observed that large number of women entrepreneurs were not actually managing their business. It was decided to include only those women entrepreneurs in our study who were managing their business personally. Information has been collected from respondents by using pre-tested well-designed questionnaire. Two stage random sampling technique has been used to choose the respondents for the above study. The classification of women entrepreneurs in different industries has been shown in Table-2.

Table 2
Industry-wise Classification of Enterprises Owned by Women Entrepreneurs

Type of Industry	*Number of Women entrepreneurs*	*Percentage*
Manufacturing	191	42.44
Trading	72	16.00
Services	145	32.22
Others	42	9.34
Total	450	100

Most of these women entrepreneurs have established their business after post-reform period i.e. after 1991. All these women entrepreneurs have employed at least 5 workers in their enterprises. Factor analytical model has been used to analyze the data.

RESULTS AND DISCUSSION

The perception of women entrepreneurs towards various entrepreneurship related issues have been subject to factor analysis technique. Varimax rotated matrix have been used for extracting the factors.

Table 3
KMO and Bartlett's Test

Kieser-Meyer-Olin Measure of Sampling Adequacy	0.660	
Bartlett's Test of Sphericity	Approx. Chi-Square	3827.059
	df	325
	Sig.	0.000

Table 3 shows the Kaiser-Meyer-Olkin (KMO) and Bartlett's test of sphericity. The KMO test measure of sampling adequacy equal to 0.660 vividly reveals that data is fit for factor analysis. Bartlett's test of sphericity (3827.039) further collaborates our finding.

Table 4 shows the varimax rotated factor matrix results for all women entrepreneurs in our study. Two factors have been extracted which altogether account for 27.161 per cent of

Table 4
Varimax Rotated Matrix

Sr. No.	*Label*	*Statement*	*Factor 1*	*Factor 2*	*Communalities*
1.	X_1	It is difficult to survive without help of husband.	0.084	0.143	0.027
2.	X_2	Women can compete with men.	-0.031	-0.199	0.040
3.	X_3	Success results in neglect of children, family and home.	-0.054	0.080	0.095
4.	X_4	Availing financial assistance from support system is a problem.	0.347	0.149	0.143
5.	X_5	Home is the right place for women.	-0.211	0.028	0.045
6.	X_6	Women become entrepreneur out of compulsion.	-0.447	-0.013	0.200
7.	X_7	Job is better than entrepreneurship.	-0.017	0.116	0.013
8.	X_8	Being a women is boon for becoming entrepreneur.	0.169	0.159	0.054
9.	X_9	Marketing of the product is a problem for women entrepreneurs.	0.158	0.163	0.051
10.	X_{10}	Ideal stage to be an entrepreneur is before marriage	0.284	0.169	0.109
11.	X_{11}	Present policy provisions are sufficient for growth of women entrepreneurship.	0.218	-0.150	0.069
12.	X_{12}	With reduction of public sector self employment is the only way.	0.409	-0.150	0.190
13.	X_{13}	Ignorance of law is an obstacle.	0.556	-0.014	0.309
14.	X_{14}	Management should be a compulsory subject at graduate level.	0.712	0.031	0.507
15.	X_{15}	Social and cultural barriers act as hindrance in the growth of business.	0.540	0.339	0.406
16.	X_{16}	Emerging areas have more scope than traditional ones.	0.513	0.047	0.266
17.	X_{17}	EDPs can act as stimulator.	0.601	-0.044	0.363
18.	X_{18}	Business family can act as motivator.	0.702	0.015	0.493
19.	X_{19}	Success stories of women entrepreneurs can act as motivator.	0.677	-0.018	0.458
20.	X_{20}	Product produced by women entrepreneurs should be given due publicity.	0.635	0.243	0.462
21.	X_{21}	Business incubators should be setup.	0.392	0.342	0.271
22.	X_{22}	Women officials should deal with women.	-0.047	0.869	0.758
23.	X_{23}	Women inspectors should deal with women.	-0.039	0.882	0.780
24.	X_{24}	Acquiring technical know how is a problem.	-0.025	0.535	0.286
25.	X_{25}	Management training is must for women.	0.097	0.438	0.202
26.	X_{26}	There should be separate support agencies for women entrepreneurs.	-0.052	0.738	0.548
Eigen value			4.180	2.882	
Percentage of variance			16.076	11.084	
Cumulative percentage of variance			16.076	27.161	

Extraction method : Principal component analysis.
Rotation Method : Varimax with Kaiser Normalization.
Rotation Converged in 3 iterations.

variance. It shows that 27.161 per cent of total variance is explained by information contained in varimax rotated matrix. The percentage of variance explained by factor 1 to 2 is 16.076 and 11.084. The communalities have been shown at the right side of the table 4, which explains the amount of variance in the variable that is accounted by two factors taken together. Large communalities indicate that a large amount of variance in a variable has been extracted by factor solution. A factor loading represents the correlation between an original variable and its factors. Factor loading is nothing but coefficient of correlation. The varimax factors solution shows that some of the variable have low factor loading values. The factor loading below 0.30 have been left. The name of factors, statements label and factor loading are summarized in Table 5.

The explanation of these two factors has been discussed below.

Table 5
Naming of factors

Factors	*Name of Factors*		*Label Statements*	*Factor Loadings*
F_1	Business related issues	X_4	Availing financial assistance from support system is a problem	0.347
		X_6	Women become entrepreneur out of compulsion.	-0.447
		X_{12}	With reduction of public sector self employment is the only way.	0.409
		X_{13}	Ignorance of law is an obstacle.	0.556
		X_{14}	Management should be a compulsory subject at graduate level.	0.712
		X_{15}	Social and cultural barriers act as hindrance in the growth of business	0.540
		X_{16}	Emerging areas have more scope than traditional ones.	0.513
		X_{17}	EDPs can act as stimulators	0.601
		X_{18}	Business family can act as motivator	0.702
		X_{19}	Success stories of women entrepreneurs can act as motivator.	0.677
		X_{20}	Product produced by women entrepreneurs should be given due publicity.	0.635
		X_{21}	Business incubators should be setup.	0.392
F_2	**Separate official machinery**	X_{22}	Women officials should deal with women	0.869
		X_{23}	Women inspectors should deal with women.	0.882
		X_{24}	Acquiring technical know-how is a problem	0.535
		X_{25}	Management training is must for women	0.438
		X_{26}	There should be separate support agencies for women entrepreneurs	0.738

BUSINESS RELATED ISSUES (F_1)

It is an important factor which accounts for maximum percentage of variance equal to 16.076. Twelve variables have been loaded on this factor. The loading of twelve variables indicates that business related issues are the main important issues before women entrepreneurs. These twelve variables have eigen value 4.180. The eigen value more than 4 further shows that these variables are main obstacles for the growth of entrepreneurship among women. The women entrepreneurs face the problem of ignorance of law, problem of publicity, infrastructure and knowledge relating to general management of small enterprises.

Problems relating to business can be tackled by increasing the awareness of various rules and regulations relating to business. This problem can further be solved by incorporating business related subjects at graduate or +2 levels. Knowledge of various business opportunities in the market economies should be enhanced by organizing workshops and seminars at colleges and universities level. Training programmes relating to entrepreneurship development should be strengthened further. It will help women entrepreneurs in solving various issues confronting them. Latest marketing techniques which can be beneficial to SMEs under new economic regime can be better understood through training programmes. Moreover, challenges faced by SMEs can be solved by hearing the views of experts in this field. NGOs, Institutes of higher education and women organizations should play a vital role in this direction.

SEPARATE OFFICIAL MACHINERY (F_2)

The second factor, which accounts for 11.084 per cent of variance consist of five variables and has been designated as separate official machinery related issues. The eigen value for these five variables is 2.882. Eigen value more than two further highlights that these variables in this factor acts as obstacles in business. Women due to male dominance society require separate supporting agencies and women officials to deal with their cases and in this process they face the problem of acquiring latest technology. This problem should be solved by creating separate cells in the various departments headed by women officials. It will help the women entrepreneurs in presenting their cases better. Separate cells will help women entrepreneurs to discuss issues relating to training and technological transfer in an effective manner. Technology transfer will also make these SMEs more competitive and profitable under new economic regime. It will also helpful to these SMEs to overcome quality related barriers faced by them.

The components plot in rotated space further shows the association between various variables into the two factors extracted through factor analysis.

SUGGESTIONS AND POLICY IMPLICATIONS

The foregoing analysis reveals that the factor analysis has clubbed various issues relating to women entrepreneurs into two factors, one is designated as business related issues and other is separate official machinery. Business related issues can be tackled by enhancing level of awareness in the field of management of small enterprises and imparting training in the field of business. Infrastructure and other facilities need to be strengthened. Requirements of separate

Component Plot in Rotated Space

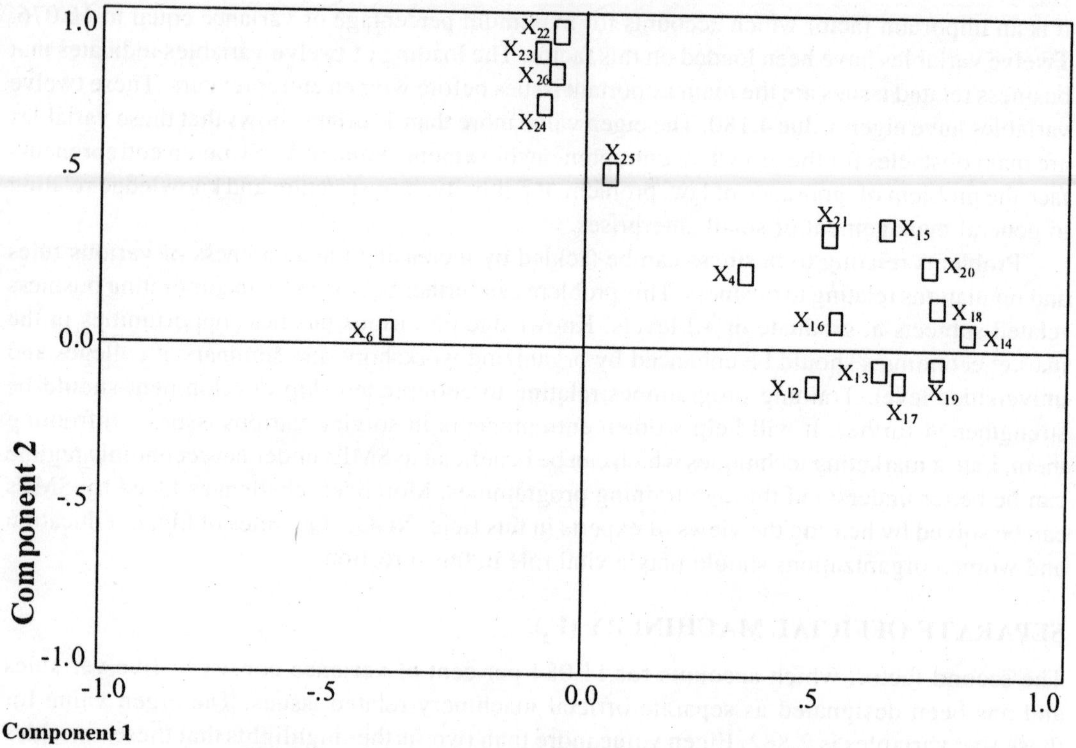

support agencies can be tackled by creating special cells under the charge of women officials within different departments. It will help women entrepreneurs in presenting their cases better.

References

Bliss R. T. and Garratt N. L. (2001), Supporting Women Entrepreneurs in Transitioning Economies, *Journal of Small Business Management*, Vol. 39 (4), pp. 336-344.

Breen *et al.* (1995), Female Entrepreneurs in Australia: An Investigation of Financial and Family Issues, *Journal of Enterprising Culture*, Vol 3, No.4, pp 445-461.

Caputo R. K. and Dolinsky Arthur (1998), Women's Choice of Pursue Self-Employment : The Role of Financial and Human Capital of Household Members, *Journal of Small Business Management*, Vol. 36 (2), pp. 8-18.

Government of India (2001-02), Third All Indian Census of SSI, DC(SSI), Ministry of SSI, New Delhi.

Mambula (2002), Perceptions of SME Growth Constraints in Nigeria, *Journal of Small Business Management*, Vol. 40, No. 1, pp 58-65.

National Foundation for Women Business Owners (NFWBO, 2001), Entrepreneurial Vision in Action: Exploring Growth Among Women and Men-owned Firms. Washington DC.

Shigeko Mitusuhasi. (2000), Access to markets. OECD Conference on Women entrepreneurs in SMEs 2000: A Major Force in Innovation and Job Creation. Synthesis, OECD 29 November-1 December, Paris, France.

Tagoe *et al.* (2005), 'Financial Challenges Facing Urban SMEs under Financial Sector Liberalisation in Ghana', *Journal of Small Business Management*, Vol. 43, No. 3, pp. 331-343.

Taylor and Brooksbank (1995), Marketing Practices Among Small New Zealand Organizations, *Journal of Enterprising Culture*, Vol 3, No.2, pp 149-160.

Watson J. (2003), Failure Rates for Female-Controlled Businesses: Are They Any Different? *Journal of Small Business Management*, Vol. 41 (3), pp. 262-277.

Workshop proceedings (2000), Second OECD Conference on Women Entrepreneurs in SMEs: A Major Force in Innovation and Job Relation. Synthesis, OECD 29 November-1 December, Paris, France.

REFUGEE CRISES: CAUSES AND POLICY RECOMMENDATIONS

*Kevin Sylwester**

Abstract

In this model, external pressure provides impetus for people to become refugees versus remaining at home. However, the nature of this pressure, war versus a natural disaster, for example, determines the nature of the refugee crisis as well as whether aid to refugees raises or lowers welfare. In some cases, aid unambiguously raises welfare. In others, the effect of aid on welfare is nonmonotonic or can even trigger a refugee crisis in the first place.

***Key Words:** Refugees, International Aid*

***JEL Classification:** O15*

1. INTRODUCTION

On many occasions, refugees have fled their homes to find safety elsewhere. Such occurrences are most prevalent in Asia or Africa although the Kosovars in 1998 demonstrate that this problem is not limited to these two continents. (See Wilkinson [2000], Weaver [1998], Schrijvers [1997], Black and Sessay [1998], and Kibreab [2003] for specific examples including the composition and effects of refugees.) Thousands and sometimes millions of people flee in mass. Unlike the migrant being attracted to better opportunities abroad, refugees are marked both by their group nature and because they are being pushed out of their homes more so than they are being pulled by foreign opportunities.

Despite past and ongoing refugee crises and despite the tremendous welfare implications involved in these mass movements, both for the refugees themselves and for the countries receiving them, little attention has been placed on this issue, at least in the economics literature. One examination is found in Stark (2004) who presents a formal model of some of the causes and consequences of refugees. Stark's model predicts that the probability of becoming a refugee is likely to lower the accumulation of human capital and so result in poorer communities. Stark also shows that small populations are more susceptible to launching a refugee crisis since the departure of one individual is more likely to trigger additional departures. Stark, however, does not consider why individuals want to leave or what might be triggering a refugee crisis in the first place. Stark writes:

---

* Department of Economics, Mailcode 4515, Southern Illinois, University, Carbondale, IL 62901, *ksylwest@siu.edu.*

> "Refugee flows typically arise from the capriciousness of nature and the ferocious hostility of fellow human beings" (page 325).

Few would doubt the truthfulness of this statement. Nevertheless, these different causes, a natural disaster as opposed to threats of violence, could hold different implications for what types of policies are most appropriate to confront the exigency. The model in this paper considers how different causes of a potential refugee crisis can lead to vastly different outcomes and why some international responses that are welfare improving in one circumstance could exacerbate problems in others. For example, policies that are welfare improving in such cases as the 2004 Indian Ocean tsunami might be detrimental in some cases of ethnic strife in Africa.

The rest of the paper is organized as follows. Section 2 presents a model where external pressure creates conditions for a refugee crisis to exist. Agents decide whether to remain at home or to relocate to a refugee camp. The model allows for different possibilities as to how this external pressure is formulated. Section 3 finds the equilibrium of the model under different types of crises and analyzes policy implications under each type. A conclusion follows in section 4.

II. THE MODEL

There is a continuum of agents totaling mass N > 0. Each agent faces the same exogenous external threat and so faces the following choice. She can stay at home or choose to go to a refugee camp. Each agent makes this choice individually. There is no coordination across agents. Furthermore, I take there to be many agents and so each agent sees himself as negligible, never considering how his choice affects others. Let N" denote the mass of agents going to the refugee camp with 0 ≤ N" ≤ N.

The return to staying at home despite this threat is given by the function s(N") where a greater threat lowers s(*) for any N". But whether the function s(*) is increasing or decreasing with N" depends on the nature of the threat and I consider more than one possibility in section 3. The return to going to a refugee camp is given by r(N"). I take r(*) to be initially increasing with N". For N" small, a larger refugee population allows an agent to make more contacts within the camp and provides a greater sense of community. As refugee camps grow, they are also more likely to attract international attention and so are more likely to receive aid thereby further raising the return of going to a refugee camp. Of course, N" could become so big that overcrowding of the camp overcomes these benefits and so further increases in the mass of refugees with N" already large could lower r(*). Therefore, I take r(*) to be increasing with N" for 0 ≤ N" < N* and to be decreasing with N" for N" > N*. Any cost of moving from home to the refugee camp is embedded in r(*). Exogenous changes in international aid to refugees shift r(*). No specific functional forms are used so as to leave the model as general as possible. I consider different cases in section 3 by considering different assumptions for s(*). The sign of s'(N") will become key in determining how aid effects the welfare of refugees.

When I analyze the effects of foreign aid allocated to refugees, I abstract away from any welfare effects that such aid has on the donors, either negatively through a loss in resources or positively from satisfaction of helping others. Furthermore, this paper does not consider how the presence of refugees affects those countries that receive them although I acknowledge that this is an important issue. With these simplifications, aggregate welfare is given by [N-N"]s(N") + N"r(N").[1]

3. SOLUTIONS

In any solution, agents depart for the refugee camp whenever the return to staying is less than the return to leaving. If the return to staying is initially greater than the return to departing, I only consider the equilibrium where agents stay even if there are other equilibria since there is no initial impetus to leave.[2] All agents unambiguously become refugees if $s(x) < r(x)$ for all $0 \leq x \leq N$ so that the return to staying is less than the return to becoming a refugee regardless of the current mass of refugees. The key to the model's solution is how s(*) evolves with N". I consider different possibilities below.

Case 1: s(N") is increasing with N" for all 0 # N" # N.

Case one captures the potential for a natural disaster to hit the community putting pressure on local resources to support local residents.[3] As people flee, the return for remaining agents increases because there are now fewer agents that need water, food, and other necessities. Provided s(0) < r(0), agents start leaving until some N" is reached such that s(N") = r(N") or until N" = N, in which case all agents become refugees. Figure 1 considers the case where an intersection exists

Figure 1

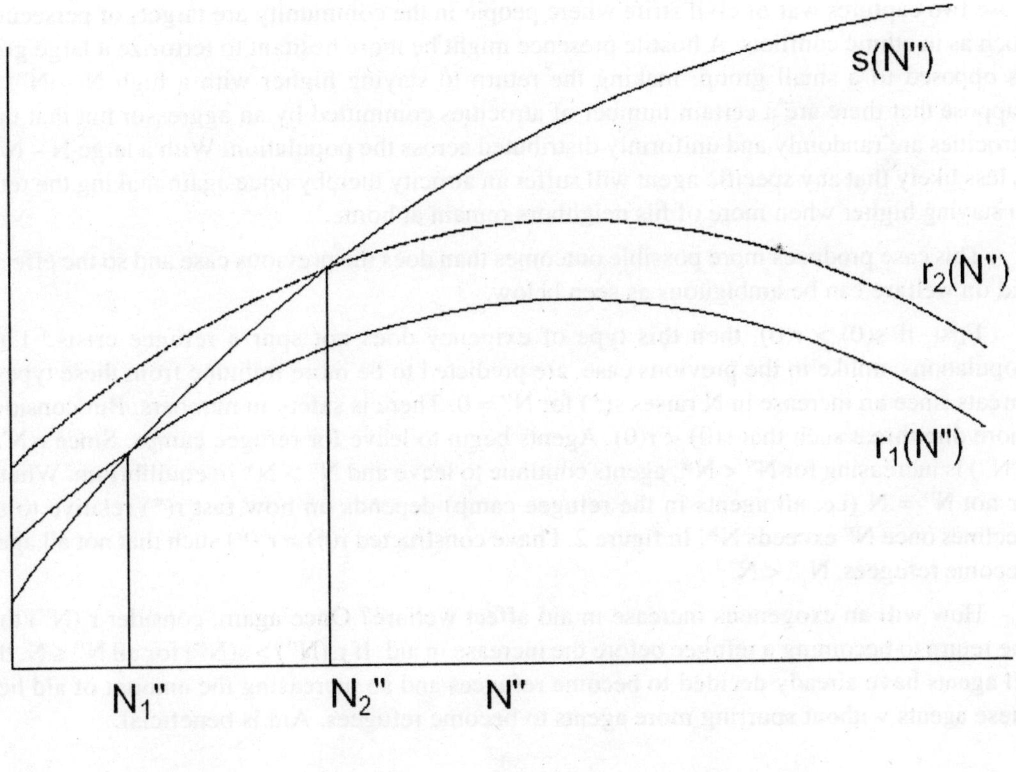

for some $N_1'' < N$ with r(*) initially given by $r_1(*)$. Given the nature of s(*), an exogenous increase in N should lower s(*) for any N". This means that larger populations are more likely to spawn refugees when these types of crises hit.

Now suppose that an exogenous increase in international aid to refugees raises the return of becoming a refugee and r(*) shifts to $r_2(*)$. N" increases to N_2'' as more agents become refugees. Both refugees and those who remain benefit. Refugees benefit because of the increase in aid and "stayers" benefit because with more refugees there are more resources per agent for those who remain. This result holds even if $N_2'' > N^*$, implying that overcrowding lowers the return of becoming a refugee given the same r(*). In other words, the upward shift in the r(*) function from $r_1(*)$ to $r_2(*)$ due to the increase in aid dominates the downward movement along $r_2(*)$ due to the greater mass of refugees. The reason that the shift must dominate in equilibrium is that as the increase in aid attracts more refugees, the return to staying at home increases. Since r(N") = s(N") in equilibrium, welfare must be higher at the refugee camp even if additional overcrowding ensues. The model shows that when the nature of the exigency is such that environmental conditions deteriorate so that the land can sustain fewer people, then providing aid to refugees so as to increase their number is unambiguously beneficial to all agents, regardless of whether these agents are refugees or not.

However, aid need not always be beneficial in other types of crises as shown below.

Case 2: s(N") is decreasing with N" for all 0 ≤ N" ≤ N.

Case two captures war or civil strife where people in the community are targets of persecution such as in ethnic conflicts. A hostile presence might be more hesitant to terrorize a large group as opposed to a small group, making the return to staying higher with a high N – N". Or, suppose that there are a certain number of atrocities committed by an aggressor but that these atrocities are randomly and uniformly distributed across the population. With a large N – N", it is less likely that any specific agent will suffer an atrocity thereby once again making the return to staying higher when more of his neighbors remain at home.[4]

This case produces more possible outcomes than does the previous case and so the effect of aid on welfare can be ambiguous as seen below.

First, if s(0) > r(0), then this type of exigency does not spur a refugee crisis.[5] Large populations, unlike in the previous case, are predicted to be more immune from these types of threats since an increase in N raises s(*) for N" = 0. There is safety in numbers. But consider a more dire threat such that s(0) < r(0). Agents begin to leave for refugee camps. Since r(N") – s(N") is increasing for N" < N*, agents continue to leave and N" > N* in equilibrium. Whether or not N" = N (i.e. all agents in the refugee camp) depends on how fast r(*) relative to s(*) declines once N" exceeds N*. In figure 2, I have constructed r(*) = $r_1(*)$ such that not all agents become refugees, $N_1'' < N$.

How will an exogenous increase in aid affect welfare? Once again, consider $r_1(N'')$ to be the return to becoming a refugee before the increase in aid. If $r_1(N'') > s(N'')$ for all N" ≤ N, then all agents have already decided to become refugees and so increasing the amount of aid helps these agents without spurring more agents to become refugees. Aid is beneficial.

But now consider the case presented in figure 2. Some agents decide to become refugees because $s(0) < r_1(0)$. However, not all agents are refugees in figure 2 as $N_1'' < N$. An increase in aid shifts $r(*)$ upwards to $r_2(*)$ and more agents become refugees. If the increase in aid is "small", however, then N" remains less than N as not all agents become refugees. But since N" remains less than N, then $s(N_2'') < s(N_1'')$ and so welfare for those who remain has decreased. Since $r(N'') = s(N'')$ in equilibrium, welfare for those in the refugee camp has also diminished.

Figure 2

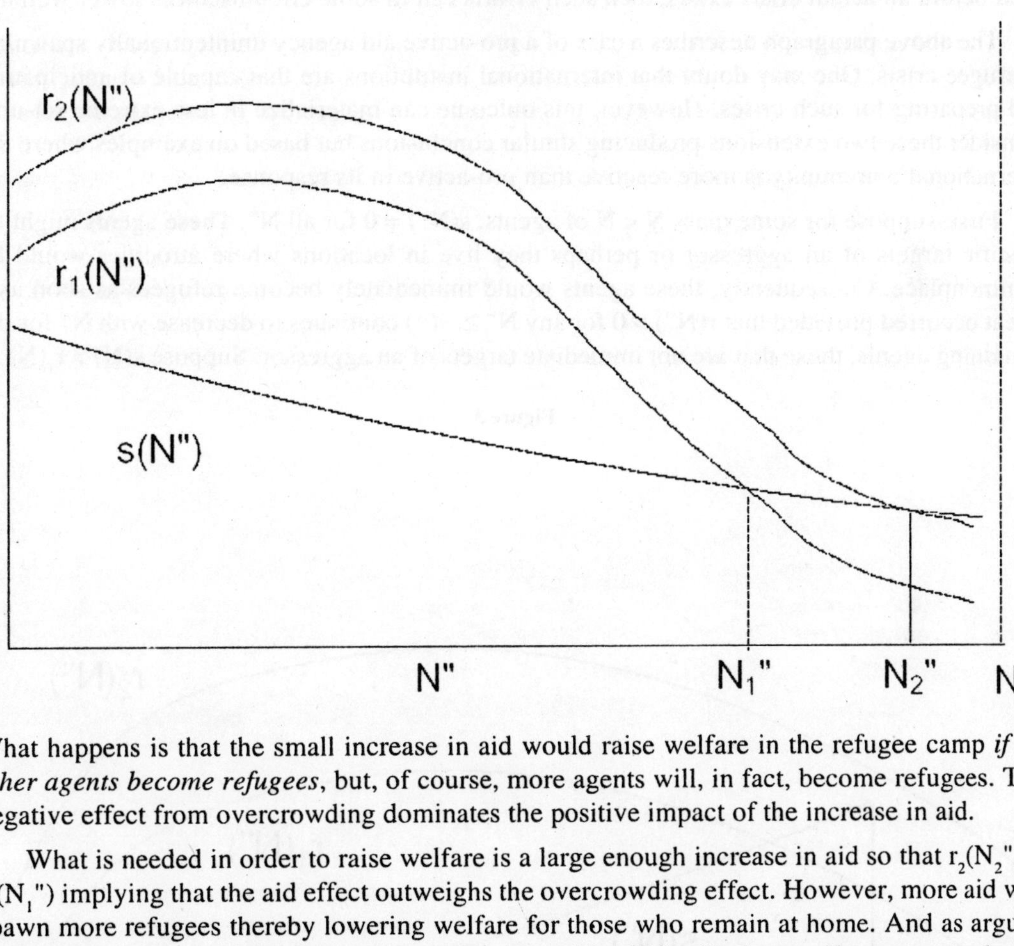

What happens is that the small increase in aid would raise welfare in the refugee camp *if no other agents become refugees*, but, of course, more agents will, in fact, become refugees. The negative effect from overcrowding dominates the positive impact of the increase in aid.

What is needed in order to raise welfare is a large enough increase in aid so that $r_2(N_2'') > r_1(N_1'')$ implying that the aid effect outweighs the overcrowding effect. However, more aid will spawn more refugees thereby lowering welfare for those who remain at home. And as argued above, if some new equilibrium, N_2'', exists where $N_1'' < N_2'' < N$, then welfare must go down. Thus, in this case where $s(*)$ is decreasing with N", a necessary condition for aid to raise welfare is for all agents to become refugees. Only at the corner solution of $N'' = N$ is it possible for $r_2(N) > s(N_1'')$. Aid then raises welfare if $r_2(N) > r_1(N_1'')$. In this situation where not all agents are initially refugees, aid has nonmonotonic effects on welfare and so the size of any aid package becomes crucial in determining whether welfare goes up or down. But once all agents are at the refugee camp, then increases in aid unambiguously raise welfare.

Finally, consider a case where $s(0) > r_1(0)$. No agents initially want to become refugees. However, suppose international aid agencies still believe that a crisis might occur and so prepare for the contingency by setting up refugee camps in advance. Given sufficient preparation, it is possible that $s(0) < r_2(0)$. Now, the act of preparing for refugees causes them to exist. Moreover, if $s(0) < r_2(N_2")$, then agents' welfare decreases. Agents would have been better served if no preparations had been undertaken. One implication is that as the world becomes more sensitive to the plight of refugees and moves to act preemptively to accommodate potential refugees even before an actual crisis exists, then such efforts can in some circumstances lower welfare.

The above paragraph describes a case of a pro-active aid agency unintentionally spawning a refugee crisis. One may doubt that international institutions are that capable of anticipating and preparing for such crises. However, this outcome can materialize in less extreme set-ups. Consider these two extensions producing similar conclusions but based on examples where the international community is more reactive than pro-active in its response.

First, suppose for some mass $\underline{N} < N$ of agents, s(N") = 0 for all N". These agents might be specific targets of an aggressor or perhaps they live in locations where atrocities would be commonplace. Consequently, these agents would immediately become refugees as soon as a threat occurred provided that r(N") > 0 for any N" ≥. s(*) continues to decrease with N" for the remaining agents, those that are not immediate targets of an aggressor. Suppose $s(\underline{N}) > r_1(\underline{N})$ as

Figure 3

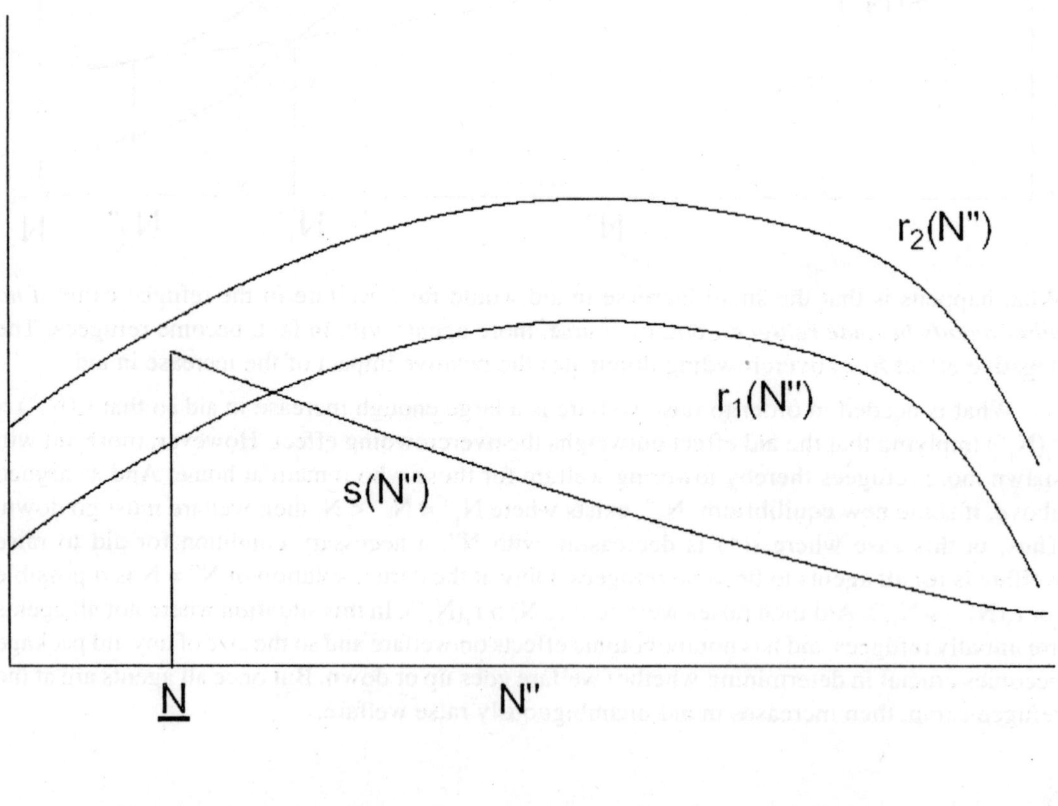

in figure 3. Then, mass $\underline{N}$ agents become refugees but no one else does. But now suppose that aid agencies choose to send more aid to these mass $\underline{N}$ refugees. If $s(\underline{N}) > r_2(\underline{N})$, then the refugee aid is beneficial and raises welfare. Mass $\underline{N}$ refugees benefit because of the increased resources at the refugee camp whereas the mass $N - \underline{N}$ agents who stay are unaffected. But if $s(\underline{N}) < r_2(\underline{N})$, then more agents become refugees and aid triggers a larger flow of refugees than would otherwise exist. More importantly, it is less clear whether aggregate welfare would increase or decrease as the analysis follows that above. The key determinant would be whether the overcrowding at the refugee camp outweighs the direct benefits that aid creates.

In a second example, the timing of aid could be a crucial factor. Suppose that an agent lives in a refugee camp for two periods, one and two, and so the return to becoming a refugee is r(N") = R(N") + bR(N") where R(*) is the return for each period.[6] More generally, periods one and two can denote the present and the future. The parameter $0 < b < 1$ denotes a discount rate. Consider an increase in aid that shifts R(*) upwards by one unit. This increase in aid will raise r(*) more if the aid arrives in period one rather than in period two because agents discount the future with $b < 1$. Depending on parameter values, it is possible that $r(0) > s(0)$ when aid arrives concurrent with the onset of a crisis in period one and that $r(0) < s(0)$ if this same level of aid is delayed until some future date. That is, values of a could exist where $R(0)[1 + ab] < s(0) < R(0)[a + b]$ where $a > 1$ denotes the upward shift in R(0) produced by the inflow of aid. The implication mirrors the conclusion when aid agencies are pro-active. As aid agencies more quickly respond to crises stemming from wars, then the more likely it is that crises will occur in the first place.

IV. CONCLUSION

Underlying causes of refugees can be quite diverse and so it should not be surprising that policy implications differ across causes. This model has taken an initial step in trying to distinguish reasons as to why people become refugees and the appropriateness of policy responses by the international community. In cases of environmental causes, aid should be more forthcoming as it is beneficial for both refugees and those who stay behind. But in cases of ethnic and civil strife, providing aid to refugees should be more circumspect. For one, the effects of aid on welfare need not be monotonic. More importantly, an outflow of aid can in some cases actually trigger a refugee crisis that would not have happened in its absence. Nevertheless, this paper does not argue that aid should never be forthcoming, only that it is sometimes less clear whether aid will raise or lower welfare.

Notes

1. To incorporate the welfare of countries receiving refugees one could denote aggregate welfare as: [N-N"]s(N") + N"r(N") - g(N}) where g'>0, g(0) = 0 accounts for the welfare loss of host countries. The welfare implications would be affected accordingly.

2. For example, some 0 < N'<N could exist where s(N') = r(N'). Such an N' would constitute and equilibrium. However, I do not analyze this equilibrium if s(0) > r(0) such that no agent has an incentive to leave for the refugee camp if all other agents remain at home.

3. Realistically, a point n (with 0 < n < N) could eventually be reached where so many people leave that remaining agents would be, in effect, isolated and so s(*) would be decreasing with N" for N">n. However,

I do not explicitly consider this case as such a point might not likely be reached until refugee flows are already large (i.e. n is near N).

4. Stark (2004) assumes a productive spillover so that individual returns increase as fewer people leave and become refugees. Such an assumption is implicitly captured by having s(*) decrease with N". In case 1 where s(*) increases with N", I implicitly assume that these positive spillovers are "small" should they exist.

5. However, this does not mean that other equilibria do not exist (see footnote 2), only that I am assuming that these equilibria will never be realized because agents have no incentive to deviate from the initial one.

6. For simplicity, I assume that N" remains the same across the two periods. In other words, no agent is allowed to re-choose whether or not to become a refugee in period two.

References

Black, Richard and Mohamed F. Sessay (1998), "Refugees and Environmental Change in West Africa: the Role of Institutions," *Journal of International Development* 10, 699-713.

Kibreab, Gaim (2003), "Rethinking Household Headship among Eritrean Refugees and Returnees," *Development and Change* 34, 311-337.

Schrijvers, Joke (1997), "Internal Refugees in Sri Lanka: the Interplay of Ethnicity and Gender," *European Journal of Development Research* 9, 62-82.

Stark, Oded (2004), "On the Economics of Refugee Flows," *Review of Development Economics* 8, 325-329.

Weaver, Jerry L. (1988), "Searching for Survival: Urban Ethiopian Refugees in Sudan," *Journal of Developing Areas* 22, 457-475.

Wilkinson, Ray (2000), "Cover Story," *Refugees Magazine* 3 (120), 6-21.

ORGANIZING WORKING WOMEN IN INFORMAL ECONOMY

*Siddhartha Sarkar**

The informal sector represents an important segment of the economy and certainly of labour market in many countries, especially developing countries and poses a challenge to policy makers with regard to issues relating to improvement of the working condition and social protection of the workers engaged in the informal sector. While the definition of social security has been made comprehensive, however little attention has been paid to the working poor in the informal sector. This paper delves into genesis of organizing different types of informalised workers through social security measurement.

INTRODUCTION

The term informal sector was first used by Keith Hart (1970) in a study of urban Ghana and it has been further refined by International Labour Organization (ILO, 1972) while studying the employment situation in Kenya. The informal sector is characterized by ease of entry, small-scale operations, family ownership of enterprise, labour intensive and adaptive technology, lack of support and recognition from the government, competitive and unregulated product market, unprotected labour market, undisclosed income or tax evasion etc. In addition to these, the other characteristics include deplorable working condition and low level of wage, low capital accumulation and reinvestment, insecure and temporary nature of employment etc. Besides, the informal sector may be classified into four categories on the basis of their nature of works namely, home based workers, self-employment workers, piece wageworkers and time wageworkers. The causes of informalisation may be of economic recession, evasion of tax as well as excessive governmental regulation of market sector.

The urban economy can be classified broadly as formal and informal sectors. As far as the contrasting characteristics of the two sectors are concerned, the entry into the informal sector labour market is unrestricted and level of earning is also very low, while that in formal sector labour market, entry is restricted and level of earning is high. Apart from the distinguishing characteristics, there exist strong direct and indirect inter-linkages between formal and informal sectors (Sarkar, 2006a).

The employment in the informal economy has risen rapidly in all regions of the developing countries and various forms of non-standard employment have emerged in most regions of the developed countries. In the developing economy, it was only the once rapidly growing economies

* Faculty, Department of Commerce, Dinhata College, Dinhata, Cooch Behar, West Bengal, India, E-mail: *siddhartha_31@yahoo.com*

that experienced substantial growth of modern sector employment. However, in the wake of the recent economic crisis, most of these countries experienced a substantial decline in formal wage employment and a concomitant rise in informal employment. How many retrenched workers have been reinstated in formal jobs as these economies have begun to recover from the crisis is not yet known. Why has the informal economy continued to expand and grow? There is no simple answer to this question as different causal factors are at work in different contexts. However, some mix of the following sets of factors would explain the persistence or expansion of the informal economy in most countries, regions, or industries. The first set of factors relates to the páttern of economic growth. Some countries have experienced little or no economic growth, while others have pursued capital-intensive growth or what some observers call jobless growth. In both such contexts, not enough jobs are created for all those seeking work. Many frustrated formal job seekers find employment or create their own work in the informal economy. Another pattern of economic growth namely high tech growth tends to create more high-skill service sector jobs than lower-skill manufacturing jobs. In such contexts, those without the skills to compete for high-tech formal jobs find work or continue to work in the informal economy. There is another, more optimistic, scenario namely, growth from below. In some countries the tiny business and micro-business sectors are more dynamic and create more jobs than the formal sector. The second set of factors has to do with economic restructuring and economic crisis. Available evidence suggests that during periods of economic adjustment whether due to economic reforms or economic crises, the informal economy tends to expand. This is because retrenched workers move into the informal economy when public enterprises are closed or the public sector is downsized. This is also because households need to supplement formal sector incomes with informal earnings in response to inflation or cutbacks in public services. The third set of factors relates to the globalization of the world economy. Global trade and investment patterns tend to privilege capital, especially companies that can move quickly and easily across borders and to disadvantage labour especially lower-skilled workers that cannot migrate easily or at all. To enhance their global competitiveness more and more investors are moving to countries that have low labour costs or shifting to informal employment arrangements. Furthermore, there has been a radical restructuring of production and distribution in many key industries characterized by outsourcing or subcontracting through global commodity chains. The net result is that more and more workers are being paid very low wages and many of them have to absorb the non-wage costs of production. Globalization also tends to privilege large companies who can capture new markets quickly and easily to the disadvantage of small and micro entrepreneurs who face difficulties gaining knowledge of much less access to emerging markets. In sum, globalization puts pressure on low-skilled workers and petty producers by weakening their bargaining power and subjecting them to increasing competition. Why should the persistence or expansion of the informal economy be of interest or concern? There is a link between working in the informal economy and being poor. Average incomes are lower in the informal economy than in the formal sector. As a result, a higher percentage of people working in the informal economy, relative to the formal sector, are poor. However, there is no simple relationship between working in the informal economy and being poor or working in the formal sector and escaping poverty (Sethuraman, 1998; Thomas, 1995). The relationship between informal employment and poverty appears only when informal workers are classified by employment status and by industry or trade. Informal incomes worldwide tend to decline as one moves across the following types of employment from employer to self-employed to informal and casual wageworkers to industrial outworker. The link between working in the informal economy and being poor is stronger for women than for men. A higher percentage of women than men worldwide work in the informal economy. Moreover, there is a gender gap in incomes and wages in the informal economy. This is because women worldwide are under-represented in higher income employment statuses in the informal economy (employer and self-employed) and over represented in the lower income statuses (casual wage worker and industrial outworker). Available evidence suggests that globalization of the economy tends to reinforce the links between poverty, informality and gender. This is because global competition tends to encourage formal firms to shift formal wageworkers to informal employment arrangements without minimum wages, assured work, or benefits and to encourage informal units to shift workers from semi-permanent contracts without minimum wages or benefits to piece-rate or casual work arrangements without either assured work; minimum wages, or benefits. This is also because globalization often leads to shifts from secure self-employment to more precarious self-employment, as producers and traders lose their market niche. With these shifts, and as more and more men enter the informal economy, women tend to be pushed to the lowest income end of the informal economy. But globalization can also lead to new opportunities for those who work in the informal economy in the form of new jobs for wageworkers or new markets for the self-employed. However, a collaborative effort on the part of grassroots organizations of those who work in the informal economy with sympathetic representatives of non-governmental, research, government, private sector and international development organizations is needed to enable the most vulnerable segments of society to seize these opportunities. There needs to be a much more detailed interpretation of who is in the informal economy and what they are doing, as well as a more comprehensive analysis of how globalization, particularly trade and investment policies, are affecting the employment arrangements and income sources of those who work in the informal economy (Sarkar, 2006b).

TYPOLOGY

All informal activity has one common feature namely the entrepreneurs who works in the informal economy perceive the benefits of doing so to offset the costs of going formal. Recent studies have identified a number of reasons why some entrepreneurial activity may take place in the shadows. The most important determinants are the prevalence of burdensome and costly government regulations and the level and administrative complexity of taxation. Informality comes at a cost, the inability to use government and some private sector services available to firms that fully comply with regulations. In countries entrepreneurs may well opt to be formal, even if regulations are many and taxes are high. In contrast, entrepreneurs in countries where the quality of public services to enterprises is poor have a much easier choice. In the absence of discernible benefits of going formal, they prefer to save their time and money and stay informal. Many transition economies have experienced surging share of entrepreneurial activity in the informal sector. Some of this activity is illegal. Such activity will not become formal, regardless of improvements in the enterprises climate. Other activities, like small production units operate merely for the subsistence of their owners and do not generate enough revenue to make their inclusion in the tax base meaningful.

However, there exists a considerable share of entrepreneurial activity that is semi-formal e.g., the organization is registered but most changes. Informal activities usually fall into three broad categories namely employees are not, and can become formal with appropriate policy underground enterprises, subsistence enterprises and unofficial enterprises.

Subsistence enterprises result from coping strategies adopted by families to compensate for low wages or external shocks e.g., unemployment etc. Unofficial enterprises generally result from the desire to escape or avoid the administrative and/or financial burden of regulation e.g., license and permit regimes, taxes, labour regulations etc. Firms around the world lie on a spectrum of entrepreneurial activity, ranging from informal to formal. A typology of the informal sector is presented in Table 1. Another typology represents categories of informal work based on the context of the work. Informal work may involve a person working for someone else or a person being self-employed and within each of the categories there are two arrangements (Table 2).

Table 1
A Taxonomy of Typology of Informal Sector

	Informal sector	
	Subsistence enterprises	*Unofficial enterprises*
Degree of informality	100 per cent	High proportion of sales and workers not registered
Type of activity	Single street traders, cottage/ micro enterprises, subsistence farmers	Small manufacturers, service providers, distributors, contractors
Technology	Labour intensive	Mostly labour intensive
Owner profile	Poor, low education, low level of skills	Poor and non-poor, well educated, high level of skills
Markets	Low barrier to entry, highly competitive, high product homogeneity	Low barrier to entry, highly competitive, some product differentiation
Finance needs	Working capital	Working capital, some investment capital, supplier credit
Other needs	Personal insurance, social protection	Personal perhaps business insurance

Source: Djankov *et al.*, 2003.

Table 2
Structure of Informal Work Typology

	Primary work for firm	*Extra work for current employer*
Person works for someone else	Works off the books Works under the table Paid in cash and not taxed	Works extra hours on weekends or evening (paid in cash and not taxed)
Person self employed	Person operate own tiny business Cash only exchange Ongoing, regular Business is seen primary income May invest income into business	Does sporadic odd jobs, services or products Works extra hours on weekends or evening (paid in cash and not taxed)

Source: ILO, 2002.

Following the worker approach workers in the informal economy can be broadly distinguished into wage employment and non-wage employment, each consisting of the components of own account workers, employers/owners of informal enterprises with at least one hired worker; unpaid family helpers in both types of informal enterprises, employees in the enterprises of informal employers, outworkers or home workers (persons working at home, or on premises of his choice other than the employer's, to produce goods or services on a contract or order for a specific employer or contractor), independent wage workers not attached to only one employer and providing services to individuals, households and enterprises, e.g., domestic workers and watchmen working for households and informal employment in formal sector enterprises (workers whose pay and benefits do not conform to existing labour regulations). This categorization is similar to that developed by Sethuraman (1998). In the literature the first four categories are generally taken to represent employment in the informal sector. The need to distinguish the category of independent wageworkers can be debated. In many Latin American countries domestic helps are distinguished in the national surveys and together with independent wageworkers are added to the informal sector (Sethuraman, 1998). The first process of informalisation of the labour force, pushing work out of formal work situations, leads to an increase in the first component, non-wage employment. It can also lead to increase in the first two varieties of the second component i.e., informal wage employment. The second process of informalisation, resulting in looser contracts and fewer benefits, leads to an increase in the last category of workers, informal employment within the formal enterprises as defined by the enterprise-based approach. Obviously it is not easy to obtain empirical estimates of these categories of workers from the national official labour statistics. However, an approximation of the first component of the informal economy can be arrived at, non-wage employment or self-employment, by the addition of employers, own account workers and unpaid family helpers in the activity status classification of the national labour force survey. While it may be relatively safe to assume that own account workers and unpaid family helpers are part of the informal economy, this assumption may not be very accurate for the category of employer. Employers, however, form a very small proportion of the workforce. The second component of the informal economy is even more difficult to demarcate from the official data since there is really a continuum in the degree of informality in the employer-employee relationships. The official data distinguish only employees. The Indian labour force surveys further classifies them into casual and regular. All regular workers do not necessarily belong to the formal economy, as they often do not receive a variety of benefits due to the formal worker such as provident funds, paid leave etc. An approximation of the second component of the informal economy can be made by assuming that all casual employees definitely constitute a part of the informal economy since they are least likely to obtain any of the benefits accruing to formal economy workers. Another indicator or measure of the nature of informality of the work status or sector is the earnings differentials. The informal economy can be distinguished by the inferior quality of work and inferior terms of employment, both remuneration and benefits. Among the non-wage component inferior technologies leads to low productivity and hence to low earnings or incomes.

Since informal sector is very diverse and it covers many types of work, so it is difficult to classify it into a specific group as uniform. However, the workers in the informal sector may be classified broadly into four categories as under:

(i) Home Based Workers

The workers in this category carry out their activities using their traditional skill and labour. The majority of the home based workers work in the privacy of their homes and they are invisible. This category of workers engages in earthen pots making, rural artisans etc.

(ii) Self Employed or Own Account Workers

Self-employed or own account workers are those who do not have any permanent place for carrying out their activities. Some of them have to change their place of activity almost on a daily basis. In this category of workers includes street vendors, hawkers, rag pickers, rickshaw pullers, sex workers etc.

(iii) Piece Wage Workers

There has been a tremendous growth of private informal manufacturing such as garment making, knitting etc. These categories of workers are employed by entrepreneurs. They are usually employed on a piece rate basis. This type of workers carries out their work independently, but employers exercise control over them by supplying raw material and sometimes advancing minimum cash. This kind of labour is often found in beedi making, carpet and mat weaving, lace industry etc.

(iv) Time Wage Workers

This type of workers sells their labour power in exchange of a low paid time rate of wage. The most of the workers in this category are quasi permanent. These workers are placed in a most disadvantageous position. Their activities rely heavily on manual labour. This category includes gardeners, cleaners, sweepers, construction labourers, bricks workers, agricultural labourers, domestic helps etc.

SOCIAL SECURITY MEASURES

Social security is both a concept as well as a structure. It represents basically a system of protection of individuals who are in need of such protection by the State as an agent of the society. Such protection is relevant in contingencies such as retirement, resignation, retrenchment, death and disablement that are beyond the control of the individual members of the society. State as a representative of the society has an important mandate to keep parity with such differences through a protective cover to the poor, the deprived and the disadvantaged. The concept of social security is now generally understood as meaning protection provided by the society to its members through a series of public measures against the economic and social distress that otherwise is caused by the stoppage or substantial reduction of earnings resulting from sickness, maternity, employment injury, occupational diseases, unemployment, invalidity, old age and death. The ILO concept of social security is based on the recognition of the fundamental social right guaranteed by law to all human beings who live from their own labour and who find themselves unable to work temporarily or permanently for reasons beyond their control. At the international level, the preamble of the charter of ILO also referred to the need and protection of workers against sickness, disease and injury arising out of their employment, pension for old age, protection of the interests of the workers who were employed in countries other than their own. Thus the right to social security was recognized officially for the first time. Social security has been recognized as an instrument for social transformation and progress and must be preserved, supported and developed as such. Furthermore, far from being an obstacle to economic progress as is often alleged, social security organized on a firm and sound basis will promote progress, since once men and women benefit from increased security and are free from anxiety will become more productive. There is considerable controversy about the social and economic effects of social security and most of the current debate is focused on its supposedly negative effects. Social security is supposed to discourage people from working and saving to reduce international competitiveness and employment creation and to encourage people to pull out from the labour market prematurely. On the other hand, social security can also be observed to have a number of very positive economic effects. It can help to make people capable of earning an income and to increase their productive potential, it may help to maintain effective demand at the national level and it may help create conditions, in which a market economy can flourish, notably by encouraging workers to accept innovation and change. A formal social security system presupposes the interventionist role of the State on redistribution grounds. Social security measures are generally income, maintenance measures intended to provide a minimum living to the people when they are deprived of the same due to invalidity, unemployment or old age. The two basic elements of social security are provision of a minimum living to those who are deprived of the same and selective redistribution of income to a target group to reduce inequalities. Social security to the workers would involve providing or framing such schemes or services or facilities and amenities, which can enable the workers to lead a decent minimum standard of life and having economic security to fall back upon in the event of loosing job for whatsoever may be the reason in the circumstances beyond their control. The workers must be given the wages and other services, which will enable them and the members of their family to lead a decent life. Thus social security is an instrument for social transformation and good governance. Social security in India was traditionally the responsibility of the community in general. Currently ongoing measures towards transformation process has added a new dimension to the issue and enhanced the requirement further towards a planned and regulated institutionalized measure in the form of social security in its common understanding. Low-income women workers constitute one of the most vulnerable groups in Indian society. Their vulnerability arises from their irregular work, their low economic status, their little bargaining power, their lack of control over their earnings, their need to balance work with care for children and homework and their lack of assets. Unequal gender relations indeed assume an important role in defining their insecurities (Dasgupta, 2003).

Social security comprises of two types of measures namely, promotional and protective. Promotional measures consist mainly of employment, training and nutrition schemes by which a person is able to work and earn a livelihood. Protective measures consist of schemes by which the State provides the means of livelihood when a person is not able to work (Subrahmanya, 2000). ILO standards relating social security are mainly protective and have been designed primarily for the formal sector. There are many possible measures for social security provision for the informal sector, but two specific models have been explored as follows (Sarkar, 2004).

Welfare funds represent one of the methods for providing social security to the workers in the informal sector in India. Welfare funds are of two types, namely, contributory and tax based. The funds set up by the central government are tax based, while those set up by the government of Kerala are mostly contributory. A contributory scheme is akin to social insurance. In India, there is only one social insurance scheme, namely, the employees' social insurance scheme. The funds may be administered departmentally or by autonomous body and are financed by the central as well as State governments. The other scheme, namely, the government of India's, tax based welfare funds cover mine workers, beedi rollers, cine workers and workers in building and construction industry. The fund is administered by the office of the director general, labour welfare, through its regional offices and financed by special levies in the forms of cess.

The State funds are mainly contributory based on contributions from employers, workers and government, and administered by labour departments of respective State governments. The funds cover wide range of facilities including health care, education for children, housing and water supply, old-age and survivor benefits, group insurance schemes and recreational facilities. The central welfare funds for mine workers and beedi rollers may be used for improvement of public health and sanitation, prevention of disease, and provision and improvement of medical facilities, water supplies and facilities for washing, educational facilities, standards of living including housing and nutrition, amelioration of social conditions and provision of recreational facilities, family welfare including family planning and other services. Although the model has been implementing successfully in India, still, mine and beedi workers have no provision for meeting the expenditure on any of the well recognized branches of social security like benefits of sickness, occupational injury, maternity, invalidity, old-age, survivor or unemployment.

Insurance corporations in India have been providing social insurance to the workers in the informal sector. With the assistance of Central and State governments, they have introduced various schemes, which are administered directly through government or more successfully through cooperatives and non-government organizations and are a combination of social assistance and social insurance. The Life Insurance Corporation (LIC) in India has developed group insurance, which is akin to social insurance based on large numbers. It has the potential to provide social security to those in the informal sector. The scheme offers life insurance cover at a premium of Rs. 10 for every Rs. 10,000 of benefits. Up to Rs. 5,000 coverage is subsidized up to 50 per cent by one time capital grant from the government. This model has been adopted by the central government, State governments and voluntary organizations to cover the life insurance of many groups of workers in the informal sector. The largest of these schemes, where the premium is contributed by the central government, is for landless agricultural workers. There are many other group insurance schemes for workers in the informal sector, for milk producers, handloom weavers, rickshaw pullers, shop assistants, sweepers, beedi workers, fish farmers and others. The scheme of the LIC provide mainly survivor benefits, some also provide old-age pensions too. Apart from the LIC, the General Insurance Corporation (GIC) of India also administers a few social security schemes such as personal accident social security scheme for poor families, the hut insurance scheme and the solatium fund. The GIC has also launched a health insurance scheme and has been monitoring the comprehensive group insurance scheme for the central government. The schemes of the GIC include invalidity benefits, health insurance and protection against loss of property.

Some other schemes of social security protection in the informal sector include:

- Childcare services to workingwomen, especially crèches for children of working mothers have been implemented by the Central Social Welfare Board.
- Under National Maternity Benefit Scheme, central assistance is provided in the form of payment of Rs.300 each to pregnant women for first two childbirths.
- Under Family Benefit Scheme, central assistance is given in the form of payment of a lump sum of Rs.5000 to families below the poverty line on the death of their breadwinner.
- Under National Old-age Pension Scheme, central assistance is extended to States for payment of old-age pension to men and women who have attained the age of 65 or more at Rs. 75 per month.
- Assistance in case of sickness, either in the form of a lump sum or reimbursement of medical expenses, assistance in case of death of bread winner and maternity assistance is provided by many voluntary organizations as well as co-operative societies.

Several State governments of India have taken initiatives to provide various protective social security measures for workers in the informal sector. A few States such as Andhra Pradesh, Gujarat, Kerala and Tamil Nadu also have special pension schemes for agricultural workers. Maternity benefits for landless agricultural labour have been introduced in Gujarat, Karnataka and Kerala to compensate loss of wage due to absence at work. However, health care as a part of the social security does not seem to exist in any State. Gujarat, Tamil Nadu and Kerala have certain welfare schemes exclusively for women and children while a number of other States offer welfare benefits for various categories of population below the poverty line.

Successive governments in Kerala have introduced a number of social security and welfare schemes in view of attaining the goal of minimizing income insecurity among the weaker sections. It has various schemes for the benefits of the informal sector (Rajan *et al.*, 1999). The most important protective type schemes in terms of coverage are old-age pensions for destitute and rural labourers. Another innovative programme in Kerala is the creation of welfare funds. In order to meet the demands of the informal sector workers, some types of social insurance and other non-wage benefits, a new institutional innovation was come into limelight in the form of welfare funds. With the active support from the trade unions, the government of Kerala took the initiative to create a fund through contributions from worker, employers and government.

Apart from the Kerala, Tamil Nadu has been a pioneer in implementing social security protection for the workers in the informal sector (Guhan, 1993). The main initiatives are liberalized pensions, accident relief scheme, new survivor benefit scheme, maternity assistance scheme and marriage grant scheme. It has been implementing protective social security for providing nutrition to vulnerable groups such as pregnant and destitute women and the aged and the like. Other States in India and developing countries can learn from the experiences of Kerala and Tamil Nadu on what can be done in the area of protective social security measures at reasonable cost to help the vulnerable groups. Some other States have also taken important initiatives in recent years, namely, employment guarantee scheme in Maharashtra, primary education in Himachal Pradesh and Madhya Pradesh, public distribution in Andhra Pradesh and land reform in West Bengal. In contrast, in States like Bihar, Uttar Pradesh, Rajasthan, there seems to be apathetic towards the necessity to build social security schemes (Mahendra Dev, 2000).

A number of State governments have also set up welfare funds for various categories of workers. The government of Kerala has set up about 35 welfare funds for different categories of occupations and sectors. These welfare funds cater to the needs of agricultural workers, auto rickshaw workers, cashew workers, coir workers, construction workers, fishermen and women, handloom workers etc.

The government of Assam has set up a statutory fund under Assam Plantation Employees Welfare Fund Act, 1959 for the benefit of the plantation workers. Similar funds have also been set up in Gujarat and Maharashtra under Bombay Labour Welfare Fund Act, 1953 and in Karnataka under Mysore (Karnataka) Labour Welfare Act, 1965 and in Punjab under the Labour Welfare Act, 1965.

The State governments of Andhra Pradesh and Uttar Pradesh have also set up welfare funds for various categories of workers. All these welfare funds however, cater to a very small segment of the total workforce. In view of the change in the perception of the social security i.e., an essential input to the productivity rather than burden on exchequer, some State governments are making concerted efforts to extend social security to the workers in the informal sector. For instance, the government of Karnataka is going to set up a social security authority of Karnataka and create a welfare board to cater to the needs of the 66 identified occupational groups shortly. Further, occupational groups can be added to it as and when the necessity arises. The welfare fund will be created by levying a cess from transport vehicles, employer's contribution, workers and the State government when there is no employer. The fund created therein will be utilized to implement schemes and programmes covering pension, health, housing, insurance in case of death and disability aspects for the benefit of workers.

Recently, the government of West Bengal initiated State Assisted Scheme of Provident Fund for Unorganized Workers. The scheme covers all wage employed and self-employed workers between the ages of 18 to 55 years in the unorganized sector having an average family income of not more than Rs.3500 per month. Each subscriber worker contributes a sum of Rs.20 per month and equal matching amount contributed by the state government. The interest on the balance at credit of subscriber is also paid by the state government annually at the rate declared by the State government. Total contribution along with interest has to be refunded to the worker on attainment of the age of 55 years. The scheme will have provision for loans and withdrawals from the fund as prescribed by the State government. The government of West Bengal had identified 50 industries in the unorganized sector and 16 self-employed occupations, of which 13 unorganized industries and 7 self-employed occupations are being covered in the first phase. These industries include tailoring shops, establishments having less than 20 workers, bakery, handloom, construction, earthen pottery, stone crushing, auto repairing, etc. The self-employed occupations include cycle rickshaw, head load workers, railway/street hawkers, auto rickshaw operators, mason and cobblers.

The Department of Agriculture of the State of Punjab implements a scheme financed from the funds available with marketing committees/boards to provide financial assistance to the farmers and labourers in case of death or injury by operating the agricultural machinery/ implements and undertaking other operations both at the level of farm since 1984. The scope of the scheme includes death or disablement to any farmer or labour working in the agricultural machinery implements or arising out of the use of the said machinery implements in the state of Punjab, death or disablement to any farmer or labour arising out of digging of tube-well in the State of Punjab or electric current while operating tube-well in the farm, death or disablement to any farmer or labour while using the insecticides or pesticides in the State of Punjab or due to snake biting while working in field or watering the field and death or disablement to labour employed in field arising out of use of agricultural machinery implements. The financial assistance provided under the scheme includes payment of Rs.75,000 in case of death, Rs.30,000 in case of partial disability such as loss of one leg, eye, arm or serious injury, Rs.45,000 in case a farmer or labour lost both eyes, arms, leg, etc. Rs.7,500 to Rs.22,500 in case of loss of fingers and Rs.30,000 in case of loss of four fingers, which is treated as loss of one arm. The group was apprised of the free medical check up camps being organized by the government of Punjab. Workers working in hazardous and dangerous process establishments come in contact with various toxic substances and other chemicals from which they are likely to contact with occupational diseases. The government of Punjab has decided to carry out free medical check up of such workers. Till date 165 medical check up camps have been organized in which 50,000 workers have been examined and medicines worth Rs. 18 lakhs were spent in these camps by the employers which generated a lot of goodwill. 3500 workers were referred to hospitals for their blood test, chest X-rays, surgical operations, skin diseases, leprosy etc. This is a very welcome step in the right direction as it demonstrates the willingness of the State to share the burden in delivery of health services.

The government of Tamil Nadu introduced Tamil Nadu Social Security and Welfare Scheme-2001. These schemes cover manual worker, auto rickshaws and taxi drivers, washer-men, hairdressers, tailoring workers, handicraft workers and palm tree workers. The State government is planning to formulate scheme for handlooms and handloom silk-weaving workers, footwear and leather goods manufacturing and tannery workers and artists. State government has set up the goal and social security and welfare fund for the respective workers. Every worker registered under the scheme for two years initially has to pay a sum of Rs.100 and every employer 3 per cent of the wages payable by him to the worker employed to the social security and welfare board. The fee for renewing the registration is Rs.10. The funds are to be utilized for paying premium towards insurance coverage having provision of compensation of Rs. 1 lakh in case of death or loss of both hands, feet, Rs.50,000 in case of loss of one hand or one foot and Rs.25,000 in case of permanent total disablement from injuries other than loss of limbs or death. The financial assistance is extended to the tune of Rs. 10,000 to the nominee of the deceased worker in case of natural death and Rs. 2,000 to meet the funeral expenses. Assistance of Rs.1,000 for the education of the son or daughters of the workers passing 10th Standard examination, Rs.1500 for passing plus two examination and studying in regular bachelor degree course and Rs.2,000 in case of post graduate course or professional course for every academic year is provided through the fund. A sum of Rs. 2,000 is extended to the applicant or his son or daughter for marriage. Further, assistance is also extended for delivery or the miscarriage or pregnancy or the termination of pregnancy by a registered female worker to the extent of Rs. 2,000.

In addition to governmental efforts, several public institutions and agencies are also providing various kinds of social security benefits to selected groups of workers. Two of the outstanding examples are those of Self-Employed Women's Association (SEWA) and the Mathadi Workers Boards in Maharashtra. The social security experiments of SEWA started in 1975 with a demand from members for a maternal protection scheme followed by health care and childcare. This was followed by starting of an insurance programme in collaboration with insurance companies. The insurance scheme started by the SEWA Bank was based on a realistic estimate of the capacity of the members to pay the premium. An Integrated Insurance Scheme introduced by SEWA for its members, offers several benefits for a consolidated annual premium of Rs.45. While SEWA itself provides some of the benefits, it works as a nodal agency to get cover under various policies separately for specific benefits from different insurance companies. The risk covered includes health costs up to Rs.1,000, maternity benefit of Rs.300 and payment of varying amounts up to Rs.10,000 in case of natural or accidental death including disablement of the member or her husband. The insurance scheme has turned out to be both popular and financially viable. The total coverage of SEWA social security scheme is about 50,000 women. The experience of SEWA reveals that in order to become effective, the social security scheme for the informal sector should be locally managed and controlled. Further, only such schemes will become viable which is need based and integrated with the economic activities of the local people. If poor people are supported through capacity building and necessary linkages are provided with their own economic activities the chances of success of social security efforts increased significantly. Further, it has demonstrated that, it is not only necessary to search new social security programmes but new social security organizations to run them.

A *mathadi* is a worker who carries a load on his head, back, neck or shoulders. Normally his work consists of loading, unloading, carrying, shifting, weighing, tapping, banding and stacking goods. In the State of Maharashtra, the Mathadi Labour Market is regulated by Mathadi Tripartite Boards set up since 1969. There are about 50,000 registered employers and 1,50,000 workers registered under 30 different boards in the State. The Mathadi Workers Boards, besides settling disputes between unions and employers, are actively involved in imparting social security benefits to their members by setting up of hospitals and dispensaries. At present there are two hospitals with an annual budget of Rs. 2 crores which are run by six Mathadi Boards. In addition to this, there are 12 dispensaries. Each of the six Boards contributes 2 per cent of their levy and each worker contributes Rs. 20 per month. These hospitals provide diagnostic services such as radiology, pathology and sonography for around 40,000 workers and their families. During the last few years, some of the Mathadi Boards have been able to get the workers registered with them insured against accident, injuries and death. For example, Mathadi Boards in Pune are paying Rs. 152 per annum as premium out of the Board's administrative account to cover workers for a benefit of Rs. 25,000 in case of injury and Rs. 2,00,000 in case of death to each worker. This scheme has been worked out by the Mathadi Board with the General Insurance Corporation. Besides organizations like Co-operative Development Foundation (CDF),

Trivandrum District Fishermen Federation (TDFF), the Association of Sarwa Sewa Farms (ASSF), the Society for Promotion of Area Resources Centre (SPARC), Voluntary Health Services (VHS) in Tamil Nadu and the Working Women's Forum have experimented for providing social security to small groups of people. The VHS in Chennai and the Association for Health Welfare in Nilgiris (ASHWINI) in the tribal areas of Gudalur in Tamil Nadu have made efforts to provide medical care to very specific target groups. The approach of these agencies is based on collecting of contribution from the beneficiaries themselves for their future contingencies in line with the insurance principles.

CONCLUSION

In the developing economies a substantial share of employment is indeed in informal category and women in all age groups depend on the informal sector more heavily than men. Women are over represented in this sector in the sense that their share in the sector is higher than their share in total labour force. Most women tend to be own account workers and only a few are heads of micro enterprises. Relatively lower level of education among women, compared to men, seems to explain, in part, this gender differential in informal employment. Discrimination in the labour market also explains in part the disproportionate concentration as it limits women's access to formal and wage employment. Women also face additional constraints because of their homemaking and childcare responsibilities, which limits their participation in formal employment.

The concept of social security has been changing with the passage of time from traditional ways to modern forms of protection. While the definition of social security has been made comprehensive, however little attention has been paid to the working poor in the informal sector. The protection that a society provides to individuals and households to ensure access to wage and working conditions in a comprehensive sense, in matters of security of employment, health care, maternity benefits, provident fund, retirement benefits, is an essential element of the safety nets that keeps working people and their families from falling into poverty. Efforts to extend social security coverage to the informal sector face a number of challenges namely, inadequate social security expenditure as well as inefficient utilization of funds under government and non-government programmes; higher transaction costs due to the additional costs arising out enforcing compliance to extend social security coverage to the informal sector in urban and rural areas; non-existence of loan facilities and sponsorship for training to the workers in informal sector in the conventional social security protection schemes; lack of contribution capability due to low income to the existing insurance schemes for their future protection ;lack of support from the workers to some non-statutory welfare funds having negligible benefits etc.

References

Dasgupta, S. (2003), Women Organizing for Socio-Economic Security, *The Indian Journal of Labour Economics*, 46 (1): 39-68.

Djankov, S., Lieberman, I., Mukherjee, J. and Nenova, T. (2003), Going Informal: Benefits and Costs, In: Boyan Belev (ed.), *The Informal Economy in the EU Accession Countries: Size, Scope, Trends and Challenges to the Process of EU Enlargement,* Center for the Study of Democracy, Sofia.

Guhan, S. (1993), Social Security for the Poor in the Unorganized Sector: A Feasible Blueprint for India, In: K. S. Parikh *et al.* (eds.), *Human Development and Structural Adjustment,* Macmillan, Madras.

Hart, K. (1970), Small-Scale Entrepreneurs in Ghana and Development Planning, *The Journal of Development Studies*, 6 (4): 104-120.

International Labour Organization (1972), *Employment, Income and Equity: A Strategy for Increasing Productive Employment in Kenya,* Geneva.

International Labour Organization (2002), *Women and Men in the Informal Economy: A Statistical Picture,* Employment Sector Paper, Geneva.

Mahendra Dev, S. (2000), *Growth-Mediated and Support-Led Social Security in the Unorganized Sector in India,* Invest India Economic Foundation.

Rajan, I., Mishra, U.S. and Sarma, P. S. (1999), *India's Elderly: Burden or Challenge,* Sage Publications, New Delhi.

Sarkar, S. (2004), Extending Social Security Coverage to the Informal Sector in India, *Social Change*, 34 (4): 122-130.

Sarkar, S. (2006a), *Theorising Informal Economy,* Abhijeet Publications, Delhi.

Sarkar, S. (2006b), *Women Struggle for Sustainability,* Serials Publications, New Delhi.

Sethuraman, S.V. (1998), *Gender, Informality and Poverty: A Global Review*, World Bank, Washington DC.

Subrahmanya, R.K.A. (2000), Support for the Unorganized Sector: Existing Social Security Measures, In: R. Jhabvala *et al.* (eds.), *The Unorganized Sector: Work Security and Social Protection,* Sage Publications, New Delhi.

Thomas, J.J. (1995), *Surviving in the City: The Urban Informal Sector in Latin America,* CT: Pluto Press, East Haven.